THE ROMANTIC MOVEMENT

GARLAND REFERENCE LIBRARY
OF THE HUMANITIES
(VOL. 778)

THE ROMANTIC MOVEMENT
A Selective and Critical Bibliography for 1986

Edited by
David V. Erdman

with the assistance of
Brian J. Dendle
Robert R. Mollenauer
Augustus Pallotta
James S. Patty

GARLAND PUBLISHING INC. • NEW YORK & LONDON
1987

ISBN 0-8240-7043-7 (alk. paper)
ISSN 0557-2738

Printed on acid-free, 250-year-life paper
Manufactured in the United States of America

This bibliography is compiled by a joint bibliography committee of the Modern Language Association representing groups General Topics II (now Comparative Studies in Romanticism and the Nineteenth Century), English 9 (English Romantic Period), French 6 (Nineteenth-Century French Literature), German 4 (Nineteenth- and Early Twentieth-Century German Literature), Italian 2 (Italian Literature, Seventeenth Century to the Present), and Spanish 4 (Eighteenth- and Nineteenth-Century Spanish Literature). It is designed to cover a "movement" rather than a period; though the English section, for example, is largely limited to the years 1789–1837, other sections extend over different spans of years.

It is our intent to include, with descriptive and, at times, critical annotation, all books and articles of substantial interest to scholars of English and Continental Romanticism. Studies of American Romanticism that relate to this interest are selectively included. We also make note of items of minor but scholarly interest, except those which may be expected to appear in the annual *MLA International Bibliography*. Major and controversial works are given what is intended to be judicious if necessarily brief review.

The approximate size of a book is indicated by report of the number of pages. Book prices are noted when available.

We continue the practice of including available current (1987) reviews of listed books.

The editorial committee gratefully acknowledges the help of its collaborators, whose names are given at the heads of the respective sections.

To ensure notice in the next issue of the bibliography, authors and publishers are invited to send review copies of relevant books or monographs and offprints of articles to: David V. Erdman, 58 Crane Neck Road, Setauket, N.Y. 11733.

CONTENTS

JOURNALS SEARCHED

All journals regularly searched are listed here. The editor
welcomes notice of omissions, to be made good in the next
annual.

AANL   *Atti dell'Accademia Nazionale dei Lincei*
ABC   *American Book Collector* (new series)
ABI   *Accademie é Biblioteche d'Italia*
    Académie d'Angers. Mémoires
AConf   *Les Annales, Conferencia*
ActaG   *Acta Germanica* (Capetown)
    Acta Musicologicae
ActaN   *Acta Neophilologica*
    Adam: International Review
AdI   *Annali d'italianistica*
ADPh   *Arbeiten zur deutschen Philologie*
    Aevum: Rassegna di Scienze Storiche, Linguistiche,
      Filologiche
AFLSHA   *Annales de la Faculté des Lettres et Sciences*
      Humaines d'Aix
AG   *Anglica Germanica*
AHR   *American Historical Review*
AHRF   *Annales Historiques de la Révolution Français*
AI   *American Imago*
AION-SG   *Annali Istituto Universitario Orientale, Napoli,*
      Sezione Germanica
AJ   *Art Journal*
AJES   *Aligarh Journal of English Studies*
AJFS   *Australian Journal of French Studies*
AKG   *Archiv für Kulturgeschichte*
    Akzente: Zeitschrift für Literatur
AL   *American Literature*
    Albion
ALittASH   *Acta Litterarica Academiae Scientiarum Hungaricae.*
      Magyar Tudomanyos Academia. Budapest.
    Allegorica
ALM   *Archives des Lettres Modernes*

American Art Journal
American Art Review
American Journal of Sociology
American Political Science Review
AmG   L'Amitié Guérinienne
AN&Q   American Notes & Queries
AnBret   Annales de Bretagne
Anglia
Annales Benjamin Constant
Annales de Bourgogne
Annales de l'Académie de Mâcon
Annales de l'Est
Annales de l'Université de Dakar
Annales de l'Université de Toulouse-le Mirail
Annales du Centre Universitaires Méditerranéen
Annales du Midi
Annales: Economies, Sociétés, Civilisations
Annales Universitaires (Avignon)
Annali della Facoltà di Lingue e Letterature
     Straniere (Bari)
L'Année Balzacienne
AnS   Annals of Science
Antaeus
Anzeiger   Anzeiger, Oesterreichische Akademie der Wissen-
     schaften, philosophisch-historische Klasse
APh   Archives Philosophiques
APhilos   Archives de Philosophie
Apollo
AQ   American Quarterly
AR   Antioch Review
Arbitrium   Arbitrium: Zeitschrift für Rezensionen zur
     germanistischen Literaturwissenschaft
Arbor: Revista General de Investigación y Cultura
L'Arc: Cahiers Méditerranéens (Aix-en-Provence)
Arcadia: Zeitschrift für vergleichenden Literatur-
     wissenschaft
Arch   Archivium
Archiv   Archiv für das Studium der neueren Sprachen und
     Literaturen
ArH   Archivo Hispalense
ArielE   Ariel: A Review of International English Litera-
     ture
ArM   Archiv für Musikwissenschaft
ArQ   Arizona Quarterly
ArtB   Art Bulletin
Art Forum
Art History
Art International

Art News
ArtQ   Art Quarterly
       Arts and Artists
       Arts Journal
       Arts Magazine
ASch   American Scholar
ASLHM   American Society Legion of Honor Magazine
       Association des Amis d'Alfred de Vigny. Bulletin
ASSR   Archives de Sciences Sociales des Réligions
AUB   Analele Universitatü, Bucuresti
AUMLA   Journal of the Australasian Universities Language
       and Literature Association
Aurora   Aurora: Eichendorff-Almanach
       L'Avant-Scène
AWR   Anglo-Welsh Review
BAAD   Bulletin de l'Association des Amis d'Alexandre
       Dumas
BAGB   Bulletin de l'Association Guillaume Budé
B&BM   Books & Bookman
BAWS   Bayerische Akademie der Wissenschaften. Philo-
       sophischhistorisch Klasse, Sitzungsberichte
BB   Bulletin of Bibliography
BBaud   Bulletin Baudelairien
BBMP   Bulletin de la Biblioteca Menéndez Pelayo
BC   Book Collector
BCLF   Bulletin Critique du Livre Français
BduB   Bulletin du Bibliophile
       Belfagor: Rassegna di Varia Umanità
       Bennington Review
       Berkshire Review (Williams College)
BF   Book Forum
BFE   Boletín de Filología Española
BGDSL   Beiträge zur Geschichte der deutschen Sprache
       und Literatur
BH   Bulletin Hispanique
BHR   Bibliothèque d'Humanisme et Renaissance
BHS   Bulletin of Hispanic Studies
       Bibliothèque de l'Ecole des Chartres
       Biblos
BIHR   Bulletin of the Institute of Historical Research
       (London)
BioC   Biologia Culturale
BIQ   Blake: An Illustrated Quarterly
BJA   British Journal of Aesthetics
BJECS   British Journal for Eighteenth Century Studies
BJHS   British Journal for the History of Science
BJRL   Bulletin of the John Rylands Library
BL   Beiträge zur Literaturkunde

	Blackwood's Magazine
BLAM	*Bulletin de la Librairie Ancienne et Moderne*
BLE	*Bulletin de Littérature Ecclesiastique*
BLR	*The Bodleian Library Record*
BM	*The Burlington Magazine*
BMMLA	*Bulletin of the Midwest MLA*
	Boletín de la Académia Argentina de Letras
	Les Bonnes Feuilles
	Boundary
BPhilos	*Bibliography of Philosophy*
BRAE	*Boletín de la Real Academia Española*
BRAH	*Boletín de la Real Academia de la Historia*
BRH	*Bulletin of Research in the Humanities*
	The British Library Journal
BRP	*Beiträge zur romanischen Philologie* (Berlin)
BSAP	*Bulletin de la Société des Amis de Marcel Proust et des Amis de Combray*
BSUF	*Ball State University Forum*
BUJ	*Boston University Journal*
	Bulletin de la Bibliothèque Nationale
	Bulletin de l'Académie Royale de Langue et de Littérature Françaises (Brussels)
	Bulletin de la Société Belge des Professeurs de Français
	Bulletin de la Société d'Histoire du Protestantisme Français
	Bulletin de la Société Jules Verne
	Bulletin de l'Association des Amis d'Alain
	Bulletin de l'Association des Amis de J.-J. Rousseau
	Bulletin de l'Association des Amis de Rabelais et de La Devinière
	Bulletin de l'Association J.-K. Huysmans
	Bulletin des Amis d'André Gide
	Bulletin des Amis de Flaubert
	Bulletin des Amis de Jules Romains
	Bulletin d'Informations Proustiennes
	Bulletin Monumental
	Bulletin of the Faculty of Literature (Kyushu University)
	Bulletin Signalétique
	Byron Journal
BYUS	*Brigham Young University Studies*
CA	*Cuadernos Americanos*
CACP	*Cahiers de l'Amitié Charles Peguy*
	Cahiers Canadien Claudel
CahiersC	*Cahiers Césairiens*
	Cahiers d'Analyse Textuelle

	Cahiers de l'Ecole Supérieure des Lettres de Beyrouth
	Cahiers des Amis de Valery Larbaud
	Cahiers d'Histoire
	Cahiers Diderotiens
	Cahiers François Mauriac
	Cahiers Internationaux du Symbolisme
	Les Cahiers Naturalistes
CahiersS	*Cahiers Staëliens*
CAIEF	*Cahiers de l'Association Internationale des Etudes Françaises*
CalSS	*California Slavic Studies*
CamR	*Cambridge Review*
CAN	*Cahiers Gérard de Nerval*
	Canadian Journal of Research in Semiotics
CB	*Cuadernos Bibliográficos*
CC	*Cultural Critique*
CE	*College English*
CentR	*Centennial Review*
CeS	*Cultura e Scuola*
CG	*Colloquia Germanica*
CH	*Crítica Hispanica*
CHA	*Cuadernos Hispanoamericanos* (Madrid)
ChLB	*Charles Lamb Bulletin*
CHR	*Catholic Historical Review*
CI	*Carte italiane. A Journal of Italian Studies*
CimR	*Cimarron Review*
CJC	*Cahiers Jean Cocteau*
CJG	*Cahiers Jean Giraudoux*
CJH	*Canadian Journal of History*
CJIS	*Canadian Journal of Italian Studies*
CL	*Comparative Literature*
CLAJ	*College Language Association Journal*
ClaudelS	*Claudel Studies*
	Clio
CLQ	*Colby Library Quarterly*
CLS	*Comparative Literature Studies*
CMen	*Cahiers Mennaisiens*
CML	*Classical and Modern Literature: A Quarterly*
CMLR	*Canadian Modern Language Review*
CollL	*College Literature*
	Colloquio (Lisbon)
	Commentary
	Commonweal
	Comparatist: Journal of the Southern Comparative Literature Association
	Comparative Criticism: A Yearbook (Cambridge)
	Comparative Literature Symposium Proceedings (Texas Tech University)

CompD	*Comparative Drama*
CompLB	*Comparative Literature Bulletin Commentary*
	Computers and the Humanities
	Computer Studies in the Humanities
	Connaissance des Arts
	The Connoisseur
	Contemporary French Civilization
	Contemporary Literature
ContR	*Contemporary Review*
Conv	*Convivium*
	Cornhill Magazine
Cos	*Costerus*
CP	*Concerning Poetry*
CPe	*Castrum Peregrini*
CQ	*Cambridge Quarterly*
CR	*Critical Review*
CRCL	*Canadian Review of Comparative Literature*
CREL	*Cahiers Romains d'Etudes Littéraires*
CritI	*Critical Inquiry*
	Criticism
	Critique: Revue Générale des Publications Françaises et Etrangères
	Critique: Studies in Modern Fiction
CritQ	*Critical Quarterly*
CrL	*Critica Letteraria*
CrS	*Critical Survey*
CSR	*Christian Scholar's Review*
	Culture Française (Bari)
	Culture Française (Paris)
Dada	*Dada/Surrealism*
	Dalhousie French Studies
	Dance Chronicle
DB	*Doitsu Bungaku: Die deutsche Literatur*
DBGU	*Deutsche Beiträge zur geistigen Überlieferung*
	Degrés
	Degré Second
	Delta
DHS	*Dix-Huitième Siècle*
	Diacritics
	Dialogue: Revue Canadienne de Philosophie
	Diderot Studies
	Dispositio
DL	*Deutsche Literatur*
DLZ	*Deutsche Literatur-Zeitung*
	Documents Stéphane Mallermé
DQR	*Dutch Quarterly Review of Anglo-American Letters*
DR	*Dalhousie Review*

DrR	*Drama Review*
DSN	*Dickens Studies Newsletter*
DSS	*XVIIe Siècle*
DU	*Deutschunterricht*
DUJ	*Durham University Journal*
DVLG	*Deutsche Vierteljahrschrift für Literatur-wissenschaft und Geistesgeschichte*
DZPhil	*Deutsche Zeitschrift für Philosophie*
EA	*Etudes Anglaises*
E&S	*Essays and Studies*
EAS	*Essays in Arts and Sciences* (University of New Haven)
ECent	*The Eighteenth Century: Theory and Interpretation*
EcHR	*Economic History Review*
ECl	*Etudes Classiques*
ECLife	*Eighteenth-Century Life* *L'Ecole des Lettres Lendemains*
ECr	*L'Esprit Créateur* (Minneapolis) *Ecrits de Paris*
ECS	*Eighteenth Century Studies*
EDH	*Essays by Divers Hand*
EdL	*Etudes de Lettres*
EG	*Etudes Germaniques*
EHR	*English Historical Review*
EIA	*Estudos Ibero-Americanos*
EiC	*Essays in Criticism* (Oxford) *Eire*
EL	*Esperienze Letterarie*
ELH	*Journal of English Literary History*
ELit	*Etudes Littéraires*
ELLF	*Etudes de Langue et Littérature Françaises* (Tokyo)
ELN	*English Language Notes*
ELWIU	*Essays in Literature* (Western Illinois University)
EM	*English Miscellany* *Encounter* *English*
EnlE	*Enlightenment Essays*
EP	*Etudes Philosophiques*
ES	*English Studies*
ESA	*English Studies in Africa* (Johannesburg)
ESC	*English Studies in Canada* *Esprit*
ESQ	*Emerson Society Quarterly*
ESR	*European Studies Review* *Essays in French Literature* *Essays in Literature*
EstF	*Estudios Filosóficos*

GQ   German Quarterly
GR   Germanic Review
      Gradiva
GRM   Germanisch-romanische Monatsschrift, Neue Folge
GSlav   Germano-Slavica
GSLI   Giornale Storico della Letteratura Italiano
GSR   German Studies Review
      Gulliver
GW   Germanica Wratislaviensia
H   History
HAHR   Hispanic American Historical Review
      Harvard English Studies
      The Hebrew University Studies in Literature
HeineJ   Heine Jahrbuch
HisJ   Hispanic Journal
      Hispania
Hispano   Hispanófila
      Historia
      The Historian
      History and Theory
      History of Religions
      Historical Methods
HJ   Historical Journal
HLB   Harvard Library Bulletin
HLQ   Huntington Library Quarterly
HöJb   Hölderlin Jahrbuch
      Horizon
HPE   The History of Political Economy
HQ   Hopkins Quarterly
HR   Hispanic Review
HSL   Hartford Studies in Literature
HT   History Today
HudR   Hudson Review
Hum   Humanities
      Humanities Association Review
      The Humanities Review (New Delhi)
I&L   Ideologies and Literature
IASL   Internationales Archiv für Sozialgeschichte der
      deutschen Literatur
Ibero   Iberoromania
IdS   Idealistic Studies
IHA   L'Information d'Histoire de l'Art
IL   L'Information Littéraire
      L'Information Historique
      International Fiction Review
      Interpretations (Memphis State University)
      Inti: Revista de Literatura Hispánica
IPQ   International Philosophical Quarterly

KuL   Kunst und Literatur
          Kunstwerk
          Das Kunstwerk
Kurbiskern Kurbiskern: Literatur und Kritik
L&H   Literature and History
L&P   Literature and Psychology
Lang&L   Language & Literature
          Language and Style
          Languages
LanM   Les Langues Modernes
          Lavoro Critico
LC   Library Chronicle (University of Pennsylvania)
LCr   Lavoro Critico
LCUT   Library Chronicle of the University of Texas
LE&W   Literature East and West
LenauA   Lenau-Almanach (Wien)
LenauF   Lenau-Forum. Vierteljahresschrift für vergleich-
          ende Literaturforschung (Wien)
          Leonardo
LetN   Lettres Nouvelles
          Letras
LHR   Lock Haven Review (Lock Haven State College, Pa.)
LI   Lettere Italiane
          Library
          The Library Quarterly
          La Licorne (Faculté des Lettres et des Langues
          de l'Université de Poitiers)
LiLi   Zeitschrift für Literaturwissenschaft und
          Linguistik
          Lingua e Stile
          Literature and Ideology
LitR   Literary Review
          Littérature
          Littératures
LJ   Library Journal
LJGG   Literaturwissenschaftliches Jahrbuch. Im
          Auftrage der Litteratur Gorres-Gesellschaft.
          N.F.
LL   Lingua e letteratura
LMFA   Literature, Music and Fine Arts
LNL   Linguistics in Literature
LR   Les Lettres Romanes
LSoc   Language in Society
LuK   Literatur und Kritik
          Lumière et Vie
LWU   Literatur in Wissenschaft und Unterricht
LY   Lessing Yearbook
MA   Le Moyen Age

M&L   Music and Letters (London)
           Marche Romane
           Master Drawings
MC   Misure Critiche
McNR   McNeese Review (McNeese State University,
           Louisiana)
MD   Modern Drama
Merkur   Merkur: Deutsche Zeitschrift für europäisches
           Denken
MFS   Modern Fiction Studies
MGS   Michigan Germanic Studies
MHG   Mitteilungen der E.T.A. Hoffmann-Gesellschaft
MichA   Michigan Academician
MidH   Midlands History
MiltonQ   Milton Quarterly
           Mime, Mask, and Marionette: A Quarterly Journal
           of Performing Arts
           Minerva
MinnR   Minnesota Review
MissQ   Mississippi Quarterly
ML   Modern Languages (London)
MLJ   Modern Language Journal
MLN   Modern Language Notes
MLQ   Modern Language Quarterly
MLR   Modern Language Review
MLS   Modern Language Studies
MMM   Mélanges Malraux Miscellany
           Modern Age
           Modern Australian Literature
Monatshefte Monatshefte: A Journal Devoted to the Study of
           Germanic Language and Literature
           Mosaic
MP   Modern Philogy
MQ   Midwest Quarterly (Pittsburg, Kansas)
MQR   Michigan Quarterly Review
MR   Massachusetts Review
MSE   Massachusetts Studies in English
MSpr   Moderna Språk
MuK   Maske und Kothurn
           Mundus Artium
MusQ   Musical Quarterly
MV   Minority Voices: An Interdisciplinary Journal
           of Literature and the Arts
NA   Nuova Antologia
           Names
N&Q   Notes & Queries
NARG   Nuovi Argumenti
NCF   Nineteenth Century Fiction

PS   *Prose Studies*
PSch   *Prairie Schooner*
        Présence de George Sand
        Psychoanalytic Review
PTL   *PTL: A Journal for Descriptive Poetics and Theory*
        Publications de l'Institut de France, Paris
        Publications of the Center for Baudelaire Studies
PULC   *Princeton University Library Chronicle*
QI   *Quaderni d'Italianistica*
QJI   *Quarterly Journal of Ideology*
QJS   *Quarterly Journal of Speech*
QL   *La Quinzaine Littéraire*
QQ   *Queen's Quarterly*
        Quaderni Francesi
RA   *Revue d'Allemagne*
RABM   *Revista de Archivos, Bibliotecas y Museos*
RANAM   *Recherches Anglaises et Américaines*
        Rapports
RBPH   *Revue Belge de Philologie et d'Histoire*
RC   *Le Ragioni Critiche*
RCEH   *Revista Canadiense de Estudios Hispánicos*
RCSF   *Rivista Critica della Storia della Filosofia*
RDM   *Revue des Deux Mondes*
RdS   *Revue de Synthèse*
RE   *Revue d'Esthétique*
        Réalités
        Recherches de Sciences Religieuses
RecL   *Recovering Literature*
REE   *Revista de Estudios Extremenos*
REG   *Revue des Etudes Grecques*
REH   *Revista de Estudios Hispanicos*
REI   *Revue des Etudes Italiennes*
REL   *Review of English Literature* (Leeds)
        représentations
RES   *Review of English Studies*
Restoration *Restoration: Studies in English Literary Culture,*
            1600-1700
RevEH   *Revue d'Histoire Ecclésiastique*
        Review
        Reviews in European History
RevR   *Revue Romane*
        Revue Belge de Musicologie
        Revue de la Bibliothèque Nationale
        Revue de l'Art
        Revue de l'Histoire des Religions
        Revue de Louisiane (Louisiana Review)
        Revue de l'Université de Bruxelles
        Revue de Metaphysique et de Morale

Revue des Etudes Juives
Revue des Etudes Slaves
Revue des Sciences Religieuses
Revue d'Esthétique
Revue de Théologie et de Philosophie
Revue d'Histoire et de Philosophie Religieuses
Revue d'Histoire Moderne et Contemporaine
Revue du Louvre et des Musées de France
Revue du Monde Russe et Soviétique
Revue du Pacifique
Revue Française de Psychanalyse
Revue Française d'Histoire de Livre
RF   Romanische Forschungen
RFE   Revista de Filologia Española
RFNS   Revista di Filosophia Neo-Scolastica
RG   Revue Générale
RGer   Recherches Germaniques
RH   Revue Historique
RHEF   Revue d'Histoire de l'Eglise de France
RHL   Revue d'Histoire Littéraire de la France
RHM   Revista Hispánica Moderna
RHT   Revue d'Histoire du Théâtre
RHV   Revue Historique Vaudoise
RI   Revista Iberoamericana
RIE   Revista de Ideas Estéticas
RiLI   Rivista di Letteratura Italiana
        Rimbaud Vivant
RJ   Romanistisches Jahrbuch
RL   Revista de Literatura
R&L   Religion and Literature
RLC   Revue de Littérature Comparée
RLI   Rassegna della Letteratura Italiana
RLM   Revue des Lettres Modernes
RLMC   Rivista di Letterature Moderne e Comparate
        (Firenze)
RLR   Revue des Langues Romanes
RLSt   Rackham Literary Studies
RLV   Revue des Langues Vivantes
RMM   Revue de Métaphysique et de Morale
RMus   Revue de Musicologie
RNL   Review of National Literatures
RO   Revista de Occidente
        Romania
        Romanica Wratislaviensis
        Romanistische Zeitschrift für Literaturgeschichte/
           Cahiers d'Histoire des Littératures Romanes
        Romantisme
RomN   Romance Notes (University of North Carolina)

Studies in Browning
Studies in the Humanities
Style
STTH Science/Technology and the Humanities
STZ Sprache im technischen Zeitalter
Sub-stance: A Review of Theory and Literary
Criticism
SuF Sinn und Form
Sur
SVEC Studies in Voltaire and the Eighteenth Century
SWJP Southwestern Journal of Philosophy
SWR Southwest Review
Symposium
SZ Stimmen der Zeit: Monatsschrift der Gegenwart
TAH The American Hispanist
TAPS Transactions of the American Philosophical Society
TCBS Transactions of the Cambridge Bibliographical
Society
TDR The Drama Review
Tel Quel
Testo
Text
Thalia: Studies in Literary Humor
Theater Heute
Theatre Quarterly
Thought: A Review of Culture and Idea
ThR Theatre Research
ThS Theatre Survey
TJ Theatre Journal
TLL Travaux de Linguistique et de Littérature
(University of Strasbourg)
TLS Times Literary Supplement (London)
TM Les Temps Modernes
TN Theatre Notebook
Topic: A Journal of the Liberal Arts (Washington,
Pa.)
TR Table Ronde
Travail Théâtral
TRI Theatre Research International
Tropos
TSE Tulane Studies in English
TSL Tennessee Studies in Literature
TSLL Texas Studies in Literature and Language
TuK Text und Kritik
TWC The Wordsworth Circle
UDR University of Dayton Review
UKPHS University of Kansas Humanistic Studies
UMSE University of Mississippi Studies in English

Unisa   Unisa English Studies
Univ   Universitas: Zeitschrift für Wissenschaft, Kunst
            und Literatur
            University of North Carolina Studies in Romantic
            Languages and Literatures
UQ   Universities Quarterly
UR   University Review (Kansas City, Missouri)
UTQ   University of Toronto Quarterly
UWR   University of Windsor Review
            Vestnik, Seria 10, Filologia (University of
            Moscow)
            Viertelsjahrhefte für Zeitgeschichte
VLang   Visible Language
VN   Victorian Newsletter
VP   Victorian Poetry
VQR   Virginia Quarterly Review
VS   Victorian Studies
WasacanaR   Wasacana Review (University of Regina, Canada)
WB   Weimarer Beiträge
WCR   West Coast Review
            Westerly: A Quarterly Review
            Westermanns Monatshefte
WCWR   William Carlos Williams Review
WHR   Western Humanities Review
W&L   Women and Literature
WLT   World Literature Today
WMQ   William and Mary Quarterly
            The World of Music
WS   Women's Studies
WuW   Welt und Wort
WVUPP   West Virginia University Philological Papers
WW   Wirkendes Wort
WZPHP   Wissenschaftliche Zeitschrift der Pädogogischen
            Hochschule Potsdam
WZUB   Wissenschaftliche Zeitschrift der Humbolt-
            Universität zu Berlin
WZUH   Wissenschaftliche Zeitschrift der Martin-Luther-
            Universität Halle-Wittenberg
WZUJ   Wissenschaftliche Zeitschrift der Friedrich-
            Schiller-Universität Jena
WZUL   Wissenschaftliche Zeitschrift der Karl-Marx-
            Universität Leipzig
YCGL   Yearbook of Comparative and General Literature
YES   Yearbook of English Studies
YFS   Yale French Studies
YR   Yale Review
YULG   Yale University Library Gazette
YWMLS   Year's Work in Modern Langauge Studies

THE ROMANTIC MOVEMENT

GENERAL

(Compiled by David V. Erdman with the assistance of Thomas
L. Ashton, Irene H. Chayes, Janice Haney-Peritz, Bishop C.
Hunt, Frank Jordan, Robert R. Mollenauer, Augustus Pallotta,
James S. Patty, Jeffrey C. Robinson, Robert M. Ryan, and
Mark T. Smith)

1. BIBLIOGRAPHY

See the respective "Bibliography" and "General" sections for
each language, below. *The Romantic Movement Bibliography* has
been published in its present form beginning with the *Bibliography* for 1979, in 1980. For previous years, see the "Bibliography of the Romantic Movement" in *English Language Notes* (*ELN*),
September supplements, 1965-1979. In 1973 a cumulative reprint
since 1936 was published in seven volumes by the Pierian Press
and R.R. Bowker, New York. For the most extensive general listing, in all languages, without commentary, see the annual *MLA
International Bibliography*, vols. 1 and 2.

Floyd, Phylis. "Documentary Evidence for the Availability of
    Japanese Imagery in Europe in Nineteenth-Centry Public Collec-
    tions." *ArtB* 68 (1986): 105-41.

    The earliest recorded acquisition by the Bibliothèque
Nationale is 1795; "Japanese prints were available in Europe
at least as early as the second quarter of the nineteenth
centry, despite Japan's seclusion from the West for over two
centuries" (126). Contains an appendix of "Japanese Art in
Public Collections in Paris" and a bibliography on "japonisme."

Harris, Laurie Lanzen, and Cherie D. Abbey, eds. (Jelena
    Obradovic Kronick and Janet Mullane, assoc. eds.). *Nineteenth-
    Century Literature Criticism: Excerpts from Criticism of the
    Works of Novelists, Poets, Playwrights, Short Story Writers,
    Philosophers, and Other Creative Writers Who Died Between
    1800 and 1900, from the First Published Critical Appraisals
    to Current Evaluations*, vols. 11, 12, 13. (Vol. 13 ed.

Cherie D. Abbey, with the same associates.) Detroit: Gale
Research, 1986. Pp. 557, 576, 531. $90.00 each.

(For other vols. see *RMB* for 1982, 1983, 1984, and 1985.)
Volume 11 includes Fredrika Bremer, Alexandre Dumas (père),
Klopstock, Lamartine, M.G. Lewis, Mill, and two others.
Volume 12 includes Byron (pp. 82) and Wordsworth (pp. 97),
as well as Fanny Burney, Herman Melville, and four others.
Volume 13 includes Austen (pp. 62), Blake (pp. 105), Novalis,
and five others.
Volume 14, dated 1987 (pp. 559; $90.00), includes Godwin,
Landor, Mary Shelley, and six others.
These are wonderful "libraries" of well-chosen quotations,
from the author's lifetime to the 1980s--with a critical
list of "additional bibliography." (D.V.E.)

Hubin, Allen J. *Crime Fiction, 1794-1980: A Comprehensive
Bibliography*. New York: Garland Publishing, 1984. Pp.
xix+712. $75.00.

Rev. by B.C. Bloomfield in *L*, 6th series, 8 (1986): 96-98.
Revised and enlarged edition of the 1979 work.

The MLA International Bibliography. New York: Modern Language
Association.

The *Bibliography* for 1986 is published in the fall of 1987.
Volume 1, *British Isles, British Commonwealth, New Zealand,
and American Literatures* (including Caribbean in English).
Prepublication $25.00, members' regular price $144.00.
Volume 2 (two-book set), *European, Asian, African, and
South American Literatures* (including Latin American and
Caribbean in French). Prepublication $25.00, regular $168.00.
Volume 4, *General Literature and Related Topics*. Prepublica-
tion $10.00, regular $72.00.
Volume 5, *Folklore*. Prepublication $10.00, regular $72.00.

2. ENVIRONMENT: ART, PHILOSOPHY, POLITICS, RELIGION, SOCIETY

Anderson, Wilma C. *Between the Library and the Laboratory:
The Language of Chemistry in Eighteenth-Century France*.
Johns Hopkins University Press, 1984. Pp. vii+190.

Rev. by Maurice Crosland in *JMH* 58 (1986): 730-31.

Berman, David. "The Jacobitism of Berkeley's *Passive Obedience*."
JHI 47 (1986): 309-19.

A useful reminder of what political philosophy meant in Wordsworth's youth. (T.L.A.)

Bertaud, Jean-Paul. "Napoleon's Officers." *P&P* 112 (1986): 91-111.

"The corps of officers was to be not only a melting pot for the elites but also a training school for pedagogues whose task would consist in passing on to all the French people the notion of *honour* taught in the camps."

Blum, Carol. *Rousseau and the Republic of Virtue: The Language of Politics in the French Revolution.* Cornell University Press, 1986. Pp. 302. $24.95.

Professor Blum attempts--successfully, one should hope--to rescue modern historiography from exclusive focus on political, social, and economic concerns and revive attention to the original texts of the French Revolution, in particular those of the Jacobins, which "were apt to invoke virtue and Jean-Jacques Rousseau" (27).
The most difficult concept for modern scholars to accept is Robespierre's association of "virtue" with "terror"! And perhaps only a complete reading of this book, as it shifts focus from Rousseau to his disciple Robespierre, will convince historians--as it has the present reviewer--that the architect of the Committee of Public Safety meant what he said when he announced that the Republic was founded on two principles, "virtue, and its emanation, terror," that "virtue without terror is impotent," and "terror without virtue is malignant." And that he was talking abut Rousseauean "virtue," as it functioned in a "popular government in revolution" (30, 259).
What immediately clouded the issue was that, soon after Thermidor, "Rousseau's virtue was wrenched away from associations with Rousseau and Saint-Just" and altered in significance by surviving cults (278). "In the years that followed, however, before Bonaparte set his foot firmly on the nation's neck, an occasional echo of the old dream was sounded" (281). (D.V.E.)

Bossenga, Gail. "From *Corps* to Citizenship: The *Bureaux des Finances* Before the French Revolution." *JMH* 58 (1986): 610-42.

Exposing the disenchantment of the privileged *corps* with the monarchy. (T.L.A.)

Cate, Curtis. *The War of the Two Emperors: The Duel Between Napoleon and Alexander of Russia, 1812.* New York: Random House, 1986. $24.95.

Rev. favorably in *NY*, March 3, 1986, pp. 106-07.
Not seen.

Cohen, I. Bernard. *Revolution in Science.* Harvard University
Press, 1985. Pp. xx+711. $25.00.

Rev. by James R. Hoffman in *QQ* 93 (1986):   443-46.
A superb historical investigation of how the descriptive
terms *revolution* and *revolutionary* were attributed to scientific developments in the past four centuries.   (T.L.A.)

Connor, Patrick.   "For Western Eyes Only: Chinese 'Export'
Painting 1780-1850."   *Apollo* 123 (1986):   325-31.

Conser, Walter H., ed.   "James Marsh and the Germans."   *NEQ* 59
(1986):   259-66.

Prints from the holograph, September 4, 1830, to the
German philosopher F.A.G. Tholuck, with reference to Coleridge's
Aids to Reflection.   (T.L.A.)

Crafts, N.F.R.   *British Economic Growth During the Industrial
Revolution* (i.e., 1700-1850).   Oxford University Press,
1986.   Paper $11.95.

Hardcover reviewed in *RMB* for 1985, p. 46.

Dahlhaus, Carl.   *Realism in Nineteenth-Century Music.*   Trans.
Mary Whittall.   Cambridge University Press, 1985.   Pp. 160.
$29.95.

Rev. by Roger Hollinrake in *M&L* 67 (1986):   212-13.

de Groer, Léo.   *Les arts décoratifs de 1790 à 1850.*   Paris:
Editions du Chêne, 1986.   Pp. 348; illus.

A survey of the decorative arts in France, England, Germany,
Italy, and Russia.

Dix, Robin.   "Addison and the Concept of 'Novelty' as a Basic
Aesthetic Category."   *BJA* 26 (1986):   383-90.

Background for the Romantic concept of originality.

Drescher, Seymour.   *Capitalism and Antislavery: British
Mobilization in Comparative Perspective.*   (Anstey Memorial
Lectures, 1984.)   London: Macmillan, 1987.   Pp. 300.   £29.50

"Les Droits de l'Homme."   *EP* no. 2 (April-June 1986).

Entire issue devoted to the concept of the "Rights of Man"
in its historical context and modern significance.

Eighteenth-Century Life n.s. 9, no. 3 (May 1985).

Edited by Robert P. Maccubbin, this special issue on
"Unauthorized Sexual Behavior During the Englightenment"
includes eighteen essays, many of which acknowledge a debt
to the work of Foucault. Indeed, seven of the essays focus
not on sexual behavior but on sexual discourse: Roy Porter
analyzes *Aristotle's Master-Piece*, a primer on sex which
"went through over twenty editions in the eighteenth century
and far more in the nineteenth"; David Coward explores the
erotic fantasies of Restif de la Bretonne; Peter Sabor compares
Cleland's *Memoirs of Fanny Hill* to its unexpurgated original;
Robert Ellrich discusses the veiling and unveiling of sexual
reference in French fiction; and Paul-Gabriel Bouce, Robert
Dawson, and Armando Marchi consider the discourse of erotica
and pornography in England, France, and Italy respectively.
Sodomy and the emergence of a male homosexual subculture
and identity are at issue in five essays, many of which note
that prosecutions for sodomy increased in the eighteenth century. In an especially noteworthy essay, Trumbach links the
development of a male homosexual identity to the new rigidity
in gender distinctions, a linking that should interest feminists.
Although Michael Rey's account of the life-style of Parisian
homosexuals includes some remarks on the class politics of
homosexuality, Vern Bullough, Jean-Pierre Guicciardi, and John
Gillis take the politics of sexuality as their main concern.
Besides documenting the social recognition of prostitution
as an economic necessity, Bullough recounts some eighteenth-
century proposals for reform, while Guicciardi relates the
demise of sovereignty suffered by Louis XVI to the sexual
transgressions of Louis XV. In what may well be the collection's most important essay, Gillis not only critiques
Lawrence Stone's evolutionary model of social change but also
makes a convincing argument that "groups just below the master
artisan and independent smallholder class were developing modes
of marriage and family life suited to the unprecedented conditions of early industrialization." In so doing, these groups
"challenged prescriptions of affective individualism ...
with a different set of moral imperatives that emphasize the
value of love and commitment in and out of marriage and
recognize the necessity of parenting and family arrangements
beyond the nuclear family." Finally, the collection also
includes three essays that set sexuality within the context
of such ideologies as libertinism, scientific materialism,
and enlightened humanism. Taken as a whole or in parts, this
collection is a valuable source of information, much of which
is relevant to an understanding of Romanticism. (J.H-P.)

Erdman, David V. *Commerce des Lumières: John Oswald and the British in Paris, 1790-1793.* University of Missouri Press, 1986. Pp. 338. $39.00.

An informative and disturbing study of the life and works of John Oswald. Based on information gleaned from extensive archival research, Erdman composes quite a full account of this Scotsman turned revolutionary, an account usefully punctuated with four "interchapters" of contextual data. From Edinburgh, Erdman follows Oswald as he becomes, in turn, a British "bloodyback" in India, a Grub Street writer in London, and a militant member of the Cercle Social, the Jabobin Club, and the British Club in Paris. Along the way, Erdman debunks a number of traditional historical interpretations, including the notion that the September Massacres made it impossible for "honest British citizens" to support the French Revolution. In November of 1792, members of the British Club in Paris celebrated and publicly toasted the French Republic, the destruction of tyrants, the National Convention, and "the coming convention of England and Ireland." Oswald, however, went further; he repeatedly urged the French to send a 60,000-member battalion to assist the British in their attempts at liberation, a proposal that Erdman considers in the context of Pitt's disinformation campaign.

Oswald and his battalion never reached England; instead, they were sent to the Vendee to put down a local rebellion against conscription and other Parisian dictates. There, in 1793, Oswald died on the battlefield. Although Erdman notes the contradiction between Oswald's "mission" in the Vendee and his "belief in direct democracy and an armed populace," he does not dwell on it, in part because his study is not intended to be "an evaluation of [Oswald's] personality and philosophy." However, by demonstrating Oswald's participation in a discursive ideology of Truth, Universality, and absolute sovereignty, and by linking this "enlightened" ideology to the practice of "philosophic war," Erdman not only provokes the reader's interest in the relation of (Oswald's) means to (Oswald's) end but also makes an informed evaluation of Oswald's kind of revolutionary discourse and practice much more possible. Historically considered, Oswald may be a minor character; but the issues his life and work raise are major ones for those of us disturbed by the fact that "philosophic war" and the arms market continue to flourish. (J.H-P.)

Finson, Jon W., and R. Larry Todd. *Mendelssohn and Schumann: Essays on Their Music and Its Context.* Duke University Press, 1984. Pp. 300. $32.50.

Rev. by Clive Brown in *M&L* 67 (1986):   179-80 as "an informative and stimulating addition to the literature." Of particular interest are two articles on literary influences, linking Mendelssohn with Ossian and Schumann with Shakespeare.

Frevert, Ute. *Krankheit als Politisches Problem, 1770-1880.* Gottingen: Vandenhoeck & Ruprecht, 1984. Pp. 469.

Rev. by Johnathan Sperber in *JMH* 58 (1986):   756-58. Giving the history of medical policy and some useful lessons. (T.L.A.)

Fuchs, Rachel. *Abandoned Children: Foundlings and Child Welfare in Nineteenth-Century France.* State University of New York Press, 1985. Pp. xvii+357.

Rev. by Bonnie G. Smith in *JMH* 58 (1986):   325-26.

Garrioch, David. *Neighbourhood and Community in Paris, 1740-1790.* Cambridge University Press, 1986. Pp. 290. $44.50.

Communities remained strong. Not seen.

Garrioch, David, and Michael Sonenscher. "*Compagnonnages*, Confraternities and Associations of Journeymen in Eighteenth-Century Paris." *EHQ* 16 (1986):   25-45.

"In eighteenth-century Paris, journeymen belonged to trade-based confraternities rather than to the *compagnonnages*." Unlike the *campagnonnages*, confraternities "were attached to a particular church and locality."

Geison, Gerald, ed. *Professions and the French State, 1700-1900.* University of Pennsylvania Press, 1984. Pp. x+319.

Rev. by Robert A. Nye in *JMH* 58 (1986):   323-24.

Giacometti, Massimo, ed. *The Sistine Chapel: Michelangelo Rediscovered.* London: Muller, Blond and White, 1986. Pp. 271; illus. £40.00.

Rev. by Charles Hope in *TLS*, Dec. 15, 1986, p. 1399, as a presentation of the restored decorations which reveal a Michelangelo we never knew, "a brilliant and very distinctive colourist." One wonders how much closer to their original state were these paintings in the days of Flaxman and Romney, when Blake's work was being compared to Michelangelo's. (D.V.E.)

Gilmore, Michael T. *American Romanticism and the Marketplace.*
University of Chicago Press, 1985. Pp. ix+177. $19.95.

  Rev. as "extremely interesting and important" by Nina Baym
  in *JEGP* 85 (1986): 600-02.

Gough, Hugh. "The Provincial Jacobin Club Press During the
French Revolution." *EHQ* 16 (1986): 47-76.

Gracyk, Theodore A. "Kant's Shifting Debt to British Aesthetics." *BJA* 26 (1986): 204-17.

Gracyk, Theodore A. "Sublimity, Ugliness, and Formlessness
in Kant's Aesthetic Theory." *JAAC* 45 (1986): 49-56.

Gray, Marion W. "Prussia in Transition: Society and Politics
Under the Stein Reform Ministry of 1808." *TAPS* 76, part 1
(1986). (Entire issue with index and bibliography.)

Grew, Raymond. "Picturing the People: Images of the Lower
Orders in Nineteenth-Century French Art." *JIH* 17 (1986),
203-31. Illus.

  Superbly written and supplemented with telling illustrations,
this essay argues that French artists of the nineteenth
century by and large refused to depict the lower classes in
their social relations. Important. (J.C.R.)

Grieder, Josephine. *Anglomania in France, 1740-1789: Fact,
Fiction and Political Discourse.* (Histoire des Idées et
Critique Littéraire, 230.) Geneva and Paris: Droz, 1985.
Pp. xii+177.

  Rev. by Malcolm Cook in *JES* 16 (1986): 143-44.

Grubb, James S. "When Myths Lose Power: Four Decades of
Venetian Historiography." *JMH* 58 (1986): 43-94.

Guest, Ivor. *Jules Perrot: Master of the Romantic Ballet.*
New York: Princeton Book Company, 1984. Pp. 383. $37.50.

  Rev. negatively by Susan Allene Manning in *ThS* 26 (1985):
205-07.

Hanson, Alice. *Musical Life in Biedermeier Vienna.* (Cambridge
Studies in Music.) Cambridge University Press, 1985. Pp.
256. $39.50.

  Rev. with faint praise by Peter Branscombe in *M&L* 67
(1986): 209-10.
  Examines the period between 1815 and 1848.

Hartle, Ann. *The Modern Self in Rousseau's Confessions, A Reply to St. Augustine.* (Revisions: A Series of Books on Ethics.) Notre Dame University Press, 1983. Pp. xiii+186. $19.95.

Rev. by Ronald Grimsley in *JHP* 23 (1985): 592–93.

Hohenberg, Paul M., and Lynn Hollen Lees. *The Making of Urban Europe, 1000–1950.* Harvard University Press, 1986. Pp. 368. $30.00.

Not received.

Hunt, Lynn, and George Sheridan. "Corporation, Association, and the Language of Labor in France, 1750–1850." *JMH* 58 (1986): 813–44.

Kennedy, Ellen, and Susan Mendus, eds. *Women in Western Political Philosophy: Kant to Nietzsche.* Brighton, England: Wheatsheaf, 1987. Pp. 215. £22.50, paper £9.95.

Not received.

Korshak, Yvonne. "*Paris and Helen* by Jacques Louis David: Choice and Judgment on the Eve of the French Revolution." *ArtB* 69 (1987): 102–16. 26 illus.

"As events unfolded, *Paris and Helen*, a painting about choice motivated by amoral attitudes and private indulgence, developed as a pendant to *Brutus*, a painting about choice motivated by moral and public concerns." An impressively successful scrutiny of the minute particulars that reveal "the complexity and depth of David's understanding of issues on the eve of the Revolution, a complexity that was to vanish ... once the Revolution began." (D.V.E.)

Krukowski, Lucian. "Hegel, 'Progress,' and the Avant-Garde." *JAAC* 44 (1986): 279–90.

Lesch, John E. *Science and Medicine in France: The Emergence of Experimental Physiology, 1790–1855.* Harvard University Press, 1984. Pp. ix+276.

Rev. by Toby Gelfand in *JMH* 58 (1986): 557–58; see also *RMB* for 1984, p. 20, under Porter.

Light, Fred, and David Finn. *Canova.* New York: Abbeville Press, 1983. Pp. 280; 312 illus., 32 color pls. $85.00.

Reviewed approvingly by Suzanne G. Lindsay in *ArtB* 68 (1986): 340–43 as "the first monograph in English on one of the foremost figures of Neoclassicism" (1757–1827).

Lindsay, Suzanne G. "Emblematic Aspects of Fuseli's Artist
in Despair." *ArtB* 68 (1986): 482-83.

   Sees the huge foot that the artist in the painting is lean-
ing on (reproduced on the dust-jacket of Bate's *The Burden of
the Past*, for example) as a rather heavy-handed (!) pun on
Fuseli's name, which means Little-Foot in Swiss-German
(Füssli).

Lossky, Boris. "Consécration internationale de l'art de Giacomo
Quarenghi." *GBA* 108 (July-Aug. 1986): 221-24. 5 illus.

   On the Italian classical architect who worked in Russia,
1780-1817.

Lovejoy, David S. *Religious Enthusiasm in the New World:
Heresy to Revolution*. Harvard University Press, 1985. Pp.
viii+291. $25.00.

   Rev. by Norman Pettit in *NEQ* 59 (1986): 277-80; rev. by
James Tanis in *PMHB* 110 (1986): 185-86.

MacDonald, Mary Lou. "The Natural World in Early Nineteenth-
Century Canadian Literature." *CL* 111 (1986): 48-65.

Markoff, John. "Literacy and Revolt: Some Empirical Notes
on 1789 in France." *AJS* 92 (1986): 323-49.

   "This study explores the relationship between levels of
literacy in rural France toward the end of the 18th century
and the extent and nature of peasant mobilization at the
beginning of the French Revolution."

Mathews, Richard K. *The Radical Politics of Thomas Jefferson:
A Revisionist View*. University Press of Kansas Press, 1986.
Pp. ix+171. $22.50.

   Rev. by Frank Shuffleton in *ECS* 20 (1986-87): 265-66.

Matthews, Denis. *Beethoven*. (Master Musicians.) London:
Dent; Totowa, N.J.: Littlefield, Adams, 1985. Pp. 288.
$25.00.

   Rev. by Julian Rushton in *M&L* 67 (1986): 419-21 as "an
engagingly written, uncontroversial account of the life and
works."

Mayr, Otto. *Authority, Liberty and Automatic Machinery in
Early Modern Europe*. (Studies in the History of Technology.)
The Johns Hopkins University Press, 1986. Pp. xviii+265.
$30.00.

Part 1, "Authoritarian Systems," pursues the rise of the
clock metaphor, from late-Gothic beginnings to the mechanical
philosophy of a clockwork universe, and finally the "rejection
of the clock metaphor in the name of liberty." Part 2,
"Liberal Systems," examines the imagery of balance and
equilibrium in politics and economics, into the realm of
the self-regulating mechanisms of practical technology as
the base of liberty conceptions. Thirty illustrations, both
symbolic and mechanical.

Melton, James Van Horn. "From Image to Word: Cultural Reform
and the Rise of Literate Culture in Eighteenth-Century
Austria." *JMH* 58 (1986): 95-124.

Ménétra, Jacques-Louis. *Journal of My Life.* Trans. Arthur
Goldhammer. Columbia University Press, 1986. Pp. 368.
$30.00.

Rev. by Victor Brombert ("Before the Deluge") in *NR*, Jan.
26, 1987.
Record of his life and times by an eighteenth-century French
glazier, covering the period from before the Revolution to the
end of the Directory. (See also "French 1. General.")

Mokyr, Joel. *Why Ireland Starved: A Quantitative and Analytical
History of the Irish Economy, 1800-1850.* London and Win-
chester, Mass.: Allen and Unwin, 1983. Pp. xi+330. £7.95;
$29.95.

Neustadt, Richard E., and Ernest R. May. *Thinking in Time:
The Uses of History for Decision-Makers.* New York: Free
Press, 1986. $19.95.

Rev. by Paul Kennedy in *The Atlantic* 248 (July 1986): 76-
78.
Not received.

Nicolson, Nigel. *Napoleon 1812.* New York: Harper and Row,
1985. $16.95.

Rev. favorably in *NY*, Jan. 27, 1986, p. 98.
Not seen.

Olausson, Magnus. "The *Désert de Retz* and King Gustavus of
Sweden." *GBA* 107 (May-June 1986): 181-90. 16 illus.

Drawings of the famous eighteenth-century French landscape
garden and plans for a *maison de plaisance* at the new Haga
Palace in Sweden.

Olsen, J.M.   "Representations of Pope Pius VII: The First
Risorgimento Hero."   *ArtB* 68 (1986):   77-93.

> Artists examined include David, Wilkie, Lawrence, Canova,
> and others.

Osborne, Charles.   *Schubert and His Vienna*.   London: Weidenfeld and Nicolson; New York: Knopf, 1985.   Pp. xii+209.
$18.95.

> Rev. with reservations by Alice M. Hanson in *M&L* 67 (1986):
> 396.

Ostwald, Peter F.   *Schumann: Music and Madness* (American title:
Schumann: The Inner Voices).   London: Gollancz; New
England University Press, 1985.   Pp. 390. $28.00.

> Rev. in *M&L* 67 (1986):   207-09 by Ronald Taylor, who finds
> the psychoanalytic study "a fascinating, infuriating and ul-
> timately self-destructive book."

Paley, Morton D.   *The Apocalyptic Sublime*.   Yale University
Press, 1986.   Pp. xii+196; 92 illus., 7 col. $35.00.

> Rev. by John Gage in *TLS*, Feb. 27, 1987, p. 211 as a lec-
> ture on Blake "which has now gathered up West, P.J. de
> Loutherbourg, Turner, and Martin" (and others); and "seeks
> to enrol Edmund Burke as the fountainhead of the Apocalyptic
> Sublime, although his *Philosophical Enquiry* showed no interest
> in the Apocalypse at all."
> Mortimer's *Death on a Pale Horse* initiates the apocalyptic
> sublime, while Poussin's *Deluge* is the forerunner of the
> apocalyptic sublime.   Paley keeps his definitions rather loose
> throughout the book so that he can include not only the
> Apocalypse and the flood but also Belshazzar's Feast (John
> Martin's version of which receives the only double-page
> spread), shipwrecks, plagues, and John the Baptist.   Although
> the commentary remains thin, it glimmers with fascinating
> facts, and the total effect of the plates is sublime.
> (M.T.S.)

Parissien, Steven.   "Thomas Jefferson and English Palladianism."
Apollo 124 (1986):   366-68.

Petschauer, Peter.   "Christina Dorothea Leporin (Erxleben),
Sophia (Gutermann) von La Roche, and Angelika Kauffmann:
Background and Dilemmas of Independence."   *SECC* 15 (1986):
127-43.

Platt, Robert. "Aesthetic Crisis and Artwork." *JAAC* 44
(1986): 339-49.

Some reference to Keats's "Urn." (T.L.A.)

PMHB 110 (1986): 1-109.

A richly illustrated single number devoted to the American
painter Rembrandt Peale (1778-1860), who traveled to England
(1808-10, 1830), and was instrumental in shaping the Anglo-
American style in portraiture. Contents: Carol E. Hevner,
"Rembrandt Peale's Life in Art" (1-31); Lillian B. Miller,
"In the Shadow of His Father: Rembrandt Peale, Charles
Willson Peale, and the American Portrait Tradition" (33-70);
Lois Marie Fink, "Rembrandt Peale in Paris" (71-90); Paul J.
Staiti, "Rembrandt Peale on Art" (91-109); plus a Peale
chronology and notes. (T.L.A.)

Pocock, J.G.A. *Virtue, Commerce, and History: Essays on
Political Thought and History, Chiefly in Eighteenth Century.*
Cambridge University Press, 1985. Pp. 321. $39.50, paper
$12.95.

Rev. by Keith Thomas ("Politics as Language") in *NYRB*,
Feb. 27, 1986, pp. 36-39.

Porter, Roy, and Mikulas Teich, eds., *Revolution in History.*
Cambridge University Press, 1986. Pp. 351. £25.00, paper
£3.95.

Not received.

Ravenswaay, Charles Van. *Drawn from Nature: The Botanical
Art of Joseph Prestele and His Sons.* Washington, D.C.:
Smithsonian Institution Press, 1984.

Rev. by Nicolas Powell in *Apollo* 123 (1986): 64.

Reich, Nancy B. *Clara Schumann: The Artist and the Woman.*
London: Gollancz; Cornell University Press, 1985. Pp. 384.
$25.00.

Rev. by Alan Walker in *M&L* 67 (1986): 409-10: "No one
who is interested in the music of the nineteenth century can
afford to overlook it."

Reinhardt, Steven. "The Selective Prosecution of Crime in
Ancien Régime France: Theft in the Sénéchaussée of Sarlat."
EHQ 16 (1986): 3-24.

"Royal justice on the eve of the French Revolution was
not the imperialistic institution of the previous century.
Instead, it had reached a modus vivendi in which royal,
seigneurial and popular justice combined to meet the varied
needs of the populace for the redress of grievances."

Representations 14 (Spring 1986).

A special issue on "Sexuality and the Social Body in the
Nineteenth Century," edited by Catherine Gallagher and
Thomas Laqueur. Of the eight essays in this issue, three
are of interest to Romanticists. In "Orgasm, Generation
and the Politics of Reproductive Biology," Laqueur examines
"the radical eighteenth-century reconstruction of female,
and more generally human, sexuality in relation to the equally
radical Enlightenment political reconstruction of 'Man'"; he
finds that "an anatomy and physiology of incommensurability
replaced a metaphysics of hierarchy in the representation
of women in relation to men," a finding evidenced by reference
to Rousseau, More, and Wollstonecraft as well as to medical
discourse. In a similar vein, Londa Schiebinger argues that
drawings of specifically female skeletons first appeared in
the late eighteenth century as part of a politically inspired
effort to give gender distinctions a scientific basis.
Finally, in "The Body Versus the Social Body in the Works of
Thomas Malthus and Henry Mayhew," Catherine Gallagher claims
that Malthus "destroyed the homological relationship between
individual and social organisms by tracing social problems to
human vitality itself." In so doing, he helped engender "the
division of the social organism into valuable (weak but productive) and problematic (strong but unproductive) bodies,"
a division that lies at the heart of Mayhew's remarks on
costermongers in *London Labour and the London Poor*.

Rigotti, Francesca. "Biology and Society in the Age of Enlightenment." *JHI* 47 (1986): 215-33.

Robson, David W. *Educating Republicans: The College in the
Era of the American Revolution, 1750-1800.* Westport, Conn.:
Greenwood Press, 1985. Pp. xvi+272. $35.00.

Rev. by Frederick Rudolph in *ECS* 20 (1986): 62-64.

Rose, Margaret A. "Theories of Nature from Hegel to Marx."
BJA 26 (1986): 150-60.

Rudowski, Victor A. "Lessing *contra* Winckelman." *JAAC* 44
(1986): 235-43.

Laokoon (1766) against Winckelmann's *Gedanken* (1755), but both in praise of Greece. (T.L.A.)

Sass, Else Kai. *Lykkens Tempel (The Temple of Fortune): A Painting by Nicolai Abilgaard*. Copenhagen: Christian Ejlers Forlag, 1986. Pp. 322. D Kr. 348.00.

Rev. by Christine Stevenson in *BM* 128 (Sept. 1986): 682. Numerous color and black-and-white illustrations.

Sellier, Philippe. "Cain (le mythe de)." *CRCL* 13 (1986): 17-28.

Only useful on the Continental background in the seventeenth and eighteenth centuries. (T.L.A.)

Seward, Desmond. *Napoleon's Family*. New York: Viking, 1986. $16.95.

Rev. in *NY*, Aug. 25, 1986, pp. 95-96. Not seen.

Shortland, Michael. "The Power of a Thousand Eyes: J.C. Lavater's Science of Physical Perception." *Criticism* 28 (1986): 379-408.

Silver, Bruce. "Clarke on the Quaker Background of William Bartram's Approach to Nature." *JHI* 47 (1986): 507-10.

Simpson, David. *The Politics of American English, 1776-1850*. Oxford University Press, 1986. Pp. xii+301. $24.95.

Rev. enthusiastically by Emory Elliott in *NCL* 41 (1986): 498-501. Not seen.

Stafford, Barbara Maria. *Voyage into Substance: Art, Science, Nature, and the Illustrated Travel Account, 1760-1840*. MIT Press, 1986. Pp. 645; illus. $39.95.

Not seen.
Reviewed by Charles Rosen in *NYRB*, Nov. 6, 1986, pp. 55-60 as "magnificently printed" but "often inaccurate, consistently obscure and unconvincing," and "profoundly mistaken."
Rosen, for our benefit, takes the occasion to offer an accurate and lucid voyage into the evidence that "reading the past into the direct experience of the present had ... become second nature to the early Romantics--not just the past, but many different kinds of past, millennial, annual, seasonal, diurnal, momentary," related to the revolution in

lyric poetry (Wordsworth, Hölderlin, and others) and in landscape painting (Constable, Friedrich), and music (landscape poetry transformed into the German *Lied*). (D.V.E.)

Taft, Richard Tomlinson. "The Relationship Between Art and Philosophy: An Examination of Hegel, Blake, Nietzsche and Heidegger." Ann Arbor, Mich.: University Microfilms International,

Dissertation.
In chapter 4 Blake and Nietzsche "are discussed because each attempts to transgress the traditionally established boundary between art and philosophy."

Tait, A.A. "Lord Findlater, Architect." *BM* 128 (Oct. 1986): 738-41. 5 illus.

Identifying the anonymous designer of the plans and elevations in *Les Plans et Desseins de la Architecture* (Leipzig and Paris, 1798).

Virtanen, Reino. "Claude Bernard's Prophecies and the Historical Relation of Science to Literature." *JHI* (1986): 275-86.

Cites two poets and a scientist who would not have argreed with C.P. Snow about the growing gap between literature and science. It was Wordsworth who foresaw the time when "the remotest discoveries of the Chemist, the Botanist, or Mineralogist, will be as proper objects of the poet's art as any"; Victor Hugo expressed similar ideas; the scientist Claude Bernard also. Yet today, for poetry, the gap is as great as ever--but not for novels. Virtanen examines several philosophers and novelists from Duhamel to Saint-John Perse. Thought-provoking. (D.V.E.)

Williams, Guy. *The Age of Agony: The Art of Healing, 1700-1800.* Academy Chicago Publishers, 1986. Pp. $15.95, paper $7.95.

Not seen.

Woloch, Isser. "From Charity to Welfare in Revolutionary Paris." *JMH* 58 (1986): 779-811.

A major work, which finds more citizen support of the poor than previously thought. (T.L.A.)

Woodcock, George. "Political Frye." *CL* 110 (1986): 153-56.

Brief but interesting review essay on David Cook, *Northrop Frye: A Vision of the New World* (New World Perspectives,

distributed by Oxford; $7.95; not seen) which discusses the
political vision, dressed in the form of literary criticism,
that animates Frye's work. "Too taxonomically generalizing
to be a good literary critic in the Arnold-Baudelaire-Wilson
league, he is a fine cultural philosopher," says Woodcock.
(B.C.H.)

Yazawa, Melvin. *From Colonies to Commonwealth: Familial
Ideology and the Beginnings of the American Republic.* The
Johns Hopkins University Press, 1985. Pp. 261. $28.50.

   Rev. by Ruth H. Bloch in *ECS* 20 (1986-87): 262-65.

Reviews of books previously listed:

ALDRIDGE, A. Owen, *Tom Paine's American Ideology* (see *RMB* for
1984, p. 5), rev. by Steven Rosswurm in *ECS* 19 (1986): 549-
51; CROW, Thomas E., *Painters and Public Life in Eighteenth-
Century Paris* (see *RMB* for 1985, p. 6), rev. by Richard
Wrigley ("Pictures at an Exhibition") in *Art History* 9 (1986):
380-88; EAGLETON, Terry, *The Function of Criticism: From
"The Spectator" to Post-Structuralism* (see *RMB* for 1985, p.
22), rev. by John Rodden in *QJS* 72 (1986): 103-06; by Gary Wihl
in *SAQ* 85 (1986): 199-202; HASKELL, Francis, and Nicholas
Penny, *Taste and the Antique* (see *RMB* for 1981, p. 10),
rev. by Frank Felsenstein in *BJECS* 5 (1982): 287-89; by
Christopher Lloyd in *EHR* 100 (1985): 415; by Hugh Plommer
in *Classical Review* 32 (1982): 264-65; by Francis Russell in
JRSA 129 (1981): 803-04; HUNT, Lynn, *Politics, Culture and
Class in the French Revolution* (see *RMB* for 1984, p. 11), rev.
by Norman Hampson in *ECS* 19 (1985-86): 297-300; KRAEHE, Enno E.,
*Metternich's German Policy 2: The Congress of Vienna 1814-
1815* (see *RMB* for 1985, p. 10), rev. by Paul W. Schroeder
in *SAQ* 85 (1986): 102-05; McGANN, Jerome J., *The Beauty of
Inflections: Literary Investigations in Historical Method*
(see *RMB* for 1984, pp. 28-29), rev. by William E. Cain in
VQR 62 (1986): 337-43; MILLER, James, *Rousseau: Dreamer
of Democracy* (see *RMB* for 1984, p. 14), rev. by Harry Payne
in *ECS* 19 (1986): 395-98 as "new and provocative"; by Jean
A. Perkins in *MP* 84 (1986): 92-94 as showing the importance
of Geneva better than it shows Rousseau's method of thinking;
PALMER, R.R., *The Improvement of Humanity: Education and the
French Revolution* (see *RMB* for 1985, p. 12), rev. by Gary
Kates in *ECS* 19 (1986): 551-53 with high praise but as "more
successful in charting the early institutional history of
French schools than in explaining the decisions taken by
revolutionary politicians in response"; POINTON, Marcia,
*The Bonington Circle: English Watercolour and Anglo-French
Landscape 1790-1855* (see *RMB* for 1985, p. 12), rev. by

Michael Rosenthal in *BJA* 26 (1986): 292-94; STAFFORD, Barbara, *Voyage into Substance* (see *RMB* for 1984, p. 16), rev. by David Allen in *LRB*, Feb. 6, 1986, pp. 9-10; by Marcia Pointon in *BJA* 26 (1986): 82-83; by Cecil J. Schneer in *ArtB* 68 (1986): 682-84; VAN KLEY, Dale K., *The Damiens Affair and the Unravelling of the Ancien Régime* (see *RMB* for 1985, p. 17), rev. by David Hudson in *ECS* 19 (1986): 401-04; YOLTON, John W., *Perceptual Acquaintance from Descartes to Reid* (see *RMB* for 1985, p. 18), rev. by John T. Stevenson in *ECS* 19 (1986): 539-41.

Composite reviews:

Crow, Thomas. *Art Bulletin* 68 (1986): 497-502.

Reviews Ronald Paulson, *Representations of Revolution (1789-1820)* (see *RMB* for 1983, p. 24); Philippe Bordes, *Le Serment du Jeu de Paume de Jacques-Louis David: le peintre, son milieu et son temps de 1789 à 1792* (see *RMB* for 1984, p. 245); and Norman Bryson, *Word and Image: French Painting of the Ancien Régime* (Cambridge University Press, 1981; pp. 299; 103 b. & w. illus.; paper $17.95; not listed here before).

Delbanco, Andrew. "Movers and Shapers." *NR*, Dec. 8, 1986, pp. 38.

A review of two books by Bernard Bailyn, both published by Knopf in 1986: *The Peopling of British North America: An Introduction* (pp. 177; $16.95), and *Voyagers to the West: A Passage in the Peopling of America on the Eve of the Revolution* (pp. 668; $30.00).

Kramer, Michael P. *ECS* 19 (1986): 450-54.

Reviewing David Epstein, *The Political Theory of The Federalist* (University of Chicago Press, 1984; pp. ix+234; $22.00); and Albert Furtwangler, *The Authority of Publius: A Reading of the Federalist Papers* (Cornell University Press, 1984; pp. 1515; paper $14.95).

Thomson, Richard. "Prime Site for Development." *Art History* 9 (1986): 108-15.

Discussing twelve books on nineteenth-century art. The following cover the earlier period: Robert Rosenblum and H.W. Janson, *Art of the Nineteenth Century, Painting and Sculpture* (London: Thames and Hudson, 1984; pp. 527; 413 illus., 8 col. pls.; £25.00); Philippe Grunchec, *The Grand Prix de Rome: Paintings from the Ecole des Beaux-Arts, 1797-*

1863 (see *RMB* for 1984, p. 209); and Patricia Condon et al.,
In Pursuit of Perfection: The Art of J.-A.-D. Ingres (Louis-
ville, Ky.: J.B. Speed Art Museum, 1983-84; pp. 25; 239
illus., 64 col. pls.; $35.00).

Review article:

Rosen, Charles. "Now Voyager." *NYRB*, Nov. 6, 1986, pp. 55-
60. 2 illus.

A severe critique of Barbara Maria Stafford, *Voyage into
Substance: Art, Science, Nature, and the Illustrated Travel
Account, 1760-1840* (see *RMB* for 1984, p. 16), whose illustrations Rosen praises but finds the text "often inaccurate,
consistently obscure and unconvincing" and the author's
attempts to separate the scientific accounts from others of
the time "specious." In order to correct what he sees as
her "distortions" and "misrepresentations," Rosen gives his
own version of parts of the topic, notably the influence of
Ramond de Carbonnières's writings about his travels in the
Alps. (I.H.C.)

3. CRITICISM

Bahti, Timothy. "Ambiguity and Indeterminacy: The Juncture."
CL 38 (1986): 159-80.

"Reading romantic poetry and its ambiguities may yield
theoretical knowledge about reading literature, and reading
per se, even if this means that their meaningfulness may lie
in the difficulty, the indeterminacy, even the impossibility
of understanding a moment of death." Includes a short analysis
of Keats's "This Living Hand."

Bidney, Martin. "Beethoven, the Devil, and the Eternal Feminine:
Masters' Goethean Typology of Redemption." *PLL* 22 (1986):
187-205.

Bishop, Jonathan. "Emerson and Christianity." *Renascence* 38
(1985-86): 183-200.

Cameron, Sharon. "Representing Grief: Emerson's 'Experience.'"
Representations no. 15 (Summer 1986): 15-41.

Cameron, Sharon. *Writing Nature: Henry Thoreau's "Journal."*
Oxford University Press, 1985. Pp. x+173. $17.50.

Rev. by Richard Bridgman in *NEQ* 59 (1986): 431-34, who

finds "much to take issue with in this severely compressed and abstract study."

Chaimowicz, Thomas. *Freiheit und Gleichgewicht im Denken Montesquieus und Burkes.* Vienna and New York: Springer Verlag, 1986. Pp. 202. $24.90.

Rev. by Paul Gottfried in *ECS* 20 (1986): 115-18.

Chase, Cynthia. *Decomposing Figures: Rhetorical Readings in the Romantic Tradition.* Johns Hopkins University Press, 1986. Pp. 234. $25.00.

A collection of nine essays, all but one of which have been previously published. Taking her point of departure from de Man's "inference" that "Romanticism ... challenges the genetic principle which necessarily underlies all historical narrative," Chase sets out to see "what happens in testing this inference in the analysis of particular works." Choosing texts by Wordsworth, Rousseau, Keats, Hegel, Baudelaire, Kleist, George Eliot, and Freud, Chase explores the workings of three figures that she believes to be "constitutive" of lyric, autobiography, and narrative: the figure of voice, the figure of face, and the figure of causality. Not surprisingly, what she repeatedly finds is "disfiguration: a theme or motif ... as well as a rhetorical effect or process" which "renders [the text] opaque or discontinuous." This finding leads her to conclude that "if there is a Romantic tradition, it would consist ... in the recurrence of an attention to problems of reading that undercut the possibility of tradition in the sense of a handing on intact of values, knowledge, function, and forms."
    Although Chase's "readings" are as painstakingly intricate and elegant as de Man's, they are much less polemical. Hence, one has to wonder what the point of all her labor is--especially nowadays when the kind of "nihilistic" reading that undermines our traditional narratives has become all too familiar. In his attempts to make nihilism active, Nietzsche not only undermined such genetic principles as aim, unity, truth, and being but also fabricated genealogies-- another kind of history. Perhaps it is time for us to follow suit. (J.-H-P.)

Coates, Paul. *Words After Speech: A Comparative Study of Romanticism and Symbolism.* New York: St. Martin's Press, 1986.

Not received.

Cohen, Michael. "Edmund Burke and the Two Revolutions." *RecL* 14 (1986): 71-86.

Comparative Literature 38,4 (Fall 1986).

An issue entitled "On Paul de Man" and dedicated to the
memory of de Man. Includes the following three essays:
Jane Marie Todd, "Framing the *Second Discourse*" (307-18);
Peggy Kamuf, "Monumental De-Facement: On Paul de Man's
The Rhetoric of Romanticism" (319-29); and Jean-Pierre
Mileur, "Allegory and Irony: 'The Rhetoric of Temporality'
Re-examined" (329-36). Whereas Kamuf is content to expli-
cate and praise de Man's rigorous way of reading "the
literary thing," Todd and Mileur leaven their praise with
critique. Todd argues that de Man's "neglect of the subject
who 'frames' the *Discourse*" leads him not only to neglect
the issue of sexual difference but also "to adopt Rousseau's
ironic and politically conservative stance." In discussing
de Man's "attempt to move beyond the impossible demands of
the Romantic subject," Mileur argues that "language is not
an inherently stronger defense against mystification than
is selfhood"; "the infinite play of signifiers, the perpetual deferral of meaning, the ironizing of ironies of
irony, is a perpetual flight" that "reveals the persistence
of Romantic desire." (J.H-P.)

Cook, Albert. *Figural Choice of Poetry and Art.*
University Press of New England, for Brown University, 1985.
Pp. ix+256. $22.50.

Rev. by James D. Carney in *JAAC* 44 (1986): 414-15.
Does not deal directly with the Romantics, but has things
to say about "The Slippery Procedures of Literature" in
thought, image, and story, that (as a few citings of Wordsworth demonstrate) should assist us in study of the poetry
of any age. (D.V.E.)
For Cook's book on the Romantics, see next entry.

Cook, Albert. *Thresholds: Studies in the Romantic Experience.*
University of Wisconsin Press, 1986. Pp. xi+308. $37.50.

"For the Romantic Poet every moment is a threshold"; the
poise of such a poem as the "Ode to Melancholy" is felt
as "a triumph of symbolic clearness under the pressure of
fluid states"-- because of Keats's control of his symbols,
and also the ode form itself. History supplied the "*anomie*
pervasive after the beginning of the Industrial Revolution,"
and psychological pressure is notable in the family circumstances of most of the poets except Blake.
"Wordsworth wandered and walked over a lonely terrain"
in a spirit comparable to "the restless displacement of
Shelley and Byron, of Gogol and Hölderlin and Nietzsche, a

state of spirit given supremely reductive expression in
the poem placed last in Baudelaire's *Les Fleurs du mal*,
'le Voyage.'" The "spots of time" in *The Prelude* are
"encountered in transit."

Cook, moving quickly over the line between psychology
and "metrical contract," can point out how within such a
contract, even the placing of a colon can establish a
critical threshold.

A fascinating voyage through the precarious grounds of
most of the European Romantics. (D.V.E.)

Davenport, Guy. "Claiming Kin: Artist, Critic, and Scholar
as Family." *Shenandoah* 36 (1986): 35-86.

Davie, Donald. "God in Recent Poetry." *TLS*, May 23, 1986,
p. 569.

Moves on from Empson's *Milton's God* (1961, to 1981).

Derre, Jean-René. *Littérature et politique dans l'Europe du
XIXe Siècle*. Presses Universitaires de Lyon, 1986. Pp.
440. Fr. 150.00.

"L'auteur s'intéresse à l'analyse des mouvements intellec-
tuels, idéologiques et sociaux dans l'Europe romantique
notamment à travers les rapports de la France et de l'Allemagne dans la première moitié du dix-neuvième siècle."
(*Les Livres du Mois*, June 1986, p. 52).
Not seen.

Dodd, Philip, ed. *The Art of Travel: Essays on Travel
Writing*. London: Frank Cass, 1982. Pp. viii+164. £9.95.

Rev. by Harold Beaver in *YES* 16 (1986): 221-23.

Dodd, Wayne. "The Art of Poetry and the Temper of the Times."
OR 37 (1986): 6-14.

With much personal reference to Keats. (T.L.A.)

Donohue, A. McNeill. *Hawthorne: Calvin's Ironic Stepchild*.
Kent State University Press, 1985. Pp. xii+359. $27.50.

Rev. by Kathleen Verduin in *NEQ* 59 (1986): 149-52.

Doudna, Martin K. "Hawthorne's Pandora, Milton's Eve, and the
Fortunate Fall." *ESQ* 31 (1985): 164-72.

Durer, Christopher S. "Melville's 'Synthesizing' Narrator,
Mardi, Fichte, and the *Fruhromantiker*." *RP&P* 10,1 (1986):
45-60.

Fink, Stephen. "The Language of Prophecy: Thoreau's 'Wild Apples.'" *NEQ* 59 (1986): 212–30.

Fried, Debra. "Repetition, Refrain, and Epitaph." *ELH* 53 (1986): 615–32.

Includes a consideration of poetry by Edgar Allan Poe.

Fried, Michael. "Antiquity Now: Reading Winckelmann on Imitation." *October* no. 36 (Summer 1986): 87–97. 1 illus.

A perceptive new look at the famous essay, *Reflections on the Imitation of the Painting and Sculpture of the Ancient Greeks* (1755). To Fried, Winckelmann's imaginary reconstruction of how Michelangelo transferred a sculptural model to marble reveals "a desire for repetition so acute, absorbing, and physically immediate as to make the perfected sculpture ... equivalent to a kind of death. (I.H.C.)

Frow, John. *Marxism and Literary History.* Oxford: Basil Blackwell, 1986. Pp. 272. £19.50.

Reviewed sympathetically but critically by Michael Sprinker in *TLS*, Jan. 16, 1986, pp. 65–66.
Not seen.

Fry, Paul. "Disposing of the Body: The Romantic Moment of Dying." *SWR* 71 (1986): 8–26.

Fry, speaking only partly historically, argues that the Romantic moment of death—contrary to myths about the nineteenth century's attitude toward death—is simple but not morbid. He concentrates on "the visible act of dying, with special attention to what the body is doing and what it looks like just before it becomes a corpse."

Fullenwider, Henry. "The Goethean Fragment 'Die Natur' in English Translation." *CLS* 23 (1986): 170–77.

Galle, Roland. "Sociopsychological Reflections on Rousseau's Autobiography." *NLH* 17 (1986): 555–71.

Gilmore, Michael T. *American Romanticism and the Market-Place.* University of Chicago Press, 1985. Pp. ix+177. $19.95.

Rev. by Philip Gura in *ESQ* 32 (1986): 68–78; by Elizabeth A. Meese in *Criticism* 28 (1986): 216–20; by Joel Myerson in *NEQ* 59 (1968): 308–10.

Gorak, Jan. "Deus Artifex: Transformations of a Topos."
ESA 28 (1985): 21–45.

Much reference to Coleridge's *Biographia*. (T.L.A.)

Grossman, Lionel. "History as Decipherment: Romantic
Historiography as the Discovery of the Other." *NLH* 18
(1986): 23–57.

Handwerk, Gary J. *Irony and Ethics in Narrative: Schlegel
to Lacan.* Yale University Press, 1986. Pp. ix+231. $21.00.

Handwerk's analysis of ironic discourse in the Romantic
and post-Romantic period "emphasizes the recuperative power
of irony [and] its role in defining and extending the idea
and experience of community." His first two chapters on
the Romantic period treat Friedrich Schlegel's irony and
the Romantic subject in *Lucinde*, *Heinrich von Ofterdingen*,
The Prelude, and *Sartor Resartus*.

Herdmann, Ute. *Die Südlichen Poeme A.S. Pushkins. Ihr
Verhältnis zu Lord Byrons Oriental Tales.* 1982.

Rev. by Ulrika Jekutsch in *Anglia* 104 (1986): 246–49.
Not seen.

Holquist, J. Michael. "The Carnival of Discourse: Bakhtin
and Simultaneity." *CRCL* 12 (1985): 220–34.

Criticism and play theory. (T.L.A.)

Howe, Irving. *The American Newness: Culture and Politics
in the Age of Emerson.* Harvard University Press, 1986.
Pp. 99. $12.50.

Rev. by Robert Coles in *NEQ* 59 (1986): 564–66.

Humphries, Jefferson. *Losing the Text: Readings in Literary
Desire.* University of Georgia Press, 1986. Pp. xiii+218.
$25.00.

Humphries' study of literary reading as "an act not of
possession but of loss" makes parenthetical reference to
Coleridge and Keats, quotes Lamb and Hazlitt as readers
of *King Lear*, and mentions Rousseau as read by Derrida.

Hundert, R.J. "A Satire of Self-Disclosure: From Hegel
Through Rameau to the Augustans." *JHI* 47 (1986): 235–48.

The path is through Mandeville rather than Hegel. (T.L.A.)

Jackson, Thomas H. "Herder, Found, and the Concept of Expression." *MLQ* 44 (1983): 374-93.

Karlinsky, Simon. *Russian Drama from Its Beginnings to the Age of Pushkin.* University of California Press, 1985. Pp. xxi+357.

   Rev. by W.G. Jones in *JES* 16 (1986): 150-51.

Kee, James M. "Narrative Time and Participating Conciousness: A Heideggerian Supplement to McGann's 'The Romantic Ideology.'" *Romanticism* 9 (1985): 51-63.

Leinwand, Theodore. *The City Staged: Jacobean Comedy, 1602-13.* University of Wisconsin Press, 1986.

   Mr. Leinwand gives us a new and extremely interesting approach to Jacobean city comedy. Taking a "new historical" approach, he breaks through our old, cliché conceptions of the relation between city comedy conventions and seventeenth-century London socioeconomic realities. For example, the formula triangle of citizen cuckold--aristocratic gallant--citizen wife used to be thought a reflection of the "attitude of the times" toward the relation among social classes. By subtle examination of the phenomenological relation between social stereotypes and theatrical conventions, Leinwand shows that city comedies function as "interrogative texts" which provoke their audiences to question the very ideological constructs they present. Using the plays of Dekker, Middleton, Chapman, Fletcher, Jonson, and others as well as extra-literary texts like sermons, socioeconomic tracts, and commentaries, the author convincingly demonstrates that "Jacobean theatre did not stand in relation to reality only as a comment on, or abstraction of, an event; it too was inscribed within reality and could fasten onto already available cultural terms. The process was truly dialectic, not hierarchical." The Jacobean theater and the social reality that it mirrored and yet by which it was inscribed were mutually modifying architects of the forms of social role and social reality.
   This is an important work, which will be of value both to scholar/critics of seventeenth-century literature and to historians of ideas. (Rose Zimbardo)

Levering, David. "The Politics of Emerson's Man-Making Words." *PMLA* 101 (1986): 38-56.

Lord, George deForest. *Trials of the Self: Heroic Ideals in the Epic Tradition.* Hamden, Conn.: Archon Books, 1983. Pp. x+249. $25.00.

Rev. by Larry D. Bouchard in *JR* 66 (1986):   222-23, who cites references to *Don Juan* and *The Prelude*.

Lucas, John.   *Romantic to Modern Literature: Essays and Ideas of Culture 1750-1900*. Brighton, England: Harvester; New York: Barnes and Noble, 1982. Pp. viii+231. £18.95.

Rev. by Terry Eagleton in *YES* 26 (1986):   273-74.

Macherey, Pierre.   "History and Novel in Balzac's *The Peasants*." Trans. Warren Montag. *MinnR* 26 (1986):   165-71.

The essay is reprinted to introduce *A Theory of Literary Production*, which Terry Eagleton has praised repeatedly. (T.L.A.)

Mahlendorf, Ursula R.   *The Wellsprings of Literary Creation: An Analysis of Male and Female "Artist Stories" from the German Romantics to American Writers of the Present*. (Studies in German Literature, Linguistics, and Culture, 18.) Columbia, S.C.:   Camden House, 1985. Pp. xx+292; 4 illus. $29.00.

Rev. by Lee B. Jennings in *JEGP* 85 (1986):   635-36. The seven writers treated are Hoffmann, Büchner, Mörike, Stifter, Kafka--and Kate Chopin and Sylvia Plath, there being no suitable German *women* to use as examples!

Manos, Nikki Lee.   "*The Ordeal of Richard Feverel*:   Bildungs-roman or Anti-Bildungsroman?" *VN* 70 (1986):   18-24.

Goethe's *Wilhelm Meister* is more the model than Carlyle's more negative version of the structure. (T.L.A.)

McDonald, Christie V.   *The Dialogue of Writing: Essays in Eighteenth-Century Literature*. (Library of the *Canadian Review of Comparative Literature*, 7.) Wilfrid Laurier University Press, 1984. Pp. xviii+109. $12.95.

Rev. by Aubrey Rosenberg in *UTQ* 56 (1986):   137-38.

McGann, Jerome J.   *The Beauty of Inflections: Literary Investigations in Historical Method and Theory*. Oxford: Clarendon Press, 1985. Pp. xii+352. £19.50.

Rev. by Maggie Berg in *RES* 37 (1986):   617-19. Not received.

McGann, Jerome J., ed.   *Textual Criticism and Literary Interpretation*. University of Chicago Press, 1985. Pp. xi+239. $22.00, paper $10.95.

Papers read at a conference in 1982 at the California Institute of Technology.

Rev. by William J. Burling in *SHR* 21 (1987): 174-77 as, from the first essay to the last, "one of the most important" recent collections" bearing on the profession of literary studies."
Not received; but we were sent an offprint of Peter Manning's Byron article (see below), the only strictly Romantic essay in the collection.

Mehlman, Jeffrey. "Writing and Deference: The Politics of Literary Adulation." *Representations* no. 15 (Summer 1986): 1-14.

The adulators are American academics; the adulated is Jacques Derrida. Parodying with a purpose, Mehlman works through a series of puns, coincidences, and floating clues to the interesting case of Gerhard Heller, the German censor in Paris during the Occupation who was a worshipful Francophile, and the French writers associated with him. (I.H.C.)

Meyer, Michel. *De la problematologie: Philosophie, Science et Langage*. Liège: Pierre Mardaga, 1986. Pp. 308. Paper Bel Fr 1.450, Fr 229.00.

Mitchell, W.J.T. *Iconology: Image, Text, Ideology*. University of Chicago Press, 1986. Pp. x+226. $20.00.

Rev. favorably by Rudolf Arnheim in *TLS*, June 27, 1986, p. 712; by James Heffernan in *Word and Image* 2 (1986): 382-83; by Mark Conroy in *SHR* 20 (1986): 365-71 (along with Christopher Norris, *The Contest of Faculties: Philosophy and Theory After Deconstruction* [London: Methuen, 1985]).
Six related essays, two of which have been published separately, on the word-versus-image problem in aesthetic theory since the eighteenth century. In the author's own words, he more specifically is "studying the complex relations between iconophobia and iconophilia, between love and fear of images, between the 'soft' and 'hard' view of ideological criticism." "Iconophobia" and "iconophilia" are terms that recur, along with such others as "idolatry," "fetishism," and "iconoclasm," sometimes in variant forms ("ideolatry," "mediolatry"), usually with special meanings.
Part 1 is occupied by the introductory "What Is an Image?" (see *RMB* for 1984, p. 30). In part 2, the positions of four representative theorists are examined in reverse historical order and close analytical detail: Nelson Goodman, "Pictures and Paragraphs"; E.H. Gombrich, "Nature and Convention"; Gotthold Lessing, "Space and Time" (see *RMB* for 1984, p. 29); and Edmund Burke, "Eye and Ear." Karl Marx follows in part 3. Also discussed along the way-- but these are by no means all of those who are cited or quoted--are Plato, Leonardo da Vinci, Rudolph Arnheim, Erwin

Panofsky, and Walter Benjamin.

The showpiece of the book is the last essay, "The Rhetoric of Iconoclasm," a study of Marx's figurative language and aesthetic concepts, in which the argument begins from the images of the camera obscura and the fetish (for "ideology" and "commodity," respectively) and concludes with an explanation of why Marxist theory, both classic and contemporary, is "embarrassed" in dealing with the arts. (It must be said that Mitchell's own understanding of ideology, as revealed in his practical comments in part 2, is disappointingly vague: a matter of "power and value," "our causes and crusades," focused on topical "race and gender" rather than on orthodox class, and identified through tenuous verbal clues which yield only a few minor examples. One could have wished for an updated version of "false consciousness," boldly applied to more than one kind of thought.) In the closing pages, Mitchell offers a "liberal" resolution to the dilemma of present-day Marxist critics which is like his resolution to the broader problem (see p. 46): "dialectical pluralism," on the two Blakean "models of dialogue" in *The Marriage of Heaven and Hell*.

Evidently the product of drastic revision, this book is an impressive intellectual achievement, in its author's command of the central texts and secondary literature alike, his own dialectical sense, and especially his skill in analyzing critically writings which themselves were presented as critical analyses. (I.H.C.)

Morris, Kevin L. *The Image of the Middle Ages in Romantic and Victorian Literature*. London: Croom Helm, 1984.

Not seen.

Mortier, Roland. "Variations in the Dialogue in the French Enlightenment." *SECC* 16 (1986): 225–40.

"It is symptomatic that it is necessary to wait for the beginning of the nineteenth century to see the resurgence of the dialogue, a form very little in vogue during the Revolution which much preferred the treatise, the pamphlet, or journalism."

Nehamas, Alexander. *Nietzsche: Life as Literature*. Harvard University Press, 1985. Pp. 234. $17.50.

Rev. by Kathleen M. Higgins in *JAAC* 45 (1986): 199–200.

Neubauer, John. *The Emancipation of Music from Language: Departure from Mimesis in Eighteenth-Century Aesthetics*. Yale University Press, 1986. Pp. ix+249. $21.50.

Challenging traditional assumptions, Neubauer examines
eighteenth-century theories of music that led to the new
aesthetic theories associated with Romanticism. Rejecting
the description of this period as a change from mimetic to
expressive art, he goes back to antiquity and traces the
evolution of verbal-rhetorical and mathematical approaches
to music, then the theorizing of the Enlightenment culminating in Diderot, Goethe, Herder, Kant, Wackenroder, and
Novalis.

A sample: in Beethoven's Fifth Symphony his "high
sobriety" expresses "to a very high degree the romanticism
of music" (says Hoffmann) and Neubauer observes that the
"double demand for emotional intensity and sober detachment
links Hoffmann's vision of Romantic music with the poetics
of Friedrich Schlegel, Novalis, Keats, and Coleridge" (206).
Further comment on the poets is not made, but the reader
who absorbs this perception of "The Emancipation" will readily think of what it means in the poetry. (D.V.E.)

Neufeldt, Leonard N., and Christopher Barr. "'I Shall Write
Like a Latin Father': Emerson's 'Circles.'" *NEQ* 59 (1986):
92-108.

Derrida helps explain Emerson's grasp of incongruity.
(T.L.A.)

Nichols, Bill. "Ideological and Marxist Criticism: Towards
a Metahermeneutics." *SLIm* 19 (1986): 83-107.

Nicholson, Linda J. *Gender and History: The Limits of Social
Theory in the Age of the Family.* Columbia University Press,
1986. Pp. 238. $27.50.

Rev. by Angela Miles in *Women's Review of Books* 4 (Nov.
1986): 17-18 as presenting "a powerful ... case for the
absolute necessity of historical awareness within feminism"
while "fall[ing] short of its goal of providing an 'initial
framework for creating a history of gender in the modern
period.'"

Rather than examining the struggles of men and women as they
produce and are produced by history, Nicholson focuses on the
emergence and changing relations of three domains: the
family, the state, and the economy. Includes critical analyses of Locke's liberalism, Marx's materialism, and radical
feminism's ahistoricism.

Norris, Christopher. "On Paul de Man's *The Rhetoric of
Romanticism*: A Review Essay." *SHR* 20 (1986): 53-69.

An admiring retrospective on the career represented by this collection of critical essays.

Orr, Linda. "The Revenge of Literature: A History of History." *NLH* 18 (1986): 1-22.

"History came to provide the main common denominator for the many hybrid genres that characterized the (Romantic) period, combining epic, utopia, political philosophy, religion, fiction, and lyricism. Poets wrote history literally (Schiller, Lamartine) and figuratively (Hugo, *La Légende des siècles*). And certain historians (especially Barante and Thierry) were heavily influenced by the novels of Walter Scott or Chateaubriand.... Between the Greeks and Germans an abyss appears to yawn" (3). Even Homer nods. (B.C.H.)

Ortega y Gasset, Jose. "Kant and the Modern German Mind." *YR* 75 (1986): 161-80.

Reprinted from 1941 for *YR*'s seventy-fifth anniversary.

Ortiz, Gloria. *The Dandy and the "Senorito": Eros and Social Class in the Nineteenth-Century Novel.* Ann Arbor, Mich.: University Microfilms International, 1986.

Dissertation.

Patterson, Mark. "Emerson, Napoleon, and the Concept of the Representative." *ESQ* 31 (1985): 230-42.

A penetrating analysis of the Man of Destiny as odd man out. (T.L.A.)

Pattison, George. "Nihilism and the Novel: Kierkegaard's Literary Reviews." *BJA* 26 (1986): 161-71.

Peckham, Morse. *Romanticism and Ideology.* Greenwood, Fla.: Penkevill Publishing, 1985. Pp. viii+381. $32.50.

Rev. by Karl Kroeber in *KSJ* 35 (1986): 223-26.

Pettersson, Torsten. "Incompatible Interpretations of Literature." *JAAC* 45 (1986): 147-61.

Some reference to "A Slumber Did My Spirit Seal." (T.L.A.)

Porte, Joel, ed. *Emerson: Prospect and Retrospect.* (Harvard Studies, 10.) Harvard University Press, 1982. Pp. vii+197. $16.50.

Rev. by Barbara L. Packer in *SiR* 24 (1985): 575-77.

Prendergast, Christopher. *The Order of Mimesis.* Cambridge
University Press, 1986. Pp. 288. £27.50.

   Rev. by Peter Brooks in *TLS*, July 11, 1986, p. 796: "It
is worth trying to rescue the 'order' of mimesis because it
provides shared forms for publicly engaging shared questions."

Rabb, J.D. "Herbert L. Stewart, Thomas Carlyle, and Canadian
Idealism." *CL* 111 (1986): 211-14.

Rajan, Tilottama. "Displacing Post-Structuralism: Romantic
Studies After Paul de Man." *SiR* 24 (1985): 451-74.

   In the first two parts of this essay the author discusses
the "intellectual origins" of de Man's early work and the
"limits" of his recent work on Romanticism; valuable comparisons and distinctions are drawn between the positions of
de Man and those of such familiar other figures as Benjamin,
Derrida, Adorno, and especially Nietzsche. Rajan's own proposal is that "Romantic language is best approached in terms
of a deconstructive phenomenology more radical then Heidegger's,"
but without the limitations imposed on language by the post-
structuralism of Derrida and of de Man alike.
   Rather surprisingly, Rajan concludes by recommending that
deconstruction "widen its boundaries" by looking to a new
conceptual source, reader-response theory. Coleridge's
"The Eolian Harp" is briefly examined in demonstration (I.H.C.)

Rigney, Ann. "Toward Varennes." *NLH* 18 (1986): 77-98.

   A "textual" study of French Revolution historiography;
the author quotes Michael de Cuteau to the effect that
"historiography itself is a legitimate object of semiotic
analysis to the extent that it is narrative or a distinct
type of discourse."

Rogerson, John. *Old Testament Criticism in the Nineteenth
Century: England and Germany.* London: Society for
Promoting Christian Knowledge, 1984. Pp. xiii+320. £15.00.

   Rev. by Joseph L. Altholz in *VS* 29 (1986): 474-75.

Rosowski, Susan. *The Voyage Perilous: Willa Cather's Romanticism.* University of Nebraska Press, 1986. Pp. xviii+284.
$22.95.

Rubin, James H. "Allegory Versus Narrative in Quatremère de
Quincy." *JAAC* 44 (1986): 383-92.

   Good on the shift from young Romantic to official classicism. (T.L.A.)

Scarry, Elaine. *The Body in Pain: The Making and Unmaking
of the World.* Oxford University Press, 1985. Pp. 385.
$24.95.

Rev. unfavorably by Peter Singer in *NYRB*, Feb. 27, 1986,
pp. 27-30 as "pretentious" and weak in logic; by Maire
Jaanus in *Critical Texts* 3 (1986):   25-28 as "a brilliantly
original meditation on the subject-object relationship";
by A.S. Byatt in *TLS*, June 13, 1986, p. 637 as "a brave
book, and worth persevering with."
An unusual and thought-provoking combination of cultural
criticism and imaginative speculation. Like Blake, Scarry
locates "the problem of suffering" within the "more expansive
frame of the 'problem of creating'" and in so doing invites
us "to attend with more commitment" to the "philosophical
and ethical import" of "the subject of making." As Scarry
represents it, the "subject of making" is a Romantic-Marxist
body whose dialectical engagement in the work of creating
the world involves two related yet distinguishable processes:
making up and making real. As artistic and cultural creation
attest, making up and making real can work to relieve the body
in pain. However, as torture and war demonstrate, the body
in pain can also be (ab)used in violent attempts to make the
made-up real. Since the devastatingly nondialectical acts
of torture and war both mime and invert the authentically
material work of human creation, Scarry argues that we must
make "the nature of creation ... conceptually available
and susceptible to description so that periodic dislocations
within its overall structure of action can be recognized
and repaired." Although this updated humanistic argument
is appealing, it behooves us to be more skeptical than
Scarry is about the relationship between conceptual "recognition" and the work of "repair." (J.H-P.)

Schwartz, Nina. "The Ideologies of Romanticism." *New Orleans
Review* 13 (1986):   84-96.

Scott, Joan W. "Gender: A Useful Category of Historical
Analysis." *AHR* 91 (L986): 1053-85.

Issues and new perspectives.

Scott, Nathan A., Jr. *The Poetics of Belief.* University of
North Carolina Press, 1985. Pp. 198. $24.00.

Rev. by David Jasper in *JR* 66 (1986):   221-22; covers
Coleridge.

Seyersted, Per. *From Norwegian Romantic to American Realist:
Studies in the Life and Writings of Jhalmar Hjorth Boyesen.*

Foreword by Marc Ratner. Appendix. Eight Essays by
Boyesen. Oslo: Solum Forlag; Atlantic Highlands, N.J.:
Humanities Press, 1985. Pp. 192. $18.45.

Rev. by Orm Øverland in *ES* 67 (1986): 374-76. "Before
his career was cut short by his early death in 1895,
[Boyesen] had 20 books to his name, had had access to the
leading journals, had married into New York society, and
was a Professor at Columbia University."

Shavit, Zohar. *Poetics of Children's Literature.* University
of Georgia Press, 1986. Pp. xiii+200. $25.00.

The focus of this study, which ranges from Perrault and
Grimm to Carroll to Blyton and includes texts mostly in English and Hebrew, is upon "*the universal structural traits
and patterns common to all children's literatures*, taking
into account the periods in which they occur and the different rates of their development" (xi).

Shields, David S. "Mental Nocturnes: Night Thoughts on Man
and Nature in the Poetry of Eighteenth-Century America."
PMHB 110 (1986): 237-58.

Shields thinks that the Revolution failed to free American
poets from anxiety about the human place in the natural environment. (T.L.A.)

Simpkins, Scott. "Romanticism and Rhetoric." *LitR* 29 (1986):
392-95.

Stam, Robert. "Film and Language: From Metz to Bakhtin."
SLIm 19 (L986): 109-30.

Steele, Peter. "*Scriptor Ludens*: The Notion and Some Instances." *CRCL* 12 (1985): 235-63.

This sharp study of literature and play touches on Byron
and Pope. (T.L.A.)

Stillinger, Jack. *JEGP* 85 (1986): 550-57.

Review essay on recent work on deconstruction, post-
structuralism, literary history, and criticism in the university. Stillinger starts out with, "As most recent
readers of this journal are aware, the brief life of American deconstruction is over; it is, rather in the manner of
the thoroughly dead bird in the Monty Python skit, a *former*
theory," and goes on from there. Somber, hilarious, and
well worth reading. (B.C.H.)

Todd, Janet. *Sensibility: An Introduction.* London: Methuen,
1986. Pp. 169. £16.95.

   Rev. by W.B. Carnochan in *TLS*, Feb. 27, 1987, p. 218, as
a failure—in discrimination of terms, and of relevant materials; as having attempted "an impossible task."

Voloshin, Beverly R. *"Wieland*: 'Accounting for Appearances.'"
NEQ 59 (1986): 341-57.

   The novel is enslaved by the Lockean paradigm. (T.L.A.)

Von Hallberg, Robert, ed. *Canons.* University of Chicago
Press, 1984. Pp. 407. $25.00.

   Rev. by Richard Shusterman in *JAAC* 45 (L986): 97-99.

Ware, Tracy. "D.C. Scott's 'The Height of the Land' and the
Greater Romantic Lyric." *CL* 111 (1986): 10-25.

   Duncan Campbell Scott, the Canadian poet; the article
discusses M.H. Abrams in some detail.

Watson, Roderick. *Macmillan History of Literature: The
Literature of Scotland.* London: Macmillan, 1984. Pp.
xiv+481. £7.95.

   Rev. by Lara Hartveit in *ES* 67 (1986): 90-91 as being
exceptionally useful, balanced, and free of hidden agenda,
and unusual in including liberal selections of *Gaelic* works
in translation which are often unfamiliar to English-speaking
readers. "Modest in its pretentions but impressive in its
scope and insight," it is "extremely readable."
   Not seen.

Watson, Stephen. "Aesthetics and the Foundation of Interpretation." *JAAC* 45 (1986): 125-38.

   Rich in its use of Hegel. (T.L.A.)

Woodcock, George. "Eros and Thanatos: Love and Death in
the Arts." *QQ* 92 (1985): 679-90.

   Delacroix's *Death of Sardanapalus* is central. (T.L.A.)

Young, Philip. *Hawthorne's Secret: An Un-Told Tale.* Boston:
David R. Godine Publishers, 1984. Pp. 3+183. $15.95.

   Rev., somewhat gingerly, by John Seelye in *SAQ* 85 (1986):
311-13 as important and substantially convincing. His
"secret," of course, is a full-blown incestuous relationship
with his sister, which Young sees as the real subject of
The Scarlet Letter; lots of references to Byron.

See also Adams ("Blake").

Reviews of books previously listed:

BAKER, Carlos, *The Echoing Green* (see *RMB* for 1984, pp.
20-21), rev. by Richard Harter Fogle in *KSJ* 35 (1986):
218-20; BANN, Stephen, *The Clothing of Clio: A Study of
the Representation of History in Nineteenth-Century Britain
and France* (see *RMB* for 1984, p. 6), rev. by Hans Kellner
in *JMH* 58 (1986): 535-36; CULLER, Jonathan, *The Pursuit of
Signs: Semiotics, Literature, Deconstruction* (see *RMB* for
1981, p. 23), rev. by Lee B. Jennings in *MP* 82 (1985): 448-
54; DE MAN, Paul, *The Rhetoric of Romanticism* (see *RMB* for
1984, pp. 22-23), rev. by Lilian R. Furst in *JEGP* 85 (1986):
90-92; by David Simpson in *SAQ* 85 (1986): 202-04; by
William Keach in *KSJ* 35 (1986): 213-18; by Mark Storey in
English 35 (1986): 67-73; EAGLETON, Terry, *The Function
of Criticism* (see *RMB* for 1984, p. 22), rev. by Robert Wess
in *MinnR* 25 (1985): 139-41; ELLISON, Julie, *Emerson's
Romantic Style* (see *RMB* for 1984, pp. 23-24), rev. by Wai-
chee Dimock in *GaR* 40 (1986): 572-76; by David Simpson in
JEGP 85 (1986): 148-50; FRY, Paul H., *The Reach of Criticism:
Method and Perception in Literary Theory* (see *RMB* for 1985,
p. 23), rev. by William Keach in *KSJ* 35 (1986): 213-18;
FURST, Lilian R., *Fictions of Romantic Irony* (see *RMB* for
1985, p. 23), rev. by Mark Kipperman in *KSJ* 35 (1986): 220-
23; by Logan Speirs in *ES* 67 (1986): 572-74; by Stuart M.
Sperry in *JEGP* 85 (1986): 134-35; HAGSTRUM, Jean H., *Sex
and Sensibility: Ideal and Erotic Love from Milton to
Mozart* (see *RMB* for 1980, pp. 19-20), rev. by Maurice Charney
in *Review of Psychoanalytic Books* 2 (1983-84): 500-01; by
Dimiter Daphinoff in *ES* 64 (1983): 71-72; by Alicia Ostriker
in *BIQ* 18 (1984): 52-53; by Peter Wagner in *ECL* 8 (1983):
108-14; HAMPSON, Norman, *Will and Circumstance: Montesquieu,
Rousseau and the French Revolution* (see *RMB* for 1983, p.
10); rev. by George Armstrong Kelly in *JMH* 58 (1986): 726-
27; HUNT, Lynn, *Politics, Culture, and Class in the French
Revolution* (see *RMB* for 1984, p. 11), rev. by Jon Klancher
in *HLQ* 49 (1986): 409-14; JAY, Paul, *Being in the Text* (see
RMB for 1984, pp. 26-27), rev. by Jane Marie Todd as "competent and coherent" in *CL* 38 (1986): 298-99; KNAPP, Steven,
Personification and the Sublime: Milton to Coleridge (see
RMB for 1985, p. 26), rev. by Lucy Newlyn in *RES* 37 (1986):
430-33; by Rosemary Ashton in *TLS*, Sept. 19, 1986, pp.
1035-36; KORSHIN, Paul J., and Robert R. Allen, eds., *Greene
Centennial Studies* (see *RMB* for 1985, p. 26), rev. by John
A. Vance in *ECS* 20 (1986): 91-94 as having "about everything
one could ask for from a festschrift"; by Harlan W. Hamilton

in *SAQ* 85 (1986):   396-99 as "remarkable among festschrifts"
[*sic*] and containing a fine essay on Jane Austen by R.F.
Brissenden; MACPHERSON, Jay, *The Spirit of Solitude: Conventions and Continuities in Late Romance* (see *RMB* for 1982,
p. 27, and *RMB* for 1984, p. 28), rev. by James Engell in
SiR 24 (1985):   578-80; by Lucy Newlyn in *RES* 37 (1986):
455-56; McGANN, Jerome J., *The Romantic Ideology: A Critical Investigation* (see *RMB* for 1985, p. 28), rev. by Michael
Fischer in *BIQ*, 18 (1984-85):   152-55; by Lilian R. Furst in
CRCL 13 (1986):   301-03, who finds that "McGann tries to exploit the socio-historical focus of Marxist criticism ...
while at the same time maintaining a critical posture towards
certain influential recent trends in Western Marxist thought
about art and literature"; by William H. Galperin in *JEGP* 84
(1985):   135-38; by H. Haeger in *RP&P* 9 (1985):   75-83; by
Beatrice Marie in *MLN* 99 (1984):   204-09; by Frederick W. Shilstone in *SHR* 19 (1985):   167-68; by James M. Kee in *RP&P* 9
(1985):   51-63 (with a reply by McGann on pp. 65-73): McGANN,
Jerome J., *A Critique of Modern Textual Criticism* (see *RMB* for
1985, p. 27), rev. by W. Speed Hill in *KSJ* 35 (1986):   229-30;
McGANN, Jerome J., ed., *Historical Studies and Literary
Criticism* (see *RMB* for 1985, p. 27), rev. by Colin Falck in
TLS, May 30, 1986, p. 599; NEMOIANU, Virgil, *The Taming of
Romanticism* (see *RMB* for 1985, p. 28), rev. by Gerhart Hoff-
meister in *YCGL* 34 (1985):   145-46; PARKER, Hershel, *Flawed
Texts and Verbal Icons: Literary Authority and American
Fiction* (see *RMB* for 1984, p. 30-31), rev. by Don L. Cook
("Textual Ignorance as a Threat to Scholarship") in *Documen-
tary Editing* 9 (1987):   5-8; PAULSON, Ronald, *Representa-
tions of Revolution (1789-1820)* (see *RMB* for 1983, p. 24);
for 15 reviews in three years, see list in *BIQ* 20 (1986-87):
98; rev. by William Walling in *YCGL* 34 (1985):   143-44; by
Hugh Witemeyer in *MLQ* 45 (1984):   204-07 as "hurried,
imprecise, and astonishingly clumsy" (N.B. This book is now
in paperback at $17.04); RAPP, Carl, *William Carlos Williams
and Romantic Idealism* (see *RMB* for 1985, p. 31), rev. by
Nancy K. Barry in *WHR* 40 (1986):   185-88; REED, Arden,
Romantic Weather: The Climates of Coleridge and Baudelaire
(see *RMB* for 1984), p. 32), rev. by Daniel Hughes in *SiR*
25 (1986):   140-46; ROGERS, Pat, *Eighteenth-Century Encoun-
ters* (see *RMB* for 1985, p. 31), rev. by Francis Doherty in
RES 37 (1986):   571-72; SCHWARTZ, Joel, *The Sexual Politics
of J.J. Rousseau* (see *RMB* for 1985, p. 15), rev. by Arthur
Mitzman in *JMH* 58 (1986):   943-48; THORSLEV, Peter L., Jr.,
Romantic Contraries: Freedom Versus Destiny (see *RMB* for
1984, p. 34), rev. by Stuart Curran in *TWC* 17 (1986):   192-
94; by James Engell, mostly favorably, in *MLQ* 46 (1985):
212-15; by Donald H. Reiman in *RP&P* 10,ii (1986):   65-69;

by Alan Robinson in *RES* 37 (1986): 269-70; by Frederick
W. Shilstone in *SHR* 20 (1986): 282-84; by John R. Reed
in *SiR* 25 (1986): 156-58; WELLBERRY, David, *Lessing's
Laocoön: Semiotics and Aesthetics in the Age of Reason*
(see *RMB* for 1985, p. 33), rev. by Robert S. Leventhal in
ECS 19 (1986): 424-29; WENDORF, Richard, ed., *Articulate
Images: The Sister Arts from Hogarth to Tennyson* (see *RMB*
for 1983, pp. 29-30), rev. by C.L. Brooks in *RES* 37 (1986):
129-30; by Stephen Leo Carr in *ECent* 26 (1984): 203-08;
by John Dixon Hunt in *Word and Image* 1 (1985): 409-20; by
Anne K. Mellor in *BIQ* 19 (1985-86): 112-13; by Bruce
Redford in *MP* 83 (1986): 316-18; by Graham Reynolds in
TLS, May 25, 1984, p. 578; WHALLEY, George, *Studies in
Literature and the Humanities: Innocence of Intent* (see *RMB*
for 1985, p. 33), rev. by Patricia Rae in *DR* 65 (1985):
312-14; WILLIAMS, Anne, *Prophetic Strain: The Greater Lyric
in the Eighteenth Century* (see *RMB* for 1985, p. 33), rev.
by Arthur J. Weitzman in *ECS* 20 (1986): 101-04 as "stimulating" in spite of its theories.

Review essay:

Bashford, Bruce. "A Contemporary Defense of Poetry." *Review*
6 (1984): 303-09.

A judicious review of an important critical work we somehow
missed when it first appeared: Charles Altieri, *Act and
Quality: A Theory of Literary Meaning and Humanistic Understanding* (University of Massachusetts Press, 1981; pp. 343).
Much of the book is concerned with meeting the deconstructionists' denial of the possibility of recovering determinate
meanings from texts. Altieri points to the flaw in Derrida's
reasoning, and turns to performance theory. "Against
theorists like Paul de Man and Frank Kermode who emphasize
indeterminacy, Altieri stresses our ability to adjudicate
among claims about the nature of the performance embodied
in a work. But he warns against critical abstraction:
"discursive statements ... can never lift the meaning off
the work." On other grounds than Shelley's, concludes
Bashford, Altieri, via literary study, can see "that the
human purposes most worth pursuing are to a significant extent
compatible."

Brooks, Peter. "Reinventing Reading." *NR*, Nov. 24, 1986, pp.
45-48.

Based on two new collections of "key texts" by Roland
Barthes, both published by Hill and Wang in 1985: *The Rustle*

of Language (pp. 373; $25.00), and *The Responsibility of Forms: Critical Essays on Music, Art, and Representation* (pp. 312; $22.95). The former is said to include Barthes's "very last text," "One Always Fails in Speaking of What One Loves," a meditation on Stendhal.

Donoghue, Denis. "The Limits of Language." *NR*, July 7, 1986, pp. 4-45.

Two books provide the occasion: Paul de Man, *The Resistance to Theory* (University of Minnesota Press, 1986; pp. 160; $25.00, paper $10.00), and Peter Brooks, Shoshana Felman, and J. Hillis Miller, eds., *The Lesson of Paul de Man* (Yale French Studies, 69; Yale University Press, 1986; pp. 333; $12.95). After a perfunctory nod in their direction, Donoghue writes his own assessment of de Man and a critique of deconstruction, both shrewdly perceptive. The conclusion offers a glimpse of possible reconciliation between rhetoric and poetics on one side and hermeneutics and history on the other. (I.H.C.)

Fitch, Raymond. *JEGP* 85 (1986): 136-39.

Review of Jerome Hamilton Buckley, *The Turning Key: Autobiography and the Subjective Impulse Since 1800*, and of Paul Jay, *Being in the Text: Self-Representation from Wordsworth to Barthes* (see *RMB* for 1984, pp. 72-73, and p. 26).

ENGLISH

(Compiled by Thomas L. Ashton, University of Massachusetts;
Irene H. Chayes, Kensington, Maryland; Janice Haney-
Peritz, Beaver College; Bishop C. Hunt, College of Charles-
ton; Frank Jordan, Miami University, Oxford, Ohio; John
E. Jordan, University of California, Berkeley; Mark Miner,
Westmar College; Charles E. Robinson, University of Dela-
ware; Jeffrey C. Robinson, University of Colorado; Robert
M. Ryan, Rutgers University; Mark T. Smith, Southwest
Missouri State University)

1. BIBLIOGRAPHY

Altick, Richard D. "Nineteenth-Century English Best-Sellers:
A Third List." *SB* 39 (1986): 235-41.

Supplement to the lists published in *The English Common
Reader* (1957) and in *SB* 22 (1969): 197-206.

Bindman, David, ed. *The Thames and Hudson Encyclopaedia of
British Art*. London: Thames and Hudson, 1985. £10.50.

Contains entries on most of the artist members of Blake's
circle (Barry, Bartolozzi, Blake himself, Calvert, Flaxman,
Fuseli, Gillray, the two classicist Hamiltons, Jeffreys,
Kauffmann, Payne Knight, Linnell, Loutherbourg, the Master
of the Giants, Mortimer, Opie, Palmer, Richmond, Romney,
the Runcimans, Stothard, Varley, and West); with short
articles on history painting, Boydell's Shakespeare Gallery,
the Industrial Revolution, neoclassicism, the Royal Academy,
Shoreham, and the sublime will make a most useful work of
reference for anybody interested in British art of Blake's--
or, in fact, any other--period." (Note in *BIQ* 20 [1986-87]:
86 by D.W. Dörrbecker.)

Bruntjen, Sven H.A. *John Boydell (1719-1804): A Study of
Art Patronage and Publishing in Georgian London*. (Outstand-
ing Dissertations in the Fine Arts.) New York: Garland

Publishing, 1985. $50.00.   (Reprint of a 1974 Stanford
University Ph.D. thesis.)

Buck, John Dawson Carl.   "The Elegance of Information:
Frontispieces for Farming, Gardening, and the Domestic
Arts." *BRH* 86 (1983–85):   430–52.

Chadwyck-Healey Inc./Ltd.   *The Anglo-American Historical
Names Database.* 1986.   1,000,000 entries, $3,750.00;
supps. of 250,000 entries, $750.00 each.

An alphabetical index of personal names in 273 British
and Irish biographical dictionaries published between 1840
and 1940; in the National Union Catalog of Manuscript
Collections and National Inventory of Documentary Sources
(in the U.S. and the U.K.); in Harvard class books and class
reports; and in other biographical sources.
Available in microfiche or computer tape; later on CD-ROM.

Cockton, Peter, comp. *Subject Catalogue of the House of
Commons Parliamentary Papers 1801-1900.* Alexandria, Va.,
and Cambridge, England: Chadwyck-Healey Inc., 1986.
$50,000.00; 46,183 microfiches, $6.00 each.

Cross, Anthony Glenn. *The Russian Theme in English Literature
from the Sixteenth Century to 1980:   An Introductory Survey
and a Bibliography.* Oxford: Willem Meeuws, 1985.   Pp. 278.

Rev. by John Slatter in *JES* 16 (1986): 303–04.

Dörrbecker, Detlef W. "Blake and His Circle: A Checklist
of Recent Publications." *BIQ* 20 (1986–87):   76–100.

Dunbar, Clement. "Current Bibliography." *KSJ* 35 (1986):
233–68.

The indispensable annual bibliography for Byron, Shelley,
Keats, Hazlitt, Hunt, and their circles.

Dunbar, Clement. *Shelley Studies, 1950-1984:   An Annotated
Bibliography.* New York: Garland Publishing, 1986.   Pp.
250. $34.00.

Supplement to Dunbar's bibliography of 1976 covering
1823 to 1950.

The English Gift Books and Literary Annuals 1823-1857.
On microfiche with a printed index of contributors.
Cambridge, England: Chadwyck Healey.   211 vols. on 697
microfiches. £1,250.00.

Rev. by Joanne Shattock in *YES* 16 (1986):   313.

Erdman, David V. "Improving the Text of *The Complete Poetry & Prose of William Blake*." *BIQ* 20 (1986): 49-52.

Followed, on p. 110, by a small list of "Errata's Errata"--which will be followed in *BIQ* 21 by a much longer list supplied by Alexander Gourlay--and a promise that both publishers of the Blake text, Doubleday and California University Press, intend to incorporate these corrections in their next printings. (D.V.E.)

Essick, Robert N. "Blake in the Marketplace, 1984." *Blake* 19 (1985): 24-38, "Blake in the Marketplace, 1985." *BIQ* 20 (1986): 12-31. 10 illus.

Feather, John. "British Publishing in the Eighteenth Century: A Preliminary Subject Analysis." *Library* 8 (1986): 32-46.

An old-fashioned statistical analysis, dividing publication into religion, social sciences, literature, history, and geography, and then providing further breakdown. Forty-seven percent of the literature was poetry, and 11 percent fiction, with a marked increase in verse in the last three decades. Between 1700 and 1800, 14,834 sermons were published, as opposed to 9,135 political pamphlets, and those pamphlets appeared in the following percentages for the ten decades: 12 (through 1810, etc.), 17, 6, 6, 9, 8, 8, 8, 9, 17--the big years being those between 1710-1720, and 1790-1800. (T.L.A.)

Finch, Jeremiah S. "The Taylor Lamb Collection." *PULC* 47 (Winter 1986): 255-61; and *ChLB* 55 (1986): 229.

Inventory of the Princeton Library's collection of books and manuscripts, the latter including letters, poems, and early drafts of some Elian essays.

Fryckstedt, Monica. *"Douglas Jerrold's Shilling Magazine."* *VPR* 19 (1986): 2-27.

Provides a comprehensive treatment in the form of *Wellesley Index*: an introductory essay followed by list of contents (1845-48) and identification of authorship. Among the contents are P.G. Patmore's "Personal Recollections of the Late William Hazlitt" (nos. 4, 18, 27) and Francis Worsley's "Poem to Leigh Hunt on His Sixtieth Birthday" (no. 371).

Gatton, John Spalding, et al. "The W. Hugh Peal Collection at the University of Kentucky." *The Kentucky Review* 4,1 (1982): 21-237.

Includes "Overview" by John Clubbe (see *RMB* for 1984, p. 40).

A full account of 17 Wordsworth, 18 Coleridge, 22 Lamb, and 20 Southey items, a few from "Other Romantics and Their Contemporaries," and some from earlier and later periods.

It is to be understood that this catalogue includes only items that have been on display; the complete Peal Collection is large.

Glock, Waldo Sumner. *Eighteenth-Century English Literary Studies: A Bibliography.* Metuchen, N.J. and London: Scarecrow Press, 1984. PP. xviii+847. $52.50.

Rev. briefly but approvingly in *ES* 67 (1986): 275. Authors covered include Addison, Akenside, Boswell, Fanny Burney, Burns, Churchill, Collins, Cowper, Crabbe, Defoe, Fielding, Gay, Goldsmith, Gray, Johnson, Pope, Prior, Richardson, Smart, Smollett, Steele, Sterne, Swift, Thomson, and Young (only major figures).

Hackett, Nan. *Nineteenth Century British Working-Class Autobiographies: An Annotated Bibliography.* New York: AMS Press, 1985. Pp. vii+241. $34.50.

Huff, Cynthia. *British Women's Diaries: A Descriptive Bibliography of Selected Nineteenth-Century Women's Manuscript Diaries.* New York: AMS Press, 1985. PP. xxvi+139. $32.50.

Kline, Sims, ed. *Literary Criticism Register (LCR). A Monthly Listing of Studies in English and American Literature.* P.O. Drawer CC, DeLand, Fla., 32721. Annual subscription $34.00, institutional rate $59.00.

Laxton, Paul, ed. *London Bills of Mortality.* Alexandria, Va., and Cambridge, England: Chadwyck-Healey, 1986. 500 microfiches, $1,800.00; guide $15.00.

The weekly bills and annual bills (all that survive) from the 1590s to 1849.

Lister, Raymond. *Great Images of British Printmaking: A Descriptive Catalogue 1789-1939.* London: Garton, 1978.

Published in conjunction with an exhibition at Garton's gallery; prints by Blake, Richmond, Calvert, Palmer, and the British neo-Romantics who were influenced by them.

Myers, Robin, and Michael Harris, eds. *Author/Publisher Relations During the Eighteenth and Nineteenth Centuries.* (Publishing Pathways Series.) Oxford: Oxford Polytechnic Press, 1984. Pp. 175. £6.75.

Not seen.

Pitcher, E.W. "Some Puzzling Reprintings of Literary Prose in the Final Years of the *Town and Country Magazine.*" *Library* 8 (1986): 159–64.

Most of the essays published in 1792–93 were reprints. No puzzles—just dead letters. (T.L.A.)

Roth, Barry. *An Annotated Bibliography of Jane Austen Studies, 1973-83.* University Press of Virginia, 1985.

Todd, Janet, ed. *A Dictionary of British and American Women Writers 1660-1800.* London: Methuen, 1985. Pp. xxiv+344. £30.00.

Rev. by Judy Simons in *RES* 37 (1986): 452–53.

Todd, William B. *A Bibliography of Edmund Burke.* 2d ed. with new notes. (St. Paul's Bibliographies, 5.) London: St. Paul's Bibliographies, 1982. Pp. 316. £16.00.

Rev. by F.P. Lock in *YES* 16 (1986): 278–79.

Uffelman, Larry K. "Victorian Periodicals 1985: A Checklist of Scholarship and Criticism." *VPR* 19 (1986): 160–64.

With indices.

Williams, Moelwyn I. *A Directory of Rare Book and Special Collections in the United Kingdom and the Republic of Ireland.* London: Library Association, 1985. £75.00.

Rev. by Joel H. Wiener as a "major publishing event" in *VPR* 19 (1986): 111–12, and well worth the praise.

See also Crossan ("Clare").

Reviews of books previously listed:

AITKEN, W.R., *Scottish Literature in English and Scots: A Guide to Information Sources* (see *RMB* for 1982, p. 35), rev. by J.H. Alexander in *YES* 16 (1986): 231–34; AVERLEY, G., et al., eds., *Nineteenth Century Short Title Catalogue 1801-1815* (see *RMB* for 1985, p. 37), rev. by Patricia Fleming in *VPR* 19 (1986): 68–69; DRABBLE, Margaret, ed.,

The Oxford Companion to English Literature (see *RMB* for
1985, p. 38), rev. by Basil Cottle in *RES* 37 (1986):   620–
23; JACKSON, J.R. de J., *Annals of English Verse, 1770–
1835:   A Preliminary Survey of the Volumes Published* (see
RMB for 1984, p. 42), rev. by Anne McWhir in *UTQ* 56 (1986):
99–101; MARRS, Edwin W., Jr., *A Descriptive Catalogue of the
Letters of Charles and Mary Lamb in the W. Hugh Peal Collection* (see *RMB* for 1985, p. 40), rev. by Winifred F. Courtney
in *KSJ* 35 (1986):   211–13; ROSENBAUM, Barbara, and Pamela
White, comps., *Index of English Literary Manuscripts*, vol.
4, *1800–1900*, part 1, *Arnold-Gissing* (see *RMB* for 1984, p.
43), rev. by Joanne Shattock in *YES* 16 (1986):   299–301;
SULLIVAN, Alvin, ed., *British Literary Magazines*, vol. 1,
The Augustan Age and the Age of Johnson, 1698–1788, vol. 2,
The Romantic Age, 1789–1836 (see *RMB* for 1983, pp. 37–39),
rev. by Pat Rogers in *YES* 16 (1986):   213–20 with criticism
and corrections.

2.   ENVIRONMENT: ART, PHILOSOPHY, POLITICS, RELIGION, SOCIETY

Abrams, Ann Uhry. *The Valiant Hero: Benjamin West and Grand-
Style History Painting.* Smithsonian Institution Press,
1985. Pp. 210; 142 b. & w. illus., 7 col. pls. $39.95.

Rev. by Henry Adams in *BM* 128 (June 1986):   435–36.

Agius, Pauline. *Ackermann's Regency Furniture and Interiors.*
The Crowood Press, 1984. £35.00.

Rev. by Frances Collard in *Apollo* 123 (1986):   66.

Altick, Richard D. *Paintings from Books: Art and Literature
in Britain, 1760–1900.* Ohio State University Press, 1986.
Pp. xxvi+527; 365 b. & w. illus. $60.00.

Rev. favorably by Peter Campbell in *LRB*, Dec. 4, 1986,
pp. 20–21; by Robert Bernard Martin ("Talking Pictures")
in *NYRB*, Feb. 12, 1987, pp. 29–30.
An encyclopedic study of English literary painting, from
its beginnings in eighteenth-century theatrical pictures
and through its phenomenal growth in response to the tastes
of a new audience, middle-class or newly rich, to its decline
after the mid-nineteenth century. Altick estimates that
some 10,000–12,000 paintings were produced in this category,
by artists major, minor, or now forgotten.
The documented information Altick has assembled is so full
that it makes for an awkward structure and a certain redun-

dancy. After his general exposition, he starts over with
summaries of the pictorial treatments of Shakespeare's plays
(part 2) and of the works of other English writers,
arranged by period (part 3). How this impressive amount of
material might be used for "historical or critical purposes"
is suggested not in a concluding chapter but at the end of
part 1.

Literary painting was at its height during the first two
Victorian decades, but because of Altick's topical organization the names of the earlier painters--Reynolds, Romney,
Stothard, Fuseli, Martin, Etty, and others less well known--
continually recur beside those of their successors. (Blake
is mentioned but technically excluded, along with D.G.
Rossetti, because he did not work in oil.) Similarly recurring are references to Thomson, Sterne, Goldsmith, Burns,
Byron, and Scott, whose works provided subjects for some
of the most popular pictures.

A running theme which is relevant to present-day critical
theory is the fate of the principle of *ut pictura poesis*.
On Altick's evidence, the two arts were increasingly confused and consequently devalued in literary painting, which
at its worst added literary tags to hackneyed scenes already
familiar to the unsophisticated audience. In later Victorian
criticism, one effect of the dominance of the genre was a new,
and defensive, theoretical separation of the "sister arts"
which is still with us. (I.H.C.)

Andrew, Patricia. "A Landscape by Joseph Wright of Derby."
BM 128 (Oct. 1986): 741-43. 4 illus.

River Landscape, with Cliffs and Houses in the Distance,
previously attributed to Richard Wilson, is now attributed
to Wright of Derby.

Archer, John W. *The Literature of British Domestic Architecture, 1715-1842.* MIT Press, 1985. Pp. 1078; 11 illus.
£99.95.

Rev. by Ben Weinreb in *BM* 128 (Oct. 1986): 751-52.

Armstrong, Gordon S. "Art, Folly, and the Bright Eyes of
Children: The Origins of Regency Toy Theater Reevaluated."
ThS 26 (1985): 121-42.

Paper cut-out theaters, with characters ranging from
Romeo and Juliet to Bluebeard and the Vampire, were popular
as toys in England from 1811 to 1830.

Barrell, John. *The Political Theory of Painting from Reynolds to Hazlitt: "The Body of the Public."* Yale University Press, 1986. Pp. viii+366; 26 illus. $30.00.

Rev. by Graham Reynolds in *Apollo* 124 (1986): 568.

The word "political" in Barrell's title refers to a theory, first enunciated by Shaftesbury, which postulated a "republic of the fine arts" (later of "taste") analogous to a political republic, and assigned a political function to painting, at first the promotion of the "public virtues." After the attenuation of the theory by mid-century, there was an effort to revive it when the Royal Academy was founded. The major contribution was made by Joshua Reynolds, who in his *Discourses* sought "to establish a public painting, whose function [would be] to confirm the audience for art as the members of a republic, or community, of taste, and, by that means, to confirm their membership also of a political public."

Barrell's nearly 100-page chapter on Reynolds is virtually a paraphrase of the *Discourses*, accompanied by a commentary more detailed than is usually given to art theory, or to critical theory of any kind. The subsequent chapters on Barry, Blake, and Fuseli trace the modifications of Reynolds's theory and the beginnings of its dissolution. In Hazlitt's writings, finally, we arrive at the "individualist" theory of art most familiar today, according to which the aesthetic is separated from the political sphere, "excellence" is achieved by "individual genius," and the "satisfactions" of art "are offered to us as we are private individuals, not public citizens." The chapter on Blake--based on his Reynolds annotations, "Descriptive Catalogue," "Public Address," and the descriptions of Chaucer's Pilgrims--should not be overlooked by Blakeists interested in making theoretical formulations of his opinions. Strongly disagreeing with Morris Eaves by name, Barrell demonstrates persuasively that in Blake's usage such terms as "original," "character," "individual," and "public" had the standard meanings of the time, the same as for the other writers discussed, rather than the present-day meanings that have been assumed. In this chapter, however, Barrell is least sure of the relevance of the political analogy; without inquiring into precisely how the "different characters of society" would be "'members' of Christ's body," he is willing to add a qualifier and accept a "religious republic of taste" as Blake's version of the political republic.

In his expositions Barrell maintains an admirable scholarly objectivity, sometimes to excess. He does not seem to appreciate the implications of his defense of Barry's

physiognomic categories in relation to society and the
"division of labor" (see chapter 2). Only on the last
page does he explicitly confess that he values the writers
he has been discussing because they tried to understand
the history and function of art in relation to "the political"
as such. The ambiguity on which Barrell exits can as easily
be read as a wish for the kind of representational and
political art the twentieth century has already disastrously
seen, as it can be read as a warning against the use of the
"republic of taste" theory as a justification. (I.H.C.)

Bate, Jonathan. "Hal and the Regent." *ShS* 38 (1985): 69-75.

A fine study using Gillray and Cruikshank, plus playbills,
that indicates just how popular was George IV's Prince Hal
allegory, as Byron, for one, knew. (T.L.A.)

Beattie, J.M. *Crime and the Courts in England 1660-1800.*
Princeton University Press, 1986. Pp. xxiv+663. $72.00,
paper $19.95.

Documentation and statistics of the kinds of offenses
and offenders and the administration of justice. Valuable
for the realities behind the novelists' and poets' perceptions of shifts in the quality of their community, especially
the London area. At the end of the American war, "the
courts and the prisons were once again overtaken ... by
another crisis of violent crime in London and, to a greater
extent than ever before, throughout the country" (582).
E.g., "no woman had been executed in Surrey for more than
twenty years"; in the next five years "twelve women were
convicted of capital offenses, of whom eight appear to have
been executed" (584). Capital punishing increased, and the
gallows were moved from Tyburn to the front of Newgate, in
December 1783, to eliminate the festive and ego-soothing
parade to the scaffold, but crimes against property were
increasingly punished by imprisonment and transportation.
To the *Gentleman's Magazine* in 1790 it was clear that a
disgraceful code of laws was a barbarous response to an
increasingly immoral and brutalized population (630).
But this is only a sampling, not a summary, of the information in this volume. (D.V.E.)

Beckett, J.V. *The Aristocracy in England 1660-1914.* London
and New York: Basil Blackwell, 1986. Pp. 528. $34.95.

How the aristocracy survived its loss of economic preeminence.

Beckett, J.V. "Elizabeth Montague: Bluestocking Turned
   Landlady." *HLQ* 49 (1986): 149-64.

   Excellent background for *Pride and Prejudice*, and based
on a new look at the manuscript correspondence. (T.L.A.)

Belchem, John. *'Orator' Hunt: Henry Hunt and English
   Working-Class Radicalism*. Oxford: Clarendon Press,
   1985. Pp. xii+304. $39.95.

   Rev. by Brian Harrison in *LRB*, June 19, 1986, pp. 17-18;
by John W. Osborne in *Albion* 18 (1986): 515-16; by William
Thomas in *TLS*, March 7, 1986, p. 238.
   An attempt to rescue the radical agitator of "Peterloo"
fame from his detractors who, while admitting his effectiveness at rallying the working classes, have finally dismissed
him as little more than a "braggart demagogue." This is,
surprisingly, the first book-length study of Hunt. Belchem
claims it to be a biography; in reality it is more a detailed
study of Hunt's career from 1803 (when at 30 he abandoned
his early loyalism) until his defeat for reelection to
Parliament in 1833, 18 months before his death. Short
beginning and ending chapters do little more than sketch in
details of his early days as a Wiltshire landowner and then
of his rapid physical decline after returning to private
life following passage of the First Reform Bill. In fact,
little information about his private life is ever given
that is not directly related to his campaigns: e.g., the
sudden appearance for the first time on p. 169 of Hunt's
son, Henry, Jr., as a mature adult helping his father run
a family business, when, so far as the reader knows to this
point, Hunt has no offspring. Belchem candidly admits Hunt's
paranoia and sometimes absurd posturing; nevertheless, he
succeeds admirably in establishing Hunt's credentials as the
only unwavering, and undoubtedly the most effective, champion of the working classes in the first three decades of
the century, whose tireless campaigning made the eventual
acceptance of universal suffrage and annual Parliaments
almost inevitable. This book, then, does what all historical
studies should: it forces us to reassess some of our long-
accepted notions about a crucial time in our recent past.
(M.M.)

Belchem, John. "'Orator' Hunt, 1773-1835: A British Radical
   Reassessed." *HT* 36 (1985): 21-27.

   Claims that Henry Hunt made a "considerable contribution
to radicalism and the making of the English working class."
As usual in *HT*, entertaining illustrations. (M.T.S.)

Berg, Maxine. *The Age of Manufactures: Industry, Innovation and Work in Britain, 1700-1820.* Totowa, N.J.: Barnes and Noble, 1985. Pp. 378.

   Rev. by John Bohstedt in *Albion* 18 (1986): 502-05 as a "rich and important book," raising intentionally more questions than it answers; with a valuable bibliography.

Bindman, David, ed. *The Encyclopaedia of British Art.* London: Thames and Hudson, 1985. £10.50.

   Rev. by Richard Kingzett in *Apollo* 123 (1986): 292.

Black, Jeremy. *The British and the Grand Tour.* London: Croom Helm; Wolfeboro, N.H.: Longwood, 1985. Pp. viii+273. $34.50.

   Rev. by A.G. Cross in *JES* 16 (1986): 138 as "a new and serious attempt to investigate every aspect of the Grand Tour experience ... from 1713 to 1793."

Black, Jeremy, ed. *Britain in the Age of Walpole.* New York: St. Martin's Press, 1985. Pp. vii+260. $27.95.

   Rev. by Linda Colley in *JMH* 58 (1986): 914-15.

Blouet, Olwyn Mary. "Sir William Reid, F.R.S., 1791-1858: Governor of Bermuda, Barbados and Malta." *NRRS* 40 (1986): 169-91.

Bogel, Frederic V. *Literature and Insubstantiality in Later Eighteenth-Century England.* Princeton University Press, 1984. Pp. 226. $22.50.

   Rev. by Bruce Redford in *ECS* 19 (1986): 414-17 as "a study of insubstantiality that mimics the phenomenon it seeks to describe" with only occasional "glimmers of insight." Not received.

Bourne, J.M. *Patronage and Society in Nineteenth-Century England.* London and Baltimore: Edward Arnold, 1986. Pp. ix+198. $54.50.

   More than you may want to know about "Old Corruption" and little about people you know. But an education in itself-- useful for any biographical study. (D.V.E.)

Bowen, Huw V. "The East India Company and Military Recruitment in Britain, 1763-71." *BIHR* 59 (May 1986): 78-90.

   The Anglo-French and Seven Years wars led to a large increase in need for troops, for which the company had to com-

pete with the regular army. Ultimately it failed because
of regular army opposition and the huge, inhospitable lands
it was trying to govern.

Brennan, Matthew C. "The Wordsworth of Landscape: Constable
or Turner?" *SAQ* 85 (1986): 252-60.

　Sees Wordsworth as having more in common, surprisingly,
with Turner than with Constable.

Brett, David. "The Aesthetical Science: George Field and the
'Science of Beauty.'" *Art History* 9 (1986): 336-50.
5 illus.

　Field was a dye and pigment chemist and aesthetic theorist,
important for his ideas on color technology, expressive form,
and "the possibility of forming a 'universal' or 'uncondi-
tioned' visual language through a 'science of art.'"

Brown, David Blayney. "Testaments of Friendship; Two New
Portraits by James Barry of Francis Douce and Joseph
Nollekens." *BM* 128 (Jan. 1986): 27-31. 2 illus.

Brown, Iain Gordon. "A Character of Lord Monboddo." *N&Q*,
n.s. 33 (Dec. 1986): 523-24.

　A newly discovered attack on Monboddo, quoted in its
entirety from a MS in the National Library of Scotland.

Burkett, Mary E., ed. *George Romney 1734-1802*. Kendal, England:
Abbot Hall Gallery, 1984.

　Catalogue of a small exhibition in 1984.

Burns, J.H. "Clio as a Governess: Lessons in History 1798."
HT 36 (Aug. 1986): 10-15.

　On the life and work of Miss Richmal Mangnall, school-
mistress and author of *Historical and Miscellaneous Questions for the Use of Young People* (1798).

Burns, James. "From 'Polite Learning' to 'Useful Knowledge'
1750-1850." *HT* 36 (April 1986): 21-29.

Cameron, Elisabeth. *Encyclopedia of Pottery and Porcelain:
The Nineteenth and Twentieth Centuries*. London: Faber, 1986.
£30.00.

　Rev. by Geoffrey Wills in *Apollo* 124 (1986): 225-26.

Campbell, Thomas J. "Penruddock Recreated: John Philip
Kemble's Alterations of Cumberland's *The Wheel of Fortune*."
ThS 25 (1984): 83-94.

Discusses Kemble's performance and the changes he made
in the 1795 melodrama that contributed to its enduring
popularity.

Canovan, Margaret. "The Un-Benthamite Utilitarianism of
Joseph Priestley." *JHI* 45 (1984): 435-50.

Chandos, John. *Boys Together: English Public Schools, 1800-
1864.* Yale University Press, 1984. Pp. 412.

Rev. by Richard Aldrich in *JMH* 58 (1986): 551-52.
Takes a realistic look. (T.L.A.)

Chappell, Miles L. "Fuseli and the 'Judicious Adoption' of
the Antique in the Nightmare." *BM* 128 (June 1986): 421-22.
3 illus.

Proposes as the source of the stricken dreamer the figure
of a reclining Maenad in a sarcophagus relief belonging to
the Farnese Collection, Rome.

Christie, Ian R. "George III and the Historians--Thirty Years
On." *H* 71 (1986): 205-21.

Although it was determined in 1966 that King George was
not psychologically insane but had a hereditary physical
illness, paraplegia, which gave him spells of delirium,
historians often still brandish "psychoanalytic" interpretations of the politics of his "insanity."

Claeys, Gregory. "'Individualism,' 'Socialism,' and 'Social
Science': Further Notes on a Process of Conceptual Formation, 1800-1850." *JHI* 47 (1986): 81-93.

The Owenite movement is the subject, in case you haven't
figured that out from the title. (T.L.A.)

Clark, Jonathan C.D. *English Society 1688-1832: Ideology,
Social Structures and Political Practice During the Ancien
Regime.* (Cambridge Studies in the History and Theory of
Politics.) Cambridge University Press, 1985. Pp. xiii+442.
$39.60.

Rev. by Jeremy Black in *New Statesman*, Jan. 24, 1986,
p. 26 as "an intelligent, stimulating, panoramic view....
In many senses his discussion of the last 30 years of his
period is the most interesting in the book"; by Alan Ryan
in *LRB*, Jan. 25, 1986, pp. 14-16.
Not seen.

Clark, J.C.D. *Revolution and Rebellion: State and Society
in England in the Seventeenth and Eighteenth Centuries.*
Cambridge University Press, 1986. Pp. 192. $34.50, paper
$9.95.

   Not seen.

Coles, Nicholas. "Sinners in the Hand of an Angry Utilitarian:
J.P. Kay(-Shuttleworth) 'The Moral and Physical Condition
of the Working Classes in Manchester (1832).'" *BRH* 86
(1983-85): 453-88.

Colley, Linda. "Whose Nation? Class and National Consciousness in Britain 1750-1830." *P&P* 113 (1986): 97-117.

   Against those historians who believe that nationalism
was "creation and tool of the ruling classes," Colley argues
that in fact the state did little to promote national
consciousness, in part because such a consciousness was
connected with politicization of the populace. Indeed, since
"almost all sectional interest groups in Britain resorted
to nationalist language and activism to advance their claims,"
nationalism must not be considered "a simple act of loyalist
conformity." An interesting and convincing argument.
(J.H-P.)

Cook, B.F. *The Elgin Marbles*. London: British Museum Publications, 1984. Pp. 72; 50 b. & w. and 36 col. illus. £4.95.

   Rev. (with books by John Boardman, *The Parthenon and Its
Sculptures* and *Greek Sculpture: The Classical Period*) by
Ellis Tinias ("Greek Marbles and Restitutionism") in *Art
History* 9 (1986): 396-400.

Corfield, P.J., and Chris Evans. "John Thelwall in Wales:
New Documentary Evidence." *BIHR* 59 (Nov. 1986): 231-39.

   Thelwall's "retreat" to Wales in 1797 was not the giving
up of radical activity, as some historians have characterized
it.

Cordingly, David. *Nicholas Pocock, 1740-1821.* Conway, Wales:
Conway Maritime Press in association with the National
Maritime Museum, 1986. Pp. 120; 77 b. & w. illus., 8 col.
pls. £12.95.

   Rev. by Martin Butlin in *BM* 128 (Nov. 1986): 834.
Said to be the first in a series of monographs on British
marine artists.

Cormack, Malcolm. *Constable: His Life and Work.* Cambridge University Press, 1986. Pp. 256. $49.50.

Rev. by Andrew Wilton in *S*, May 31, 1986, pp. 25–26.

Corrigan, Philip, and Derek Sayer. *The Great Arch: English State Formation as Cultural Revolution.* Oxford and New York: Basil Blackwell, 1986. Pp. viii+304. $34.95, paper $15.95. (Listed last year: see *RMB* for 1985, p. 45.)

A book that breathes Marxist fire in its introductory and concluding sections, while offering in between a somewhat more conventional history of the evolution of the English state from Norman times to the nineteenth century. The earlier historical chapters are vigorously written syntheses of current knowledge, whereas the later ones, increasingly militant in tone, become at the same time progressively less coherent. Hence the chapter most relevant to us may disappoint because it is often vague, confused, and contradictory. The authors' thesis is that "the state" came to have cultural as well as political meaning because governmental regulation was increasingly made to serve both incipient capitalism and patriarchal social relations. This is a fair, albeit a controversial, argument, but the authors mar its development with dreary diatribes and fractured logic. A nineteenth-century example on p. 151 quotes Gladstone as expressing sympathy with the working classes while insisting he couldn't have meant it because, after all, he wasn't a worker. For those who wish an expert review of the formation of the English state as it affected (and was affected by) the development of English culture, this book will do nicely up to the mid-eighteenth century; but as a cogent Marxist critique of England from 1750 on, it is something of a disappointment. (M.M.)

Coslett, Tess, ed. *Science and Religion in the Nineteenth Century.* Cambridge University Press, 1984. Pp. 249. £22.50, paper £7.95.

Not seen.

Cowling, Maurice. *Religion and Public Doctrine in Modern England.* (Cambridge Studies in the History and Theory of Politics, 2.) Cambridge University Press, 1985. Pp. 403. $49.50.

Rev. by John Selwyn Gummer in *S*, Jan. 18, 1986, pp. 23–24 as "nobly attempted and always instructive."

Volume 2 focuses on the eighteenth and nineteenth centuries.

Crafts, N.F.R. *British Economic Growth During the Industrial
Revolution.* Oxford University Press, 1985.

  Reviewed in *RMB* for 1985, p. 46; now available in paperback at $11.95.

Crimmins, James E. "Bentham on Religion: Atheism and the
Secular Society." *JHI* 47 (1986): 95–110.

  On Bentham the Atheist with an upper-case *A*. (T.L.A.)

Crimmins, J.E. "Bentham's Unpublished Manuscripts on Subscription to Articles of Faith." *BJECS* 9 (1986): 33–44.

  Bentham's unpublished manuscripts of 1773 attack the
practice of making university students subscribe to the Thirty-
Nine Articles of the Anglican Church. Hence, his critiques
of religion published between 1809 and 1823 do not indicate
a change in his views occasioned by a frustration with reform.

Dawson, Aileen. *Masterpieces of Wedgwood in the British
Museum.* London: British Museum Publications, 1984. £7.95.

  Rev. by Geoffrey Wills in *Apollo* 123 (1986): 68.

Dawson, Aileen. "Two Napoleonic Sèvres Ice-Pails: A Present
for the Emperor: A New Acquisition for the British Museum."
Apollo 124 (1986): 328–33.

Deis, Elizabeth J., and Lowell T. Frye. "'London or Else the
Back-Woods': Some British Views of America in the 1830s."
SAQ 85 (1986): 374–87.

  Has a "Selected Bibliography" at the end.

Denvir, Bernard. *The Early Nineteenth Century: Art, Design
and Society, 1789–1852.* (Longman's *Documentary History of
Taste in Britain* series.) London: Longman's, 1984. Pp.
316. Paper £6.95.

  Rev. by Ian Small in *BJA* 26 (1986): 83–84 as useful but
flawed; an anthology of original documents, with introductions.

Dickey, Laurence. "Historicizing the 'Adam Smith Problem':
Conceptual, Historiographical, and Textual Issues." *JMH* 58
(1986): 579–609.

  An important update on the issue of reconciling the *Theory
of Moral Sentiment* and the *Wealth of Nations*. (T.L.A.)

Dickinson, H.T. *British Radicalism and the French Revolution 1789-1815*. New York: Basil Blackwell, 1985. Pp. 96. Paper $6.95.

   Rev. by Clara K. Gandy in *Albion* 18 (1986): 513-15 as a valuable contribution to the historiography of English radicalism.
   Not received.

Digby, Anne. *Madness, Morality and Medicine: A Study of the York Retreat 1796-1914*. Cambridge University Press, 1985. Pp. 320. $39.50.

   Rev. by Mark Philp in *LRB* April 3, 1986, pp. 17-19.
   Not seen.

Dinwiddy, J.R. *From Luddism to the First Reform Bill: Reform in England 1810-1832*. (Historical Association Studies.) London and New York: Basil Blackwell, 1986. Pp. 96. Paper $7.95.

   Not seen.

Dyson, Anthony. *Pictures to Print: The Nineteenth-Century Engraving Trade*. London: Farrand Press, 1984. Pp. xxx+234. £15.00. (Distributed in the U.S. by The Book Press, Ltd., Williamsburg, Va.; $15.00.)

   Rev. by Helene E. Roberts in *VPR* 19 (1986): 75-76.

Egerton, Judy. "George Stubbs: Two Rediscovered Enamel Paintings." *BM* 128 (Jan. 1986): 24-27. 3 illus.

   Portrait of Mrs. French's Lap-Dog (1782) and *Lion on a Rock* (1775), both rediscovered in 1984.

Ehrlich, Cyril. *The Music Profession in Britain Since the Eighteenth Century: A Social History*. New York: Clarendon Press, 1985. Pp. viii+269. $39.95.

   Rev. by Steven Norquist in *VS* 30 (1986): 132-33; by Philip Waller in *M&L* 67 (1986): 411-12.
   Not received.

Engen, Rodney K. *Dictionary of Victorian Wood Engravers*. Cambridge, England: Chadwyck-Healey, 1985. £45.00.

   Rev. by Barbara Quinn Schmidt in *VPR* 19 (1986): 74.

Erffa, Helmut von, and Allen Staley. *The Paintings of Benjamin West*. Yale University Press, 1986. Pp. xii+606; 525 b. & w. illus., 111 col. pls. £75.00.

Rev. by Brian Allen in *Apollo* 124 (1986): 455; by
William L. Pressly in *BM* 128 (Oct. 1986): 753-54.

Ertl, Heimo. "'The Manner Wherein God Has Dealt With My Soul':
Methodistiche 'Lives' im 18. Jahrhundert." *Anglia* 104
(1986): 63-93.

Ford, Trowbridge H. "Political Coverage in *The Times*, 1811-
41: The Role of Barnes and Brougham." *BIHR* 59 (May 1986):
91-107.

An important article, demonstrating that much of the existing commentary about this era concerning *The Times* is in
error. Contrary to received opinion, *The Times* was not a
government organ but "such a powerful, consistent voice for
reform and justice that governments not only moderated reactionary policies but were encouraged to take up reform"
(95). Much valuable information on the paper's coverage
of Pentridge, Peterloo, and the Queen Caroline affair.
(M.M.)

Fraser, Flora. *Beloved Emma: The Life of Lady Hamilton.*
London: Weidenfeld and Nicolson, 1986. Pp. 410. £14.94.

Rev. by Roy Porter in *TLS*, Dec. 5, 1986, p. 1380.

Frew, John, and Carey Wallace. "Thomas Pitt, Portugal, and
the Gothic Cult of Batalha." *BM* 128 (Aug. 1986): 582-86.
4 illus.

On the "first ever account in English of a sizeable body
of Iberian architectural antiquities," written by the nephew
of William Pitt on a visit to Lisbon in 1760. This was the
precedent for the later highly influential architectural
drawings of the same church by James Cavanah Murphy in
1792-95.

Gallagher, Catherine. "The Body Versus the Social Body in
the Works of Thomas Malthus and Henry Mayhew." *Representations* no. 14 (Spring 1986): 83-106.

Included in the special issue, "Sexuality and Social Body

in the Nineteenth Century." Malthus (first *Essay on the Principles of Population*, 1798) and Mayhew (*London Labour and London Poor*, 1861) are considered in relation to the traditional "homology" of the individual human body and the body of society, which they transformed into opposition. Against both Adam Smith and the Utopians Condorcet and Godwin, Malthus "valorized" the sexual and laboring body and implied that the problems of overpopulation could be diminished by "making the production of productive bodies the telos of exchange." Mayhew revised and extended Malthus's theory and the "Malthusian problem" by "physicalizing" the marketplace in the bodies of the active but nonproducing costermongers, in whom he saw the danger that society would reduce human value to "its most primitive biological needs."

The author's skillful interpretation of these "representations" is a model of the critical construction of seemingly intractable, nonliteray material, which so far appears to be the only acceptable, or at least accepted, alternative to the opposite treatment of literature proper. (I.H.C.)

Gascoigne, John. "Anglican Latitudinarianism and Political Radicalism in the Late Eighteenth Century." *H* 71 (1986): 22-38.

"The Established Church ... has generally been dismissed as being too complacent and too bound up with the existing order to offer any challenge to the *status quo*--a view this paper seeks to qualify."

Gelling, Margaret. *Place-Names in the Landscape*. London: Dent, 1984. Pp. ix+326.

Rev. by W.F.H. Nicolaisen in *Names* 33 (1985): 100-02.

Gowing, Lawrence. *The Originality of Thomas Jones*. London: Thames and Hudson, 1985. Pp. 64; 52 b. & w. illus. £4.95.

Rev. by Judy Egerton in *BM* 128 (July 1986): 509. 1 illus.

Harris, John. *The Design of the English Country House 1620-1920*. London: Trefoil, 1985. £19.95.

Rev. by John Martin Robinson in *Apollo* 123 (1986): 368.

Harrison, Mark. "The Ordering of the Urban Environment: Time, Work and the Occurrence of Crowds 1790-1835." *P&P* 110 (1986): 134-68.

"The existence in Bristol of both ordered work time and ordered crowd-forming time seems inconsistent with any notion of an unruly popular culture and a chaotic urban environment in the early nineteenth century."

Hartman, Mark. "Hobbes's Concept of Political Revolution." *JHI* 47 (1986): 487–95.

Hayley, B. *Carleton's Traits and Stories and the Nineteenth-Century Anglo-Irish Tradition*. London: Colin Smythe, 1983. Pp. xiv+432. £14.75.

> Rev. by Hilary Pyle in *RES* 37 (1986): 109–10.

Hemlow, Joyce, with Althea Douglas and Patricia Hawkins, eds. *The Journals and Letters of Fanny Burney (Madame d'Arblay)*, vol. 11, *Mayfair 1818-1824, Letters 1180-1354*, vol. 12, *Mayfair 1825-1840, Letters 1355-1529*. Oxford: Clarendon Press, 1984. £85.00.

> Rev. by R.L. Brett in *RES* 37 (1986): 424–25.

Herrmann, Luke. *Paul and Thomas Sandby*. London: Batsford, in assoc. with Victoria and Albert Museum, 1986. Pp. 175; 98 b. & w. illus., 11 col. pls. £14.95.

> Rev. by Judy Egerton in *BM* 128 (Oct. 1986): 755.

Hill, B.W. *British Parliamentary Parties 1742-1832: From the Fall of Walpole to the First Reform*. London: Allen and Unwin, 1985. £18.00.

> Not seen.

Hillyard, Brian. "William Scott, Edinburgh Bookbinder." *Library* 8 (1986): 269.

Hodnett, Edward. *Image and Text: Studies in the Illustration of English Literature*. London: Scolar Press, 1982. Pp. 280; 42 illus. $35.00.

> Rev. by Karl Kroeber in *BIQ* 19 (1985): 75 as ridiculous.

Huntington Library Quarterly 49 (1986): 1-90. Special issue on "English Narrative Art."

> Being the papers presented at the library's Hunt Symposium (1986): David H. Solkin, "Portraiture in Motion: Edward Penny's *Marquis of Granby* and the Creation of a Public for English Art" (1-24), is useful on the frustration of the narrative painters by Royal Academy preference for the grand style; David Bindman, "The Consolation of Death: Roubiliac's

Nightingale Tomb" (25-46), a keen and penetrating study of mid-eighteenth century tomb sculpture, searches for cultural transition in attitudes toward death, with illustrations that call to mind Keats's "sculptured dead"; Norman Bryson, "Enhancement and Displacement in Turner" (47-66), shifts the focus of the papers by concentrating on light and visual information; and Martin Meisel, "Seeing It Feelingly: Victorian Symbolism and Narrative Art" (67-90), takes a brilliant look at the favorite stories told by Victorian paintings, and particularly Holman Hunt's *Scapegoat*. Certainly a provocative group of essays. (T.L.A.)

Journal of British Studies (*JBS*) 25,4 (Oct. 1986). Special issue on "Re-Viewing the Eighteenth Century."

Linda Colley, "The Politics of Eighteenth-Century British History" (359-79): "The significance ... of the state, of war, of empire, of nationalism, of demography, of geography, and, indeed, of gender stands in need of rigorous yet confident analysis"; Joanna Innes and John Styles, "The Crime Wave: Recent Writing on Crime and Criminal Justice in Eighteenth-Century England" (380-435); Robert Allan Houston, "British Society in the Eighteenth Century" (436-66): "England was well on the way to becoming a class society by the time of the Napoleonic Wars but had not yet become one"; T.H. Breen, "An Empire of Goods: The Anglicization of Colonial America, 1690-1776" (467-99).
For a review essay by John A. Phillips, see below.

Jupp, Peter. *Lord Grenville 1759-1834.* Oxford University Press, 1985. Pp. 516. $45.00.

Rev. as "well written and scholarly" by Richard Mullen in *ContR* 248 (1986): 107-08.

Kauffmann, C.M. *John Varley 1778-1842.* (British Watercolours.) London: Batsford, and the Victoria and Albert Museum, 1984. Paper £7.95.

Kent, Christopher. "More Critics of Drama, Music and Art." *VPR* 19 (1986): 99-105.

Supplements two previous lists and contains brief information on John Payne Collier, Thornton Hunt, and a few others—but mainly Victorian and later.

Kestner, Joseph. *Protest and Reform: The British Social Narrative by Women 1827-1867.* University of Wisconsin Press, 1985. Pp. x+242. $21.50.

Rev. by Patrick Brantlinger in *JEGP* 85 (1986):   575 as "useful to anyone interested in resurrecting a number of nearly forgotten women writers."

Kiernan, Kevin S.   "Madden, Thorkelin and MS Vitellius/ Vespasian A XV." *Library* 8 (1986):   127–32.

By carefully tracing Madden's scholarship, Kiernan shows that Thorkelin's transcript of *Beowulf* was more likely to have been made in 1789 than 1787.   (T.L.A.)

Kinch, Michael P.   "The Meteoric Career of William Young, Jr. (1742–1785), Pennsylvania Botanist to the Queen." *PMHB* 110 (1986):   359–88.

Young was back and forth from Pennsylvania to England with American plants for Kew Gardens.   (T.L.A.)

Kingzett, Richard.   "Fyvie and Its Treasures." *Apollo* 124 (1986):   342–44.

Klein, Milton W., and R.W. Howard.   *The Twilight of British Rule in Revolutionary America: The New York Letter Book of General James Robertson, 1780–83.* Cooperstown: New York State Historical Association, 1984.   Pp. xi+274. $17.50.

Rev. by Don Higginbotham in *NEQ* 59 (1986):   459–61. A scholarly study newly based on the manuscript in the Scottish Record Office.   (T.L.A.)

Kramnick, Isaac.   "Eighteenth-Century Science and Radical Social Theory: The Case of Joseph Priestley's Scientific Liberalism." *JBS* (Jan. 1986):   1–30.

Lesser, Margaret.   *Clarkey: A Portrait in Letters of Mary Clarke Mohl* (1793–1883).   Oxford University Press, 1984. Pp. 235.   £15.00.

Levere, Trevor H.   "Magnetic Instruments in the Canadian Arctic Expeditions of Franklin, Lefroy, and Nares." *AnS* 43 (Jan. 1986):   57–76.

Royal Navy expeditions from 1815 on to discover a North-west Passage and general knowledge about the Arctic.

Mabey, Richard.   *Gilbert White: A Biography of the Author of the Natural History of Selborne.*   London: Century; North Pomfret, Vt.:   David and Charles, 1986.   Pp. 224. $29.95.

Rev. by Oliver Rackham in *S*, July 19, 1986, pp. 31–32.

MacDonald, Michael. "The Secularization of Suicide in England
1660–1800." *P&P* 111 (1986): 50–100.

Based on his examination of "coroners' juries, local
institutions composed of ordinary men whose verdicts determined what their community's legitimate public reaction
to suicidal deaths would be," MacDonald concludes that "men
of middling rank responded to cultural polarization by
gradually giving the rites of desecration a new function
that was at once consistent with elite opinion ... and
responsive to the moral values of their communities."

MacLaine, Allan H. *Allan Ramsay*. Boston: Twayne Publishers,
1985. Pp. xii+160. $21.95.

Rev. by Thomas Crawford in *RES* 37 (1986): 574–75.

Maclarnon, Kathleen. "W.J. Bankes in Egypt." *Apollo* 124
(1986): 116–20.

Marks, Patricia. "Harriet Martineau: *Fraser's* 'Maid of
[Dis]Honour.'" *VPR* 19 (1986): 28–34.

McConnell, Anita. "The Scientific Life of William Scoresby,
Jnr., with a Catalogue of His Instruments and Apparatus in
the Whitby Museum." *AnS* 43 (May 1986): 257–86.

Scoresby (1789–1857), a whaler, then clergyman, studied
the Greenland Sea, magnetism, compasses. Helpful information
on the state of scientific knowledge of the Arctic, 1807–
1822.

McCusker, John J. "The Business Press in England Before
1775." *Library* 8 (1986): 205–31.

On the rise of the newspaper. (T.L.A.)

McDowell, R.B., and D.A. Webb. *Trinity College Dublin 1592–
1952: An Academic History*. Cambridge University Press,
1982. Pp. xxiv+580. £35.00.

Rev. by J.C. Beckett in *YES* 16 (1986): 249–50.

McGowen, Randall. "A Powerful Sympathy: Terror, the Prison,
and Humanitarian Reform in Early Nineteenth-Century Britain."
JBS 25 (1986): 312–34.

McNamara, Ruth Ann. "The Theme of the Learned Painter in
Eighteenth-Century British Self-Portraiture." Ann Arbor,
Mich.: University Microfilms International, 1984.

Dissertation. Summarized in *BIQ* 20 (1986): 87.

McPhee, Peter. "Electoral Democracy and Direct Democracy
in France 1789-1851." *EHQ* 16 (1986): 77-96.

An interesting essay that critiques "modernization" theory
and trickle-down explanations of social change. McPhee begins
by noting that "the image of the French Revolution as a time
of massive political mobilization sits awkwardly with the
fact of low participation rates in national elections after
1789." "How could it be that in August-September 1792 ...
fewer than 20 percent of adult males bothered to vote ...
[while] in the National Assembly elections of April 1848,
no fewer than 84 percent of adult males voted?" McPhee
answers that "people may not perceive electoral participation as being the only or even the best way of exercising
popular control." (J.H-P.)

Meehan, Michael. *Liberty and Poetics in Eighteenth Century
England*. London: Croom Helm, 1985.

Not seen.

Miller, Harold. "John Whittaker's *Ceremonial of the Corona-
tion of His Most Sacred Majesty King George the Fourth*."
ABC 36 (Dec. 1986): 17-23.

One of the most sumptuous books ever published, of which
no definitive copy exists because each copy contained
different contents according to the wishes of its buyer.
"Copies" in the Pierpont Morgan and New York Public libraries,
among others. "We will not see the like of these books again."

Morris, David, and Barbara Milner. *Thomas Hearn 1744-1817:
Exhibition Catalogue, Bolton Museum and Art Gallery, South
hampton Art Gallery, Victoria Art Gallery, Bath* (1985-86).
£5.50.

Rev. by Graham Reynolds in *Apollo* 123 (1986): 288.

Neale, R.S. *Writing Marxist History: British Society, Economy and Culture Since 1700.* London and New York: Basil Blackwell, 1985. Pp. xxii+319. $34.95.

A witty and wicked scrutiny of British history and the historians' fitting and misfitting its images. Sterne's attempt at "a tolerable straight line" is presented as the proper path. The "bourgeoisie" is found not to have existed as "a class for itself." Literature is only glanced at—except for a delightful chapter on "Property and Alienation" in Austen's *Mansfield Park* in which David Lodge's "Morris Zapp" is effectively "zapped." Important. (D.V.E.)

Nieli, Russell. "Spheres of Intimacy and the Adam Smith Problem." *JHI* 47 (1986): 611-24.

Once again on reconciling the *Theory of Moral Sentiments* (1759) and the *Wealth of Nations* (1776). (T.L.A.)

Norie, John. "A Billingsley-Decorated Service." *Apollo* 123 (L986): 242-45.

"William Billingsley (1758-1828), generally acknowledged the finest ever flower painter on English porcelain."

Pal, Pratapaditya, and Vidya Dehejia. *From Merchants to Emperors, 1757-1930.* Cornell University Press, 1986.

Rev. by Mildred Archer in *Apollo* 124 (1986): 453-54.

Patey, Douglas L. "Johnson's Refutation of Berkeley: Kicking the Stone Again." *JHI* 47 (1986): 139-45.

Useful for its comments on Hartley's *Observations on Man* (I749). (T.L.A.)

Peacock, John. "Inigo Jones and the Arundel Marbles." *JMRS* 16 (1986): 75-90.

Transplanting "old Greece into England" well ahead of Lord Elgin. (T.L.A.)

Porter, Roy. "Before the Fringe: Quack Medicine in Georgian England." *HT* 36 (Nov. 1986): 16-22.

Powell, David. *Tom Paine: The Greatest Exile*. London:
   Croom Helm; New York: St. Martin's Press, 1985. Pp. 320.
   $22.50.

   Rev. by Brian Martin in *New Statesman*, May 23, 1986, p. 29.

Pressly, Nancy L. *Revealed Religion: Benjamin West's Com-
   missions for Windsor Castle and Fonthill Abbey*. San Antonio,
   Tex.: San Antonio Museum of Art, 1983.

   Rev. by Allen Staley in *BIQ* 19 (1985-86): 120-21.
   Catalogue of an exhibition.

Pry, Kevin. "The Opera House Petition of 1799." *TN* 40
   (1986): 101-06.

   When the opening of the London opera season was delayed
   by a labor dispute, the king intervened on behalf of the
   performers.

Rainbow, Bernarr. "The Rise of Popular Music Education in
   Nineteenth-Century England." *VS* 30 (1986): 25-49.

Raquejo, Tonia. "The 'Arab Cathedrals': Moorish Architecture as Seen by British Travellers." *BM* 128 (Aug. 1986):
   555-63. 14 illus.

   On writers, architects, and painters who traveled in Spain
   during the period 1770-1850 and their theories about the
   Moorish cathedrals. Among those discussed are David Urquhart,
   James Cavanah Murphy, Thomas Hartwell Horne, David Roberts,
   and Owen Jones.

Redford, Bruce. "'A Peep Behind the Curtain at Drury Lane':
   The Richard Brinsley Sheridan Archive at Princeton." *PULC*
   46 (Spring 1985): 249-68.

   An appreciation of "the finest Sheridan archive in the
   world" calling attention to documents illuminating his
   "three careers--dramatic, managerial, and political."

Reid, Robert. *Land of Lost Content: The Luddite Revolt, 1812*.
   London: Heinemann, 1986. Pp. xiii+334. £15.00.

   Rev. by Paul Foot as "a grand book about a grand subject"
   in *S*, Sept. 13, 1986, pp. 28-29.
   Robert Reid is not a scholar, but he has made excellent
   use of scholarly sources in this journalistic retelling of
   the Luddite outbreak. We do not gain from his book's re-
   organization of events, which creates a dramatic focus--
   the incident at Rawfolds--and a rebel hero, George Mellors.

But we do gain immensely from Reid's awareness of the
contemporaneous canvas on which he paints the workingman's
struggle--the Peninsula War, the assassination of Spencer
Perceval, etc. This is a stimulating read, despite its
attempt to seek parallels in modern labor struggle and
technological displacement, and its "televised" vignettes--
Byron comes off as a stock figure of dissipation. Government's inability to see change coming, and the intractability
of its response, make for a tragic tale. (T.L.A.)

Reynolds, Graham. "William Mulready and John Sheepshanks."
Apollo 124 (1986): 358-61.

Richetti, John Jay. *Philosophical Writing: Locke, Berkeley,
Hume.* Harvard University Press, 1983. Pp. 287. $25.00.

Rev. by Ralph S. Pomeroy in *ECS* 20 (1986): 68-70.
Not received.

Riddell, Richard. "Neo-Classical Designs for Medals by C.H.
Tatham." *Apollo* 123 (1986): 116-22.

Ritvo, Harriet. "Animal Pleasures: Popular Zoology in
Eighteenth- and Nineteenth-Century England." *HLB* 33 (1985):
239-79.

A fine essay on the success of Thomas Bewick's *General
History of Quadrupeds* (1790) and much else of interest.
(T.L.A.)

Rogers, Katherine M. *Feminism in Eighteenth-Century England.*
Brighton, England: Harvester, 1982. Pp. viii+291.

Rev. by Douglas Brooks-Davies in *YES* 16 (1986): 264-68.

Rosenfeld, Sybil. *The Georgian Theatre of Richmond, Yorkshire,
and Its Circuit: Beverley, Harrowgate, Kendal, Northalleron,
Ulverston, and Whitby.* London: Society for Theatre Research, 1984. Pp. 122; illus. £3.50.

Rev. by Edward Langhans in *ThS* 26 (1985): 97-99.
History of a provincial theater and traveling company from
1749 to 1830 and beyond.

Rudé, George. *Criminal and Victim: Crime and Society in Early
Nineteenth-Century England.* Oxford University Press, 1986.
Pp. 146. $26.00.

Rev. by Geoffrey Pearson in *TLS*, March 28, 1986, p. 335,
along with Philip Priestley's *Victorian Prison Lives:*

English Prison Biography 1830-1914 (London: Methuen, 1986);
$25.00).   To be recommended "for its warmth and vitality, no
less than for its thought-provoking observations on whether
crime can be counted as a disguised form of 'class war.'"

Sambrook, James. *The Eighteenth Century: The Intellectual
and Cultural Context of English Literature, 1700-1789.*
London: Longman's, 1986. $29.95, paper $14.95.

   Rev. favorably by Pat Rogers in *LRB*, Nov. 6, 1986, pp.
   20-21.
   Not seen.

Schwartz, Richard B. *Daily Life in Johnson's London.*   University of Wisconsin Press, 1984.   Pp. xix+196. $25.00, paper
   $9.95.

   Rev. by Max Byrd in *BIQ* 19 (1985-86):   110-11.
   Not seen.

Scott, Barbara.   "The Duchess of Berry as a Patron of the Arts."
   Apollo 124 (1986):   345-53.

Searle, C.E.   "Custom, Class Conflict and Agrarian Capitalism:
   The Cumbrian Customary Economy in the Eighteenth Century."
   P&P 110 (1986):   106-33.

   "The consolidation of capitalist class relations was, in
   fact, a complex and protracted process, which owed more to
   the volatility of commodity markets and the unintended consequences of inheritance practices than it did to the *Sturm
   und Drand* of the class struggle."

Shadwell, Wendy.   "Britannia in Distress."   *ABC* 11 (Jan.
   1986):   3-12; (March 1986):   11-22.

   A survey of the wealth of caricatures concerning the
   opposition in Britain to the loss of the American colonies,
   with many reproduced here.

Sheridan, Richard B. *Doctors and Slaves: A Medical and
   Demographic History of Slavery in the British West Indies,
   1680-1834.*   New York: Cambridge University Press, 1985.
   Pp. xxii+420. $42.50.

   Rev. by Todd L. Savitt in *WMQ* 43 (1986):   499-501.
   Not seen.

Smith, Olivia. *The Politics of Language, 1791-1819.*   Oxford:
   Clarendon Press, 1984.   Pp. xiii+269. $27.95.

Rev. by David Simpson in *BIQ* 20 (1986):   63-64:   "Its
six chapters deal with ... the *Rights of Man* controversy,
the pamphlet wars (Eaton, Spence, Hannah Moore), Horne Tooke,
the Hone trials, Wordsworth, Coleridge and Cobbett."   "The
main thesis ... is that by 1815 there had occurred a 'weakening of the hegemony of the concept of vulgarity'...."
Not seen.

Stafford, William. *Socialism, Radicalism and Nostalgia:
Social Criticism in Britain 1775-1830*. Cambridge University
Press, 1985. $39.50, paper $13.95.

Not received.

Thorne, R.G. *The House of Commons 1790-1832*. London: Secker and
Warburg, 1986. 5 vols. £225.00.

Reviewed as "an essential tool for any historian of those
years," by Robert Blake in *The London Times*, Aug. 7, 1986,
p. 11.

Townsend, Joseph. *A Dissertation on the Poor Laws: By a
Well-Wisher to Mankind*. University of California Press,
1985. Paper $6.95.

von Erffa, Helmut, and Allen Staley. *The Paintings of
Benjamin West*. Yale University Press, 1986. Pp. 606.
$75.00.

Rev. by Martin Butlin in *S*, June 28, 1986, p. 33.

Walker, John. "Maria Cosway: An Undervalued Artist." *Apollo*
123 (1986):   318-24.

Walker, Richard. *Regency Portraits*. National Portrait
Gallery/HMSO, 1986. Vol. 1, pp. 720; vol. 2, pp. 432.
£85.00.

Rev. by Kenneth Garlick in *Apollo* 134 (1986):   65-66;
by Graham Reynolds in *TLS*, March 28, 1986, p. 328.
Poets were as concerned about their public image as were
politicians. Thomas Moore "despaired of finding a painter
capable of rendering the play of intellect in his features;
Byron thought that Bartolini's bust made him look like a
superannuated Jesuit. The most sensitive of all was Robert
Southey."
An "excellent compendium."

Wallech, Steven. "'Class Versus Rank': The Transformation
of Eighteenth-Century English Social Terms and Theories of
Production." *JHI* 47 (1986):   409-31.

By 1821 the class concept had captured the British imagination, thanks to Ricardo. (T.L.A.)

Warrington, Bernard. "William Pickering and the Book Trade
in the Early Nineteenth Century." *BJRL* 68 (1985): 247-66.

Whelan, Frederick G. *Order and Artifice in Hume's Political
Philosophy*. Princeton University Press, 1985. Pp. xii+393.
$35.00.

Rev. by John Robertson in *ECS* 20 (1986-87): 238-41.

White, James. "An Irish Romantic: James Arthur O'Connor."
Apollo 123 (1986): 132.

Wind, Edgar. *Hume and the Heroic Portrait: Studies in
Eighteenth-Century Imagery*. Ed. Jaynie Anderson. Oxford:
Clarendon Press, 1986. Pp. 139; 124 b. & w. illus. £29.50.

Rev. by John Gage in *BM* 128 (Dec. 1986): 906-07.

Woloch, Isser. "Napoleonic Conscription: State Power and
Civil Society." *P&P* 111 (1986): 101-29.

"With bureaucratic routine and coercion, [the Napoleonic
regime] broke a pattern of draft resistance that had long
seemed endemic" and in so doing "emboldened Napoleon to
adopt his suicidal ways."

Womersley, D.J. "The Historical Writings of William Robertson." *JHI* 47 (1986): 497-506.

Robertson's *History of America* (1777) was the certain
reading of the Romantic poets to a man, and Womersley is
interested in Robertson's shift in style brought on by the
New World as subject, which makes him "almost a Romantic
historian." (T.L.A.)

Young, Hilary. "A Further Note on J.J. Boileau, 'a Forgotten
designer of Silver.'" *Apollo* 124 (1986): 334-37.

See also Reynolds ("English 4. Reynolds"); Southey ("English 4.
Southey").
Reviews of books previously listed:

BRADY, Frank, *James Boswell: The Later Years, 1769-1795* (see
RMB for 1985, p. 43), rev. by David Daiches in *ECS* 19 (1986):
412-14; by Claire Lamont in *RES* 37 (1986): 422-24;
BRANTLEY, Richard E., *Locke, Wesley, and the Method of
Romanticism* (see *RMB* for 1984, pp. 71-72), rev. by Leopold

Damrosch, Jr., in *ECS* 19 (1986):   438-41 as missing much;
BUTLER, Marilyn, ed., *Burke, Paine, Godwin, and the Revolution Controversy* (see *RMB* for 1984, p. 47), rev. by D.A.N.
Jones in *LRB*, Sept. 6-19, 1984, pp. 18-19; by Don Locke
in *TLS*, Sept. 21, 1984, p. 1061; CHRISTIE, Ian R., *Stress
and Stability in Late Eighteenth-Century Britain* (see *RMB*
for 1984, p. 48), rev. by Isaac Kramnick in *ECS* 19 (1986):
534-35; CROSS, Nigel, *The Common Writer: Life in Nineteenth-
Century Grub Street* (see *RMB* for 1985, p. 46), rev. by
Louis James in *VPR* 19 (1986):   159; DUTTON, H.I., *The Patent
System and Inventive Activity During the Industrial Revolu-
tion, 1750-1853* (see *RMB* for 1985, p. 47), rev. by Moureen
Coulter in *VS* 29 (1986):   316-17; EHRMAN, John, *The Younger
Pitt: The Reluctant Transition* (see *RMB* for 1983, p. 43),
rev. by Wm. Kent Hackmann in *ECS* 19 (1986):   433-34; FRUCHTMAN,
Jack, Jr., *The Apocalyptic Politics of Richard Price and
Joseph Priestley: A Study in Late Eighteenth-Century
English Republican Millennialism* (see *RMB* for 1983, p. 43),
rev. by Martin Fitzpatrick in *British Journal for Eighteenth-
Century Studies* 8 (1985):   236-28; by A. Thomson in *DHS* 17
(1985):   474; HEMPTON, David, *Methodism and Politics in
British Society, 1750-1850* (see *RMB* for 1985, p. 48), rev.
by Jeffrey Cox in *JMH* 58 (1986):   916-17; HONT, Istvan,
and Michael IGNATIEFF, eds., *Wealth and Virtue: The Shaping
of Political Economy in the Scottish Enlightenment* (see *RMB*
for 1984, p. 54), rev. by Isaac Kramnick in *JMH* 58 (1986):
301-03; INKSTER, Ian, and Jack Morrell, eds., *Metropolis
and Province: Science in British Culture, 1780-1850* (see
RMB for 1983, p. 48), rev. by James Paradis in *VS* 29 (1986):
328-30; PAULSON, Ronald, *Literary Landscape: Turner and
Constable* (see *RMB* for 1982, p. 50), rev. by Kathleen
Nicholson in *ArtB* 68 (1986):   343-45 as disappointing and
weighed down by a "heavily freighted conceptual framework"
and "metaphorical gynmnastics"; REARDON, Bernard, *Religion
in the Age of Romanticism* (see *RMB* for 1985, p. 13), rev.
by Harry J. Ausmus in *AHR* 91 (1986):   1185-86 as "scholarly
and informative" even though its "structure ... lacks co-
hesiveness"; by W.R. Ward in *JEH* 37 (1986):   477-78 as
"useful" though "old-fashioned"; SALES, Roger, *English
Literature in History, 1780-1830* (see *RMB* for 1983, pp.
65-66), rev. by J.R. Dinwiddy in *EHR* 101 (1986):   256-57 as
"crude and self-indulgent"; STEWART, Robert, *Henry Brougham
1778-1868;   His Public Career* (see *RMB* for 1985, p. 55);
rev. by Asa Briggs in *S*, Feb. 1, 1986, pp. 25-26; by J.H.
Burns in *LRB*, March 20, 1986, pp. 17-18; by Richard Mullen
as "a most useful account" in *ContR* 249 (July 1986):   53-54;
THOMIS, Malcolm I., and Jennifer Grimmett, *Women in Protest
1800-1850* (see *RMB* for 1983, p. 54), rev. by Deirdre Beddoe

in *VS* 29 (1986):   331-32; TWITCHELL, James B., *Romantic Horizons: Aspects of the Sublime in English Poetry and Painting, 1770-1850* (see *RMB* for 1984, pp. 63-64), rev. by Lucy Newlyn in *RES* 37 (1986):   430-33; by William Walling in *TWC* 15 (1984):   108-09.

Composite reviews:

Gandy, Clara K.   *Albion* 18 (1986):   513-15.

Reviews F.P. Locke, *Burke's Reflections on the Revolution in France* (see *RMB* for 1985, p. 99) and H.T. Dickinson, *British Radicalism and the French Revolution 1789-1815* (New York: Basil Blackwell, 1985).   Locke is said to place Burke squarely "in the role of spokesman for the Rockingham Whig party" but to emphasize "that full understanding of the *Reflections* must come from study of it as a work of political rhetoric."   The Dickinson book is recommended as a valuable contribution to the historiography of English radicalism.

Greenfield, John.   *SAR* 51,2 (May 1986):   140-44.

Reviews Richard E. Brantley, *Locke, Wesley, and the Method of English Romanticism* (see *RMB* for 1984, pp. 71-72) and Paul Hamilton, *Coleridge's Poetics* (see *RMB* for 1983, pp. 101-02).

Phillips, John A.   "Peers and Parliamentarians Versus Jacobites and Jacobins: Eighteenth-Century Stability?" *JBS* 25 (1986):   504-14.

Reviews Brian Hill, *British Parlimentary Parties, 1742-1832* (see *RMB* for 1985, p. 42), H.T. Dickinson, *British Radicalism and the French Revolution* (see *RMB* for 1985, p. 46), and two books of 1984 we seem to have missed.   One of these, John Cannon, *Aristocratic Century: The Peerage of Eighteenth-Century England* (Cambridge University Press, 1984, pp. x+193; $34.50), is said to be witty and erudite but "synthetic" rather than "pioneering," and often wide of the mark—partly from the narrow focus on the nobility.   The other, Jeremy Blake, ed., *Britain in the Age of Walpole* (New York: St. Martin's Press, 1984, pp. viii+260; $27.95), is described as a collection of essays "by an extremely talented cluster of scholars" but not further discussed.

Powell, Cecilia.   "Terra Firma for Constable and Turner." *Art History* 9 (1986):   99-107.

Reviews the following: Ian Fleming-Williams and Leslie Parris, *The Discovery of Constable* (see *RMB* for 1984, p. 135); David Hill, *In Turner's Footsteps: Through the Hills and Dales of Northern England* (London: John Murray, 1984; pp. 128; ca. 150 col. and b. & w. illus.; maps; £12.95); Graham Reynolds, *The Later Paintings and Drawings of John Constable* (see *RMB* for 1984, p. 135); and Martin Butlin and Evelyn Joll, *The Paintings of J.M.W. Turner*, rev. ed. (see *RMB* for 1984, pp. 171-72).

Review essays:

Himmelfarb, Gertrude. "The Group: Bourgeois Britain and Its Marxist Historians." *NR*, Feb. 10, 1986, pp. 28-36.

On the contemporary historians, the best known of whom is E.P. Thompson, who once composed the so-called Historians' Group of the British Communist Party; books by and about them are cited in passing—e.g., Harvey J. Kaye, *The British Marxist Historians* (Cambridge: Polity Press, 1984). Himmelfarb raises questions about party loyalty and scholarly responsibility, and calls for "a historical account of Marxism and Communism in our time, written by historians who were personally involved in these movements." "Such a confrontation with the recent past might ... even inspire them to liberate themselves from the theories and assumptions they have applied to the [more distant] past." (I.H.C.)

Perkin, Harold. *JMH* 58 (1986): 886-89.

Reviews M.L. Bush, *The English Aristocracy: A Comparative Synthesis* (Manchester University Press, 1984; pp. 224; $27.00), John Conron, *Aristocratic Century: The Peerage of Eighteenth-Century England* (Cambridge University Press, 1985; pp. x+193; $34.50), and Jonathan Powis, *Aristocracy* (London: Basil Blackwell, 1984; pp. 110). A suggestive review. (T.L.A.)

3. CRITICISM

Abrams, M.H. *The Correspondent Breeze: Essays on English Romanticism.* New York: Norton, 1986. Pp. 296. £19.95.

Rev. by Chris Baldick in *TLS*, Dec. 27, 1985, p. 1484 as offering, in the volume of his collected essays, "more than enough ... to sustain his standing as a literary historian in the best of humanist traditions," even though in some respects "an inadvertent precursor of deconstruction."

Alexander, J.H.   "Literary Criticism and the Later 'Noctes
   Ambrosianae.'"   *YES* 16 (1986):   17-31.

   These "Noctes," appearing in *Maga* (1822-1835), were
primarily the work of John Wilson.

Alexander, Meena.   "Sarojini Naidu: 'Romanticism and
   Resistance.'"   *ArielE* 17,4 (1986):   49-61.

   The first Indian woman elected president of the National
Congress (1925) and friend of Gandhi and Nehru, Naidu first
gained fame as a poet who espoused "a mellifluous if dated
English diction." Her first book of poetry, *The Golden
Threshold*, was published in London in 1905, with a frontis-
piece by J.B. Yeats. Very interesting. (B.C.H.)

Applewhite, James. *Seas and Inland Journeys: Landscape and
   Consciousness from Wordsworth to Roethke.* University of
   Georgia Press, 1986. Pp. viii+236. $25.00.

   Applewhite explores what he terms the "elegiac compromise"
of Romantic and modernist poetry, whereby the poet must
recover contact with the collective unconscious in order to
maintain his inspiration, yet knows that if he comes too
close to it he will be submerged in madness or death. The
compromise is elegiac because the poet inevitably finds himself farther away from the pure form of the unconscious each
day that he lives. Hence, according to Applewhite, the
frequent image in Romantic and modernist poetry of the
fragile boat navigating perilously on a wide sea (e.g., in
Coleridge, Shelley, Hopkins); the house or tower erected
near the sea or the dark forest (e.g., in Wordsworth, Keats,
Poe, Yeats), where the man-made object represents the rational, conscious self, and the surrounding nature figures
forth the irrational, collective unconscious. Poets who
find ways to recover contact with the unconscious without
neglecting the conscious life are the successful compromisers;
those who fail to navigate the perilous sea will fail as
poets. Applewhite concludes that Wordsworth, Coleridge,
Yeats, and Roethke come off best because they found the
balance between separation and absorption. Shelley and
Hopkins have only mixed success: their despair in the
later stages of their careers was a sign that once they
approached the unconscious they could not maintain their
separation from it. Poe and Eliot fail almost totally--
the hysteria and destructiveness of their "waste land"-
scapes being a sign of their inability to achieve the
integration of individual conscious and collective unconscious necessary to poetic inspiration. But it is difficult

to summarize this engaging study without sounding unfairly
reductive. Applewhite's detailed and ingenious Jungian
readings of "Tintern Abbey" and "The Ancient Mariner"
(prototypes of successful integration because the poet in
each case emerges enriched from his contact with the unconscious) and of Coleridge's "Dejection" (prototype of the
failure to integrate) remain fair to the complexity of these
poems while avoiding the temptation to see one-to-one
relationships between landscape objects and psychic states.
All in all, a book well worth perusing, even if you aren't
Jung enough to buy the whole argument. (M.M.)

Auerbach, Nina. *Romantic Imprisonment, Women and Other
Glorified Outcasts.* Columbia University Press, 1985. Pp.
xxiv+315. $25.00.

Only listed last year (see *RMB* for 1985, p. 61).
Despite the title, *Romantic Imprisonment* is a collection
of sixteen disparate essays (all but two of which have been
previously published), the chief unity of which is authorial--
the kind of thing university presses used to be reluctant
to publish. This book appeared in a Gender and Culture
series, and the author's frank introduction declares that
the essays, which were written over a period of 17 years,
fall into periods of the author's development and contain
what she now recognizes as errors which she is not correcting
because "the essays herein do not aim at immutable truths
about their subjects; they are rather my own psychic translations of the cultural life I felt I was living during
their composition"--i.e., they reflect the history of
feminism. Noting all this, the reader need not be a male
chauvinist pig to dismiss the volume as an indulgent cult
production. Such a dismissal would, however, be a mistake,
because of the real power demonstrated in the essays. One
is struck by the range of the book: three pieces on Jane
Austen, two each on Carroll, Brontë, and George Eliot, one
each on Browning and Dickens, a stimulating if little-
developed investigation of literary orphans, a critical
survey of Dorothy Sayers which takes off from the Amazons,
and a knowledgeable biographical/iconographic piece on Ellen
Terry. True, the same comparisons tend to be made again
and again; true, one is sometimes more impressed by the
ingenuity--as of an imagistic connection of Maggie Tulliver
to the Gothic--than convinced by the argument. But there
is throughout a wealth of fresh perceptions and a significant
power of unexpected relationships that makes one glad to have
the pieces conveniently brought together. Professor Auerbach says in her introduction, "All these essays are concerned with the sorts of power the apparently alien and

excluded snatch from and wield over citizens who think they
are safe." One suspects this is a slightly strained afterthought, but if there are any who feel safe, it might give
them to think. (J.E.J.)

Baer, Cynthia M. "'Lofty Hopes of Divine Liberty': The Myth
of the Androgyne in 'Alastor,' 'Endymion,' and 'Manfred.'"
Romanticism 9 (1985): 25-49.

Barker, Gerard A. *Grandison's Heirs: The Paragon's Progress
in the Late Eighteenth-Century English Novel*. University
of Delaware Press; London and Toronto: Associated University Presses, 1985. Pp. 187. $26.50.

   From Richardson's Grandison to Austen's Darcy, the
evolution of the "paragon" is traced--through Sheridan's
Faulkland, and Burney's Orville, and Inchbald's Dorriforth,
to Holcroft's Henley; thence to Godwin's and Austen's more
realistically examined heroes. Godwin, even in his early
Italian Letters, dealt in psychological realism that ran
counter to Richardson's idealization of human nature (129).
And in *Pride and Prejudice* "the mellowing of Darcy's
astringent character ... represents a decisive departure from
Austen's predecessors, signaling the emergence of a more
psychologically realistic Grandisonian hero." (D.V.E.)

Bate, Jonathan. *Shakespeare and the English Romantic Imagination*. Oxford: Clarendon Press, 1986. Pp. xvi+276. $39.00.

   Reviewed by T.W. Craik in *ChLB* 57 (Jan. 1987): 29-32 as
"a wide-ranging, well-written, and highly intelligent study."

Behrendt, Stephen C. "'The Consequence of High Powers':
Blake, Shelley, and Prophecy's Public Dimension." *PLL* 22
(1986): 254-75.

   "Both authors recognize the public imperative of prophetic
art. The Romantic prophet is a socially committed leader,
not the detached elitist he is often take for"--so concludes
an analysis that fails to indicate how men are to be "wrought"
to sympathy by a sublime poetic. (T.L.A.)

Bidney, Martin. "Faulkner's Variations on Romantic Themes:
Blake, Wordsworth, Byron, and Shelley in *Light in August*."
MissQ 37 (1985): 277-86.

   "[T]here can be little doubt that all four Romantics have
helped deepen the resonances."

Blum, Antoinette. "The Uses of Literature in Nineteenth- and Twentieth-Century British Historiography." *L&H* 11 (Fall 1985): 176-202.

> Evaluates the work of E.P. Thompson, Raymond Williams, Peter Laslett, E.J. Hobsbawm, and R.H. Tawney, as well as of some leading Victorian and early twentieth-century historians for their use of literary evidence.

Bridgman, Richard. "From Greenough to 'Nowhere'" Emerson's *English Traits*." *NEQ* 59 (1986): 469-85.

> Useful in calling our attention to the essay, which makes reference to Wordsworth and Carlyle, and which is seen to portray a conflict between hope and a realistic appraisal of the American character (T.L.A.)

Burgan, Mary. "Heroines at the Piano: Women and Music in Nineteenth-Century Fiction." *VS* 30 (1986): 51-76.

Cafarelli, Annette. *Narrative Sequence, and Biography: Johnson and Romantic Prose*. Ann Arbor, Mich.: University Microfilms International, 1986.

> Dissertation.

Cave, Richard Allen, ed. *The Romantic Theatre: An International Symposium*. Totowa, N.J.: Barnes and Noble, 1986. Pp. 130. $24.50.

> Essays by Timothy Webb, "The Romantic Poet and the Stage: A Short, Sad History"; Giorgio Melchiori, "The Dramas of Byron"; Stuart Curran, "Shelleyan Drama"; and Richard Allen Cave, "Romantic Drama in Performance"; with "a short bibliography" on the Romantics and the theater, by Christina Gee and Judith Knight--short but helpful, with good sections on Coleridge, Keats, and Wordsworth as well as Byron and Shelley. (D.V.E.)

Cook, David. *Northrop Frye: A Vision of the New World*. Toronto: New World Perspectives, 1986. Pp. 122. $7.95.

> Rev. by Ramsay Cook in *UTQ* 56 (1986): 157-59.
> According to reviewer Cook, author Cook sets out to "caricature" Frye's "pastoral liberalism" and "technological humanism"; Frye's "recreative imagination" is seen both rejecting "Blake's revolutionary vision" and departing from "Locke's sensual materialism."
> Not received.

Cordasco, Francesco. "An Unrecorded Bensley Edition of
Junius." *N&Q*, n.s. 33 (March 1986): 84.

In the New York Public Library.

Cottom, Daniel. *"The Civilized Imagination": A Study of Ann
Radcliffe, Jane Austen and Sir Walter Scott.* Cambridge
University Press, 1985.

Cross, Nigel. *The Common Writer: Life in Nineteenth-Century
Grub Street.* Cambridge University Press, 1985. Pp. vi+266.
$39.50.

Rev. by David Montrose in *New Statesman*, Jan. 17, 1986,
p. 33; by James L. West, III, in *PBSA* 79 (1985): 591-98.
Not received.

Curran, Stuart. *Poetic Form and British Romanticism.* Oxford
University Press, 1986. Pp. ix+265. $29.95.

Curran attempts no less than a history of British Romantic
poetry, taking genre as his focus. He contends that the
Romantics' claims to be writing whatever sprang spontaneously
from their imaginations have obscured their heavy dependence
on genre. The author's brilliance and originality and the
broad sweep of his knowledge are everywhere evident. An
important thread throughout is the notion of genre as
liberation from and defense against the reactionary forces
of the age. For example, he sketches the revival of interest in medieval and Renaissance poetry as an appeal by
both the left and the right to the greatness of England's
past during the intense repression of dissent after 1795.
In his treatment of the sonnet, he reminds us that Shakespeare's sonnets were popular only with Keats. The discussion of the hymn and the ode offers a compelling reading
of Coleridge's "Dejection," though Curran slips when he
tries to deal with "Tintern Abbey" as an ode. The chapter
on the pastoral is in many ways the most original. Curran
sees its essence as a tension between the values of retreat
and the knowledge of its impossibility. Pastoral, he claims,
became an ally of revolution: a defense of the workers
against repression. In this light Curran finds *Lyrical
Ballads* to be all pastoral and no ballad--an inversion not
just of the linguistic but also of the generic hierarchy.
All the major Romantics, he contends, psychologize the
pastoral: Keats wishes to eroticize it, Wordsworth to
localize it in Grasmere, Coleridge to Christianize it,
Shelley to test its limits by mentalizing it; this applies
even to Blake and Byron, who oppose it. Curran then argues

the instability of romance because, like the pastoral, it
has impossible desires at once for entropy and for total
liberation. Chapter 7 shows how the epic was used by
conservatives to bolster renewed nationalism and by radicals
to celebrate revolution without penalty. Thus he explains
how Byron, who opposed many of the cultural assumptions of
his day, could write in genres (epic, mock-epic, and satire)
which imply stable and widely accepted cultural norms. The
chapter on "composite orders" demonstrates the mixture of
epic, pastoral, and romance in *The Prelude*, and that poem's
surprisingly extensive use of epic machinery. These are
only a few examples of how focusing on genre enables Curran
to achieve new and arresting insights. His wisest decision
was to try to be thorough but not comprehensive; this
enables him to "cover' all the important ground while remaining free to pursue his theses. Occasionally one feels that
he is either using genre to explain too many things or
defining it so generally as to include too much. Never
mind: we will all be absorbing what he has to teach us
for a long time to come. (M.M.)

Cushing, James Byers. "The Figure of the Poet: Self-Representation in Young, Blake, and Wordsworth." Ann Arbor,
Mich.: University Microfilms International, 1984.

Treats Blake's *Night Thoughts* designs as critical comment
on Young, and *The Four Zoas* as responding to *Night Thoughts*
in the poem's "focus on the figure of the poet, Los, and
his struggle to represent himself."

Doody, Margaret Anne. *The Daring Muse: Augustan Poetry
Reconsidered*. Cambridge University Press, 1985. Pp. 288;
28 illus. Paper $12.95.

Rev. by Francis Doherty in *BJECS* 9 (1986): 251-52 as
"the best single book on the range of Augustan poetry";
by Howard Erskine-Hill in *TLS*, March 14, 1986, p. 280
as making good use of unacknowledged sources, effective in
its reformulations, and achieving its own emphasis.
Doody defines "Augustan" generously, not only in terms
of whom it includes--everyone from Rochester through Blake--
but also in terms of its "peculiar or characteristic"
qualities. Traditionally, Augustan poetry has been associated
with a concern for genre, a dedication to Ovid, Horace,
and Virgil, an interest in satire, and a commitment to the
couplet. Although Doody explores each of these traditional
associations, she argues that the "characteristic" qualities
of Augustan poetry are ambition, daring, restless desire,
self-consciousness, experimentalism, originality, paradox,

power, metaphoricity, sublimity, and--most important--vision:
"[Augustan] poets not only see beyond the real--they see
into the real, they see something else, wonderful or frigh-
tening. 'To see a World in a Grain of Sand'; Blake could
have come only in this period, with the experience of
Augustan imagination at his back."
    In emphasizing these qualities, Doody makes it possible
for us to see the links not only between Blake and a poet
like Pope but also between the Romantics and the Augustans.
However, since the qualities she emphasizes are so often
presumed to be the essential qualities of all literature,
one soon begins to wonder what, if anything, makes Augustan
poetry different. Doody drops some hints along the way;
she describes the poetry as "free-trading," attributes to
the Augustans the belief that "some profit can be made of
almost everything," and associates the literature's double
voice with a two-party system. But Doody never develops
these hints, in part because she seems to assume that to
historicize or politicize would defeat her declared purpose: "to restore the sense of excitement that can come
from reading Augustan poetry." It may be time to question
this assumption as well as a "sense of excitement" based on
a desire for the same. (J.H-P.)

Eagleton, Terry. "Marxism, Structuralism and Poststructuralism."
    Diacritics 15 (1985): 2-12.

Eaves, Morris, and Michael Fischer, eds. *Romanticism and
    Contemporary Criticism*. Cornell University Press, 1986.
    Pp. 246. $29.95, paper $8.95.

    Contains essays by Northrop Frye, "The Survival of Eros in
Poetry"; W.J.T. Mitchell, "Visible Language: Blake's
Wond'rous Art of Writing"; J. Hillis Miller, "On Edge: The
Crossways of Contemporary Criticism"; M.H. Abrams, "Construing and Deconstructing"; and Stanley Cavell, "In Quest
of the Ordinary: Texts of Recovery." Following each essay
is a transcript of a question-answer session from a series
of lectures in a course on "The Romantic Self" given at the
University of New Mexico in 1983.
    Tracing the presence of Eros in literature from the Bible
to the Romantics, Northrop Frye associates--with reference
to Blake as formative to his thinking--the function of the
"god" in our literature as a hopefully liberating representation of psychic force.
    Says W.J.T. Mitchell, "the specifically political charac-
ter of Blake's commitment to making language visible can
best be seen by reflecting on his 'graphocentrism,' his

tendency to treat writing and printing as media capable of
full presence, not as mere supplements to speech."

This essay, along with the subsequent questions and
Mitchell's answers, is--I believe--a major document of "late"
criticism of Blake in relation to contemporary (particularly
deconstructive) literary theory. Along with James Chandler's
Wordsworth's Second Nature (chapter 10) and remarks in
Marilyn Butler's *Romantics, Rebels, and Reactionaries*, this
piece opens out the complexities of writing as occasions of
both politics and vision, both the written/pictorial artifact and the historical/psychological liberation of the
reading/viewing subject. In the discussion, Mitchell uses
his essay to tease clean the lasting--and to Mitchell truly
subversive and liberating--features of Derrida's deconstruction from the easier and consoling and fashionable uses that
have been made of him (Derrida). This is a major essay,
written with passion and vision as well as historical and
textual precision.

J. Hillis Miller discusses "A Slumber Did My Spirit
Seal" as a poem that dismantles the logos of the poem, as
an example of current critical thinking that tries to enter
the "strangeness" of the poem more fully by moving beyond
traditional hierarchical and oppositional and unitary
impulses in criticism.

Deconstruction, Miller says, is simply very good reading,
reading that admits or *submits* to the "coerciveness" of the
work--interesting, in light of the Yale claim for criticism's
co-primacy with literature. But the critic also assumes
the solidity of the "self" while he deconstructs it, that
is, perceives it as a problem. Like Blake with his pas-
sionately complex study (in his poetry) of written versus
spoken language, Miller presents a similar complexity about
the self as a problem for criticism and writing. Miller
here appears, curiously, as liberating as Blake.

Abrams gives an exceedingly helpful summary of Derrida's
Of Grammatology in order to do the same for J. Hillis
Miller's deconstructive reading of Wordsworth. Ultimately
the deconstruction of Wordsworth's poem is found ingenious
but not particularly helpful.

Wonderfully in this volume, Miller answers Abrams answering Miller. The latter claims that Abrams's distinction
between a "construing" of recognizable reading and a subsequent, superadded, and implicitly gratuitous deconstructive
reading is false: that no such distinction exists or can
exist. If not so persuasive in practice (as Abrams suggests),
Miller is very persuasive in theory.

Cavell--picking up the theme of philosophical skepticism
in Miller's and Abram's essays--extends it to brief, rather
fluffy, discussions of "The Ancient Mariner" and "The Intima-

tions Ode" in an effort to say something about the Romantics' efforts to battle and confront their own skepticism about the "ordinary," what I take to be "otherness," and their effort to "acknowledge" or participate in it.

The book as a whole disappoints but partly for a potential not fully realized. Mitchell's essay integrates current excitement about the historical understanding of Romanticism with an acknowledged debt to deconstruction. Miller, moving the other way, openly anticipates the possibilities of an essay like Mitchell's even though his (Miller's) deconstruction doesn't reach that far; furthermore Miller can offer an incisive critique of Abrams's traditionalist, humanist critique of deconstruction. But Frye's, Abrams's, and Cavell's essays contribute little to what is a potentially powerful and currently important dialogue. (J.C.R.)

Edmundson, Mark Wright. *Towards Reading Freud: Moments of Self-Representation in Milton, Wordsworth, Keats, Emerson, Whitman and Sigmund Freud.* Ann Arbor, Mich.: University Microfilms International, 1986.

Dissertation.

Egan, Susanna. *Patterns of Experience in Autobiography.* University of North Carolina Press, 1984. PP. xi+226. $19.95.

See the review essay by Robert Bell, at end of this section.

Engell, James, ed. *Johnson and His Age.* (Harvard English Studies, 12.) Harvard University Press, 1985. Pp. xii+574. $25.00, paper $8.95.

Received in 1987. A festschrift in honor of W. Jackson Bate; 23 essays, beginning with Lawrence Lipking on "Johnson and the Meaning of Life" (1-28) and including these specifically Romantically relevant essays: John L. Mahoney, "The Anglo-Scottish Critics: Toward a Romantic Theory of Imitation" (255-84); Jean H. Hagstrum, "'What Seems to Be: Is': Blake's Idea of God" (425-58); Ralph W. Rader, "From Richardson to Austen: 'Johnson's Rule' and the Development of the Eighteenth-Century Novel of Moral Action" (461-83); Alex Page, "'Straightforward Emotions and Zigzag Embarrassments' in Austen's *Emma*" (559-74). No index.

Engelburg, Karsten, ed. *The Romantic Heritage; A Collection of Critical Essays.* (Publications of the Department of English, University of Copenhagen, 12.) University of Copenhagen, 1983. Pp. 229.

Not seen.

Everett, Barbara. *Poets in Their Time: Essays on English Poetry from Donne to Larkin*. London: Faber, 1986. Pp. 264. £15.00.

> Not seen.
> The review by Peter Porter, in *TLS*, Dec. 26, 1986, p. 1441, does not make the book sound interesting; the weakest essays are said to be those on Browning, Keats, and Pope.

Falck, Colin. "A Defence of Poetry." *JAAC* 44 (1986): 393-403.

> In using Shelley (and other Romantics) for his own purposes, Falck quickly shifts from a defender of modernism to a defense of the Romantic tradition. (T.L.A.)

Ferguson, Moira, ed. *First Feminists: British Women Writers 1578-1799*. Indiana University Press and The Feminist Press, 1985. Pp. 461. Paper $12.95.

> A valuable resource for scholars and an excellent text for the classroom. Working from an initial list of 71 women who "wrote explicitly feminist works in English" between 1578 and 1799, Ferguson selects writings by 28 to represent both the range and depth of the period's "mainstream" feminist polemic. Recognizing "that what we would define as feminist is dependent upon and changes within different historical periods," Ferguson seems to have used a broad definition to amass her initial list, which includes not only women who "advocate[d] women's just demands and rights" but also those who "counter[ed] or offset *at any level* the socio-cultural, sexual, and psychological oppression and economic exploitation of women." However, Ferguson's selections from this initial list seem to be based on more specific principles. First, she is mainly interested in "feminist polemicists" who write "to urge or to defend a pro-woman point of view which includes resistance to patriarchal values, convention, and domination or a challenge to misogynous ideas." Second, she is intent on emphasizing two kinds of resistance and challenge: the adumbration of antipatriarchal arguments and the expression of a romantic friendship between women. And finally, Ferguson is committed to representing writings by women from three different classes: the aristocracy, the bourgeoisie, and the working class. Although I believe that these three principles for selection are wise as well as sound, I also suspect that some readers will be disturbed to find their particular favorites—be they male or female—excluded from a collection entitled *First Feminists*. Perhaps "Feminist Polemics" would have been a better title.

Besides short biographical sketches, the collection includes a valuable introduction in which Ferguson not only describes various kinds of feminist polemic but also places this polemic within the context of a society that was changing from "feudal-agricultural to bourgeois-industrial," a change that coincided with an ideological shift from misogynistic attacks on "sexually rampaging unnatural women" to "protective advice about maintaining proprieties and staying in a subordinate place." Given this introduction as well as the selections, we are now in a better position to analyze and understand the ideological, rhetorical, and stylistic dimensions of early British feminist polemic. (J.H-P.)

Findlay, L.M. "Paul de Man, Thomas Carlyle, and 'The Rhetoric of Temporality.'" *DR* 65 (1985): 159-81.

A reading of de Man's influential essay, an essay "tested for equity and suasiveness against Carlyle's ... rhetoric of temporality." Findlay concludes that "it is not allegory alone but allegory as it is apprehended in the rhetorical *agon* of discourse that 'unveil[s] an authentic temporal destiny.'"

Fite, David. *Harold Bloom: The Rhetoric of Romantic Vision.* University of Massachusetts Press, 1985. Pp. xiv+230. $25.00.

Reading *Harold Bloom*, I have experienced an unexpected nostalgia for the days of first discovering Bloom's apparently provocative pronouncement on the Romantics in passionate, and thus provocative, language. Fite does us the considerable service of presenting Bloom's career with careful summaries of each of his books placed in cultural context. So much of Bloom already, I suspect, has either been suppressed or subsumed in more recent criticism or acknowledged in telling gestures ("precursor poet," "anxiety of influence," "swerve") meant to stand for a whole argument that it is good to see it all spelled out in a handy way.

Fite, like Bloom a critic of other writers, "appreciates" his subject, but unlike Bloom does not wrestle with it. He is a cautious critic, making sure that Bloom's critics get their due. But this, too, is all right since it serves as a summary portrait of the climate in which Bloom's passionate writing has thrived. (J.C.R.)

Frank, Lawrence. *Charles Dickens and the Romantic Self.* University of Nebraska Press, 1985. Pp. 283. $23.95.

Rev. by Charles J. Rzepka in *SiR* 25 (1986): 585–89 as deserving to be read "by every student of romanticism."

Fraser, Hilary. *Beauty and Belief: Aesthetics and Religion in Victorian Literature.* Cambridge University Press, 1986. Pp. xii+287. $34.50.

Traces the influence of Romantic aesthetic theory from the Tractarians to the Aesthetes.

Fruman, Norman. "Ozymandias and the Reconciliation of Opposites." *SLIm* 19 (1986): 71–87.

Fruman is entertaining and illuminating as he oversimplifies, reduces, and otherwise misconstrues the idea of "the reconciliation of opposites" which "*should* strike one as illogical and an affront to one's actual experience of the arts and to common sense." Fruman's questionable standard of common sense seems to blind him to the value of an "illogical" experience which is the "actual experience" of many.

Blaming the New Critics, especially Brooks in "The Language of Paradox," for the popularity of German Romantic theories of opposites, Fruman sighs with relief that fashions change as he happily quotes Wellek: "the German romantics have almost disappeared from the horizon and seem to have become almost incomprehensible in their specific philosophical suppositions."

Along the way Fruman engages in his energetic and witty Coleridge-bashing. For example, contemplating the marvelous *Biographia* passage of the water-insect winning its way upstream, Fruman shrugs his wise-guy shoulders: "Without a previous knowledge of Kant and Schelling, few readers of the *Biographia* can have the vaguest notion of what this mystifying statement can possibly mean." Feigning (?) ignorance of the illumination of Coleridge's brilliancies, Fruman guesses that the "strange and totally unexpected connection between the imagination and oppositions" may have been learned by Coleridge from Schelling.

After delighting in the Germans' blunder that the admired Juno Ludovisi bust was not even Greek, as they had supposed, Fruman undercuts Empson's analysis of Keats's "Ode to Melancholy": "Empson's 'opposites' are not in the poem but in his own suppositions, just as the Juno Ludovisi's beauty and terror and celestial self-sufficienty were not in an antique bust but in the dialectical assumptions of Friedrich Schiller."

Fruman's blindnesses hardly detract from the corrective force of his attacks. He does know how to kick 'em while they're down. (M.T.S.)

Frye, Northrop. *Northrop Frye on Shakespeare.* Ed. Robert
Sandler. Yale University Press, 1986. Pp. vi+186. $17.95.

"We have to keep the historical Shakespeare always present
in our minds, to prevent us from trying to kidnap him into
our own cultural orbit," announces Frye in his introduction,
and indeed this book does not move Shakespeare into the
Romantic period. But any Romantics scholar will appreciate
the relevant historical audience allusions, as well as
finding Frye's Shakespeare delightful between-semesters
reading.

The book has no index, but the *Kirkus* review mailed with
it notes that Frye considers *Hamlet* the central play for
nineteenth- and twentieth-century audiences and *Lear*, with
its sense of the world's "absurdity," apt for the present,
while *Antony and Cleopatra* may suit the twenty-first
century "because of its investigations of the uses and abuses
of power."

Gallagher, Catherine. *The Industrial Reformation of English
Fiction: Social Discourse and Narrative Form 1832-1867.*
University of Chicago Press, 1985. Pp. xiv+320.

Rev. by Jeremy Hawthorn in *English* 25 (1986): 273-78.

Goslee, Nancy M. *"Uriel's Eye": Miltonic Stationing and
Statuary in Blake, Keats and Shelley.* University of Alabama
Press, 1985.

Griffin, Dustin. *Regaining Paradise: Milton and the Eighteenth
Century.* Cambridge University Press, 1986. Pp. xi+299.
$29.95.

The Romantic period and a few of the poets are but briefly
cited; yet all of us can benefit from the improved precision
of this account of the responses of the major eighteenth-
century poets to "Milton as a resource to be drawn on,
re-created, transformed." And we may also benefit from
Dustin's success in distancing his study from the "influence"
studies of W.J. Bate and Harold Bloom as well as the
earlier naively empirical surveys.

"Though it may seem attractive to us to imagine that every
writer's life is filled with literary anxiety ... I do not
find this to be true of writers in the ages of Dryden, Pope,
and Johnson; rather, "a sense of detachment, friendly
rivalry, and literary possibility" (ix). (D.V.E.)

Gunner, Jeanne. *T.S. Eliot's Romantic Dilemma: Tradition's
Anti-Traditional Elements.* New York: Garland Publishing,
1985. $33.00.

Hagstrum, Jean H. *The Romantic Body: Love and Sexuality in
Keats, Wordsworth, and Blake.* University of Tennessee
Press, 1985. Pp. xvi+177. $14.95.

In his magisterial *Sex and Sensibility: Ideal and Erotic
Love from Milton to Mozart*, Professor Hagstrum voices the
need for its sequel in Romanticism, which has become the
present volume (the latest of the Hodges Lectures at the
University of Tennessee). That earlier book, a model of
traditional scholarship informed by Blakean and Freudian
insight, surveyed literature from the Restoration through
Goethe in order to mark the emergence of the opposing im-
pulses--in literature--of sex and its evasion or transcendence, sensibility (or *angelisme*). Similar opposition
appears in the following generations of the Romantics except
that Hagstrum argues that in most instances the literary
representation of sex in Romanticism gets absorbed into the
representation of the larger category, love. That is, the
two forces that previously opposed each other now exist
hierarchically, one contained within the other. But I
believe that only secondarily (or perhaps implicitly) does
Hagstrum wish to propose this hierarchical relationship.
Primarily he wants to show that, contrary to most readings
of Romantic poetry, the poems often maintain and carry elements of sex and sensuousness into the transcendence, the
Romantic love, that gives the poems ultimate shape and
purpose.
This is a very important corrective contribution, one that
all readers of Romanticism should find useful. Readers of
Wordsworth will benefit the most, since that poet's work has
suffered most from the dominant critical tradition's predisposition to spiritualization. Wordsworth's poetry lends
itself most naturally among the Romantic poets to this
hierarchical vision, sex and passion ultimately being absorbed into the larger, more "ennobling" structure of (often
domestic) love.
The question of the success or failure of Hagstrum's
hypothesis emerges most dramatically in the discussion of
Keats. Although some of Keats's poems exhibit a version of
the Wordsworthian structure, many do not. Put differently,
Keats tests the values and political implications of sex
more radically and, I think, with differing results for
art. Hagstrum mentions Foucault but does not take seriously
the latter's proposal that in the early post-Enlightenment
period the representation of sexuality needs to be considered
in terms of power. As a result, the "look" of Romantic
poetry, dynamically speaking, does not significantly change
in Hagstrum's reading. Those elements that, in this period,

ought to be considered potentially subversive seem happily
to arrange themselves amidst a dialectics of transcendence.
Oddly, the book that ought to have inserted into our paradigm of the Romantic poem the dissonance of sex ends up as
a new angle on Abrams's "natural supernaturalism." (J.C.R.)

Haney-Peritz, Janice. "Refraining from the Romantic Image:
Yeats and the Deformation of Metaphysical Aestheticism."
SiR 25 (1986): 3-37.

One of "Yeats's favorite, though apparently minor, formal
supplements: the refrain" is taken as a clue to the
formalism in Yeats which "seems to owe so much to at least
one strain of romantic aesthetics." Examining Yeats's
formalism naturally involves "displaying and exploring" his
"capacity for deformity" (6).
Noting that several critics have seen a curious connection
between Coleridge's use of "a small water-insect" to refute
associationism and Yeats's poem "Long-Legged Fly," Haney-
Peritz illuminates the critical metaphysics of both poets
while finding in the refrain of Yeats's "Fly" poem "an un-
canny cross between a Coleridgean-like body and a Nietzschean-
like ghost" (31). (D.V.E.)

Harker, Dave. *Fakesong: The Manufacture of British "Folksong"
1700 to the Present Day.* Milton Keynes: Open University
Press, 1985. Pp. xviii+297. £8.95.

Rev. by D.K. Wilgus in *VS* 30 (1986): 133-34.

Harvey, Geoffrey. *The Romantic Tradition in Modern English
Poetry: Rhetoric and Experience.* New York: St. Martin's
Press, 1986.

Not seen.

Hill, James L. "Experiments in the Narrative of Consciousness:
Byron, Wordsworth, and *Childe Harold,* Cantos 3 and 4." *ELH*
53 (1986): 121-40.

Hoagwood, Terence Allan. *Prophecy and the Philosophy of Mind:
Traditions of Blake and Shelley.* University of Alabama
Press, 1985. $23.50.

"Prior relations subsisted between Christian biblical
commentaries and secular philosophies of mind, but the poets'
splendid unification of these traditions is revolutionary."
Not seen.

Homans, Margaret. *Bearing the Word: Language and Female
Experience in Nineteenth-Century Women's Writing.* University of Chicago Press, 1986. Pp. 326. $22.00.

According to Homans, a "myth of language" lies "at the heart
of nineteenth-century European culture." After pointing to
Wordsworth's account of language acquisition in *The Prelude*
as an embodiment of this myth, Homans turns to Lacan for
"the most compelling contemporary formulation" of the myth
of a symbolic order founded on the absence or death of the
mother, the loss of the referent, the recognition of the
law of the father, and the emergence of a desire for figurative substitutions. Since this myth puts woman in the
position of being the lost referent and/or the figurative
object of the desiring subject's quest, it was bound to cause
problems for nineteenth-century women writers. However, as
Homans sees it, those problems were complicated by the
difference between male and female experience. Appealing
to the authority of Nancy Chodorow, Homans argues that
because women do not perceive the mother as irrevocably
lost, they do not embrace the symbolic order as wholehearted-
ly as men do. Instead, they retain some relationship with
a presymbolic, preoedipal mother, a relationship that child-
bearing quite literally reproduces. On the basis of this
controversial model of female experience, Homans links the
reproduction of mothering to a "structure of literalization,"
distinguishes the structure of literalization from "the
structure of figuration" mandated by the symbolic law of the
father, and sets out to explore how six nineteenth-century
women dealt with the conflict of being both daughters and
writers. Choosing mostly well-known texts by Dorothy
Wordsworth, Emily Brontë, Charlotte Brontë, Mary Shelley,
George Eliot, and Elizabeth Gaskell, Homans structures her
interpretations around "instances of 'bearing the work,'"
textual moments in which "a shift from relatively figurative
to relatively literal" is "connected to the thematics of
female experience." The result is a series of readings that
should prove useful not only to scholars intent on contributing to feminist criticism but also to teachers interested
in dealing with the thematics of female experience in their
literature classes. Indeed, even though I question Homans's
rendition of Lacan as well as her theoretical approach to
women's experience, I believe that her concern with instances
of "bearing the work" makes her study a major contribution
to our understanding of the nineteenth century. (J.H-P.)

Hutchings, Bill. *The Poetry of William Cowper.* London: Croom-
Helm, 1983.

Rev. by Richard Bradford in *Notes and Queries* 32 (1985):
398; by Pierre Danchin in *English Studies* 66 (1985): 69-72.

Jann, Rosemary. *The Art and Science of Victorian History.*
Ohio State University Press, 1985. Pp. xxviii+272. $27.00.

Material on Carlyle.

Kestner, J. *Protest and Reform: The British Social Narrative
by Women, 1827-1867.* London: Methuen, 1985. Pp. x+242.
£15.00.

Rev. by Penny Bonmelha in *RES* 37 (1986): 585-86.

King, James. *William Cowper: A Biography.* Duke University
Press, 1986. Pp. xiv+340. $35.00.

Rev. by W.B. Carnochan ("Pathos and Pathology") in *TLS*,
July 11, 1986, p. 765 as "less ingratiating than Charles
Ryskamp's study" but "full, diligent, authoritative, reti-
cent, and moving."
This carefully researched biography is useful for the quantity of factual information it provides, even though King's
decision to avoid criticism of the poetry excludes from
consideration what was most vital in Cowper's singularly
uneventful life--a life that is here made to seem even more
reclusive than it actually was. For example, King says
almost nothing about Cowper's response to the French Revolution, to which (as one sees in the letters) his Whig principles kept him well disposed until 1793. King's ventures
into psychoanalysis do not seem particularly well grounded
in theory, but he is persuasive and illuminating in his
argument that Cowper's religious despair was a symptom
rather than a cause of his mental illness and that his Evan-
gelical beliefs were more often a comfort than a torment. Of
particular interest to students of the Romantic period is the
discussion of Cowper's relationship with William Hayley
and a detailed account of the composition and publication
of the translation of Homer (with Henry Fuseli acting as
press reader and reviser for Joseph Johnson) that provides
useful insight into how such things were managed by publishers
in the early 90s. (R.M.R.)

MacQueen, John. *The Enlightenment and Scottish Literature.*
Vol. 1, *Progress and Poetry.* Edinburgh: Scottish Academic
Press, 1982. Pp. viii+158. £7.50.

Rev. by J.H. Alexander in *YES* 16 (1986): 231-34.

Mahony, John L. *The Whole Internal Universe: Imitation and the New Defense of Poetry in British Criticism 1660-1830.* Fordham University Press, 1986. Pp. 166. $25.00.

Rev. by Howard Erskine-Hill in *TLS*, Dec. 26, 1986, p. 1441 as a "cautious but useful survey" of the concept of *mimesis* from Aristotle through Sidney and into the English Romantics-- unhappily neglecting Pope as a major critic at the center of a "cultural moment" fulfilled by Keats.
Not seen.

McCarthy, William. *Hester Thrale Piozzi: Portrait of a Literary Woman.* University of North Carolina Press, 1986. $28.00.

Rev. in *NY*, April 14, 1986, p. 110 as "witty and persuasive." Not seen.

McCormack, W.J. *Ascendancy and Tradition in Anglo-Irish Literary History from 1789 to 1939.* Oxford: Clarendon Press, 1985. £27.50.

Rev. by Hilary Pyle in *RES* 37 (1986): 598-99.

McFarland, Thomas. "Imagination and Its Cognates: Supplemen- tary Considerations." *SLIm* 19 (1986): 35-50.

In this follow-up to his recent *Originality and Imagina- tion* (see *RMB* for 1985, pp. 66-67) McFarland often quotes from that book, as in this central statement: "Originality symbolizes the mystery of *principium individuationis,* which in its most idealized form is the concept of soul; ultimately that is its only function."
Examples from Hartman, Addison, Hazlitt, Rousseau, Keats, and Emerson further bolster the book's contention that the terms "imagination" and "originality" are synonymous. (M.T.S.)

McMullen, Lorraine. *An Odd Attempt in a Woman: The Literary Life of Frances Brooke.* University of British Columbia Press, 1983. Pp. 243. $29.95.

Rev. by Mary Jane Edwards in *ECS* 19 (1986): 430-33.

Meehan, Michael. *Liberty and Poetics in Eighteenth Century England.* London, Sydney, and Dover: Croom Helm, 1986. Pp. vi+190. $31.00.

Parts 1-4 take us into the 1760s "and beyond"; part 5, "William Wordsworth," is brief but pithy, focusing on the *Convention of Cintra* and illustrating "a number of ways in which political ideas shaped his poetic interests through

the years 1800-1815." Meehan assumes that Wordsworth has
"earned little attention either as a thinker or as an effective polemicist." The attention given here is fairly
slapdash. (D.V.E.)

Mendilow, Jonathan. *The Romantic Tradition in British Political
    Thought.* Totowa, N.J.: Barnes and Noble, 1986. Pp. 267.
    $31.50.

Mendilow "begins with the effect produced on the thought
of the Romantic writers by the French Revolution and its
aftermath, ... proceeds to consider their influence throughout the century on the development of the peculiarly British
varieties of conservatism and socialism, and ends with their
contribution, largely at second or third hand, to what
virtually amounts to a philosophy of empire."
    A shrewdly argued and tightly woven discourse, beginning
with "The Political Message of Wordsworth's *Prelude*." "His
interpretation of the nature and function of the poet ...
had a tremendous influence.... It gives point ... to the
final sentence of Shelley's 'Defence of Poetry' ... it
illuminates Disraeli's quotation of Shelley's sentence....
It may too have prepared the ground for Carlyle's assertion ... that the men of letters are a 'perpetual priest-
hood.'" The Romantic movement Shelley led "had a major
impact on ... the peculiar British varieties of both socialism
and conservatism" (42).
    Chapter 2 examines "Robert Southey and the Communal Values
of Politics," with Coleridge involved in the discussion.
But Southey remains more prominent in the rest of this book.
Chapter 3, "The History Shelley Never Wrote," a history that
germinated in *Mont Blanc*, develops a thesis similar to
Carlyle's, but would remain committed to revolution, "whereas
Southey, Carlyle and Disraeli believed that revolution could
and should be prevented" (107). Chapter 4 is thought-pro-
vokingly called "Thomas Carlyle's 'Marriage of Heaven and
Hell'"-- e.g., "what Marx described as 'the muck of ages'
Southey and Carlyle saw as the repositor of the great tradition" (143). In chapter 5, "Three Shades of Tory Radicalism,"
we pursue the "influence of the romantic tradition" (i.e.,
mainly Carlyle) on three shades of Tory radicalism, those of
Disraeli, Kingsley, and Ruskin. Disraeli, by "bringing the
romantic tradition into the service of Toryism, ... was instrumental in bringing the party up to date to suit the needs
of the modern world" (170).
    With chapter 6, "The Working Man as Hero...," we swing
back to "the Socialist faith," deriving from Carlyle, Ruskin,
and Morris--with Marx long untranslated into English; and

then, in chapter 7, "The Romantic Tradition in British
Imperialist Ideology," we examine the other prong of the
inheritance "bequeathed by Carlyle and his school to British
political thought." Components, we find, are derived even
from Shelley; and we are to "take Wordsworth as a paradigm"
(with *The Excursion* offering both the brighter and the darker
sides of industrialism and national expansion). (D.V.E.)

Mudge, Bradford. "Burning Down the House: Sara Coleridge,
Virginia Woolf, and the Politics of Literary Revision."
TSWL 5 (1986): 229-50.

An important essay which everyone involved in studying
and teaching literature should read--whether or not s/he
is interested in Sara Coleridge or Virginia Woolf. In
Woolf's response to Sara Coleridge as well as in Sara
Coleridge's 1851 memoir, Mudge uncovers a series of crucial
dilemmas that lead him to "raise serious questions about
the evaluative paradigms that continue to structure our critical practice." Indeed, if our attempts at historical revision are to succeed, then it seems that we will have to
expand our focus, change our critical values, and practice
a new kind of analysis which Mudge, following Berger, calls
"functional analysis." Not only do I agree with Mudge but
I also applaud the way he engages in a dialogue with women
writers. If this is what a "functional analysis" entails,
then surely we need more of it. (J.H-P.)

Murphy, Peter T. "Fool's Gold: The Highland Treasures of
MacPherson's Ossian." *ELH* 53 (1986): 567-91.

Nabholtz, John R. *"My Reader, My Fellow-Labourer": A Study
of English Romantic Prose*. University of Missouri Press,
1986. Pp. viii+134. $22.00.

As Nabholtz admits, he has been anticipated both by himself and by other scholars in exploring how the Romantics
sought to retrain the reader of prose no less than of poetry.
Scholarship on *The Friend* is a case in point: the work that
might have received the most extensive analysis is treated
only briefly. But students of the subject will appreciate
Nabholtz's graceful rhetorical analyses of essays by Lamb
and Hazlitt and will do well to attend carefully to his
argument (and most important point) that "the success or the
failure of the 'Preface' [to *Lyrical Ballads*] as prose document must be considered" in terms of Wordsworth's objective--
"the creation of a mutually understanding and beneficial
relationship between reader and writer"--and the rhetorical
means he employed to realize it. (F.J.)

Newlyn, Lucy. *Coleridge, Wordsworth, and the Language of
  Allusion.* Oxford: Clarendon Press, 1986. Pp. xvii+214.
  $37.00.

   Rev. by Rosemary Ashton in *TLS*, Sept. 19, 1986, pp. 1035-
36.
   A detailed examination of the hidden (and sometimes open)
allusions of Coleridge and Wordsworth to each other in their
works, taking "the specially allusive poetry of 1802 as a
centrepiece, flanked on one side by a reinterpretation [mostly
new here] of the Alfoxden period, in which differences first
emerge; on the other by a discussion of major allusive texts
in the years 1804-7" (ix). The author confesses "an especial
anxiety" about Harold Bloom, having found his work helpful
yet quarreled with his findings. (Next, perhaps, we should
all read Newlyn's study alongside Rzekpka's [see below]).
   Newlyn's unpacking of the Wordsworthian echoes in Coleridge's
"Letter to Sara Hutchinson" is exemplary. In "a poem that
so consistently explores literary relationship, one can
hardly ignore ambiguity in the words, 'Leaves & Fruitage,
not my own, seem'd mine!' The metaphor can be followed on
two related levels" (77). On the conscious level the vine
is Hope; on the unconscious it is Wordsworth.
   One sharp criticism: in chapter 4 on the "Radical Difference" between Wordsworth and Coleridge, a good deal of
significance is wrung from "the ludic poetry of *The Barberry
Tree*" (107); yet the assumption that the poem is Wordsworth's,
rather than Coleridge's, is a very shaky assumption indeed.
(See below: John Beer, under "Wordsworth.") Can't win 'em
all! (D.V.E.)

Norris, Christopher. "On Paul de Man's 'The Rhetoric of
  Romanticism.'" *SHR* 20 (1986): 53-69.

Parkinson, Kathleen, and Martin Priestman, eds. *Peasants
  and Countrymen in Literature: A Symposium Organized by the
  English Department of the Roehampton Institute in February
  1981.* London: English Department of the Roehampton
  Institute, 1982. Pp. vi+210. £2.00.

   Rev. by Shelagh Hunter in *YES* 16 (1986): 309-10, who
mentions discussions of Clare, Wordsworth, and Scott.

Patey, Douglas Lane. *Probability and Literary Form:
  Philosophical Theory and Literary Practice in the Augustan
  Age.* Cambridge University Press, 1984. $44.50.

   Rev. by Maxmillian E. Novak in *VQR* 62 (1986): 156-62 as
the most "learned" book on eighteenth-century criticism in

a generation. According to Novak, Patey "finds the essential change to romantic literature in the 'fusion' of external and internal perception. Objects seem to melt together in the poetry of Wordsworth and Coleridge. But to his credit, he perceives much of Coleridge's criticism not so much as a revolutionary development as an attempt to solve the problems raised by the Augustan critics within the framework created by those critics" (159).

Also rev. by Eric Rothstein in *ECS* 19 (1986): 421-24.

Patrides, C.A., and Joseph Wittreich, eds. *The Apocalypse in English Renaissance Thought and Literature: Patterns, Antecedents, and Repercussions.* Cornell University Press, 1984. Pp. viii+452. $49.50.

Rev. by Morton D. Paley in *BIQ* 20 (1986): 53-56. Illus. Essays by M.H. Abrams, Bernard McGinn, Marjorie Reeves, Jaroslav Pelikan, Barnard Capp, Michael Murrin, Florence Sandler (tracing the Legend of Holiness in *The Faerie Queene* to the Revelation pattern); by the two editors; by Paul Korshin, on Restoration and post-Restoration traces; nothing on the Romantic period; a jump to America (but "could Blake in calling his Milton 'the Awakener' have had in mind the Awakening in America?" asks Paley); then two essays on the post-Romantic period; and an elaborate and helpful bibliography by Wittreich.

Not seen.

Perkins, David. "Johnson and Modern Poetry." *HLB* 33 (1985): 303-12.

Peterson, Carla L. *The Determined Reader: Gender and Culture in the Novel from Napoleon to Victoria.* Rutgers University Press, 1986. Pp. 246. $25.00.

Rajan, Tilottama. "The Supplement of Reading." *NLH* 17 (1986): 573-94.

Concerned with Romantic *fragments* (e.g., *Christabel*) and what the author calls "the disappearance of narrative, dramatic, or conceptual actualization, a phenomenon which results in the absence from Romantic texts of embodied or achieved meaning as opposed to discarnate meaning" (573). Wagner's music is better than it sounds. Lots of diagrams about signifier/signified, reader/receiver, etc. (B.C.H.)

Richardson, Alan. "The Dangers of Sympathy: Sibling Incest in English Romantic Poetry." *SEL* 25 (1985): 737-54.

Roberts, Marie. *British Poets and Secret Societies*. London:
Croom Helm, 1986. Pp. 181. £17.95.

    Rev. by Christopher MacLachlan in *SLJ* 13 (1986), supp.
25: 10-13.
Freemasonry in Burns, Rosicrucianism in Shelley.

Rogers, W.E. *The Three Genres and the Interpretation of
Lyric*. Princeton University Press, 1983. Pp. vii+277.
$23.50.

    Rev. by E.D. Blodgett in *CRCL* 13 (1986): 287-92.

Rzepka, Charles J. *The Self as Mind: Vision and Identity in
Wordsworth, Coleridge, and Keats*. Harvard University Press,
1986. Pp. ix+286. $22.50.

    An absorbingly detailed and carefully organized attempt
to redefine "the structures of consciousness and self-
consciousness that are central to Romanticism." Previous
major critics are drawn upon, with both periphrastic accuracy
and fresh applications.
    Studies of Wordsworth and Coleridge easily shed light from
the two poets' interactions; introducing Keats brings out
both contrasts and similarities of problem. E.g., all
three (the critic notes) "were orphaned by the age of ten.
Keats alone seems to have overcome, without excessive dependence on external surrogates, the resulting, recurring
feelings of self-dispersion that both exhilarated and
frustrated him, inspired and limited his poetic ambitions.
It can plausibly be argued that Wordsworth, like his friend
Coleridge, failed to internalize a strong self-affirming
presence during his childhood and young manhood, and that
this lack of an assured source of maternal love, recognition,
and affection within the psyche, this 'abyss of idealism,'
encouraged in Wordsworth the displacement of desire through
projections of maternal care and solicitude onto the natural
world, as well as feelings of self-dispersion" (161). And
on and in, deeper and deeper. (D.V.E.)

Schulz, Max F. *Paradise Preserved: Recreations of Eden in
Eighteenth- and Nineteenth-Century England*. Cambridge
University Press, 1986. Pp. xv+368. $39.50.

The mystique of an earthly paradise is ever with us, but
in the two centuries under scrutiny here it assumed an
unusually rich diversity of symbolic representation, appearing in gardens, painting, literature, urban centers, and in
technology and engineering. The pattern Schulz detects in
the images of paradise from 1710 to 1900 is dialectical:
Eden is first associated with gardens, then with urban
centers, and finally (and synthetically) with aesthetic
forms. For instances of Eden as literal garden Schulz selects
Stowe, Stourhead, and Hafod (the Welsh garden of Thomas
Johnes), but unaccountably he provides no visual images--no
photographs or drawings--of them. To the virtually uncir-
cumscribed and largely mental and spiritual Eden of the
Romantics "Capability Brown" pointed the way. None of the
Romantic poets (Keats is not included [?] but Crabbe and
Clare are), for all their strong will and potent creativity
to conjure Eden, succeeded in imagining an untroubled paradise. With the Romantics Schulz comes into his own, showing
in detail how the efforts of Blake, Coleridge, and Wordsworth especially were vulnerable to their experience of lapse
as well as to their code of sincerity. By 1830 the old
hope of finding or making the earthly paradise was less
alive than ever except in the visual art of Bewick, Constable,
and Palmer, of which Schulz has provided examples.

To the Victorian substitution of the Heavenly City for Eden
as image of the earthly paradise John Clare and John Martin
were the transitional figures. For the outward and secular
turn of the Victorian imagination proper Schulz chooses the
Crystal Palace and Whistler's Peacock Room as points of
greatest expansion and contraction, both representing perfectly the effort to "align--update, refashion, and repre-
sent--an unending spiritual ideal with a constantly changing
reality." A multidisciplinary study, beautifully produced,
that does honor to the term. (F.J.)

Schwartz, Nina. "The Ideologies of Romanticism." *New Orleans
Review* 13 (1986): 84-95.

Seymore, Barbara. *A Radiant Trail: The Extension of the Conceit Through Eighteenth-Century English Poetry.* Ann Arbor, Mich.: University Microfilms International, 1986.

  Dissertation.

Shattock, Joanne. "Politics and Literature: Macaulay, Brougham, and the *Edinburgh Review.*" *YES* 16 (1986): 32-50.

Simpson, Roger. "Epics in the Romantic Period." *N&Q*, n.s. 33 (June 1986): 160-61.

  Adds to the survey of titles published in A.D. Harvey's book and in recent *N&Q* articles.

Smith, Olivia. *The Politics of Language 1791-1819.* Oxford: Clarendon Press, 1984. Pp. xiv+272. $27.95.

  Rev. by Jon Klancher in *HLQ* 49 (1986): 409-14; by David Simpson in *BIQ* 20 (1986): 63-64.

Smith, Peter. *Public and Private Value: Studies in the Nine- teenth-Century Novel.* Cambridge University Press, 1984. Pp. 244. $29.95.

  Rev. by Patricia Alden in *MinnR* 25 (1985): 136-38.

Spacks, Patricia Meyer, and W.B. Carnochan. *A Distant Prospect: Eighteenth-Century Views of Childhood.* Papers Read at a Clark Library Seminar, October 13, 1979. Los Angeles: William Andrews Clark Memorial Library, University of California, 1982. Pp. vi+50.

  Rev. by A.J. Sambrook in *YES* 16 (1986): 255-56, who mentions an essay by Carnochan on Blake.

Spencer, Jane. *The Rise of the Woman Novelist: From Aphra Behn to Jane Austen.* New York: Basil Blackwell, 1986. Pp. 225. $50.00, paper $14.95.

  An extraordinarily ambitious and informative study. Spencer addresses more than a century of women's writing, comments on at least twenty women novelists, and refers to well over a hundred novels. Happily, however, the book does not read like a survey. Spencer argues that even though men and women are not essentially different, eighteenth- century attitudes toward the female sex put women novelists in a special position, a position that significantly affected their writing. Dividing her study into two parts, Spencer first describes the position of the eighteenth-century woman novelist as it was constituted by the literary marketplace,

by an ideology of femininity, by the self-representations
of women writers, and by the critical terms on which women's
literary authority was accepted (and occasionally acclaimed)
as a sociocultural good. Although much of this description
impressed me as "what oft was thought but ne'er so well expressed," I did find Spencer's analysis of Behn's, Manley's,
and Barker's novelistic self-representations especially
astute and her attention to ideological contradictions,
individual differences, and historical variations unusually
judicious.

In the second part of her study, Spencer divides women's
novelistic responses to their position into three separate
yet related traditions: a tradition of protest which makes
much of seduction; a didactic tradition which conforms by
plotting the heroine's reform; and a tradition of escape
which offers the heroine of romance a fantasy of female
power. As she analyzes each of these traditions, Spencer
discusses a wide range of novels, including such protest
novels as *The British Recluse*, *The Countess of Dellwyn*, and
Maria: Or the Wrongs of Woman; such conforming novels as
The Reform'd Coquet, *Evelina*, and *Emma*; and such romantic
novels as *The Recess* and *The Romance of the Forest*. However,
by including so many novels, Spencer is more or less forced
to treat them as illustrations of her categories; the result
is something that comes perilously close to being a survey.
In the chapters on the didactic tradition and the tradition
of escape, this problem seems especially acute as Spencer
tends to mute rather than to articulate each tradition's
ideological contradictions. But such is not the case with
her discussion of the figure of seduction, a discussion that
deserves to be developed more fully in another book. Indeed,
the best thing about this book may just be that it is likely
to provoke many more studies of eighteenth- and nineteenth-
century women novelists, studies in which individual differences, ideological contradictions, and historical variations can be emphasized without fear that the larger picture
will be lost. By framing her study in terms of the woman
novelist's position, Spencer has enabled us to see that
there is a larger picture at issue. (J.H-P.)

Starzyk, Lawrence J. "The Non-Poietic Foundations of Victorian
    Aesthetics." *BJA* 26 (1986): 218-27.

    "Poietic" is borrowed from Hannah Arendt and refers to our
sense of the world as something made or created; considerable
discussion of Carlyle, Coleridge, Blake, and other Romantics.

Twitchell, James. *Forbidden Partners: The Incest Taboo in
    Modern Culture*. Columbia University Press, 1986. Pp. 311.
    $24.95.

Watson, J.R. *English Poetry of the Romantic Period, 1789-
1830.* London: Longman's, 1985.

   Not seen.

Watson, Roderick. *Macmillan History of Literature: The
Literature of Scotland.* London: Macmillan, 1984. Pp.
xiv+481. £25.00, paper £7.95.

   Rev. by Thomas Crawford in *SLJ* 13 (1986): supp. 25:
27-32 (see also correspondence between Watson and David
Groves, objecting to the characterization of Hogg's politics on pp. 53-59, ibid.); by Kathryn Sutherland in *RES* 37
(1986): 425-26.

Weiskel, Thomas. *The Romantic Sublime: Studies in the
Structure and Psychology of Transcendence.* The Johns Hopkins
University Press, 1986. Pp. 240. Paper $8.95.

   Paperback of the 1976 edition; new foreword by Harold
Bloom.
   We reviewed it in the "RMB" in *ELN* 15 (1977): 25; and
listed further reviews in *ELN* 16 (1978): 27.
   Bloom finds Weiskel's criticism "at once moral or primary,
and de-idealizing or antithetical. The kind may not be
possible to attain.... " A poignant personal introduction
by Weiskel's wife gives us glimpses of daily life, especially
of Weiskel's life outside the academy before he was drowned
in 1974. She tells us that he came to his working definition
of the sublime--"it is that moment when the relation between
the signifier and signified breaks down and is replaced by
an indeterminate relation"--while he was cutting wood.
   Hypothesizing that the literary, "rhetorical" sublime is
structurally cognate with the "natural" sublime encountered
in landscape, Weiskel willingly pays the price of using
economic principles ("roughly calculating gain and loss")
to close his theories to "mystical" explanations. In Fact,
Robert Barth's 1977 review in *ELN* faulted the book for its
Blake's rejection of the sublime which Weiskel is trying to
define.
   Weiskel defines a negative (metaphorical_ sublime "in
which the absence of determinate meaning becomes significant'
and leads to substitution and a positive (metonymical)
sublime in which "the mind recovers by displacing its excess
of signified into a dimension of contiguity.... The positive
sublime suggests immanence, circularity, and a somewhat regressive resistance to alienation of all kinds.... The negative sublime seems to offer to the poet the truly primary
power of the god."

After valuable explanations of Burke, the Oedipus complex, and Collins, the book ends with a brilliant discussion of Wordsworth's Simplon Pass episode: "I propose ... that the remembered disappointment--'*that we had crossed the Alps*'-- is in fact a screen memory drastically inflated (if not created) in order to block the emergence of the deeper, more terrifying and traumatic memory of Gondo Gorge." Thus Words-worth maintains the consciousness of self which the sublime threatens. (M.T.S.)

Wesling, Donald. *The New Poetries: Poetic Form Since Coleridge and Wordsworth.* Bucknell University Press, 1985. Pp. 228. $32.50.

Light is shed on the whole process of poetry; Coleridge and Wordsworth get a good deal of attention, but the other Romantics are barely mentioned. They and the Augustans are taken as sufficiently familiar to the reader--and this is a proper focus--that critical attention can be given to historical generalizations. Chapter 1, "The Transformation of Premises," begins with "The Literary Transition at 1795"; gives us a table of six categories that distinguish "Augustan Form" from "Romantic Form"; and leads us through a cleverly guided tour under such headings as "Romantic Form as Proceed-ing" and "In Cognition: Poem and Reader After 1795." Chapter 3 helps us leap to "The Crisis of Versification, 1855-1910."
Even determinedly focused Romantics will find themselves led on to the end. (D.V.E.)

Whiteley, Paul. "Beattie, More, and Hayley." *The Late Augustans and the Origins of English Romanticism.* London: Croom Helm, 1985. £15.95.

Not seen.

Wilkie, Brian. "The Romantic Ideal of Unity." *SLIm* 19,2 (1986): 5-21.

This is a reasonable and clever way to try to bring to-gether two camps in Romantic criticism. One camp sees unity and the other sees self-contradiction. Wilkie wants it both ways: "Since the Romantics were indeed obsessed with unity but were also aware of the enormous complexity of experience, they coped with the need to satisfy both the obsession and the awareness by creating in their most characteristic work what I shall call overlays, or superimpositions. These overlays do not fuse; they cling together and cohere while also retaining a high degree of independence, competing with

each other sometimes to the point of contradiction." The
epitome of these overlays, which are compatible with organicism, is Beethoven's quotation from Schiller's "Ode to Joy"
in his Ninth Symphony: "O Freunde, nicht diese Töne!"

Leaving aside the easy cases of Keats and Byron and the
difficult one of Austen, Wilkie explores Coleridge, Shelley,
and above all Blake, who created the most "dazzling and
complex set of overlays" in written text and accompanying
illumination. In this argument *The Visions of the Daughters
of Albion* is not a continuation of *The Book of Thel*, but an
overlay. "The result is the kind of simultaneity widely
recognized as essential to Blake's vision of time and experience. In terms of his individual literary works, this
means that we have neither something executed over erasure
nor a sequential thread but a set of superimposed visions,
or overlays."

"It is, precisely, this understanding [in Blake's "On
Homers Poetry"] of unity in terms of existence rather than
of abstract essence that defines the Romantic version of
organic form as achieved through overlays. This is the mode
of unity they realized in the most distinctive and most
important of their works. Whether anything that so nearly
borders on self-contradiction can be called unity at all may
be questioned; clearly, I believe it can be meaningfully
called that." And so do I. (M.T.S.)

Williams, Anne. *Prophetic Strain: The Greater Lyric in the
Eighteenth Century.* University of Chicago Press, 1984.
Pp. x+186.

   Rev. by David Womersley in *RES* 37 (1986): 572-73.
   Not seen.

Festschrift: "Homage to Carl Woodring." *SiR* 25 (Fall 1986).

   Six essays (listed below in "English 4. Studies of
Authors"): Jerome J. McGann on Blake; Donald H. Reiman on
Coleridge; Peter J. Manning and Kenneth R. Johnston on
Wordsworth; Stuart M. Sperry and Stuart Curran on Shelley.

See also Matlock ("Wordsworth").

Reviews of books previously listed:

ABRAMS, M.H., *The Correspondent Breeze: Essays on English
Romanticism* (see *RMB* for 1984, pp. 69-70), rev. by Karl
Kroeber in *KSJ* 35 (1986): 223-26; ADAMS, Hazard, *Philosophy
of the Literary Symbolic* (see *RMB* for 1983, p. 58), rev. by
Daniel T. O'Hara in *MLQ* 45 (1984): 311-14; by William Keach

in *KSJ* 35 (1986): 213-18; ALBRIGHT, Daniel, *Lyricality
in English Literature* (see *RMB* for 1985, p. 60), rev. by
Anne Williams in *BIQ* 19 (1986): 144-46; AUERBACH, Nina,
Romantic Imprisonment: Women and Other Glorified Outcasts
(see *RMB* for 1985, p. 61), rev. by Marcia Gordon in *Novel:
A Forum on Fiction* 19 (1986): 278-82; BOGEL, Frederic V.,
*Literature and Insubstantiality in Later Eighteenth-Century
England* (see *RMB* for 1985, p. 62), rev. by Wallace Jackson
in *BIQ* 20 (1986): 57-60, who notes that the book "is
specifically grounded on the perception ... of the last
half of the century as 'an ontological field in which
questions of being ... take precedence over other kinds
of question" (the book was never received for our reviewing);
rev. by Bruce Redford in *ECS* 19 (1986): 414-17; BORGMEIER,
Raimund, *The Dying Shepherd. Die Tradition den englischen
Ekloge von Pope bis Wordsworth* (see *RMB* for 1980, p. 51),
rev. by Dietrich Rolle in *Anglia* 104 (1986): 237-39; BRANT-
LEY, Richard E., *Locke, Wesley, and the Method of English
Romanticism* (see *RMB* for 1984, pp. 71-72), rev. very
critically by Leopold Damrosch, Jr., in *ECS* 19 (1986): 438-
41; by James Chandler in *JR* 66 (1986): 106-08; BRISMAN,
Leslie, *Romantic Origins* (see *ELN* 17, supp. 51); rev. by
Heide N. Rohloff in *Anglia* 103 (1985): 220-24; BUCKLEY,
Jerome Hamilton, *The Turning Key: Autobiography and the
Subjective Impulse Since 1800* (see *RMB* for 1984, pp. 72-73),
rev. by A.F.T. Lurcock in *RES* 37 (1986): 299-301; by Eugene
L. Stelzig in *KSJ* 35 (1986): 207-11; CANTOR, Paul A.,
Creature and Creator: Myth-Making and English Romanticism
(see *RMB* for 1984, p. 73), rev. by T. Hoagwood in *Choice* 22
(1984): 421-22; by Iain McGilchrist in *TLS*, Aug. 3, 1984,
p. 862; by Mark Roberts in *RES* 37 (1986): 103-05; HOLMES,
Richard, *Footsteps of a Romantic Biographer* (see *RMB* for
1985, p. 65), rev. by Robert M. Adams ("False Scents") in
NYRB, April 10, 1986, pp. 36-37; COCKSHUT, A.O.J., *The Art
of Autobiography in Nineteenth- and Twentieth-Century
England* (see *RMB* for 1984, p. 73), rev. by A.F.T. Lurcock
in *RES* 37 (1986): 299-301; COHEN, Ralph, ed., *Studies in
Eighteenth-Century British Art and Aesthetics* (see *RMB* for
1985, pp. 62-63), rev. by Ann Bermingham as "thoughtful and
provocative" in *ECS* 20 (1986): 104-07; by Christopher
MacLachlan in *BJA* 26 (1986): 396-97; COTTOM, Daniel, *The
Civilized Imagination: A Study of Ann Radcliffe, Jane Austen,
and Sir Walter Scott* (see *RMB* for 1985, pp. 63-64), rev.
by Kathleen L. Fowler in *TWC* 17 (1986): 235-37; DAICHES,
David, *Literature and Gentility in Scotland* (see *RMB* for
1984, p. 75), rev. by J.H. Alexander in *YES* 16 (1986):
250-51; ELLIS, Steve, *Dante and English Poetry: Shelley to
T.S. Eliot* (see *RMB* for 1984, p. 75), rev. by K.M. Lea in

RES 37 (1986):   134-35; FREISTAT, Neil, *The Poem and the Book: Interpreting Collections of Romantic Poetry* (see *RMB* for 1985, p. 64), rev. by Don H. Bialostosky in *TWC* 17 (1986):   232-33; by Dinah Birch in *RES* 37 (1986):   433-34; by Mary Quinn in *KSJ* 35 (1986):   226-28; HEFFERNAN, James A.W., *The Re-Creation of Landscape: A Study of Wordsworth, Coleridge, Constable and Turner* (see *RMB* for 1985, p. 64), rev. by Anne K. Mellor in *RP&P*, 10,2 (1986):   83-84; HILL, Christopher, *The Experience of Defeat: Milton and Some Contemporaries* (see *RMB* for 1985, p. 49), rev. by Perez Zagorin in *JMH* 58 (1986):   549-51; HOAGWOOD, Terence Allen, *Prophecy and the Philosophy of Mind: Traditions of Blake and Shelley* (see *RMB* for 1985, p. 65), rev. by Alan Robinson in *RES* 37 (1986):   576-77; JACK, R.D.S., and Andrew Noble, eds., *The Art of Robert Burns* (see *RMB* for 1984, p. 78), rev. by David W. Lindsay in *YES* 16 (1986):   288-89; KORSHIN, Paul J., *Typologies in England, 1650-1820* (see *RMB* for 1983, p. 62), rev. by G.S. Rousseau in *JEGP* 85 (1986):   125-28; LEAVIS, Q.D., *Collected Essays: The Englishness of the English Novel*, ed. G. Singh (see *RMB* for 1985, p. 66), rev. by Thomas L. Jeffers in *WHR* 40 (1986):   83-89; McFARLAND, Thomas, *Originality and Imagination* (see *RMB* for 1985, pp. 66-67), rev. by James C. McKusick in *TWC* 17 (1986):   194-96; by Lucy Newlyn in *RES* 37 (1986):   613-15; by Rudolf F. Storch, in *ELN* 23 (1986):   58-60; McGUIRK, Carol, *Robert Burns and the Sentimental Era* (see *RMB* for 1985, p. 67); rev. by Elizabeth Hedrick in *SAR* 51, (Nov. 1986):   144-46; MEISEL, Martin, *Realizations: Narrative, Pictorial, and Theatrical Arts in Nineteenth-Century England* (see *RMB* for 1984, pp. 80-81), rev. by Joseph Viscomi in *SiR* 25 (1986):   561-67; MILLER, J. Hillis, *The Linguistic Moment: From Wordsworth to Stevens* (see *RMB* for 1985, pp. 67-68), rev. by Michael Fischer in *JEGP* 85 (1986):   572-74 as trailing "clouds of theoretical speculation"; by Michael Hancher in *TWC* 17 (1986): 179-200; MILLER, Karl, *Doubles: Studies in Literary History* (see *RMB* for 1985, p. 68), rev. by Vincent Newey in *RES* 37 (1986):   615-17; MORGAN, Peter F., *Literary Critics and Reviewers in Early Nineteenth-Century Britain* (see *RMB* for 1983, p. 63), rev. by Joanne Shattock in *YES* 16 (1986): 301-02; MORRIS, Kevin L., *The Image of the Middle Ages in Romantic and Victorian Literature* (see *RMB* for 1985, p. 69), rev. by Bernard Richards in *RES* 37 (1986):   434-36; NEWEY, Vincent, *Cowper's Poetry: A Critical Study and Reassessment* (see *RMB* for 1984, p. 82), rev. by A.J. Sambrook in *YES* 16 (1986):   279-80; POOVEY, Mary, *The Proper Lady and the Woman Writer: Ideology as Style in the Works of Mary Wollstonecraft, Mary Shelley, and Jane Austen* (see *RMB* for 1984, pp. 82-84), rev. by Nancy Armstrong in *MLN* 99 (1984):   1251-57;

by Mary Hughes Brookhart in *SAR* 51 (1986):   133; by Robert
A. Colby in *NCF* 39 (1984):   339-44; by April London in *RES*
37 (1986):   267-71; by M.E.S. in *Prose Studies* 8 (1985):
100-01; by James Thompson in *ECT&I* 27 (1986):   101-06; by
Judith Wilt in *MP* 83 (1986):   434-37 as omitting a key passage from *Emma* but otherwise picking its examples "wonderfully well"; REED, Arden, ed., *Romanticism and Language*
(see *RMB* for 1984, pp. 84-88), rev. by Mark Storey in *English*
35 (1986):   67-73; RAJAN, Balachandra, *The Form of the
Unfinished: English Poetics from Spenser to Pound* (see *RMB*
for 1985, pp. 69-70), rev. by Ann Janowitz in *TWC* 17 (1986):
233-35; REED, Arden, ed., *Romanticism and Language* (see *RMB*
for 1984, pp. 84-88), rev. by Marshall Brown in *TWC* 17 (1986):
200-02; by Stuart Peterfreund in *JEGP* 85 (1986):   464-67;
ROGERS, Pat, *Literature and Popular Culture in Eighteenth-
Century England* (see *RMB* for 1985, p. 71), rev. by Francis
Doherty in *RES* 37 (1986):   571-72; by Denis Donoghue in
LRB, Feb. 6, 1986, pp. 11-12; SCHAPIRO, Barbara A., *The
Romantic Mother: Narcissistic Patterns in Romantic Poetry*
(see *RMB* for 1983, pp. 66-67); rev. by John Howard in *SAR*
50,1 (Jan. 1985):   105-08; SCHEUERMANN, Mona, *Social Protest
in the Eighteenth-Century English Novel* (see *RMB* for 1985,
p. 71), rev. by John P. Zomchich in *ECS* 20 (1986):   79-82;
SUMMERFIELD, Geoffrey, *Fantasy & Reason: Children's
Literature in the Eighteenth Century* (see *RMB* for 1985, pp.
72-73), rev. by Isaac Kramnick in *ECS* 20 (1986-87):   260-62
as "a new and most welcome addition" to this field of study;
THORSLEV, Peter L., Jr., *Romantic Contraries: Freedom
versus Destiny* (see *RMB* for 1984, p. 34), rev. by David
Punter in *BIQ* 20 (1986):   60-63.

Composite reviews:

Ackiss, Davis L.   *SAR* 51,2 (May 1986):   136-40.

   Reviews Miriam Allott, *Essays on Shelley* (see *RMB* for 1982,
   pp. 139-40), and Terence Allen Hoagwood, *Prophecy and the
   Philosophy of Mind: Traditions of Blake and Shelley* (see
   RMB for 1985, p. 65).

Bell, Robert.   "Autobiography and Literary Criticism."   *MLQ*
46 (1985):   191-201.

   Reviews A.O.J. Cockshut, *The Art of Autobiography in Nine-
   teenth- and Twentieth-Century England* (see *RMB* for 1984,
   p. 73) and Susanna Egan, *Patterns of Experience in Autobiography* (not previously listed: see above in this section).

Monsman, Gerald. "Recent Studies in the Nineteenth Century."
   SEL 26 (1986): 777-813.

   The first 15 pages of the annual roundup are devoted to the
   Romantics (Wordsworth, Hazlitt, Coleridge, Keats, Mary
   Shelley) and the Gothic, with thoughtful reflections by
   the reviewer and comments on the current trends in scholarship and criticism.

Kamuf, Peggy. "Monumental De-Facement: On Paul de Man's
   The Rhetoric of Romanticism." *CL* 38 (1986): 319-28.

   Kamuf praises de Man's "deconstruction of the concept of
   romanticism" for its "ability to encounter repeatedly 'the
   inability to read' without erecting this repetition into
   a system or method of reading."

4. STUDIES OF AUTHORS

AUSTEN

Allen, Dennis W. "No Love for Lydia: The Fate of Desire in
   'Pride and Prejudice.'" *TSLL* 27 (1985): 425-43.

Bertelsen, Lance. "Jane Austen's Miniatures: Painting,
   Drawing, and the Novels." *MLQ* 45 (1984): 350-72.

Boren, Lynda S. "The Performing Self: Psychodrama in Austen,
   James and Woolf." *CentR* 30 (1986): 1-24.

   Boren argues that Austen, Woolf, and James share an understanding of "the human condition" which leads them to use
   "dramatic conventions and devices" to portray the self.
   The remarks on Austen are concerned with *Persuasion* as a
   novel about "the evolution of self and its close resemblance
   to the creative act itself." Based on a "knowledge of [her]
   own nothingness," Anne develops a performing self, a self
   "sustained by an indomitable spirit and nurtured through
   the eyes of love."

Davies, J.M.Q. "*Emma* as Charade and the Education of the
   Reader." *PQ* 65 (1986): 231-42.

Flavin, Louise Ann. *The Aesthetic Effects of Free Indirect
   Discourse in the Novels of Jane Austen.* Ann Arbor, Mich.:
   University Microfilms International, 1985.

   Dissertation.

Gillie, Christopher. *A Preface to Jane Austen.* London: Longman's, 1985.

    Not seen.

Grey, J. David, ed. *The Jane Austen Companion.* London: Macmillan, 1986.

    Not seen.

Gunn, Daniel P. "In the Vicinity of Winthrop: Ideological Rhetoric in *Persuasion.*" *NCL* 41 (1986): 403-18.

Halperin, John. "Jane Austen's Lovers." *SEL* 25 (1985): 719-36.

Heydt, Jill. "'First Impressions' and Later Recollections: The Place of the Picturesque in *Pride and Prejudice.*" *Studies in the Humanities* 12 (1985): 115-24.

Heyns, Michiel. "Shock and Horror: The Moral Vocabulary of 'Mansfield Park.'" *ESA* 29 (1986): 1-18.

    Fanny's success is part Austen's moral lapse. (T.L.A.)

Jones, Kathleen Anne. *Jane Austen's Fictional Parents.* Ann Arbor, Mich.: University Microfilms International, 1986.

    Dissertation.

Kaufman, David. "Closure in *Mansfield Park* and the Sanctity of the Family." *PQ* 65 (1986): 211-29.

Kirkham, Margaret. *Jane Austen, Feminism and Fiction.* London: Methuen, 1986. Pp. 187. Paper $10.95.

    A polemical study which is intent on upholding Austen's greatness by defending her work from charges of limited vision and sociopolitical conservatism. According to Kirkham, the subject matter and argument of Austen's novels prove that she was a feminist moralist in the Enlightenment tradition of Astell, Macaulay, and Wollstonecraft. Like these earlier feminists, Austen believed "that women share the same moral nature as men, ought to share the same moral status, and exercise the same responsibility for their own conduct." However, unlike her avowedly feminist precursors, Austen wrote after the Wollstonecraft scandal of 1798 which made an open declaration of feminism dangerous. Hence, Austen experimented with various modes of indirection

until she discovered the best solution to her rhetorical
problem: the coupling of irony and allusion with an "indirect free style" of narration that makes the heroine the
novel's central intelligence from beginning to end.

Kirkham cites nothing from the letters or the life that
clearly indicates Austen's approval of--or interest in--
the works of Astell, Macaulay, and Wollstonecraft. Nor
does she find that the novels contain verbal echoes of or
direct allusions to avowedly feminist works. Lacking such
material evidence, Kirkham builds her argument on the
dubious proposition that for women of Austen's period, "to
become an author was, in itself, a feminist act." This
proposition leads her to dismiss as unimportant class and
sociopolitical differences among women writers, to present
enlightened feminism as a totalizing and noncontradictory
ideology, to represent Austen's work as a unified whole,
and finally, to sever the link between Austen's morality
and conservatism. Yet even though Kirkham overstates her
case, this book is well worth reading, not only for its
local insights but also for its general attempt to deal with
the problematic relations among such discourses as moralism,
feminism, radicalism, and conservatism. (J.H-P.)

Liotta, Christine M. *"Quite in the Line of Lovelaces": The
Nature and Function of the Rake in Jane Austen's Novels.*
Ann Arbor, Mich.: University Microfilms International,
1985.

  Dissertation.

Litvak, Joseph. "The Infection of Acting: Theatrical and
Theatricality in *Mansfield Park*." *ELH* 53 (1986): 331-55.

McKenzie, Alan T. "The Derivation and Distribution of
'Consequence' in *Mansfield Park*." *NCF* 40 (1985): 281-96.

Merrett, Robert James. "The Life of Writing." *DR* 65 (1985):
122-28.

Meyers, Kate B. "Jane Austen's Use of Literary Allusion in
the Sotherton Episode of *Mansfield Park*." *PLL* 22 (1986):
96-99.

  Psalm 118:20 adds to the significance of the narrow gate
at Sotherton. (T.L.A.)

Natoli, Joanna Bartosik. *The Idea of Home in "Mansfield Park,"
"Jane Eyre," and "Tess of the D'Urbervilles."* Ann Arbor,
Mich.: University Microfilms International, 1985.

  Dissertation.

Perry, Ruth. "Interrupted Friendships in Jane Austen's
Emma." *TSWL* 5 (1986): 185-202.

In *Emma*, "Austen uses the marriage plot to comment on the
situation of women in her society and not merely to rein-
scribe it." The "essentials of that commentary" constitute
a second story, the story of how "women's relations to each
other are affected by their need to negotiate heterosexual
relations." Although Austen repeatedly provokes her readers
to desire a friendship between Emma and Jane Fairfax, she
pointedly refuses to let such a friendship materialize. In
this provocative refusal, Perry reads a "subversive message"
that "constitutes" a social critique of a culture that
"devalues women." The argument that Austen comments on the
situation of women in her society is certainly convincing.
But the notion that her commentary is "subversive" and thus
constitutive of a far-reaching sociocultural critique is
more problematic; I, for one, am not yet convinced. (J.H-P.)

Pickrel, Paul. "Lionel Trilling and 'Emma': A Reconsidera-
tion." *NCF* 40 (1985): 297-311.

Smith, Mack. "The Document of Falsimilitude; Frank's Epistles
and Misinterpretation in *Emma*." *MSE* 9 (1984): 52-70.

Spender, Dale. *Mothers of the Novel: 100 Good Women Writers
Before Jane Austen.* London: Pandora; New York: Methuen, 1986.

Not seen.

Stewart, Maaja A. "The Fools in Austen's *Emma*." *NCL* 41
(1986): 72-86.

Struever, Nancy S. "The Conversable World." In *Rhetoric
and the Pursuit of Truth: Language Change in the Seventeenth and Eighteenth Centuries.* Los Angeles: William
Andrews Clark Memorial Library, 1985. $12.50.

Rev. by T. Conley in *QJS* 72 (1986): 483-86.
Discusses Jane Austen at some length.
Not seen.

Tanner, Tony. *Jane Austen.* London: Macmillan, 1986. Pp.
291. £20.00, paper £6.95.

Rev. by John Bayley in *LRB*, Feb. 5, 1987, pp. 15-16 as
"Yawning and Screaming."
Not seen.

Thompson, James. "Jane Austen and the Limits of Language."
    JEGP 85 (1986): 510-31.

    Connects Austen with eighteenth-century notions of in-
    expressibility, with many interesting parallels in Words-
    worth. Valuable. (B.C.H.)

Trickett, Rachel. *"Mansfield Park."* *TWC* 17 (1986): 87-95.

Zelicovici, Dvora. "Reversal in 'Pride and Prejudice.'"
    Studies in the Humanities 12 (1985): 106-14.

See also Roth ("English 1. Bibliography"); Neale, Beckett
    ("English 2. Environment"); Auerbach, Barker, Cottom, Engell,
    Spencer ("English 3. Criticism"); Wilkie ("Coleridge").

Reviews of books previously listed:

BARFOOT, C.C., *The Thread of Connection: Aspects of Fate
    in the Novels of Jane Austen and Others* (see *RMB* for 1982,
    p. 72), rev. by Joan H. Pittock in *YES* 16 (1986): 296-97;
    GILSON, David, *A Bibliography of Jane Austen* (see *RMB* for
    1982, p. 73), rev. by David L. Vander Meuler in *PBSA* 79
    (1985): 435-42 as "the preeminent reference work for Austen
    studies" and "a model for the treatment of works of other
    authors"; by Brian Southam in *YES* 16 (1986): 293-96;
    HALPERIN, John, *The Life of Jane Austen* (see *RMB* for 1985,
    pp. 78-79), rev. unfavorably by Anita Susan Grossman in
    ASch 55 (1986): 272-75; by Carolyn Heilbrun in *Novel: A
    Forum on Fiction* 19 (1986): 183-85; by Karen B. Mann in
    SAQ 85 (1986): 301-03; by Robert W. Rogers in *JEGP* 85
    (1986): 569-71 as "generally judicious"; by Deirdre LeFaye
    in *RES* 37 (1986): 426-30; by James Merett in *DR* 65 (1985):
    122-28; by James Thompson in *SAR* 51 (1986): 138-40; HARDY,
    John, *Jane Austen's Heroines: Intimacy in Human Relation-
    ships* (see *RMB* for 1984, p. 93), rev. by Juliet McMaster in
    NCF 40 (1986): 476-79; KIRKHAM, Margaret, *Jane Austen:
    Feminism and Fiction* (see *RMB* for 1983, p. 71), rev. by
    Frederick M. Keener in *YES* 16 (1986): 297-98.

BARRY

Allan, D.G.C. "Barry and Johnson." *Journal of the Royal
    Society of Arts* 133 (1985): 628-32.

Barrell, John. "The Functions of Art in a Commercial Society:
    The Writings of James Barry." *ECent* 25 (1984): 117-40.

Brown, David Blayney. "Testaments of Friendship: Two New Portraits by James Barry of Francis Douce and Joseph Nollekens." *BM* 128 (1986): 27-31.

BECKFORD

Kann, Roger, trans. *Journal intime: au Portugal et en Espagne, 1787-1788*. Paris: José Corti, 1986. Pp. 333. Fr. 150.00.

Rev. by Jean-Jacques Mayoux in *QL* 470, Sept. 16-30, 1986, pp. 15-16.

Orlando, F. "Vathek o la dannazione dell' 'Enfant gâté.'" *Saggi e Recerche di letteratura francese* 23 (1984): 277-303.

Roberts, Hugh. "Beckford, Vulliamy and Old Japan." *Apollo* 124 (1986): 338-41.

BEDDOES

Thompson, James R. *Thomas Lovell Beddoes*. Boston: Twayne Publishers, 1985. Pp. 137. $18.95.

Rev. by Leonidas M. Jones in *KSJ* 35 (1986): 188-90.

See also King-Hele ("Darwin").

BLAKE

Adams, Hazard. "The Dizziness of Freedom; or Why I Read William Blake." *CE* 48 (1986): 431-43.

"Literary study through examination of the particular goes beyond [specialists' interests] ... into questions of the critique of society and culture, questions of ethics, and questions of the role of language in life." "On each of these matters," Adams finds that Blake is "exemplary" as well as "inspirational." Indeed, Adams believes that Blake offers us the contrary we need in order to work ourselves out of the negations produced by contemporary critical theory. More specifically, he argues that Foucault's "reborn sociology" makes resistance impossible since it disregards "the individual will and with it the notion of power as inherent in those imaginative acts Blake regards as the ground of culture-making." As I see it, the problem with this argument is that it relies on an individual/society negation, the very negation to which Foucault's work stands

as a contrary. Perhaps the issue should not be who is more
contrary--Blake or Foucault--but which negations are most
important to undo these days. (J.H-P.)

Adkins, Camille. "In Adam's Room: Incarnation of the Divine
Image in *Paradise Lost* and *Jerusalem*." Ann Arbor, Mich.:
University Microfilms International, 1984.

> Dissertation.
> ("Milton perceives a God who is all light, whereas Blake
> recognizes light and darkness in divinity.")

Baine, Rodney, with Mary R. Baine. *The Scattered Portions:
William Blake's Biological Symbolism*. University of Georgia,
English Department, 1986. Pp. xx+260. $24.95.

> Beginning with the belief that "no other English poet or
> artist used biological images and symbols ... more often or
> more meaningfully than did William Blake," Baine presents
> a firmly researched, carefully applied commentary on
> carnivorous, herbivorous, and granivorous animals, birds
> of prey, insects, reptiles, marine life, trees, and plants.
> Baine insists that Blake almost always follows traditional
> emblematic symbolism and is ironic only in *The Marriage of
> Heaven and Hell*. The book's conclusion reminds us of the
> gauntlet Baine throws down: "The Tyger, as we can now
> perceive, is neither Christ militant nor creative energy,
> but an ugly and malevolent manifestation of the Selfhood.
> 'The Clod and the Pebble,' as the symbols help us to per-
> ceive, does not suggest that a conflation of selfish and
> unselfish love is necessary; rather it rejects the inferior,
> selfish view for the superior, unselfish one." However, in
> the earlier section where he discusses "The Clod and the
> Pebble," the reason Baine thinks that the Clod's view is
> favored is that the Clod and the patient cattle take up more
> than half the illustration! In a similar questionably dog-
> matic interpretation, the illustrated Tyger "is an ugly and
> foolish-looking beast."
> This militant insistence that there is almost no ambiguity
> in Blake's animal symbolism seems unnecessarily rigid, but
> it does not detract from the value of the myriad details.
> (M.T.S.)

Behrendt, Stephen. "'This Accursed Family': Blake's *America*
and the American Revolution." *ECent* 27 (1986): 26-51.

> *America: A Prophecy* "marks a transition in Blake's work
> from the narrative topicality of *The French Revolution* to
> the encyclopedic epic mythology of *Europe* and the later

prophecies." Central to this transitional work is the
"metaphor of the family," a metaphor that enables Blake to
represent "the psychological dilemma underl[ying] the revolution as a particular historical event." That dilemma
hinges on the perversions of desire produced by a patriarch
whose "jealous and selfish restrictions upon another's
liberty" tyrannically oppress both the "mother country"
and its children. Drawing on Lawrence Stone's work,
Behrendt argues that Blake's use of the family metaphor
not only indicates "his sensitivity to the changing form
and function of the family at the end of the eighteenth
century" but also bespeaks his vision of "the egalitarian
companionate family unit" as a model of liberation, a model
appropriate for the state as well as the sexes.

However, if Blake was as sensitive to changes in the
family as Behrendt claims he was, then how could he possibly
believe that the domesticated nuclear family constituted
a viable model for liberation? Did he really imagine that
the squirearchy--among whom the "egalitarian, companionate
family unit" had become the ideal--were free of patriarchical
perversions? I am not convinced that we do justice to Blake
when we read his metaphor of the family along the (political)
lines set down by Lawrence Stone. (J.H-P.)

Bellin, Harvey, and Darrel Ruhl, et al., eds. *Blake and Sweden-
borg, Opposition Is True Friendship: The Sources of William
Blake's Arts in the Writings of Emanuel Swedenborg: An
Anthology.* London: Swedenborg Foundation, 1985.

Not received.

Bentley, G.E., Jr. "A New *America*." *BIQ* 20 (1986): 37-33.
Illus.

A newly discovered copy of *America* proves to be "an excellent photographic facsimile ... made about 1885." Proof
lies in an "1885" watermark! Otherwise the matter might
remain moot.

(G.E.B. and D.V.E., however, don't see the same details.
In *America* 5 I see a grapevine and a man and a sprout of
wheat shooting up; Bentley doesn't mention the wheat but
keeps talking about the grapevine as a *tree*.) (D.V.E.)

Bentley, G.E., Jr. "From Sketch to Text in Blake: The Case
of *The Book of Thel*." *BIQ* 19 (1986): 128-41. 11 illus.

Bentley, G.E., Jr. "Keynes and Blake at Cambridge." *BIQ* 19
(1985): 69-71.

Bentley, G.E., Jr. "'The Triumph of Owen': William Owen
Pughe and Blake's 'Ancient Britons.'" *National Library of
Wales Journal* 24 (1985): 248-61.

Not seen.

Bentley, G.E., Jr. "Thomas Sivright and the Lost Designs for
Blair's Grave." *BIQ* 19 (1985-86): 103-06.

Bentley, G.E., Jr. "The Way of a Papermaker with a Poet:
Joshua Gilpin, William Blake, and the Arts in 1796."
"[Same title] ... A Postscript." *N&Q*, n.s. 33 (March 1986):
80-84; (Dec. 1986): 525.

The March note speculates that Gilpin's important diary
reveals a visit to Blake the poet; the December note corrects
that, recognizing that a William Staden Blake was meant.

Bidney, Martin. "Solomon and Pharaoh's Daughter: Blake's
Response to Wordsworth's Prospectus to *The Recluse*." *JEGP*
85 (1986): 532-49.

Billigheimer, Rachel V. "The Eighth Eye: Prophetic Vision
in Blake's Poetry and Design." *CLQ* 22 (1986): 93-110.

Bindman, David. "Samuel Palmer's 'An Address to the Electors
of West Kent, 1832.'" *BIQ* 19 (Fall 1985): 56-59.

Bindman, David. "William Blake and Popular Religious Imagery."
BM 128 (Oct. 1986): 712-18. 13 illus.

Bindman proposes that certain Blake designs were influenced
by pictures in the tradition of seventeenth-century anti-
Catholic polemic, which survived in his own time in "cheaply
printed and often very crude form." Others suggested are the
so-called "Hieroglyphicks," a term that had come to mean
any "visual puzzle"; Bindman cites prints of "The Tree of
Life," for *Jerusalem* 76, and "Daniel's Great Image," for
Blake's engraving of the Laocoön.
    In these instances, however, the only elements in common
with Blake's designs are not overall compositions or images,
as in his borrowings from mainstream art, but ideas or
devices of representation: the Pope enthroned, Christ crucified on a living tree, a human figure combined with inscribed text. The critical questions raised pertain to more
than Blake's relation to a particular religious tradition.
(I.H.C.)

Blondel, Jacques. "L'Eros Blakien." Pp. 7-16 in *Romanticism anglais et Eros*. Université de Clermont-Ferrand 2, 1982.

Bloom, Harold, ed. *William Blake*. (Modern Critical Views.) New York: Chelsea House Publishers, 1985. Pp. vi+209. $17.95.

An introduction by Harold Bloom; reprinted articles by David V. Erdman (1951); Robert F. Gleckner (1957); Northrop Frye (1966); W.J.T. Mitchell (1970); Harold Bloom (1971); Thomas R. Frosch (1974); Thomas Weiskel (1976); Susan Fox (1976); Leslie Brisman (1978); Leopold Damrosch, Jr. (1980); David Wagenknecht (1973); and Diana Hume George (1980).
Not seen until 1987. A convenient selection; the authors were not all consulted--some may have wished to revise. (D.V.E.)

Brown, James Boyd. "The History of an Illusion: The Meaning of the Four Zoas in Blake's *The Four Zoas*." Ann Arbor, Mich.: University Microfilms International, 1984.

Dissertation.
Brown's main thesis is quite new, that the Nights of the poem treat of a sequence of historical epochs. He manages to establish a consistent and plausible historical pattern of interpretation--though at times with very little solid evidence. And again and again he makes the text yield valuable insight into the complex meanings of the Zoa figures. (D.V.E.)

Butlin, Martin. *William Blake*. Rev. ed. Salem, N.H.: Salem House-Merrimack, 1985. $6.95.

Revised edition of Butlin's guide to the Tate Gallery's Blake collection. Not seen.

Chayes, Irene H. "Fallen Earth and Man in Nature: William Blake in Iconographic Tradition." *Studies in Iconography* 10 (1984-86): 169-95. 12 illus.

An impressively successful attempt to give Blake "a place in spite of himself in the long historical continuity of European art." Focusing on the visual evidence that relates two sculptural poses variously employed by Blake--a sleeping or reclining hermaphrodite, Fallen Earth, and Man in Nature on all fours, as in Nebuchadnezzar or the Beast with the Whore--Chayes identifies with a thoroughness hitherto lacking in Blake studies the specific sources in antique sculpture and successive adaptations over the centuries: "Unknowingly, in taking over the poses of the Sleeping Herma-

phrodite and/or the Reclining Venus for his original figures
of Fallen Earth, and of St. John Chrysostom and/or Aristotle
Mocked for his original figure of Man in Nature, Blake was
making a place for himself in the particular iconographic
traditions that have been traced by Millard Meiss and Edgar
Wind, both of whom could justifiably have added his name
to their lists of artists"--as we can add to their names
that of Irene Chayes.

Sadly, this essay has been not only delayed in the press
but very badly printed. I should like to pass along the
most serious corrections of the printers' omissions, indicated by the author in the copy sent to me. Footnote 31,
missing but belonging two lines after note 30, should read:
"Hewlett of course was confusing two saints' names. Dürer's
'The Penance of St. John Chrysostom' (ca. 1496-97) is now
usually accepted as the source of Blake's Nebuchadnezzar
in the color print and, by extension, of Nebuchadnezzar's
prototype in *Marriage* 24. Yet there are several other
versions of the same penitential scene by German engravers
who were followers of Dürer."

In footnote 24, the Ziegler title should read: "François
Beaufelaire (1759-1827): Peintre et amateur d'Art," *Gazettes
des Beaux-Art* 93 (March 1979): 120, fig. 13, and 121.

A most impressive opening chapter of the book we are impatiently awaiting. (D.V.E.)

Crossan, Greg. "'Infant Sorrow' and Robert Greene's *Menaphon*."
BIQ 19 (1986): 142-43.

A "minute particular."

Dörrbecker, Detlef W. "Fläche, Linie, Figur und Raum:
Grundzüge der Bildform bei William Blake." *Unijournal:
Zeitschrift der Universität Trier* 12,2 (1986): 6.

A dissertation abstract; University of Trier, West Germany.

Egerton, Judy. "William Blake at Wildenstein." *BM* 128 (Aug.
1986): 619-21. 4 illus.

Report on the exhibition, *William Blake and His Contemporaries*, at the Wildenstein Gallery, London, June-July 1986,
featuring selections from the Blake Collection at the Fitz-
william Museum.

Ellis, Helen. "Blake's 'Bible of Hell': *Visions of the
Daughters of Albion* and the Song of Solomon." *ESC* 12 (1986):
23-36.

"In reworking the Song of Solomon for his Bible of Hell,
Blake evidently intended to use the idyllic, unfettered

sexuality of Bride and Bridegroom as a standard for the
human sexual relationships of his own day. But both his
own ambivalence toward sexuality and his model betrayed
him."

Essick, Robert N. "Blake's *Job*: Some Unrecorded Proofs and
Their Inscriptions." *BIQ* 19 (1985-86): 96-102. 5 illus.

In *Job*, plate 1, the family have books open but are not
playing their musical instruments; in plate 21, they have
all risen and are playing and singing: a dramatic contrast,
we've often noted. But Essick now finds proofs of these
plates with inscriptions that praise *both* postures: plate
1, "Prayer to God is the Study of Imaginative Art"; plate
21, "Praise to God is the Exercise of Imaginative Art."
Ahah! (D.V.E.)

Essick, Robert N. "Dante Gabriel Rossetti, Frederic Shields,
and the Spirit of William Blake." *VP* 24 (1986): 163-72.

The name of Robert Essick on an article promises lively
scholarly revelation. Working with his habitual precision
and insight, Essick carefully presents evidence and judicially
draws conclusions. This article features reproductions of
five versions of Frederic Shields's sketches of Blake's
room overlooking the Thames. The sonnet which Rossetti
dedicated to Blake in his 1881 *Ballads and Sonnets* was based
on Shields's sketches, not on a visit to the room (which
Rossetti apparently never made). Even more surprisingly
the sonnet was not based on any of Blake's poetry, even that
in the *Notebook*, which Rossetti owned. Essick concludes
that Blake's material, textual presence and his insistence
on determinate outline threatened Rossetti, the least linear
of the Pre-Raphaelites, who then chose Blake's life as subject of his sonnet. "Rossetti joins with Shields and Gil-
christ to celebrate Blake's death as a passing into the
heaven of Victorian sensibility." (M.T.S.)

Essick, Robert N. "Variation, Accident, and Intention in
William Blake's *The Book of Urizen*." *SB* 39 (1986): 230-35.

Suggests that the omission of plate 4 from several copies
of *Urizen* resulted from an error in alignment during printing
that Blake was apparently unable to correct. Essick speculates that other significant textual variations "may have as
much to do with the contingencies of Blake's presswork as
[with] his transcendental ideas."

Essick, Robert. "William Blake, William Hamilton, and the
Materials of Graphic Meaning." *ELH* 52 (1985): 833-72.

Fenske, Siglinde, ed. *William Blake 1757-1827*. (Maler:
Leben, Werk und ihre Zeit, 15.) Hamburg: Marshall Cavendish
International, 1986. DM 4.90.

> An illustrated pamphlet in a popular series; an English
> version has probably been published in the U.K. and the U.S.
> Not seen.

Finch, G.J. "Romantic Poetry and the Limits of Explication."
Ariel 16,1 (1986): 27-42.

> For a discussion of these limits in the interpretation of
> Blake, see pp. 37-41.

Forster, Harold. *Edward Young: The Poet of the Night Thoughts*.
Alburgh, England: Erskine Press, 1986. Pp. 434. £29.95.

> Rev. by Pat Rogers in *TLS*, March 20, 1987, pp. 287-88 as
> fairly successful as biography but misconceived and erroneous
> as critical evaluation.
> Neither Forster (presumably) nor Rogers mentions Blake's
> interest in Young's poem.
> Not seen.

Gaddy, Holly C. "The Poet as Monk." *MSE* 9 (1984): 1-12.

> On Thomas Merton's 1938 master's thesis, "Nature and
> Art in William Blake." (T.L.A.)

Gardner, Stanley. *Blake's Innocence and Experience Retraced*.
London: Athlone Press; New York: St. Martin's Press, 1986.
Pp. xviii+211; 60 illus. $27.50.

> The retracing is both geographic--through St. James's
> parish, where Blake grew up, and later Lambeth, where he
> lived from 1791 to 1800--and historical, centered on the
> change in community care for paupers' children from the
> spontaneous social concern of the early 1780s (the school
> set up by Blake's neighbors in King Street is taken as the
> standard) to the suspicion, self-interest, and retrenchment
> of the 1790s, when the "schools of industry" were established.
> Gardner provides documentary information which in itself
> is interesting, often moving, and which does illuminate
> such obviously relevant poems as "The Chimney Sweeper" and
> "Holy Thursday," in both sequences.
> With others, even in *Innocence*, his approach is less
> successful; in the chapters on *Experience* he resorts to
> circumstantial biography and anticipations of the Lambeth
> books to supplement the social and moral commentary that be-
> comes increasingly inadequate as he advances. Thus written

in chains, because Gardner will accept no other context for
the Songs, some of the interpretations of individual texts
and designs take bizarre turns or seem almost willfully
uncomprehending. (I.H.C.)

Glausser, Wayne. "A Note on the Twenty Years of Blake's
Spectre." *ELN* 24 (1986): 43-44.

Godard, Jerry C. *Mental Forms Creating: William Blake
Anticipates Freud, Jung and Rank.* University Press of
America, 1985.

Not seen.

Gourlay, Alexander S. *Blake's Sisters: A Critical Edition,
with Commentary, of "The Book of Thel" and "Visions of the
Daughters of Albion."* Ann Arbor, Mich.: University Microfilms International, 1986.

Dissertation.

Greco, Norma A. "Blake's 'Laughing Song': A Reading." *CP*
19 (1986): 67-72.

Greco, Norma A. "Mother Figures in Blake's *Songs of Innocence*
and the Female Will." *RP&P* 10,i (1986): 1-16.

Gresham, Gwendolyn Holloway P. *The Voice of Honest Indigna-
tion: William Blake's Critique of the Polity, Liturgy,
Ethics, and Theology of the Church of England.* Ann Arbor,
Mich.: University Microfilms International, 1986.

Dissertation.

Gross, David. "Infinite Indignation: Teaching, Dialectical
Vision, and Blake's *Marriage of Heaven and Hell*." *CE* 48
(1986): 175-86.

This Marxist analysis of Blake's link between the voice
of God and the voice of honest indignation emphasizes the
dialectic between reality and imagination. Gross concludes
that Blake works well in the classroom because he forces
active engagement with cultural assumptions. (M.T.S.)

Gross, David. "'Mind-Forg'd Manacles': Hegemony and Counter-
Hegemony in Blake." *ECent* 27 (1986): 3-25.

According to Gross, "to see Blake's work in the light of
Gramsci's ideas and formulations [concerning hegemony] is
to contribute to an understanding of his significance as a

poet in ways ignored and/or distorted by traditional Blake
criticism" which has interpreted Blake "either politically
or spiritually, as concerned primarily with society *or*
psychology." Rather than participate in this critical
either/or, Gross would like to read in a way that realizes
the dialectical interpenetration of the political and the
personal in Blake's works. But is it really the case that
traditional Blake criticism has ignored this interpenetration? I think not. And what about the issue of distortion? Although it may indeed be the case that critics have
distorted the conjuncture of the personal and the political
in Blake's work, Gross's appeal to "hegemony" doesn't really
clarify matters. On the one hand, Gross reifies hegemony,
writing as if it were some *thing* that Blake could definitely
be against. On the other hand, Gross fails to give hegemony
any specificity, defining it as a system of values, a set
of attitudes, a world view, and a common sense which "is
in one way or another supportive of established order and
class interests." Yes, we do need a way of representing
Blake's dialectic that is less indebted to idealism and/or
empiricism. But no, Gross's "hegemony" is not the way; as it
is used here, it merely repeats prevailing distortions.
(J.H-P.)

Groves, David. "Blake, Thomas Boston, and the Fourfold Vision."
BIQ 19 (1986): 142.

   A "minute particular."

Haigwood, Laura Ellen. "Eve's Daughters: The Subversive
   Feminine in Blake and Wordsworth." Ann Arbor, Mich.:
   Unviersity Microfilms International, 1985.

   Dissertation.
   Argues, from the Milton illustrations and *Visions of the
   Daughters of Albion*, that Oothoon's "free love" arguments
   are "embedded in sexist assumptions" and "may be an example
   of Blake's skill at dramatic irony rather than a simple
   enunciation of his own views on free love."

Hall, Carol Louise. *Blake and Fuseli: A Study in the Trans-
   mission of Ideas*. New York and London: Garland Publishing,
   1985. (Garland Publications in Comparative Literature.)
   Pp. xi+171; illus. $33.00.

   Hall's *Blake and Fuseli* is a marvelous compendium of facts
about connections between the two artists. Fuseli (Füssli)
was sent to London in 1764 as an emissary between German
and English intellectual worlds. Coincidentally, although

Fuseli was sixteen years older than Blake, they began their careers as artists at about the same time in 1779. In 1781 Fuseli moved to 1 Broad Street; since Blake was still officially living at 28 Broad Street, they may have known each other that early.

The centerpiece of the book is a list of documentary evidence of Blake's and Fuseli's knowledge of each other. There are 16 documents between the 1770s and 1810. Blake's first recorded comment on Fuseli, in a letter to Flaxman on September 12, 1800, indicates that they knew each other well in 1787. Fuseli never mentioned Blake's poetry but stated his high regard for Blake's designs.

After details about Fuseli's European background and literary activities--plenty of poetry in his theological training--Hall gives us chapters on Winckelmann, Rousseau, and above all Lavater, whose *Aphorisms on Man*, translated into English by Fuseli, were annotated by Blake. These aphorisms may well have provided the direct impetus for the Proverbs of Hell. (M.T.S.)

Heppner, Christopher. "Blake's 'The New Jerusalem Descending': A Drawing (Butlin no. 92) Identified." *BIQ* 20 (1986): 4-11. 3 illus.

Heppner, Christopher. "The New Jerusalem Defended." *BIQ* 20 (1986-87): 102-04.

Reply to criticism by Tolley, listed below.

Hilton, Nelson, and Thomas A. Vogler, eds. *Unnam'd Forms: Blake and Textuality.* University of California Press, 1985. Pp. xiii+267; 28 illus. $34.00.

Nine essays, plus an Envoi by Geoffrey H. Hartman, "So Many Things," attempting to react to both "what is known and understood" and "what is known and not understood."

David Simpson writes of "Reading Blake and Derrida--Our Caesars Neither Praised nor Buried" (11-25); Gavin Edwards of "Repeating the Same Dull Round" (26-48)--discussing first Blake's "performative" utterances, then his "proverbs." Paul Mann discusses "*The Book of Urizen* and the Horizon of the Book" (49-68): if the book "is an ontological horizon," will "any book ... itself be implicated and bound within the horizon"?

Nelson Hilton, "An Original Story" (69-104), notes many close links between Blake's *Visions of the Daughters of Albion* and the related lives and works of Wollstonecraft and Fuseli. One convincing detail, among many: on Blake's title page, Oothoon is flying from Blake's adaptation of

Fuseli's idea for *The Fertilization of Egypt*--beside a
dancing group borrowed from Fuseli's *The Shepherd's Dream*.
Eye-opening!

Donald Ault, "Re-Visioning *The Four Zoas*" (105-39), offers
interesting samples of the sort of narrative processes and
textual features he analyzes in his forthcoming book. (Ault
has a problem about sequences. No one knows what order the
leaves were in when Blake died. We know what Ellis and Yeats
did conjecturally in sorting them, and the changes Keynes,
who added folio numbers, made. We have to find what clues
we can to achieve the most probable sequences--even assuming
that Blake himself made no final decision, e.g., which of
two "Night the Seventh" headings to use and where to go from
there.)

Thomas A. Vogler, "Re:Naming MIL/TON" (140-76), does a
rigorous job of responding to Blake's invitation to open
up his text and pictures to multiple readings.

A simple example appears in the "emphatically chirographic
splitting represented on the title-plate ... as Milton's (?)
own hand is shown reaching *through* and 'breaching' the
name." The question mark invites *us* to see that the hand
may be that of "The Author and Printer W. Blake" inscribed
beside the other hand!

Stephen Leo Carr, "Illuminated Printing: Toward a Logic
of Difference" (177-96) is not impressively logical; several
footnotes cite but push aside attempts by Robert Essick at
critical assistance!

Robert N. Essick, "How Blake's Body Means" (197-217),
responds more fully to Carr--and others including Erdman--
and insists that "the only 'Blake' actually existing in this
world now is the various, recalcitrant, and material body
of the manufactured objects he had a role in producing."

V.A. De Luca, "A Wall of Words: The Sublime as Text"
(218-41), shrewdly sums up the philosophical implications
of these discussions. "The terminology of our present-day
discourse on textuality easily lends itself to the discussion
of Blake," and Blake "would recognize much in our current
discourse as part of the vocabulary of sublimity," *but* he
"would see this vocabulary as stuck in the intermediate
or deprivative phase of the sublime moment.... For Blake
Presence is available.... In that sublimity we breathe
heaven's air, but as a gift to sustain us in our return to
the continuities of the common day." (D.V.E.)

Holloway, John. *Blake*. (The Open University/Arts. A Third-
Level Course, ser. A362: "Romantic Poetry," units 2-3.)
Milton Keynes, Bucks, England: Open University Press, 1984.

A coursebook up to *The Song of Los*; 57 pages, complete
with text extracts.

Holmes, John. *William Blake's Place in the Mystical Tradition.*
Ann Arbor, Mich.: University Microfilms International, 1986.

   Dissertation.

Imaizumi, Yoko. *Brotherhood in Blake: Psychology and Poetics.*
Ann Arbor, Mich.: University Microfilms International.
1986.

   Dissertation.

John, Donald. "Blake and Forgiveness." *TWC* 17 (1986):   74-80.

Johnston, John H.   "Thomson, Jago, Cowper, Blake, and Seward."
Pp. 56-82 in *The Poet and the City: A Study in Urban Perspectives*. University of Georgia Press, 1984.

   Not seen.

Kamusikiri, Sanda Darlene. *"A Building of Magnificence":
Blake's Major Prophesies and Eighteenth-Century Conceptions
of the Human Sublime*. Ann Arbor, Mich.: University Microfilms International, 1986.

   Dissertation.

Kauvar, Elaine M.   "The Sorrows of Thel: A Freudian Interpretation of *The Book of Thel*." *JEP* 5 (1984):   210-22.

Kemeny, Tomaso, ed. *Seminario sull'opera di William Blake.*
Florence: Università di Pavia, 1983.   L. 10,000.00.

   Proceedings of a 1982 conference at Pavia, including
   Claudia Corti on Blake's "poetical iconism"; Marcella Quadri
   on word and image in Blake's work; Carla Locatelli on
   "tautology" in the *Songs*; Roberto Sanesi on Blake and Newton;
   Rossana Bossaglia on Blake and the "problem of the predecessors of symbolism"; and the editor on Blake and Joyce.
   Not seen.

La Belle, Jenijoy. "A Pencil Sketch for Blake's Dante Illustrations." *BIQ* 19 (1985):   73-74.

Larrissy, Edward.   "Blake and the Hutchinsonians." *BIQ* 20
(1986):   44-47.

   More about Blake's apparent indebtedness to the "main
   school of anti-Newtonians," especially the Hutchinsonians.

Of considerable interest; yet, though note 4 says "there
is evidence that Blake had read" *An Abstract ... of John
Hutchinson*, no specific evidence is cited. (D.V.E.)

Lee, Judith. "Scornful Beauty: A Note on Blake and Ariosto."
ELN 23,4 (1986): 35-38.

Lesser, Harry. "Blake and Plato." *Philosophy* 56 (1981):
223-30.

Lincoln, Andrew. "Blake and the Natural History of Creation."
E&S 39 (1986): 94-103.

Discussion of the contrasting visions of creation as a
delusion and as an act of mercy that are presented in Nights
1 and 2 of *The Four Zoas*.

Linkin, Harriet Kramer. "The Language of Speakers in *Songs of
Innocence and of Experience*." *RP&P* 10 (1986): 5-24.

"Blake encodes many innocent voices with idiolects that
fail to contain the disruptive knowledge of Experience,"
and decoding proceeds apace. "Critics who have previously
commented on the function of point of view and context ...
rarely comment on idiolectic variation among Blake's
speakers."

Linkin, Harriet Kramer. "The Search for a Transcendent
Language: Linguistic Strategies in Herbert and Blake."
Ann Arbor, Mich.: University Microfilms International,
1985.

Dissertation.

Marvel, Laura. "Blake and Yeats: Visions of Apocalypse."
CollL 13 (1986): 95-105.

Masterson, Donald, and Edward O'Shea. "Code Breaking and Myth
Making: The Ellis-Yeats Edition of Blake's *Works*." *Yeats
Annual* 3 (1985): 53-80.

Matsushima, Shoichi. *Koko no Geijutsuka William Blake*. Tokyo:
Hokuseido, 1984. ¥ 5,000.00.

McCord, James. "Mixed Motives and Deadly Acts: Historical and
Dramatic Character in William Blake's *King Edward the Third*."
ECS 19 (1986): 480-501.

Comparing and contrasting Blake's play with its sources,
especially David Hume and Rapin de Thoyras, McCord counters

previous interpretations, especially Gleckner's and Erdman's.
The characters are fuller and Blake is more sensitive to
Shakespearean achievements than previously thought. We need
to be "sensitive to ambiguity in character and to the perceptual conflicts in Shakespeare's plays, and aware of the
fallacy of historical 'truth.'" (M.T.S.)

A reading of the play in the light of Blake's likely sources,
especially the historical accounts by Hume and Rapin. Like
those two authors, Blake is said to have been aware of the
difficulties of interpreting historical character; "their
works ought to be regarded as inquiries into the nature
of historical identity rather than as didactic treatises."
A rare view of Blake as *not* in opposition to eighteenth-
century trends of thought. (I.H.C.)

McCord, James. "West of Atlantis: William Blake's Unromantic
View of the American War." *CentR* 30 (1986): 383-99.

In *America: A Prophecy*, Blake is "unable to grasp enough
joyful images to affirm that the American war was, in typical
Romantic fashion, a spiritual prelude to the French Revolution or a genuine prelude to apocalypse." McCord considers
the omission of "apocalyptic images associated with America,"
the numerous illustrations of "the horrors of war," and the
three cancelled title plates. All of these indicate Blake's
"ambivalence," his concern "that the American dream of freedom and justice might be sacrificed on the altars of power
and ambition after the war."

McGann, Jerome J. "The Idea of an Indeterminate Text: Blake's
Bible of Hell and Dr. Alexander Geddes." *SiR* 25 (1986):
303-24.

Interesting information about Geddes, a radical Bible
scholar and Roman Catholic priest associated with the publisher Joseph Johnson, whose "fragment hypothesis" concerning the books of the Old Testament McGann believes was known
to and influenced Blake. (In his background account McGann
unfortunately blurs the distinctions between syncretic
mythology and the new textual scholarship of the time, as
well as between Gnosticism and Neoplatonism.) The argument
is that the various textual problems posed by *The Book of
Urizen*--including the plate order in the existing copies,
which were made over a period of years--"represent deliberate
acts on Blake's part," designed to parody the Book of Genesis
"along lines opened up by the new biblical criticism,"
especially that of Geddes.

McGann's thesis is based on assumptions about Blake's
intentions and his power to act upon and sustain them which

are open to question. Not the least is the initial assumption (still uncritically accepted by others as well) that,
because of the rhetorical promise by one of the personae
in *The Marriage of Heaven and Hell*, *Urizen* was part of an
actual "Bible of Hell" planned by Blake himself and carried
forward into *Ahania* and *Los*. (I.H.C.)

McHenry, Henry Davis, Jr. "1: Prolegomenon for a Complete
    Angler: The Social Conditioning of Learning; 2: Reference
    and Exuberance: Blake's Idea of Language." Ann Arbor,
    Mich.: University Microfilms International, 1985.

    Dissertation.

Meller, Horst. "Audens 'As I Walked Out One Evening' und
    Blakes 'London': Zwei Epiphanien großstädtischer Unheim-
    lichkeit." *Anglistik und Englischunterricht* 26 (1985):
    107-25.

Meller, Horst. "Gedichstruktur und die ungelösten Antagonismen
    der Realität: Blakes 'London'-Gedicht." *Zum Verstehen
    englischer Gedicht.* (Literaturstudium 2/Uni-Taschenbücher
    1070.) München: UTB-Fink, 1985. Pp. 169-84.

Miller, Dan. "Contrary Revelation: *The Marriage of Heaven
    and Hell.*" *SiR* 24 (1985): 491-509.

    A close analysis of *Marriage* which repeatedly emphasizes
    the presence of contrariety--as incommensurability, separa-
    tion, incomparability--in the very means by which the
    "principle" is stated, argued, illustrated, or mythicized.
    Miller's point is ultimately that Blake's "major figures
    and concepts" are "tropes whose meaning cannot be separated
    from the terms of their representation. Reading [this] and
    later works is less a matter of translating narrative into
    consistent doctrine than it is describing the figures govern-
    ing both myth and logic." (I.H.C.)

Mitchell, W.J.T. "Visible Language: Blake's Wond'rous
    Art of Writing." Pp. 46-86 in Morris Eaves and Michael
    Fischer, eds., *Romanticism and Contemporary Criticism.*
    Cornell University Press, 1986.

    A lecture complete with questions and answers (86-95).

Mulhallen, Karen. "The Crying of Lot 318; or, Young's *Night
    Thoughts* Colored Once More." *BIQ* 19 (1985): 71-72.

Nanavutty, Piloo. "The River of Oblivion." *AJES* 11 (1986): 93-97.

A drawing, hitherto unidentified, to illustrate Dante's *Purgatory*, Canto 18. (Said to be "reproduced here for the first time" but, alas, not bound in the copy received.) "The two central figures of the composition are Dante and Beatrice. Dante is seated on a stone, and turns his back upon Beatrice who is standing beside him. He stretches out longing arms into the distance. His brows are contracted in anguish, and the eyes, half closed, gaze into futurity."

"News and Comment." *BC* 35 (1986): 362-365.

Announces the publication by the Blake Trust of the *Job* illustrations, which will complete the whole set.

Ostriker, Alicia. "Reply to Hagstrum." *BIQ* 18 (1985): 238.

See Hagstrum ("English 3. Criticism") above.

Ott, Judith Lynn. "The Illuminations of William Blake's *Jerusalem, The Emanation of the Giant Albion*: What Are Those Golden Builders Doing?" Ann Arbor, Mich.: University Microfilms International, 1985.

Dissertation. Emphasis on "establishing the perimeters of his multiple sources."

Phipps, Frances. "Let Me Be Los: Codebook for *Finnegans Wake*." *Toth-Maatian Review* 3,5, suppl. (1985). (503 W. Indiana Ave., Urbana, IL 61801.)

Hundreds of illustrations of Egyptian artifacts and Blake's designs.

Piquet, François. "Quelques aspects de l'Eros chez Blake." *Romantisme anglais et Eros* (1982): 17-28.

Piquet, François. "L'Infini qui nait au creux de la paume ou Edward Gordon Craig et William Blake." *RHT* 36 (1984): 227-46.

Powell, Nicholas. "Bizarre Brotherhood." *Apollo* 123 (1986): 429-31.

A "Round the Galleries" article on the exhibition "William Blake and his Contemporaries" at the Wildenstein Gallery.

Raine, Kathleen. "The City in William Blake." *AJES* 11 (1986): 75-97.

A lively survey of Blake's life in and visionary recognition

of the city as "the tragic and terrible scene of human
struggle and suffering ... of the heavens and hells of human
experience ... the total expression of the human imagination, in its heights and in its depths."

Rix, Donna S. "*Milton*: Blake's Reading of Second Isaiah."
Pp. 106-18 in Jan Wojcik and Raymond-Jean Frontain, eds.,
Poetic Prophecy in Western Literature. Fairleigh Dickin-
son University Press; Associated University Presses, 1984.

   Not seen.

Rose, Edward J. "Blake's *Jerusalem*, St. Paul, and Biblical
Prophecy." *ESC* 11 (1985): 396-412.

Rothenberg, Molly Anne. "Blake's Higher Criticism: Rhetoric
and Re-Vision in *Jerusalem*." Ann Arbor, Mich.: University
Microfilms International, 1985.

   Dissertation. ("Blake wrote *Jerusalem* in order to teach
his readers to recognize the rhetorical strategies by which
sacred texts are constructed.")

Ryskamp, Charles. "Paul Mellon and William Blake." Pp. 329-
37 in John Wilmerding, ed., *Essays in Honor of Paul Mellon:
Collector and Benefactor*. Washington, D.C.: National
Gallery of Art, 1986.

Schiff, Gert. "William Blake: Anarchist, Haeretiker und
Moralist." *Forma et subtilitas: Festschrift für Wolfgang
Schöne zum 75. Geburtstag*. Ed. Wilhelm Schlink and Martin
Sperlich. Berlin: de Gruyter, 1986. Pp. 229-48.

Shaviro, Steven. "'Striving with Systems': Blake and the
Politics of Difference." *Boundary* 2,10.3 (1982): 229-50.

Shortland, Michael. "The Power of a Thousand Eyes: Johann
Caspar Lavater's Science of Physiognomical Perception."
Criticism 28 (1986): 379-408.

   Full bibliography.

Singh, Gurbhagat. *Poetry as Metaconsciousness: Readings in
William Blake*. Atlantic Highlands, N.J.: Humanities Press,
1983. $16.00.

   Not seen.

Sosnowski, T. Ford. "Meter and Form in Blake's 'The Lamb'
and 'The Tyger.'" *Kwartalnik Neofilologiczny* 31 (1984):
407-16.

Spector, Sheila A. "Death in Blake's Major Prophecies."
Studia Mystica 7,3 (1984): 3-28.

Taylor, Dena Bain. "The Visual Context of 'Joseph of
Arimathea Among the Rocks of Albion.'" *BIQ* 20 (1986):
47-48. Illus.

"Unlike the Druids of the antiquaries ... Blake's Joseph
bears no symbols of power or authority.... He has no warm
clock [cloak?], no sandals, no rolling hills and established
settlement behind him."

Tolley, Michael J. "The *Allegorical Female Figure*: She Cometh
With Clouds." *BIQ* (1986-87): 101-02.

Reply by Heppner, listed above.

van Schaik, Pam. "The 'Divine Image' and 'Human Abstract' in
a Selection of William Blake's Illustrations to Edward
Young's *Night Thought*." *del Arte* (Pretoria: University of
South Africa) 33 (Sept. 1985): 4-22. 12 illus. (2 in col.).

Arranged in the sequence NT 446, 512, 69, 87, 53, 200,
206, 409, 162, 142, 317, the plot unfolds from "Majestic
Night: Muse, and Ancestor of Nature," to "The 'Human
Harvest' rising from death's 'dark Vale.'" An impressive
and valuable scrutiny of key designs. (D.V.E.)

Viscomi, Joseph. "Recreating Blake's Illuminated Prints:
The Facsimiles of the Manchester Etching Workshop." *BIQ*
19 (19850: 4-23.

Waxler, Robert P. "The Virgin Mantle Displaced: Blake's
Early Attempt." *MLS* 12,1 (1982): 45-53.

Not previously noted.
"Blake keeps the Biblical and Miltonic structure in the
background, but they help define the relationship between
Oothoon and Thel.... They are the inner form of the works
themselves or the latent content that will be revealed in
Blake's later work." Valuable insight. (D.V.E.)

Welch, Dennis M. "Blake's Critique of Election: *Milton* and
the *Comus* Illustrations." *PQ* 64 (1985): 509-53.

The article is preceded by 16 black-and-white illustrations.

Welch, Dennis M. "'Cloth'd with human beauty': *Milton* and
Blake's Incarnational Aesthetic." *R&L* 18,2 (1985): 1-16.

Welch, Dennis M. "Imitation in Blake's *Night Thoughts*
Illustrations." *CLQ* 22 (1986): 165-84.

Werner, Bette Charlene. *Blake's Vision of the Poetry of Milton:*
Illustrations to Six Poems. Bucknell University Press, 1986.
Pp. 319; 79 illus. $45.00.

Keeping her predecessors (including two thus far in the
1980s) in respectful view, Werner compares Milton's verse
and Blake's designs once more and cautiously revises
previous emphases on the illustrator's disagreements with
his poet. She argues, in general convincingly, that in
later versions of the same designs and later series of illustrations to different poems Blake's interpretations were
increasingly affirmative and increasingly in sympathy with
Milton's [Blakean] theme of the "testing" of the soul by
experience. Her close attention to the details of the
drawings in relation to Milton's texts often produces valuable
insights. As she proceeds, too, she becomes less dependent
on received interpretations, so that her "testing" thesis
applies at least to her own experience in writing the book.
On the debit side, Werner is weakest in dealing with
Blake's drawings as pictorial art. When she mentions their
relation to earlier art, it is nearly always only incidentally
and at second hand, by way of other Blake scholars. Her
descriptions tend to be impressionistic or moralizing, less
in response to the images on the page than to the subject,
or an advance conception of it. When she is concerned with
states of mind, Werner looks for evidence not only in gesture
and attitude but also in the supposed facial expressions of
the figures represented—despite the variables of competence
and accident, and often the practical difficulties of
determining what if any expression Blake may have intended.
On the other hand, more conspicuous and even intrusive
effects, such as the exaggerations that come perilously
close to caricature in the series for *Paradise Regained*,
are left unremarked.
As her main title indicates, Werner shares the common
assumption in the literary reading of Blake's designs that
they are transparent windows for meanings which need only
be packaged in words. By now, that is an assumption it is
surely time to reconsider, at least in the specific cases
that repeatedly attract new studies. (I.H.C.)

Witke, Joanne. *William Blake's Epic: Imagination Unbound*.
New York: St. Martin's Press, 1986. Pp. viii+231. $27.50.

Although *William Blake's Epic* is strong in some details,
especially in links with Berkeley's *Siris* and with Reynolds,

it consistently sets up a simple war between two forces--
the "naturalistic" and the "imaginative"--and ignores most
complexities in *Jerusalem*. Witke especially fails to take
into account Blake's tensions between expansion and contraction: the subtitle and the entire book imply that the
imagination need take on no wiry bounding line.

She does provide some intriguing arguments which identify
Coban, Hyle, and Hand with Bacon, Locke, and Newton. For
example, Hand equals Newton because Blake is "utilizing
the ellipsis for 'hand of God,' [to show that] Newton denies
the power of spirit; imposing his law upon the world, he
usurps the divine prerogative."

However, most of the book is oversimplified or obvious.
The following two statements are typical: "Because a vital,
creative eternal spirit underlies Blake's system of art,
the existence and nature of God are related issues," and
"Blake ... has a high estimate of all art. He regards it
objective and true, having equal place with other kinds
of knowledge."

The oversimplifications are often accompanied by clichés
and other weak diction: "Albion suffers the supreme outrage:
he is crucified by his own sons. They have taken vengeance,
which belongs to God alone. Near death, Albion has second
thoughts about the doctrines he has accepted and asks profound philosophical questions."

About halfway through, Witke abandons most pretenses to
interpretation; she simply paraphrases "the narrative" of
chapters 3 and 4, occasionally repeating generalizations
from earlier chapters. (M.T.S.)

Yoshimura, Masakazu. "Blake and the Cycle Symbolism." *Studies
in English Literature* (Tokyo) 60 (1983): 47-59.

Summary in English in 61 (1984): 116-17.

See also Erdman, Paley, Taft ("General 2. Environment");
Cook, Mitchell, Scarry ("General 3. Criticism"); Bindman,
Dorrbecker, Erdman, Essick, Lister ("English 1. Bibliography");
Barrell, Behrendt, Bidney, Curran, Cushing, Eaves and
Fischer, Engell, Goslee, Hagstrum, Hoagwood, Spacks, Wilkie
("English 3. Criticism"); McFarland ("Coleridge"); Walker
("Cosway"); Colp, King-Hele ("Darwin"); Klemm ("Fuseli");
Curran ("Shelley"); Zach ("German 2. General").

Reviews of books previously listed:

BRACHER, Mark, *Being Form'd: Thinking Through Blake's
Milton* (see *RMB* for 1985, p. 83), rev. by Nelson Hilton in
RP&P 10 (1986): 67-70; BUTLIN, Martin, *The Paintings and*

Drawings of William Blake (see *RMB* for 1981, pp. 78-79),
rev. by Morris Eaves in *SiR* 25 (1986):   pp. 147-54 in a
critical history of the *catalogue raisonné* as a genre;
CREHAN, Stewart, *Blake in Context* (see *RMB* for 1984, p. 101),
rev. by Stuart Peterfreund in *BIQ* 19 (1985-86):   113-16,
foolishly misconstruing Crehan's approach (see the strong
response to Peterfreund by Crehan, "Blake, Context and Ideology," *BIQ* 20:   104-07 and the reply by Peterfreund in *ibid.* 20:
108-09); by Paul Hamilton in *TLS*, June 15, 1984, p. 674;
by T. Hoagwood in *Choice* 22 (1984):   266; DEEN, Leonard W.,
*Conversing in Paradise: Poetic Genius and Identity-as-
Community in Blake's Los* (see *RMB* for 1983, p. 77), rev. by
Mary Lynn Johnson in *BIQ* (1985-86):   107-10; by Edward J.
Rose in *TWC* 15 (1984):   111-12; by Charlene Werner in *Mil-
tonQ* 18 (1984):   35-36; DISALVO, Jackie, *War of Titans:
Blake's Critique of Milton and the Poetics of Religion* (see
RMB for 1983, pp. 78-79), rev. by Jacques Blondel in *EA* 39
(1986):   97; by Anne Ferry in *RQ* 37 (1984):   671-72; by
Robert F. Gleckner severely, in *BIQ* 19 (1986):   146-50; by
Andrew Lincoln in *RES* 37 (1986):   105-07; DOSKOW, Minna,
*William Blake's "Jerusalem":   Structure and Meaning in
Poetry and Picture* (see *RMB* for 1983, pp. 79-80); rev. by
V.A. deLuca in *BIQ* 18 (1984):   56-58; by Paul Hamilton in
TLS, June 15, 1984, p. 674; by Donald John in *RES* 36 (1985):
434-36; DOWDEY, Landon, ed., *The Four Zoas: The Torments
of Love and Jealousy in the "Death and Judgment of Albion
the Ancient Man"* (see *RMB* for 1983, p. 80), rev. by W.J.T.
Mitchell in *The Library Quarterly* 55 (1985):   115-17; EAVES,
Morris, *William Blake's Theory of Art* (see *RMB* for 1982, pp.
83-84), rev. by Stephen D. Cox in *ECS* (1985):   391-405; by
Raymond Lister in *JRSA* 132 (1983):   86-87; by Thomas A. Vogler
in *SIR* 24 (1985):   289-300; ESSICK, Robert N., *The Separate
Plates of William Blake: A Catalogue* (see *RMB* for 1983, pp.
80-81), rev. by David Scrase in *BIQ* 20 (1986):   64-66; ESSICK,
Robert N., and Morton D. Paley, eds., *Robert Blair's "The
Grave," Illustrated by William Blake* (see *RMB* for 1982,
p. 85), rev. by Andrew Wilton in *BIQ* 18 (1984):   54-56;
FERBER, Michael, *The Social Vision of William Blake* (see *RMB*
for 1985, pp. 85-86), rev. by G.Z. Cevasco in *Choice* 23:
867; by Jenijoy La Belle in *RP&P* 10 (1986):   63-66; by
Karen Shabetai in *Criticism* 28 (1986):   343-46; FRYE,
Northrop, *The Great Code: The Bible and Literature* (see *RMB*
for 1981, p. 25), rev. by Paul-Gabriel Bouce in *EA* 37 (1984):
449-50; GLECKNER, Robert F., *Blake and Spenser* (see *RMB* for
1985, pp. 86-87), rev. by Stephen C. Behrendt in *ECS* 20
(1986):   257-60 as "a rich and complex book" worth more than
a single reading; GLECKNER, Robert F., *Blake's Prelude:
Poetical Sketches* (see *RMB* for 1983, pp. 81-83); rev. by

Thomas J. Corr in, *CollL* 11 (1984): 286-89; by Stephen D. Cox
in *ECS* 18 (1985): 391-405; by Paul Hamilton in *TLS* June 15,
1984; p. 674; by Nelson Hilton in *SIR* 23 (1984): 409-13;
by François Piquet in *EA* 38 (1985): 237-38; by Dennis M.
Welch in *MLQ* 45 (1984): 301-02; by Joseph Wittreich in
TWC 15 (1984): 113-14; GLEN, Heather, *Vision and Disenchantment: Blake's Songs and Wordsworth's Lyrical Ballads*
(see *RMB* for 1984, p. 102), rev. by Avril Horner in *PNReview*
11 (1985): 54-56; by François Piquet in *EA* 38 (1985):
465-66; by David Simpson in *BIQ* 18 (1985): 227-31; by
John Williams in *L&H* 10 (1984): 272; by M.A. Williams in
UNISA English Studies 23 (1985): 41-42; HILTON, Nelson,
Literal Imagination: Blake's Vision of Words (see *RMB* for
1983, p. 83), rev. by Stephen D. Cox in *ECS* 18 (1985): 391-
405; by Michael Ferber in *Criticism* 26 (1984): 397-99; by
David Wagenknecht in *BIQ* 19 (1985-86): 117-20); LARISSY, Edward, *William Blake* (see *RMB* for 1985, pp. 89-91), rev. by Nel-
son Hilton in *BIQ* 20 (1986): 66-68 as "at turns provoking, re-
warding, irritating, and disappointing"; PALEY, Morton D., *The
Continuing City: William Blake's Jerusalem* (see *RMB* for 1983,
pp. 85-86), rev. by Stephen D. Cox in *Eighteenth-Century
Studies* 18 (1985): 391-405; by Paul Hamilton in *TLS*, June
15, 1984, p. 674; by Mary Lynn Johnson (very favorably) in
JEGP 85 (1986): 275-78; by François Piquet in *Etudes
Anglaises* 38 (1985): 237-39; RAINE, Kathleen, *The Human
Face of God* (see *RMB* for 1982, p. 89), rev. by Glyn Hughes
in *New Statesman*, April 2, 1982, p. 23; by Bo Ossian Lindberg
in *BIQ* 19 (1986): 151-55; still not seen; SINGH, Charu
Sheel, *The Chariot of Fire* (see *RMB* for 1981, p. 88), rev.
by Pamela Dunbar in *MLR* 80 (1985): 129; STOCK, R.D., *The
Holy and the Daemonic from Sir Thomas Browne to William
Blake* (see *RMB* for 1982, p. 90), rev. by Jacques Blondel in
EA 37 (1984): 327; by Pat Rogers in *RES* 35 (1984): 377-78;
by Patricia Meyer Spacks in *MP* 82 (1984): 206-09; by L.J.
Swingle in *MLQ* 44 (1983): 80-91; by D.R.M. Wilkinson in
YES 16 (1986): 286-88; TANNENBAUM, Leslie, *Biblical Tradi-
tion in Blake's Early Prophecies* (see *RMB* for 1982, pp. 90-
91), rev. by Stephen C. Behrendt in *TWC* 15 (1984): 106-08;
by Michael J. Tolley in *SiR* 24 (1985): 300-07; by D.R.M.
Wilkinson in *YES* 16 (1986): 286-88; VISCOMI, Joseph, et al.,
"An Island in the Moon," videotape (see *RMB* for 1985, pp.
94-95), rev. by Tim Hoyer in *BIQ* 20 (1986), pp. 68-70, along
with a Swedenborg Foundation docudrama of "The Marriage of
Heaven and Hell"; WARK, Robert R., ed., *Essays on the Blake
Followers. Huntington Library Quarterly* 1 (1983-84);
listed without Wark's name in *RMB* for 1983, pp. 83-84; rev.
by Raymond Lister in *BIQ* 19 (1985): 80-83; WARNER, Janet A.,
Blake and the Language of Art (see *RMB* for 1984, pp. 108-09),

rev. by John Dixon Hunt in *Word and Image* 1 (1985): 409–
20; by L.R. Matteson in *Choice* 22 (1985): 1486; by Karen
Mulhallen in *TWC* 17 (1986): 202–04 as "a rich and fascinating
introduction"; by Peter A. Taylor in *QQ* 92 (1985): 859–60;
WEBSTER, Branda S., *Blake's Prophetic Psychology* (see *RMB*
for 1984, pp. 109–10), rev. by Stephen D. Cox in *ECS* 18
(1985): 391–405; by Kelvin Everest in *British Journal for
Eighteenth-Century Studies* 8 (1985): 106–07; by Paul
Hamilton in *TLS*, June 15, 1984, p. 674; by François Piquet
in *EA* 38 (1985): 466–67.

Review Essay:

Hilton, Nelson. "The Moment of Implosion." *EC* 27 (1986):
106–12.

Reviews Behrendt, Stephen, *The Moment of Explosion: Blake
and the Illustration of Milton* (see *RMB* for 1983, pp. 74–75).
Mocking a "critical fundamentalism" which claims to arbi-
trate questions of Truth, Hilton accuses Behrendt of ignoring
"contemporary theory and interpretation" in his "cliché-
ridden, Church of Blake orthodoxy."

BURKE

Cohen, Michael. "Edmund Burke and the Two Revolutions."
RecL 14 (1986): 71–86.

Conniff, James. "Edmund Burke's Reflections on the Coming
Revolution in Ireland." *JHI* 47 (1986): 37–59.

"While the French Revolution was accelerating and hardening
Burke's resistance to reform in England, it was having the
opposite effect of confirming him in his reformism in regard
to Ireland," concludes a careful study of much importance.
(T.L.A.)

Hampsher-Monk, Iain. *The Political Philosophy of Edmund
Burke*. (Documents in Political Ideas series.) Harlow:
Longman's, 1986. Pp. 284. Paper £5.95.

Howes, Craig. "Burke, Poe, and 'Usher': The Sublime and
Rising Woman." *ESQ* 31 (1985): 173–89.

An interesting study of the sublime, and how "Poe embodies
Burkean understanding in the narrator." (T.L.A.)

Lock, F.P. *Burke's Reflections on the Revolution in France.*
London: Allen and Unwin, 1985. Pp. 228. $27.95.

Listed in *RMB* for 1985, p. 99; rev. by Clara K. Gandy in
Albion 18 (1986): 513-15 as placing Burke squarely "in
the role of spokesman for the Rockingham Whig party" but also
emphasizing that full understanding of the *Reflections* must
come from a study of its political rhetoric.

A readable and judicious account of the context, composition, ideology, structure, style, and reception of Burke's
Reflections on the Revolution in France. Unlike the Victorian liberal John Morley or the contemporary conservative
Peter Stanlis, Lock represents Burke as primarily a party
politician; as a member of Lord Rockingham's group, Burke
tried to remain true to "what he believed to be the political
ideas and ideals" of aristocratic Whiggism. Of these ideas
and ideals, the most important to Burke was the notion that
the 1688 Revolution had established a stable social order
based on the power of property. It was this order that Burke
sought to protect from the vagaries of circumstance, including, of course, such political circumstances as the debates
on the American Colonies, the India Bill, the Regency Crisis,
and the French Revolution. Before 1789, Burke seems to have
believed that the King and his cronies posed the most serious
threat to the 1688 settlement. However, after 1789, he saw
the major threat as emanating from those Dissenters and radical Whigs who not only advocated reform at home but also
celebrated the French Revolution as a promise of political
equality abroad. Since Burke considered ideas of political
equality a major threat to the property rights upon which
English society was founded, he embarked on a critique of
Price and the French Revolution.

Yet *Reflections* is more than a critique; it is also a
defense of aristocratic Whiggism as the true inheritance
of the 1688 Revolution. With Rockingham's death in 1782,
the failure of the Fox-North coalition, Fox's compromise
with Pitt during the Regency Crisis, and the emergence of
Sheridan as the party's major rhetorician, Burke had become
a rather marginal figure. The party seemed to be going in
a new direction, moving away from the aristocratic Whiggism
which Burke espoused. In part, *Reflections* was designed to
put the party back on its proper course, to persuade the
Whigs that reform and revolution were bad deviations from
the good liberties achieved in 1688.

Since Lock considers *Reflections* to be a work of persuasion
rather than a philosophical disquisition, he not only

emphasizes Burke's political context but also devotes a
chapter to an analysis of the text's rhetoric. Following
the method of the classical rhetoricians, Lock discusses
the arguments, the disposition, and the style of *Reflections*.
The problem, however, is that this approach minimizes the
importance of style, representing it as a "dress" which has
little or no bearing on the text's fundamental ideology.
Yet, as Lock points out, Burke's "eloquence" made him much
admired, even by those like Godwin and Hazlitt who seem
to reject his ideas. Furthermore, Lock also shows that
over the past hundred years or so, Burke has been used to
support a number of seemingly incompatible political positions. How could this happen? To answer this question
something less classical needs to be done with Burke's
rhetoric. Lock makes a convincing case for interpreting
the *Reflections* as the work of a party politician. But
if we want to understand the power this text has exerted,
then we must recognize that politics is more than a party
game; it is also a rhetorical struggle. (J.H-P.)

Rashid, Salim. "Forum--Economists and the Age of Chivalry:
    Notes on a Passage in Burke's *Reflections*." *ECS* 20 (1986):
    56-61.

    The background of Burke's hostile reference to "oecono-
    mists," i.e., Physiocrats.

Ritchie, Daniel E.C. *Edmund Burke's Nineteenth-Century
    Literary Significance*. Ann Arbor, Mich.: University Micro-
    films International, 1986.

    Dissertation.

Wells, G.A. "Burke on Ideas, Words, and Imagination."
    BJECS 9 (1986): 45-51.

    Burke's views on words, ideas, and their relation are a
    mixture of blindness and insight. Burke errs in believing
    that each idea must be associated with one specific image;
    that words stand in for objects; and that a word produces
    the same effect as the object it putatively represents.
    These errors lead Burke to assume that the pleasures of the
    imagination are constituted by resemblances rather than by
    differences.

See also Erdman, Paley ("General 2. Environment"); Chaimowicz,
    Cohen, Mitchell ("General 3. Criticism"); Gandy ("English
    2. Environment"); Wheeler ("Carlyle"); Whale ("Hazlitt").

BURNEY

Epstein, Julia L. "Writing the Unspeakable: Fanny Burney's
  Mastectomy and the Fictive Body." *Representations* no. 16
  (Fall 1986): 66. 5 illus.

  In 1811, with only a wine cordial as anesthetic, Fanny
  Burney underwent a "simple mastectomy of the right breast."
  While she was recovering, she wrote for her friends and
  family a detailed account of her experience in which she
  "channeled her fear and anger into a medical history,
  reenacted in her own 'case,' and thereby defused the framework of dominance that she found as oppressive as the physical pain." In similar detail Epstein compares the autobiographical narrative to episodes of violence in Burney's
  novels, to her physicians' descriptions of the operation,
  and to later nineteenth-century medical discussions of cancer
  surgery. (I.H.C.)

Hemlow, Joyce, Althea Douglas, and Patricia Hawkins, eds.
  The Journals and Letters of Fanny Burney, vols. 11 and 12.
  Oxford: Clarendon Press, 1984. Pp. xii and vi+530. $19.95
  both vols.

  Rev. by G.E. Bentley, Jr., in *UTQ* 56 (1986): 101-03.

BURNS

Brown, Mary Ellen. *Burns and Tradition*. University of
  Illinois Press, 1984. Pp. xv+176. $19.95.

Daiches, David. *Literature and Gentility in Scotland*. Edinburgh University Press; Columbia University Press, 1982.
  Pp. vii+114. $14.00.

Ferguson, J. De Lancey, ed. *The Letters of Robert Burns*,
  vol. 1, *1780-89*, vol. 2, 2d ed., ed. G. Ross Roy. Oxford
  University Press, 1986. Pp. 493, 521. $79.00 each.

  Rev. by Douglas Dunn in *TLS*, July 25, 1986, pp. 803-04.

Grimble, Ian. *Robert Burns*. P. Bedrick, 1986.

  Not seen.

Macqueen, John. "Synthesis and Transcendence; Robert Burns."
  Pp. 132-54 in his *The Enlightenment and Scottish Literature*,
  vol. 1, *Progress and Poetry*. Edinburgh; Scottish Academic
  Press; Columbia University Press, 1982.

  Not seen.

Roy, G. Ross, ed. *The Letters of Robert Burns*, vol. 1,
   1780-89, vol. 2, *1790-96*. 2d ed. Ed. by J. DeLancey
   Ferguson. Oxford: Clarendon Press, 1985. £45.00 each.

   Rev. by K.G. Simpson in *SLJ* 13, supp. 25 (1986):   6-10.

See also Erdman ("General 2. Environment"); Roberts ("English
   3. Criticism"); Groves ("Hogg").

Reviews of book previously listed:

   McGUIRK, Carol, *Robert Burns and the Sentimental* (see *RMB*
   for 1985, p. 67), rev. favorably by Ian Campbell in *RP&P*
   10 (1986):   61-62; by Cynthia L. Caywood in *SAQ* 85 (1986):
   408-09.

Review essay:

MacLachlan, Christopher. Untitled Review Essay. *SLJ* 13,
   supp. 25 (1986):   10-13.

   Recent work on Burns is discussed with special reference
   to: Mary Ellen Brown, *Burns and Tradition* (University of
   Illinois Press, 1984; pp. xv+176; $19.95); and Donald A.
   Low, ed., *Robert Burns; The Kilmarnock Poems* (London:
   Everyman Classics, 1985; pp. xxxiv+188; £3.50).

BYRON

Adams, Hazard. "Byron, Yeats and Joyce: Heroism and Technic."
   SiR 24 (1985):   399-412.

Baker, Mark. *Byron "Epistolaris."* Ann Arbor, Mich.:   University Microfilms International, 1985.

   Dissertation.

Baum, Joan. *The Calculating Passion of Ada Byron*. Hamden,
   Conn.:   Archon Books, 1986. Pp. xix+123. $21.50.

   Designed to waste library budgets, this frothy study bills
   Byron's daughter as the human adding machine, and calls
   her upbringing her "programming." It ought to sell well
   because its heroine is an early lady scientist with a Romantic past, unless you remember that last year we had a better
   book on the same subject that I subtitled: *Byron's Daughter
   Meets the Computer* (see *RMB* for 1985, p. 108). And before
   that we had one on the Byron women. Fingers crossed that
   they're taping the video somewhere right now, and if we're

lucky we'll find out that Lady Byron was really Mary
Shelley. (T.L.A.)

Beatty, Bernard. *Byron's Don Juan*. Totowa, N.J.: Barnes
and Noble; London: Croom Helm, 1985. Pp. iii+239. £22.50.

Rev. (mostly favorably) by Peter Morgan in *BJ* 14 (1986):
571-72; by J. Drummond Bone in *BJ* 14 (1986): 67-68.

Bone, in his precise and intelligent review, calls
Beatty's work "a subtle way of presenting the ontology of
Don Juan as a poem whose being is process (not content),
and yet is also something quite specific, and quite
specifically developing (it is not merely a continual eater
of its own tail)."

It is clear that Beatty knows his *Don Juan* very well
indeed, and that it has lived in his mind in the course of
long literary studies which have enriched his understanding
of the poem. This follows from his frequent reference to
Byron's other works, to the best of Byron scholarship, and
to English and Continental works whose parallel structures
do enlarge our understanding of Byron's poem. "The four
chapters" of his study, he tells us, "could be crudely
subtitled *Death*, *Thought*, *Sex* and *Holiness* in *Don Juan* ...
but this would mislead for the book is about literary
procedures not concepts." This indicates not a thematic
study, but one that aims at the chief question for post-
Ridenour readers, the question framed in McGann's *Don Juan
in Context*, but unanswered there. Beatty asks: "Does
the course of the poem pare away everything external to it
on which we may ground a comic view of life?" This is a
very subtle question indeed, and if we say yes to it, then
we must accept *Don Juan* as a self-destructive artifact that
is the essence of *nothing*. When Gleckner wrote of *Don Juan*,
"Fundamentally, it has to do not with morality or immorality
but with nothingness," this is what he had in mind. But
Beatty's rejection is explicit: "I cannot agree with this."
His "argument is that the poem's persistence in [its]
impossible mode ... is evidence not of 'sceptical tradition'
but of an original, Romantic revaluation of comic process."

"*Don Juan* is a comedy not simply because it evidences much
of the proper life of comedy but also because it engages in
a redefinition of that life." This is evidence of what I
long ago called the poem's joyful symmetry, and Beatty's
detailed reading makes for both a surprising and enriching
experience: Aurora Raby "represents too that blend of
fiction and real, trusted space which the poem discloses as
its own proper life and to which the narrator is brought to
say 'Yes.' This is not a familiar Romance or Romantic ideal

but a discovery in the midst of satire, farce and festivity
of an indestructible spiritual reality on which comedy's
celebration of the contingent rests." Beatty's analysis
is as valuable as the wisdom of these words. His book has
made a quiet debut, but it deserves some very important
reviews. (T.L.A.)

Byron Journal 14 (1986).

Paul Douglas, "Hebrew Melodies as Songs" (12-21) is an
initial argument for more musicological work on the settings,
which recognizes the appeal of the songs from decade to
decade. Susan Bassnett, "Byron and Translation" (22-32) takes
the latter as its subject, but praises the quality of Byron's
translation of Pulci. Michael Gassenmeier, "Private Licen-
tiousness and Political Morality in *Don Juan*" (33-43) discusses "the relationship between narrator and reader in *Don
Juan* (33-43) against the background of the Augustan satire
of Dryden and Pope." The goal is "not a new one," but our
understanding of epic satire is somewhat enlarged. Next
comes Patricia A. LaCerva, "Byron and the Pseudepigrapha:
A Re-examination of the Mystery Plays" (44-51), a note on
obscure sources which Byron *may* have known: "Given Byron's
knowledge of Syncellus and the Book of Enoch ... the poet
probably was familiar with the writings of the Jewish Sibyl-
lists." This depends on whether or not Byron read Richard
Laurence's 1821 translation of the Book of Enoch, which
the current author's "given" does not establish—in light
of E.H. Coleridge's doubts. Selby Whittingham's "Byron and
the Two Giorgiones" (52-55) is correct to note that "the
subject of this article has also been dealt with by Dr. Hilary
Gatti [see *RMB* for 1984, p. 116] ... I had not read her
article when I wrote mine: we come to the same conclusion."
Robert Harregar, "Byron and Cricket" (57-58) is a note on
Byron to Charles David Gordon, August 4, 1805, on the Eton-
Harrow match. Book reviews are separately listed. All in
all, not the best that can be expected. (T.L.A.)

Christensen, Jerome. "'Marino Faliero' and the Fault of
Byron's Satire." *SiR* 24 (1985): 313-33.

Corr, Thomas J. "Byron's 'Werner': The Burden of Knowledge."
SiR 24 (1985): 375-98.

Dando, Joel A. *The Poet as Critic: Byron in His Letters and
Journals.* Ann Arbor, Mich.: University Microfilms International, 1986.

Dissertation.

Elledge, W. Paul. "Byron's Harold at Sea." *PLL* 22 (1986): 154-64.

A subtle study introducing a concern with Byron's psychological structures: "Harold's avoidance of ceremonial leave-taking, that is, while defensively setting distance between Self and Other, may also minister to an anxiety which perpetuates the illusion of continuity by pretending that severance has not occurred." The notes indicate, and the next listing as well, an intention to use separation anxiety as a fulcrum in a larger study of definite future interest. (T.L.A.)

Elledge, W. Paul. "Divorce Italian Style: Byron's *Beppo*." *MLQ* 46 (1985): 29-47.

Elledge, W. Paul. "Talented Equivocation: Byron's 'Fare Thee Well.'" *KSJ* 35 (1986): 42-61.

Continues Elledge's new study of separation anxiety by focusing on another goodbye poem with wit and talent. (T.L.A.)

Findley, L.M. "Culler and Byron on Apostrophe and Lyric Time." *SiR* 24 (1985): 335-53.

Goldberg, Leonard S. "Center and Circumference in Byron's *Lara*." *SEL* 26 (1986): 655-73.

"The sense of fragmentation encoded into the image of the circle suggests that any promise of integration must remain beyond its limits, in horizonless modes of experience. To pierce the circle is to violate the necessary conditions—among them perceptual—imposed upon existence and that Lara can no longer tolerate.... But as long as the circle remains the foundation for human sight, ... we must witness the fact of self-division." Clearly on *Lara* and self-division. (T.L.A.)

Gordon, Archie. *A Wild Flight of Gordons*. London: Weidenfield and Nicolson, 1985. £10.95.

Rev. by J. Drummond Bone in *BJ* 14 (1986): 66-67. On the family tree of Byron's mother, and interesting. (T.L.A.)

Graham, Peter W. "Byron and Disraeli." *VN* 69 (1986): 26-30.

A sketch of Byron's influence on Disraeli, and "how and why the [Victorian] writer outgrew it." Though it is unlikely that the author first terms Byron's effect "unlikely," given what is generally known of the scope of his influence on the

next generation. Certainly Graham is right to find what he
calls the "moral ambiguity" of *Don Juan* in *Vivian Grey* (1826).
But the claim that Byron drowns in *Venetia* (1837) proves as
much continuing influence as rejection. (T.L.A.)

Hill, James L. "Experiments in the Narrative of Consciousness:
    Byron, Wordsworth, and *Childe Harold*, Cantos 3 and 4." *ELH*
    53 (1986): 121-40.

    An early concentration on the dissolution of Byron's main
characters and consequent emergence of the narrator's consciousness, doesn't quite set the stage for a reexamination
of the influence of "Tinern Abbey" on *Childe Harold*, which
concludes: "Byron is using a procedural strategy very much
like Wordsworth's to present an environmental psychology
that is the obverse of Wordsworth's in its insistence on the
negative effects of environment on the development of personality, and on the virtual helplessness of the individual
consciousness to shape or control its own development."
Such a Wordsworthian view of Byron does not escape Byron's
own view of Wordsworth. (T.L.A.)

Koprince, Susan. "The Clue from *Manfred* in *Daisy Miller*." *ArQ*
    42 (1986): 293-304.

Levine, Alice, and Jerome J. McGann, eds. *Poems in the Auto-*
    graph of Lord Byron Once in the Possession of the Countess
    Guiccioli: Poems 1807-1818, a Facsimile of the Manuscripts
    in the Pierpont Morgan Library, vol. 1, *The Manuscripts of*
    the Younger Romantics. Gen. ed. Donald H. Reiman. New York
    and London: Garland Publishing, 1986. Pp. xx+250. $90.00.

    Dr. Donald Reiman is to be congratulated for launching a
series which will make facsimile copies of the manuscripts
of Byron, Keats, and Shelley widely available, and raise
the level of scholarly and critical interpretation of the
works of these poets by bringing a new textual standard to
bear. This first volume of the Byron poetry manuscripts
with an "introduction and notes by Alice Levine" makes frequent reference to Prof. McGann's OET Byron, though in itself
it provides no transcript of the included poems, and its notes
are largely concerned with physical matters on the manuscripts.
(Some of the watermarks which trouble Levine are recorded
in Continental catalogues.)
    The contents are: *Manfred*, *Beppo*, and *Mazeppa*, a small
fragment of *Oscar of Alva*, the corrected galley proofs of
Hints from Horace, and the fair copy of *Imitation of Martial,*
VI.34. The MSS of the major poems are all first draft, making

this volume extremely valuable, and the quality of reproduction is generally excellent. Here and there a minor error
has escaped correction--on p. 249, *Shelley and His Circle*,
vol. 2, should be vol. 7--but the high standards rarely fail.
Further volumes are eagerly anticipated. (T.L.A.)

Manning, Peter J. "The Hone-ing of Byron's Corsair." Pp. 107-
26, 221-24 in McGann's *Textual Criticism and Literary Interpretation* (listed above in "General 3. Criticism").

Comparing Byron's *The Corsair* with the text revised and
pirated by the radical publisher William Hone is amusing and
"has the larger merit of directing attention to the influences
that shape the significance of a poem."

Marshall, L.E. "'Words Are Things': Byron and the Prophetic
Efficacy of Language." *SEL* 25 (1985): 801-22.

McGann, Jerome J., ed. *Byron.* (The Oxford Authors.) Oxford
University Press, 1986. Pp. xxviii+1081. $45.00, paper
$16.95.

Back when this series was the Oxford Standard Authors
and affordable, individual volumes consisted of "the complete
works" of the selected authors. The print was a source of
eye-strain, but almost everything was included, to the advantage of students with an inquiring mind. Therefore it
comes as a shock to find that this classroom-intended one-
volume *Byron* is a selection! I have no quarrel with McGann's
introduction and notes, and the text is based on the Oxford
English Texts' *Byron* which he is in the course of editing.
(Since this one-volume edition prints poems that have yet
to appear in the OET *Byron*, McGann is at pains to assure us
that these come from the OET-prepared texts.) There is a
mini-selection of Byron's correspondence, which is ludicrous
and a waste of space that might have enclosed more poetry.
But in the end, McGann gives us *Childe Harold* and *Don Juan*
complete, which means he can't give much else. From the plays
it's *Manfred* and *Cain*; from the tales *The Giaour*, *Mazeppa*,
and *Beppo*. You will not find the *Prisoner of Chillon*, the
Lament of Tasso, or *Sardanapalus*; much else is absent from
this volume. Particularly frustrating is the absence of
satiric works, and the productions of the Italian period.
Giving *Don Juan* and *Childe Harold* whole is an important step,
which represents a difficult decision, but a more balanced
selection would have better served *Byron's poetic development*--
a phrase found in the title of McGann's early critical study.
(T.L.A.)

McGann, Jerome J., ed. *Lord Byron. The Complete Poetical
    Works.* Oxford: Clarendon Press, 1986. Vol. 4, pp. xxi+568,
    £50.00. Vol. 5, pp. xxiv+771, £60.00.

Volume 4 extends the definitive edition from 1816 to 1820,
and includes *The Prisoner of Chillon, Manfred, The Lament of
Tasso, Beppo, Mazeppa, The Prophecy of Dante, Marino Faliero,*
and the shorter poems of this period. Volume 5 is McGann's
edition of *Don Juan.* One is always indebted to this
progressing definitive edition of Byron's poetry and drama,
most of all for the energy with which Professor McGann has
organized his task. There is no escaping the debt we owe
him for his ability to bring together the varied and varying
sources of Byron's text. At the same time, however, a torrent
of literary criticism has also sprung from McGann's pen, and
that has taken its toll in the current volumes. If every
reviewer of these volumes will find some corrections necessary,
that does not slight the whole of McGann's efforts. But volume
5 shows him heavily in the debt of Steffan and Pratt's variorum
Don Juan (though why he fails to mention its second edition
in addition to the Penguin revisions is a mystery), and in
volume 4 we are told that *Marino Faliero* has been edited by
Barry Weller. We are not, however, told just what Weller's
credentials for this task are, despite the fact that his name
doesn't appear in the *RMB* Byron section in at least the past
five years. We must therefore surmise that McGann, who had
access to my own transcript of the Pforzheimer fair copy of
Marino Faliero, as well as an incomplete transcript from a
xerox copy of the Morgan manuscript, somehow "collaborated"
in Weller's editing. If that's the case, it's somewhat
troubling to note that we are told that the play's motto was
added by Byron to the proof—as a photograph indicates—without being told that the motto is also given at the conclusion
of the fair copy. If we are to think of it only as an addition to the proofs, we will not understand that Murray cancelled and Byron restored a motto whose meaning would have
been very clear from the italics of the word *"Dux,"* all of
which gets no explanation here. Simply to translate *dux* as
master here also misses the point. And to write "for more
extended discussion of the political context, see" E.D.H.
Johnson's 1940 essay is insulting and ludicrous in light of
Carl Woodring's subsequent *Politics in English Romantic Poetry*
and my own political interpretation published in *Studies in
Romanticism,* both of which go far beyond Johnson. Furthermore,
the list of nine additional manuscript sources (521-22) appears
not to include Byron's holograph letter in the William Andrews
Clark Library, which also provides an addition to the text.
I'm not going to correct many other errors in this volume,

but if Weller "will now assume complete responsibility" for editing the plays that will be published in volumes 6 and 7 of the edition, McGann will have to rethink his abdication. (T.L.A.)

Murphy, Peter T. "Visions of Success: Byron and Southey." *SiR* 24 (1985): 355-73.

Sharp, Michael Stewart. *'Freedom's Battle': War and Revolution in Byron's Major Poetry.* Ann Arbor, Mich.: University Microfilms International, 1986.

Dissertation.

Sullivan, Ernest W., II. "A Fragment of a Possible Byron Poem in Manuscript." *PBSA* 80 (1986): 55-73.

A minutely detailed argument for Byron's authorship of an 18-line poem apparently addressed to his daughter Ada shortly after her birth.

Ulmer, William A. "The Dantean Politics of *The Prisoner of Chillon.*" *KSJ* 35 (1986): 23-29.

Bonivard as Ugolino neatly resolves the conflict of positive politics and incarceration despair. Byron would have known that George III was a Guelph. (T.L.A.)

Watkins, Daniel P. "Social Relations in Byron's 'The Giaour.'" *ELH* 52 (1985): 873-92.

Wilson, Carol Shiner. *The Banquet of Life: Gustatory Metaphors in Byron's "Don Juan."* Ann Arbor, Mich.: University Microfilms International, 1985.

Dissertation.

See also Erdman ("General 2. Environment"); Herdmann, Lord, Steele ("General 3. Criticism"); Dunbar ("English 1. Bibliography"); Altick, Bate, Reid, Walker ("English 2. Environment"); Baer, Bidney, Cave, Hill, Wilkie ("English 3. Criticism"); Musty, Robinson ("Clare"); Gates ("Hunt"); Bromwich ("Jeffrey"); Marquess ("Keats"); Dowden ("Moore"); Bann ("Scott"); Barker-Benfield, Burling, Robinson, Reiman ("Shelley, P.B."); Johnson-Cousin ("French 2. Staël"); Zach ("German 2. General"); Bonadeo ("Italian 2. General").

Reviews of books previously listed:

BEATY, Frederick L., *Byron the Satirist* (see *RMB* for 1985,

pp. 100–01), rev. by Bernard Beatty in *BJ* 14 (1986): 65–66;
by W. Paul Elledge in *TWC* 17 (1986): 240–42; by Clement T.
Goode in *ELN* 24,2 (1986): 71–73; CROMPTON, Louis, *Byron and
Greek Love: Homophobia in Nineteenth-Century England* (see
RMB for 1985, p. 103), rev. by Kenneth Dover in *BJ* 14 (1986):
63–64 who finds "big questions unanswered"; by Leslie A.
Marchand (favorably) in *KSJ* 35 (1986): 190–93; by Peter L.
Thorslev in *TWC* 17 (1986): 220–32, who praises Crompton's
subject while ignoring the lack of concern with Byron;
GRAHAM, Peter W., ed., *Byron's Bulldog: The Letters of John
Cam Hobhouse to Lord Byron* (see *RMB* for 1984, p. 117), rev.
favorably and very interestingly, by Robert F. Gleckner in
SAQ 85 (1986): 209–12; by Leonidas M. Jones in *KSJ* 35 (1986):
188–90; HOFFMEISTER, Gerhart, *Byron und der Europäische
Byronismus* (see *RMB* for 1984, p. 117–18), rev. by Frederick
Garber in *YCGL* 34 (1985): 146–48; by Heidi Rohloff in
Anglia 104 (1986): 240–46; MARCHAND, Leslie A., ed., *Byron's
Letters and Journals*, vol. 11, "The Trouble of an Index (see
RMB for 1982, p. 98), rev. by Andrew Nicholson in *YES* 16 (1986):
302–04; PAGE, Norman, ed., *Byron: Interviews and Recollections*
(see *RMB* for 1985, p. 108), rev. by Neil Berry in *TLS*, Jan.
23, 1987, p. 80; by Ian Scott-Kilvert in *BJ* 14 (1986): 68;
ROBINSON, Charles E., ed., *Lord Byron and His Contemporaries:
Essays from the Sixth International Byron Seminar* (see *RMB*
for 1983, p. 92), rev. by Andrew Nicholson in *YES* 16 (1986):
305–06; VASSALLO, Peter, *Byron: The Italian Literary Influence* (see *RMB* for 1984, p. 120), rev. by Frederick L. Beaty
in *TWC* 17 (1986): 242–44.

CARLYLE

Baker, Lee C.R. "The Diamond Necklace and the Golden Ring:
   Historical Imagination in Carlyle and Browning." *VP* 24
   (1986): 31–46.

Baker, Lee C.R. "The Open Secret of *Sartor Resartus*: Carlyle's
   Method of Converting His Reader." *SP* 83 (1986): 218–35.

   The key to the Editor (and therefore to *Sartor Resartus*)
is an understanding of the Romantic irony pervasive in the
work. The Editor is not a rhetorical strategy in the usual
sense—not, say, an Imlac—but rather a type of midwife who
helps to elicit the reader's own understanding of the Clothes
Philosophy, helps him to discover it for himself. Hence
the multiform ironies encountered. Baker labels Carlyle's
method maieutic instead of rhetorical. Editor, Professor,
reader—all are, or become in the process of reading, Romantic ironists, precisely the result to which Carlyle's
creative energies are directed. A useful article. (F.J.)

Bossche, Chris R. Vanden. "Desire and Deferral of Closure in Carlyle's *Sartor Resartus* and *The French Revolution*." *JNT* 16 (1986): 72-78.

Bossche uses recent narrative theory to understand Carlyle's narrative forms, which characteristically both seek and evade an ending, and at the same time uses Carlyle's narrative practice to "provide a new perspective on the significance and limits of modern narratology." Metaphors of revolution in the narratologists and in Carlyle are the common ground that brings the two aims together. (F.J.)

Chapman, David Wayne. "The Essay as a Literary Form." Ann Arbor, Mich.: University Microfilms International, 1986.

Includes Carlyle. Dissertation.

Clausson, Nils. "Disraeli and Carlyle's 'Aristocracy of Talent': The Role of Millbank in *Coningsby* Reconsidered." *VN* 70 (1986): 1-5.

Millbank, contrary to the customary view, is not a Carlylean captain of industry, a natural aristocrat, because Disraeli was not as receptive to industrialism as Carlyle. Rather in the character of Millbank Disraeli anticipated Arnold's criticism of the middle classes in *Culture and Anarchy*. (F.J.)

Cumming, Mark. "Carlyle, Whitman, and the Disimprisonment of Epic." *VS* 29 (1986): 207-26.

Cumming details the "important relationship of Whitman and Carlyle," using *The French Revolution* and *Leaves of Grass* to focus a thoroughgoing comparison which reveals striking similarities: "Both *The French Revolution* and *Leaves of Grass* dedicate themselves to an accurate representation of modern facts within the framework of a disimprisoned epic vision." Solid work. (F.J.)

Davies, James A. "The Effects of Context: Carlyle and the *Examiner* in 1848." *YES* 16 (1986): 51-62.

Carlyle published three articles in the 1848 *Examiner*, providing Davies with the occasion to study the relationship between an essay and its context. By attending to the formal literary characteristics of the periodical he seeks to describe the total effect of an issue. (F.J.)

Egan, Susanna. *Patterns of Experience in Autobiography*. University of North Carolina Press, 1984. Pp. xi+226. $19.95.

Rev. by Robert Bell in *MLQ* 46 (1985): 197-201.

By patterns of experience Egan means the dominant narrative patterns—the archetypal ones—commonly found in autobiography. Carlyle, in *Sartor Resartus*, relies on the journey pattern, adhering "more fully than the others [Wordsworth, Rousseau, George Moore] to the detailed possibilities of the metaphor." (F.J.)

Findlay, L.M. "Paul de Man, Thomas Carlyle, and 'The Rhetoric of Temporality.'" *DR* 65 (1985): 159-181.

Carlyle's reading and rhetoric of temporality in *Sartor Resartus* are the test for Findlay's "fair reading (or strong misreading) of de Man." By Findlay's account de Man is shrewd, challenging, but unconvincing, because through a selective endorsement of language he underestimates temporality and falsely aligns symbol with simultaneity and the spatial: "In the intersts of re-writing literary history and re-habilitating allegory, de Man refuses to see that nothing is impervious to time; that all categories and sets of categories can be considered categories of language, and, as such, bear with them the inscription and employment of language-as-temporality." Findlay has chosen the right test. (F.J.)

Finley, C. Stephen. "'Greater than Tongue Can Tell': Carlyle and Ruskin on the Nature of Christian Heroism." *Christianity & Literature* 34 (1985): 27-40.

Goldberg, Michael K., and Jules P. Siegel, eds. *Carlyle's Latter-Day Pamphlets*. Toronto, Ontario: Canadian Federation for the Humanities, 1983. Pp. 594.

Not seen.
Rev. by Ellen Lane in *SSL* 21 (1986): 365-67.

Johnson, Wendell Stacy. *Sons and Fathers: The Generation Link in Literature, 1780-1980*. Peter Lang, 1985. Pp. viii+237.

Includes Carlyle.
Not seen.

Juckett, Elizabeth Cox. "The Art of the Tightrope Dancer: Thackeray's Response to Carlyle." Ann Arbor, Mich.: University Microfilms International, 1986.

Dissertation.

Landow, George P. *Elegant Jeremiahs: The Sage from Carlyle
to Mailer.* Cornell University Press, 1986. Pp. 198.
$17.50.

Carlyle is a founding father of the genre of the sage,
which Landow teaches us how to read by identifying the
techniques that distinguish it from both the novel (or the
New Journalism, as the case may be) and wisdom literature.
By Landow's account the genre invented by Carlyle, Ruskin,
Arnold, and Thoreau, with some differences, flourishes today
in the writings of Mailer, Didion, and Tom Wolfe especially.
At most points Landow recognizes and credits the Romantic
roots of the genre as he goes about providing us with the
requisite critical tools to read a large body of obviously
important prose as literature. For those who all along
have inclined so to read it, he makes it easier to recognize
and name the tools. (F.J.)

McGowan, John P. *Representation and Revelation: Victorian
Realism from Carlyle to Yeats.* University of Missouri Press,
1986. Pp. vi+206. $26.00.

Carlyle is the subject of McGowan's third chapter, "Carlyle's
Characteristics," and a touchstone throughout the book, which
argues that the Victorians' approach to reality is a synthesis of the empiricists'--through representation or in-
directly--and the Romantics'--through revelation or directly.
Carlyle "oscillates between his strong desire for direct,
unmediated, and intuitive knowledge of the real and his
understanding that such revelation is impossible." Carlyle's
theory of the symbol is a response to this understanding--
to the necessity of approaching the real indirectly--but
because he resists this necessity even as he devises a strategy
for responding to it he is mentor to later writers who subscribe to models of immediate perception and direct knowledge.
The chapter includes a useful distinction between Coleridge's
symbols and Carlyle's--one of many such useful clarifications
in this earnest and forthright book. (F.J.)

Rosenberg, John D. *Carlyle and the Burden of History.* Oxford:
Clarendon Press; Harvard University Press, 1985. Pp. x+209.
£19.50; $20.00.

The American edition was listed, but not reviewed, in *RMB*
for 1985, p. 112 (where it is described as having 220 pages).
Rev. by Peter Allan Dale in *NCL* 41 (1986): 485-90 as the
most important study of Carlyle in many years, and as utterly
free of what the author refers to as the "quackery" of deconstruction, etc.; by D.R.M. Wilkinson, unfavorably, in *ES*

67 (1986):   458-59 ("will be read only by those already
convinced of the greatness of Carlyle as a writer and the
continuing importance of his message"); by Gerald Monsman
in *SEL* 26 (1986):   794-96.

If Carlyle ultimately sank under the burden of writing
history as he conceived it--and Rosenberg argues that he
did, the burden of reading Carlyle all but vanishes in this
lucid study. *The French Revolution* is Rosenberg's especial
subject, and it has rarely, if ever, been scrutinized with
a sharper eye. Deft comparisons with Milton, Wordsworth,
Gibbon, Scott, Dickens, and Eliot, among others, speed
Rosenberg on his way to marking the path whereby Carlyle
arrived at his descendental vision of history. And with
the same keen but balanced eye with which he examines
Carlyle's "great decade"--from *Sartor Resartus* to *Past and
Present*--Rosenberg reviews the later writings, where Carlyle's
fear of losing his powers of speech--of the onset of silence--
is movingly exposed. The parallels with Wordsworth's career
are plain to see, but it is Rosenberg's Keatsian view of
Carlyle's life as "lived allegory" that gives this book its
power. (F.J.)

Surtees, Virginia. *Jane Welsh Carlyle*. Salisbury: Michael
Russell, 1986. Pp. 294. £12.95.

Rev. by Alethea Hayter in *TLS*, Dec. 5, 1986, p. 138, along
with volumes 10, 11, and 12 of *The Collected Letters of
Thomas and Jane Welsh Carlyle* (Duke University Press, 1986;
$35.00 per vol.).

"'Groping through the sepulchral caverns of our being'
was a habitual indulgence [of Carlyle's]; if he would only
have taken his wife exploring with him, it might have prevented
Mrs. Carlyle's keenest disappointment in their marriage."
Not seen.

Tarr, Rodger L., and Fleming McClelland, eds. *The Collected
Poems of Thomas and Jane Welsh Carlyle*. Greenwood, Fla.:
Penkevill Publishing, 1986. Pp. liv+232. $30.00.

Rev. by Gerald Monsman in *SEL* 26 (1986):   797. These poems
are described as "the compositions of innocents who were
struggling to survive the Byronic temper that had become a
part of the post-Regency psyche." Neither the editors nor
the author of the foreword, G.B. Tennyson, make extravagant
claims for the 42 (possibly 51) poems and 12 translations by
Thomas or the fragment of a play, 11 poems, and 4 translations by Jane. Even so, they are offered here with full
scholarly apparatus--44 pages of introductory material and
100 pages of notes and index. Those who read the apparatus
and skip the poems will have the right idea. (F.J.)

Timko, Michael. "Carlyle, Sterling, and the Scavenger Age."
SSL 20 (1985): 11-33.

The context for an unpublished fragment related to both
the *Life of Sterling* and *The Scavenger Age* and thus written
between 1844 and 1851. (F.J.)

Wasko, Jean Kay. "The Familiar Letter as a Literary Genre
in the Nineteenth Century." Ann Arbor, Mich.: University
Microfilms International, 1986.

Includes the Carlyles. Dissertation.

Wheeler, Elizabeth. "Great Burke and Poor Boswell: Carlyle
and the Historian's Task." *VN* 70 (1986): 28-31.

"By looking at both men and both books (*Reflections on the
Revolution in France* and *Life of Johnson*), Carlyle came
to his own understanding of the historian's task." Burke
proved to be the negative example, Boswell the positive one.
(F.J.)

See also Erdman ("General 2. Environment"); Handwerk, Manos,
Rabb ("General 3. Criticism"); Findlay ("English 2. Environment"); Bridgman, Jann, McGowan, Mendilow ("English 3. Criticism"); Harris ("Coleridge").

Reviews of books previously listed:

DRESCHER, Horst W., ed., *Thomas Carlyle 1981: Papers Given
at the International Carlyle Centenary Symposium* (see *RMB* for
1985, p. 112), rev. in *EA* 39 (1986): 355-56; KAPLAN, Fred,
Thomas Carlyle: A Biography (see *RMB* for 1984, p. 123), rev.
by David R. Sorensen in *RES* 37 (1986): 112-13; by Frank M.
Turner in *JMH* 58 (1986): 303-05 who finds it "a major contribution"; by Chris R. Vanden Bossche in *MLQ* 45 (1984):
303-05; SANDERS, Charles Richard, Kenneth J. Fielding, et al.,
eds., *The Collected Letters of Thomas and Jane Welsh Carlyle*,
vols. 10, 11 and 12 (see *RMB* for 1985, pp. 112-13), rev. by
Alan Bell in *S*, Jan. 18, 1986, p. 28; by Alethea Hayter in
TLS, Dec. 5, 1986, p. 1380; by Gerald Monsman in *SEL* 26
(1986): 796-97; by Carlisle Moore in *SSL* 21 (1986): 295-

310; VIJN, J.P., *Carlyle and Jean Paul: Their Spiritual
Optics* (see *RMB* for 1984, p. 36), rev. by G.B. Tennyson in
SSL 20 (1985): 271-76.

Composite review:

Tarr, Rodger L., "Truth and Fiction: Carlyle edited and Reedited." *Review* 7 (1985): 239-58.

The three works under review--Goldberg and Seigel's edition
of Carlyle's *Latter-Day Pamphlets*, Cate's edition of the
Carlyle-Ruskin correspondence; and Kaplan's biography--testify
to a birth of interest in Carlyle stimulated by the centenary
of his death in 1981. Tarr has mostly praise for the editors
but little good to say about the biographer, who has reedited
Carlyle, in the process converting fact into fiction. To
prove his point Tarr focuses on Kaplan's treatment of the
Carlyles' love life. Given his conclusion--that Kaplan's
work is regressive, returning Carlyle studies to the school
of psychoanalytic biography that at the turn of the century
nearly destroyed Carlyle's reputation--it is difficult to
understand how at the outset he can assert that the three
items under review attest to a "promising future for Carlyle
studies." (F.J.)

CLARE

Blackmore, Evan. "John Clare's Psychiatric Disorder and Its
Influence on His Poetry." *VP* 24 (1986): 209-28.

Almost all of the conclusions in this article are stated
very cautiously. After tracing despondency and fluctuating
moods in Clare's letters (while admitting that many people
less insane may have written similar letters), Blackmore
speculates about causes, which could have been familial,
organic (probably not), or environmental. Clare's manic-
depressiveness (not schizophrenia) *may have* made him write
more verses, *may have* aggravated his sexism. It probably
had "various complex influences" but not on his nature
poetry. (M.T.S.)

Crossan, Greg. "Some Fugitive John Clare Items, 1820-1977."
N&Q, n.s. 33 (June 1986): 167-70.

Items missed in Dendurent's 1978 bibliography (see also
RMB for 1981, p. 105).

The John Clare Society Journal 5 (1986).

Contents: June Counsel, "Coming to Clare" (5-8); John Lucas, "The Flitting" (9-13); J.R. Watson, "John Clare" (14-15): Rodney Lines, "John Clare and Herbal Medicine" (16-21); Richard L. Gillin, "Minute Particulars and Imaginative Forms" (22-29); R.K.R. Thornton, "The Nature of *The Parish*" (30-35); Neil Philip, "To John Clare" (36); Greg Crossan, "The Nine *Lives* of John Clare" (37-46); and reviews of books by and about Clare by Edward Storey, Marghanita Laski, and R.K.R. Thornton. Lucas offers a not entirely convincing political reading of "The Flitting"; Gillin analyzes the sonnets in Clare's first volume; Thornton argues the unity of *The Parish*; Crossan assesses the available biographies and autobiographies of Clare. (M.M.)

Musty, John. "Collecting Country Writers." *Antiquarian Book Monthly Review* 13,141 (Jan. 1986): 4-15.

Concerns Clare, Duck, and Bloomfield. The portrait reprinted here, purportedly of the poet Clare, is actually of John Fitzgibbon, second earl of Clare and a friend of Byron's. And the answer is: no, I didn't invent the name of the author of this article, but I wish I had. (M.M.)

Robinson, Eric, ed. *John Clare: The Parish, A Satire*. Notes by David Powell. Harmondsworth and New York: Viking, 1985. Pp. 96. Paper $5.95. Penguin Books, £2.50. Hardcover not available.

Rev. by R.L. Brett in *RES* 37 (1986): 455.
The publication of this poem in its entirety for the first time should be a cause for satisfaction among Romanticists (the longest excerpt hitherto in print consisted of fewer than half of its some 2,200 lines). A narrative satire in heroic couplets, *The Parish* is essentially two poems intermingled; one in which Clare pillories (or occasionally celebrates) particular village types--"Dandy Flint, Esq.," "Dr. Urine," "Bumtagg the Bailiff," etc.--and another in which he makes more general comments on the hypocrisy, cant, and oppression of overseers, justices of the peace, wealthy farmers, and traveling preachers. The latter passages are relatively less successful because in them the narrative line is sometimes confused--perhaps because Clare let his anger control him. But the individual type-portraits can be enormously entertaining, and reveal much about life on the bottom of the heap in rural England of the time. Critics will (perhaps inevitably) compare Clare to Pope and Byron; while his satire lacks Pope's polished brilliance and Byron's

exuberance, that is in part because Clare had other things in mind, as well as because the poem is unfinished. Clare can be blunt and crude, but his insight into the motivations of those classes "above" him rarely falters. Provided readers allow Clare to be himself in this poem, they will find him unfailingly interesting. (M.M.)

Schulz, Max F. "Crabbe's and Clare's Enclosured Vales." Pp. 137-51 in *Paradise Preserved: Recreations of Eden in Eighteenth and Nineteenth-Century England*. Cambridge University Press, 1986.

A shrewd evaluation of Clare's strengths and weaknesses as a poet. (M.M.)

Storey, Mark, ed. *The Letters of John Clare*. Oxford: Clarendon Press, 1985. Pp. xliii+705. $74.00.

Rev. by Tom Paulin in *TLS*, June 20, 1986, pp. 675-76.
Prints all known Clare letters, plus 22 *to* him, almost doubling the number of the former now published, with a much superior editing job over the old and notoriously unreliable Tibble edition of 1951. It is a shame to find any fault with the superb editing and annotating Storey has done, but one has to wonder why the index contains no topical references. Do users of the letters of writers really want to know only what persons and places they referred to? (M.M.)

Williams, Merryn, and Raymond Williams, eds. *Selected Poetry and Prose of John Clare*. (Modern English Texts.) London: Methuen, 1986. Pp. 242. Paper £14.95.

Not received.

See also Parkinson, Schulz ("English 3. Criticism").

Reviews of books previously listed:

BROWNLOW, Timothy, *John Clare and Picturesque Landscape* (see *RMB* for 1983, p. 97), rev. by P.M.S. Dawson in *MLR* 81 (1986): 178-81; GRAINGER, Margaret, ed., *The Natural History Prose Writings of John Clare* (see *RMB* for 1984, p. 124), rev. by April London in *RES* 37 (1986): 108-09; ROBINSON, Eric, David Powell, and Margaret Grainger, eds., *The Later Poems of John Clare 1837-1864* (see *RMB* for 1984, pp. 126-27), rev. by R.L. Brett in *RES* 37 (1986): 278-79; by Mark Minor in *SiR* 25 (1986): 576-82; STOREY, Edward, *A Right to Song* (see *RMB* for 1983, pp. 97-98), rev. by Edward Strickland in *SiR* 25 (1986): 154-57.

CORBETT

Review of book previously listed:

SPATER, George, *William Cobbett: The Poor Man's Friend* (see
RMB for 1982, p. 108), rev. by A.J. Sambrook in *YES* 16 (1986):
281-82.

COLERIDGE

Avis, Paul. "Coleridge on Luther." *ChLB* 56 (1986): 249-55.

Barth, J. Robert, S.J. "Theological Implications of Coleridge's
Theory of Imagination." *SLIm* 19,2 (1986): 23-33.

   In another of his penetrating contributions to Romantic,
religious, and Coleridgean theory, Barth insists that
"Coleridgean polarity ... is not simply a tension between two
essentially antagonistic forces; it is rather a fruitful
sharing between two 'forces' of one 'power.'"
   "Only imagination ... can bring us--including the theologian--
to the full encounter with religious reality, because it is
only symbolic language that resists the human drive for
clarity and determinateness." (M.T.S.)

Bate, Jonathan. "'Kubla Khan' and 'At a Solemn Music.'" *ELN*
24,1 (1986): 71-73.

Beer, John. "Coleridge, Hazlitt, and 'Christabel.'" *RES* 37
(1986): 40-54.

Beer, John. "Coleridge's Originality as a Critic of Shakespeare."
SLIm 19 (1986): 51-69.

   This article defends, especially against assault from
Norman Fruman, Coleridge's claims to originality in his
theories of organic form, especially as applied to Shakespeare.
For example, Hazlitt heard Coleridge apply his own philosophical ideas to *Hamlet* as early as 1798. After quoting Coleridge's
and Schlegel's comments on several other Shakespeare plays,
Beer concludes that Coleridge's version of organic terminology
was more subtle than Schlegel's. (M.T.S.)

Benzon, William. "Articulate Vision: A Structuralist Reading
of 'Kubla Khan.'" *Literature and Society* 18 (1985): 3-29.

   Elaborate diagrams. A method that "yields a description of
the path in semantic space that generates the object text"
(27).

Bidney, Martin. "*Christabel* as Dark Double of *Comus*." *SP* 83 (1986): 182-200.

Christensen, Jerome. "'Like a Guilty Thing Surprised': Deconstruction, Coleridge, and the Apostasy of Criticism." *CritI* 12 (1986): 769-87.

    Once again Coleridge attracts deconstruction. Ostensibly in reply to an attack (by Frank Lentricchia) on younger deconstructionists who in the 1960s were political activists and are so no longer, Christensen reads Coleridge and Paul de Man together, interweaving their concepts and preserving their respective terminologies, with excursions into the political apostasies of the two Burkes, Edmund and Kenneth, as well as of Coleridge himself. Given the method, the last step in the argument is predictable: "No doubt the tacit political agenda of deconstruction is apostasy, but ... that apostasy is the imaginative reflex, or trope, that constitutes modern criticism." (I.H.C.)

Coleman, Dierdre. "Coleridge, Quakerism, and 'The Friend.'" *TWC* 17 (1986): 134-42.

De Paolo, Charles. "Coleridge and the History of Western Civilization, c. 4004 B.C.-500 A.D." *Clio* 14 (1985): 181-203.

    Coleridge's planned attempt at a coherent Christian historiography would have reconciled the Bible with anthropology. Giving us glimpses of Coleridge's notes made between January 1818 and February 1819, De Paolo emphasizes Coleridge as Christian historian, idealist, conservative moralist, and synthesizer of knowledge. (M.T.S.)

De Paolo, Charles. "The Lessons of Wisdom and Caution: Coleridge's Periodization of Western History." *TWC* 17 (1986): 119-30.

Farness, Jay. "Strange Contraries in Familiar Coleridge." *ELWIU* 13 (1986): 231-45.

    In *The Rime of the Ancient Mariner* and chapter 13 of the *Biographia*, Coleridge "exemplifie[s] ... a sense of the weave of the 'creative' and the 'critical' that prefigures both the 'Arnoldian Concordat' and the breaches it has since suffered in the name of reformation."

Ferris, David S. *Transfigurations (on Coleridge's 'Biographia Literaria')*. Ann Arbor, Mich.: University Microfilms International, 1986.

    Dissertation.

Fruman, Norman. "Ozymandias and the Reconciliation of Opposites." *SLIm* 19,2 (1986): 71-87.

"What is historically crucial to realize is that the linking of opposites to the fundamental processes of an 'imaginative' faculty is [a mere] espisode in the history of transcendental idealism"; reassessment of Coleridge's theory "could hardly come at a more difficult time for literary theories of any kind.... This generation's eager theorists have pressed on to fresh fanes and postures new."

Gallant, Christine, ed. "Coleridge's Theory of the Imagination as Critical Method Today." *SLIm* 19 (Fall 1986).

Editor's comment, pp. 1-2; essays by Brian Wilkie, J. Robert Barth, Thomas McFarland, John Beer, and Norman Fruman, published in that order, are here listed alphabetically (see above and below). Readers familiar with the work of these critics won't find much that is new here (except perhaps in Wilkie's engaging essay introducing the concept of "overlays," a conception that deserves more development. (J.H-P.)

Greenberg, Martin. *The Hamlet Vocation of Coleridge and Wordsworth.* Iowa University Press, 1986.

Not seen.

Harris, Kenneth Marc. "Reason and Understanding Reconsidered: Coleridge, Carlyle and Emerson." *ELWIU* 13 (1986): 263-81.

Although Harris does not contend that Coleridge is a "Kantian" he does argue that "his appreciation of Kant is more knowledgeable than is generally conceded" and that "his divergences from Kant should not be dismissed as thoughtless or tendentious distortions but evaluated as substantive attempts to arrive at a new position."

Jackson, H.J. "'Turning and turning': Coleridge on Our Knowledge of the External World." *PMLA* 101 (1986): 848-56.

Coleridge's contemporaries saw him as "a poet who dwindled into a philosopher"; we have so much of his previously unpublished work that we can recognize him as "a thinker who happened to be a poet." Jackson finds his originality "in deep structures" evident in "a series of spacial images each in turn displaced by a more satisfying model." The movement of spiraling ascent, which Coleridge called the "compass of nature," is examined in its spiraling through Coleridge's writings.

Jang, Gyung-Ryul. "The Imagination *Beyond* and *Within* Language:
An Understanding of Coleridge's Idea of Imagination."
SiR 25 (1986): 505-20.

   Argues that "all attempts at de-mystifying Coleridge's
primary and secondary Imagination seem to have gone astray";
concludes that "human imagination is, in a sense, a '*dim*' ...
not a lucid 'Analogue of [God's] creation, as Coleridge
puts it."

Jasper, David. *Coleridge as Poet and Religious Thinker.*
London: Macmillan; Allison Park, Pa.: Pickwick, 1985.
Pp. xii+195. $19.90.

   Not received.
   Rev. by Martin Jarrett-Kerr in *DUJ*, n.s. 47 (June 1986):
379; by Paul Hamilton in *TLS*, Dec. 27, 1985, p. 1484, as
debatable, but clearly argued, condensing "much of the best
of recent Coleridgean scholarship" (quite a tall order).

Lefebure, Molly. *The Bondage of Love: A Life of Mrs. Samuel
Taylor Coleridge.* London: Gollancz; New York: Norton,
1986. Pp. 287; illus. £15.95; $17.95.

   Reviewed sympathetically and critically (and sometimes
inaccurately) by Norman Fruman in *TLS*, Aug. 22, 1986, pp.
910-11; by Anthony Storr in *S*, Aug. 23, 1986, pp. 22-23;
favorably by John Bayley in *LRB*, Oct. 23, 1986, pp. 19-20.
   This is "must" reading for anyone truly interested in the
complex interrelations of Coleridge, Wordsworth, Southey,
and DeQuincey and their families and associates, for central
to their varying friendships and hostilities was Sarah Fricker
Coleridge, a "most extraordinary character" (epithet of
Dorothy Wordsworth's) who, as Molly Lefebure richly and
beautifully demonstrates, "must surely rank among the most
maligned of great men's wives."
   To protect *her husband's* reputation, Mrs. Coleridge burned
a lifetime accumulation of letters from him--and thus delayed
until now the rescue of her own. Fortunately so much Coleridgean, Southeyan, and Wordsworthian material survived that th
present work is able to rescue the truth about her from "a
view based upon morphine distortion, sour Grasmere gossip,
and the sensation-seeking 'revelations' of journalism." An
expert on the psychology of drug addiction, and living close
enough to Greta Hall to realize its neglected importance
for this subject, Molly Lefebure turns out to be the perfect
scholar to restore Mrs. Coleridge to light. What relief she
brings to many dark areas! (D.V.E.)

A fascinating and important book, the gem of the year in Romantic studies. The author has proved beyond a shadow of a doubt that Sara Coleridge *mère* was not the mousey, rather unpleasant mediocrity pictured by tradition, but a person of great strength of character in her own right, whose personality and activities were systematically buried in oblivion by Coleridge, or misinterpreted by the Wordsworth circle, who believed what Coleridge said about her. According to the dust jacket, Molly Lefebure "is well qualified to write of drug addiction, having worked for years as private secretary to the late Professor Keith Simpson, Home Office pathologist and head of the Department of Forensic Medicine at Guy's Hospital. She also worked for a period of years at first hand with drug addicts and projects connected with their problems." This experience led her to see Coleridge's behavior to his wife as part of a standard pattern afflicting morphine addicts: blaming one's problems, and the fact of addiction itself, on those nearest and dearest to the addict. (This would explain, at least in part, the quarrel with Wordsworth, too.) Really, Coleridge's treatment of Sara as revealed here makes an appalling story, all the more damaging since the author lets the facts speak for themselves. Thus, in a letter written in February 1799, while STC was of course in Germany, Sara tells Poole of the death of Berkeley: "Oh! my dear Mr. Poole, I have lost my dear dear child! at one o'clock on Sunday Morning a violent convulsive fit put an end to his painful existence, myself and two of his aunts were watching by his cradle. I wish I had not seen it, for I am sure it will never leave my memory; sweet babe! what will thy Father feel when he shall hear of thy sufferings and death!" (112). Yet, in the same letter, she goes on to agree to Poole's demand that she *not tell* Coleridge about the child's death, because it might interfere with the Great Man's productivity at Gottingen—even though her "money is nearly gone; could you supply me untill Samuel makes me some provision ... perhaps he may think I have enough to last untill his return not knowing my situation" (113). The Archangel is further damaged by all this; in fact, he emerges as almost criminally irresponsible, and the Wordsworths as pretty well hoodwinked by their one-sided devotion to a cad (or, as we say, a real stinker). The mystery of Coleridge's luminous genius deepens and acquires, through Lefebure's study, an additional and tragic dimension. Even if the case is occasionally overstated, we can never look at the Wordsworth circle in its entirety in quite the same way again. A remarkable achievement. (B.C.H.)

Lefebure, Molly. "Consolation in Opium: The Expanding
Universe of Coleridge, Humphrey Davy and 'The Recluse.'"
TWC 17 (1986): 51-60.

Lowes, John Livingstone. *The Road to Xanadu: A Study of the
Ways of the Imagination.* Princeton University Press, 1986.
Paperback reprint $14.95.

  The famous detective investigation of Coleridge's sources
  and alchemical processes. Good to have it kept in print.
  Excellent to have an appreciative "Foreword: John Living-
  ston Lowes and Coleridge's Poems" (ix-xviii) by Thomas
  McFarland. (D.V.E.)

Luis, Keith Alan. *Family Relationships in Coleridge's Poetry.*
Ann Arbor, Mich.: University Microfilms International, 1985.

  Dissertation.

Luther, Susan N. "'The Hidden Fire': Samuel Taylor Coleridge
and the Daughers of Memory." Ann Arbor, Mich.: University
Microfilms International, 1986.

  Dissertation.

Mays, J.C.C. "Coleridge's Borrowings from Jesus College
Library, 1791-94." *TCBS* 8, part 5 (1985): 557-81.

  Annotated list of 33 borrowings (the record is incomplete
  because mutilated) along with useful remarks on what the
  pattern of borrowing reveals about STC's life at Cambridge.

McFarland, Thomas. "Imagination and Its Cognates: Supplementary Considerations." *SLIm* 19,2 (1986): 35-50.

  Having, in his recent book, *Originality and Imagination*
  (see *RMB* for 1985, pp. 66-67), argued that historically
  Romanticism transferred "mental energy from the weakening
  concept of soul to an alternative vehicle, Imagination,"
  McFarland presents some corroborating data--finding a good
  deal in Hazlitt, also Rousseau and Keats and Emerson, and
  concluding triumphantly with Blake's usage as "normative for
  his time."

McFarland, Thomas. "So Immethodical a Miscellany: Coleridge's
Literary Life." *MP* 83 (1986): 405-13.

McKusick, James C. *Coleridge's Philosophy of Language.* (Yale
Studies in English, 195.) Yale University Press, 1986.
Pp. xiv+175. Paper $15.95.

A packed and valuable monograph (recently a dissertation)
that turns out to be less forbidding than its title suggests.
Also, despite the location of the publisher, it is a work
of traditional literary scholarship, historically based, and
not much dependent on semiotics, etc., etc. Rather, it is
indebted to "revisionist" historians of linguistics such as
Hans Aarsleff, who have emphasized the French connection
rather than the Germanic. "Rather than seeing Coleridge as
a forerunner of modern philology, or semantics, or structuralism," the author says in his introduction, "I have
attempted to situate him within the linguistic controversies
of his own period." There follow chapters on the concept of
"natural language" in the eighteenth century; on STC's relationship with Horne Tooke and the "noun-verb controversy";
"Coleridge's Response to German Philology"; "The Role of
Linguistic Theory" in his literary criticism; and a concluding
chapter on Coleridge's *Logic* (only made available in 1981!)
as embodying a systematic philosophy of language. McKusick
has interesting things to say about the problem of "poetic
diction": "The entire controversy between [W and STC]
arises from their very different concepts of natural language.
For Wordsworth, 'natural language' is synonymous with
'ordinary language'; only in everyday conversation can the
referents of words be determined sufficiently to make communication possible. This process of rectification requires the
presence of unchanging natural objects to provide standards
of usage. For Coleridge, on the other hand, natural language
is entirely the result of individual acts of creation ... his
predilection for individual forms of expression stands in
strong opposition to Wordsworth's dream of a common language"
(114-15). Wordsworth is thus the true heir of eighteenth-
century language theory, and STC the innovator and the
Romantic. In contrasting Coleridge with Kant, the author
makes what seems to me a very perceptive comment: Coleridge's
"philosophy of language is an open one. [He] regards
language as existing at the forefront of cultural progress,
and he resists the urge to impose a false closure upon it.
Indeed, one way of describing the difference between the
Logic and the *Critique of Pure Reason* is that the former
sees itself as contributing to an ongoing conversation, while
the latter sees itself as getting in the last word" (148).
Touché! (B.C.H.)

Milne, Fred L. "Coleridge's 'Kubla Khan': A Metaphor for the
Creative Process." *SAR* 51,4 (Nov. 1986): 17-29.

In the mental landscape of Xanadu, the stream of thought
rises from and sinks into the unconscious, while Kubla presides
as the creative imagination.

Moon, Kenneth. "Lowry's *Under the Volcano* and Coleridge's
   Kubla Khan." *Explicator* 4,2 (Winter 1986): 44-47.

Morrow, John. "The National Church in Coleridge's *Church and
   State*." *JHI* 47 (1986): 640-52.

   A strong and careful refutation of Peter Allen's essay
   on Coleridge's tract (see *RMB* for 1985, p. 118), which finds
   any connection to the thought of Gramsci "misleading."
   "Coleridge's support for the Church of England, like his
   rejection of the 1799 Constitution, depended upon the use of
   Country Party arguments about the importance of independent
   forms of property in mixed and balanced constitutions," and
   therefore his position was without break. (T.L.A.)

Newlyn, Lucy. "Parodic Allusion: Coleridge and the 'Nehemiah
   Higginbottom' Sonnets, 1797." *ChLB* 56 (1986): 255-59.

   Sharp focus on the "layering" of allusions to Lamb and
   Wordsworth.

Nye, Eric W. "Coleridge and the *Berkshire Chronicle*: A New
   Manuscript Letter and 'A Tale of Horror.'" *PQ* 64 (1985):
   584-92.

   Includes a previously unknown poem by Coleridge, ten lines
   long, and probably dating from 1828, called "A Tale of Horror:
   Dedicated to Lord Byron and Sir Walter Scott." It is a mildly
   scatological parody, and not particularly clever or funny.
   (B.C.H.)

Pradhan, S.V. "The Historiographer of Reason: Coleridge's
   Philosophy of History." *SiR* 25 (1986): 39-62.

   "Judging from the standard works on the subject, it is
   clear that Coleridge hasn't received the recognition due to
   him as a philosopher of history" (39).
   "In short, Coleridge's philosophy of history is idealistic
   and elitist and belongs to the Christian tradition of historiography. Its passion for principles can be interpreted as
   a passion for regularities, without the assumption of which
   history may be possible but philosophy of history ... is
   impossible."
   "Toynbee is perhaps the only English historian who could
   be looked upon as Coleridge's worthy heir and successor"
   (62).

Reiman, Donald H. "Coleridge and the Art of Equivocation."
   SiR 25 (1986): 325-50.

If Blake has largely been protected from literary psychoanalysis, Coleridge has become the object of too much, which
can degenerate into moralistic indictment, Protestant rather
than Freudian, with little enlightenment about the workings
of his mind. Presenting the child Coleridge once again as
father to the mature poet and critic, Reiman cites instances
in both the poetry and the prose of apparent revelation
which masks concealment, attack in the guise of praise, confession as a means of reiteration. *Biographia Literaria* is
the main exhibit, with equivocations identified at the
strategic points of title, subtitle, epigraph, and first
chapter. Reiman's most arresting critical suggestion is that
Coleridge is imitating Sterne, assuming a "Shandean" persona
of "bemused self-condescension" in order to "outsmart" his
readers as well as his friends.

The heavy emphasis throughout on conscious intention allows
little room for the unconscious and Coleridge's own sporadic
recognition of its operations, always a complicating factor
in assessments of this kind. An assumption of conscious intention persists in the background when Reiman transforms
the sibling rivalry of the nursery into a "Biblical urge to
fratricide," expressed not only in *The Ancient Mariner* but
also in Coleridge's public confessions of guilt, which Reiman
regards as "symbolic fratricide: depredations of brother
writers, at once confessed, repented, and reenacted." (I.H.C.)

Roe, Nicholas. "Coleridge, Wordsworth, and the French Invasion
Scare." *TWC* 17 (1986): 142-48.

Rookmaaker, H.R., Jr. *Towards a Romantic Conception of Nature:
Coleridge's Poetry up to 1803.* (A Study in the History of
Ideas. Utrecht Publications in General and Comparative
Literature, 20.) Amsterdam and Philadelphia: John
Benjamins, 1984. Pp. 214. $39.00, paper $24.00.

Not seen.

Rzepka, Charles J. "Christabel's 'Wandering Mother' and the
Discourse of the Self: A Lacanian Reading of Repressed
Narration." *RP&P* 10,1 (1986): 17-43.

Simons, John. "Coleridge and the Sublime: 'This Lime-Tree
Bower My Prison.'" *ChLB* 56 (1986): 260-63.

Stansfield, Dorothy. "A Note on the Genesis of Coleridge's
Thinking on War and Peace." *TWC* 17 (1986): 130-34.

Wallen, Martin. "Return and Representation: The Revisions
of 'The Ancient Mariner.'" *TWC* 17 (1986): 148-56.

Watson, Kenneth V. *Coleridge's Marginal Dialectics*. Ann
   Arbor, Mich.: University Microfilms International, 1986.

   Dissertation.

See also Couser, Erdman ("General 2. Environment"); Gorak,
   Humphries, Rajan, Scott ("General 3. Criticism"); Smith
   ("English 2. Environment"); Applewhite, Cave, Cook, Curran,
   Fruman, Haney-Peritz, McGowan, Mudge, Nabholtz, Newlyn,
   Rzepka, Schulz, Wesling, Wilkie ("English 3. Criticism");
   McGowan ("Carlyle"); King-Hele ("Darwin"); Snyder ("DeQuincey");
   Beer ("Lamb"); Beer et al., Eilenberg ("Wordsworth").

Reviews of books previously listed:

   GRAVIL, Richard, et al., eds., *Coleridge's Imagination* (see
   RMB for 1985, pp. 120), rev. by Mary Wedd in *ChLB* 57 (1987):
   32-34; HARDING, Anthony John, *Coleridge and the Inspired
   Word* (see *RMB* for 1985, pp. 121-22), rev. by Rosemary Ashton
   in *TLS*, Sept. 19, 1986, p. 1035; by Robert N. Essick in *RP&P*
   10 (1986): 71-75; by John Spencer Hill in *TWC* 17 (1986):
   204-06; JACKSON, H.J., ed., *Samuel Taylor Coleridge* (Oxford
   Authors) (see *RMB* for 1985, p. 122), rev. by Rosemary Ashton
   in *TLS*, Sept. 19, 1986, pp. 1035-36; MODIANO, Raimonda,
   Coleridge and the Concept of Nature (see *RMB* for 1985, p.
   124), rev. by Rosemary Ashton in *TLS*, Sept. 19, 1986, pp.
   1986-87; by Laurence Lockridge in *TWC* 17 (1986): 222-24;
   VLASOPOLOS, Anca, *The Symbolic Method of Coleridge, Baudelaire,
   and Yeats* (see *RMB* for 1984, p. 134), rev. by Barbara Hull
   in *RP&P* 10 (1986): 77-81 as a "triumph" in explaining
   Coleridge, to whose work she should have devoted her entire
   book; WHALLEY, George, ed., *The Collected Works of Samuel
   Taylor Coleridge: Marginalia*, vol. 2 (see *RMB* for 1984, p.
   134), rev. by Anthony John Harding in *TWC* 17 (1986): 217-19;
   by W.J.B. Owen in *UTQ* 56 (1986): 103-06; WHEELER, Kathleen M.,
   The Creative Mind in Coleridge's Poetry (see *RMB* for 1982,
   p. 114), rev. by John O. Hayden in *Genre* 17 (1984): 435-38.

Review essay:

McFarland, Thomas. "So Immethodical a Miscellany: Coleridge's
   Literary Life." *MP* 83 (1986): 405-13.

   After a brief discussion of some of the paradoxes of the
   Biographia, McFarland praises the "magisterially" edited
   recent edition by Bate and Engell. McFarland is especially
   impressed by the handling of Coleridge's foreign language
   sources. To show this edition's superiority to Shawcross's,
   he quotes at length one example of Bate and Engell's uncovering

of Coleridge's plagiarism of Leibniz, not directly but by way of a translation by Jacobi. (M.T.S.)

CONSTABLE

Cormack, Malcolm. *Constable*. Phaidon, 1986. £35.00.

Rev. by Graham Reynolds in *Apollo* 134 (1986): 140-41.

Hill, David. *Constable's English Landscape Scenery*. London: John Murray, 1985. £15.95.

Rev. by Graham Reynolds in *Apollo* 123 (1986): 288.

See also Stafford ("General 2. Environment"); Brennan ("Wordsworth").

Review of book previously listed:

REYNOLDS, Graham, *The Later Paintings and Drawings of John Constable* (see *RMB* for 1984, p. 135), rev. by Louis Hawes in *ArtB* 68 (1986): 172-74 as "a truly magnificent achievement."

COSWAY, MARIA

Walker, John. "Maria Cosway: An Undervalued Artist." *Apollo* 123 (1986): 318-24.

CRABBE

Spiegelman, Willard. "Peter Grimes: The Development of a Hero." *SiR* 25 (1986): 541-60.

Attempts to clarify the relationship between the hero of Benjamin Britten's first opera, in 1945, and "the distinctly less than titular figure in George Crabbe's 1810 series of verse epistles." Although "it has become conventional to think of one Peter or both as 'Byronic' in character, I hope to show that the label 'Wordsworthian' might be a more accurate one."

See also Schulz ("English 3. Criticism"); Schulz ("Clare").

Review of book previously listed:

FAULKNER, Thomas C., *Selected Letters and Journals of George Crabbe* (see *RMB* for 1985, p. 128), rev. by Irene Simon in *ES* 67 (1986): 570-71.

DARWIN, E.

Colp, Ralph, Jr.   "The Relationship of Charles Darwin to the
Ideas of His Grandfather, Dr. Erasmus Darwin." *Biography* 9
(1986):   1-24.

King-Hele, Desmond. *Erasmus Darwin and the Romantic Poets.*
London: Macmillan, 1986. Pp. 294. £27.50.

Rev. by Gillian Beer in *TLS*, Sept. 19, 1986, p. 1036, as
a "learned, instructive, and mildly monomaniac enterprise"--
which discovers Darwin's presence everywhere among the
Romantics--yet "in the end, convincing." This includes not
only Blake, Coleridge, Wordsworth, Shelley, and Keats, but
such neglected Romantics as Brooke Boothby, Thomas Lovell
Beddoes, Mary Tighe, Anna Seward, and Eleanor Porden. I
agree. (D.V.E.)

King-Hele, Desmond.   "Erasmus Darwin: Master of Interdisciplinary Science." *Interdisciplinary Science Reviews* 10
(1985):   170-91.

A useful introduction to Darwin's career and many-faceted
scientific achievements.

DE QUINCEY

Lindop, Grevel, ed. *Confessions of an English Opium-Eater and
Other Writings.* (World's Classics.) Oxford University
Press, 1985. Pp. 304. $5.95.

Includes, as well, "On the Knocking at the Gate in Macbeth,"
"The English Mail-Coach," and the *Suspira de Profundis.*

May, Claire B. *Fall and Redemption: A Mythic Interpretation
of Thomas de Quincey's Imaginative Prose.* Ann Arbor, Mich.:
University Microfilms International, 1985.

Dissertation.

Schwob, Marcel, trans. and ed. *Les derniers jours d'Emmanuel
Kant.* Paris: Ombres, 1986.

Rev. by Ghislain Sartoris in *NRF* 401 (June 1, 1986):   92-94.

Snyder, Robert Lance.   "De Quincey's Literature of Power: A
Mythic Paradigm." *SEL* 26 (1986):   691-711.

Snyder, Robert Lance, ed. *Thomas De Quincey: Bicentenary
Studies.* University of Oklahoma Press, 1986. Pp. xxiv+375.
$29.50.

Thomas De Quincey was born in 1785, but it is appropriate
for someone who had the reputation, in Dorothy's Wordsworth's
phrase, of being "eaten up by the spirit of procrastination"
that the bicentenary volume should actually appear at the
beginning of 1986. The papers are independent of each other,
and the same passages from De Quincey's "impassioned prose"
tend to appear again and again. But there is a substantial
range, including De Quincey's "icons of Apocalypse," his
journalistic practices, his relationship to Freudian theory,
his "dark sublime," his use of Romantic irony, the canon--
with some suggested additions--and characteristics of his
fiction, his "dynamic of supplementarity," his use of the
concepts of nexus and gravitation, and his cosmology.
De Quincey, who liked to think of himself as a "polyhistor,"
would have been delighted to be taken so seriously.

The three illustrations show us De Quincey in painting,
sketch, and daguerreotype. Seventeen essays (including the
editor's introduction) open up so many attractive reading
possibilities that some of us may be tempted to prepare a
graduate--or even an undergraduate--course in De Quincey.

Here are the essay topics: E. Michael Thron, "Thomas
De Quincey and the Fall of Literature"; V.A. de Luca, "De
Quincey's Icons of Apocalypse: Some Romantic Analogues";
John C. Whale, "'In a Stranger's Ear': De Quincey's Polite
Magazine Context"; Michael Cochise Young, "'The True Hero
of the Tale': De Quincey's *Confessions* and Affective Auto-
biographical Theory"; Martin Bock, "De Quincey's Retrospec-
tive Optics: Analogues of Intoxication in the Opium-Eater's
'Nursery Experiences'"; Charles L. Proudfit, "Thomas De
Quincey and Sigmund Freud: Sons, Fathers, Dreamers--Pre-
cursors of Psychoanalytic Developmental Psychology"; Robert M.
Maniquis, "The Dark Interpreter and the Palimpsest of
Violence: De Quincey and the Unconscious"; A.S. Plumtree,
"The Artist as Murderer: De Quincey's Essay 'On Murder
Considered as One of the Fine Arts'"; John Beer, "De Quincey
and the Dark Sublime: The Wordsworth-Coleridge Ethos";
John E. Jordan, "Grazing the Brink: De Quincey's Ironies";
Grevel Lindop, "Innocence and Revenge: The Problem of De
Quincey's Fiction"; Jan B. Gordon, "De Quincey as Gothic
Parasite: The Dynamic of Supplementarity"; Frederick Burwick,
"Nexus in De Quincey's Theory of Language"; Arden Reed,
"'Booked for Utter Perplexity' on De Quincey's *English Mail-
Coach*"; Joel D. Black, "Confession, Digression, Gravitation:
Thomas De Quincey's German Connection"; and "'The Loom of
Palingenesis': De Quincey's Cosmology in 'System of the
Heavens.'"

See also Whitmore ("Scott"); Wordsworth ("Wordsworth").

Review of book previously listed:

DEVLIN, D.D., *De Quincey, Wordsworth and the Art of Prose*
(see *RMB* for 1983, p. 111), rev. by Joshua Wilner in *SiR* 25
(1986): 590-94.

EDGEWORTH

Bour, Isabelle. "Une autre écriture: les contes moraux de
Maria Edgeworth." *EA* 39 (1986): 129-38.

Edgeworth, Maria. *Belinda*. Intro. by Eva Figes. London,
Boston, and Henley: Pandora Press, 1986. Pp. xi+434.
£4.95.

   Written in 1801, this is the story of Belinda and the two
men who court her. Around this conventional literary cliché,
Edgeworth weaves a complex and powerful narrative, so that a
romantic comedy of manners becomes a rich and subtle counter-
point of themes--love, fidelity, passion, cynicism, and the
position of women in society. In balancing the problem of a
young woman choosing a partner for life with a young man
faced with the same dilemma, Edgeworth joins Mary Wollstonecraft in attacking Rousseau's ideas on the education of women.
(Helen Cooper)

Edgeworth, Maria. *Patronage*. Intro. by Eva Figes. London,
Boston, and Henley: Pandora Press, 1986. Pp. xi+631.
£6.95.

   Though flawed, this was Edgeworth's most commercially
successful novel. Published in 1814, *Patronage* is an astute
and humorous portrayal of the British class system and the
different ways in which men and women make their way in the
world. It is both a novel of manners and a meditation on
the concept of "patronage," both financial and sexual. In
attempting to deal with moral issues affecting the working
world of the upper and middle classes in society, Edgeworth's
novel was ahead of its time. (Helen Cooper)

EDINBURGH REVIEW

Fontana, Biancamaria. *Rethinking the Politics of Commercial
   Society: The Edinburgh Review 1802-1832.* Cambridge University Press, 1985. Pp. 264. $34.50.

   Not received.

See also Bromwich, Morgan ("Jeffrey").

EDINBURGH WEEKLY JOURNAL

See Garside ("Scott").

THE EXAMINER

See Davies ("Carlyle").

FERRIER

Cullinan, Mary. *Susan Ferrier.* (English Authors Series.)
Boston: Twayne Publishing, 1984. Pp. xii+135. $18.95.

> Rev. by W.A. Craik in *SLJ* 13, supp. 24 (1986): 13-15.
> Liberation has finally gotten around to one of the most
> interesting and unstudied romantic novelists (1782-1854).
> Thank Twayne for the resurrection, if not the life. (T.L.A.)

Ferrier, Susan. *Marriage.* Intro. by Rosemary Ashton. London:
Virago Press, 1985. Pp. xvi+513. £4.50.

> Rev. by Jean Ann Scott Miller in *SLJ* 13, supp. 25 (1986):
> 17-19.
> For the reviewer's information, the novel was published
> in 1818. (T.L.A.)

FUSELI

Klemm, Christian. *Johann Heinrich Füssli: Zeichnungen.*
(Kunsthaus Zürich: Sammlungsheft 12.) Zurich: Kunsthaus
Zürich, 1968.

> Catalogue of Fuseli drawings exhibited in 1986.

GALT

Galt, John. *Annals of the Parish.* Ed. James Kinsley. (World's
Classics.) Oxford University Press, 1986. Pp. xxvii+242.
Paper $13.95.

> Kinsley's 1967 edition for Oxford English Novels, with an
> updated list of biographical and critical studies by Ian C.
> Gordon. (F.J.)

Graham, Robert J. "John Galt's *Bogle Corbet*: A Parable of
Progress." *SLJ* 13 (1986): 31-47.

> A major attempt to resuscitate the literary failure based
> on Galt's experience in Canada. (T.L.A.)

Scott, P.H. *John Galt*. (Scottish Writers Series.) Edinburgh:
Scottish Academic Press; Columbia University Press, 1985.
Pp. vi+130. Paper £4.50; $7.50.

Rev. by W.R. Aitken in *RES* 37 (1986): 579-80; rev. with
Patricia Wilson's edition of Galt's *Ringan Gilhaize; or,
The Covenanters*, listed below, by Ian Campbell in *NCL* 41
(1986): 233-34.

Waterston, Elizabeth, ed. *John Galt: Reappraisals*. University
of Guelph, Ontario. $10.00.

Rev. by A.A. Den Otter in *CL* 109 (1986): 139-40.
Not seen.

Wilson, Patricia J., ed. *Ringan Gilhaize, or The Covenanters
by John Galt*. Edinburgh: Scottish Academic Press; Columbia
University Press, 1984. Pp. xxviii+370. £8.50; $25.00.

Rev. by W.R. Aitken in *RES* 37 (1986): 579-80.

GODWIN

Marshall, Peter, ed. *The Anarchist Writings of William Godwin*.
London: Freedom Press, 1986. Pp. 182. £3.50.

Rev. by Nicolas Walter in *New Statesman*, March 14, 1986,
p. 28, as a useful introductory anthology.

Philp, Mark. *Godwin's Political Justice*. Cornell University
Press, 1986. Pp. x+278. $29.95.

Although marred by redundancy and a rather heavy-handed
analytical style, Philp's study makes a significant contribution to our understanding of both *Political Justice* and
"the nature of radicalism in the 1790s." According to Philp,
Godwin's faith in anarchy and the perfectibility of man is
neither as groundless nor as quirky as one might suppose.
Besides being rooted in the intellectual tradition of Rational
Dissent, Godwin's faith was reinforced by his ongoing participation in a radical community whose existential "integrity"
was based on the joint practices of private judgment and
public debate. In line with changes in this community,
Godwin revised *Political Justice*, replacing his originally
rationalist arguments with arguments "drawn from the work
of the British Moralists and the literature of Sensibility."
However, Godwin's newfound appreciation for the affections
involved him not only in a revision of arguments but also
in a novel personal experience: an affair with Mary Wollstonecraft that eventually led to marriage, fatherhood, and
social scandal.

As the scandal provoked by Godwin's *Memoirs* indicates, the radical community was full of internal contradictions. However, Philp argues that Godwin's "fall from public grace" as well as his privately recorded recantations of political justice were not the product of radical contradictions; rather, they were the by-products of a governmental repression that destroyed the existential "integrity" of Godwin's community. Of all Philp's arguments, I found this one the least convincing, not only because it rests on a nondialectical conception of the relationship between internal and external but also because it implies that internal contradictions are incompatible with radical integrity as well as community. Philp believes that his conceptions of integrity, community, and repression are necessary in order to defend the "radical intellectual culture" of the 1790s from E.P. Thompson's charge of "extremism divorced from correlative action or actual social commitment." But are they really so necessary? I think not. (J.H-P.)

Scheiber, Andres. "Falkland's Story: *Caleb Williams'* Other Voice." *SNNTS* 17 (1985): 255-66.

See also Erdman ("General 2. Environment"); Gallagher ("English 2. Environment"); Barker ("English 3. Criticism"); Reiman, Watson ("Shelley, P.B.").

Reviews of book previously listed:

MARSHALL, Peter H., *William Godwin* (see *RMB* for 1984, p. 139), rev. by David McCracken in *MP* 84 (1986): 99-101 as better than Locke's biography of Godwin; by Ralph M. Wardle in *KSJ* 35 (1986): 205-07.

Review essay:

Tysdahl, B.J. *ECS* 19 (1986): 435-37.

Reviews Marshall's *William Godwin*, comparing it with other recent books on Godwin, including some that "undermine any view," such as Marshall's, "of Godwin as a consistent, rational thinker," e.g., the books of Don Locke, D.H. Monro, and Jean de Palacio. And, of course, Tysdahl's own (see *RMB* for 1981, pp. 113-14).

THE GOTHIC

Day, William Patrick. *In the Circles of Fear and Desire: A Study of Gothic Fantasy.* University of Chicago Press, 1985. Pp. xi+208. $17.50.

Rev. by Patrick Brantlinger in *Criticism* 28 (1986): 220-22.

Fowler, Kathleen. "Hieroglyphics in Fire: *Melmoth the Wanderer*." *SiR* 25 (1986): 521-39.

Maturin's novel is generally found "disturbing, but compelling," but its power must be recognized as deriving from "the urgency of Maturin's religious message." It grew out of a sermon by the author and skillfully dives to link the powers of "keen and thoughtful social criticism" with religious urgency.

Harwell, Thomas Meade, ed. *The English Gothic Novel: A Miscellany in Four Volumes*. (*SSEL* issue on Romantic Reassessment, 33,1). University of Salzburg Press, 1986.

Volume 1, *Contexts*: This miscellany includes twenty-five selections from previously published works and is organized into six sections: "Pre-Gothic," "Gothic," "Anti-Gothic," "Post-Gothic," "Varma Gothic," and "Bibliography." Although the introduction suggests that cost and copyright laws had much to do with the choice of selections, Harwell also claims that the selections represent "the best" material he has read on the Gothic, if only because they provide "mythic, symbolic, surreal and socio-economic meanings" for this literature. Yet only one of the twenty-five selections--Wylie Sypher's 1945 essay on "Social Ambiguity in a Gothic Novel"--interprets the Gothic as a social text, an interpretation the editor takes care to categorize as "Marxist." Most of the remaining selections--many of whch were originally published between 1957 and 1969--describe the general psychological and formal characteristics of the Gothic novel. The work of Devendra Varma is emphasized (eight of the twenty-five selections are by Varma) while contemporary critical approaches to the fantastic, the sublime, terror, and horror are totally ignored. As for the bibliography, it is a reprint of two of Jakob Brauchli's three lists of English novels of terror: the quasi-chronological List 1 and the topical List 2. On the whole, this is a disappointing volume, a miscellany which is unlikely to be of much use in the classroom or in scholarly research. (J.H-P.)

Volume 2, *Texts* (p. 353) reprints essays on Walpole's *The Castle of Otranto* by Walter Scott, Elizabeth MacAndrew, Martin Kallich, and Devendra Varma; on William Beckford's *Vathek* by Robert Kiely, Andre Parreaux, and James Henry Reiger; on Ann Radcliffe's *The Mysteries of Udolpho* by Robert Kiely, Sir Thomas Noon Talfourd, and Devendra P. Varma; on Matthew Gregory Lewis's *The Monk* by John Berryman and Peter Brooks;

on Mary Shelley's *Frankenstein* by William F. Axton and
Robert Kiely; and contains an extensive bibliography, 1764-
1824, by Maurice Levy.
Volume 3, *Collateral Gothic 1* (pp. 241) begins with bits
by Fielding (18) and Smollett (9-11); quotes essays by
Robert Arnold Aubin, Montague Summers, J.M.S. Tompkins, and
Paul Yvon (all under the heading "Pre-Gothic to Gothic"
(8-80). The next section, "Gothic," reprints bits by Clara
Reeve, Walter Scott, and Devendra Varma (81-87)--a group
headed "Genre"; then bits by Summers, Raymond D. Havens,
Georges Meyer, and Michael Sadleir, headed "Idea"; an essay
by Eino Railo under "Characterization"; and one by Joel
Porte under "Effect."
The last section, "Anti-Gothic," quotes Maurice Levy, Scott,
Parreaux, Scott again, Garber, Birkhead, and Juliet Becket.
Volume 4, *Collateral Gothic 2* (pp. 317) is divided into
sections "Before 1832" and "After 1832," featuring bits and
essays by Fernand Baldensperger, Marcon A. Christensen,
Leslie Fiedler, Karl S. Guthke, Robert B. Heilman, and Allice
Mary Killen; also Birkhead, MacAndrew, Parreaux, and Railo;
then, under the heading "Underpinnings," an essay by Maurice
Levy on "Structures Profondes."
A prefatory essay in each volume, by editor Harwell, sets
the stage. (D.V.E.)

McGuire, Karen. "The Artist as Demon in Mary Shelley, Stevenson, Walpole, Stoker, and King." *Gothic* 1 (1986): 1-5.

Sedgwick, Eve Kosofsky. *The Coherence of Gothic Conventions.*
London: Methuen, 1986. Pp. 150. Paper $6.95.

Reprint of 1980, with new introduction clarifying the
connections between literary and sociopolitical implications.

See also Frew and Wallace ("English 2. Environment"); Schork,
Watkins ("Lewis").

Reviews of books previously listed:

SIEBERS, Tobin, *The Romantic Fantastic* (see *RMB* for 1985,
p. 130), rev. by Frederick Burwick in *RP&P* 10,2 (1986):
72-76, with a shrewd critique of the rival theories of
Siebers and Todorov; TWITCHELL, James B., *Dreadful Pleasures:
An Anatomy of Modern Horror* (see *RMB* for 1985, p. 131), rev.
by Jonna G. Semeiks, *Criticism* 28 (1986): 467-70.

HAZLITT

Gates, Payson G. "Hazlitt's *Select British Poets*: An American
Publication." *KSJ* 35 (1986): 168-82.

This essay, though unrevised and unpublished since Gates's
death in 1955, represents the best kind of literary detective
work. Gates convincingly argues that Hazlitt's suppressed
Select British Poets was imported into America by the
American "publisher" William C. Hall and that the ornate title
page was probably printed in Boston. (C.E.R.)

Heller, Janet Ruth. "Hazlitt's Appeal to Readers in His
Dramatic Criticism." *ChLB* 57 (Jan. 1987): 1-16.

An extensive and rigorous critique: Hazlitt "is as concerned with the reader's responses to literature as he is
with the poet's creative powers." (D.V.E.)

Jones, Stanley. "First Flight: Image and Theme in a Hazlitt
Essay." *Prose Studies* 8 (1985): 35-47.

Concerns "My First Acquaintance with Poets."

Jones, Stanley. "A Hazlitt Anomaly." *Library* 7 (L985): 60-63.

Hitherto unnoticed examples of careless proofreading by
Hazlitt of "My First Acquaintance with Poets," probably due
to fatigue. These mistakes have resulted in as many as
three different versions of the same sentence appearing in
separate modern editions of this essay.

Jones, Stanley. "The Hazlitts at the Mitre Court 'Wednesdays'
in 1808: Hidden Implications of a Mary Lamb Letter." *ChLB*
57 (Jan. 1987): 17-19.

Corrects the Hazlitts' whens and wheres.

Neve, Michael, ed. *Liber Amoris*. London: Chatto and Windus
(Hogarth Press), 1985. Paper £3.95.

Rev. by Michael Foot, in a long essay in *ChLB* 55 (1986):
224-28, richly evaluating Hazlitt's embrace of Rousseau's
"flaming redhot revolutionary politics but [also] his no
less revolutionary idea of love-making." And Foot reminds
us of the "elaborate discussion of the book" by Marilyn
Butler in *YES* 14 (1984): 209-25 (see *RMB* for 1984, p. 142).

Uphaus, Robert W. *William Hazlitt*. Boston: Twayne Publishing,
1985.

Not seen.

Whale, John. "Hazlitt on Burke: The Ambivalent Position of
a Radical Essayist." *SiR* 25 (1986): 465-81.

Finds--as most readers of Hazlitt do--"an important
opposition within Hazlitt's writing between the radical and
the essayist."

See also Humphries ("General 3. Criticism"); Fryckstedt
("English 1. Bibliography"); Barrell, McFarland, Nabholtz
("English 3. Criticism"); Beer, McFarland ("Coleridge");
Bromwich ("Jeffrey").

Review of books previously listed:

BROMWICH, David, *Hazlitt: The Mind of a Critic* (see *RMB* for
1984, pp. 141-42), rev. by Martha Del Sapio in *YES* 16 (1986):
298-99; KEYNES, Geoffrey, Kt., *Bibliography of William Hazlitt*,
rev. thoroughly, with important supplementary notes and precise dates of publication, by Stanley Jones in *Analytical and
Enumerative Bibliography* 6 (1982): 272-76.

HOGG

Groves, David. "James Hogg, Leigh Hunt, and the 'New Poetic
Mirror.'" *TWC* 17 (1986): 249-50.

Has discovered a new parody (very funny, in fact) by James
Hogg, this time of Leigh Hunt, called "Hamatory Verses to a
Cow," making fun of Hunt's cockneyisms and other propensities.
The verses, 64 lines in all, are printed here for the first
time. 'Ot stuff! (B.C.H.)

See also Massie ("Scott, W.").

HUNT

Gates, Eleanor M. "Leigh Hunt, Lord Byron, and Mary Shelley:
The Long Goodbye." *KSJ* 35 (1986): 149-67.

Dealing with the available facts from the period of June
and July 1823, Gates ably defends Leigh Hunt against the
prejudiced judgments of Doris Langley Moore. Moore (and
others) have been misled by Mary Shelley's unsigned *copy* of
a letter that was actually written by Leigh Hunt to Lord
Byron on July 13, 1823. The original letter is here tran-
scribed and reproduced in facsimile. (C.E.R.)

Reiman, Donald H. "Leigh Hunt and American Readers." *TLS*,
    May 23, 1986, p. 561.

    In response to a review by William St. Clair, April 18,
    1986, of recent books on Hunt, Reiman traces the greater
    enthusiasm in America for Hunt to Americans' relatively
    egalitarian social principles.

Stam, David H. "The Doors and Windows of the Library: Leigh
    Hunt and Special Collections." *BC* 35 (Spring 1986): 67-75.

    Concludes that Hunt should have been a librarian because
    he was one of the great bibliomaniacs.

See also Dunbar, Fryckstedt ("English 1. Bibliography");
    Groves ("Hogg"); Marquess ("Keats"); Quinn, Reiman ("Shelley,
    P.B.").

Reviews of books previously listed:

    BLAINEY, Ann, *Immortal Boy: A Portrait of Leigh Hunt* (see
    RMB for 1985, pp. 133-34), rev. by David R. Cheney in *KSJ*
    35 (1986): 199-201; McCOWN, Robert A., ed., *The Life and
    Times of Leigh Hunt: Papers Delivered at a Symposium* (see
    RMB for 1985, pp. 135-36), rev. by David R. Cheney in *KSJ*
    35 (1986): 199-201.

JEFFREY

Bromwich, David. "Romantic Poetry and the *Edinburgh* Ordinances."
    YES 16 (1986): 1-16.

    Deals with Jeffrey, John Scott, Hazlitt, and others on Byron,
    Shelley, and Keats.

See also Fontana ("*Edinburgh Review*").

Review of book previously listed:

    MORGAN, Peter F., ed., *Jeffrey's Criticism: A Selection* (see
    RMB for 1985, pp. 136-37), rev. by J.H. Alexander in *YES* 16
    (1986): 292-93.

KEATS

Aske, Martin. *Keats and Hellenism: An Essay.* Cambridge
    University Press, 1985. Pp. 193. $32.50.

    Starting off with a useful chapter on what Hellenism had
    come to mean in Keats's time, Aske devotes the rest of his

book to an application of Harold Bloom's theory of poetic
influence to Keats's relationship with his Greek forebears,
in a somewhat predictable narrative which has the belated
ephebe struggling with a tyrannical classical Muse who
threatens his very survival as a modern poet until she is
finally (and rather easily, in the guise of Lamia) exorcized
from his imagination. The critical play yields its quota
of insights, among them some striking observations on how
the statuesque figures of "Hyperion" obstruct and immobilize
the poem's progress. But Aske's argument would be more persuasive if he had substantiated rather than assumed his
basic premise that Keats's Hellenism was "an anxious and
hazardous affair" involving such momentous consequences as
poetic "self-immolation." Did Keats really set out to
"recuperate" Greek antiquity or merely to exploit it for
specific effects? Did his classical muse actually pose any
greater threat to his creative life than, say, his *trecento*
muse--the one that inspired "Isabella"? "Hyperion" certainly
shows the anxiety of influence, but the challenge of Milton
makes that of Hesiod seem negligible. When Homer is "displaced and screened" by Chapman, the problem is not so much
Keats's belatedness as his linguistic inadequacy. A better-
educated contemporary like Shelley wouldn't have had the
same difficulty.

One occasionally has the sense that Aske's argument is being
inflated rather than reasoned. His own anxiety of influence
(the avatars are Bloom, Hartman, and Derrida) shows in his
apparent need to validate his perceptions by translating
them into other people's terminology. When he employs
Derrida's language of presence, absence, plenitude, supplement, and *parergon* simply to reiterate Francis Jeffrey's
remarks on the attenuation of "Endymion," achieving thereby
no increase of clarity or subtlety over what Jeffrey himself
expressed in better English, one is reminded of how much of
contemporary criticism amounts to this kind of dutiful exercise in translation. Aske is a competent reader: he should
not need to trick out his critical intuitions in borrowed
clothing. (R.M.R.)

Baker, Jeffrey. *John Keats and Symbolism.* Sussex: Harvester;
New York: St. Martin's Press, 1986. Pp. 212. $27.50.

The title doesn't adequately suggest the scope of this
consistently interesting revisionary study of the poetry.
Baker rejects any view of Keats's development as a passage
from Romantic escapism to tragic realism, arguing instead
that the poet progressed from a simplistic aestheticism to
a more mature and fully integrated sensibility involving a
broadened if more puzzled awareness of the conflicting

blessings and miseries of earthly existence. The great odes
in particular represent "sophisticated art springing from
radical bewilderment"--an "aporetic" vision of reality that
is more comprehensive than tragic vision and finds expression
in the kind of oxymoronic symbols that characterize Keats's
later poetry, symbols like Lamia and Autumn, presenting a
vision of reality as a complex of pleasure and pain.

  This "perception that good and evil are permanently and
inseparably present together in the world" undermined the
idiosyncratic religious faith the younger Keats had constructed
for himself, but Baker detects in all his verse "the plane-
tary tug exercised by orthodox religious tradition." His
alertness to religious tension in the poetry bears surprisingly
abundant fruit: Baker is very convincing on the religious
significance of "Hyperion," and his notion of the "Grecian
Urn" as an agnostic's ikon is brilliantly suggestive--a
surprisingly original reading of that well-read poem.

  But Baker is almost always original, or trying to be. He
takes nothing for granted, reads every line as though for the
first time, and will not allow his perceptions to be bullied
by other critics, even the most prestigious. He is secure
enough to complain of the "expository muddle" of "The Fall
of Hyperion" and to insist that "Ode on Melancholy" is a
seriously flawed poem. The positive results--multiple fresh
insights where one didn't expect to find them again--more
than compensate for the occasional lapse (e.g., his reading
of "To Autumn" as a critique of a Godwinian order). All this
in clean and accurate prose of a kind that is not natural
in an age like this. (R.M.R.)

Bewell, Alan J. "The Political Implications of Keats's Classicist Aesthetics."

   See Wolfson, below.

Bromwich, David. "Keats's Radicalism."

   See Wolfson, below.

Dickstein, Morris. "Keats and Politics."

   See Wolfson, below.

Elliot, Nathaniel Y. "Keats's 'To Solitude.'" *Explicator* 44
   (1986): 29-31.

Fry, Paul H. "History, Existence, and 'To Autumn.'"
   See Wolfson, below.

Harding, Anthony John. "Speech, Silence, and the Self-Doubting Interpreter in Keats's Poetry." *KSJ* 35 (1986): 83-103.

"On Seeing the Elgin Marbles," "Endymion," "Ode on a Grecian Urn," and "The Fall of Hyperion" seen as dramatizing a tension between the poet's sense of his limited (because belated) powers and the obligation to articulate an authentic poetic response when his creativity is challenged. An interesting (if somewhat hypersensitive and inflated) discussion of a recurrent Keatsian situation. (R.M.R.)

Hofman, Ulrich. *Die erdichtete Idenität: Subjekt des Autors und auktoriales Subjekt in den Briefen und einigen Gedichten von John Keats.* Tübingen: Max Niemeyer Verlag, 1984. Pp. 247. DM 74.00.

Not seen.

Hopkins, Brooke. "Keats's 'Ode on a Grecian Urn': The Use of the World." *AI* 43 (1986): 121-31.

In accordance with D.W. Winnicott's explanation of how "transitional objects and transitional phenomena" function, Keats's poem is interpreted as a "process whereby the urn is viewed first as an ideal object, later becomes the object of the speaker's destructive impulses, and finally ends as his 'friend,' as something he can use."

Keach, William. "Cockney Couplets: Keats and the Politics of Style."

See Wolfson, below.

Kerner, David. "The Problem of Evil in the 'Ode on a Grecian Urn.'" *TSLL* 28 (1986): 227-49.

To the unspoken question about the meaning of life that is deflected by the urn's concluding statement, the poem's submerged answer is a kind of tragic evolutionism: we are the products of an endlessly creative but unconscious power of beauty that brings us indifferently to life and then to death. A strikingly original reading of the poem, enriched at every step by Kerner's command of the rest of the poetry and the letters. (R.M.R.)

Kirchhoff, Frederick. "Keats's Nightingale, the Process of Writing, and the Self of the Poet." *ELWIU* 13 (Spring 1986): 29-41.

Through the act of writing, the poet recovers the individual selfhood that was lost in identification with the bird's non-

representational song. A subtle, impressive argument.
(R.M.R.)

Lau, Beth. "Further Corrections to Amy Lowell's Transcriptions of Keats's Marginalia." *KSJ* 35 (1986): 30-38.

In a necessary supplement and corrective to Norman Anderson's
earlier "Corrections" (*KSJ* 23 [1974]: 25-31), Lau supplies
the annotations and marked passages that Lowell omitted in
her transcriptions from *The Fairie Queene*, *The Rogue*, and
Palmerin of England and corrects some other errors.

Lau, Beth. "Keats's Eagles and the Creative Process." *RP&P*
10,2 (1986): 49-63.

An errata sheet recording more than twenty errors in this
article, none of Lau's making, was sent to all subscribers
in December 1986.

Marquess, William Henry. *Lives of the Poet: The First Century
of Keats's Biography*. Pennsylvania State University Press,
1985. Pp. 134. $20.00.

A succinct survey of the biographies by Milnes, Rossetti,
Colvin, and Lowell, with some attention along the way to the
"extrabiographical life of a poet's image" as it developed
in the critical attitude of nonbiographers like Arnold and
Swinburne. We see how the Victorian biographers dealt with
Keats's sexual experience and his religious skepticism, and
how they shaped the poet's life to suit their differing
cultural agendas, the products ranging from Milnes's "manly"
poet to Rossetti's morbid one. It is instructive to watch
our own current conception of Keats taking recognizable form
as the stream is fed by various tributaries and to observe
how a "biographical" event like the publishing of Keats's
letters to Fanny Brawne can help create the critical attitude
that Keats's poems show (in Rossetti's words) a "want of
manful thew and sinew and of mental balance." While Marquess
is not given to abstract reflection on the art of biography,
he provokes some theoretical objections when he asserts, for
example, that "Hunt can hardly be called a biographer" and
ignores the impact of *Lord Byron and Some of His Contemporaries*
as a catalyst provoking the first critical assessment of
English Romanticism as a movement and as the context of Keats's
poetic life. The book concludes with an epilogue discussing
the major biographies of the 1960s--those by Ward, Bate, and
Colvin. (R.M.R.)

O'Rourke, James L. *Persona and Voice in the Odes of Keats.*
Ann Arbor, Mich.: University Microfilms International,
1986.

Dissertation.

Peterfreund, Stuart. "The Truth About 'Beauty' and 'Truth':
Keats's 'Ode on a Grecian Urn,' Milton, Shakespeare, and
the Uses of Paradox." *KSJ* 35 (1986): 62–82.

The "polysemous paradoxicality" of the urn's concluding
statement acknowledges and celebrates the tension between
mortality and immortality, following the lead of Shakespeare
in Sonnet 101. Peterfreund's delight in "pun, paradox, and
lexicographical instability" isn't completely infectious,
but one enjoys watching his keen mind going through its
paces. (R.M.R.)

Robinson, Dwight E. "Maritime Antecedents of John Keats:
Supplementary Note." *KSJ* 35 (1986): 38–41.

Brief additions to Robinson's 1985 article (see *RMB* for
1985, p. 141).

Scherr, Barry J. "Lawrence, Keats and *Tender Is the Night*:
Loss of Self and 'Love Battle' Motifs." *RecL* 14 (1986):
7–17.

Shepko, Carol. *"The Shore of Tangled Wonder": Apprehensions
of Space in Keats's Poetry.* Ann Arbor, Mich.: University
Microfilms International, 1986.

Dissertation.

Schor, Esther. *Developments and Transformations of Pastoral
Melancholy in Some Poems of Keats, Tennyson, and Hardy.*
Ann Arbor, Mich.: University Microfilms International,
1986.

Dissertation.

Vantine, Diane L. *Imagination and Myths in John Keats's Poetry.*
Ann Arbor, Mich.: University Microfilms International,
1986.

Dissertation.

Ward, Aileen. *John Keats: The Making of a Poet.* 2d ed.
New York: Farrar, Straus and Giroux, 1986. Pp. xiv+459.
Paper $11.95.

Except for minor corrections in the text, the revisions in this new edition of Ward's 1963 biography are confined to the notes and bibliography, which acknowledge more recent developments in biographical and textual scholarship. After 23 years Ward's book remains a useful introduction to Keats; perhaps time has even increased its stature, restoring some of the value denied to it when it was published in the same year as Walter Jackson Bate's biography of the poet. In that autumn of the New Criticism, there was some negative reaction to Ward's psychoanalytic approach, the fruitfulness of which has since been demonstrated by critics who have acknowledged Ward's influence. The influence is hereby made accessible to yet another generation of readers. (R.M.R.)

Watts, Cedric. *A Preface to Keats*. London and New York: Longman's, 1985. Pp. xiv+185.

This is one of the better introductory studies of Keats intended for students. It does not entirely avoid the inaccuracies, simplifications, and vulgarities of perception and diction that seem inevitable in such popularizations, but its flaws are more than made up for by useful features. The biographical section tells a good story, balancing compression with such generosities as long excerpts from the *Endymion* reviews. The "critical discussions" are usually reliable when Watts confines his remarks to Keats; when formulating larger generalizations he can be a menace, as in his judgment that Milton's example inspired the Romantics to "waste huge amounts of time and energy" on futile efforts like Blake's prophecies and *The Prelude*. One senses that Watts has boned up on Keats criticism but is not particularly familiar with the period. In addition to basic biography and criticism we are given a generously detailed history of Keats's reputation and influence, a surprisingly successful essay defining Romanticism with a checklist of 12 criteria, useful observations on tangential figures like Chatterton and Constable, a helpful commentary on *Otho the Great* in the context of contemporary drama, a discussion of the sensuous in poetry, and, for lagniappe, a concluding essay on Keats's persistent concern with thresholds—liminal or transitional situations. There are appended glossaries of proper names in the poetry and in Keats's biography, and a gazetteer of geographical locales. (R.M.R.)

Wolfson, Susan, intro. "Keats and Politics: A Forum." *SiR* 25 (1986): 171-229.

This collection of short pieces might be subtitled "Six Critics in Search of a Topic." Current critical ideology is

uncomfortable with an apolitical Keats; so it becomes necessary to find in his poetry traces of the "fine and subtle
alertness to the political issues of his age" that Susan
Wolfson claims for Keats in her introduction. The real challenge is to find political content in "To Autumn," where
Jerome McGann provocatively said there was none (see *RMB* for
1980, p. 106). The present discussion was instigated by
Morris Dickstein in an MLA paper reprinted here ("Keats and
Politics") insisting that, despite the absence of overt
political reference, "To Autumn" aims at social renovation
by way of "the disinterested exertions of art." Picking up
the baton, William Keach's "Cockney Couplets: Keats and the
Politics of Style" argues that the political circumstances
and public discourse of September 1819 are detectable in
"To Autumn," finding evidence therein of the "stylistic
instincts" observable earlier in Keats's more overtly political
Huntian period. David Bromwich in "Keats's Radicalism"
offers perceptive comments on passages in *Endymion*, *Isabella*,
and *Hyperion* and goes on to consider "To Autumn" in the context of Keats's meditations on current events, concluding
that the freedom he found in poetry did not exclude awareness of the value of other freedoms being fought for in his
time. After an abortive attempt to link *Hyperion*'s "Egyptian"
Titans with Napoleon's Eastern expedition, Alan Bewell ("The
Political Implication of Keats's Classicist Aesthetics")
retreats to the position that the very absence in Keats's
poetry of a political voice associates him politically with
the voiceless classes of society. But Paul Fry remains un-
convinced. In "History, Existence, and 'To Autumn,'" he
reads the ode as an encounter with mortality in a state of
detachment from the ephemera of contemporary politics. All
in all, the forum is an amusing and often impressive demonstration of what scholarly imagination and critical ingenuity can do when "straining at particles of light in the midst
of a great darkness." (R.M.R.)

See also Platt ("General 2. Environment"); Bahti, Chase, Dodd,
Humphries, Neubauer ("General 3. Criticism"); Dunbar ("English
1. Bibliography"); *Huntington Library Quarterly* ("English 2.
Environment"); Applewhite, Baer, Cave, Curran, Edmundson,
Everett, Fruman, Goslee, Hagstrum, Mahony, McFarland,
Rzepka ("English 3. Criticism"); McFarland ("Coleridge");
King-Hele ("Darwin"); Bromwich ("Jeffrey"); Reiman ("Shelley,
P.B."); Zachs ("German 2. General").

Reviews of books previously listed:

GOELLNICHT, Donald C., *The Poet-Physician: Keats and Medical Science* (see *RMB* for 1984, pp. 145-46), rev. by Jeffrey C. Robinson in *KSJ* 35 (1986): 198-99; PEDERSON-KRAG, Geraldine, *The Lurking Keats* (see *RMB* for 1984, pp. 147-48), rev. by Susan Wolfson in *KSJ* 35 (1986): 193-97; POLLARD, David, *The Poetry of Keats: Language & Experience* (see *RMB* for 1985, pp. 140-41), rev. by Dinah Birch in *RES* 37 (1986): 433-34; by Colin Murry in *BJA* 26 (1986): 179-81, favorably; by Susan Wolfson in *KSJ* 35 (1986): 193-97; RHODES, Jack Wright, *Keats's Major Odes: An Annotated Bibliography of the Criticism* (see *RMB* for 1984, p. 148), rev. by Dinah Birch in *RES* 37 (1986): 110-12; VENDLER, Helen, *The Odes of John Keats* (see *RMB* for 1983, pp. 120-21), rev. by John Bayley in *SiR* 24 (1985): 551-65; by Dinah Birch in *RES* 37 (1986): 110-12; by Herbert J. Levine in *Genre* 17 (1984): 419-21; by Robert Ryan in *MP* 83 (1986): 319-21 as "superior," "essential," and "useful"; WALDOFF, Leon, *Keats and the Silent World of Imagination* (see *RMB* for 1985, pp. 143-44), rev. by Barbara Schapiro in *ELN* 24,2 (1986): 74-76; by Susan Wolfson in *KSJ* 35 (1986): 193-97.

LAMB

Beer, John. "Did Lamb Understand Coleridge?" *ChLB* 56 (Oct. 1986): 232-49.

"From the first, Lamb must have known that Coleridge did not simply want to save the world but to solve the universe into the bargain." A delightful, insightful essay. (D.V.E.)

Courtney, Winifred F. "New Light on the Lambs and the Burneys." *ChLB* 57 (Jan. 1987): 19-27.

Day, W.D. "Charles Lamb and 'The Anatomy of Melancholy.'" *ChLB* 52 (1985): 111-19.

Phillips, Adam, ed. *Charles Lamb: Selected Prose.* Penguin Classics, 1985. £4.95.

Rev. by Mary Wedd in *ChLB* 57 (Jan. 1987): 27-29 with great disappointment about the editor's superficial attitude and his meager selection of essays. The Viking edition of *The Portable Charles Lamb* remains a much better choice.

Sutherland, Kathryn. "The Coming of Age of the Man of Feeling: Sentiment in Lamb and Dickens." *ChLB* 55 (1986): 196-210.

Watson, J.R. "Lamb and Food: The Crowsley Memorial Lecture."
   ChLB 54 (1986): 160-74.

See also Humphries ("General 3. Criticism"); Finch ("English
   1. Bibliography"); Nabholtz ("English 3. Criticism"); Newlyn
   ("Coleridge").

Reviews of books previously listed:

   MONSMAN, Gerald Cornelius, *Confessions of a Prosaic Dreamer:
   Charles Lamb's Art of Autobiography* (see *RMB* for 1985, pp.
   146-47), rev. by Jane Aaron in *RES* 37 (1986): 276-78; by
   Michael Cochise Young in *SAR* 50 (Sept. 1985): 107-10; by
   Fred V. Randel in *JEGP* 85 (1986): 272-75; by Eugene L.
   Stelzig in *KSJ* 35 (1986): 207-11; PRANCE, Claude A., *Com-
   panion to Charles Lamb* (see *RMB* for 1983, p. 124), rev. by
   Winifred F. Courtney in *KSJ* 35 (1986): 211-13.

LEWIS

Schork, R.J. "Lewis' *The Monk*." *Explicator* 44 (1986): 26-29.

Watkins, Daniel. "Social Hierarchy in Matthew Lewis's *The Monk*."
   SNNTS 28 (1986): 115-24.

   Interprets *The Monk* as a social text whose implications are
   "highly conservative," if not "reactionary." Lewis locates
   the sources of horror in violations of the established
   hierarchical structures of class, religion, family, and sex.
   So, for example, Ambrosio is represented not as an aristocratic villain but as a horrifying abomination engendered by
   his parents' transgression of class boundaries. On the whole,
   this is an interesting and convincing reading. (J.H-P.)

See also "The Gothic."

MOORE

Dowden, Wilfred S., ed. *The Journal of Thomas Moore*, vol. 3,
   1826-1830. University of Delaware Press, 1986. Pp. 895-
   1360. $60.00.

   Rich in references to Byron, Hobhouse, the Hollands, the
   Lansdownes; publisher Longman; the Moores, John Murray,
   James Power (Moore's music publisher), Rogers, Lord Russell,
   Mary Shelley (not Percy), *The Times*, and Wellington.

See also Walker, Richard ("English 2. Environment'); Ogle,
Reiman ("Shelley, P.B.").

Reviews of book previously listed:

DOWDEN, Wilfred S., ed., *The Journal of Thomas Moore*, vol. 2
(see *RMB* for 1984, p. 152), rev. by Peter J. Manning in *KSJ*
35 (1986): 201–03; by Leslie A. Marchand in *SiR* 25 (1986):
567–71; vols. 1 and 2 rev. by Peter W. Graham in *TWC* 17
(1986): 219–21.

OPIE

Opie, Amelia. *Adeline Mowbray, or, The Mother and Daughter*,
intro. by Jeanette Winterson. London, Boston, and Henley:
Pandora Press, 1986. Pp. viii+275. £4.95.

Mrs. Mowbray brings up her daughter as a free thinker
but is horrified when Adeline stands by those principles,
refuses marriage, and lives with the man she loves. After
escaping a planned rape by her stepfather, losing her friends,
and being disowned by her mother, Adeline finds herself in
the modern dilemma of belonging to a supposedly progressive
society that refuses help or respect to anyone living outside
its terms. First published in 1804 and set in the Libertarian
aftermath of the French Revolution, *Adeline Mowbray* is based
on the life of Mary Wollstonecraft. The novel makes no moral
judgments, and in that sense is closer to a modern novel than
its Victorian successors. (Helen Cooper)

PALMER

Palmer, Samuel. "An Address to the Electors of West Kent,
1832." *BiQ* 19 (Fall 1985): 60–68.

Reviews of book previously listed:

LISTER, Raymond, *The Paintings of Samuel Palmer* (see *RMB*
for 1985, pp. 148–49), rev. by David Blayney Brown in *BM*
128 (June 1986): 436–37; by Martin Butlin ("Connoisseurship
and the Palmer Fakes") in *BIQ* (1986): 155; by Graham
Reynolds in *Apollo* 123 (1986): 288.

PEACOCK

Bachinger, K.E. "How Sherwood Forest Became the Valley of
Many-Colored Grass: Peacock's *Maid Marian* as a Source for
Poe's 'Eleanora.'" *AN&Q* 24 (1986): 72–75.

Burns, Bryan. "The Classicism of Peacock's *Gryll Grange*."
  KSMB 36 (1985): 89-101.

Burns, Bryan. *The Novels of Thomas Love Peacock.* London:
  Croom Helm; New York: Barnes and Noble, 1985. Pp. 256.
  $27.50.
    Rev. by Bill Ruddick in *CritQ* 27,3 (Fall 19850: 91.
    Not seen.

Butler, Marilyn. "Druids, Bards and Twice-Born Bacchus:
  Peacock's Engagement with Primitive Mythology." *KSMB* 36
  (1985): 57-76.

Dawson, Carl. "Peacock's Comedy: A Retrospective Glance."
  KSMB 36 (1985): 102-13.

Joukovsky, Nicholas A. "Peacock Before *Headlong Hall*: A New
  Look at His Early Years." *KSMB* 36 (1985): 1-40.

The Keats-Shelley Memorial Bulletin 36 (1985). Special issue
  on Thomas Love Peacock. Pp. 126. £4.00.

  Except for a review of a production of *The Cenci*, the body
of this issue of the *Keats-Shelley Memorial Bulletin*, edited
by Timothy Webb with Peter Garside as guest joint-editor, is
devoted to Peacock, printing six papers given at a Peacock
"bicentenary" conference at Gregygnog Hall, Powys, on July
16-18, 1984. The pieces are by recognized Peacock scholars:
Bryan Burns, Marilyn Butler, Carl Dawson, Nicholas Joukovsky,
Lionel Madden, and Howard Mills. They cover a range from
the factual to the speculative. At one end are Joukovsky's
harvest from his work on Peacock's letters of a scrupulously
detailed survey of "Peacock before *Headlong Hall*" and Madden's
examination of "The Welsh Dimension in Peacock's Life and
Work"; at the other are the personal and critical reflections
of Dawson's "Peacock's Comedy: A Retrospective Glance."
Mills considers "Peacock and Music"; Burns examines "The
Classicism of Peacock's *Gryll Grange*"; Butler offers a
learned discussion of "Peacock's Engagement with Primitive
Mythology," placing his use of myth illuminatingly in the
context of the work of contemporary primitivists and its
religious and political implications. Despite the commemorative background, these essays are not effusions of enthusiasts;
the tone is scholarly and moderate. But the writers obviously
feel and make a plausible case for the importance of Peacock.
(J.E.J.)

Madden, Lionel. "'Terrestrial Paradise': The Welsh Dimension in Peacock's Life and Work." *KSMB* 36 (1985): 41-56.

Mills, Howard. "The Dirty Boots of the Bourgeoisie: Peacock on Music." *KSMB* 36 (1985): 77-88.

Mulvihill, James. "A Tookean Presence in Peacock's *Melincourt*." *ES* 67 (1986): 216-20.

   Argues that Mr. Sarcastic is modeled on John Horne Tooke.

Simpson, Roger. "A Source for Peacock's *The Misfortunes of Elphin*." *N&Q* 33 (June 1986): 165-66.

   Actually three places from which Peacock could have derived the "Melvas" episode.

See also Reiman ("Shelley, P.B.").

PORDEN

See King-Hele ("Darwin").

RADCLIFFE

See Cottom ("English 3. Criticism").

REYNOLDS

Auty, Giles. "Reconsidering Reynolds." *S*, Feb. 1, 1986, pp. 32-33.

   Thoughts on an exhibition at the Royal Academy.

Hayes, John. "Reflecting on Reynolds at the Royal Academy: Two Hundred Years On." *Apollo* 123 (1986): 246-53.

Penny, Nicholas, ed. *Reynolds*. London: Royal Academy of Arts, in assoc. with Weidenfeld and Nicolson, 1986. Pp. 408; 151 col. pls. £20.00, paper £10.95.

   Rev. (with books on Degas and Pompeo Batoni) by Francis Haskell ("What's in a Portrait?") in *NYRB*, March 27, 1986, pp. 7-10; by Oliver Millar ("Reynolds at the Royal Academy") in *BM* 128 (March 1986): 228-30 and Duncan Robinson ("Reynolds Reviewed"), *ibid.*: 230-32.
   Rev. by Pat Rogers in *TLS*, Jan. 31, 1986, p. 117 as a "superb catalogue" with "the best short introduction current-ly available."
   Exhibition catalogue.

Penny, Nicholas. "Reynolds and Picture Frames." *BM* 128 (Oct. 1986): 810-24. 25 illus.

   The first of a series of "occasional articles on the history of frames."

Tschern, Nadia. "Reynolds' Streatham Portraits and the Art of Intimate Biography." *BM* 128 (Jan. 1986): 4-10. 10 illus.

   The subjects of the portraits include Oliver Goldsmith, Samuel Johnson, Charles Burney, and Reynolds himself.

Waterhouse, Ellis K. "Reynolds, Angelica Kauffmann and Lord Boringdon." *Apollo* 122 (1985): 270-74.

See also Altick, Barrell, Hayes ("English 2. Environment").

Review of book previously listed:

   JONES, Leonidas M., *The Life of John Hamilton Reynolds* (see *RMB* for 1984, p. 154), rev. by Ralph M. Wardle in *KSJ* 35 (1986): 205-07.

SCOTT, J.

Review of book previously listed:

   O'LEARY, Patrick, *Regency Editor: Life of John Scott* (see *RMB* for 1983, p. 127), rev. by J.H. Alexander in *YES* 16 (1986): 292-93; by John O. Hayden in *SLJ* 12, supp. 23 (1985): 54-56.

See also Bromwich ("Jeffrey").

SCOTT, W.

Alexander, J.H. "Scott's 'The Chase' and Wordsworth's 'Hart-Leap Well.'" *Scott Newsletter* 9 (1986): 10-13.

   Wordsworth's poem may have been influenced by Scott's anonymous translation of Bürger's ballad.

Alexander, J.H. "The Year's Work in Scottish Literary and Linguistic Studies 1983: Scott." *SLJ*, supp. 23 (1985): 27-30.

   Review of some 20 notes and articles.

A.S.B. "Scott for Scotland." *BC* 35 (Fall 1986): 281-92.

   Celebrates the return of valuable Scott material to the National Library of Scotland: the long-lost set of the

Waverley novels in which Scott entered late revisions, plus
various manuscripts, mostly of the novels and letters. The
Pforzheimer sold them to Scotland because they are "thinning
down" in order to concentrate more on Shelley and his circle.

Bann, Stephen. *The Clothing of Clio: A Study of the Representation of History in Nineteenth-Century Britain and France.*
Cambridge University Press, 1984. Pp. xii+196. $42.50.

Chapter 5, entitled "The Historical Composition of Place:
Byron and Scott," proposes that by comparing Scott's relation
to Abbotsford (and Melrose and Dryburgh) and Byron's to
Newstead Abbey we can explain the great contrast between the
two contemporary poets' attitudes toward history--between
Byron's ironic view, which characteristically decomposes
history into fragments, and Scott's naive view, which recovers
and recreates the wholeness of history from its ruins. Both
Washington Irving and Melanie Klein inform Bann's fascinating
analysis of the way in which architecture can figure in the
poetic resistance to or appropriation of the past. (F.J.)

Beckett, Ruth. "Another Shakespearean Influence in *Waverley.*
Scott Newsletter 9 (1986): 2-7.

The debt of Scott's Colonel Talbot to Shakespeare's John
Talbot in *I Henry VI.*

Beiderwell, Bruce John. "Civil Punishment in the Waverley
Novels." Ann Arbor, Mich.: University Microfilms International, 1986.

Dissertation.

Beiderwell, Bruce. "The Reasoning of Those Times: Scott's
Waverley and the Problem of Punishment." *Clio* 15 (1986):
15-30.

Locke's *Second Treatise* and the "contemporary debate over
the reform of the criminal laws" provide the context for an
exploration of the "unevenness of justice" in *Waverley.*

Bell, Alan, et al. "Scott for Scotland." *BC* 35 (1986): 281-
92.

The National Library of Scotland now has the set of
Waverley novels marked with Scott's revisions for the Magnum
Opus edition and also Scott's manuscripts which were previously
held by the Pforzheimer Library.

Criscuola, Margaret M. "Constancy and Change: The Process of
   History in Scott's *Redgauntlet*." *SSL* 20 (1985):   123-36. ✓

   Scott's fictions explore the common pattern within historical change--constancy to a code--which he saw within distinct historical events. They do not, however, suggest
   that history has direction.

Dryden, Edgar A. "*Waverley* and American Romance: The Thematics
   of a Form." *Genre* 13 (1985);   335-61.

Garside, Peter. "Scott as a Political Journalist." *RES* (1986):
   503-17.

   On Scott's participation in the *Edinburgh Weekly Journal*
   "as a *sequential* process." Garside uncovers Scott's role
   in the journal by identifying his contributions, putting them
   in political context, and showing how they tended to play
   off against Ballantyne's editorship. (F.J.)

Garside, P.D. "Scott's First 'Letter on Reform': An Edited
   Version." *Scott Newsletter* 8 (1986):   2-14.

   The first of two letters intended for the *Edinburgh Weekly
   Journal*. When edited the "result is a surprisingly coherent
   and sometimes fluent critique of the political situation late
   in 1830, one which involves expression of some of Scott's
   most fundamental political beliefs."

Gordon, Robert C. "The Marksman of Ravenswood: Power and
   Legitimacy in *The Bride of Lammermoor*." *NCF* 41 (1986):
   49-71.

   "In one distinctive act [Edgar Ravenswood] exemplified
   all the virtues of action that landed possession could
   bestow ... his deed is romantically attractive in part because
   for more than a century before Scott, British polemicists
   had been engaged in a debate whose subject was ... the
   relationship between property and the capacity for action."
   Gordon's essay is an attempt to complete Alexander Welsh's
   line of argument in *The Hero of the Waverley Novels*, making
   use of the Antaeus myth to explain the significance of Edgar's
   rescue of Sir William Ashton and Lucy from the charging bull.
   (F.J.)

Groves, David. "'Lines Addressed to Miss Jarman, of the
   Theatre-Royal': A Poem by Walter Scott." *Scott Newsletter*
   9 (1986):   13-14.

Groves, David. "Sir Walter Scott to Thomas Pringle: A Letter."
    Scott Newsletter 7 (1985): 15-16.

Hewitt, David. "The Magnum Opus and the Pforzheimer Manuscripts."
    Scott Newsletter 8 (1986): 18-20.

Hewitt, David. "The New Edinburgh Edition of the Waverley
    Novels." *Scott Newsletter* 8 (1986): 18-20.

    A progress report.

Hurst, Clive. "The Dunston Collection." *BLR* 12 (1986): 177-
    203.

    This collection was discovered to contain "nearly a thousand
    volumes of early editions of Scott's novels."

Inboden, Robin Louise. "'The Music in My Heart I Bore': The
    Ballad Revival, Scott, and Wordsworth." Ann Arbor, Mich.:
    University Microfilms International, 1986.

    Dissertation.

Kerr, James P. "Fiction Against History; The Uses of Romance
    in the Waverley Novels." Ann Arbor, Mich.: University
    Microfilms International, 1986.

    Dissertation.

Kerr, James. "Scott's Dream of the Past: *The Bride of
    Lammermoor* as Political Fantasy." *SNNTS* 18 (1986): 125-42.

    The central critical problem posed by *The Bride* is "to
    establish the motives, at once aesthetic and political,
    which have generated the form of the novel and to understand
    why *The Bride* should appear to the readers as an attempt to
    fuse conflicting representational modes and how the novel's
    formal strategies work to resolve the very conflicts they
    enact." (By "political fantasy" Kerr means "the form in and
    through which history is retextualized in fiction.") What
    oft was thought but differently expressed. (F.J.)

Kerr, James. "Scott's Fable of Regeneration: *The Heart of
    Midlothian*." *ELH* 53 (1986): 801-20.

    Kerr attributes the mix of genres and the tensions that
    result from them in *Heart of Midlothian* to "Scott's effort,
    ultimately unsuccessful, to write an ambitious political
    fable"--one that shows through Jeanie Deans's pilgrimage to
    London and interview with Queen Caroline how a corrupt,
    oppressive society--a society where truth has no language--

might be redeemed. Kerr's comparison of Jeanie's language
first with Staunton's and then with the Queen's is the meat
of this substantial article. (F.J.)

Lamont, Claire, ed. *Waverley; or 'Tis Sixty Years Since.*
(World's Classics.) Oxford University Press, 1986.
Pp. xxxii+474. Paper $4.95.

Based on Lamont's 1981 edition for Clarendon Press.

Massie, Allan. "James Hogg and Sir Walter Scott: A Study in
Friendship." *EDH* 44 (1986): 63-85.

A lecture given to the Royal Society of Literature com-
memorating the 150th anniversary of Hogg's death (in 1985).
Hence the emphasis falls on Hogg. Of special interest is
Massie's explanation "for the failure of [the] friendship
to develop as one would ideally wish to see a friendship
between two men of genius develop." Massie's view of Hogg
as a postmodern will come as a surprise to many. (F.J.)

Mitchell, Jerome. "Scott Holdings in the Library at Schloss
Corvey." *Scott Newsletter* 8 (1986): 14-17.

Mitchell surmises that this is "the largest cache of Scott's
works in first (or early) editions and of early works about
him that one is likely to find in West Germany or in any
other German-speaking country." (F.J.)

Overton, W.J. "Scott, the Short Story and History: 'The Two
Drovers.'" *SSL* 21 (1986): 210-25.

Scott's short stories "enable a more radical view of
history than do Scott's novels" because stories are less
available than novels to "a progressive, Whig interpretation
of history. Instead they present history as the product
of basic economic and cultural tensions." A strong article.
(F.J.)

Smith, Janet Adam. "Scott's Magnum Opus Returns." *TLS*, April
18, 1986, p. 421.

Brief account of how Scott's own corrected copy of the Magnum
Opus, which left Britain in 1929, returned (along with several
manuscripts belonging to the Pforzheimer Collection) to the
National Library in time for the editors of the forthcoming
Edinburgh edition of the Waverley novels to benefit from it.
(F.J.)

Smith, Louise Z. "Dialectic, Rhetoric, and Anthropology in
    Scott's *Waverley.*" *SSL* 21 (1986): 43-52.

    The newer elements in Scott's fictions--dialectical
    rhetoric and anthropological historicism--are what distin-
    guishes them from eighteenth-century fiction. The essay
    includes an instructive comparison of Scott's fictions with
    those of Charlotte Smith. (F.J.)

Sroka, Kenneth M. "Scott's Aesthetic Parable: A Study of
    Old Mortality's Two-Part Structure." *ELWIU* 10 (1983): 183-
    97.

    By emphasizing the historical in part 1 and the fictional
    in part 2, the form "implicitly instructs the reader in the
    independence of and interdependence between fiction and
    history in the historical novel."

Sutherland, Kathryn. "Travel Books, Fishing Manuals, and
    Scott's *Redgauntlet.*" *SLJ* 13 (1986): 20-30.

    Skillfully demonstrates the influence of the travel book,
    particularly Richard Franck's *Northern Memoirs,* which Scott
    edited in 1821, but also Johnson's *Journey to the Western
    Islands of Scotland,* on *Redgauntlet,* "arguably Scott's most
    topographical novel." Sutherland does not neglect the in-
    fluence of Scott's own traveling in Northumberland and,
    subsequently, Liddesdale when a young man. (F.J.)
    Championing salmon spearing against the new stake net
    fishing in the manner of the Luddites. (T.L.A.)

Tait, Margaret. "*The Surgeon's Daughter*: Possible Sources."
    Scott Newsletter 9 (1986): 7-10.

Tulloch, Graham. "Imagery in *The Highland Widow.*" *SSL* 21
    (1986): 147-57.

    The imagery supports "a complex but consistent view of
    historical change in the Highlands." (F.J.)

Valente, Joseph. "Upon the Braes: History and Hermeneutics
    in *Waverley.*" *SiR* 25 (1986): 251-76.

    At the center of the novel's structure is the antithesis
    of history ("not a given in *Waverley*") and romance: "Every
    pertinent aspect of the novel rests upon the braes [the
    border] between historical fact and romantic fancy." By
    marrying a "protostructuralist hermeneutic to a proto-histo-
    rical one" (the principle innovation in *Waverley*) Scott took
    a step that makes him fully contemporary. (F.J.)

Whitmore, Daniel. "Bibliolatry and the Rule of the Word:
A Study of Scott's *Old Mortality*." *PQ* 65 (1986): 243-62.

Bibliolaters or literalists are important figures in Scott.
Marginal in most novels, where they are accommodated or ex-
pelled from community, in *Old Mortality*, where they occur in
both camps, they are destroyed. Whitmore explores the nexus
between literalism and tragedy, with results that enable him
to answer most of the objections to the novel's concluding
chapters. By this reading *Old Mortality* is a more impressive
performance than even its greatest admirers had thought it
to be. First-rate piece of work. (F.J.)

Whitmore, Daniel. "Fagin, Effie Deans, and the Spectacle of
the Courtroom." *Dickens Quarterly* 3 (1987): 132-34.

The trial scene in the penultimate chapter of *Oliver Twist*
has been traced, in certain aspects, to De Quincey's *Confessions*; an equally probable source is noted—in convincing
detail—in chapter 22 of Scott's *The Heart of Midlothian*.

See also Altick ("English 2. Environment"); Cottom, Parkinson
("English 3. Criticism"); Rosenberg ("Carlyle"); Harwell
("The Gothic"); Bottoni, Chandler ("Italian 3. Manzoni").

Reviews of books previously listed:

ALEXANDER, J.H., and David Hewitt, eds., *Scott and His
Influence* (see *RMB* for 1983, pp. 128-30), rev. by Ian Campbell
in *SSL* 21 (1986): 318-19; ANDERSON, James, *Sir Walter Scott
and History, with Other Papers* (see *RMB* for 1982, pp. 129-
30), rev. by Peter Garside in *YES* 15 (1985): 307-09;
CRAWFORD, Thomas, *Walter Scott* (see *RMB* for 1982, p. 130),
rev. by J.H. Alexander in *YES* 16 (1986): 231-34; McMASTER,
Graham, *Scott and Society* (see *RMB* for 1982, pp. 133-34),
rev. by Peter Garside in *YES* 16 (1986): 290-92 as "an
important book"; MILLGATE, Jane, *Walter Scott: The Making
of the Novelist* (see *RMB* for 1984, pp. 157-59), rev. by
S. Monod in *EA* 39 (1986): 98-99 as "un livre élégant et
distingué, remarquable en particulier par sa cohérence et
par sa clarité!"; by Kathryn Sutherland in *RES* 37 (1986):
425-26; by Edward Wagenknecht in *SiR* 25 (1986): 159-61;
SHAW, Harry E., *The Forms of Historical Fiction: Sir Walter
Scott and His Successors* (see *RMB* for 1983, pp. 131-32, and
RMB for 1984, p. 160), rev. by Kenneth M. Sroka in *SLJ*,
suppl 24 (1986): 7-9 as helping to "establish Scott as the
source and centre rather than the predecessor, of all subsequent great historical fiction."

Composite review:

Whitmore, Daniel. *MP* 84 (1986): 94-99.

Reviews Millgate's *Walter Scott* and Shaw's *Forms of Historical Fiction* (see above) as, taken together, "a significant advance."

SEWARD

See King-Hele ("Darwin").

SHELLEY, Mary

Forrey, Steven Earl. "The Hideous Progenies of Richard Brinsley Peake: Frankenstein on the Stage, 1823 to 1826." *ThR* 11 (1986): 13-31.

McGavran, James Holt, Jr. "Shelley, Virginia Woolf, and *The Waves*: A Balcony of One's Own." *SAR* 48,4 (Nov. 1983): 59-73.

Finds evidence in the novel of Woolf's ambivalent attitude toward Shelley. One senses that McGavran's own knowledge of the poet is second-hand, not quite adequate to grasp the complexities of Woolf's response. (R.M.R.)

McGuire, Karen. "The Artist as Demon in Mary Shelley, Stevenson, Walpole, Stoker, and King." *Gothic* 1 (1986): 1-5.

Newman, Beth. "Narratives of Seduction and the Seductions of Narrative: The Frame Structure of Frankenstein." *ELH* 53 (1986): 141-53.

Pitcher, Edward W.R. "*Frankenstein* as Short Fiction: A Unique Adaptation of Mary Shelley's Novel." *SSF* 20 (1983): 49-52.

Describes an 1825 adaptation called *The Monster Made by Man; or, the Punishment of Presumption.*

Roberts, Robin Ann. *A New Species: Female Tradition in Science Fiction from Mary Shelley to Doris Lessing.* Ann Arbor, Mich.: University Microfilms International, 1985.

Dissertation.

Vasbinder, Samuel. *Scientific Attitudes in Mary Shelley's "Frankenstein."* Ann Arbor, Mich.: University Microfilms International Research Press, 1985.

Not received.

Veeder, William. *Mary Shelley and Frankenstein: The Fate of
Androgyny.* University of Chicago Press, 1986. Pp. ix+277.

    This important book, as the late James Rieger noted in
a dust-jacket blurb, will provoke: after it is read, "neither
the Shelleys nor [*Frankenstein*] will look quite the same
again." Veeder is a good reader of the text of *Frankenstein*,
an equally good reader of that text in the contexts of Mary
Shelley's novels and letters and journals (no tales of stories
used, however), and a provocative and sometimes rash reader
of *Frankenstein* in the context of Mary Shelley's life. The
net effect of Veeder's book is a renewed, indeed increased,
conviction that Mary (as she is called by Veeder) was a
brilliant artist who combined innumerable themes, motifs,
patterns, and relationships into a novel that deserves a
greater accolade than George Levine's earlier remark that
Frankenstein is "the most important minor novel in English."
    Veeder's thesis is that Mary was passionately concerned
in her life and fiction with the psychological ideal of
androgyny and the frequent and painful reality of its de-
generation into bifurcation. He believes that Mary's exploration of that conflict between the ideal and the reality,
between selfless Agape and selfish Eros, was caused by a
discordant relation with Shelley that was perceptible to her
as early as 1816, a discord contextualized by the other dis-
cords that both Mary and Shelley experienced separately in
their lives with their own parents and families. No easy
task before him, Veeder attempts to read *Frankenstein* as a
novel that reflects Mary's relations with Shelley and their
circles (Byron, Claire, etc.), with her own parents and family,
and with Shelley's parents and family. Veeder succeeds when
his thesis embraces and illuminates the generalities of Mary's
personal experiences; he does not always succeed, however,
when he too rigidly reads (and sometimes overreads) the
specifics of *Frankenstein* as an allegorical narrative of the
life of Shelley, especially when the evidence of that life
is provided by hearsay from the likes of Hogg, Medwin, and
Trelawny or by post-*Frankenstein* events and poems after 1818.
    All of the by now familiar ingredients of *Frankenstein* are
subsumed here: doubling, motherless children, head killing
heart, trips north and south, ice and snow, and the like.
What Veeder adds is a sensitivity to the language of the novel,
a passionate conviction to counter incorrect readings by
earlier critics, and an eagerness to address new issues.
Most readers of Veeder will enjoy and agree with the analyses
of the meanings behind the characters' names in *Frankenstein*;
will be bemused and possibly angered by the extremes of his
one liners (e.g., "Mary as domestic feminist portrays her husband as domestic assassin"); will tolerate but not readily

accept a view of life and art so intertwined that Shelley
in 1822 in the Lerici strangling episode could be "acting
out four years after *Frankenstein* events in the novel which
reflected his murderous will before 1818"; will applaud
chapter 5 on "The Divided Self and Man" that analyzes the
important father-child relations in the novel, in the Shelleys
personal experiences, and in Shelley's poetry; and, finally,
will welcome answers to questions about the death of Alphonse,
the survival of Ernest, and the moral culpability of both
Walter and Victor—for the latter, Veeder notes that even
"Frankenstein has missed the point of *Frankenstein*." (C.E.R.)

Womersley, David. "Hume and Mary Shelley." *N&Q*, n.s. 33 (June
19860: 164-65.

   The influence of Hume on a passage from *Frankenstein*
describing the Monster's response to books.

See also Homans ("English 3. Criticism"); Hartwell, McGuire,
   and other entries under "The Gothic"; Gates ("Hunt"); Veeder
   ("Shelley, P.B."); Sauer ("German 2. General").

SHELLEY, P.B.

Barker-Benfield, B.C. "The Honeymoon of Joseph and Henrietta
   Chichester, with Daniel Roberts' Memories of Byron and
   Shelley." *The Bodleian Library Record* 12 (1986): 119-41.

   On honeymoon on the Continent from January 1827 through
August 1829, the Chichesters recorded in their diary for
13 September 1828 the dinner conversation of Daniel Roberts,
who had been with Byron and Shelley in 1822. Hearsay evidence
is here provided on such matters as the two poets' wager
of £1000 and its aftermath, Leigh Hunt and the *Liberal*,
Shelley's first marriage, Captain Hay and Fletcher, the two
poets at billiards and on *Beppo*, Trelawny, and Shelley's death.
Barker-Benfield, as always, provides exceptionally detailed
contexts for this new document, which Charles Cox sold to
the Bodleian in 1985. (C.E.R.)

Behrendt, Stephen C., ed. *Percy Bysshe Shelley: Zastrozzi and
   St. Irvyne.* (The World's Classics.) Oxford University Press,
   1986. Pp. xxxi+206. Paper $3.95.

Blank, G.K. "Shelley's Wind of Influence." *PQ* 64 (1985):
   475-91.

Blank, G.K. "Shelley's Wordsworth; The Dessicated Celandine."
   ESA 29 (1986): 87-96.

Shelley's little-known "Verses Written on a Celandine" (they're not in the Norton edition, nor the OXSA 1970 revision) show the poet "usurping Wordsworth's own imagery to disclaim yet credit the older poet." Good work. (T.L.A.)

Brinkley, Robert A. "On the Composition of 'Mont Blanc': Staging a Wordsworthian Scene." *ELN* 24,2 (1986): 45-57.

Burling, William J. "New Light on Shelley's 'Lines to--.'" *KSJ* 35 (1986): 20-23.

A Sotheby's catalogue text of Shelley's "Sonnet to Byron" seems to confirm the authority of Mary Shelley's fair copy of this sonnet in Bodleian MS Shelley adds. d.7 (printed in Robinson, *Shelley and Byron*, pp. 201-02).

Cason, Robert Ernst. *Shelley, Pindar and the Ideology of the Ode*. Ann Arbor, Mich.: University Microfilms International, 1986.

Dissertation.

Cave, Richard Allen. *"The Cenci* in Performance." *KSMB* 36 (1985): 114-18.

Praise for Debbie Sherwell's production at the Bristol Old Vic. Yet Cave (and possibly Sherwell and Leonie Mellinger, who played Beatrice) seem to have misunderstood Beatrice in the last acts: Shelley's Beatrice does *not* "shift from victim to a visionary who finds in crime a clarity of insight"; although "suffering and guilt can shape the imagination for good," such shaping does not occur in Shelley's *The Cenci*. Nevertheless, even if Shelley's intentions were misread, Cave's encomia make us wish we were there. (C.E.R.)

Crisman, William. "Psychological Realism and Narrative Manner in Shelley's 'Alastor' and 'The Witch of Atlas.'" *KSJ* 35 (1986): 126-48.

Although a little heavy-handed in tracing the Poet's and the Witch's psychological problems to their childhood experiences, Crisman illuminates many relations in and between these two poems, both of which contain psychologically complex *characters*, whose motivations and actions are worth fuller study. Denied a mother's love in their youth, both the Poet and the Witch, Crisman argues, deny others as a consequence; and both physically dissipate within settings and plots that likewise dissolve. (C.E.r.)

Curran, Stuart. "The Political Prometheus." *SiR* 25 (1986):
  429-55. 3 illus.

  Curran discovers meaningful parallels and verbal links
  with *Prometheus Unbound* in contemporary works, mostly literary,
  in which Prometheus is "an avatar of revolution against specific oppressions: civil, racial, sexual, and religious."
  One of these "representative examples" is Blake's *Visions of
  the Daughters of Albion*. Another is a ballet, *Prometeo*,
  choreographed by Salvatore Vigano, which Curran believes
  Shelley may have learned of in Milan. (I.H.C.)

Dutt, Anjali. *Images of Solitude in Shelley's Poetry*. Ann
  Arbor, Mich.: University Microfilms International, 1985.

  Dissertation.

Essick, Robert N. "'A Shadow of Some Golden Dream': Shelley's
  Language in *Epipsychidion*." *PLL* 22 (1986): 165-75.

  "Reading *Epipsychidion* as a proleptic allegory of certain
  modern issues in the philosophy of language," the essay
  strikes chords, but leaves the third sphere pilotless at
  times. (T.L.A.)

Freedman, William. "Postponement and Perspectives in Shelley's
  'Ozymandias.'" *SiR* 25 (1986): 63-73.

  "No less than the judgment of Ozymandias ... Shelley's and
  our own is subject to the ravages of time" (73).

Gold, Elise M. "*King Lear* and Aesthetic Tyranny in Shelley's
  The Cenci, *Swellfoot The Tyrant*, and *The Witch of Atlas*."
  ELN 24,1 (1986): 58-70.

Gutschera, Deborah A. "The Drama of Reenactment in Shelley's
  The Revolt of Islam." *KSJ* 35 (1986): 111-25.

  Subsuming recent articles on the structural patterns in
  Shelley's epic, Gutschera also notes the repetition or reenactment of Shelley's theme in the four successive parts
  of the poem: the discursive essay of the preface; the
  dedicatory stanzas to Mary; the introductory vision of
  Canto 1; and the narratives of Laon and Cythna in the remaining cantos.

Hoagwood, Terence Allan. "Shelley, Milton, and the Poetics
  of Ideological Transformation: *Paradise Lost* and the Prologue to *Hellas*." *RP&P* 10 (1986): 25-48.

Houlihan, James W. "Lyrico-Narrative in Pindar and Shelley."
Ann Arbor, Mich.: University Microfilms International, 1986.
Dissertation.

Kearney, Martin F. "Hawthorne's Beatrice Rappaccini: Unlock-
ing Her Paradoxical Nature with a Shelleyan Key." *CLAJ* 29
(1986): 309-17.

Points out some obvious parallels with Shelley's Beatrice,
but the reading of *The Cenci* is superficial at best. (R.M.R.)

Ogle, Robert B. "Shelley's Whirlwind Imagery in *Prometheus
Unbound*: A Segment of Its Evolution." *ELN* 23,3 (1986):
36-41.

Brief consideration of possible antecedents in the Bible,
Milton, Addison, Pope, and Moore.

Quinn, Mary A. "'The Daemon of the World': Shelley's Antidote
to the Skepticism of 'Alastor.'" *SEL* 25 (1985): 755-74.

Quinn, Mary A. "Leigh Hunt's Presentation Copy of Shelley's
Alastor Volume." *KSJ* 35 (1986): 17-20.

With Shelley's emendation, line 443 of *Alastor* reads
"Of desperate hope convulsed his curling lip."

Rees, John. *Shelley's Jane Williams*. London: William Kimber,
1985. Pp. 226.

Reider, John. "The 'One' in 'Prometheus Unbound.'" *SEL* 25
(1985): 775-800.

Reiman, Donald H., ed. *The Mask of Anarchy: Facsimiles of the
Intermediate Fair-Copy Holograph in the Ashley Collection,
the British Library, the Press-Copy Transcription by Mary W.
Shelley (with Additions and Corrections by P.B. Shelley) in
the Library of Congress, Proofs of the First Edition, 1832
(Corrected by Leigh Hunt) in the Luther A. Brewer Collection,
University of Iowa, and A Holography Addition to Leigh Hunt's
Preface in the Ashley Collection, the British Library*. (The
Manuscripts of the Younger Romantics: Percy Bysshe Shelley,
2.) New York: Garland Publishing, 1985. Pp. xxiii+157.
$75.00.

Reiman, Donald H., ed. *Peer Bell the Third: A Facsimile of
the Press-Copy Transcript by Mary W. Shelley, with Additions
and Corrections by Percy Bysshe Shelley (Bodleian MS Shelley
adds. c. 5, folios 50-69) and The Triumph of Life: A Facsimile*

*of Shelley's Holograph Draft (Bodleian MS Shelley adds. c.
4, folios 18-58) Together with Fragments in the Carl H.
Pforzheimer Library and in the Collection of Lord Abinger.*
(The Bodleian Shelley Manuscripts: Percy Bysshe Shelley,
1.) New York: Garland Publishing, 1986. Pp. xiii+347.
$90.00.

Reiman, Donald H., ed., and Doucet Devin Fischer, assoc. ed.
Shelley and his Circle 1773-1822, vols. 7-8. Harvard
University Press, 1986. Pp. xlvii+1228.

Reading the latest volumes of *Shelley and his Circle* is
like listening to a favorite aunt and uncle, whom we haven't
seen since 1973 (they visited in 1961 and 1970 as well),
tell us more about the family of which we are a part. At
the same time that they bring the history of our family more
up to date (volume 8 advances the history seven months, from
January through July 1820), they retrospectively fill in the
details provided in their earlier visits (volume 7 provides
new information on the period from 1815 through the end of
1819)--and, as always, they occasionally look back even
farther to provide the contexts for the family history. Consequently, anyone interested in the facts of Shelley, Byron,
Godwin, and their circles should take the time to listen to
the whole of this latest discourse, should be willing to
take the latest facts and correct those given earlier (since
the last visit, over 1300 new MS items have been acquired),
and should patiently await future visits when this "*pro-
sopography*" (8: xxxvii) will be continued.

My task here is to provide enough information to encourage
those who know *Shelley and his Circle* to read the two latest
volumes and to make others aware that the volumes are as
fundamental to research on the Romantics as the *DNB*, as collected editions of poetry and letters, and as all of those
other comprehensive tools that we use (or should use) so often.
Those unable to purchase the eight volumes thus far published
should at least keep xeroxes of the four indices at hand in
order to take advantage of the extensive literary research
of Kenneth Neill Cameron, Donald H. Reiman, Doucet Devin
Fischer, and their assistants, all of whom evidence a love
and respect for truth that makes these volumes so valuable.
To indicate the contents of volumes 7-8, I turn to Shelley
first and find authoritative texts for thirteen Shelley
letters: to Peacock of July 17, 1816, May [2?], 1820,
and July 12, 1820; to Lackington, Allen and Co. of October
23, 1817; to English, English & Becks of March 10, 1820;
to Horace Hall of March 19, 1820, March 24, 1820, and May
26, 1820; to Hogg of April 20, 1820 and July 1, 1820; to

Charles Ollier of May 14, 1820; to Byron of May 26, 1820;
and to Samuel Hamilton of July 1, 1820. Of these letters,
four (those to English and to Hall) are not in Jones's
edition of Shelley's letters; eight are printed by Jones
from previously printed and usually inaccurate texts; and
only one (to Lackington) was printed by Jones from MS.
Hence the need to use *Shelley and his Circle* itself as a
standard edition to supplement Jones and, in the process,
to benefit from the extensive commentary on these letters
and the other documents here printed. In the case of the
letter to Hogg of April 20, 1820, for example, Reiman is at
his finest, correcting errors in Jones's earlier text,
glossing Shelley's "P.S." on the Boinvilles with extensive
comments on the later life of Harriet de Boinville and her
daughter Cornelia Turner, punctuating that essay with
transcriptions of unpublished letters from Harriet de Boinville and Clair Clairmont that are among the Abinger MSS,
and linking Shelley's love of women with his love for classical antiquities and his attempts to understand historical
process (8: 977-1001). Commentaries on the other letters
reveal equally important items: a reminder that "no scholar
can afford to rely solely on the most recent edition or
biography" (7: 39n.); a long essay on "Shelley and the
Upholsterers of Bath" (8: 827-42) that explains Shelley's
indebtedness of over £1000.00 to the upholsterers English,
English, & Becks, who had furnished Albion House at Great
Marlow in 1817 (this essay concludes with a list of the documents on this matter, forty-three dated from February 4, 1820,
to December [? 1828], that are in the Pforzheimer Collection);
an account of Shelley's business relations with an "H. Hall"
at Kleiber's bank in Florence (8: 890-97, 915-22, 1058-63)
that contains such diverse items as remarks on the Shelleys'
relationship with Madame Merveilleux du Plantis, important
corrections to the Jones edition (1061n. in Jones, "a fragment tentatively dated '?November-December 1819'[2: 160]--
is clearly the end of the incomplete letter of January 17,
1820 [2: 169-70]"), and a conjecture (1062n.) that Medwin
contacted Charles Ollier in June 1819 (evidence assembled
by this reviewer confirms this conjecture); an important
emendation (1016 and n.) of a phrase in Shelley's letter to
Hunt of April 10, 1822 (from "time has corrected me" in
Jones [2: 405] to "time has corrupted me"); and the increasing evidence that both Shelley's and Peacock's satires were
ideological rather than personal, even in the case of *Peter
Bell the Third* (8: 1027).

Among the other Shelley documents printed in these two
volumes, the most important is "Athanase: A Fragment," the
holograph press-copy MS that Reiman dates ?December 1819 in

his provocative essay "Shelley as Athanase" (7: 110-60).
Reiman convincingly argues for the importance and the
separateness of this 124-line "Fragment" (what is normally
printed as part 1 of a text that Mary Shelley and other
editors have enlarged), which concludes with "And so his
grief remained--let it remain--untold," a line reminiscent
of Shelley's narrative strategies in *Julian and Maddalo*.
According to Reiman, the "portrait of Athanase shows the
reuniting of Shelley's inner and outer selves embodied in
the maniac and Julian"; the good, moral, unhappy, and reti-
cent Athanase contrasts the earlier Shelleyan poet-heroes
who were often men of "great moral fortitude and resource-
fulness"; and the "poem represents, perhaps, Shelley's deepest
poetic exploration of his own motivations" in the context
of moral action and good works that would "bring him no
ultimate reward." As in the case of all such extended essays
on Shelley's poetry in *Shelley and his Circle*, they represent
the *sine qua non* of all subsequent research: dates are provided for first, intermediate, and final texts; personal,
historical, and social contexts are interwoven to provide
carefully reasoned explication; and comprehensiveness of
research and fullness of thinking are evident at every turn
of the page.

Shelley is, of course, not the only figure represented in
these two volumes. In fact, much of the two volumes is made
up of Byron and Guiccioli papers, prefaced by two excellent
essays by Doucet Devin Fischer, "'Countesses and Cobblers'
Wives': Byron's Venetian Mistresses" (7: 163-214) and
"Countess Guiccioli's Byron: 'Mio Byron'" (7: 373-487).
These essays and the approximately 150 letters, most from
Guiccioli to Byron, are essential reading for an understanding
of Byron's life in Italy, his amatory relationships with
Marianna Segati, Margherita Cogni, and Arpalice Taruscelli,
and his last attachment with Guiccioli.

The extensive archive upon which Fischer based her second
essay includes not only the numerous Guiccioli letters but
also "several important Byron letters, two Shelley letters,
letters written by Francesca Silvestrini, manuscripts relating
to the Guiccioli separation ... , Pietro Gamba's papers, a
series of letters written to La Guiccioli by (among others)
Mary Shelley, Charles Barry, and Thomas Moore, Teresa Guiccioli
transcripts of Byron's poems, holograph accounts of her own
early life and the life she shared with Byron, and contemporary
biographies marked with her angry marginalia" (7: 376). Among
the other important Byron documents in this volume is a press-
copy MS of *Beppo*, which is preceded by Jerome J. McGann's
essay "'Mixed Company': Byron's *Beppo* and the Italian Medley"
(7: 234-57), which dates the MS, outlines various influences

on the poem, and claims that "*Beppo* is a crossroads in Byron's career as an artist, and is probably the most crucial single work in the entire canon." Elsewhere, Reiman argues that *The Lament of Tasso* shows "Byron at a great turning point in his life and poetry"--see the commentary on Byron to Murray, April 23, 1817 (7: 223). Space prevents me from detailing other contents of these two volumes. Suffice it to say that MSS of Trelawny, Sir Timothy Shelley, Peacock, Keats, Hunt, and Godwin make these two volumes essential reading for students of the Romantics. Upon reading the volumes, many will encounter important materials, including footnotes that record MSS and books in the Pforzheimer Collection that will not be published in *Shelley and His Circle*. Someone will certainly be interestd in learning the whereabouts of thirty-six letters that Charles Barry wrote to Guiccioli between 1823 and 1831 (7: 449n.), of over sixty letters and MSS by or relating to Thomas Campbell (7: 470n.), and a fair-copy MS of an unpublished three-volume novel by Lady Mount Cashell (8: 909). (C.E.R.)

Robinson, Charles E. "Shelley to Byron in 1814: A New Letter." *KSJ* 35 (1986): 104-10.

Robinson argues that this new ten-word letter ("Mr Shelley begs Lord Byron's acceptance of the inclosed poem"), dated June 2, 1814, probably concerns Shelley's "Feelings of a Republican on the Fall of Bonaparte."

Shawcross, John T. "Further Remarks on Milton's Influence: Shelley and Shaw." *MiltonQ* 20 (1986): 85-92.

Finds influence without anxiety in Shelley's response to Milton, but "negative reaction, even rebellion" in Shaw's.

Shealy, Ann. *The Ravaged Garden: A Critical Study of Shelley's "Epipsychidion."* Pompano Beach, Fla.: Exposition Press of Florida, 1985. Pp. x+86. $15.00.

Sperry, Stuart M. "The Ethical Politics of Shelley's *The Cenci*." *SiR* 25 (1986): 411-27.

Veeder, William. "The Negative Oedipus: Father, *Frankenstein*, and the Shelleys." *CritI* 12 (1986): 365-90.

Integrating "the traditional disciplines of biographical and close textual analyses," Veeder sets out not only to "confirm the prominence of father for the Shelleys but also [to] establish the ideal against which their most subversive

and important art was created." *The Revolt of Islam,*
Prometheus Unbound, and *The Cenci* are considered along with
Frankenstein. (I.H.C.)

Watson, George. "The Reckless Disciple: Godwin's Shelley."
HudR 39 (1986): 212-30.

The disciple was "reckless" in his misunderstanding of the
master's political theory.

Welburn, Andrew. *Power and Self-Consciousness in the Poetry
of Shelley.* New York: St. Martin's Press, 1986.

Not seen.

Welch, Dennis M. *"Queen Mab* and *An Essay on Man:* Scientific
Prophecy Versus Theodicy." *CLAJ* 29 (1986): 462-82.

"Shelley reworked several ideas and images from the *Essay*
in an effort to replace Pope's theodicy and its emphasis on
order, hierarchy, and submission with a scientific prophecy
based on Necessity, human potential, and evolutionary progress."

See also Dunbar ("English 1. Bibliography"); Mendilow ("English
2. Environment"); Applewhite, Baer, Bidney, Cave, Clausen,
Curran, Falck, Goslee, Hoagwood, Holmes, Piper, Roberts,   );
Schell, Wilkie ("English 3. Criticism"); Bidney ("Blake");
King-Hele ("Darwin"); Bromwich ("Jeffrey"); Veeder ("Shelley,
P.B."); Zach (German 2. General"); Klabes ("German 3.
Hölderlin").

Reviews of books previously listed.

EVEREST, Kelvin, ed., *Shelley Revalued: Essays from the
Gregygnog Conference* (see *RMB* for 1983, p. 135), rev. by
Daniel Hughes in *SiR* 24 (1985): 565-72; KEACH, William,
Shelley's Style (see *RMB* for 1984, pp. 165-66), rev. by
Stephen C. Behrendt (favorably) in *PQ* 65 (1986): 134-36;
rev. by Jerrold E. Hogle in *KSJ* 35 (1986): 183-88; by
Frederick Kirchoff in *ELN* 25,1 (1986): 102-03; by Stuart M.
Sperry (favorably) in *TWC* 17 (1986): 238-40; SCRIVENER,
Michael Henry, *Radical Shelley: The Philosophical Anarchism
and Utopian Thought of Percy Bysshe Shelley* (see *RMB* for
1982, pp. 143-45), rev. by Stuart Curran in *MLQ* 45 (1984):
91-94 (mixed); by P.M.S. Dawson in *YES* 16 (1986): 306-08;
by Morton D. Paley in *SiR* 24 (1985): 572-74.

Review article:

Newlyn, Lucy. "Shelley's Ambivalence." *EiC* 36 (1986): 263-
68.

Reviews William Keach's *Shelley's Style* (see *RMB* for 1985, pp. 165-66). Shelley emerges as "canny" and "duplicitous," and Keach as "a little remorseless."

SOUTHEY

Manogue, Ralph Anthony. "Robert Southey's *Wat Tyler*." *TN* 37 (1983): 22-24.

Brief discussion of a possible provincial production in 1817, with a reproduction of the playbill.

Southey, Robert. *Mr. Rowlandson's England*. Ed. John Steel. Antique Collectors' Club, 1985. Pp. 202; 250 illus. £14.95.

Rev. by Celina Fox in *BM* 128 (Dec. 1986): 90.
According to reviewer Fox, the text is condensed from "three volumes of *Letters from England*, written by Southey in the guise of a Spanish nobleman, Don Manuel Alvarez Espriella, and published in 1807"; "nearly all" the illustrations are after drawings and watercolors by Rowlandson.

See also Mendilow ("English 2. Environment"); Murphy ("Byron").

STUART, LOUISA

Rubinstein, Jill, ed. Lady Louisa Stuart, *Memoirs of Frances, Lady Douglas*. London and Edinburgh: Scottish Academic Press; Columbia University Press, 1985. Pp. xxii+106. $18.00.

Rev. enthusiastically (and anonymously) in *QQ* 93 (1986): 717 as a fine work by a largely unknown writer who was virtually unpublished in her lifetime. The book has a preface by J. Steven Watson; Lady Douglas lived from 1750 to 1817.

TIGHE

See King-Hele ("Darwin").

TURNER

Lindsay, Jack. *Turner: The Man and His Art*. London: Granada, 1985. Pp. 179; 13 col. pls., 13 b. & w. illus. £10.05.

Rev. by Graham Reynolds in *Apollo* 123 (1986): 288.

Rodner, William S. "Humanity and Nature in the Steamboat Paintings of J.M.W. Turner." *Albion* 18 (1986): 455-74. 6 illus.

"Turner's interest in this theme has been interpreted as a
clear indication of 'sympathy' with the Industrial Revolution,"
but he could see the steamer rendered helpless in the grip
of a storm system; he "captured the dramatic struggle between
human and environmental forces."

Stainton, Lindsay. *Turner's Venice.* London: British Museum
Publications, 1985. Pp. 77; 18 figs., 112 col. pls. £16.95.

Rev. by Richard Kingzett in *Apollo* 123 (1986): 218-19.

See also Paley ("General 2. Environment"); *Huntington Library
Quarterly* (Bryson); Barrell ("English 2. Environment");
Brennan ("Wordsworth").

Composite review:

Hartley, Craig. *BM* 128 (May 1986): 363-64.

Reviews the Jack Lindsay and Lindsay Stainton books listed
above.

WOLLSTONECRAFT

Harasym, S.D. "Ideology and Self: A Theoretical Discussion
of the 'Self' in Mary Wollstonecraft's Fiction." *ESC* 12
(1986): 163-77.

Although the focus, point, and aim of this essay are by no
means clear, it seems that Harasym intends to analyze the
problematic relations of self, writing, and feminist ideology
in Wollstonecraft's *Maria or The Wrongs of Woman.* The analysis,
however, proceeds by way of Hegel and Lacan and is punctuated
with numerous appeals to the authority of such writers as
Benveniste, Derrida, de Man, and Jameson. Since these writers
appear to be the ones who know, Harasym uses their terms not
only to define Wollstonecraft's intentions but also to expose
her failure to realize those intentions. On the one hand,
we are told that *Maria* was intended as a "Hegelian work of
art"--a self-conscious realization of the unified self whose
presence would enable Wollstonecraft to substantiate her
"paradoxically feminist, yet monolithic, ideology." On the
other hand, Harasym calls on Derrida, de Man, and Lacan to
explain why and how the realization of this intention is
"endlessly deferred and sutured between imaginary reconcilia-
tions and their symbolic representations."

Harasym's devotion to the contemporary theorists of signification slights Wollstonecraft's discursive and ideological

struggles, so much so that *Maria* appears to be little more
than evidence in support of a masterful set of truths--a
contemporary ideology. Although our readings of Wollstonecraft should be informed by a knowledge of contemporary
critical theory, they should not be swamped--or vamped--
by that knowledge and its good terms. Surely, there is room
for dialogue on such matters as the self, writing, and
ideology; and certainly there is still a need for feminist
struggle. (J.H-P.)

See also Erdman ("General 2. Environment"); Kirkham ("Austen");
Philp ("Godwin"); and Opie ("Opie").

Reviews of books previously listed:

FERGUSON, Moira, and Janet Todd, *Mary Wollstonecraft* (see
RMB for 1984, pp. 172-73), rev. in *Choice* 21 (1984): 1605;
HARDT, Ulrich H., ed., *A Critical Edition of Mary Wollstonecraft's "A Vindication of the Rights of Women"*: *With Stric-
tures on Political and Moral Subjects* (see *RMB* for 1984,
p. 173), rev. by J.D.F. in *N&Q* 31 (1984): 137-38; PENIGAULT-
DUHET, Paule, *Mary Wollstonecraft* (see *RMB* for 1985, p. 162),
rev. by Emily W. Sunstein in *KSJ* 35 (1986): 203-05.

WORDSWORTH, D.

Gittings, Robert, and Jo Manton. *Dorothy Wordsworth*. Oxford:
Clarendon Press; New York: Oxford University Press, 1985.
$17.95.

　　Rev. as a "scrupulous and sensitive biography" by Isabel
Colegate in *S*, March 30, 1985, pp. 24-25; as "distressingly
narrow, sexist, and ... outmoded" by Beth Darlington in *TWC*
17 (1986): 227-29; as "a disappointment, offering little
that is new" by Park Honan in *ContR* 247 (Sept. 1985): 165-
66.

Ruddick, Bill. "Dorothy Wordsworth's Life and Letters Reconsidered." *CritQ* 27 (1985): 45-49.

Woof, Pamela. "Dorothy Wordsworth, Writer." *TWC* 17 (1986):
95-110.

Wordsworth, Dorothy. *The Greens of Grasmere: A Narrative*.
Wolverhampton, England: Clark and Howard Books. Pp. 60.
Paper £1.50.

　　First published in 1936.
Not received.

See also Chase ("General 3. Criticism"); Homans ("English 3. Criticism").

Review of book previously listed:

HOMANS, Margaret, *Women Writers and Poetic Identity: Dorothy Wordsworth, Emily Brontë, and Emily Dickinson* (see *RMB* for 1981, p. 145), rev. by Anne K. Mellor in *RP&P* 10 (1986): 77-78.

WORDSWORTH, W.

Anderson, Erland. "Mean Objects, Not Ignoble Ends." *TWC* 17 (1986): 184-86.

   Reflections on the raven's nest episode in *Prelude* 1, brought on by hearing a lecture by a member of the Royal Society for the Protection of Birds delivered at the annual Bald Eagle Conference in Klamath Falls, Oregon. The author notes that "egg collecting, a typical English vice, is now outlawed" but remains a serious problem. The speaker "showed slides of the Lake District which he said he didn't dare to show in his own country for fear that an egg collector might be in the audience and, thus, recognize the location of the yet unprotected nest. One of the illegal collections he confiscated with the aid of a local constable contained over 22,000 eggs." The early worm gets the bird. (B.C.H.)

Bartlett, Brian. "'Inscrutable Workmanship': Music and Metaphors of Music in *The Prelude* and *The Excursion*." *TWC* 17 (1986): 175-80.

Beer, John, et al. "'The Barberry-Tree': Three 'Blithesome Blossoms.'" *RES* 37 (1986): 348-83.

   A reexamination, with new evidence, of the mysterious authorship of "The Barberry-Tree," discovered in 1964 and attributed to Wordsworth. John Beer opens the discussion with "Who Wrote 'The Barberry-Tree'?" presenting the case for Coleridge's authorship (349-59). J.C.C. Mays, in "The Authorship of 'The Barberry-Tree'" (360-70) demonstrates convincingly that the new evidence, proving it to be a parody, rules out Wordsworth as author; he suggests other possible authors, cautiously. Then Jonathan Wordsworth, "'The Barberry-Tree' Revisited" (371-77), briefly and dismissively rejects the parodic argument, to let "the vast majority" of the lines of the poem "scream out 'Wordsworth'" to him--thus evading any discussion of evidence.

The text of the poem found in *Felix Farley's Bristol Journal* of October 17, 1897 is given (376-383) beside the manuscript version. The case for Coleridge's authorship of this parody, however, seems to me conclusiveness. (D.V.E.)

Bidney, Martin. "'The Common Day' and the Immortality Ode: Cheever's Wordsworthian Craft." *SSF* 23 (1986): 139-51.

Purports to show that in his story "The Common Day" John Cheever attempts to "re-make Wordsworth's ode in the image of his own perceived world" by muting the metaphysics and adding wry whimsy while he gives us images of sun, prison-house, heart, and nature. (M.T.S.)

Bidney, Martin. "Radiant Geometry in Wordsworthian Epiphanies." *TWC* 16 (1985): 114-20.

Birdsall, Eric. "Unmerited Contempt, Undeserved Praise: More on Wordsworth's Earliest Reviews." *TWC* 17 (1986): 247-49.

The author means reviews *of* Wordsworth, not *by* him (English should be kept up, as Keats said). Birdsall has discovered several unnoticed "notices" of *Ev. W.* and *Des. Sk.*--in the *English Review*, the *Scots Magazine*, and the *New Annual Register*--and concludes that "we must reevaluate our notion that Wordsworth's early works received a bad press." (B.C.H.)

Blake, Kathleen. "Elizabeth Barrett Browning and Wordsworth: The Romantic Poet as a Woman." *VP* 24 (1986): 387-98.

This article contrasts *Aurora Leigh* and *The Prelude* to expose "the difference that sex makes to the development of the female as compared to the male poet." It centers especially on one critical difference: a love story provides the basic narrative line of *Aurora Leigh* but not of *The Prelude*.
Browning is the refutation that the Victorians were seeking objectivity to avoid solipistic romanticism. "In fundamental ways she seems quite Wordsworthian," although relations between people were more important to her than was the relation between man and nature. "Within the same romantic progression from human love to love of nature, she must deal with the first very much as a problem before she can have any chance of resolving what is problematic in the second. The double distance she must travel makes the halfway mark a sufficient point of closure in *Aurora Leigh*." (M.T.S.)

Bloom, Harold, ed. *William Wordsworth* (Modern Critical Views.) New York: Chelsea House Publishers, 1985. Pp. viii+206. No price given.

Part of the editor's vast project is gathering together
"views" on just about everything; the first page lists 150
authors, from Homer to Hazlitt to Geoffrey Hill, adding
ominously, "these and other titles in preparation." The
volume contains a short (eight pages), slightly breathless,
and wonderfully goofy introduction by Bloom that sets up
"The Old Cumberland Beggar" as the great unsung Wordsworthian
masterpiece. This is followed by a reprinting of ten essays
and excepts from books: Frederick A. Pottle, "The Eye and
the Object in the Poetry of Wordsworth"; Paul de Man, "Intentional Structure of the Romantic Image"; Geoffrey Hartman,
"The Romance of Nature and the Negative Way"; John Hollander,
"Wordsworth and the Music of Sound"; M.H. Abrams, "Two Roads
to Wordsworth"; Thomas Weiskel, "Wordsworth and the Defile
of the Word"; Harold Bloom, "The Scene of Instruction: *Tintern
Abbey*"; Frances Ferguson, "The 'Immortality Ode'"; Thomas
McFarland, "The Wordsworthian Rigidity"; and Kenneth R.
Johnston, "'Home at Grasmere' in 1800." By now most of this
will be familiar to everyone, except perhaps the essay by
Frances Ferguson, which the editor introduces as "a distinguished instance of the deconstructive criticism fostered
by de Man and by Jacques Derrida." (B.C.H.)

Borno, Horiya A. "The 'Matthew' Poems." *DUJ*, n.s. 47 (Dec.
1985): 95-105.

Stanza-by-stanza commentary on "Wordsworth's most neglected
great lyrics."

Bragg, Melvyn. *The Maid of Buttermere*. London: Hodder and
Stoughton, 1987. Pp. 414. £10.95.

A fiction--not seen. Do the poets get into the fiction,
one wonders?

Brennan, Matthew C. "The Wordsworth of Landscape: Constable,
or Turner." *SAQ* 85 (1986): 252-60.

Brinkley, Robert A. "Vagrant and Hermit: Milton and the
Politics of 'Tintern Abbey.'" *TWC* 16 (1985): 126-33.

Chavkin, Allan. "Wordsworth's Secular Imagination and 'Spots
of Time.'" *CLAJ* 26 (1983): 452-64.

The secular imagination cannot ignore or transcend mundane
reality, though it can vitalize and renovate it. The "spots"
include *Prelude* 4: 369-468 and "Resolution and Independence."
Nothing much new here. (R.M.R.)

Coombs, James H. *Wordsworth and Milton: Prophet-Poets.* Ann Arbor, Mich.: University Microfilms International, 1986. Dissertation.

Dangerfield, Anthony. "'The Faded Plain': Memory and Experience in Wordsworth's *An Evening Walk.*" *TWC* 17 (1986): 164-68.

Davis, Nora S. "Wordsworth, Haydon and Beaumont: A Change in the Role of Artistic Patronage." *ChLB* 55 (1986): 210-24.

Egri, Peter. "The Romantic Form of the Sonnet and Sonata: Wordsworth and Hubert Parry." *CLS* 22 (1985): 455-71.

Technical analysis shows that the Romantic sonnet and the Romantic sonata both moved toward emotional homogeneity and cyclic tightness.

Eilenberg, Susan Ruth. *Strange Power of Speech: Usurping Voices in Wordsworth and Coleridge.* Ann Arbor, Mich.: University Microfilms International, 1986.

Dissertation.

Eldridge, Richard. "Self-Understanding and Community in Wordsworth's Poetry." *P&L* 10 (1986): 273-94.

"To be a person at all, Wordsworth's example shows us, is to be engaged with others in an unending activity of the interpretation of oneself as objectively directed to certain ends." In support of this thesis, Eldridge weaves quotations from *The Prelude* into a discussion of "personhood," a discussion that initially depends on such collocations as "action-guiding self-understanding" and "self-conscious end-directed beings." Given this beginning, one has to be grateful that Eldrige discovered Wordsworth's poetry. (J.H-P.)

Fertel, R.J. "The Wye's 'Sweet Inland Murmer.'" *TWC* 16 (1985): 134-35.

Foster, Mark. "'Tintern Abbey' and Wordsworth's Scene of Writing." *SiR* 25 (1986): 75-95.

"Thomas Weiskel argues correctly that 'Tintern Abbey' is 'always in danger of coming to a dangerous halt,' this 'in reaction to a hidden sense of presence which cannot be signified.' ... The Wordsworthian originates from this ambiguity."

Galperin, William H. "Anti-Romanticism, Victorianism, and the
Case of Wordsworth." *VP* 24 (1986): 357-71.

  Since Wordsworth spanned both the Romantic and Victorian
ages, he "has been subject not surprisingly to misreadings
and misappropriations." According to Galperin, calling the
Victorians un-Romantic makes sense only if we read by the
narrowed aesthetic humanism of Pater and Arnold.
  In Galperin's reading, the Victorians saw Wordsworth whole,
allowing him the un-Wordsworthian poems which we deny him.
As part of his argument, he reverses modern critical standards
by giving *The Excursion*, which the Victorians saw as Wordsworth's greatest poem, priority over the unfinished, unpublished (by the poet), unnamed *Prelude*. (M.T.S.)

Galperin, William H. "Authority and Deconstruction in Book V
of *The Prelude*." *SEL* 26 (1986): 613-31.

Gardiner, Lorne. "Grasmere, 1979." *QQ* 93 (1986): 497-98.

  Not a scholarly article, but a scholarly *poem* about Wordsworth; 56 lines, and quite moving. (B.C.H.)

Gast, Marlene. *Wordsworth and Milton: Varieties of Connection*.
Ann Arbor, Mich.: University Microfilms International, 1985.

  Dissertation.

Gervais, David. "Wordsworth and Modern Criticism." *CQ* 15
(1986): 148-56.

  Review of J.P. Ward, *Wordsworth's Language of Men*, and of
David Ellis, *Wordsworth, Freud, and the Spots of Time* (see
RMB for 1984, pp. 187-88; for 1985, pp. 165-66).

Gill, Stephen. "'Affinities Preserved': Poetic Self-Reference
in Wordsworth." *SiR* 24 (1985): 531-49.

Gill, Stephen. "'The Brays of Yarrow': Poetic Context and
Personal Memory in Wordsworth's 'Extempore Effusion Upon
the Death of James Hogg.'" *TWC* 16 (1985): 120-25.

Goslee, Nancy M. *Uriel's Eye: Miltonic Stationing and
Statuary in Blake, Keats, and Shelley*. University of Alabama
Press, 1985.

  Not seen.

Graver, Bruce E. "Wordsworth and the Language of Epic: The
Translation of the *Aeneid*." *PQ* 83 (1986): 261-85.

Sees Wordsworth's translation as "remarkably subtle and complex," and much better as poetry than has been thought. "To preserve the moving power of Virgil's poetry, he must approximate the complex interaction of the physical properties of language--its sounds and rhythms--with patterns of syntax and idea. This method of translation suggests that Wordsworth considered the power of great poetry to reside in the physical properties of language as much as in the ideas it represents" (26). I don't think Wordsworth's Virgil is as good as the author suggests, but it is nice to see the translations taken seriously. (B.C.H.)

Graver, Bruce. "Wordsworth and the Romantic Art of Translation." *TWC* 17 (1986): 169-74.

Enthusiastic and original, but there is some exaggeration; Wordsworth did not produce "an enormous quantity" (169) of translated verse, as the author claims, and it is doubtful whether "Wordsworth has recreated a sense of what it is like to read Horace more fully than did any earlier translator" (173). (B.C.H.)

Graver, Bruce E. "Wordsworth, St. Francis, and Lady Charlotte Bury." *PQ* 65 (1986): 371-80.

A new source for "The Cuckoo at Laverna."

Hall, Spencer, ed., with Jonathan Ramsey. *Approaches to Teaching Wordsworth's Poetry*. (Approaches to Teaching Masterpieces of World Literature, ed. Joseph Bigaldi.) New York: The Modern Language Association of America, 1986. Pp. x+182. $30.00, paper $16.50. 20 percent discount to members.

A valuable guide to the state of the art. A long section on editions and readings (for students *and* teachers) is followed by 30 "Pedagogical Approaches" discussed by that many pedagogues--beginning with Herbert Lindenberger on "Teaching Wordsworth from the 1950s to the 1980s" and Peter J. Manning "On Failing to Teach Wordsworth." To be read, week after week, with a fixed grin. (D.V.E.)

Harris, Wendell. "Romantic Bard and Victorian Commentators: The Meaning and Significance of Meaning and Significance." *VP* 24 (1986): 455-69.

Gleaning Bauer's 1978 bibliography to trace Wordsworth's reputation, Harris finds many notices of Wordsworth during the Victorian Age, but only six great statements--by Pater, Mill, Hutton, Brooke, Stephen, and Arnold--that begin to make

the effort toward interpretation, not just meaning.
Harris concludes: "If one wished, then, to state the
differences in criteria which most deeply underlay nineteenth-
century disagreements about Wordsworth, one might say that
those who looked to the moral development of the individual
as the fundamental ground for the improvement of human
happiness celebrated Wordsworth, while those who required
the improvement of the social structure as a whole ... were
dubious." (M.T.S.)

Hoskins, Robert. "Greene and Wordsworth: *The Ministry of
Fear.*" *SAR* 48,4 (Nov. 1983): 32-42.

The novel uses a series of allusions to Wordsworth as ironic
enforcement of Graham Greene's "dark vision of an anti-pastoral
and un-Romantic world in which lost innocence can never be
re-captured.

Howard, William. "Narrative Irony in *The Excursion.*" *SiR* 24
(1985): 511-30.

Jarvis, Robin. "Shades of Milton: Wordsworth at Vallombrosa."
SiR 25 (1986): 483-504.

Johnston, Kenneth R. "Philanthropy or Treason? Wordsworth
as 'Active Partisan.'" *SiR* 25 (1986): 371-409.

Superbly marshals, with careful avoidance of overreading,
the increasingly clear evidence that Wordsworth was, indeed,
"an active partisan" in the cause of radical reform in those
obscure London years. Either the legend is true that he
worked on the radical journal *The Philanthropist*, or something
very much like that occurred. Brilliant! (D.V.E.)

Jump, Harriet. "Tendencies in Wordsworth's *Prelude* Revisions."
ChLB 54 (1986): 175-85.

Jump, Harriet. "'That Other Eye': Wordsworth's 1794 Revisions
of *An Evening Walk.*" *TWC* 17 (1986): 156-63.

Kelliher, W.H., ed. *The Manuscripts of William Wordsworth's
Poems, in Two Volumes (1807): A Facsimile with an Introduction.* London: British Library Publications, 1984; Wolfeboro,
N.H.; Longwood Publishing Group, 1986. Pp. 328. £75.00,
$112.50. $92.75 for Wordsworth-Coleridge Members.

Rev. favorably by A.R. Jones in *Library* 8 (1986): 184-86.
Much of the photography is very faint, but the examination
of evidence as to every detail of writing and publication is

very thorough. (Jones recommends using the 1983 transcript
by Jared Curtis.)

   "At first sight," the editor tells us, the manuscripts
from which the 1807 *Poems* was prepared "may seem to be one
of the most oddly-assorted collections of material ever to
be sent by a poet to his publisher, and some will doubtless
be disappointed at the relatively haphazard appearance of such
an important literary document" (1). Not just at first
sight, however; the reader would require second sight to make
sense out of the photographs, which are so faintly reproduced
as to be quite useless for scholarly purposes. The introduction is learned, but long-winded (more than 70 pages
measuring 9 by 14 inches) and the editor's conclusions, by
his own admission, differ in only "a few small points" from
what Jared Curtis had to say in his Cornell edition of the
same material (*Poems, in Two Volumes, and Other Poems, 1800–
1807*) published the year before (1983). Why, then, bother
with this version? I don't get it. (B.C.H.)

Kishel, Joseph F., ed. *"The Tuft of Primroses" with Other
Late Poems for "The Recluse" by William Wordsworth*. Cornell
University Press, 1986. Pp. xiv+394; 131 illus. $42.50.

   This is the twelfth volume in the Cornell series. It presents
"reading texts" of "The Tuft of Primroses" (1808) and "St.
Paul's" (1808); parallel reading texts of "To the Clouds"
(1808, 1842) and of "Composed when a probability existed of
our being obliged to quit Rydal Mount as a Residence" (early
and late versions, both dating from 1826); and, in keeping
with earlier volumes in the series, photographs and transcriptions of most of the mss. on which the poems are based. The
titles of all of these, in the table of contents and throughout, are given in italics rather than in quotation marks.
This is slightly misleading. Like many of the reconstructions
in the Cornell series, the poems gathered together here were
of course not published as separate, independent works by
Wordsworth. The "Tuft" and "St. Paul's" were not published
by him at all; "St. Paul's" is De Selincourt's title, devised
for *PW* 4: 374. The use of full italics thus lends these
editorial assemblages an air of textual authority which they
simply do not possess. Be this as it may, the texts presented
here are once again minor miracles of patient research and
devoted scholarship. "This edition," in the editor's words,
"provides a complete textual history of the late *Recluse*
poems, presenting the 1808 poems as a group, the way they
stood in manuscript before portions of *The Tuft of Primroses*
were adapted for use in *The Excursion* and *The Prelude* and
before *To the Clouds* was revised for publication. The early

version of *To the Clouds*, here printed for the first time,
emerges as a far more confident poem, vastly different from
the one published in 1842; Wordsworth's final intentions in
The Tuft of Primroses are established; and *St. Paul's* is
put back into the context of the poems that surround it in
manuscript. Full, annotated transcriptions of all of the
surviving manuscripts allow the reader to trace the many
states by which each poem grew, clarifying, for the first
time, the shape of *The Recluse* in 1808 and revealing the
way in which portions of it were reworked and salvaged for
later use" (x). And the "early version" of the 1826 "Composed when a probability existed" is reconstructed here for
the first time. It "appears, surprisingly, as a 101-line
'conversation poem,' roughly modeled on Coleridge's *This
Lime-Tree Bower My Prison*. In its final form, the poem has
grown to a length of more than 200 lines, largely through
the addition of a substantial passage on Joan of Arc—modeled
on an episode in Robert Southey's *Joan of Arc*, written in
collaboration with Coleridge nearly thirty years earlier"
(x-xi). This is fascinating, and adds another chapter to
the growing complexity of Wordsworth's relationship with
Coleridge. So does the editor's discovery of the sources
for the "Tuft" in William Cave's *Life of St. Basil* (1716);
the introduction quotes extensively from Cave and suggests
that the letters of Basil and Gregory provided Wordsworth
with a model (in 1808) of his relationship with Coleridge
(see 20-27). All this is fascinating. Well done, editor;
well done, Cornell! (B.C.H.)

Kneale, Douglas. "Milton, Wordsworth, and the 'Joint Labourers'
   of the *Prelude*." *ESC* 12 (1986): 37-54.

   Variations on the theme of "joint labourers," beginning
with the Miltonic echo of I.14, moving through an analogy
between Adam's relation to Eve and Wordsworth's relation
to Providence, shifting to a discussion of Wordsworth's
friendship with Coleridge, and concluding with some coments
on the necessary collaboration of reader and text.

Kneale, J. Douglas. "Wordsworth's Images of Language: Voice
   and Letter in *The Prelude*." *PMLA* 101 (1986): 351-61.

   "Wordsworth's meeting with the blind Beggar strikingly
illustrates the interpenetration of voice, self, and text."

Knoepflmacher, U.C. "Revisiting Wordsworth: Lewis Carroll's
   'The White Knight's Song.'" *Victorians Institute Journal*
   14 (1986): 1-20. Illus.

A fascinating comparison of a sequence of Carroll's ironic revisions of "Resolution and Independence," in 1856, again in 1864, and finally in 1871. Sheds corrective light on Anne K. Mellor's "inadequate understanding of the romantic-ironic operations of parody" (2).

Kramer, Lawrence. "Victorian Sexuality and 'Tintern Abbey.'" *VP* 24 (1986): 399-410.

"Tintern Abbey" offered a difficulty and a solution to the Victorians, who read it as a model of human erotic desire; they took the difficulty (inner loss) but not the solution (recuperative power).

Levinson, Marjorie. *Wordsworth's Great Period Poems*. Cambridge University Press, 1986. Pp. x+170. $32.50.

The author means, not great "period" poems (poems about history?) but poems *of* Wordsworth's great period, the "great decade" as it used to be called. Included are four essays, on "Tintern Abbey," *Michael*, the Ode, and "Peele Castle." But the book is not really about Wordsworth; its real concern is the comings and goings of American scholarship on the Romantics over the last 25 years or so. As such, it will only be of interest to those who find such matters intriguing. The author's sheer insensitivity to language, shown in the title, weakens whatever claim the book might have to be taken seriously. Another example, from the preface: "Jerry McGann is the first and last influence on all my thinking" (x). From chapter 1: "'Tintern Abbey' does *allude*, although it does not attend, to the dimension designated by its title. Lines 1-22--to all appearances, a series of timeless, spiritually suggestive pastoral impressions--in fact represent a concretely motivated attempt to green [*sic*] an actualized political prospect and to hypostatize the resultant fiction, a product of memory and desire" (15). From the introduction: "That silence of 'unspeakable' (Jameson's 'logical scandal,' Macherey's 'rupture' and 'fissure,' Bakhtin/Volosinov's 'intonation,' Della Volpe-McGann's 'quid') inheres within the work and can determine its peripheral contours as well.... The omission of the picture of the *place* (as opposed to 'mind') from 'Tintern Abbey' is a contradiction of this kind, a thematic/iconic bind. The syntactic contradiction in line 33 of 'Peele Castle' ('So once it would have been,--'tis so no more': opposition of a past conditional to a present indicative, thereby suppressing the *unconditional* past, i.e., the so once it *was*), locates another such node. Precisely where the work blurs its manifest representations and where its smooth surface thickens, invaginates, or breaks open, is where its ideological situation can begin to take shape for us. These places—quite literally, spots of time, or deposits of historicity—are where the privatized 'world' of the poem (Abrams's 'heterocosm') confesses its possession by the *world*, 'the place where, in the end, / We find our happiness, or not at all'" (9).

One might be willing to wade through this gobbledegook if there were light at the end of the tunnel—"invaginated" or not—if, that is to say, the book had anything real to say about Wordsworth. But it doesn't, and we aren't. Twaddle. (B.C.H.)

Loukides, Michael Kosta. *The World's Metrics: Repetitive Modelling in Wordsworth's Poetry*. Ann Arbor, Mich.: University Microfilms International, 1986.

    Dissertation.

Manning, Peter J. "Placing Poor Susan: Wordsworth and the New Historicism." *SiR* 25 (1986): 351-69.

A disagreement with the discussion of Wordsworth's poem "Poor Susan" by Heather Glen in *Vision and Disenchantment* (see *RMB* for 1984, p. 102) which in the main would not have been out of place in the same journal a generation ago. Manning pays his respects to the 1980s when he notes that (in the original version) Susan "is herself a text for the ... speaker to write upon," and that her "seeing" is "a microcosm of the reading process," in which "questions about the status of her vision play out questions of the status we accord texts." (I.H.C.)

Matlak, Richard E. "Classical Argument and Romantic Persuasion in 'Tintern Abbey.'" *SiR* 25 (1986): 97-129.

"'Tintern Abbey' seeks to acquire its pedagogical authority through an ethos of romantic sincerity within a framework of classical argumentative structure, thereby wedding a traditional, public form of argumentation with romantic persuasion. The tentativeness ... that seems to undermine its affirmations betrays not a poet at odds with himself, but an assertive poet concerned with persuasion" (98-99).

Coleridge and Dorothy are very much involved in this discussion—as are innumerable modern critics, from Abrams to Zall.

Milstead, John. "Tragedy in the Intimations Ode." *PMLA* 101 (1986): 858-59.

A comment on Sitterson (see below): tragedy is another genre "that makes its presence felt."

Morgan, Thaïs E. "Rereading Nature: Wordsworth Between Swinburne and Arnold." *VP* 24 (1986): 427-39.

   Swinburne judges Wordsworth for his "failure to admit the
inadequacy of his own vision and confront the facts" and
replaces him with Arnold, whose *Empedocles on Aetna* is the
right reader of nature. However, "Swinburne himself falls
short of revolt and re-signs the Romantic metaphor of reading
nature into his own discourse." (M.T.S.)

Moss, Carolyn J. "Wordsworth's Marginalia in John Davis's
Travels ... in the United States." *PBSA* 79 (1985): 539-41.

   Five notes of marginal interest.

Owen, W.J.B. "The Ascent of the Mind." *TWC* 17 (1986): 60-73.

   Interesting study, together with a reconstructed text, of
a passage of about 240 lines in MS "Y" of *The Prelude*, mostly
omitted from the 1805 and later texts. (B.C.H.)

Owen, W.J.B. "Wordsworth's Chanticleer." *TWC* 17 (1986): 246-
47.

   Brief but useful note on connections between the *Nun's
Priest's Tale* and various versions (including MS revisions
printed in Averill's text) of *An Evening Walk*. (B.C.H.)

Page, Judith W. "Wordsworth and the Psychology of Meter."
PLL 21 (1985): 275-94.

Palumbo, Linda J. "The Later Wordsworth and the Romantic
Ego: Bede and the Recreant Soul." *TWC* 17 (1986): 181-84.

Prickett, Stephen. "Macaulay's Vision of 1930: Wordsworth
and the Battle for the Wilderness." *E&S* 39 (1986): 104-17.

   Macaulay foresaw agriculture on Helvellyn; Wordsworth
campaigned to keep the neighborhood undeveloped.

Purkis, John A. *A Preface to Wordsworth*. London: Longman's,
1985.

   Not seen.

Rapf, Joanna E. "'Visionaries of Dereliction': Wordsworth
and Tennyson." *VP* 24 (1986): 373-85.

   Compares, among other poems, *In Memoriam* XCV with "Tintern
Abbey" to show that Tennyson never emerged from the "sunless
gulfs of doubt" as Wordsworth did. "Like Shelley, but unlike
Wordsworth, the roots of Tennyson's imaginative strength do

not come from the self in solitude, but from the emotional
intensity of relationship. Consequently, much of his poetry
is about the paralysis of a mind left alone with itself....
There is a bleak honesty to the struggles in Tennyson's
poems that gives them an exiting directness that Wordsworth's
do not have.... Tennyson's doubt is our doubt." (M.T.S.)

Ready, Robert. "Lines Written in Wordsworth." *MLS* 15 (1985):
225-31.

Ross, Marlon. "Naturalizing Gender: Woman's Place in Wordsworth's Ideological Landscape." *ELH* 53 (1986): 391-410.

Scarfone, Suzanne. *The Architectonics of Fate: Equilibrium
and the Process of Creation in the Work of William Wordsworth
and Virginia Woolf.* Ann Arbor, Mich.: University Microfilms
International, 1986.

    Dissertation.

Sexton, Mark S. *"Of Time and the River*: A Wordsworthian Unity."
SAR 51,4 (Nov. 1986): 79-93.

    Ideas from the 1800 preface to *Lyrical Ballads* influenced
"not only Wolfe's portrait of Eugene Gant as a young artist,
but ... also the aesthetic that governs much of the novel's
narrative presentation."

Simpson, David. "What Bothered Charles Lamb About Poor Susan?"
SEL 26 (1986): 589-612.

Sitterson, Joseph C., Jr. "The Genre and Place of the Intimations Ode." *PMLA* 101 (L986): 24-37.

    Proposes seeing the Intimations Ode, which was placed at
the end of Wordsworth's collected poetry, as part of a larger
narrative plot in which the author included lyric, "an inclusion that also occurs within the [poem] itself." This helps
us to understand that "its uneasy coexistence of statement
and uncertainly, which many critics consider its greatest
weakness, is actually its greatest strength."
See response by John Milstead (listed above).

Taylor, Anya. "Religious Readings of the Immortality Ode."
SEL 26 (1986): 633-54.

Taylor, Dennis. "Hardy and Wordsworth." *VP* 24 (1986): 441-54.

    Treating only "plausible debts," Taylor adds to the already
discovered parallels and specific mentions of Wordsworth by

Hardy. After investigating the influence in the context
of the larger tradition of Romantic lyric and Romantic
sensibility, Taylor concludes: "Hardy was extremely responsive to Wordsworth and extremely critical of him. He also
brings the Wordsworthian lyric to remarkably un—Wordsworthian
conclusions in language and meter." (M.T.S.)

Thomas, Gordon K. "Surprised by Joy: Wordsworth and the Princes
of Serendip." *TWC* 17 (1986): 80–87.

Timko, Michael. "Wordsworth and Clough: Divine Reflections
and Obvious Facts." *VP* 24 (1986): 411–25.

Quoting Carlyle, Eliot, Browning, and above all Clough on
Wordsworth, Timko reveals significant differences between
the Romantics and the Victorians. "To Clough and other
Victorians, then, Wordsworth is guilty of pride and, even
worse, falsity. He is for them, ironically, guilty of the
very same faults that Wordsworth ascribed to others, avoiding
the real, the truth." (M.T.S.)

"Waiting for the Palfreys: The Great *Prelude* Debate." *TWC*
17 (1986): 1–38.

An issue of *The Wordsworth Circle* devoted entirely to a
debate, held at the Wordsworth Summer Conference in the Lake
District in 1984, "on the relative merits" of the 1805 and
1850 texts. Both texts were found to be relatively meritori-
ous, and there was much to be said on both sides. The sayers
included Herbert Lindenberger and Norman Fruman (pro–1805)
and Robert Barth and Jeffrey Baker (pro–1850). Jonathan
Wordsworth chaired the discussion.

Walker, Eric C. "Wordsworth's 'Third Volume' and the Collected
Editions, 1815–20." *PBSA* 80 (1986): 437–53.

An account of Wordsworth's plan for an addition to the 1815
Poems bringing together in one volume the poetry published
in *Thanksgiving Ode, Peter Bell, The Waggoner,* and *The River
Duddon.*

Ward, J.P. "'Came from Yon Fountain': Wordsworth's Influence
on Victorian Educators." *VS* 29 (1986): 405–36.

Winberg, Christine. "Wordsworth's Preface of 1815: In Defence
of Fancy." *Unisa* 23 (1985): 11–18.

Wordsworth, Jonathan. "The Dark Interpreters: Wordsworth and
De Quincey." *TWC* 17 (1986): 40–50.

See also Erdman, Stafford, Virtanen ("General 2. Environment");
Cook, Handwerk, Lord, Pettersson ("General 3. Criticism");
Brennen, Mendilow ("English 2. Environment"); Applewhite,
Bidney, Bridgmen, Cave, Curran, Eaves and Fischer, Edmund-
son, Hagstrum, Hill, McGowan, Meehan, Nabholtz, Newlyn,
Parkinson, Rzepka, Schulz, Weiskel, Wesling, Wilkie ("English
3. Criticism"); Thompson ("Austen"); Bidney ("Blake"); Hill
("Byron"); Egan, Rosenberg ("Carlyle"); Greenberg, Lefebure,
Newlyn, Roe ("Coleridge"); King-Hele ("Darwin"); Snyder
("De Quincey"); Alexander Inboden ("Scott"); Blank, Brinkley
("Shelley"); Goodson ("German 3. Hölderlin").

Reviews of books previously listed:

BIALOSTOSKY, Don H., Making Tales: The Poetics of Wordsworth's
Narrative Experiments (see RMB for 1984, p. 176), rev. by
Peter J. Manning in MLQ 46 (1985): 96-98 ("impressive," but
the use of Bakhtin is "a bit of a Red herring"); by W.J.B.
Owen in RES 37 (1986): 273-76; DAVIS, Philip, Memory and
Writing: From Wordsworth to Lawrence (see RMB for 1985, p.
165), rev. by Karen McLeod Hewitt in RES 37 (1986): 140;
ELLIS, David, Wordsworth, Freud, and the Spots of Time: Interpretation in "The Prelude" (see RMB for 1985, pp. 165-66),
rev. by Richard E. Matlak in TWC 17 (1986): 224-27 (lukewarm);
by John Woolley in English 35 (1986): 73-78; HEFFERNAN,
James A.W., The Re-Creation of Landscape: A Study of Words-
worth, Coleridge, Constable, and Turner (see RMB for 1985,
pp. 166-67), rev. by William Walling in TWC 17 (1986): 197-
98; JOHNSTON, Kenneth R., Wordsworth and "The Recluse" (see
RMB for 1984, pp. 182-83), rev. by Michael Baron in English
34 (1985): 157-62; JORDAN, John E., ed., "Peter Bell" by
William Wordsworth (see RMB for 1985, pp. 168-69), rev. by
W.J.B. Owen in RES 37 (1986): 578-79; McCRACKEN, David,
Wordsworth and the Lake District: A Guide to the Poems and
Their Places (see RMB for 1984, pp. 184-85), rev. by Mary
Wedd in RES 37 (1986): 107-08; OSBORN, Robert, ed., "The
Borderers" by William Wordsworth (see RMB for 1983, pp. 152-
53), rev. by Robert Langbaum in SiR 25 (1986): pp. 571-76;
OWEN, W.J.B., The Fourteen-Book "Prelude," by William Words-
worth (see RMB for 1985, pp. 170-71), rev. by Susan J.
Wolfson in TWC 17 (1986): 209-13 (an especially thorough
and informative review, well worth reading for its own sake
[B.C.H.]); SIMPSON, David, Wordsworth and the Figurings of the
Real (see RMB for 1983, p. 156), rev. by Susan Wolfson in
SiR 25 (1986): 131-40 as "consistently engaging and provocative"; WARD, J.P., Wordsworth's Language of Men (see RMB for
1984, pp. 187-88), rev. by James Chandler in TWC 17 (1986):
207-09 as "confused and unpersuasive"; by W.J.B. Owen in RES

37 (1986): 273–76; WATSON, J.R., *Wordsworth's Vital Soul:*
The Sacred and Profane in Wordsworth's Poetry (see *RMB* for
1984, pp. 188–89), rev. by Peter Larkin in *YES* 16 (1986):
289–90.

Composite reviews:

Mudge, Bradford K. *SAR* 50,4 (Nov. 1985): 116–20.

Reviews Don H. Bialostosky, *The Poetry of Wordsworth's*
Narrative Experiments (see *RMB* for 1984, p. 176) and James
K. Chandler, *Wordsworth's Second Nature: A Study of the*
Poetry and Politics (see *RMB* for 1984, pp. 177–78).

Sheats, Paul D. *The Wordsworth Circle* 17 (1986): 214–16.

Reviews the Cornell Wordsworth editions of *An Evening Walk*,
ed. James Averill, and *Descriptive Sketches*, ed. Eric Birdsall
(see *RMB* for 1984, pp. 174–75 and 176–77).

YEARSLEY

Ferguson, Moira. "Resistance and Power in the Life and
Writings of Ann Yearsley." *ECent* 27 (1986): 247–68.

An appreciative account of the life and writings of Ann
Yearsley, the milkwoman poet "who fought for artistic
recognition and economic independence; who supported the
French Revolution and the rights of the British peasants;
who allied with, fought on behalf of, and showed compassion
for abused men and women around the world, with a message,
always, to fight back." Ferguson emphasizes Yearsley's
discursive confrontations with Hannah More, with the Bristol
slave traders, and with Levi Eames (the mayor of Bristol)
and his "gentlemen" friends, finding in these confrontations
proof of Yearsley's staunch resistance to oppressive power
as well as reasons why we should vindicate her struggles by
recognizing her as "a woman far ahead of her time."

FRENCH

(Compiled by Mary Ellen Birkett, Smith College; Eugene F. Gray, Michigan State University; Jon B. Hassel, University of Arkansas; Danielle Johnson-Cousin, Vanderbilt University; James S. Patty, Vanderbilt University; Albert B. Smith, Jr., University of Florida; Emile J. Talbot, University of Illinois at Urbana-Champaign.

1. GENERAL

Agard, Brigitte, et al. *Le XIXe siècle en littérature.* (Perspectives et Confrontations.) Paris: Hachette-Littérature, 1986. Pp. 544. Fr. 115.00.

According to *BCLF* (Oct. 1986), an "excellent manuel."

Albert, Pierre. "Le *Journal des connaissances utiles* de Girardin (1831-1836 ...) ou la première réussite de la presse à bon marché." *Revue du Nord* 66 (1984): 733-44.

A forerunner of the mass press, whose birth is normally dated from 1836. Albert provides a general history of this and other periodicals aiming at the same market.

Alocco-Bianco, L. *Dal re al buffone. Parabola d'artista (1820-1857).* Trieste: Deganutti, 1983. Pp. 209.

A symposium on the theme of the function and image of the poet in the first half of the nineteenth century in France, treating Lamartine, Hugo, Vigny, Gautier, Borel, Nerval, Musset, Saint-Simon *(L'Organisateur)*, and George Sand. See brief résumé of the volume by Annarosa Poli in *SFr* 29 (1985): 401.

Armogathe, Daniel. "Les origines de l'art social en France: du saint-simonisme au romantisme." Pp. 132-43 in *Analyses et réflexions sur l'art.* Paris: Ellipses Marketing, 1984. Pp. 224. Fr. 90.00.

Athanassoglou-Kallmyer, Nina Maria. "*Imago Belli*: Horace
Vernet's *L'Atelier* as an Image of Radical Militarism Under
the Restoration." *ArtB* 68 (1986): 268–80.

Aymes, Jean-René. *La déportation sous le Premier Empire: les
Espagnols en France (1808–1814)*. Pref.· by Jean Tulard.
Paris: Publications de la Sorbonne, Université de Paris
4, 1983. Pp. 568. Fr. 150.00

> Rev. by Christian Hermann in *RHMC* 33 (1986): 509–11; by
> Antonio Molinar Prada in *Hispania* (Madrid) 160 (1985): 458–
> 62.
> A comprehensive study of the fate of the 50,000 deportees
> (who included Alcalá Galiano and Mora) imprisoned in
> Napoleonic France. Bibliography; onomastic index.

Beaud, Marie-Josèphe, et al., eds. *Lectures et lecteurs au
XIXe siècle: la bibliothèque des amis de l'instruction*.
(Actes du colloque, 10 novembre 1984, Paris, Bibliothèque
des amis de l'instruction du 3e arrondissement.) Paris:
Bibliothèque des amis de l'instruction du 3e arrondissement,
1985. Pp. x+124. Fr. 45.00.

Becq, Annie. "Esthétique et politique sous le Consulat et
l'Empire: la notion du beau idéal." *Romantisme* 51 (1986):
23–37.

> Texts by Emeric-David, Quatremère de Quincy, N. Ponce,
> Chaussard Sobry, Andrieux, Millin, Madame de Staël, and
> Cabanis show signs of "bien des idées-forces du XIXe siècle:
> promotion de l'individuel et de l'historique qui accèdent
> au discours théorique de l'idéal, valorisation de l'intimité
> subjective où se dessinent les lois de l'univers, accent
> sur l'imagination dont les créations jouissent d'une logique
> spécifique et passent par l'annulation du réel."

Becq, Annie. *Genèse de l'esthétique française moderne: de la
raison classique à l'imagination créatrice 1680–1814*. 2 vols
Paris: Pacini, 1984. Pp. 939. £40.00.

> Rev. by Nicholas Cronk in *FS* 40 (1986): 469–70.

Bellet, Roger, ed. *L'aventure dans la littérature populaire
au XIXe siècle*. (Colloque sur "Le Livre d'aventures dans
la littérature populaire," 1983, Ecole nationale supérieure
des bibliothèques de Villeurbanne, France.) Presses
universitaires de Lyon, 1985. Pp. 220. Fr. 90.00.

Berchet, Jean-Claude. "Et in Arcadia Ego!" *Romantisme* 51
    (1986):   85-104.

    On the renewal of the image of Arcadia (a province of the
Peloponnese), thanks to actual travel accounts in the region
starting at the end of the eighteenth century (e.g.,
Chateaubriand's *Itinéraire*). Other important documents
are Barthélemy's *Voyage du jeune Anarchasis* (1788), Castel-
lan's *Lettres sur la Morée* (1808), Pouqueville's *Voyage en
Morée* (1805), and the Stephanopoli brothers' *Voyage* (An 8).

Berchet, Jean-Claude, ed. *Le Voyage en Orient, Anthologie des
    voyageurs français dans le Levant au XIX*^{e} *siècle*. (Bouquins.)
    Paris: Robert Laffont, 1985. Pp. 1108. Fr. 120.00.

Bergmann, Karl Hans. *Blanqui. Ein Rebell im 19. Jahrhundert*.
    Frankfurt: Campus Verlag, 1986. Pp. 640; illus.

Berthier, Patrick. *Le Théâtre au XIX*^{e} *siècle*. (Que sais-je?,
    2327.) Paris: Presses universitaires de France, 1986. Pp.
    128. Fr. 22.40.

Bertier de Sauvigny, Guillaume de. *La France et les Français
    vus par les voyageurs américains*, vol. 2, *1815-1848*. Paris:
    Flammarion, 1985. Pp. 344. Fr. 160.00.

    Rev. by Henri Dubief in *BSHPF* 132 (1986): 641-42; by
Jean Vidalenc in *RH* 558 (April-June 1986): 495-97.
    See *RMB* for 1984, p. 196, for treatment of volume 1.

Besnier, Patrick. "Le dernier mot (Maistre, Ballanche, Nodier)."
    RLMC 39 (1986): 235-46.

    On the "statut du livre" in these three authors. "De
façons très diverses, ils manifestent tous trois le rêve et
l'exigence du livre somme; et tous trois se heurtent à des
formes de l'incomplétude, comme s'il devenait difficile ou
impossible de poser le dernier mot." For Maistre and
Ballanche, Besnier focuses on *Les Soirées de Saint-Petersbourg*
and *La Vision d'Hébal*; "chez Nodier, le livre et son image
sont très fortement menacés ... Nodier rêve parfois d'un
livre absolu, au-delà des contradictions--mais c'est pour
en nier la possibilité.... Donc le bibliomane en ce monde
n'accède pas à l'Un; il est voué plutôt à la prolifération
malsaine des volumes, au pluriel épuisant des bibliothèques.
Son rêve conduit Nodier bibliothécaire et bibliophile à
rêver suicidairement de la 'mort du livre,' qui serait la
sienne aussi."

Biermann, Karlheinrich. "Die Anfange der frühsozialistischen
    Kunst- und Literaturkritik: *Le Globe* (1830-1832)."
    Lendemains 37 (1985): 9-17.

Blüher, Karl Alfred. *Die französische Novelle*. Tübingen:
    Francke Verlag, 1985. Pp. 358.

Boigne, Louise de. *Mémoires*, vol. 1; *Du règne de Louis XVI à
    1820*, vol. 2; *De 1820 à 1848*. Intro. by Jean-Claude Berchet.
    (Le Temps retrouvé, 23-24.) Paris: Mercure de France,
    1986. Pp. 560, 556. Fr. 149.00 each vol.

Böker, Uwe. "Die französische Kritik an der 'industriellen
    Literatur' und am Wandel des schriftstellerischen Berufbildes
    zur Zeit der Julimonarchie." *Wolfenbütteler Notizen zur
    Buchgeschichte* 10 (Dec. 1985): 93-112.

Bollème, Geneviève. *Le Peuple par écrit*. Pref. by Jacques Le
    Goff. Paris: Editions du Seuil, 1986. Pp. 285. Fr. 95.00.

    Rev. by George Rudé in *TLS*, July 4, 1986, p. 729.
    A study of the word and concept of "the people," this book
    is not centered on the French Romantic period; still, Michelet
    figures prominently in it (the other major figures involved
    being Simone Weil and the Chinese poet Luxun).

Bonvallet-Mallet, Nicole. "Ben Jonson et la critique française
    au XIXe siècle. Quelques opinions." *LR* 38 (1984): 205-40.

    The critics cited include, notably, Villemain, A. Pichot,
    Chasles, A. Mézières, and Taine.

Bowman, Frank Paul. "Symbole et désymbolisation." *Romantisme*
    50 (1985): 53-60.

    On "desymbolization," "préoccupation fondamentale de la pensé
    romantique, ... activité fort répandue dans la théorie du
    droit, de la religion et de l'herméneutique dans le deuxième
    quart du dix-neuvième siècle," as revealed in texts from
    Michelet, Quinet, Cousin, Ballanche, Flaubert, and a number
    of less-important thinkers. Looming behind a lot of this
    is the figure of Hegel.

Bury, J.P.T., and R.P. Tombs. *Thiers 1797-1877. A Political
    Life*. London: Allen and Unwin, 1986. Pp. 307. £27.50.

    Rev. by David H. Pinkney in *TLS*, Dec. 19, 1986, p. 1417.

Caffort, Michel. "Un Français 'nazaréen': Emile Signol."
    Revue de l'Art 74 (1986): 47-54.

Based on a study of three religious works by Signol from the period 1834-37. Caffort claims that Signol achieved originality despite the influence of Overbeck.

Casenave, Jean. *Ecrivains romantiques sur la côte basque.* (Le Petit Format.) Biarritz: L'Auteur, 1985.

Chaudonneret, Marie-Claude. "Jeanron et 'l'art social': *Une scène de Paris.*" *La Revue du Louvre* 36 (1986): 315-19.

Inspired by the acquisition of this picture (from the Salon de 1833) by the Musée des Beaux-Arts at Chartres. "L'artiste donne, au-delà de la représentation du concret, une méditation sur le thème du héros anonyme déchu, de l'ingratitude à l'égard de ceux qui se sont battus pour un idéal."

Chovly, Gérard, and Yves-Marie Hilaire. *Histoire religieuse de la France contemporaine,* vol. 1: *1800-1880.* (Bibliothèque historique.) Toulouse: Privat, 1985. Pp. 351. Fr. 170.00.

Rev. by René Epp in *RSR* 60 (1986): 123-24; by Pierre Petit in *ETR* 61 (1986): 456-57; by Daniel Robert in *BSHPF* 132 (1986): 331-32.

Claudon, Francis. *Le voyage romantique: des itinéraires pour aujourd'hui.* (Le Voyage différent.) Paris: Philippe Lebaud, 1986. Pp. 246. Fr. 120.00.

"L'auteur nous invite à flâner en compagnie de voyageurs illustres: Chateaubriand, Wagner, G. Sand."

Cogman, P.W.M. "From *Les Soirées de Médan* to *Les Soirées de Neuilly.*" *French Studies Bulletin* 18 (Spring 1986): 10-11 [18-19].

Rehabilitates the almost forgotten *scènes historiques* of "M. de Fongeray" (i.e., Adolphe Dittmer and Edmond Cavé) and the model they provided for the 1880 collection. "All highlight ... uncomfortable aspects of the recent past."

Couprie, Alain. *La Nature, Rousseau et les romantiques.* (Profil littéraire, 94.) Paris: Hatier, 1985. Pp. 78. Fr. 14.60.

Crouzet, François. "Girardin, quel roman!" *Le Spectacle du Monde/Réalités* 286 (Jan. 1986): 70-75.

Inspired by Pierre Pellissier's biography of Emile de Girardin (see *RMB* for 1985, p. 193). This attractive, popularizing article recounts Girardin's career. Crouzet

finds Pellissier's view of the *Presse* lord entirely too rosy;
he sees Girardin as driven by an "arrivisme forcené," but
admits: "Dans trente-six domaines, Girardin a été un ex-
traordinaire semeur d'idées" and, as a journalist, "un mag-
nifique professionnel." His great monument is the law of
July 29, 1881, on freedom of the press.

Darmon, Pierre. *Damning the Innocent: A History of the Perse-
cution of the Impotent in Pre-Revolutionary France*. Trans.
Paul Keegan. New York: Viking, 1986. Pp. 234. $18.95.

Rev. by Robert Darnton ("Pop Foucaultism") in *NYRB*, Oct. 9,
1986, pp. 15-16.

Darnton, Robert. "The Forgotten Middlemen." ("The Perils of
Publishing," 4.) *NR*, Sept. 15 and 22, 1986, pp. 44-50.

The "middlemen" Darnton has in mind are those engaged in
the production and distribution of eighteenth-century books:
not only publishers and booksellers but also rag-pickers,
papermakers, typesetters, salesmen, porters. Darnton discusses
several such figures and their experiences, drawing his information from the papers of the Société typographique de
Neuchâtel (STN), a major publisher and wholesaler of French
books during the last two decades of the Old Regime. We are
urged to "rethink" our notion of literature by studying the
forgotten but highly popular books of the period in connection with the system he describes. (I.H.C.)

Davillier, Jean Charles. *Viaje por España*. Madrid: Adalia,
1984. Pp. 558.

Copiously illustrated with prints by Doré. The original
appeared in 1874 as *L'Espagne*.

Le Débat 39 (March-May 1986): "Figures et légendes de la Contre-
Révolution."

Relevant contents: François Furet, "Burke ou la fin d'une
seule histoire de l'Europe"; Mona Ozouf, "Ballanche, l'idée
et l'image du régicide"; Massimo Boffa, "Joseph de Maistre:
la défense de la souveraineté"; Gérard Gengembre, "Bonald:
la doctrine pour et contre l'histoire"; Bronislaw Baczko,
"Robespierre-roi ou comment sortir de la Terreur."

De Jean, Joan. *Literary Fortifications: Rousseau, Laclos,
Sade*. Princeton University Press, 1984. Pp. 355. $36.50.

Rev. by James Creech in *ECS* 20 (1986): 230-32.

Delatte, Dom Paul. *Dom Guéranger, abbé de Solesme*. Nouvelle
édition revue et augmentée. Solesmes: L'Abbaye, 1984.
Pp. iv+946.

   Rev. by Emile Poulat in *ASSR* 60,2 (1985): 247.
   This biography was originally published in 1909-10. The
   reviewer finds the new edition not very different from
   earlier ones.

Delon, Michel. "'Celui qui a vécu le plus.' L'idéal de la vie
intense dans le récit romanesque de l'*Emigré* (1797) à *Jean
Sbogar* (1818)." *Romantisme* 51 (1986): 73-84.

   Examples of this ideal are noted in the fiction of Sénac
   de Meilhan, Madame Cottin, Madame de Krüdener, Madame de
   Staël, Chateaubriand (*Les Martyrs*), and Nodier. "On voit
   comment la thématique de la relativité du temps et de la
   vie intense s'approfondit dans le double débat entre morale
   athée et éthique religieuse d'une part, entre monde de la
   dépense et monde de la gestion de l'argent d'autre part....
   Une époque s'essaie à une sacralisation du transitoire, à
   une valorisation de la vie brève."

De Paz, Alfredo. *La rivoluzione romantica. Poetiche, estetiche,
ideologie*. Naples: Liguori, 1984.

Diesbach, Ghislain de. *Histoire de l'émigration (1789-1814)*.
Paris: Librairie académique Perrin, 1984. Pp. 624. Fr.
140.00.

   A revised edition.

Donoso Cortés, Juan. *Essai sur le catholicisme, le libéralisme
et le socialisme*. Pref. by Arnaud Imatz. Bouère, Grez:
Dominique Martin Morin, 1986. Pp. 416. Fr. 160.00.

   A facsimile reprint of the 1851 edition.

Drost, Wolfgang. "Das neue Selbstbewusstsein der Arbeiter-
klasse und ihr Kampf für das Beau social. Zur Kunstkritik in
L'Atelier (1841-1846)." *Lendemains* 37 (1985): 27-36.

Duchet, Claude. "Aspects et fonctions de la parodie chez les
petits romantiques." Pp. 135-42 in Groupar, *Le Singe à la
porte: vers une théorie de la parodie*. New York: Peter
Lang, 1984. Pp. 177. $18.50.

Encrevé, André. "Les Protestants de l'âge romantique." In
André Encrevé, *Les Protestants en France de 1800 à nos jours.
Histoire d'une réintégration*. Paris: Stock, 1985. Pp. 282.
Fr. 98.00.

Etlin, Richard. *The Architecture of Death: The Transformation
of the Cemetery in Eighteenth-Century Paris.* MIT Press,
1985. Pp. 441. $37.50.

   Rev. by Jean Starobinski ("Burying the Dead") in *NYRB*,
Jan. 16, 1986, pp. 16-20; 2 illus.

Felkay, Nicole. "Dans les coulisses du théâtre romantique."
RHT 35 (1983): 442-53; 36 (1984): 78-91, 276-83.

Felkay, Nicole. "Le *Musée des Antiques* du libraire Nicolle."
BduB 2 (1986): 236-43.

   On the difficulties, especially financial, encountered in
the publication of the sumptuous art book with engravings
by Pierre Bouillon of the finest antique sculptures in the
Louvre in the days of Napoleon and the restored Bourbons.
The three volumes appeared from 1818 to 1827 (fascicules began
coming out in 1806). A letter of Chateaubriand (March 7, 1823)
to the Marquis de Lauriston and the latter's reply are included.

Fétis, François-Joseph. *Music Explained to the World.* Intro.
by Peter Bloom. New York: Da Capo Press, 1986. Pp. xvi+320.
$32.50.

   In his introduction, which is reprinted in *NCM* 10 (1986-87):
84-88, Bloom states that Fétis's reputation as "the spirit
of regression and as a ghost of the past" is undeserved.
(Fétis's book was originally published in 1830 as *La Musique
mise à la portée de tout le monde.*)

Finney, Gail. *The Counterfeit Idyll. The Garden Ideal and
Social Reality in Nineteenth-Century Fiction.* Tübingen:
Max Niemeyer Verlag, 1984. Pp. 161.

   Rev. by Beverly Seaton in *NCFS* 14 (1985-86): 188-90.
Treats, *inter alia, Le Rouge et le noir, Eugénie Grandet*,
and *Le Lys dans la vallée.*

Finoli, A.M. "Immagini del Medio Evo nei romanzi popolari
francesi dell'Ottocento." Pp. 143-58 in *Letteratura
popolare di espressione francese dall''ancien régime'
all'Ottocento. Roland Barthes e il suo metodo critico.*
(Quaderni della Società Universitaria per gli studi di
lingua e letteratura francese, 4.) Fasano: Schena, 1983
[1984].

   See résumé by Carlo Cordié in *SFr* 29 (1985): 394.

Floury, Jeanne. "Naissance de la presse à Fougères." *Bulletin
et Mémoires de la Société archéologique et historique de*

l'arrondissement de Fougères 23 (1984):   29-37.
Deals with the period from 1837 on.

Fontaine, Pierre-François-Léonard.   Journal: 1799-1853.
2 vols.   Paris: Ecole nationale supérieure des Beaux-Arts,
1986.   Pp. 1,500.   Fr. 1,700.00.

Fontaine was a leading architect of the nineteenth century.

Forbes, Elizabeth.   Mario and Grisi: A Biography.   London:
Gollancz, 1985.   Pp. 225. $26.00.

    Rev. (somewhat unfavorably) by Thomas G. Kaufman in The
Opera Quarterly 4 (1986):   123-26.
    The two singers "reign[ed] together for almost twenty years
(from 1843 to 1861)" over the world of singing in London and
Paris (mostly London).

Foucart, Bruno.   "La résurrection de la peinture religieuse."
Connaissance des Arts 417 (Nov. 1986):   78-85.

    A foretaste of a book Foucart was about to publish, this
article surveys the period 1800-1860, with good color
reproductions of works by Corot, Delacroix, Chassériau,
Hippolyte Flandrin, and others.

Frycer, Jaroslav.   "Le roman noir--le roman frénétique."
Sborník Praci filozofické Fakulty Brnenské Univerzity.
Series scientiae litterarum D 31 (1984):   23-30.

    On Janin, Charles Lassailly, and Borel.

Furet, François.   La Gauche et la Révolution française au milieu
du XIXe siècle.   Paris: Hachette, 1986.   Pp. 317.   Fr.
119.00.

    Rev. by Tony Judt in TLS, Sept. 26, 1986, pp. 1069-70.

Gaehtgens, Thomas.   Versailles.   De la résidence royale au
musée historique.   Antwerp: Fons Mercator, 1984.   Pp. 407;
illus.

    Rev. by Pierre Vaisse in Romantisme 51 (1986):   115-16.

Gascar, Pierre.   Le Boulevard du Crime.   Paris: Hachette,
1980.   Pp. 158; 231 illus.   Fr. 149.82.

Gasnault, François.   Guinguettes et lorettes: bals publics et
danse sociale à Paris: 1830-1870.   (Collection historique.)
Paris: Aubier-Montaigne, 1986.   Pp. 352.   Fr. 120.00.

Rev. by Jean-Yves-Mollier in *Bulletin de la Société d'Histoire de 1848 et des Révolutions du XIXe Siècle* 3 (1987): 131-32.

Gassier, Pierre. "Léopold Robert: *La Mère malheureuse* et *La Mère heureuse.*" *La Revue du Louvre* 36 (1986): 308-10.

Inspired by the acquisition of these two pictures by the Musée Rolin at Autun. Gassier provides a general view of the life and work of Robert (1794-1835) (he committed suicide). Several black-and-white plates.

Gautier, Théophile, et al. *Paris qui s'en va et Paris qui s'en vient.* (Paris insolite.) Paris: Editions de Paris, 1985. Pp. 156. Fr. 180.00.

"Une évocation du vieux Paris écrite par des journalistes et écrivains de la première moitié du 19e siècle dont Théophile Gautier" (*Les Livres du Mois*, Jan. 1986, no. 01395).

Gerbod, Paul. "La langue anglaise en France au XIXe siècle (1800-1871)." *RH* 557 (1986): 109-27.

Primarily on the "insertion" of English into the lycée curriculum. Only in 1838 did foreign languages become a required subject; before that, English had little currency in France (despite eighteenth-century Anglomania and the vogue of Shakespeare, Scott, and Byron in the Restoration period). English had a hard time at first, but pedagogy advanced and manuals appeared. Still, much progress remained to be made after 1871.

Gerbod, Paul. "Les touristes étrangers à Paris 1800-1850." *BSHPF* 129 (1983):

About 500,000 foreigners, mostly English, visited Paris in the period studied.

Géricault, Théodore. *Des écoles de peinture et de sculpture et du Prix de Rome.* Caen: L'Echoppe, 1986. Pp. 20. Fr. 18.00.

The only surviving reflections on art by the painter (first published in 1868).

Gidel, Henri. *Le Vaudeville.* (Que sais-je?, 2301.) Paris: Presses universitaires de France, 1986. Pp. 127. Fr. 22.40.

A good *mise au point* on the definition and development of this famous genre. Chapter 3, "Le vaudeville de 1800 à 1870," is the one most relevant to this bibliography. It reveals that, except for parodies of Romantic dramas, the *vaudeville* has little direct relationship to French Romanticism. Still, it is good to know what sort of plays provided the daily fare of a number of the most popular theaters of the time. Scribe, of course, is the preeminent author of *vaudevilles* in this period.

Godechot, Jacques. *La Contre-Révolution (1789-1804)*. (Quadrige, 63.) Paris: Presses universitaires de France, 1984. Pp. 426. Fr. 49.40.

Rev. by Emile Poulat in *ASSR* 60,2 (1985): 255.

Gontard, Maurice. *L'Enseignement secondaire en France, de la fin de l'Ancien Régime à la loi Falloux*. Aix-en-Provence: Edisud, 1984. Pp. 256. Fr. 98.00.

Rev. by Pierre Zind in *RHEF* 71 (1985): 179-80.

Goodden, Angelica. *'Actio' and Persuasion: Dramatic Performance in Eighteenth-Century France*. Oxford: Clarendon Press, 1986. Pp. 200. $38.00.

Gossman, Lionel. "History as Decipherment: Romantic Historiography and the Discovery of the Other." *NLH* 18 (1986-87): 23-57.

Gough, Austin. *Paris and Rome: The Gallican Church and the Ultramontane Campaign 1848-1853*. Oxford: Clarendon Press, 1986. Pp. 267. $49.95.

Rev. by John McManners in *TLS*, Jan. 30, 1987, p. 117.
A heavily documented study of the Gallican-Ultramontane conflict in mid-nineteenth-century France. Veuillot and *L'Univers* necessarily loom large in this account.

Goulemot, Jean-Marie. "Notes sur la mémorisation de la Révolution française à la fin du dix-huitième siècle." *Romantisme* 51 (1986): 17-22.

Grandville, J.-J. *Les Fables de La Fontaine*. Paris: Marabout, 1986. Pp. 448; illus. Fr. 30.00.

Greco, Raymond. "Picturing the People: Images of the Lower Orders in Nineteenth-Century French Art." *JIH* 27 (1986-87): 203-31.

Mostly on the period 1815 to ca. 1860.

Grunchec, Philippe. *Master Drawings by Géricault*. Paris: Ecole Nationale Supérieure des Beaux-Arts, 1985. Pp. 212. Fr. 250.00.

Text in English.

Grunewald, Antoinette. "Paul Chenavard et la donation Dufournet." *La Revue du Louvre* 36 (1986): 80-86.

A general sketch of the life and work of Chenavard. The author emphasizes the philosophical and ideological implications of his work and his relationship with the writers of his time.

Guichard, Léon. *La Musique et les lettres au temps du romantisme, avec bibliographie et index*. (Les Introuvables.) Plan-de-la-Tour: Editions d'Aujourd'hui, 1984. Pp. 424. Fr. 180.00.

A reprint of the edition of Paris, 1955.

Guiral, Pierre. *Adolphe Thiers*. Paris: Fayard, 1986. Fr. 160.00.

Head, Brian William. *Ideology and Social Science: Destutt de Tracy and French Liberalism*. Dordrecht and Boston: Martinus Nijhoff, 1985. Pp. 238. $45.00.

Hubert, Nicole. "A propos de portraits consulaires de Napoléon Bonaparte: Remarques complémentaires." *GBA* 108 (July-Aug. 1986): 23-30. 9 illus.

Drawings and paintings related to the consular portraits by Gros, Greuze, and Dufou.

Incisa, Ludovico, and Alberica Trivulzio. *Cristina di Belgioioso, la principessa romantica*. Milan: Rusconi, 1984. Pp. 543; illus. L. 28,000.00.

Rev. by Antonietta Sardi in *Letture* 39 (Nov. 1984): 839-40.

Jaton, Anne-Marie. *Entre le "réalisme" et la "voyance." Lavater et la littérature française*. (Università degli studi di Pisa; Facoltà di Lettere e Filosofia, Istituto di Lingue e Letterature francese.) Pisa: Goliardica, 1984. Pp. 72.

Rev. by Carlo Cordié in *SFr* 29 (1985): 591.
On Madame de Staël, Balzac, Girodet, Henri Meister, Senancour, Nodier, Stendhal, Vigny, George Sand, Fourier, Nerval, and others.

Jechová, Hana. "Le personnage et ses contours. Quelques
approches littéraires et picturales au seuil du Romantisme."
Neohelicon 10,1 (1983): 177-202.

Jones, Russell M. "Americans in Paris, 1825-1848: The Resi-
dents." *Laurels* 57 (1986-87): 37-46.

On "the three hundred or so members of the American colony."

Jones, Russell M. "Americans in Paris, 1825-1848: The
Tourists." *Laurels* 56 (1985-86): 83-94.

A broad-brushed picture of the American tourists and their
visits to Paris.

Juden, Brian. "Visage romantiques de Pan." *Romantisme* 50
(1985): 27-40.

A fine study following the multifaceted evolution of the
myth of Pan in French Romanticism, culminating in Hugo's
"Le Satyre" (*La Légende des siècles*), with considerable
attention to Nerval.

Kaenel, Philippe. "Le buffon de l'humanité: la zoologie
politique de J.-J. Grandville (1803-1847)." *Revue de l'Art*
74 (1986): 21-28.

Emphasizes the links between Granville's caricatures (e.g.,
Un autre monde [1844]) and the scientific ferment about zoology
and biology in his time. Kaenel insists on Grandville's
close relation with Balzac.

Kelley, Donald R. *Historians and the Law in Postrevolutionary
France*. Princeton University Press, 1984. Pp. 192. $22.50.

Rev. by Frank Paul Bowman in *Romantisme* 51 (1986): 107-11.

King, Norman. "Romantisme et Opposition." *Romantisme* 51
(1986): 63-71.

Uses the Groupe de Coppet as evidence in favor of the
Napoleonic period as one in which Napoleon's very repression
created the necessary conditions for Romanticism as an
opposition movement—on every level.

Knight, Philip. *Flower Poetics in Nineteenth-Century France*.
(Oxford Modern Languages and Literature Monographs.) Oxford:
Clarendon Press, 1986. Pp. 320. $45.00.

Köhler, Erich. *Romantik*, vol. 1: *Das 19. Jahrhundert*.
(Vorlesungen zur Geschichte der französischen Literatur.)
Stuttgart: Kohlhammer Verlag, 1985. Pp. 200.

Kornicker, Vera. "L'épopée d'une maison d'édition." *Le Figaro*,
April 24, 1986, p. 35.

On the exhibition at the Bibliothèque Nationale on the
150th anniversary of the founding of the house of Calmann-
Lévy. (See the book by Jean-Yves Mollier, listed in *RMB* for
1984, p. 213.)

Krakovitch, Odile, comp. *Les Pièces de théâtre soumises à la
censure (1800-1830)*. *Inventaire des manuscrits des pièces
(F^{18} 581 à 668) et des procès-verbaux des censeurs (F^{21} 966
à 995)*. Avant-propos par Jean Favier. Paris: Archives
Nationales, 1982. Pp. 335.

Rev. by Jean Vidalenc in *RH* 554 (April-June 1985): 496.

Lacassagne, Jean-Pierre. "Lectures romantiques de la Bible."
Pp. 211-28 in *Le Monde contemporain et la Bible*. (Bible de
Tous les Temps, 8.) Paris: Beauchesne, 1985.

Lalitte, Philippe. "*Robert le Diable* au XIXe siècle."
Médiévales 6 (Spring 1984): 95-108.

Lamarck et son temps, Lamarck et notre temps. (Colloque
international (CERIC) organisé par le Centre de Recherches
sur l'Histoire des Idées de l'Université de Paris.) Paris:
J. Vrin, 1982. Pp. 252. Fr. 84.00.

Rev. by Jean-Louis Fischer in *Revue d'Histoire des Sciences*
37 (1984): 326-27; by Jacques Roger in *ibid*. 36 (1983):
370-71.

Lasserre-Vergne, Anne. *Les Pyrénées centrales dans la littérature française entre 1820 et 1870*. Illustrations hors-texte,
gouaches originales de Edouard Wallon. Toulouse: Eché,
1985. Pp. 254. Fr. 160.00.

This volume offers a useful mass of information drawn from
a large body of documents, but the organization of the
material leaves something to be desired. The author loiters
too fondly over touristic travel accounts and guide books--
these provide most of the "literature" she analyzes--while
quotations from Hugo, George Sand, Baudelaire, Michelet, and
other writers are treated in passing. Still, it is good to
be able to follow the rise of the central Pyrénées region as
a focus of tourism, from the vogue of its watering-places

(e.g., Cauterets) to an appreciation of its scenery (the Cirque de Gavarnie, the Lac de Gaube, etc.) and, ultimately, the emergence of mountain climbing as a major sport. The score or so gouaches by Wallon are pleasant enough, but suffer from mediocre reproduction; furthermore, their bibliographical source is never made clear. This book, then, is not entirely satisfactory, but it is an advance on previous works in the field. (J.S.P.)

Laveissière, Sylvain. *Prud'hon: La Justice et la Vengeance poursuivant le Crime.* (Dossiers du Département des Peintures, 32.) Paris: Musées nationaux, 1986. Pp. 120. Fr. 55.00.

Leduc-Adine, J.-P. "Paysan de dictionnaire, paysan de roman, ou un modèle textuel pour une représentation sociale de la paysannerie au milieu du XIXe siècle." Pp. 185-200 in *Letteratura popolare di espressione francese dall''ancien régime' all'Ottocento. Roland Barthes e il suo metodo critico.* (Quaderni della Società Universitaria per gli studi di lingua e letteratura francese, 4.) Fasano: Schena, 1983 (1984).

See résumé by Carlo Cordié in *SFr* 29 (1985): 595.

Lendemains 8 (1983): "Musik in Paris im XIX. Jahrhundert."

Several of the articles in this special issue of *Lendemains*, as might be expected, deal with the Romantic phase of Parisian musical life in the nineteenth century: S. Döhring on Meyerbeer's four major works, N. Miller and H. Hofer on Berlioz (the former on the place of the "Lied" in Berlioz's work, the latter on his treatment of the Faust theme), J.O. Fischer on the "chanson politique, sociale et révolutionnaire" in the nineteenth century (mostly on Béranger and E. Pottier). See the review of this issue by Karl Leich-Galland in *RMus* 71 (1985): 208-41.

Lloyd, Rosemary. "Un peintre et ses critiques: Dominique Papety." *Romantisme* 50 (1985): 104-10.

Surveys the critical reaction to Papety's Fourierist paintings of the 1840s and 1850s, with emphasis on Baudelaire and Gautier. A black-and-white reproduction of the *Rêve de bonheur* (Salon de 1843) is given.

Lyons, Martyn. "Oral Culture and Rural Community in Nineteenth-Century France: The *veillée d'hiver.*" *AJFS* 23 (1986): 102-14.

This "brief examination of the purpose and social function of the *veillée*" seeks to revise Robert Mandrou's interpretation

(*De la culture populaire aux XVIIe et XVIIIe siècles* [1964]).
Lyons, for instance, downgrades the amount of communal reading
that went on. "The *veillée* resisted attempts made by an
élite culture both to assimilate it and to destroy it."

Macchia, Giovanni. *Le Rovine di Parigi*. Milan: Arnoldo
Mondadori, 1986. Pp. 417. L. 30,000.00.

    Rev. by Benedetta Craveri in *TLS*, Oct. 3, 1986, p. 1097.
Some of the essays deal with the transformation of Paris
in the nineteenth century, and at least one is on Hugo.

Madec, Philippe. *Boullée*. (Architecture.) Paris: Fernand
Hazan, 1986. Fr. 150.00.

Magnanini, Emilia. "La teoria del dramma romantico fra Russia
ed Europa." *RLMC* 39 (1986): 213-33.

    On the first impact of western European Romanticism in
Russia immediately after Napoleon. The polemic period ended
in the mid-1830s. The ideas of Schlegel and Madame de Staël,
not surprisingly, figure in this account. The literary debate
of Classicism versus Romanticism foreshadows the all-important
struggle later on of Slavophiles and Westernizers.

Martin, Henri-Jean, and Roger Chartier, eds. *Histoire de l'édition française*, vol. 3: *Le temps des éditeurs. Du romantisme
à la Belle Epoque*. Paris: Promodis, 1985. Pp. 540. Fr.
802.00.

    Rev. in *BduB* 1 (1986): 66-74; in *BCLF* 490 (1986): 1357;
by Eugen Weber in *TLS*, May 2, 1986, p. 483.

Martineau, Gilbert. *Franz Liszt*. (Figures de Proue.) Paris:
Tallandier, 1986. Pp. 252. Fr. 107.00.

[Ménétra, Jacques-Louis.] *Journal de ma vie: Jacques-Louis
Ménétra, Compagnon vitrier au 18e siècle*. Intro. by Daniel
Roche. Paris: Montalba, 1983. Pp. 431. Fr. 90.00.

    Rev. by Raymond Birn in *ECS* 19 (1986): 404-06.
For English translation, see "General 2. Environment."

Métayer, Léon. "L'Espagne et les Espagnols dans les mélodrames
parisiens (1830-1848)." *Recherches et Etudes comparatistes
ibéro-françaises de la Sorbonne Nouvelle* 5 (1983): 46-62.

    "La finalité de ces pièces 'espagnoles' n'est pas d'éclairer
le public sur l'Espagne réelle. Œuvres militantes, écrites
par des auteurs préoccupés par la politique intérieure

française, elles confirment l'image de l'Eglise espagnole
comme institution réactionnaire orientée vers la conquête
du pouvoir" (*Bulletin signalétique* 39,4, no. 4285).

Michaud, Stéphane. "Dogmes et cauchemars dans l'apologétique
romantique." *Romantisme* 52 (1986): 69-75.

Not attempting a complete history of the subject, Michaud
wishes to draw attention to the ardent defense of private
property and the almost panic fear of woman and sexuality
to be found in some leading Romantic apologists for Catholicism, some of them well known (Chateaubriand, Maistre, Dom
Guéranger), some now little known but once much read (e.g.,
l'abbé Gaume).

Michaud, Stéphane. *Muse et Madone. Visages de la femme, de
la Révolution française aux apparitions de Lourdes.* Paris:
Editions du Seuil, 1985. Pp. 242. Fr. 95.00.

Rev. by Max Milner in *Romantisme* 50 (1985): 125-26.
Contents: "Introduction" (9-16); "L'immaculée: le culte
marial 1" (17-55); "L'immaculée victorieuse des révolutions:
le culte marial 2" (56-78); "Liane et Sophie: Jean-Paul et
Novalis" (79-110); "Délier, dit-elle: Goethe" (111-44);
"La rédemption sociale: les socialistes français" (145-72);
"Isis et Marie: Gérard de Nerval" (173-204); "La femme
rédemptrice: Wagner" (205-30); "Conclusion" (231-35);
"Notes" (236-43).

Miquel, Pierre. *Le Paysage français au XIXe siècle. L'école
de la nature:* vols. 4-5. Maurs-la-Jolie: Editions de la
Martinelle, 1985. Pp. 800. Fr. 1,980.00.

Volume 5 rev. by Pierre Georgel in *Revue de l'Art* 73
(1986): 68.

Moes, Jean, and Jean-Marie Valentin, eds. *De Lessing à Heine:
un siècle de relations littéraires et intellectuelles entre
la France et l'Allemagne.* Actes du colloque de Pont-à-
Mousson, septembre 1984. (Publications de l'Université de
Metz, Département d'allemand.) Paris: Didier-Erudition,
1985. Pp. 340. Fr. 250.00.

Mollier, Jean-Yves. *Dans les bagnes de Napoléon III: mémoires
de Charles-Ferdinand Gambon.* Paris: Presses universitaires
de France, 1983. Pp. 296. Fr. 350.00.

Mongrédien, Jean. *La Musique en France des Lumières au romantisme: 1789-1830.* (Harmoniques.) Paris: Flammarion, 1986.
Pp. 376. Fr. 140.00.

Mongrédien, Jean. "Variations sur un thème: Masaniello.
Du héros de l'histoire à celui de La Muette de Portici.
Jahrbuch für Opernforschung (1985): 90-121.

Mortier, Roland. "Les retards et les obstacles à la révélation
de la littérature allemande en France." CS 37 (1985-86):
1-9.

Several documents from the eighteenth century and early
nineteenth (i.e., before De l'Allemagne)--Charles de Villers,
Vanderbourg, Degérando--are studied to reveal French smugness
and ignorance. Translators and others made serious efforts,
but the upheaval of the Revolution created a precarious
political situation.

Muray, Philippe. "L'affaire Satan." SFR 10 (1986): 237-57.

On the "réhabilitation" of Satan in the nineteenth century,
a development Muray regards as "sensationnel ... un événement
inouï dans la pensée." Satan is not merely a falsely accused
criminal: "C'est du suprême Bourreau ... qu'ils entreprennent
la défense."

Nathan, Michel, ed. Anthologie du roman populaire: 1836-1918.
(10/18, no. 1700.) Paris: Union Générale d'Editions, 1985.
Pp. 373. Fr. 34.00.

Organized thematically ("La misère"; "La vie de château";
"Filles flétries"; "Femmes à vendre"; "Les drames de l'adul-
tère"; "Goupillons, sabres et juifs allemands"; "Les crimes
de la calotte"; "Exploits patriotiques, aventures rocambolesques
hauts faits et faits divers"), this anthology provides extracts, usually just a few pages long, from authors like
Eugène Sue, Paul de Kock, Paul Féval and less well-known
figures.

Neuschäfer, Hans-Jörg. "Die Krise der Vernunft und die
Opposition des Gefühls in französischen Feuilleton-roman der
achtziger Jahre." Pp. 133-42 in Michael Rössner and Birgit
Wagner, eds., Aufstief und Krise der Vernunft: Kompara-
tistischen Studien zur Literatur der Aufklärung und des Fin-
de-siècle. Vienna, Cologne, and Graz: Bohlau, 1984. Pp. 480.

Newman, Edgar Leon. Historical Dictionary of France from the
1815 Restoration to the Second Empire. Westport, Conn.:
Greenwood Press, 1986.

Nora, Pierre, ed. Les Lieux de mémoire, vol. 1, La République,
vols. 2-4, La Nation. Paris: Gallimard, 1984. Pp. 674, 610,
662, 669. Fr. 859.00.

Rev. by Stefan Collini in *TLS*, Jan. 16, 1987, pp. 51-52.

Oehler, Dolf. "Uber einige Paris-Motive im Arbeiterlied nach dem Juni 1848." *Lendemains* 35 (1984): 32-42.

Pageard, Robert. "L'Espagne vue par un érudit français au printemps de 1852: *Voyage pittoresque en Espagne et au Portugal d'Emile Bégin*." *Recherches et etudes comparatistes ibéro-françaises de la Sorbonne Nouvelle* 5 (1983): 68-79.

Peltzer, Marina. "Imagerie populaire et caricature: la graphique politique antinapoléonienne en Russie et ses antécédents pétroniens." *JWCI* 48 (1985): 189-221. 40 illus.

Pendle, Karin. "A Night at the Opera: The Parisian Prima Donna, 1830-1850." *The Opera Quarterly* 4 (1986): 77-89.

A useful survey of the situation of female singers in the period covered, with some attention to the major figures, e.g., Damoreau, Falcon, Stoltz, plus several appendices showing "The Repertory of Selected French Prima Donnas, circa 1830-1850" (Boulanger, Colon, Damoreau, Dorus-Gras, Falcon, Stoltz) and "Selected List of Women Singers in Paris, circa 1830-1850."

Peterson, Carla. *The Determined Reader: Gender and Culture in the Novel from Napoleon to Victoria*. Rutgers University Press, 1986. Pp. 270. $25.00.

A solid discussion of the importance of reading in the lives of nineteenth-century female protagonists, which broadens into an inquiry into their reading of themselves, of others, and of reality. The examples are English and French, although the Romantics considered are all French. Peterson sees the book reading of the French protagonists as exacerbating an impulse to control and to dominate (whereas English protagonists seek acceptance into the community). Madame de Staël's Corinne is seen as increasingly abandoning an oral mode associated with "communality, immediacy, flexibility, exchange, and 'femininity,'" to adopt the "male" mode of writing characterized by "rigidity, fixity, distance, and death." Balzac's Louis Lambert is seen as "feminized" by reading, for the activity turns him inward and leads him to a passive attitude toward life. Stendhal's Julien Sorel models his life on his readings as do Mathilde and Lamiel, both of whom are also Dionysian characters who express their passions with excess. Some occasional errors of fact. (E.J.T.)

Petit, Nicolas. "Inventaire des collections Hetzel." *Arts et Métiers du Livre* 139 (May 1986): 70-79.

"Notice sur les diverses collections publiées par Hetzel à Paris au cours de sa carrière, de 1837 à 1886" (*BduB* 4 (1986): 597).

Pierssens, Michel. "Littérature et tables tournantes." *Critique* 473 (Oct. 1986): 999-1015.

Takes off from Philippe Muray, *Le XIXe siècle à travers les âges* (see *RMB* for 1984, p. 213), to discourse on occultism and especially "le spiritisme" in French literature since Romanticism, dealing at some length with Gautier's *Spirite*.

Pingeot, Anne, ed. *La Sculpture française au XIXe siècle.* Paris: Editions de la Réunion des Musées nationaux, 1986. Pp. 472.

Catalogue of an exhibition at the Grand Palais (see Marc Jordan, "Models of Propriety," *TLS*, June 27, 1986, p. 709).

Pinkney, David H. *Decisive Years in France, 1840-1847.* Princeton University Press, 1986. Pp. xii+235. $30.00.

In chapter 6 ("New Departures in the Arts"), Pinkney highlights the architectural innovations of Labrouste, the restorations of Viollet-le-Duc, the rise of realism in painting (Courbet), "modernist" interest in technology in literature, the emergence of photography, the seminal early work of Flaubert and Baudelaire, the birth of the mass press (with its *romans-feuilletons*), and the invention of the comic strip (Töpffer).

Pitwood, Michael. *Dante and the French Romantics.* (Histoire des Idées et Critique littéraire, 234.) Geneva: Droz, 1985. Pp. 336. Sw. Fr. 60.00.

Rev. by Steve Ellis in *FS* 40 (1986): 471.
A thorough study, in a traditional mode, of the subject. (J.S.P.)

Pointon, Marcia. "'Vous êtes roi dans notre domaine': Bonington as Painter of Troubadour Subjects." *BM* 128 (Jan. 1986): 10-17. 8 illus.

On paintings (in the 1820s) of figures and scenes from French history. "Bonington exploits an alternative history painting which earlier Troubadour painters like Révoil and Ingres had established but he also undermines it by ironic overtones and by subtle deviations from the expected convention."

Pompili, Bruno. *Licantropi e meteore. Saggi sul romanticismo francese. Contrappunti.* (Nuova Biblioteca Dedalo, 45; Serie Nuovi Saggi.) Bari: Dedalo, 1984. Pp. 132.

Rev. by P.A. Borgheggiani in *SFr* 30 (1986): 150-51.

Contains: "Tre articoli di Pétrus Borel sulla condizione dello scrittore"; "Le arti, *Robinson Crusoe*, *Antigone* nel 'tradurre' di Borel"; "'Mademoiselle, je vous aime comme la République.' Frenetismo e ironia in Charles Lassailly"; "Il genio malvaggio dello stato: Trialph e Lassailly"; "*Star* di Defontenay: crogiolo, crocevia, viaggia"; "Frammenti dello stesso sguardo: Lassailly e Lautréamont"; "Il viaggio nella bottiglia. Contrappunto baudelairiano."

Popkin, Jeremy D. "Conservatism Under Napoleon: The Political Writings of J. Fiévée." *History of European Ideas* (1984): 385-400.

Queffelec, Lise. "Inscription romanesque de la femme au XIXe siècle: le cas du roman-feuilleton sous la Monarchie de Juillet." *RHL* 86 (1986): 189-206.

Author's résumé: "A travers les multiples figures de femmes qu'inventent les romans-feuilletons de la Monarchie de Juillet se dessine le rôle idéologique et imaginaire de la femme à cette époque. Peu caractérisée socialement, si ce n'est pour noter son appartenance exclusive à la vie privée, elle est dans l'action l'enjeu du désir de l'homme et l'instrument de son pouvoir. A cette passivité fonctionnelle correspond sa définition comme 'nature'. Miroir du désir masculin affronté à la Loi, elle en joue, dans son ambivalence (femme fatale/femme idéale) et ses ambiguités, les contradictions internes. Gardienne de la Loi, elle doit aussi, en effet, être celle qui permet de la transgresser. Mais elle reste, double rassurant dans sa fictive altérité, l'espace d'inscription du pouvoir masculin—ce que démontre *a contrario* la figure de la femme fatale, mortelle et mortifère parce que semblable à l'homme et son concurrent."

Queffelec, Lise. "Le lecteur du roman comme lectrice: stratégies romanesques et stratégies critiques sous la Monarchie de Juillet." *Romantisme* 53 (1986): 8-21.

In this period, with its dominant "liberal" ideology, the novel comes to be seen as a feminine genre; hence a feminization of the reading public: women read novels because they are excluded from power; men write novels—and control politics. Five novels of Sue, Dumas, and Soulié are studied to to suggest how novelists and critics handled this situation (e.g., the hero incarnates the masculine author as narrator, "maître de la parole," "confesseur," "diplomate," and "magnétiseur").

Raser, Timothy. "The Fate of Beauty in Romantic Criticism." *NCFS* 14 (1986): 251-59.

Kant, Baudelaire, Ruskin, and especially Hugo ("O strophe du poëte ...") on the relationship between philosophy and poetry (knowledge and beauty).

Ravaisson, Félix. *Métaphysique et morale.* Pref. by Jean-Michel Le Lannou. (Vrin Reprise.) Paris: J. Vrin, 1986. Pp. 88. Fr. 54.00.

Reardon, Bernard M. *Religion in the Age of Romanticism: Studies in Early Nineteenth-Century Thought.* Cambridge University Press, 1985. Pp. 320. $39.50, paper $14.95.

Rev. by W.R. Ward in *JEH* 57 (1986): 477-78.

Reedy, W. Jay. "Art for Society's Sake: Louis de Bonald's Sociology of Aesthetics and the Theocratic Ideology." *PAPS* 130 (1986): 101-29.

Rémond, René. *L'Anticléricalisme en France de 1815 à nos jours.* Brussels: Editions Complexe, 1985. Pp. 389.

Rev. by Jean Baubérot in *ASSR* 61,2 (1986): 304-05.

Rieger, Dietmar, ed. *Das französische Chansons. Von Béranger bis Barbara.* Ditzingen: Philipp Reclam jun., 1986(?). Pp. 450. DM 23.80.

A bilingual anthology of the *chanson.*

Rioux, Jean-Claude. "Crime, nature et société dans le roman de la Restauration." *Romantisme* 52 (1986): 3-18.

Seeks to discover how crime and the criminal are "represented" in the novels of the Restoration period. Answers are found in the names bestowed on criminals (e.g., names with foreign endings, especially Italian), the physical portrait of the criminal, the nature of plots, the ways of relating crime to social problems, and the consensus view of human nature projected. On the surface, differences are apparent (pitting monarchists and Catholics against liberals), but only apparent: "le réflexe dominant est encore de croire ou de laisser croire ... que le bien et le mal, le crime et la vertu, n'ont rien à voir avec les différences de classes et se ramènent à de pures différences sociales."

Rubin, James Henry. "Allegory Versus Narrative in Quatremère de Quincy." *JAAC* 44 (1986): 383-92.

"To those who know him best as a pedantic archaeologist," the author says, "it may come as a surprise that in the early 1800s, Antoine-Chrysostôme Quatremère de Quincy was the most consistent advocate of ideas that exemplify the early moments of Romanticism in France" (383).

Rychner, Jacques. *Genève et ses typographes vus de Neuchâtel, 1770-1780.* Geneva: Christian Braillard, 1984. Pp. 221. Sw. Fr. 67.00.

Rev. by David Smith in *ECS* 19 (1986): 429-30.

Saffle, Michael. "Liszt Research since 1936: A Bibliographical Survey." *Acta Musicologica* 58 (1986): 231-81.

The sections on "Liszt's Travels and International Activities" (246-48); "Liszt's Intellectual and Religious Interests" (248-50); and "Other Specialized Studies" (250-52) give a useful bibliography on the composer's relationships—personal, musical, and literary—with French Romanticism, notably with Berlioz, Saint-Simonisme, Marie d'Agoult, Balzac, Hugo, and Lamennais.

Saint-Gérand, Jacques-Philippe. "Lorsqu'une critique en cache une autre: littérature, langage et société d'après le *Journal grammatical* (1826-1840)." Pp. 415-35 in *Mélanges de langue et de littérature française offerts à Pierre Larthomas.* Paris: Ecole Normale Supérieure de Jeunes Filles, 1985. Pp. 512. Fr. 180.00.

Savart, Claude. *Les Catholiques de France au XIXe siècle: le témoignage du livre religieux.* (Théologie historique, 73.) Paris: Beauchesne, 1985. Pp. 718.

Rev. by René Epp in *RSR* 60 (1986): 274-75; by E. Goichot in *RHPR* 66 (1986): 372.
A study of the religious book industry and its public (excluding religious fiction).

Scaiola, Anna Maria. *Percorsi romantici: su una tipologia femminile nella cultura francese dell'Ottocento.* Rome: Edizioni di Storia e Letteratura, 1984. Pp. 186.

Rev. by Ivanna Rosi in *RLMC* 39 (1986): 71-75.

Treats Madame de Staël, Adèle Hugo, the Beatrice Cenci
theme (Shelley, Custine, Stendhal, Dumas), Sainte-Beuve,
the theme of "La Belle Inconnue," and Flaubert.

Schamber, Ellie N. *The Artist as Politician: The Relationship
Between the Art and the Politics of the French Romantics.*
Lanham, Md.: University Press of America, 1984. Pp. 248.

Rev. by S. Petrey in *RHL* 86 (1986): 770-71.
Thumbnail biographies of Chateaubriand, Lamartine, and
Constant, with shorter reference to Borel, Hugo, Dumas,
Mérimée, et al. The book is much too brief to achieve the
author's goal of determining how an artist's historical
milieu is reflected in his or her work, whether artists from
the same social circumstances produce art with similar characteristics, and whether a particular artistic genre derives
from specific historical conditions. The bibliography is out
of date and the book contains a few errors (e.g., Constant's
death is given as both 1829 and 1830). (E.F.G.)

Scott, Barbara. "Imperial Splendour at Fontainebleau." *Apollo*
124 (1986): 444-45.

Scott, Barbara. "Nineteenth-Century French Sculpture at the
Grand Palais." *Apollo* (July 1986): 54-55.

Valuable for the reproduction of Prosper Lafaye's painting
of Princess Marie d'Orléans in her studio in the Tulleries,
"one of the most evocative representations of a 'Gothic'
interior inspired by Sir Walter Scott's novels."

Scott, Clive. *A Question of Syllables: Essays in Nineteenth-
Century French Verse.* (Cambridge Studies in French.)
Cambridge University Press, 1986. Pp. 227. £27.50.

La Sculpture française au XIXe siècle. Grand Palais, Paris,
10 avril-28 juillet 1986. Paris: Musées nationaux, 1986.
Pp. 470. Fr. 220.00.

Catalogue of the exhibition.

Seigel, Jerrold. *Bohemian Paris: Culture, Politics, and the
Boundaries of Bourgeois Life, 1830-1930.* New York: Viking,
1986. Pp. 464. $20.00.

Rev. by Loren Goldner in *French Politics and Society* 14
(1986): 39-43.

Sells, Christopher. "After the 'Raft of the Medusa': Géricault'
Later Projects." *BM* 1001 (Aug. 1986): 567-71.

On the dating of Géricault's *Traite des nègres*, *Ouverture des portes de l'Inquisition*, *Reddition de Parga*, and *La Peste de Barcelone*.

Sells, Christopher. "New Light on Géricault, His Travels and His Friends, 1816-23." *Apollo* (June 1986): 390-95.

Facts dug out of archives covering the artist's travels lead Sells to revise dates of several pictures.

Senelier, Jean. "Le voyage d'Italie." Pp. 5-12 in H. Gaston Hall et al., eds., *Mélanges à la mémoire de Franco Simone*, vol. 3, *XIXᵉ et XXᵉ siècles*. Geneva: Slatkine, 1984. Pp. 822.

Simons, Katrin. *Jacques Réattu, Peintre de la Révolution Française*. Paris: Arthena, 1985. Pp. 210; 174 b. & w. illus., 1 col. pl. Fr. 400.00.

Rev. by Philippe Bordes in *BM* 128 (June 1986): 436.

Sjödén, Karl-Erik. *Swedenborg France*. (Acta Universitatis Stockholmiensis. Stockholm Studies in the History of Literature, 27.) Stockholm: Almqvist & Wiksell, 1985. Pp. 203. Fr. 285.00.

Sorel, Philippe. "Les Dantan du Musée Carnavalet: portraits-charges sculptés de l'époque Romantique." *GBA* 107 (Jan. 1986): 1-38, 156 illus.; and *ibid.* (Feb. 1986): 87-102, 134 illus.

Illustrated catalogue, with introductory text, of all 345 items of the "Musée Dantan": caricature portraits (busts and statuettes) of contemporary public figures by the sculptor Jean-Pierre Dantan.
Among those caricatured: Berlioz, Dumas père, Hugo, Liszt, Meyerbeer, Henri Monnier, Paganini, Jules Rességuier, Rossini, Johann Strauss, and Verdi.

Statues de chair: sculptures de James Pradier, 1790-1852. Exposition, Musée d'art et d'histoire, Genève, 17 octobre 1985-2 février 1986; Musée du Luxembourg, Paris, 28 février-4 mai 1986. Paris: Musées nationaux, 1986. Pp. 404. Fr. 170.00.

Catalogue of the exhibition.

Steinmetz, Jean-Luc. *Le Champ d'écoute: essais critiques. Nodier, Gautier, Borel, Rimbaud, Mallarmé, Zola, Verne.* (Langages.) Neuchâtel: La Baconnière, 1985. Pp. 304. Fr. 237.00.

Rev. by Jean-Charles Gateau in *Europe* 691-92 (Nov.-Dec. 1986): 229.

Stocker, Mark. "'Delicious Marble Dreams': The Sculpture of James Pradier." *Apollo* (June 1986): 396-403.

Stresses Pradier's cautious evolution toward Romanticism ("his work contains Romantic elements"). His relationships with various authors are mentioned (Hugo, Flaubert, Gautier). A portrait of Pradier and 15 of his sculptures are reproduced.

Storey, Robert. *Pierrots on the Stage of Desire: Nineteenth-Century French Literary Artists and the Comic Pantomime.* Princeton University Press, 1986. Pp. xxiv+351. $37.50.

Examines artists who either wrote or wrote about pantomimes, including Champfleury, Nodier, Baudelaire, Verlaine, Gautier, Flaubert, Edmond de Goncourt, Huysmans, Margueritte, and Mallarmé.
Rev. by Jacques O. Burdick in *TJ* 38 (1986): 120-21; by Alain Montandon in *Romantisme* 52 (1986): 127-28.

Strick, Jeremy. "Connaissance, classification et sympathie: les cours de paysage et la peinture du paysage au XIXe siècle." *Littérature* 61 (Feb. 1986): 17-33.

Sutherland, D.M.G. *France, 1789-1815: Revolution and Counter-revolution.* (Fontana History of Modern France.) London: Fontana Press, 1985. Pp. 493. £5.95.

Rev. (briefly) by John B. Guarino in *Church History* 55 (1986): 401.

Szambien, Werner. "Les origines du musée d'architecture en France." *GBA* 108 (Oct. 1986): 135-40. 4 illus.

The first such museum was founded in Paris by Léon Dufourny and Louis-François Cassas at the time of the (first) Empire.

Szyfman, Léon. *Jean-Baptiste Lamarck et son époque.* Pref. by P.-P. Grassé. Paris: Masson, 1982. Pp. xxiii+448. Fr. 205.00.

Rev. by Jean-Louis Fischer in *Revue d'Histoire des Sciences* 37 (1985): 327-28.

Wagener, Françoise. *Madame Récamier: 1777-1849.* Paris: Lattès, 1986. Pp. 544; illus. Fr. 155.00.

Rev. by Michel Delon in *QL* 477 (Jan. 1-15, 1987): 13.

Walch, Jean. *Les Maitres de l'histoire: 1815-1850. Augustin Thierry, Mignet, Guizot, Thiers, Michelet, E. Quinet.* Geneva: Slatkine, 1986. Pp. 307. Fr. 338.00.

A useful summary of the contribution to historiography of each of the historians mentioned in the subtitle. Although no chapter is specifically devoted to him, Saint-Simon and his influence receive a good deal of emphasis. (J.S.P.)

Weisberg, Yvonne M.L., and Gabriel P. Weisberg. *The Realist Debate: A Bibliography of French Realist Painting, 1830-1885.* New York and London: Garland Publishing, 1984. Pp. 213.

Rev. by Pierre Georgel in *Revue de l'Art* 72 (1986): 93.

Welch, C. "Jansenism and Liberalism: The Making of Citizens in Post-Revolutionary France." *History of Political Thought* 7 (1986): 151-65.

On the "bizarre revival--the obsession among post-Revolutionary French liberals with the vocabulary and symbolism of Port-Royal, even as institutional Jansenism decayed rapidly around them." In addition to those commonly associated with early nineteenth-century Jansenism (Grégoire, Lanjuinais, Royer-Collard), Welch is interested in those outside the tradition--Rémusat and Stendhal--"who helped to create a sympathetic portrait of Jansenism." The Jansenists provided models of moral constancy and social discipline, welcome to many in post-Revolutionary France.

Woronoff, Denis. *L'Industrie sidérurgique en France pendant la révolution et l'Empire.* (Civilisations et Sociétés, 71.) Paris: Editions de l'Ecole des Hautes Etudes en Sciences Sociales, 1984. Pp. 592.

Rev. by J.-M. Goger in *RdS* 107 (1986): 177-81.

See also Olausson ("General 2. Environment").

Reviews of books previously listed:

AIME-AZAM, Denise, *Géricault: l'énigme du peintre de la "Méduse"* (see *RMB* for 1983, p. 161), rev. by Peter Byrne in *SFr* 29 (1985): 191-92; ALLEN, James Smith, *Popular French Romanticism* (see *RMB* for 1981, pp. 157-58), rev. by Peter Byrne in *SFr* 29 (1985): 345-47; BAILLY-HERZBERG, Janine, *Dictionnaire de l'estampe en France: 1830-1950* (see *RMB* for 1985, p. 178), rev. by Pierre Georgel in *Revue de l'Art* 73 (1986): 68-69; BANN, Stephen, *The Clothing of Clio* (see *RMB* for 1984, pp. 194-95), rev. by Lionel Gossman in *MLR* 81 (1986): 203-07; by Hans Kellner in *JMH* 58 (1986): 535-36; BERENSON,

Edward, *Populist Religion and Left-Wing Politics in France,
1830-1852* (see *RMB* for 1984, p. 195), rev. by Sandra Horvath-
Peterson in *Church History* 54 (1985):   134-35; by George J.
Sheridan, Jr., in *CHR* 71 (1986):   302-04; BISHOP, Lloyd,
The Romantic Hero and His Heirs in French Literature (see
RMB for 1985, pp. 178-79), rev. by Aleksandra Gruizinska
in *NCFS* 14 (1986):   352-53; by Louisa Jones in *French Forum*
11 (1986):   114-15; by Bettina L. Knapp in *FR* 59 (1985-86):
787-88; by Hans Peter Lund in *RHL* 86 (1986):   1146-47;
BOLSTER, Richard, *Documents littéraires de l'époque romantique*
(see *RMB* for 1984, pp. 196-97), rev. by Joseph-Marc Bailbé
in *RHL* 85 (1985):   1074-75; by David Bryant in *MLR* 81 (1986):
1009-10; BORDES, Philippe, *Le Serment du jeu de paume de
Jacques-Louis David* (see *RMB* for 1984, p. 245), rev. by Donna
M. Hunter in *BM* 127 (Feb. 1985):   101-02; BRESSOLETTE, Claude,
Le pouvoir dans la société et dans l'Eglise (see *RMB* for
1984, p. 197), rev. by Richard F. Costigan, S.J., in *CHR* 71
(1986):   325-26; by Gérard D. Guyon in *RHEF* 71 (1985):   377;
by Anthony W. Novitsky in *Church History* 54 (1985):   540-41;
BROOKS, Peter, *The Melodramatic Imagination* (see *ELN* 16,
supp. 90), rev. by Ross Chambers in *French Forum* 11 (1986):
116-17; BROWN, James W., *Fictional Meals and Their Function
in the French Novel, 1789-1848* (see *RMB* for 1985, p. 180),
rev. by Colin Dickson in *FR* 60 (1986-87):   397-98; by Alexander Fischler in *NCFS* 15 (1986-87):   199-201; by Diana Knight
in *FS* 40 (1986):   346-47; CHARLTON, D.G., ed., *The French
Romantics* (see *RMB* for 1984, p. 198), rev. by Hans Peter
Lund in *Canadian Modern Language Review* 42 (1985-86):   999-
1000; CROW, Thomas E., *Painters and Public Life in Eighteenth-
Century Paris* (see *RMB* for 1985, p. 183), rev. by Richard
Wrigley in *Art History* 9 (1986):   380-88; ETLIN, Richard A.,
*The Architecture of Death: The Transformation of the Cemetery
in Eighteenth-Century Paris* (see *RMB* for 1984, p. 202), rev.
by James A. Leith in *JMH* 58 (1986):   728-29; GOSSEZ, Remi,
Un ouvrier en 1820 (see *RMB* for 1984, p. 204); GROSSIR,
Claudine, *L'Islam des romantiques, 1811-1840* (see *RMB* for
1984, p. 204), rev. by Giovanni Bonaccorso in *RHL* 86 (1986):
155; GUEST, Ivor, *Jules Perrot* (see *RMB* for 1984, p. 205),
rev. by Susan Allene Manning in *Theatre Survey* 26 (1985):
205-07; HAGAN, Dorothy Veinus, *Felicien David, 1810-1876* (see
RMB for 1985, p. 186); rev. by Christopher Hatch in *The Opera
Quarterly* 4 (1986):   122-23; HARTMAN, Elwood, *French Romantics
on Progress* (see *RMB* for 1984, p. 205), rev. by Pier Antonio
Borgheggiani in *SFr* 29 (1985):   592-86:   788; by James P.
Gilroy in *NCFS* 14 (1985-86):   165-66; IKNAYAN, Marguerite,
The Concave Mirror (see *RMB* for 1984, p. 206), rev. by Frank
Paul Bowman in *Romantisme* 51 (1986):   111-13; by Marian
Hobson in *FS* 40 (1986), by Brian Juden in *RHL* 86 (1986):   765;

by James S. Patty in *RQ* 33 (1986): 492-93; by Patricia A. Ward in *NCFS* 14 (1986): 350-51; JONES, Louisa E., *Sad Clowns and Pale Pierrots* (see *RMB* for 1985, p. 188), rev. by Gita May in *FR* 59 (1985-86): 619-20; by Alain Montandon in *Romantisme* 52 (1986): 126-27; by Marilyn Gaddis Rose in *Comparative Drama* 20 (1986): 175-77; by Rosemary Sorenson in *AUMLA* 64 (Nov. 1985): 258-59; by Robert Storey in *NCFS* 14 (1985-86): 179-81; by C.W. Thompson in *MLR* 81 (1986): 486-87; LANGE, Wolf-Dieter, ed., *Französische Literatur des 19. Jahrhunderts* (see *RMB* for 1980, p. 156), rev. by René Comoth in *Marche romane* 34,1-2 (1984): 70-71; LUBAC, Henri de, *La Postérité spirituelle de Joachim de Flore*, vol. 2 (see *RMB* for 1982, p. 169), rev. by Corrado Rosso in *SFr* 29 (1985): 401-02; MARTIN, Henri-Jean, and Roger Chartier, with Jean-Pierre Vivet, gen. ed., *Le Livre triumphant, 1660-1830*, vol. 2 of *Histoire de l'édition française* (see *RMB* for 1984, p. 212), rev. by Robert L. Dawson in *ECS* 20 (1986): 97-100; MILL, John Stuart, *Essays on France and French Historians* (see *RMB* for 1985, p. 191), rev. by Tony Judt in *FS* 40 (1986): 485-86; MOSES, Claire Goldberg, *French Feminism in the Nineteenth Century* (see *RMB* for 1984, p. 213), rev. by Michael Hanagan in *JMH* 58 (1986): 733-35; by Michèle Sarde in *Contemporary French Civilization* 11 (1987): 118-20; by Margaret Collins Weitz in *FR* 60 (1986-87): 406-09; by Marilyn Yalom in *NCFS* 14 (1986): 397-98; MURAY, Philippe, *Le Dix-neuvième siècle à travers les âges* (see *RMB* for 1984, p. 213), rev. by Jean-François Furny in *SFR* 9 (1985): 437-39; by L. Rasson in *RBPH* 64 (1986): 675-78; PALANQUE, Jean-Rémy, ed., *Une catholique libérale du XIXe siècle: la marquise de Forbin d'Oppède* (see *RMB* for 1984, p. 214), rev. by Christoph Weber in *Zeitschrift für Kirchengeschichte* 97 (1986): 420-21; PARENT-DUCHATELET, Alexandre, *La Prostitution à Paris au XIXe siècle* (see *RMB* for 1981, p. 168), rev. by Anne-Christine Faitrop in *Paideia* 39 (1984): 276-77; PARENT-LARDEUR, Françoise, *Les Cabinets de Lecture* (see *RMB* for 1982, p. 173, and *RMB* for 1983, pp. 172-73), rev. by Peter Byrne in *SFr* 29 (1985): 345-47; PAULSON, Ronald, *Representations of Revolution (1789-1820)* (see *RMB* 1984, p. 214), rev. by Thomas Crow in *ArtB* 68 (1986): 497-502; PETERSON, Carla L., *The Determined Reader* (see *RMB* for 1985, p. 193), rev. by Joan C. Kessler in *NCFS* 15 (1986-87): 231-33; PRADIER, James, *Correspondance* (see *RMB* for 1984, p. 215), rev. by Michel Brix in *ECl* 54 (1986): 188; by Françoise Salnicoff in *SFr* 30 (1986): 155; by Brian Juden in *MLR* 81 (1986): 202-03; PRIOLLAUD, Nicole, ed., *La Femme au 19e siècle* (see *RMB* for 1983, p. 174), rev. by Albert Gier in *Archiv* 222 (1985): 448-50; PUPIL, François, *Le Style troubadour* (see *RMB* for 1985, pp. 193-94), rev. by

John Goodman in *Oxford Art Journal* 9 (1986): 76-78; by
Alain Mérot in *Revue de l'Art* 71 (1986): 79; RACHMAN,
Odette-Adina, *Un périodique libéral sous la Restauration*
(see *RMB* for 1984, p. 216), rev. by Alain Nabarra in *FR* 59
(1985-86): 980-81; RAYMOND, Marcel, *Romantisme et rêverie*
(see *RMB* for 1979, p. 152), rev. by Yves Vadé in *RHL* 85
(1985): 329-31; RENOUVIER, Charles, *Manuel républicain de
l'homme et du citoyen, 1848* (see *RMB* for 1981, p. 169),
rev. by Carlo Cordié in *Paideia* 39 (1984): 265-66; ROSSARD,
Janine, *Pudeur et romantisme* (see *RMB* for 1982, p. 175),
rev. by Annarosa Poli in *SFr* 29 (1985): 401; SCHÖNING, Udo,
Literatur als Spiegel (see *RMB* for 1985, p. 195), rev. by
Rosemary Lloyd in *FS* 40 (1986): 344-45; SEGALINI, Sergio,
Meyerbeer, diable ou prophète? (see *RMB* for 1985, p. 195),
rev. by Martine Cadieu in *Europe* 683 (March 1986): 206-07;
THOMASSEAU, Jean-Marie, *Le Mélodrame* (see *RMB* for 1984, pp.
218-19), rev. by Pierre Frantz in *RHL* 86 (1986): 930;
TULARD, Jean, *Napoleon: The Myth of the Saviour* (see *RMB* for
1984, p. 220), rev. by Andrew Martin in *FS* 40 (1986): 347-
48; VAJDA, György M., ed., *Le Tournant du siècle des Lumières,
1760-1820* (see *RMB* for 1984, p. 220), rev. by Dezsö Baróti in
ALittASH 28 (1986): 227-33; by Frederick Gerson in *KRQ* 32
(1985): 440-42; by David Williams in *FS* 39 (1985): 481-82;
WELCH, Cheryl B., *Liberty and Utility* (see *RMB* for 1984, p.
221), rev. by James Smith Allen in *EHQ* 16 (1986): 110-12;
by Michael P. Fitzsimmons in *The Historian* 48 (1985-86):
590-91; by George Armstrong Kelly in *French Politics and
Society* 13 (March 1986): 32-36; by Emmet Kennedy in *ECS* 18
(1985): 561-65; WILLIAMS, Huntington, *Rousseau and Romantic
Autobiography* (see *RMB* for 1984, p. 221), rev. by James F.
Hamilton in *FR* 60 (1986-87): 123-24.

Composite review:

Scott, William. "Things Fall Apart." *TLS*, Feb. 13, 1987,
p. 158.

Reviews David P. Jordan's *The Revolutionary Career of
Maximilien Robespierre* (Free Press, 1986; pp. 308; £17.95);
Hubert C. Johnson's *The Midi in Revolution*; Timothy Tackett's
*Religion, Revolution and Regional Culture in Eighteenth-
Century France: The Ecclesiastical Oath of 1791* (Princeton
University Press, 1986; pp. 425; £432.50); T.C.W. Blanning's
The Origins of the French Revolutionary Wars (London: Long-
man's; pp. 226; paper £6.95); William J. Murray's *The Right-
Wing Press in the French Revolution: 1780-1792* (Boydell and
Brewer; pp. 349; £29.50).

2. STUDIES OF AUTHORS

AGOULT

Desanti, Dominique, ed. *Histoire de la Révolution de 1848.*
Paris: Balland, 1985. Pp. 752. Fr. 169.00.

Rev. by Henri Guillemin in *Le Monde des Livres,* Feb. 15,
1985, p. 19.

Dupêchez, Charles F., ed. *Nélida.* Paris: Calmann-Lévy, 1986.
Pp. 258. Fr. 89.00.

See also Martineau, Saffle ("French 1. General"); *Friends of
George Sand Newsletter* 6,1-2 ("Sand").

BALLANCHE

Fornasiero, F.-J. "Balzac et Ballanche: autour du *Médecin de
campagne.*" *L'Année Balzacienne* (1985): 137-49.

Adds to an already substantial body of evidence indicating
a strong influence by Ballanche on Balzac. After reviewing
suggestive parallels in the social, religious, and political
ideas of the two authors, Fornasiero shows that Balzac built
his character, Father Janvier, on Ballanche himself.

Michel, Arlette. "La pensée politique de Ballanche d'après
Le Vieillard et le jeune homme." *Mémoires de L'Académie des
sciences, arts et belles-lettres de Lyon* 37 (1983): 99-100.

Paulson, William R. "Fragment et autobiographie dans l'oeuvre
de Ballanche: étude et textes inédits." *NCFS* 15 (1986-87):
14-32.

On eight "Fragments" published in *Le Bulletin de Lyon* in
1808 and 1809. Paulson also discusses and presents the MS
texts of a ninth fragment.

See also Besnier, Bowman, *Le Débat* ("French 1. General");
L'Année Balzacienne 1985 ("Balzac"); *Société Chateaubriand,
Bulletin* 28 ("Chateaubriand").

BALZAC

Adhémar, Jean. "Balzac, sa formation artistique et ses initi-
ateurs successifs." *GBA* 1391 (Dec. 1984): 231-42.

L'Année Balzacienne. Paris: Presses universitaires de France, 1985. Pp. 414.

Contents: J.-P. Galvan, "Documents nouveaux sur quelques oeuvres de Balzac" (7-18); René Guise, "'L'Excommunié.' Les enseignements du manuscrit" (19-30); René Guise, ed., "Manuscrit de L'Excommunié de Balzac" (31-104); Charles Dédéyan, "A propos d'une photographie inédite: Balzac, la princesse Belgiojoso et Mme Jaubert" (105-18); Ronnie Butler, "Balzac et Talleyrand" (119-36); F.-J. Fornasiero, "Balzac et Ballanche. Autour du 'Médecin de campagne'" (137-50); Jeannine Guichardet, "Athanase Granson, corps tragique" (151-60); Chantal Massol-Bedoin, "Secret et énigme dans 'Le Curé de village'" (161-74); Juliette Frolich, "'Le phénomene oral': l'impact du conte dans le récit bref de Balzac" (175-92); Raymond Trousson, "L'imitation de Rousseau dans 'Sténie'" (193-210); Nicole Mozet, "La mission du romancier ou la place du modèle archéologique dans la formation de l'écriture balzacienne" (211-28); Arlette Michel, "Le pathétique bal-zacien dans 'La Peau de chagrin,' 'Histoire des Treize' et 'Le Père Goriot'" (229-46); Franc Schuerewegen, "'Un épisode sous la Terreur': une lecture expiatoire" (247-64); Catherine Nesci, "Etude drolatique de femmes. Figures et fonction de la féminité dans les 'Contes drolatiques'" (265-84); Mireille Labouret, "L'aristocrate balzacienne: du blason au bestiare" (285-98); Anne-Marie Baron, "La double lignée du père Goriot ou les composantes balzaciennes de l'image paternelle" (299-312). Notes, reviews, bibliography, information.

Autour du 'Chef d'œuvre inconnu' de Balzac. Paris: Ecole nationale supérieure des arts décoratifs, 1985. Pp. 204.

L'Avant-Scène 783-84 (Feb. 1-15, 1986).

Special issue on the adaptation of Vautrin, with several articles on Balzac.

Beizer, Janet L. Family Plots. Balzac's Narrative Generations. Yale University Press, 1986. Pp. 224. $16.75.

Borowitz, Helen Osterman. "Balzac's Sarrasine: The Sculptor as Narcissus" and "Balzac's Unknown Masters." Pp. 117-29, 130-46 in Helen Osterman Borowitz, The Impact of Art on French Literature. From de Scudéry to Proust. University of Delaware Press, 1985.

The former chapter discusses Sarrasine using the Narcissus myth, both the Ovidian original and the German Romantics' retelling of it, as the basis for the discussion; the latter explores the problems of the sources for Balzac's discussion of painting in Le Chef d'œuvre inconnu.

Brooks, Peter. "Narrative Desire." Pp. 37-61 in Peter Brooks, Reading for the Plot: Design and Intention in Narrative. New York: Knopf, 1985.

Passing references to Le Père Goriot, Illusions perdues, and an interesting analysis of Le Peau de chagrin. (J.B.H.)

Cahiers de l'Université. Special issue: "Le monde de l'enseignement dans l'œuvre romanesque de Balzac." Paris: Didier-Erudition, 1986. Pp. 166. Fr. 70.00.

Chambers, Ross. "Gossip and the Novel: Knowing Narrative and Narrative Knowing in Balzac, Madame de Lafayette and Proust." AJFS 23 (May-Aug. 1986): 212-33.

Citron, Pierre. Dans Balzac. Paris: Editions du Seuil, 1986. Pp. 301. Fr. 120.00.

According to the publicity of the publisher, we have "une biographie intérieure qui renouvelle notre connaissance de Balzac.... Sans s'opposer à la plupart des vues déjà admises, cette étude fait plus que s'y ajouter en les complétant: elle les approfondit et appelle à les repenser. La Comédie humaine y gagne en humanité et en complexité douloureuse."

Diengott, Nilli. "Goriot vs. Vautrin: A Problem in the Reconstruction of Le Père Goriot's System of Values." NCFS 15 (1986-87): 70-76.

Discusses the polarization within the novel between society/ corruption versus a-society (both Goriot and Vautrin) and concludes that the ambivalent feelings generated by the novel are the result of an unrealized positive value system within the novel.

Festa-McCormick, Diana. "Linguistic Deception in Balzac's Princesse de Cadignan." NCFS 14 (1986): 214-24.

Interesting analysis of Les Secrets de la Princesse de Cadignan in terms of an atypical narrative discourse. Instead of telling the readers what is going on, Balzac intentionally deceives and manipulates them in order that they must finally participate in the creation of the meaning of the text. (J.B.H.)

Fortassier, Rose. "Un pape de la modiphilie: l'auteur de 'la comédie humaine.'" *CAIEF* 38 (1986): 157-71.

Gallagher, Edward J. "'Différent de soi-même': The Altered Self in Balzac, Flaubert and Zola." *French Studies Bulletin* 20 (1986): 9-11.

Brief mention of the split personality of Rastignac in *Le Père Goriot.*

Guichardet, Jeannine. *Balzac 'Archéologue de Paris.'* Paris: C.D.U. et S.E.D.E.S., 1986. Pp. 504. Fr. 350.00.

Imbert, Patrick. "De l'influence à l'intertexte: la littérature canadienne-française et la littérature québécoise face à Balzac." *CRCL* 13 (1986): 35-63.

Knapp, Bettina L. "Balzac's 'Gambara': Music Is a Science and an Art." *NCFS* (1986-87): 62-69.

Reading of "Gambara" in light of the future development of music.

Lambert, Deborah G. "*S/Z*: Barthes' Castration Camp and the Discourse of Polarity." *MLS* 16 (1986): 161-71.

Interesting rereading or alternative reading of *Sarrasine* which substitutes for the binary opposition (and implied sexual ideology) of Barthes an ideology of reconciliation grounded in the idea of androgyny. (J.B.H.)

Mathieu, Jean-Claude, ed. *Territoires de l'imaginaire. Pour Jean-Pierre Richard.* Paris: Editions du Seuil, 1986. Fr. 120.00.

"Essais autant dans le style de Jean-Pierre Richard que sur Jean-Pierre Richard lui-même, selon l'occasion.... Diderot, Balzac, Fromentin, Proust, Baudelaire."

Moyal, Gabriel. "La mise en pli: *Les Employés* de Balzac." *Etudes Littéraires* 19,1 (1986): 95-102.

Mozet, Nicole. "La femme-auteur comme symptôme." *Cahiers de Récherches* 13 (1984): 35-41.

See *SFr* 29 (1985): 401.

Neefs, Jacques. "Figure dans le paysage: *Le Curé de Tours.* *Littérature* 61 (Feb. 1986): 34-48.

Œuvres et Critiques 11 (1986).

    Part 3 of this "triple numéro, volume d'anniversaire" is
devoted to Balzac.

Paulson, William. "Le cousin parasite: Balzac, Serres et le
   démon de Maxwell." *SFR* 9 (1986): 397-414.

    Reading of *Le Cousin Pons* in light of Serres's *Le Parasite*.

Peterson, Carla L. "*Corinne* and *Louis Lambert*: Romantic Myth
   Making." Pp. 37-81 in Carla L. Peterson, *The Determined
   Reader. Gender and Culture in the Novel from Napoleon to
   Victoria.* Rutgers University Press, 1986. Pp. 270. $25.00.

    Discusses the similarities of the two novels in which both
protagonists use reading as a central element in their quest
for self-understanding and their elaboration of theories of
art, culture, and history, but also contrasts the novels in
terms of their final statements. In *Corinne*, there emerges
a narrator who escapes the madness and asserts her superiority
as an artist, whereas in *Louis Lambert*, the narrator is
finally caught up in the madness.

Prendergast, Christopher. "Balzac: Narrative Contracts."
   Pp. 83-118 in Christopher Prendergast, *The Order of Mimesis:
   Balzac, Stendhal, Nerval, Flaubert.* Cambridge University
   Press, 1986. Pp. vii+288. $39.50.

    Rev. by Ann Jefferson in *FS* 40: 482-84; by Peter Brooks
in *TLS*, July 11, 1986, p. 769; by J. Roach in *British Book
News* (June 1986): 368.
    For the Flaubert chapter, see below under "Flaubert."
    Although Balzac is central to Prendergast's discussion
throughout the book, chapter 3 focuses specifically on Balzac
and provides a rich and stimulating reading of the Rubempré
cycle, particularly the contractual relationship between
narrator and reader. Prendergast sees Balzac's conservatism
as a response to the linguistic and economic "individualism"
of a particular historical moment. He studies the effort
of Balzac to maintain authorial control in a system that is
increasingly out of control, where the relationship between
word and meaning is increasingly in doubt. Discussion could
be read profitably with Terdiman, below. (J.B.H.)

Prybos, Julia. "L'épistolarité déchiffrée: étude sur *Le Lys
dans la vallée* de Balzac." *MLS* 16 (1986): 62-70.

    A study of the use of letters in the novel, to be distin-
guished from classical epistolary novels. Letters are used

as means of controlling the process of reading. Balzac's use of this technique provides an insight into the nature of his creative process.

Schuerewegen, Franc. "La toile déchirée: texte, tableau et récit dans trois nouvelles de Balzac." *Poétique* 65 (Feb. 1986): 19-27.

Sitbon, Yvan. "Balzac et la terre promise de l'opéra rossinien." *34/44* no. 18 (1986): 15-24.

Terdiman, Richard. "Discourse of Initiation: On Some Contradictions in Balzac's Encounter with the Sign." Pp. 85-116 in Richard Terdiman, *Discourse/Counter-Discourse. The Theory and Practice of Symbolic Resistance in Nineteenth-Century France.* Cornell University Press, 1985. Pp. 362.

Of interest *passim* but especially chapter 1. Trying, yet dense and rich discussion of the *roman d'éducation* in which it is shown that the process of initiation, rather than liberating the individual and granting access to the dominant ideology, binds the individual because no one will, however acute (be it Vautrin), can master the regulatory structures of the system. Read with Prendergast, above. (J.B.H.)

Wetherhill, P.M. "The Novel and Historical Discourse: Notes on a Nineteenth-Century Perspective." *JES* 15 (1985): 117-30.

Young, Michael. "Beginnings, Endings and Textual Identities in Balzac's *Louis Lambert.*" *RR* 77 (1986): 343-58.

See also Finney, Kaenel, Leduc-Adine, Petit, Saffle ("French 1. General"); Fornasiero ("Ballanche"); *Société Chateaubriand, Bulletin* 28 ("Chateaubriand"); Baudry ("Dumas").

Review of books previously listed:

BROWN, James, *Fictional Meals* (see *RMB* for 1986, p. 202), rev. by Colin Dickson in *FR* 60 (1986-87): 397-98; by Alexander Fischler in *NCFS* 15 (1986-87): 199-201; by Christopher Prendergast in *FS* 40 (1986): 346-47; BUTLER, Ronnie, *Balzac and the French Revolution* (see *RMB* for 1983, p. 185), rev. by J.-H. Donnard in *RHL* 86,2 (1986): 153-54; by Annemarie Kleinert in *GRM* 36 (1986): 244-46; DARGAN, Joan, *Balzac and the Drama of Perspective* (see *RMB* for 1985, p. 202), rev. by Lawrence R. Schehr in *NCFS* 15 (1986-87): 195-96; GAUTHIER, Henri, *L'Image de l'homme* (see *RMB* for 1984, p. 227), rev. by David Bellos in *FS* 40 (1986): 475-77;

by Gretchen Rous Besser in *FR* 59 (1985-86): 981-82; JUNG, Willi, *Theorie und Praxis* (see *RMB* for 1984, p. 228), rev. by David Bellos in *FS* 40 (1986): 475-77; by Donna Rounsaville in *NCFS* 15 (1986-87): 196-98; by A. Vanoncini in *RHL* 86 (1986): 299-300; McCARTHY, Susan, *Balzac and His Readers* (see *RMB* for 1984, p. 228), rev. by Peter Brooks in *RHL* 86 (1986): 767-68; MILEHAM, James W., *The Conspiracy Novel* (see *RMB* for 1983, p. 187), rev. by Gretchen Rous Besser in *FR* 60 (1986-87): 125-26.

BARBARA

Kameya, Nori, ed. *Un conteur méconnu: Charles Barbara, 1817-1866.* (La Thèsothèque, 15.) Paris: Minard, 1986. Pp. x+259. Fr. 215.00.

Kameya, Nori. "Louis-Charles Barbara: un ami de Baudelaire." *ELLF* 46 (1985): 36-41.

BARBEY D'AUREVILLY

Contre Diderot. Pref. by Hubert Juin. (Le Regard littéraire, 3.) Paris: Complexe, 1986. Pp. 149. Fr. 49.00.

Dodille, Norbert. "Les femmes de l'écrivain." *Romantisme* 52 (1986): 45-56.

   On the women in Barbey's life.

Malicet, Michel, ed. *Hommages à Jacques Petit.* 2 vols. (Centre de récherches J. Petit, 41. Annales littéraires de l'Université de Besançon, 300.) Paris: Les Belles Lettres, 1985. Pp. 974. Fr. 500.00.

Tranouez, Pierre, ed. *Du dandysme et de George Brummell.* Paris: Balland, 1986. Pp. 142. Fr. 69.00.

BAUDELAIRE

Clements, Patricia. *Baudelaire and the English Tradition.* Princeton University Press, 1986. Pp. 442. $33.50.

   Rev. by Denis Bouchard in *UTQ* 56 (1986): 140-42.

Lloyd, Rosemary, trans. and ed. *Selected Letters of Charles Baudelaire: The Conquest of Solitude.* University of Chicago Press, 1986. Pp. 268. $24.95.

Rev. by Julian Barnes ("How Unpleasant to Meet Mr. Baudelaire!") in *NYRB*, Nov. 20, 1986, pp. 18-20, and by Frederick Brown ("The Conquest of Solitude") in *NR*, Dec. 8, 1986, pp. 38-41.

Shiff, Richard, and Michael Fried. "Critical Response." *CritI* 12 (1986): 439-52.

Shiff ("Remembering Impressions") and Fried ("Forget It: A Response to Richard Shiff") discuss Fried's earlier essay, "Painting Memories: On the Containment of the Past in Baudelaire and Manet" (see *RMB* for 1984, p. 232).

See also Chase ("General 3. Criticism").

BERANGER

King, Norman. "Constant et Béranger: un monarchiste s'explique à un républicain." *Annales Benjamin Constant* 5 (1985): 95-103.

First publication of the full text of Constant's apologia of January 29, 1829, addressed to Béranger, then in prison for having published his *Chansons inédites*. The relationship between the two writers is surveyed, by way of introduction to Constant's work.

See also Lendemains 8 ("French 1. General").

BERBIGUIER

See also Steinmetz ("French 1. General").

BERLIOZ

Husson, Thérèse. "La première édition critique de l'oeuvre littéraire d'Hector Berlioz." Pp. 165-69 in Hélène Charnassé, ed., *Aspects de la recherche musicologique du C.N.R.S.* Paris: Editions du C.N.R.S., 1984. Pp. 220. Fr. 110.00.

Lott, R. Allen. "A Berlioz Premiere in America: Leopold De Meyer and the *Marche d'Isly*." *NCM* 8 (1984-85): 226-30.

The Austrian virtuoso played his *Marche d'Isly* (orchestrated by Berlioz) in Philadelphia on November 10, 1848. Lott conjectures that a score of this work in the Paris Opera library must be Berlioz's orchestration.

See also Lendemains 8, Saffle ("French 1. General"); *La Revue Musicale* 378 ("Hugo"); Locke ("Saint Simon").

BERTRAND

Blanc, Réjane. *La Quête alchimique dans l'oeuvre d'Aloysius Bertrand*. Paris: Nizet, 1986. Pp. 217. Fr. 107.00.

Traces of esoteric philosophy not only in Bertrand's text of *Gaspard de la nuit* but also in his meticulous attention to composition, which has a parallel in the alchemist's effort to perfect matter and, by so doing, to achieve truth. Extensive bibliography.

BONALD

Bastier, Jean. "Une relecture: la pensée de Louis de Bonald confrontée aux théories de Marcel Jousse, M. Foucault, G. Dumézil." *Mémoire 2* (May 1985): 33-56.

Klinck, David. "Aux origines intellectuelles du catholicisme social: la critique de la révolution industrielle par Bonald et Lamennais." Pp. 55-68 in *Etat et pouvoir: La Corse dans la pensée politique*. Actes du colloque de Bastia (26, 27, 28 avril 1984). Presses universitaires d'Aix-Marseille, Faculté de droit et de science politique, 1985. Pp. 218. Fr. 140.00.

See also Le Débat, Reedy ("French 1. General").

BOREL

Coniglio, Angela. "Le metamorfosi della libertà. Crudeltà, ironia e rivolta nel romanzo frenetico in Francia." *Annali della Facoltà di Lettere e Filosofia dell'Università di Bari* 25-26 (1982-83): 407-31.

On *Madame Putiphar* and *L'Ane mort*.

Pompili, Bruno. *Licantropi et meteore. Saggi sul romanticismo francese. Contrappunti*. (Nuova Biblioteca Dedalo, 45.) Bari: Dedalo, 1984. Pp. 132.

Rev. by Rosemary Lloyd in *FS* 40 (1986): 474.

Steinmetz, Jean-Luc. "L'ouïe du nom." Pp. 79-103 in Jean-Luc
Steinmetz, Le Champ d'écoute: essais critiques. (Langages.)
Neuchâtel: La Baconnière, 1985. Pp. 298.

Published previously in Littérature 33 (1979): 86-99. This
reissue contains one or two new footnotes.

Steinmetz, Jean-Luc. Pétrus Borel, un auteur provisoire.
(Objet.) Presses universitaires de Lille, 1986. Pp. 224.
Fr. 85.00.

Brief review in BCLF 488-89 (Aug.-Sept. 1986): 1199.
Attempts to rehabilitate Borel, too often seen as a subversive. For Steinmetz, Borel was a man whose words serve
particularly in the most trying times, when the future of
humankind is most threatened by madness and destruction,
when "plagues" like that represented by Camus impend. Borel's
voice expresses our universal dread—and a salutary ironic
attitude.

See also Frycer, Pompili ("French 1. General").

Reviews of book previously listed:

STEINMETZ, Jean-Luc, ed., Champavert. Contes immoraux (see
RMB for 1985, p. 209), rev. by Ross Chambers in NCFS 14
(1986): 355; by R. Pearson in FS 40 (1986): 473-76; by
Jacques-Philippe Saint-Gérand in Romantisme 51 (1986): 126-
27.

CABET

Mosele, Elio. "Alla ricerca di Icaria." Studi di Letteratura
Francese 10 (1985): 224-43.

CHARRIÈRE

Dubois, Simone, and Pierre H. Dubois. "Isabelle de Charrière-
Belle de Zuylen, 1740-1805. A la recherche d'un art de
vivre. The Quest for a Philosophy of Life." Exposition,
Bibliothèque Publique et Universitaire de Neuchâtel. Con-
ception générale, textes et illustrations: S. et P.H.
Dubois. Neuchâtel: Bibliothèque Publique et Universitaire.
Pp. 48.

"The initiative for this exhibition has been taken by the
Belle de Zuylen/Isabelle de Charrière Associations of
Switzerland and the Netherlands, to mark the publication of
her collected works."

Labadie, Robert. "Belle et Benjamin." Pp. 57-70 in Robert
Labadie, *Comme un arbre aime le vent* (Extraits de la *Gazette
des Tribunaux du Midi*). Toulouse: Chez l'Auteur, 1984.

"Lettre de Zuylen et du Pontet." *Bulletin de l'Association
Belle de Zuylen-Isabelle de Charrière et de l'Association
Suisse des Amis de Madame de Charrière* 10 (Sept. 1985).
Pp. 24.

Contents: Anon., "Aan onze lezers; à nos lecteurs" (1-2);
C.P. Courtney, "Belle de Zuylen and la nouvelle Paméla" (2);
"Accueil des participants par M. Pierre Mahillon, président
de l'Association [The Hague, Oct. 20, 1984]" (3); "Ouverture
de l'exposition par Pierre Mahillon" (in Dutch, with French
conclusion; The Hague, Oct. 19, 1984) (4); "Toelichting bij
de tentoonstelling door Simone Dubois" (5-6); C.P. Courtney,
"Samuel de Constant and William Godwin's *Caleb Williams*"
(5); Simone Dubois, "L'exposition Belle de Zuylen en voyage"
(6-7); anon., "Ouverture de l'exposition par Simone Dubois"
(7); J. Winteler, "Ouverture de la quatrième assemblée générale
de l'Association suisse, 30 novembre 1984" (8); Dennis Wood,
"Isabelle de Charrière and Benjamin Constant: Work in
Progress" (9-10; 16); P.J. Buijnsters, "Een monument voor
Belle van Zuylen" (11-13); Joke van der Meer, "Le Pontet,
vroeger en nu" (13-15); C.P. Courtney, "Belle de Zuylen
in Boswell's *Life of Johnson*" (16); Michel Gilot, "Quelques
remarques sur la langue d'Isabelle de Charrière" (17-18);
J.-D. Candaux, "Belle de Charrière décrite par Rosette de
Bosset (vers 1801)" (19); "Portrait de Madame de Charrières
[*sic*]" (19); Patrice and Margaret Higonnet, "Belle in de
litteraire adelstand verheven: In the Evanescent Mode" (see
TLS, May 17, 1985) (20-22); A.C. Cosijn-Gouda, "Nieuwe
aanwinsten: 1984-1985" (22-23); anon., "Au fin de la correspondance" (23); "Jaarlijkse herdenking van de geboortedag van
Belle de Zuylen--Réunion anniversaire Belle de Zuylen" (24).
(D.J.C.)

Lettre de Zuylen et du Pontet 11 (Sept. 1986). Pp. 16.

Contents: Red., "Aan onze lezers" (1); J. Winteler, "A
nos lecteurs" (1); Red., "Rectificatie" (1); Alix S. Deguise,
"Letter from the United States" (2); Ceri Crossley, "Matthew
Arnold lecteur de Mme. de Charrière" (2); Paul Delbouille,
"Benjamin Constant entre deux règnes" (3-5); J.D.P. Wolff,
"Over de ziekte en het overlijden van Belle's moeder" (6);
Guy de Chambrier, "Madame de Charrière à travers le Journal
de Chambrier d'Oleyres (1788-1790)" (*Lettre de Zuylen et du
Pontet* 8 (7-8, 15); anon., "Deuxième partie: Chambrier

d'Oleyres commente les ouvrages de Madame de Charrière (1788
à 1790)" (9-11); Jan Willem Aschenbrenner, "Excursie
Association Isabelle de Charrière" (11); anon., "Contributie-
Cotisation" (11); Hanna Stouten, "Personen en personages
bij Belle van Zuylen" (12-14); anon., "Jaarlijkse herdenking
van de geboortedag van Belle de Zuylen--Réunion anniversaire
Belle de Zuylen" (16).

Vercruysse, Jeroom.   "Histoire et théâtre chez Isabelle de
Charrière." RHL 85 (1985): 978-987.

     By the editor of the volume on Mme. de Charrière's Théâtre,
in her Œuvres complètes (vol. 7, 1979), a brief insightful
discussion of seven comedies belonging to the second period
(1793-96), which Mme. de Charrière wrote or sketched within
a one-year span. Two of these take place in France and deal
with the Revolution (L'Auteur embarrassé; La Parfaite liberté
ou les vous et les tu). The five others (L'Emigré; L'Incon-
solable François; Marianne d'Erbac; Les Modernes caquets)
show Mme. de Charrière's concern with the emigration issue--
both aspects of one and the same question--and take place in
Switzerland.
     What might be called "théâtre d'actualité et de personnalité"
(our expression), or, in its own way, "théâtre et son double,"
Mme. de Charrière's drama bears the impact of French political
events as she intensely lived them, even at a distance. But,
as one might expect from such an incisive mind, it also reveals
Mme. de Charrière's own judgment of them (not devoid of irony),
and her own proposed social and political ideas for the
building of a modern society. This is "experimental" drama,
if not in form, in its contents.
     To quote Vercruysse: "Le théâtre d'Isabelle de Charrière
est celui de son temps: il décrit les situations, analyse
des comportements, bref il est enté sur l'événement historique
mais il sert également à proclamer un jugement et à formuler
un espoir ... se dégage de ces comédies une leçon beaucoup
plus générale qui incite le lecteur à l'humanité, à la fra-
ternité, à la liberté." (D.J.C.)

Reviews of books previously listed:

CANDAUX, Jean-Daniel, et al., eds., Œuvres complètes, vols.
1-3 (see RMB for 1980, p. 180), rev. by Bernard Bray in RLC
60 (1986): 103-06; vol. 4 (see RMB for 1985, p. 210), rev.
by Michèle Mat-Hasquin in RHL 85 (1985): 306; vol. 5 (see
RMB for 1983, pp. 192-93), rev. by M. Mat-Hasquin in RHL 86
(1986): 153; vol. 6 (see RMB for 1985, pp. 210-211), rev.
by Patrice and Margaret Higonnet in TLS, May 17, 1985, pp.
535-36; vols. 4-6 (see RMB for 1985, p. 210; for 1983, pp.

192-93; for 1985, pp. 210-11), rev. by Kurt Kloocke in *RF* 97 (1985): 477-78; DEGUISE, Alix S., *Trois femmes* (see *RMB* for 1981, p. 185), rev. by Arnold Miller in *Monatshefte* 3 (1984): 361.

CHASLES

See Bonvallet-Mallet ("French 1. General").

CHATEAUBRIAND

Baladier, Louis. "Chateaubriand, *Le génie du christianisme* (première partie, livre 5, chap. 12). Explication de texte." *L'Ecole des Lettres* (Paris) 77 (Sept. 15, 1985): 27-36.

Bardon, H. "La latinité dans les *Mémoires d'outre-tombe*." *EC1* 53 (1985): 415-23.

Chateaubriand's solid training in Latin and his love of Latin authors are evidenced in explicit references, in citations, even (for Bardon) in the cadence of his prose.

Benrekassa, Georges. "Chateaubriand et le refus du politique: le moment de l'*Essai sur les Révolutions*." *Romantisme* 51 (1986): 5-16.

Chateaubriand's jaded views on systems of government, whatever their ideology.

Berne-Joffroy, André, ed. *Vie de Rancé*. (Folio, 1769.) Paris: Gallimard, 1986. Pp. 379. Fr. 24.50.

Berthier, Philippe. "Rêverie sur une rêverie." *Recherches et Travaux. Université de Grenoble. Bulletin* 26 (1984): 139-41.

Chateaubriand and Venice.

Buron, Pierre-Emile. "Une énigme résolue: Chateaubriand et Madame Récamier." *Annales de la Société d'Histoire et d'Archéologie de l'A^{rrt} de St-Malo* (1983): 219-31.

Diniz, Marité. *Lucile, ou la nostalgie du génie*. Paris: Presses de la Renaissance, 1984. Pp. 257.

Romanticized story of Chateaubriand's sister, in the form of an imagined memoir.

Durry, Marie-Jeanne. *La Vieillesse de Chateaubriand (1830-1848)*. Paris: Champion; Geneva: Slatkine, 1986. Pp. 601. Reprint of edition of 1933.

Gourdin-Servenière, Malaka. "Désir de la mort dans *René* et *Les Natchez*: constantes du tourment romantique de l'âme." Pp. 109-20 in Gilles Ernst, ed., *La Mort en toutes lettres*. Pref. by Louis-Vincent Thomas. Presses universitaires de Nancy, 1983. Pp. 302.

Goux, Jean-Paul. "La passion de l'encre et du papier." *Digraphe* 37 (Oct. 1985): 105-13.

Remarks on *Les Mémoires d'outre-tombe*. Chateaubriand's ambition was "l'invention de sa vie par l'écriture." Aspects of the *Mémoires* which strike Goux are the heterogeneity of the manner and temporal confusion. The unity of the work lies in the subject himself.

Guiton, Micheline. *Politique et personnalité: Chateaubriand*. Paris: Nizet, 1986. Pp. 39. Fr. 42.80.

Argues that Chateaubriand's troubled public life was the result of behavior that had its roots in a number of childhood emotional traumas.

Hamilton, James F. "The Ideology of Exoticism in Chateaubriand's *Atala*: An Eighteenth-Century Perspective." Pp. 28-37 in *Exoticism in French Literature*. (French Literature Series, 13.) Department of Foreign Languages and Literatures, University of South Carolina, 1986.

Le Yaouanc, Moïse. "Stendhal et les *Mémoires* de M. de Chateaubriand." *SC* 28 (1986): 239-54, 311-25.

Argues, with heavy circumstantial evidence, for Stendhal's familiarity with the *Mémoires d'outre-tombe*, despite the absence of references to them in his works. In the second part of his article, Le Yaouanc proposes that Stendhal's *Vie de Henri Brulard* (and possibly *Souvenirs d'égotisme*) is a direct negative response to questions of style and sincerity raised by the *Mémoires*.

Markale, Jean. *Chateaubriand au-delà du miroir*. Paris: Imago, 1986. Pp. 206. Fr. 108.00.

Chateaubriand has always fascinated--literally--because he had the "magical" power to go beyond the limits of the ordinary, psychologically and creatively.

Martin, Andrew. "Chateaubriand." Pp. 100-17 in Andrew Martin, *The Knowledge of Ignorance from Genesis to Jules Verne.* Cambridge University Press, 1985. Pp. x+259. $39.50.

Chateaubriand's view of *l'Orient.*

O'Neil, Mary Anne. "Typological Symbolism in Chateaubriand's *Atala*." *SFR* 9 (1985): 335-50.

Pollmann, Leo. "Die Waldmünchen-Episode in den *Mémoires d'outretombe*." Pp. 229-41 in Angel San Miguel, Richard Schwaderer, and Manfred Tietz, eds., *Romanische Literaturbeziehungen im 19. und 20. Jahrhundert: Festschrift für Franz Rauhut zum 85. Geburtstag.* Tübingen: Gunter Narr, 1985. Pp. 358.

On Chateaubriand's representation of an unexpected stopover in the Bavarian village while traveling to Prague and Vienna (spring and early summer of 1833) on a secret mission to Charles X.

Redman, Harry, Jr. "Flaubert's *Educations Sentimentales,* Particularly the First, and Chateaubriand's *Vie de Rancé*." *Degré Second* 10 (Sept. 1986): 17-21.

Flaubert's likely familiarity with the *Vie de Rancé*, seen in parallels of theme and manner.

Riberette, Pierre, ed. *Correspondance générale,* vol. 5, 1er *avril 1822-31 décembre 1822.* Paris: Gallimard, 1986. Pp. 582. Fr. 180.00.

Riberette, Pierre. "On Editing Chateaubriand's Correspondence." *YFS* 71 (1986): 131-47.

An expert notes the pleasures and pains of editing and gives advice on the art.

Richard, Noël. *Chateaubriand: le paradis de la rue d'Enfer.* Toulouse: Chez l'Auteur, 1985. Pp. 171.

Société Chateaubriand, Bulletin 28 (1985).

Contents: Jacques Gury, "Un adolescent à Brest en 1783" (6-12); Jean Dubu, "Chateaubriand mélode, ou la prosodie de *Moïse*" (13-19); André Wartelle, "*Moïse* poème biblique" (20-24); Jean-Maurice Gautier, "Chateaubriand aux eaux de Néris (1841-1842)" (25-30); Odette Croux, "Aulnay, val d'histoire" (36-39); Pierre Riberette, "Latouche, Chateaubriand et Madame Récamier, avec des lettres inédites de Latouche [43 letters, from 1825 to 1847]" (40-58); Georges Buisson, "Henri de

Latouche, éditeur d'André Chénier" (59-68); Edouard Guitton,
"Latouche 'élève secret' d'André Chénier?" (69-74); Renée
Lemaître, "Latouche et Balzac" (75-80); Georges Lubin,
"Latouche et George Sand" (81-86); Fernand Letessier, "Henri
de Latouche, Charles et Marie Nodier" (87-91); Fernand
Letessier, "Un jugement inconnu de Latouche sur Juliette
Récamier" (91-92); Pierre Riberette, "Le modèle d'*Olivier*
[novel by Madame de Duras]" (93-100); Joseph-Marc Bailbé,
"A propos de *Léo* [by Latouche]: un épisode d'une vie d'artiste" (101-06); Jean-Claude Berchet, "Latouche romancier
de la Révolution: *Fragoletta*" (107-15); André Wartelle, "Le
sentiment religieux dans la 'Correspondance de Clément XIV et
de Carlo Bertinazzi' imaginée par Henri de Latouche" (116-
20); "Revue des autographes" (lists letters and manuscripts
by Chateaubriand; judgments on him; letters by and to
Chênedollé; letters by and to Fontanes; letters by Joubert,
Ballanche, Astolphe de Custine, Mme. de Duras, Latouche,
and Mme. Récamier; and "Lettres inédites de Chateaubriand
publiées en 1984") (121-30).   Contents also include news
of book auctions and a Colloque Joubert; "Notes de lecture
[book reviews]" (133-35); and a bibliography of recent
articles and books relating to the period (136-38).

See also Berchet, Claudon, Felkay, Michaud ("French 1. General");
Printz, Wagener ("Staël"); Le Yaouanc ("Stendhal"); Fido
("Italian 2. General").

Reviews of books previously listed:

BARBERIS, Pierre, ed., *Voyage en Amérique* (see *RMB* for 1983,
p. 193), brief rev. by Maria Rosaria Ansalone in *SFr* 29
(1985): 403; RIBERETTE, Pierre, ed., *Correspondance générale*
4 (see *RMB* for 1984, p. 238), rev. by Fernand Letessier in
BAGB no. 3 (1984): 326-27.

COLET

Bood, Micheline. *L'Indomptable Louise Colet*. Paris: Horay,
1986. Pp. 256. Fr. 99.00.

Bruneau, Jean. "Louise Colet, Maxime Du Camp, Gustave Flaubert
... et Garibaldi." Pp. 469-83 in H. Gaston Hall et al.,
eds., *Mélanges à la mémoire de Franco Simone*, vol. 3, *XIXe
et XXe siècles*. Geneva: Slatkine, 1984. Pp. 822.

   Explores the complicated story of Louise Colet's involvement in the liberation of Naples (1860), where Du Camp glimpsed
her ("je l'aperçus à Naples et je me détournai").   Flaubert

and even George Sand figure in this imbroglio. (Seven brief letters of Garibaldi to Louise Colet are appended.)

Clébert, Jean-Paul. *Louise Colet: la muse.* Paris: Presses de la Renaissance, 1986. Pp. 365. Fr. 98.00.

Flaubert, Gustave. *Lettere a Louise Colet.* Trans. and ed. M.T. Giaveri. Milan: Feltrinelli, 1984. Pp. xxviii+260. L. 15,000.00.

   Rev. by Alberto Carrara in *Letture* 40 (Feb. 1985): 129-30.

Rose, Marilyn Gaddis, trans. *Lui: A View of Him.* University of Georgia Press, 1986. Pp. xxiii+317. $24.95.

   In her foreword, the translator sketches Colet's life, then discusses *Lui* (1859) in terms of its biographical sources, i.e., her affairs with Musset and Flaubert. Rose is sympathetic to her.

See also Azar ("Cousin").

COMTE

Gouhier, Henri. *La Philosophie d'Auguste Comte: esquisses.* (Vrin Reprise.) Paris: J. Vrin, 1986. Pp. 82. Fr. 99.00.

   A collection of Gouhier's previously published articles on Comte.

Lenzer, Gertrud, ed. *Auguste Comte and Positivism: The Essential Writings.* University of Chicago Press, 1984. Pp. xxiv+506. $16.00.

Levy, David W. *Herbert Croly of "The New Republic": The Life and Thought of an American Progressive.* Princeton University Press, 1986. Pp. 335.

   Rev. by Hugh Brogan in *TLS*, Feb. 21, 1986, p. 182.
   "Croly [1869-1930] was one of the very few Americans to receive infant Baptism in the positivist church.... Auguste Comte was to the end of his life the chief influence on his thought." (The above review devotes a good deal of space to the influence of Comte on Croly.)

Sacquin, Michèle. *Auguste Comte 1798-1854. Correspondance conservée aux Archives Positivistes de la Maison d'Auguste Comte.* Intro. by Sybil de Acevedo. Inventaire établi d'après le fichier des archives Positivistes par Michèle Sacquin. Paris: Bibliothèque Nationale, 1984. Pp. 53. Fr. 25.00.

Wright, T.R. *The Religion of Humanity: The Impact of Comtean Positivism on Victorian Britain.* Cambridge University Press, 1986. Pp. 306. £27.50.

Rev. by Peter Clarke in *TLS*, May 23, 1986, p. 564.

CONSTANT

Alexander, Ian W. "La morale 'ouverte' de Benjamin Constant." Pp. 39-59 in Ian W. Alexander, *French Literature and the Philosophy of Consciousness: Phenomenological Essays.* Ed. A.J.L. Busst. New York: St. Martin's Press, 1985.

Reprint of essay that appeared on pp. 395-410 in *Studi in onore di Carlo Pellegrini*, Turin: 1963 (see *ELN* 4, supp., p. 65, listed with no comment). "Toute la morale, individuelle et politique, de Constant réside dans l'appel fait aux sentiments durables."

Amprimoz, Alexandre L. "*Adolphe* de Benjamin Constant: un roman engendré par son axe thermique." *RR* 75 (1984): 443-52.

In *Adolphe*'s letters to Ellénore one can discern the notion of literariness, exemplified by Constant's use of the opposition hot-cold. An innovative approach. (E.F.G.)

Berberis, Mauro. "Benjamin Constant: inediti e questioni di metodo." *Materiali per una Storia della Cultura giuridica* 14,i (June 1984): 73-109.

Berberis, Mauro. *Il liberalismo empirico di Benjamin Constant. Saggio di storiografia analitica.* (Università di Genova. Quaderni dell'Istituto di filosofia e sociologia del diritto.) Genoa: ECIG, 1984. Pp. 202.

Coman, Colette. "Le monde inanimé dans *Adolphe*: 'bons' et 'mauvais' objets." *RR* 77 (1986): 33-41.

An aspect of the pathetic fallacy: the narrator perceives the world as good, reassuring or as bad, persecuting, perceptions whose traces are found in the vocabulary of the text.

Cordié, Carlo. "Umanità e intelligenza di Benjamin Constant." *L'Albero* 36 (1983): 88-92.

Courtney, C.P. "Benjamin Constant in 1817: A Contemporary Pen-Portrait." *RLC* 59 (1985): 287-90.

A portrait of Constant at 50, written by an American, Augustus Lucas Hillhouse.

Courtney, C.P. *A Bibliography of the Editions of the Writings of Benjamin Constant to 1833. A Supplement.* Cambridge, England: Christ's College, 1984. Pp. 21.

Courtney, C.P. *A Guide to the Published Works of Benjamin Constant.* (SVEC, 239.) Oxford: Voltaire Foundation, 1985. Pp. 330.

Delbouille, Paul. "Benjamin Constant entre deux règnes." *Lettre de Zuylen et du Pontet* 11 (Sept. 1986): 3-5.

Summary of a talk given on October 19, 1985 at the Slot Zuylen concerning Constant's transition from the "reign" of Mme. de Charrière to that of Mme. de Staël.

Delbouille, Paul. "Constant." Pp. 516-27 in Jean-Pierre de Beaumarchais et al., eds., *Dictionnaire des littératures de langue française*, vol. 1, *A-F.* Paris: Bordas, 1984.

Rev. by Bernard Frank in *Le Matin*, July 17, 1984, p. 24.

Fontana, Biancamaria. "The Shaping of Modern Liberty: Commerce and Civilisation in the Writings of Benjamin Constant." *Annales Benjamin Constant* 5 (1985): 3-15.

The renewed interest in Constant's liberal thought occasioned by the publication of previously inaccessible manuscript material has led as well to a reassessment of classical liberal theory. The author lists some aspects of Constant's thought and shows their similarity to the thought of Scottish writers such as Hume, Smith, and Stewart.

Guggenheim, Michel. "Adolphe l'Etranger." *NCFS* 14 (1985-86): 238-50.

Although the resemblances between Camus's Meursault and Constant's Adolphe are numerous--nonconformity, desire for solitude, rejection of contemporary social values, feelings of alienation--they differ in important respects. Meursault, faced with death, discovers links to the world and to life, whereas Adolphe's indifference to life persists to the end.

Higgonet, Margaret. "Writing from the Feminine: Lucinde and Adolphe." *Annales Benjamin Constant* 5 (1985): 17-35.

"Both Schlegel and Constant achieve a radical departure in novelistic technique by 'writing *from* the feminine.'"

Hofer, Hermann. "Constant." Pp. 128-30 in Klaus Heitmann, ed., *Neues Handbuch der Literaturwissenschaft*, vol. 15,

Europäische Romantik 2. Wiesbaden: Akademische Verlags-
gesellschaft Athenaion, 1982.

Rev. by Ulrich Schulz-Buschhaus in *RJ* 34 (1983): 247-54.

Hofmann, Etienne. "Necker, Constant et la question consti-
tutionnelle (1800-1802)." *CahiersS* 36 (1985): 66-84.

Compares Necker's *Dernières vues de politique et de finance*
and Constant's unpublished *Fragments d'un ouvrage abandonné
sur la possibilité d'une constitution républicaine dans un
grand pays*. Constant's respect for Necker did not prevent
him from differing with the elder statesman. Whereas Necker's
document speaks in terms relative to the Consulat à vie,
Constant's manuscript is more general, objective, and scientific. Where Necker does not worry about an excessively
strong executive branch, placing his faith in "les lois
politiques qui établissent un sage équilibre entre les pouvoirs,
Constant is concerned about abuses of power in both the
legislative and executive branches of government. Restrictions on the powers of government are the only way to avoid
abuses.

Jones, Grahame C. "Ellénore's Letter. Its Bearing on Adolphe."
Essays in French Literature 20 (1983): 12-19.

As a caution to those who would find in Adolphe an unam-
biguous moral lesson, the author examines the psychological
games that Ellénore allegedly plays in her final letter to
Adolphe.

Kloocke, Kurt. "Benjamin Constant, *De la religion* et Georg
Creuzer, *Symbolik und mythologie der alten Völker*, une étude
épistémologique." *CahiersS* 37 (1985-86): 107-16.

Creuzer's and Constant's similarities lie in their common
roots (Kant, Schleiermacher, Protestantism), but they differ
in their concept of religion. For Creuzer, religion was a
charismatic discourse whose truth must be discovered by returning to the pure and primitive revelations of the divinity.
Constant's conception was more modern and more complex,
firmly anchored in the Enlightenment.

Kloocke, Kurt, and Christian Viredaz, eds. "Les *Livres de
dépenses* de Benjamin Constant. Second article." *Annales
Benjamin Constant* 5 (1985): 105-61.

Covers the period 1816-20.

Mistler, Jean. "Benjamin Constant, prophète du libéralisme."
Historia 460 (April 1985): 32-41.

A revised version of a talk published in *Annales Conferencia* 911 (Feb. 1968).

Mizuta, Hiroshi. "Adam Smith and Benjamin Constant." *SVEC* 216 (1983): 430-32.

Olzien, Otto. "Göttinger Laudationes: Benjamin Constant Schrifsteller." *Gottinger Jahrbuch* 32 (1984): 253-54. Text of a speech given on the occasion of affixing a commemorative plaque on the house where Constant lived.

Pavel, Thomas. "Convention et représentation." *Littérature* 57 (Feb. 1985): 31-47. A longer version of the next item.

Pavel, Thomas. "Representational Games: Constant and Flaubert." Pp. 783-89 in Herman Parret and Hans-George Ruprecht, eds., *Exigences et perspectives de la sémiotique*, vol. 2. Recueil d'hommages pour Algirdas Julien Greimas. 2 vols. Amsterdam: Benjamins, 1985. Pp. lxxxv+1065.

Constant's *Adolphe* represents the classical practice of psychological schematism (dubbed the "classical shortcut") whereas the details of Flaubert's *Madame Bovary* make the text rather opaque, a technique dubbed "the realist detour." The detour, however, leads back to moral notions. Based on only one example for each novel, the argument is much too short to be convincing. (E.F.G.)

Reymond, Françoise, ed. "Un manifeste inédit de Benjamin Constant en faveur de l'Empereur en 1815." *Annales Benjamin Constant* 5 (1985): 81-93.

Dated June 12, 1815, this text was written at Napoleon's request just before he left to join his troops in Belgium.

Seylaz, Jean-Luc. "Le portrait d'Ellénore et le jeu des pronoms." *Annales Benjamin Constant* 5 (1985): 75-79.

Because of the presence of the pronoun 'on,' Ellénore's portrait in chapter 2 lacks a definite point of view, one of the few places in the novel where this occurs.

Verrey, Dominique, and Jean-François Thomas. "Benjamin Constant. Chronologie et catalogue des manuscrits." *Uni-Lausanne* 42 (March 1985): 22-23.

Vialet, Michèle. "*Adolphe*: échec en amour ou temporisation politique." *Annales Benjamin Constant* 5 (1985): 53-73.

Recent studies of *Adolphe* call into question the three principal readings of the novel: 1) that it is autobiographical; 2) that it is a study of the human heart of classical purity; and 3) that it is a novel devoid of any contemporary historical, political, or ideological traces. The author pursues a sociohistorical tack, examining the "marginalisation" of the protagonist. The subject of the novel is "l'échec d'une insertion socio-professionnelle ardemment souhaitée." For the author, this failure is inextricably interwoven with the failure of Adolphe's affair with Ellénore.

Violi, Carlo. *Benjamin Constant. Per una storia della riscoperta. Politica e religione*. (Studi e testi filosofici.) Rome: G. Ganemi, 1985. Pp. 247.

Viredaz, Christian. "Bibliographie: parutions récentes 1983-1985." *Annales Benjamin Constant* 5 (1985): 167-74.

Winkler, Markus. "Quelques remarques de Madame de Staël et de Benjamin Constant sur le 'genre naïf' dans la littérature allemande." *CahiersS* 37 (1985-86): 23-44.

In this article, devoted mainly to Mme. de Staël, the author points out Constant's reaction to a passage in Voss's "naïve" poem "Louise," in which Constant perceives a modern attitude. For Constant "le genre simple" only has charm when confronted by its contrary, "le coeur usé," which is quite different from Mme. de Staël's view.

Wood, Dennis. "Constant in Edinburgh: Eloquence and History." *FS* 40 (1986): 151-66.

On Constant's experiences in public speaking and on his formal university studies in Edinburgh. Contains extracts from the minutes of the Speculative Society from 1783 to 1785, when Constant was a member. The author suggests, quite plausibly, that Constant's interest in religions may have sprung from his attendance at the lectures of Alexander Fraser Tytler. (E.F.G.)

Wood, Dennis. "Constant's *Cahier rouge*: New Findings." *FS* 38 (1984): 13-29.

Wood, Dennis. "Isabelle de Charrière and Benjamin Constant: Work in Progress." *Lettre de Zuylen et du Pontet* 10 (Sept. 1985): 9-10, 16.

See also King ("Béranger"); Dubois, Labadie ("Charrière"); Cahiers Staëliens 37, King, Poniatowski, Sato, Viredaz, Wagener ("Staël").

Reviews of books previously listed:

ALLEN, Robert F., *A Stylo-Statistical Study of "Adolphe"* (see *RMB* for 1985, p. 217), rev. by C.P. Courtney in *FS* 40 (1986): 218-19; COURTNEY, Cecil P., *A Bibliography of the Writings of Benjamin Constant* (see *RMB* for 1982, p. 200), rev. by A. Anninger in *PBSA* 78 (1984): 512-14; DANIELS, Barry V., *Revolution in the Theater* (see *RMB* for 1984, p. 200), rev. by Norman King in *ThR* 10 (1985): 179-81; DENTAN, Michel, *Le Texte et son lecteur* (see *RMB* for 1984, p. 241), rev. by P. Carrard in *French Forum* 10 (1985): 245-46; by M. Picard in *RHL* 86 (1986): 168-69; HOFMANN, Etienne, ed., *Benjamin Constant, Madame de Staël et le Groupe de Coppet* (see *RMB* for 1982, p. 261), rev. by J.-P. Aguet in *Revue Suisse d'Histoire* 34 (1984): 155-56; by S. Balayé in *CS* 31-32 (1982): 134-35; by Raymond Trousson in *DHS* 16 (1984): 423-24; HOLDHEIM, W. Wolfgang, *The Hermeneutic Mode* (see *RMB* for 1985, pp. 218-19), rev. by H. Bertens in *RLC* 40 (1986): 98-99; by J. Goodliffe in *Philosophy and Literature* 10 (1986): 105-06; by M. Danahy in *NCFS* 14 (1985-86): 348-49; by V. Nemoianu in *MLN* 100 (1985): 1148-51; KLOOCKE, Kurt, *Benjamin Constant* (see *RMB* for 1984, p. 241), rev. by Carlo Cordié in *SFr* 29 (1985): 186; by P. Delbouille in *RBPH* 63 (1985): 668-70; by C. Marazza in *Paideia* 40 (1985): 107-09; OMACINI, Linda, *La porta chiusa: Lettere a Juliette Récamier (1814-1816)* (see *RMB* for 1984, p. 242), rev. by Carlo Cordié in *Paideia* 39 (1984): 273-75; TODOROV, Tzvetan, "Benjamin Constant, politique et amour" (see *RMB* for 1983, p. 199), rev. by Carlo Cordié in *Paideia* 40 (1985): 112-13.

CORBIERE

Brosse, Monique. "Vrais ou faux gémeaux. Frederick Marryat et Edouard Corbière." *EA* 90 (1984): 205-13.

COURIER

Laurencin, Michel. "La terreur blanche en Touraine et le premier pamphlet politique de Paul-Louis Courier: l'affaire de Luynes (1816)." *Bulletin trimestriel de la Société archéologique de Touraine* 39 (1981): 1029-39.

Martin, Paul. "Un lecteur de Paul-Louis Courier: H.-F.
Amiel." *Cahiers Paul-Louis Courier* 13 (June 1985): 4-25.

Viollet le Duc, Geneviève, ed. *Correspondance générale*, vol.
3, *1815-1825*. Paris: Nizet, 1986. Pp. 510. Fr. 321.00.

COUSIN

Azar, Amine A. "Le cas Victor Cousin. Un étrange observateur
de la pensée germanique pendant le début du XIXe siècle."
Critique 473 (Oct. 1986): 981-98.

On Cousin's role in the intellectual life of the Restoration
and July Monarchy: Cousin as victim of Restoration repression; Cousin as "interpreter" of German philosophy in France
(Kant, Schelling, Hegel); Cousin's alleged paternity of
Louise Colet's daughter Henriette; his contributions to the
Revue des Deux Mondes. In general, the author seeks to show
in Cousin a loss of nerve and a tendency to compromise with
those in power. Good bibliography of modern studies on Cousin
at the end. (J.S.P.)

Janicaud, Dominique. "Victor Cousin et Ravaisson, lecteurs
de Hegel et Schelling." *Les Etudes philosophiques* (Oct.-
Dec. 1984): 451-66.

Vermeren, Patrice. "'La philosophie populaire' suivi de 'La
philosophie de l'égalité ou l'énigme du sphinx.'" *Le Cahier*
1 (Oct. 1985): 173-82.

Vermeren, Patrice. "Une politique de l'institution philosophique:
Quinet et Cousin." *Corpus* 1 (May 1985): 104-33.

Vermeren, Patrice. "Les vacances de Cousin en Allemagne, la
raison du philosophe et la raison d'Etat." *Raison Présente*
63 (1982): 77-97; 64 (1982): 101-19.

See also Bowman ("French 1. General").

CUSTINE

Rubino Campini, Anna Maria. "Astolphe de Custine e l'Italia."
Pp. 161-76 in H. Gaston Hall et al., eds., *Mélanges à la
mémoire de Franco Simone*, vol. 3, *XIXe et XXe siècles*.
Geneva: Slatkine, 1984. Pp. 822.

A general survey of Custine's relationship with Italy,
especially his travels in Italy and their influence on him.

Tarn, Julien-Frédéric. "Une liaison 'romantique' (lettres inédites de Custine)." *BduB* 4 (1986): 473-84.

On Custine's correspondence with Sophie Gay (about 500 of his letters to her survive, covering a half-century). Two extensive passages and a number of brief extracts are quoted. She was a second mother to him; she sponsored him socially and literarily (but their relationship was a far from simple one).

Tarn, Julien-Frédéric. *Le Marquis de Custine ou les malheurs de l'exactitude.* Paris: Fayard, 1985. Pp. 816. Fr. 180.00.

Originally intended to be a study of Custine's prose fiction, this impressive work turned into a *vie et oeuvres.* Still, the long chapters on Custine's novels--running up to 100 pages each--form the core of the book; in them, Tarn applies a variety of techniques, mostly quite traditional, to the literary analysis of Custine's fiction. The life of Custine is superbly documented, but is sometimes related in a somewhat offhand manner, as if the reader already knew the details (e.g., the crucial episode on the road to Saint-Denis). Tarn denies any effort to rehabilitate Custine, but he is sympathetic to Custine the man, seeing in him an island of integrity in a world gone coarse and vulgar. This book should remain the standard work on Custine for a long time or, in any case, serve as the starting point for most future work on him. (J.S.F.)

See also Scaiola ("French 1. General"); *Société Chateaubriand, Bulletin* 28 ("Chateaubriand").

Review of book previously listed:

MARGERIE, Diane de, ed., *Aloys* (see *RMB* for 1984, p. 244), rev. by Peter Byrne in *SFr* 29 (1985): 598.

DAVID

Germer, Stefan, and Hubertus Kohle. "From the Theatrical to the Aesthetic Hero: On the Privatization of the Idea of Virtue in David's *Brutus* and *Sabines.*" *Art History* 9 (1986): 168-84. 6 illus.

With David's two paintings as examples, the author's aim is to investigate the consequences for the "production and reception of 'history painting'" of Rousseau's conception of the public sphere as "the generalization of personal experience." The father in *Brutus* at first was seen as a tragic victim; after the Revolution he became a virtuous hero, sacrificing his sons for the sake of the fatherland." In *Sabines*, through its stylization and borrowing from tradition, the historical event was transformed into an "aesthetic presence." "The renunciation of a specific content is the result of the privatization of the interpretation of works of art which discards politics as possible subject matter." (I.H.C.)

Johnson, Dorothy. "Desire Demythologized: David's *L'Amour Quittant Psyché.*" *Art History* 9 (1986): 450-70. 9 illus.

Defends David's late painting (Brussels, 1817), his first major work after his banishment, which she says should be seen in "the context of romanticism rather than of a bankrupt neoclassicism." Along with parody, "anti-classical elements" are used "to involve the spectator in a psychosexual exploration of ... innocence and experience (ugliness defiling purity) combined with a rather dark eroticism."

DELACROIX

Des critiques en matière d'art. Caen: L'Echoppe, 1986. Pp. 16. Fr. 18.00.

Reprints an article published in the *Revue des Deux Mondes* in May 1829.

Forestier, Sylvie. "Delacroix: peintures et dessins d'inspiration religieuse." *La Revue du Louvre* 36 (1986): 225-26.

Review of an exhibition put on at Nice in the Musée National Message Biblique Marc Chagall, July 5-Oct. 6, 1986.

Johnson, Lee. "Delacroix's *Christ Healing the Blind Man of Jericho*: Poussin Reviewed." *BM* 128 (Sept. 1986): 672-74. 2 illus.

A drawing (ca. 1820) of the figure being healed in Poussin's *The Blind Man of Jericho*; later adapted in Delacroix's own unfinished version of the same subject (ca. 1862-63).

Johnson, Lee. *The Paintings of Eugène Delacroix: A Critical Catalogue 1832-1863 (Movable Pictures and Private Decorations),* vol. 3, *Text,* vol. 4, *Plates.* Oxford: Clarendon Press, 1986. £140.00 (the set).

Knapp, Bettina L. *Word/Image/Psyche.* University of Alabama Press, 1985. Pp. 247.

Includes a chapter on Baudelaire and Delacroix.

See also Foucart ("French 1. General").

DE SADE

See De Jean ("French 1. General").

DESBORDES-VALMORE

Dimić, Colette. "La maturité de Marceline Desbordes-Valmore: une percée des attitudes Biedermeier." *Romantistisch Zeitschrift für Literaturgeschichte/Cahiers d'Histoire des Littératures Romanes* 10 (1986): 83-101.

Review of book previously listed:

MOULIN, Jeanine, *Marceline Desbordes-Valmore* (see *RMB* for 1984, p. 247), rev. by Jacques Crickillon in *Marginales* 40 (Jan.-March 1985): 55-56.

DESCHAMPS

Gandilhon, René. "Le poète Emile Deschamps, Pierre Biston et le comte Pellegrino Rossi." *Revue de l'Histoire de Versailles et des Yvelines* 67 (1983): 99-104.

DESLOGES

Goblot, Jean-Jacques. "Un mystérieux rédacteur du *Globe*: Marcelin Desloges." *RHL* 85 (1985): 234-47.

DESNOYERS

Felkay, Nicole. "Louis Desnoyers et *Le Charivari*." *L'Année Balzacienne* 5 (1984): 107-31.

DUCRAY-DUMINIL

See Inagaki ("Hugo").

DUMAS

Avni, Ora. "Ils courent, ils courent les ferrets. Mauss, Lacan et Les Trois Mousquetaires." *Poétique* 16 (1985): 215-35.

A semiotic study of the peregrinations of the diamond-studded ribbon given by the king to the queen. (An English version was published in *MLN* 100 [1985]: 728-57.)

Backvall, Hans. "Dumas dans un récit suédois du XIXe siècle." *Cahiers Alexandre Dumas* 13 (1984): 30-34.

Bassan, Fernande. "Le cycle des Trois Mousquetaires--du roman au théâtre." *SN* 17 (1985): 243-49.

Compares the novels of the musketeer trilogy to the dramas derived from them. *Vingt ans après* gave rise to *Les Mousquetaires* in 1845, *Les Trois Mousquetaires* gave birth to *La Jeunesse des Mousquetaires* in 1849, and *Le Vicomte de Bragelonne* was transformed into three different dramas.

Bassan, Fernande. "Deux lettres de Dumas père à Eugène von Nordhausen." *RHL* 86 (1986): 887-91.

Two letters of November and October 1864, responding to a request that Dumas go to New York in order to publish a book from which part of the proceeds would be used for the benefit of Union war wounded. Includes interesting background information. (E.F.G.)

Bassan, Fernande, and Claude Schopp, eds. "Correspondance de Dumas." *Cahiers Alexandre Dumas* 13 (1984): 44-49, 56-62.

Baudry, Robert. "Tradition mythique et initiatique dans *Les Travailleurs de la mer* et récits parallèles." *Mbegu* (Lubumbashi) 13 (Feb. 1985): 19-37.

Brugnière, Marie-Bernadette. "Antiquité, révolution et romantisme: *La San Felice* d'Alexandre Dumas." Pp. 69-83 in Ecole de commerce de Toulouse, *Mélanges offerts à Max Cluseau*. Toulouse: I.E.P., 1985. Pp. 715. Fr. 500.00.

— "Calendrier Dumasien (1830-1831)." *Cahiers Alexandre Dumas* 13 (1984): 69-79, 84-92.

Chanteur, Isabelle, and Claude Schopp, eds. *Mes Mémoires*. Texte choisis par Isabelle Chanteur. Présentation et notes de Claude Schopp. Préface de Alain Decaux. Paris: Plon, 1986. Pp. 1034. Fr. 230.00.

Felkay, Nicole. "La Méditerranée de Dumas." *Cahiers Alexandre Dumas* 13 (1984): 17-22.

Godenne, René. "Lire les nouvelles de Dumas." *Cahiers Alexandre Dumas* 13 (1984): 4-5.

Goetschel, Marie-Thérèse. "De Coblence à Mayence, voyager, écrire, lire." *Cahiers Alexandre Dumas* 13 (1984): 25-28.

La Barre de Raillicourt, D. de. "La romanesque généalogie des Dumas." *La Revue Française de Généalogie* (Feb.-March 1985): 18-23.

⌐ Munro, Douglas. *Alexandre Dumas: A Secondary Bibliography of French and English Sources to 1983, with Appendices.* (Garland Reference Library of the Humanities, 512.) New York and London: Garland Publishing, 1985. Pp. ix+173.

Rev. by F.W.J. Hemmings in *FS* 40 (1986): 225-26 and Barbara T. Cooper in *NCFS* 14 (1985-86): 392-93.

Munro, Douglas. "Two Missing Works of Alexandre Dumas, Père." *BJRL* 66 (1983): 198-212.

Neave, Christiane. "Le Château d'If dans tous ses états." *Cahiers Alexandre Dumas* 13 (1984): 64-75.

Reymond, Evelyne. "Dumas à la Grande-Chartreuse." Pp. 77-80 in Evelyne Reymond, *Les Heures dauphinoises des écrivains français.* Paris: Didier-Richard, 1984. Pp. 134.

Ritchie, Adrian C. "Bibliographie." *Cahiers Alexandre Dumas* 13 (1984): 64-66.

Schopp, Claude, ed. *Une Aventure d'amour.* Paris: Plon, 1985. Pp. 302.

Listed in *RMB* for 1985, p. 226, without comment. Concerns Dumas's 1835 trip to Italy and his torrid, albeit brief, affair with the Hungarian singer Caroline Ungher. "Une aventure d'amour," Dumas's own account of the affair, in which the singer's name is disguised, appeared in *Le Monte-Cristo* at the end of 1859. Two other fragments, dealing with other aspects of the voyage, sometimes humorous, are extracted from *Le Monte-Cristo* of 1860 and *La Revue et Gazette musicale de Paris* of January 1836. Included as well are numerous unpublished letters from Caroline Ungher to Dumas. Appended is a helpful chronology of the trip, beginning with Dumas's departure from Paris on May 12, 1835, and ending with his return on December 27, 1835.

Schopp, Claude, ed. "Notes de voyage." *Cahiers Alexandre Dumas* 13 (1984): 35-55.

Concerns Dumas's visit to Switzerland in 1863.

Schopp, Claude, ed. "Le Simplon et la Lombardie, Album de voyage." *Cahiers Alexandre Dumas* 13 (1984): 4-16.

Vingt ans après. 2 vols. Paris: Hachette, 1985. Pp. 389 each. Fr. 57.50 each.

Review of books previously listed:

SCHIFANO, Jean-Noël, ed., *Le Corricolo* (see *RMB* for 1984, p. 249), rev. by A. Bourin in *RDM* (Jan.-March 1985): 439-42; by V. Del Litto in *SC* 27 (1984-85): 2296-97; by Claude Schopp in *Cahiers Alexandre Dumas* 13 (1984): 23-24; SCHOPP, Claude, *Alexandre Dumas* (see *RMB* for 1985, p. 226), rev. by Hubert Juin in *Magazine Littéraire* 226 (Jan. 1986): 65-66; SCHOPP, Claude, ed., *Lettres à Mélanie Waldor* (see *RMB* for 1982, p. 208), rev. by A. Zatloukal in *Cahiers Alexandre Dumas* 13 (1984): 81-82; ULLRICHOVA, Maria, *En suivant les traces d'Alexandre Dumas père en Bohème* (see *ELN* 15, supp. 105), rev. by A.C. Ritchie in *AJFS* 22 (1985): 98-100.

DURAS

Riburette, Pierre. "Le modèle d'*Olivier*." *Société Chateaubriand, Bulletin* 28 (1985): 93-100.

See also Société Chateaubriand, Bulletin 28 ("Chateaubriand").

DUVAL

See Cooper ("Mérimée").

ECKSTEIN

Review of book previously listed:

LE GUILLOU, Louis, ed., *Lettres inédites du baron d'Eckstein* (see *RMB* for 1984, pp. 250-51), rev. by Jean Gaulmier in *RHL* 86 (1986): 303-04.

ESQUIROS

Zielonka, Anthony. *Alphonse Esquiros (1812-1876): A Study of His Works*. Geneva: Slatkine, 1985. Pp. 304. Fr. 215.00.

Rev. by Jean-Claude Caron in *Bulletin de la Société d'Histoire de la Révolution de 1848 et des Révolutions du XIXᵉ Siècle* 3 (1987):   114-15.

See also Michaud ("French 1. General").

FAURIEL

Carpentari Messina, Simone.   "Manzoni dramaturge et la France: le manifeste de Fauriel."   Pp. 250-76 in H. Gaston Hall et al., eds., *Mélanges à la mémoire de Franco Simone*, vol. 3, *XIXᵉ et XXᵉ siècles*. Geneva: Slatkine, 1984.   Pp. 822.

On the role Manzoni's own theatrical efforts (e.g., *Le Comte de Carmagnole* and *Adelghis*), now largely forgotten, played in the controversy over Romanticism during the Restoration, via the impact of his *Lettre à Chauvet* (published in 1823 thanks to Fauriel).   The author calls this manifesto "un exemple rigoureux et cohérent--le seul dans les années 1820--de poétique 'idéologue.'"

Sansone, Mario.   "Manzoni francese."   *CeS* 24 (April-June 1985): 17-44.

More on Manzoni and Fauriel.

See also Ragusa ("Italian 3. Manzini").

FIEVEE

Tulard, Jean.   *Joseph Fiévée, conseilleur secret de Napoléon.* (Les Inconnus de l'Histoire.)   Paris: Fayard, 1985.   Pp. 250.   Fr. 75.00.

Rev. by Jacques Godechot in *AHRF* 263 (Jan.-March 1986): 116.

FLAUBERT

Anderson, Mary R.   *Art in a Desacralised World: Nineteenth-Century France and England.*   Lanham, Md.:   University Press of America, 1984.

Beaumont, Barbara, ed.   *Flaubert and Turgenev: A Friendship in Letters.*   New York: Norton, 1986.   Pp. 197. $197.95.

Rev. by Frederick Brown ("Dear Genius") in *NR*, Feb. 17, 1986, pp. 34-38.

Butler, R. "Flaubert et Boileau." *RHL* 86 (1986): 856-64.

Flaubert"s attitude to Boileau evolved from scorn during his Romantic youth to admiration in his maturity. Flaubert's aesthetic views in the latter period, e.g., that the ultimate value of a work depends on its conception and therefore that one must think before writing comes directly from the *Art poétique*.

Castelein, Machteld. "*Novembre* de Gustave Flaubert: un récit funèbre." *LR* 40 (1986): 133-45.

Novembre is a novel of literary discovery, an intermediary work between the first-person expansions of *Les Mémoires d'un fou* and the third-person narration of the first *Education sentimentale*. We're on familiar ground here. (E.F.G.)

Czyba, Lucette. "Flaubert et 'La Muse' ou la confrontation de deux mythologies incompatibles." Pp. 43-57 in Roger Bellet, ed., *Femmes de lettres au XIXe siècle*. Presses universitaires de Lyon, 1982. Pp. 318.

Remarks on the lack of understanding between Flaubert and Louise Colet.

Douchin, Jacques-Louis. *La Vie érotique de Flaubert*. Paris: Carrère/J.J. Pauvert, 1984. Pp. 324.

Rev. by Roger Bismut in *RHL* 86 (1986): 938-41; by Pierre Kyria in *Magazine Littéraire* 220 (June 1985): 68-69; by Maurice Nadeau in *QL*, Feb. 1-15, 1985, p. 4.
Occasionally a book appears that challenges ideas held without question for decades. This is such a book. Laid to rest forever (except perhaps for details) is the legend, created out of whole cloth by Gérard-Gaillly, of Elisa Schlesinger as the lifelong, platonic love of Flaubert and inspiration for *Les Mémoires d'un fou* and *L'Education sentimentale*. Douchin shows convincingly that far from being obsessed with the memory of Elisa, Flaubert went for long periods of time without mentioning her, even to his closest friends, and that, after his return from the Middle East in 1851, and especially during the composition of the novel supposedly inspired by her, Flaubert made no attempt to see her, although numerous occasions presented themselves. How then to explain the famous reference in the first scenario of *L'Education sentimentale* ("un collégien--Mme Sch--M Sch--moi")? Flaubert's lifelong love was a "sylphide," for which sometimes Elisa, sometimes others served as material stimulus or focal point for his nostalgic reveries. One might add that Flaubert's practice here was quite in keeping with his notion

of the "tremplin."

The deflation of the legend of Elisa Schlesinger is the highlight of this book devoted to chronicling Flaubert's relationships to women. Louise Colet of course occupies a prominent place, as do Juliet and Gertrude Herbert, Caroline Heuland, Eulalie de Langlade, and countless others. At times the list of conquests becomes a wee bit tedious, yet one must realize that such was an aspect of the Victorian era seldom acknowledged by the Victorians (but exposed for example by Zola in *Pot-Bouille*). As a final bonus, Couchin reviews the question of Guy de Maupassant's paternity, presenting interesting, albeit circumstancial evidence, that Flaubert may indeed have been the father. Essential reading for students of Flaubert. (E.F.G.)

Hilliard, Aouicha. "Le rythme de 'Smarh': deux modes contrastés du vœu de désintégration chez Gustave Flaubert." *RR* 77 (1986): 56-70.

A basic paradigm of the tale is constituted by Smarh's futile search for balance as he moves between the two extremes represented by Satan and Yuk. This symbolizes Flaubert's struggle against the temptation of disintegration, that is, madness. Depends on Sartre and R.D. Laing for theoretical support and thus accepts Sartre's view of the origin of Flaubert's illness. The paradigm is also applied, briefly, to *La Tentation de Saint Antoine*, *L'Education sentimentale*, and *Bouvard et Pécuchet*.

Kashiwagi, Kayoko. *La Théâtralité dans les deux "Education sentimentale."* Tokyo: France Tosho; Paris: Nizet, 1985. Pp. v+194. Fr. 171.20.

This revised thesis is a rather pedestrian survey of the appearance in the two novels of characters from the world of the theater and of dramatic techniques, such as the use of the double protagonist. (E.F.G.)

Knight, Diana. *Flaubert's Characters: The Language of Illusion.* (Cambridge Studies in French.) Cambridge University Press, 1985. Pp. 125. £19.50.

Rev. by P.M. Wetherill in *FS* 40 (1986): 226-27.

Lowe, Lisa. "The Orient as woman in Flaubert's *Salammbô* and *Voyage en Orient*." *CLS* 23 (1986): 44-58.

Eighteenth-century travel literature treats the Orient as other, but in spatial terms. In the nineteenth century this otherness becomes gendered: the Orient is depicted as woman. Correction: Flaubert did not write *Salammbô* upon his return

from the Orient (June 1851) but began it over six years
later.

Parke, Tim. "Flaubert devant la critique britannique."
RLC 59 (1985): 299-308.

Piccioni Borri, Anna. *Espressioni e forme del culto cattolico
nell'opera di Flaubert.* Siena: Università degli studi,
1983. Pp. 127.

    Rev. by Gisèle Séginger in *RHL* 86 (1986): 311.

Prendergast, Christopher. "Flaubert: The Stupidity of
Mimesis." Pp. 180-211 in Christopher Prendergast, *The Order
of Mimesis: Balzac, Stendhal, Nerval, Flaubert* (listed above
under "Balzac").

    This chapter is an admirable demonstration of the para-
doxical (on the model of the Cretan liar paradox) nature of
Flaubert's use of *bêtise.* Commonplaces embedded within the
text, generally interpreted as ironic, may at the same time
be taken literally. Flaubert's technique, referred to at
one point as "a peculiarly radical form of the uncertainty
principle" is more correctly viewed, however, as an anticipa-
tion of the logical problem studied in Kurt Gödel's well-
known paper, "On Formally Undecidable Propositions." (E.F.G.)

Redman, Harry, Jr. "Flaubert's *Educations sentimentales,*
Particularly the First, and Chateaubriand's *Vie de Rancé.*"
Degré Second 10 (1986): 17-21.

    Parallels between the two versions of *L'Education senti-
mentale* and *La Vie de Rancé.* Suggestive but not convincing.
(E.F.G.)

Tétu, Jean-Jacques. "Ton image (...) apparaît entre les
phrases que je cherche." Pp. 21-41 in Roger Bellet, ed.,
Femmes de lettres au XIXe siècle. Presses universitaires
de Lyon, 1982. Pp. 318.

    Three themes are prominent in Flaubert's letters to Louise
Colet: 1) Flaubert declares that his love for Louise surpasses
all his previous loves; 2) Flaubert expresses great distrust
in the happiness that love might procure; and 3) Flaubert
speaks of his love for Louise during periods of relaxation
after his literary labors. Flaubert sought in Louise a
reflection of himself, a role that she was unable or unwilling
to play.

Wild, Ingetraut. *Das Experiment der "première Education sentimentale": zur Künstler-Bürger-Problematik und zur Genese des modernen Künstlers bei Gustave Flaubert.* (Europäische Hochschulschriften, series 13, 97.) Frankfurt am Main, Bern, and New York: Peter Lang, 1985. Pp. 250.

Traces Flaubert's attitudes toward bourgeois society and the life of the artist in the first *Education sentimentale.* The author sees the opposition between the two characters Jules and Henry as a representation of the autobiographical opposition between the life of the artist and the middle-class life represented by Doctor Flaubert.

Zito, Marina. "Lo spirito del disordine e la condizione dell'uomo ne *La Tentation de Saint-Antoine.*" *AION-SR* 25 (1983): 519-38.

See also Bowman ("French 1. General"); Redman ("Chateaubriand"); Pavel ("Constant").

Reviews of books previously listed:

BERNHEIMER; Charles, *Flaubert and Kafka* (see *RMB* for 1983, p. 207), rev. by D. Faber in *RLC* 59 (1985): 360-61; by Naomi Schor in *RR* 76 (1985): 218-20; CZYBA, Lucette, *Mythes et idéologie de la femme dans les romans de Flaubert* (see *RMB* for 1983, p. 207), rev. by G. Mombello in *SFr* 29 (1985): 200-01; by G. Sagnes in *RHL* 86 (1986): 308-11; by Simone Vierne in *Romantisme* 51 (1986): 122-23; DOUCHIN, Jacques-Louis, *Le Bourreau de soi-même* (see *RMB* for 1984, p. 251), rev. by Arlette Michel in *IL* 38 (1986): 50; by P. Cogny in *RHL* 86 (1986): 937-38; SEGINGER, Gisèle, *Le Mysticisme dans "La Tentation de saint Antoine"* (see *RMB* for 1985, p. 227), rev. by Arlette Michel in *IL* 38 (1986): 50; by G. Sagnes in *RHL* 86 (1986): 936-37; WETHERILL, P.M., *Flaubert: la dimension du texte* (see *RMB* for 1983, pp. 207-08), rev. by J. Bem in *RHL* 85 (1985): 688-90.

FOURIER

Beecher, Jonathan. "Parody and Liberation in *The New Amorous World* of Charles Fourier." *History Workshop* 20 (Fall 1985): 125-33.

Pellegrino Ceccarelli, Alba. "La 'modesta proposta' di Fourier." Pp. 55-70 in *Problemi di semantica e di storia del lessico franco-italiano.* (Quaderni della Società Universitaria per gli studi di lingua e lettèratura francese, 5.) Milan: Cisalpino-Goliardica, 1984.

Romeo, C. *Introduzione a Charles Fourier*. Messina: Samperi, 1983. Pp. 133.

Rev. by Néréma Zuffi in *SFr* 29 (1985): 596-97.

Stenzel, Hartmut. "Eine Ästhetik des 'Vorscheins': Grundpositionen der Literatur- und Kunstkritik der fourieristischen 'Ecole sociétaire.'" *Lendemains* 37 (1985): 18-26.

Tundo, Laura. "Profilo di un ventennio della critica fourieriana." *Note su Socialismo e Cristianesimo* 6-7 (Oct. 1983-March 1984): 33-38.

See also Lloyd ("French 1. General").

Review of book previously listed:

NATHAN, Michel, *Le Ciel des Fouriéristes* (see *RMB* for 1981, pp. 198-99), rev. by Philippe Desan in *FR* 59 (1985-86): 1007-09.

GAUTIER

Cockerham, Harry, ed. *Poésies (1830)*. (The Athlone French Poets.) London: Athlone Press, 1985. Pp. 168.

Rev. by John Van Eerde in *NCFS* 14 (1986): 357-61. Reprint of Cockerham's edition of 1973 (see *ELN* 12, supp. 92).

Contes fantastiques. Paris: José Corti, 1986. Pp. 226. Fr. 75.00.

Fifth reprinting of the edition of 1962.

Deudon, Eric Hollingsworth. "*Mademoiselle de Maupin* rescappée de la censure orléaniste." *Les Amis de Flaubert* 66 (May 1985): 18-24.

Eigeldinger, Marc. "L'intertextualité dans *Mademoiselle Dafné* de Gautier." *RLMC* (39): 143-56.

Only five pages of this article deal with the announced subject, the first eight being devoted to a definition of intertextuality and a review of strategies for tracking it. Eigeldinger notes the obvious cases of intertextuality in the tale and attempts to demonstrate their functions. His discussion is superficial, so less than convincing. The value of the article lies in the neat synopsis of intertextuality. (A.B.S.)

Gaudair, Jean-Michel, ed. *Le Roman de la momie.* (Folio, 1718.) Paris. Gallimard, 1986.

Holt, Eileen. "Gautier's 'Carmen.'" *Parnasse* 2,2 (1984): 35-42.

An explication.

Kars, Henk. "Le sein, le char et la herse: description, fantastique et métadiscours dans un récit de Théophile Gautier." Pp. 86-109 in Leo H. Hoek, ed., *La Littérature et ses doubles.* Groningen: Inst. voor Romaanse Talen, 1985. Pp. 146.

On *Arria Marcella.*

Knapp, Bettina L. "Gautier: Aestheticism versus Asceticism in the Paintings of Ribera and Zurbarán." Pp. 6-28 in Bettina L. Knapp, *Word/Image/Psyche.* University of Alabama Press, 1985.

Gautier's diurnal spirit caused him to find the stark paintings of the Spaniards distasteful. Knapp shows little knowledge of the scholarship on Gautier and Spanish painting. (A.B.S.)

Lacoste-Veysseyre, Claudine, ed. *Correspondance générale,* vol. 2, *1843-1845.* Sous la direction de Pierre Laubriet et avec la collaboration de: Marianne Chermakian, Jean-Claude Fizaine, Andrew Gann, Jean Richard, et Jean Rose. (Histoire des Idées et Critique Littéraire, 238.) Geneva: Droz, 1986. Pp. 383. Fr. 310.00.

Brief review in *BCLF* 487 (July 1986): 1014; rev., with volume 1, by Victor Brombert in *TLS*, Sept. 26, 1986, p. 1051.

Laszlo, Pierre. "Que la fête recommence!" *SFR* 9 (1985): 47-59.

On *La Cafetière*, Gautier's fantastic tale of 1831. The story confirms the image (fading lately) of Gautier as an innovator in the art of transposition.

Lloyd, Rosemary. "Gautier est-il aussi partisan de la doctrine de l'art pour l'art qu'on veut nous le faire croire:" *Bulletin des Etudes Parnassiennes* 7 (1985): 1-13.

Lloyd, Rosemary. "Rereading *Mademoiselle de Maupin.*" *OL* 41 (1986): 19-32.

Studies structures and allusions. Finds in Gautier a mature observer of the psyche, especially insofar as love is con-

cerned. Points out also--though without substantiation--that
in *Maupin* Gautier creates a "modern myth in which beauty,
poetic inspiration and love can coincide only in a being who
is both Apollo and Aphrodite" (29). One regrets Professor
Lloyd's indifference to American--and some continental--
scholarship on *Maupin*. (A.B.S.)

Lloyd, Rosemary. "Speculum amantis, speculum artis: The
    Seduction of Mademoiselle de Maupin." *NCFS* 15 (1986-87):
    77-86.

    Two isotopes, the erotic and the aesthetic, overlap, but
    the novel ultimately favors the latter, guiding the reader
    to favor aestheticism, too.

Mickel, Emanuel J., Jr. *The "Parnassian" Legacy of Gautier's
    "Symphonie en blanc majeur."* (Occasional Papers in Language,
    Literature, and Linguistics, A30.) Iowa State University,
    1985. Pp. 11.

Puleio, M.-T. "Le thème du 'château Louis XIII' dans la
    géographie mythique de Théophile Gautier." Pp. 71-80 in
    *La letteratura e l'immaginario: problemi di semantica e di
    storia del lessico franco-italiano.* (Atti dell'XI convegno
    della Società Universitaria per gli studi di lingua e
    letteratura francese.) *Società Universitaria ... Quaderni*
    5 (1984): Special issue.

Rizza, Cecilia, ed. *Les Grotesques.* (Biblioteca della
    Ricerca: Testi Stranieri, 7.) Fasano: Schena; Paris:
    Nizet, 1985. Pp. 475. Fr. 214.00.

    Rev. by Jean Dubu in *XVIIe Siècle* 38 (1986): 310.
    The introduction is useful in evoking Gautier's poetic out-
    look in the 1830s and in emphasizing the originality of his
    relativistic historical perspective. Rizza bases her edition
    on the texts of the original articles that Gautier published
    in *La France Littéraire, Le Monde Dramatique,* and *La Revue
    des Deux Mondes,* adding the "Post-face" which he wrote for
    the 1844 edition of *Les Grotesques.* (A.B.S.)

Rossiter, Andrew. "Sens de l'amour dans *Mademoiselle de Maupin*
    de Gautier." Pp. 735-42 in Michel Malicet, ed., *Hommages à
    Jacques Petit,* vol. 2. (Annales Littéraires de l'Université
    de Besançon, 300; Centre de Recherches Jacques Petit, 41.)
    Paris: Les Belles Lettres, 1985. Pp. 977.

    Maupin marks a turning point in Gautier's search for happi-
    ness: he gives up any prospect of happiness in the concrete

world and situates his ideal rather in dream, *le rêve.*
A secondary conclusion--that, after *Maupin,* Gautier no
longer represents a search for happiness--is groundless.
(A.B.S.)

Steinmetz, Jean-Luc. "Gautier, Jensen et Freud." Pp. 45-56
in Jean-Luc Steinmetz, *Le Champ d'écoute: essais critiques.*
(Langages.) Neuchâtel: La Baconnière, 1985. Pp. 298.

Published previously in a special issue of *Europe* devoted
to Gautier (601 [May 1979]). See *RMB* for 1979, p. 182.

Willis, Pauline Wahl. "*Armance* de Stendhal et *Spirite* de
Gautier." Pp. 112-23 in V. Del Litto and Kurt Ringger, eds.,
*Stendhal et le romantisme. Actes du XVᵉ Congrès inter-
national stendhalien (Mayence, 1982).* Aran (Switzerland):
Editions du Grand-Chêne, 1984. Pp. 360.

Surprising--and surprisingly obvious--parallels between
the two novelettes. But the respective treatments of the
material confirm differing attitudes in Stendhal and Gautier.
The former appears as more "modern," with his ironic stance;
while the latter seems more traditionally Romantic because
he apparently takes his story seriously.

Zenkin, S.N. "Teatr i akterskaia igra v khudozhestvennoi
proze Teofilia Got'e." *Vestnik Moskovskogo Universiteta,*
seria 9, *Filologiia* 9,3 (May-June 1986): 50-57.

Translation of the title: Theater and Acting in the
Artistic Prose of Theophile Gautier.

See also Lloyd, Pierssens, Steinmetz, Stocker ("French 1.
General"); Gardelles ("Stendhal").

Reviews of books previously listed:

EIGELDINGER, Marc, ed., *Mademoiselle Dafné* (see *RMB* for 1984,
p. 256), rev. by Harry Cockerham in *FS* 40 (1986): 340-41;
by Ulrich Döring in *RF* 97 (1985): 482-83; by Andrew G. Gann
in *NCFS* 14 (1986): 355-57; LACOSTE-VEYSSEYRE, Claudine, ed.,
Correspondance générale, vol. 1 (see *RMB* for 1985, p. 230),
briefly rev. in *BCLF* 481 (Jan. 1986): 1814; rev. by Serge
Fauchereau in *QL* 472 (Oct. 16-31, 1986): 17; by I.H. Smith
in *AUMLA* 65 (1986): 125-26; by Peter Whyte in *MLR* 81 (1986):
747-48 (and see review by Victor Brombert in this *RMB* under
Lacoste-Veysseyre, Claudine, ed., *Correspondance générale,*
vol. 2; SCHAPIRA, M.-C., *Le Regard de Narcisse* (see *RMB* for
1984, p. 257), rev. by Peter Whyte in *MLR* 81 (1986): 748-
50; SNELL, Robert, *Théophile Gautier, a Romantic Critic* (see

RMB for 1982, pp. 215-16), rev. by R.M. Dineen in *NZJFS* 6 (1985): 68-72.

GENLIS

Virolle, Roland. "Madame de Genlis, Mercier de Compiègne: gothique anglais ou gothique allemand?" *Europe* 659 (March 1984): 29-38.

On the Gothicism in her *Les Chevaliers du cygne* and Mercier's *Rosalie et Gerblois*.

Review of book previously listed:

GENLIS, Madame de, *Inès de Castro* (see *RMB* for 1985, p. 232), rev. by Alain Clerval in *NRF* 397 (Feb. 1, 1986): 93-95.

GERICAULT

Sells, Christopher. "After the *Raft of the Medusa*: Géricault's Later Projects." *BM* 128 (Aug. 1986): 563-71. 5 illus.

The projects, left unfinished at the artist's death, were all "large-scale figure subjects with a moral dimension." Titles: *The African Slave-Trade, The Opening of the Doors of the Spanish Inquisition, The Reddition of Parga*, and *The Barcelona Plague*.

GIRARDIN (Delphine de)

Vissière, Jean-Louis, ed. *Chroniques parisiennes, 1836-1848.* Paris: Des Femmes, 1986. Fr. 125.00.

Rev. by Delphine Perret in *Journal Français d'Amérique*, April 24-May 7, 1987, p. 20.

GOBINEAU

André, Sylvie. "'Mundus imaginalis': la rencontre spirituelle de Gobineau avec le Chiisme." *Romantisme* 52 (1986): 57-68.

The impact of Gobineau's contact with Shiite religion (he was in Persia in 1855-58, 1861-63). In his travels, he discovered that the Orient had already explored and conceptualized a "metaphysical substratum" which satisfied the Romantics' "expérience vécue de l'Imaginaire." "Aussi parvint-il à construire une philosophie originale permettant de dépasser l'angoisse existentielle qui habitait déjà la conscience occidentale."

Boissel, Jean. *Gobineau.* (Le Spectacle du Monde.) Paris:
Compagnie française de librairie, 1981. Pp. 384. Fr. 175.00.

Gaulmier, Jean. "A propos de Gobineau et l'Italie: quelques
problèmes à résoudre." Pp. 425-31 in H. Gaston Hall et al.,
eds., *Mélanges à la mémoire de Franco Simone*, vol. 3, *XIXe*
et XXe siècles. Geneva: Slatkine, 1984. Pp. 822.
The problems that Gaulmier points to as needing research
are: 1) Gobineau's friendship with Charles de Barral; 2)
"l'affaire Melzi"; and 3) Gobineau's possible correspondence
with his Italian friends in the last years of his life.

Malliarakis, Jean-Gille, ed. *L'Inégalité des races.* Paris (?):
Editions du Trident, Librairie Française, 1984.

Néry, Alain. "Gobineau et la succession d'Henri V." *Mémoire*
2 (May 1985): 57-70.

Raymond, Jean-François de. "La décadence selon Gobineau."
Pp. 53-58 in *La Décadence. Réalite, mythe ou idéologie?*
Actes du colloque, 28 et 29 avril 1983. (Equipe de recherche
'Herméneutique et critique des idéologies.') Université
des Sciences Sociales de Grenoble, 1984.

Raymond, Jean-François de. *La Grèce de Gobineau. Correspondance*
politique d'Arthur de Gobineau, ministre de l'empereur à
Athènes, 1864-1868. (Les Textes français.) Paris: Les Belles
Lettres, 1985. Pp. 645.

Toda, Michel. "Arthur de Gobineau. Une épopée de la décadence."
Présent, July 12, 1985, p. 6.

Reviews of books previously listed:

BEZIAU, Roger, ed., *Etudes critiques 1842-1847* (see *RMB* for
1984, pp. 258-59), rev. by Jean Boissel in *RLC* 60 (1986):
247-49; by Peter Byrne in *SFr* 29 (1985): 414-15; by Simon
Jeune in *RHL* 86 (1986): 775-76; by Murray Sachs in *FR* 60
(1986-87): 128-29; by Françoise M. Taylor in *NCFS* 15 (1986-
87); 207-09; GAULMIER, Jean, and Jean Boissel, eds., *Œuvres*,
vol. 2 (see *RMB* for 1983, p. 214), rev. by J. Hervier in
RLC 59 (1985): 355-57; by Mario Richter in *SFr* 29 (1985):
199-200; SMITH; Annette, *Gobineau et l'histoire naturelle*
(see *RMB* for 1984, p. 259), rev. by Roger Béziau in *RHL* 86
(1986): 774-75; by Michael Biddiss in *FS* 40 (1986): 477;
by Robert T. Denommé in *FR* 60 (1986-87); 127-38; by Arlette
Michel in *IL* 38 (1986): 51; by Françoise M. Taylor in *NCFS*
14 (1985-86): 190-91; by P. Winston in *MLN* 100 (1985): 899-
901.

GUÉRIN (M. DE)

L'Amitié Guérinienne 149 (1986).

Contents: "Aux amis des Guérin" (51); Pierre Hirissou, "A la rencontre de Mauriac et des Guérin" (52-69); Albert Roux, "Sur 'Glaucus'" (70-84); Henri Maynard, "A l'occasion du 175ᵉ anniversaire de la naissance de Maurice de Guérin" (85); G.L., "Journée guérinienne. Dimanche 21 juillet 1985, Château du Cayla" (86-87); Dr Robert Maurice-Raynaud, "Rectificatif" (88); G. Laflaquière, "A travers l'imprimé" (89-90); P. Vedel, *"Vie d'Eugénie de Guérin.* Edition remaniée et mise à jour par Gilbert Vezin" (91).

L'Amitié Guérinienne 150 (1986).

Contents: Jacques Bonnardot, "Affinités; éloge de l'Esquilo" (3-7); James Vest, "Les textes retrouvés: un épithalame de Maurice de Guérin pour un ami" (8-11); Guy Sabin, "Hérédité et environnements: Levains du génie de Maurice de Guérin (deuxième partie)" (12-27); "Les chroniques de l'Amitié guérinienne" (28); P. Vedel, "Les Guérin et les âmes modernes" (28-30); G. Laflaquière, "Journée guérinienne du 20 Juillet 1896" (31); "Nouvel appel à nos amis" (32).

Review of book previously listed:

FUMAROLI, Marc, ed., *Le Centaure; Le Cahier vert; Glaucus; Pages sans titre* (see *RMB* for 1984, p. 260), rev. by Claude Gély in *RHL* 86 (1986): 1130-31.

GUIZOT

Even, Pascal. "Guizot après 1848 d'après la correspondance inédite avec Piscatory, 1848-1870)." *Revue d'Histoire Diplomatique* 100 (1986): 65-111.

Follows the correspondence more or less chronologically, but, under the different headings ("Retour d'exil," "Guizot et le Second Empire," etc.), groups Guizot's remarks by subject. Even wishes to stress the human side of Guizot.

See also Walch ("French 1. General").

Review of book previously listed:

ROSENVALLON, Pierre, *Le Moment Guizot* (see *RMB* for 1985, p. 235), rev. by Pascalis M. Kitromilides in *French Politics and Society* 13 (March 1986): 30-32.

HUGO

Albouy, Pierre, ed. *Les Chants du crépuscule; Les Voix intérieures; Les Rayons et les ombres.* (Poésie.) Paris: Gallimard, 1983.

Rev. by Arlette Michel in *Il* 36 (1984): 228-29.

Allard, René. "1985 ... Année Victor Hugo: un essai généalogique." *La France Généalogique* (Oct. 1985): 225-48.

Alluin, Bernard, Pierre Dhainaut, Michèle Hirsch, and Claire Suard, eds. "Victor Hugo, Nord de la France et Belgique: textes et dessins." *Nord* 5, supp. (1985).

Amiot, Anne-Marie. "Les fondements théologiques de la Révolution française dans *La Fin de Satan* de Victor Hugo." Pp. 137-64 in Anne-Marie Amiot, *Philosophes de la Révolution française.* Paris: J. Vrin, 1984.

Ancelet, Daniel. "Hugo, mon grand oncle." *Cerf-volant* 125 (1985): 64-65.

Arámburu Alana, Mercedes. "Homenaje a Víctor Hugo." *Letras de Deusto* 15 (1985): 175-80.

Arico, Santo L. "Madame Juliette Adam and Victor Hugo: An Unpublished Souvenir." *RomN* 26 (1985): 109-14.

History of their friendship and transcript of one of her reminiscences about Hugo.

B.D., ed. "Du sommeil et du réveil." *Revue de la Bibliothèque Nationale* 20 (Summer 1986): 59-65.

Probably part of the last version of *Libres Méditations d'un solitaire inconnu.*

Backès, Jean-Louis. "Sur un usage métaphorique du mot 'tyrannie' dans l'histoire des doctrines littéraires: à propos de la Préface de *Cromwell.*" *Cahiers de Philosophie Politique et Juridique* 6 (1984): 263-74.

Backès, Jean-Louis. "Survivances et résurgences dans l'histoire littéraire selon Hugo." Pp. 105-19 in Marc-Mathieu Münch, ed., *Recherches sur l'histoire de la poétique.* (Faculté des lettres et sciences humaines, Centre de Recherche "Littérature et Spiritualité" de l'Université de Metz.) Nancy and New York: Peter Lang, 1984.

Bailbé, Joseph-Marc. "Victor Hugo et les romanciers normands."
Etudes Normandes 34,2 (1985): 5-12.

Barrère, Jean-Bertrand. Victor Hugo: l'homme et l'oeuvre.
Paris: C.D.U.-S.E.D.E.S., 1984. Pp. 180.
    Rev. by Lloyd Bishop in RR 76 (1985): 217-18; by Marius-
François Guyard in RHL 85 (1985): 1075.

Baudry, Robert. "Tradition mythique et initiatique dans Les
Travailleurs de la mer et récits parallèles." Mbegu 13
(Lubumbashi) (Feb. 1985): 19-37.

Bellanger, Jean-Claude. "Une autre façon d'ouvrir les livres."
Le Français d'Aujourd'hui 73 (March 1986): 51-55.
    Study of 14 "Projets d'Actions éducatives" presented by
various schools in the Académie de Caen in an effort to integrate literature and living culture in the teaching of
Victor Hugo's works.

Bellosta, Marie-Christine. "Hugo, tant mieux!" Magazine
littéraire 214 (Jan. 1985): 22-24.

Bellosta, Marie-Christine. "Victor Hugo: l'image et l'histoire."
Magazine Littéraire 214 (Jan. 1985): 18-53.

Bem, Jeanne. "'Châtiments' ou l'histoire de la France comme
enchaînement de parricides." RLM 693-97 (1984): 39-51.

Bernard, Claudie. "De l'architecture à la littérature: la
topographie parisienne dans 'Notre-Dame de Paris.'" RLM 693-
97 (1984): 103-38.

Berrettini, Célia. "Victor Hugo, no centenário de sua morte."
MGS 20 (1985): 6-8.

Betz, Dorothy M. "Bibliographie commentée des études de
l'édition Massin des 'Oeuvres complètes' de Victor Hugo."
RLM 693-97 (1984): 189-223.

Biermann, Karlheinrich. Literarische-politische Avantgarde
in Frankreich 1830-1870: Hugo, Sand, Baudelaire und andere.
Stuttgart: Kohlhammer, 1982. Pp. 256.
    Rev. by Wolfgang Drost in GRM 36 (1986): 247-49.

Billaz, André. "Diderot - Hoffmann - Hugo: Le Neveu de Rameau,
Prinzessin Brambilla, L'Homme qui rit, ou les métamorphoses

du buffon des Lumières au Romantisme." *BRP* 24 (1985): 305-10.

While the Enlightenment seems to have no need of the buffoon to think about its own limitations, Romanticism integrates this figure into its quest for totality.

Blanc, Anita. "1985: Année Victor Hugo: un phénomène d'édition." *Livres-Hebdo*, Jan. 7, 1985, pp. 87-89.

Blanchard, Gérard. "Victor Hugo et les graveurs de son temps." *Communication et Langages* 62 (1984): 66-85.

Blewer, Evelyn, Sheila Gaudon, Jean Gaudon, Gabrielle Malandain, Jean-Claude Nabet, Guy Rosa, Carine Trevisan, and Anne Ubersfeld, eds. *Victor Hugo raconté par Adèle Hugo.* (Les Mémorables.) Paris: Plon, 1985. Pp. 863. Fr. 230.00.

Abundant notes clarify this edition. Three different introductions focus on Madame Hugo's personality, the problem of veracity, and the composition of this text.

Blin, J.P., ed. Victor Hugo, *Lettres et dessins de Picardie.* Amiens, 1985. Pp. 44.

Bondeville, Emmanuel. "Victor Hugo face à l'art musical." *Institut de France* 17 (1985): Pp. 3.

Bounoure, Gabriel. "Abîmes de Victor Hugo." *QL* 448 (Oct. 1-15, 1985): 14-15.

Bourin, André. "Victor Hugo cent ans après: les rééditions." *RDM* (April 1985): 185-91.

Bourlard-Collier, Simone, and Georges Guarracino. *Année Victor Hugo: une famille ... les Hugo.* (Exposition.) Marseille: Château Borély, 1985.

Bourg, Tony, and Frank Wilhelm, eds. *Le Grand-duché de Luxembourg dans les carnets de Victor Hugo.* Luxembourg: RTL, 1985.

Bouyeure-Ménager, Edith. "Victor Hugo, l'homme de l'essentielle déchirure." *Résurrection* 76 (1985): 61-75.

Brett, Vladimir, ed. *In Memoriam Victor Hugo 26-2-1802 - 22-5-1885.* Prague: Melantrich, 1985.

Brezu, Constandina. "Centenar Victor Hugo." *Luc* 25 (June 22, 28, 1985): 8.

Brombert, Victor. "Hugo, Shakespeare, the Promontory." Pp. 71-81 in Mary Ann Caws, ed., *Writing in a Modern Temper: Essays on French Literature and Thought in Honor of Henri Peyre*. Saratoga, Calif.: Anma Libri, 1984.

Brombert, Victor. "Victor Hugo: la fin du héros ou l'éclipse du père." *RLM* 693-97 (1984): 9-23.

Brosse, Monique. "Rituel et fonction de la mort dans les drames de Victor Hugo." Pp. 121-29 in Gilles Ernst, ed., *La Mort en toutes lettres: actes du colloque organisé par le département de littérature comparée de l'Université de Nancy-II, 2 au 4 octobre 1980*. Presses de l'Université de Nancy, 1983.

Brown, James W. "Sue and Hugo: An Alimentary Portrait of the Ghetto. The Meal as a Signal for Reform." Pp. 91-130 in James W. Brown, *Fictional Meals and Their Function in the French Novel 1789-1848*. University of Toronto Press, 1984. Pp. viii+215. $25.00.

Brown, John L. "Victor Hugo et le nouveau monde." *QL* 448 (Oct. 1-15, 1985): 19-21.

Brown, Nathalie Babel. *Hugo and Dostoevsky*. Ann Arbor, Mich.: Ardis, 1978. Pp. 186. $13.00.

> Rev. by Marike Findlay in *CRCL* 12 (1985): 163-70.

Caamaño, Mª. Angeles. "Unidad, correspondencias e inversiones en *Les Contemplations*." *Insula* 461 (April 1985): 4-5.

Caird, John. "Making a Musical." *Drama* 159 (1986): 7-9.

> On his production of *Les Misérables*.

Canivec, Pierre. "Modernité et actualité de Victor Hugo." *Revue du Tarn* 117 (1985): 101-03.

Canivec, Pierre. "Le personnage du roman dans 'L'Homme qui rit.'" Pp. 295-300 in *Le Personnage en question: Actes du IVe colloque du S.E.L., Toulouse, 1-3 décembre 1983*. (Travaux de l'Université de Toulouse-le-Mirail, série A, vol. 29.) Université de Toulouse-le-Mirail, 1984.

Carneiro, Maria do Nascimento Oliveira. "Victor Hugo écrit au Portugal." *Europe* 674-75 (1985): 148-55.

The text of letters written by Victor Hugo between 1859 and 1870 to the poet António Feliciano de Castilho, the journalist and biographer Brito Aranha, the writer and critic of society José Palmela, and the polemicist Guilherme Braga.

Cauna, Jacques. "Les sources historiques de 'Bug-Jargal': Hugo et la Révolution haïtienne." *Conjonction* 166 (June 1985): 21-36.

Cazaumayou, H. *Hauteville House, Maison d'éxil de Victor Hugo.* Paris: Maison de Victor Hugo, 1984.

Centenaire de la mort de Victor Hugo, jeudi 10 octobre 1985. Institut de France 10 (1985). Pp. 38.

Contents: Alain Decaux, "Victor Hugo: la vie et l'œuvre" (1-16); Maurice Rheims, "Victor Hugo et le Moyen-Age" (17-23); André Roussin, "Victor Hugo et le théâtre" (25-31); Maurice Schumann, "Victor Hugo, homme politique" (33-37). Overview of Victor Hugo by four academicians.

Chaitin, Gilbert. "Châtiment et scène primitive: le contresens de 'L'Expiation.'" *RLM* 693-697 (1984): 25-37.

Chambure, Alain de. "Hugo-Symphonie." *Magazine Littéraire* 214 (Jan. 1985): 39.

Chimot, Jean-Philippe. "Victor Hugo plasticien." *La Pensée* (May-June 1985): 70-79.

Chiron, Yves. "Victor Hugo poète, mage et bourgeois." *Ecrits de Paris* 456 (April 1985): 58-63.

Chla, L. "Victor Hugo (1802-1885)." *Inostrannye Iazyki v Shkole* (Nov. 1985): 106-08.

Chotteau, Jean-Marc. *Vive Hugo!* Illus., François Boncq; music, Erik Dehenne. Paris: Chemins de papier, 1985. Pp. 58. Fr. 150.00.

"Livre-cassette, livre-spectacle."

Cleyet-Michaud, Marius. "Victor Hugo et les mathématiques." *Cerf-volant* 123 (1985): 7-13.

Cogman, Peter. *Hugo: Les Contemplations.* (Critical Guides to French Texts, 41.) London: Grant and Cutler, 1985. Pp. 82. £2.40.

Rev. by Brian Rigby in *FS* 40 (1986): 85-86; by Marisa
Gatti-Taylor in *NCFS* 14 (1985-86): 363-65.

Collot, Michel. "Rimbaud lecteur de 'L'Homme qui rit.'"
Parade Sauvage (April 1985): 94-96.

Combes, Claudette. *Paris dans "Les Misérables."* Nantes:
Cid Editions, 1981. Pp. 338.

Combet, Georges. "Les parallélismes de 'Booz endormi.'"
RLM 693-97 (1984): 81-99.

Cosme-Damien. "L'énigme Adèle Hugo." *Ecrits de Paris* 470
(July 1986): 65-70.

Biographical sketch of Hugo's youngest daughter, with
emphasis on her affair with Albert Pinson.

Croisille, Christian. "Quelques lettres inédites de Lamartine."
Bulletin de la Société Théophile Gautier 7 (1985): 41-65.

Letters to Victor Hugo, 1829-1863.

Crouzet, François. "Victor Hugo journaliste." *Le Spectacle
du monde* 284 (Nov. 1985): 90-94.

Dabadie, Maïté. "Hugo encore?--Hugo toujours." *Cerf-volant*
125 (1985): 60-63.

Activities in Marseille.

Dalbin, Geneviève, ed. *Hugo--banlieue: Victor Hugo en Val-de-
Marne.* Préface de Jean Gaudon; avant-propos de Michel Germa.
Paris: Conseil Général du Val-de-Marne, 1985. Pp. 323.
Fr. 85.00.

Anthology.

Dällenbach, Lucien. "L'aveu et la veuve ou l'autobiographie
impossible: notes sur 'Le Dernier jour d'un condamné.'"
Versants 8 (1985): 77-79.

Dällenbach, Lucien, and Laurent Jenny, eds. *Hugo dans les
marges.* (A l'Epreuve.) Geneva: Zoe, 1985. Pp. 202.

Contents: Jacques Dubois, "L'affreux Javert, the champ
you love to hate" (9-34); Jean Rousset, "'Le Dernier Jour
d'un condamné' ou l'invention d'un genre littéraire" (35-
50); Lucien Dällenbach, "Le vide plein ou les révélations de
l'homme sans tête" (51-90); Jacques Neefs, "Marges d'ombres"

(91-117); Ross Chambers, "De la marge à la marge: le poème 'Le Pont' et 'Eclaircie'" (118-38); Charles Grivel, "Hugo: les 'Han' de l'écriture" (139-65); and Michel Butor, "L'Espérance de l'encre" (166-77); Laurent Jenny, "Tombeau" (178-202).

Daniels, Barry. "Victor Hugo." Pp. 151-98 in Barry Daniels, *Revolution in the Theater: French Romantic Theories of Drama*. (Contributions in Drama and Theatre Studies, 7.) Westport, Conn.: Greenwood Press, 1983. Pp. 251.

Rev. by Norman King in *TRI* 10 (1985): 179-81.

Dassau, P., and H. Focillon. *Victor Hugo*. Dessins mis en page par A. Avila, assisté de J.-P. Camargo. (L'Art.) Paris: Autrement, 1983. Pp. 93.

Rev. by Jean-Claude Fizaine in *FS* 86 (1985): 410.

Dauvin, Sylvie, and Jacques Dauvin. *Hernani: 1830; Ruy Blas: 1838*. (Profil d'une Oeuvre.) Paris: Hatier, 1986. Pp. 80. Fr. 15.40.

Decaux, Alain. "La France tout entière va redevenir 'hugolâtre.'" *Le Figaro* 272 (Dec. 8, 1984): 110-20.

Delacroix, Mireille. "Victor Hugo sous le signe de Saturne." *Triades* (Spring 1985): 42-59.

Derosier, Marcel. *Victor Hugo et les Hautes-Pyrénées*. (Archives Départementales, Tarbes.) Société Académique des Hautes-Pyrénées, 1985. Pp. 144. Fr. 81.00.

The names of some 50 places in the Hautes-Pyrénées found in Hugo's works. Numerous illustrations, including 15 drawings by Hugo himself.

Descotes, Maurice. *Victor Hugo et Waterloo*. (Archives Victor Hugo, 10; Archives des Lettres Modernes, 214.) Paris: Lettres Modernes-Minard, 1985. Pp. 78. Fr. 46.00.

Rev. by Keith Wren in *MLR* 81 (1986): 208-09.

Des Trébuchet à Victor Hugo. (Exposition: Châteaubriant, Bibliothèque Municipale, Archives Municipales, 1985.) Mairie de Châteaubriant, 1985. Pp. 60. Fr. 50.00.

Dezalay, Auguste. "Lecture du génie, génie de la lecture: 'Germinal' et 'Les Misérables.'" *RHL* 85 (1985): 435-46.

Dhainaut, Pierre. "Du pittoresque à la vision: Victor Hugo en Flandre." *Nord* 5, supp. (June 1985): 7-14.

Domecq, Jean-Philippe. "L'oeil regardait Victor Hugo." *QL* 448 (Oct. 1-15, 1985): 8-9.

Dubreuil, Richard. "Victor Hugo au Panthéon: le sacre du poète républicain." *L'Histoire* 77 (April 1985): 88-90.

Ducat, Robert. "Victor Hugo en milieux scolaire et adulte." *Résonance* 22 (Sept. 1985): 11-15.

Dulmet, Florica. "Les funérailles de Victor Hugo." *Ecrits de Paris* 459 (July 1985): 64-70.

Dupuy, Emile. "En marge d'un centenaire: Victor Hugo et l'Aveyron." *Revue du Rouergue* (Spring 1985): 3-8.

Letter of F. Fabié, June 1885.

Edwards, Peter J. "Six lettres retrouvées de Victor Hugo." *SFr* 29 (1985): 500-03.

Letters published by *L'Artiste* from 1859 to 1868.

Fayolle, Roger. "Victor Hugo à l'école." *Magazine Littéraire* 214 (Jan. 1985): 42-44.

Fizaine, Jean-Claude. "La cuisinière et son maître: religions et philosophies chez Victor Hugo." *Romantisme* 50 (1985): 5-26.

Florenne, Yves. "Victor Hugo dans toute sa candeur." *Corps Ecrit* 11 (1984): 189-91.

On *Angelo, tyran de Paduoue*.

Fongaro, Antoine. "Eluard et Hugo, encore." *SFr* 28 (1983): 302-04.

Fontaine, Jean-Paul. "Familles célèbres: Victor Hugo." *La Revue française de généalogie* (Aug. 1985): 31-33.

Fouchet, Max-Pol. *Victor Hugo imagier de l'ombre*. Paris: Actes Sud, 1985. Pp. 60. Fr. 50.00.

Republication of Fouchet's 1967 essay on the exhibition of Hugo's drawings held that year at the Bibliothèque Nationale.

Friedel, Christine. "Hugo--Métro." *Magazine Littéraire* 214 (Jan. 1985): 25.

Galanteris, Christian. "Cent visages." *Magazine Littéraire* 214 (Jan. 1985): 26-28.

Gamarra, Pierre. *La Vie prodigieuse de Victor Hugo.* Paris: Messidor/Temps Actuels, 1985.

Gamarra, Pierre. "Présence de Hugo ou Hugo en complet-veston?" *Europe* 673 (May 1985): 177-81.

Reviews of Georges Piroué's *Victor Hugo romancier ou les dessus de l'inconnu* (1984) and Hubert Juin's biography *Victor Hugo (1844-1870).*

Garasa, Delfín Leocadio. "Victor Hugo cien años después." *La Nación,* supp. (June 1985).

Gasiglia, Danielle. *Victor Hugo, sa vie, son oeuvre.* Paris: Frédéric Birr, 1984.

Rev. by L. Petroni in *Francofonia* 9 (Autumn 1985): 147-48.

Gaudon, Jean. "Autoportrait [d'après les carnets et la correspondance]." *Magazine Littéraire* 214 (Jan. 1985): 32-33.

Gaudon, Jean. "'L'Homme qui rit' ou la parole impossible." *IL* 36 (1984): 197-204.

To survive society's power politics, poets and philosophers are forced to adopt the least poetic language there is: irony. Society's corruption necessitates this degraded language-- which is politically efficient--or its alternative--silence.

Gaudon, Jean, ed. *Odes et Ballades. Les Orientales.* (G.-F., 439.) Paris: Garnier-Flammarion, 1985.

Gaudon, Jean. *Victor Hugo et le théâtre: stratégie et dramaturgie.* Paris: Suger, 1985. Pp. 192. Fr. 69.00.

Rev. by P.W. Cogman in *FS* 40 (1986): 339-40.
Discerns what place dramatic considerations hold in Hugo's work, examines "la bataille d'*Hernani*," shows how as a writer of tragedy Hugo incorporates conventions of melodrama that create an aura of metaphysical fatality.

Gaudon, Jean, ed. *Victor Hugo: Le Rhin: Lettres à un ami.* 2 vols. (Lettres Françaises.) Paris: Imprimerie Nationale, 1985. Pp. 449, 455.

Rev. by André Bourin in RDM (Oct. 1985): 179-83; by P.W.
Cogman in FS 40 (1986): 86-87; by Bernard Leuilliot in
Romantisme 51 (1985): 115-18, QL 448 (Oct. 1-15, 1985):
13.

Gélineau, Alain-René. Victor Hugo et l'expérience de la
transcendance. Paris: Argel, 1984. Pp. 144.

Gély, Claude. "Lettres inédites de Gaspard de Pons à Victor
Hugo." Bulletin de la Société Théophile Gautier 7 (1985):
13-39.

Twenty-seven items from Hugo's correspondence with a
companion from his early poetic career.

Gerhardi, Gerhard C. "Fonction du poète: Die Metaphorik
der politischen Mission bei Victor Hugo." Lendemains 10,37
(1984): 51-58.

Georgel, Pierre. "La gloire de Victor Hugo: propos recueillis
par Annette Rosa." Magazine Littéraire 214 (Jan. 1985): 19-
51.

Georgel, Pierre. Les Dessins de Victor Hugo pour "Les
Travailleurs de la mer." Intro. by Roger Pierrot. Paris:
Bibliothèque Nationale, 1985. Pp. 128; 44 col. pls., 32
b. & w. illus.

Georgel, Pierre. "Photogénie" (Victor Hugo et la photographie).
Magazine Littéraire 214 (Jan. 1985): 30-31.

Ghigo Bezzola, Rosa. "Una lettera autografia inedita di Hugo
(30 dicembre 1869)." Pp. 107-09 in Ottocento francese:
seconda seria. (Quaderni dell'Istituto di Lingue e Letterature neolatine, Sezione francese. Università di Milano,
Facoltà di Lettere, 3.) Milan: Cisalpino-Goliardica, 1983.

Gier, Albert. "Bildnis des Dichters als junger Mann: Die
Effekte im Theater Hugos." Neue Zürcher Zeitung 112 (May
18, 1985): 54.

Ginestier, Paul. "L'anti-théâtre de Victor Hugo." RHT 37
(1985): 174-92.

Explores the ways in which verbal delirium in Hugo's plays
dislocates and destroys, much as it does in the theater of
Beckett and Ionesco.

Gohin, Yves, ed. *L'Année terrible* [avec des extraits de *Actes et Paroles*, 1870, 1871, 1872]. (Poésie, 193.) Paris: Gallimard, 1985.

Gohin, Yves. "Peuple, individu, humanité dans l'oeuvre de Victor Hugo." *La Pensée* (May 1985): 19–27.

Greenberg, Wendy N. "Symbolization and Metonymic Chains in Hugo." *NCFS* 13 (1984–85): 224–37.

After a discussion of theories of symbolization, the author shows that *Notre-Dame de Paris* goes against Jakobson's hypothesis that poetry is the domain of associative properties, and analyzes two short didactic poems from *Les Rayons et les ombres* that provide excellent examples of continuity through symbolization.

Greenberg, Wendy Nicholas. *The Power of Rhetoric: Hugo's Metaphor and Poetics*. (American University Studies, 2,35.) New York: Peter Lang, 1985. Pp. 143. $23.00.

   Rev. by Louis Marvick in *ECr* 26 (1986): 101–02.

Grimm, Jürgen. "Victor Hugo als Theaterautor." *Neue Zürcher Zeitung* 112 (May 18, 1985): 53–54.

Grinevald, Paul-Marie. "Victor Hugo, partisan du livre." *Impressions* 29 (April 1985): 7–14.

Guichard, Daniel. "Victor Hugo, 'Le Pont' [*Les Contemplations*, 6,1]." *L'Ecole des Lettres: Revue Pédagogique du Second Cycle* 76 (May 1, 1985): 13–20.

Guillemin, Henri. *L'Engloutie: Adèle fille de Victor Hugo (1830-1915)*. Paris: Editions du Seuil, 1985. Pp. 160.

   Rev. by Janine Aeply in *NRF* 388 (May 1985): 97–99; by Jean Mambrino in *Etudes* 368 (July 1985): 417–18.

Haroche, Charles. "Un centenaire: exégètes tous azimuths de Victor Hugo." *Cahiers du communisme* (Feb. 1985): 94–102.

Heitman, Klaus. "Mütterliches Deutschland: Zu Hugo's Heidelberg-Erlebnis." *Romanistische Zeitschrift für Literaturgeschichte/Cahiers d'Histoire des Littératures Romanes* 8 (1984): 177–203.

Hellberg, Clemens, Lislott Pfaff, and Brigitte Weidmann, trans. *Vom Leben und Sterben des armen Mannes Gueux: Erzählungen.*

Mit einem Nachwort von Willi Hirdt. Glossar. Olten und
Freiburg: Walter, 1985. Pp. 238.

Henry, Pierre. *Dieu/Victor Hugo/Pierre Henry.* (Théâtre
sonore.) Paris: Actes Sud, 1986. Pp. 44. Fr. 98.00.

Herbillon, Jules. "Pour le centenaire de Victor Hugo: *Cosette.*"
Bulletin de la Société Royale Le Vieux-Liège 229-30 (April
1985): 79.

Huas, Jeanine. *Juliette Drouet: le bel amour de Victor
Hugo.* Paris: Lachurié, 1985. Pp. 256.

Hue, Jean-Louis. "Bibliographie." *Magazine Littéraire* 214
(Jan. 1985): 52-53.

✝ Holdheim, William Wolfgang. "The History of Art in Hugo's
'Notre-Dame de Paris.'" Pp. 93-109 in *The Hermeneutic Mode:
Essays on Time in Literature and Literary Theory.* Cornell
University Press, 1984. Pp. 274.

Rev. by Michael Danahy in *NCFS* 14 (1986): 348-49; by Virgil
Nemoianu in *MLN* 100 (1985): 1148-51.

Hrbata, Zdenek. "En hommage à Victor Hugo." *Philologica
Pragensia* 29 (1986): 36-38.

Review of *In Memoriam Victor Hugo* (Prague: Melantrich,
1985) treating Victor Hugo's influence in Bohemia.

Hugo et Baudelaire devant Dieu. (*Atlantis* 342.) Paris:
Atlantis, 1986. Pp. 191. Fr. 48.00.

"Hugo et moi: Questions [à Leonardo Sciascia, Danièle Sallenave,
Jacques Réda, Claude Simon, Alain Badiou, Jean Cayrol]."
QL 448 (Oct. 1-15, 1985): 6-8.

Hugo, Victor. *Pour un soldat.* Paris: Res Universalis, 1986.
Pp. 13. Fr. 40.00.

Facsimile reproduction of the Paris 1875 edition.

Inagaki, Naoki. "Fusion du livresque et du vécu: influence
de Ducray-Duminil sur la genèse et la structure double de
l'histoire d'amour dans *Han d'Islande* de Victor Hugo." *ELLF*
44 (1984): 53-70.

Because of its similarity to Hugo's obsessive sentiments
for his fiancée, Adèle, the story of Ducray-Duminil's popular
heroine Adèle's kidnapping influenced the structure of personal
relationships in Hugo's novel.

Ionesco, Eugène. *Vita grottesca e tragica di Victor Hugo.*
Trans. Anna Zanon. Milan: Spirali, 1985. Pp. 126.
L. 16,000.00.

Rev. by Alberto Carrara in *Letture* 40 (Oct. 1985): 721-22.

Iranzo de Ebersoke, Carmen. "El alma de España en Giuseppe
Verdi y Hugo [*Hernani*]." *Actas del 4º Congreso inter-
nacional de hispanistas* (Salamanca: Universidad) 1 (1982):
457-65.

Janc, John J., ed. *Les Deux Trouvailles de Gallus.* Lanham,
Md.: University Press of America, 1983. Pp. 259.

Jarrety, Michel. "Liberté de 'L'Homme qui rit.'" *RHL* 85
(1985): 41-53.

Jean-Nesmy, Dom Claude. "Le centenaire de Hugo." *Esprit et
Vie* 96 (Jan. 23, 1986): 33-36.

An "état présent" inspired by the principal publications
resulting from or coinciding with the Hugo centennial.

Juin, Hubert. "Victor Hugo et les Flandres." *Septentrion*
(Sept. 1985): 55-57.

Kaselioniene, Nijole. "Pirmieji Viktoro Hugo poezijos
vertimai i lieutuviu kalba." *Literatūra* 27 (1985): 42-51.

On Lithuanian language translation.

Kaselioniene, Nijole. "Viktor Hugo rysiai su isveiviais is
Lietuvos." *Literatūra* 26 (1984): 50-57.

Treatment of Lithuanians.

Kelley, David. "Onward and Upward." *TLS*, Oct. 11, 1985, pp.
1123-24.

Klein, Patrick, and Roger Gaillard. "Victor Hugo: genèse
d'un message politique." *Conjonction* 166 (June 1985):
47-63.

Klotz, Roger. "Le Midi dans la vie et le souvenir de Jean
Hugo." *Marseille* 137-38 (1984): 136-41.

Kruse, Joseph A., and Bernd Körtlander, pres. *Victor Hugo 1802-1885: Ein französischer Dichter am Rhein.* (Exposition.) Düsseldorf: Heinrich-Heine-Institut, 1985. Pp. 16.

Kunzle, David. "'Les Misérables' de Victor Hugo lus, médités, commentés et illustrés par Cham (1862-1863)." *GBA* 106 (July 1985): 22-34.

Lafargue, Jacqueline. *Victor Hugo: dessins et lavis.* Paris: Hervas, 1983. Pp. 159.

Rev. by Jean-Claude Fizaine in *SFr* 29 (1985): 411; by Leo H. Hoek in *LV* (1985): 89.

La Fin du siècle: tombeau de Victor Hugo. Pref. by Henri Guillemin. Paris: Quintette, 1985.

Laffly, Georges. "Hugo, la bouche d'ombre." *Ecrits de Paris* 457 (May 1985): 60-70.

Laforgue, Pierre. "Mythe, révolution et histoire: la reprise des *Misérables* en 1860." *La Pensée* (May 1985): 29-40.

Lagarde, Jean. "Lamartine et Hugo: deux parlementaires défenseurs de la Normandie maritime." *Etudes Normandes* 34,1 (1985): 73-79.

Lambert, Hervé-Pierre. "Les maisons de Victor Hugo à Paris." *Ville de Paris* 65 (May 1985): 54-58.

Lassegue, Laurence Joselyn. "La femme dans l'œuvre romanesque de Victor Hugo." *Conjonction* 166 (June 1985): 39-46.

Laster, Arnaud. "L'adieu d'Apollinaire: un hommage à Hugo?" *Que Volove?* 10 (April 1984): 11-16.

Latta, Claude. "Marie H. (1834-1906), Carmélite à Tulle, Cousine et correspondante de Victor Hugo." *Lemouzi* (Oct. 1985): 282-91.

Le Guillou, Louis. "Victor Hugo à Brest en 1834." *Cahiers de l'Iroise* 32 (1985): 61-72.

Leube, Eberhard. "L'ère du drame? Anmerkungen zum Fortwirken eines romantischen Gattungsmodells." Pp. 221-30 in Michael Rössner and Birgit Wagner, eds., *Aufstieg und Krise der Vernunft: Komparatistische Studien zur Literatur der Auf-klärung und des Fin-de-Siècle. (Hans Hinterhauser als Fest-*

schrift zum 65. Geburtstag gewidmet von seinen Freunden, Kollegen und Schülern.) Vienna: Böhlau, 1984.

Leuilliot, Bernard, ed. L'Art d'être grand-père. (G.-F., 438.) Paris: Garnier-Flammarion, 1985. Pp. 256.

López Fanego, Otilia. "Los dramas españoles de Victor Hugo." Cuadernos hispanoamericanos (Dec. 1985): 117-38.

Lureau, Serge. "Une fiction qui dit la vérité." Le Français d'Aujourd'hui 73 (Histoire Littéraire 2) (March 1986): 56-60.

How "Réponse à un acte d'accusation" can be used biographically, historically, and literarily in teaching Romanticism.

Magrini, Giacomo. "Dagli 'Châtiments' di Hugo (Saggio di traduzione)." Paragone 412 (June 1984): 31-45.

Magrini, Giacomo. "Il partitivo di Hugo." Il Confronto letterario 2 (1985): 135-51, 361-72.

Malavié, Jean. "La Vierge Marie dans l'œuvre de Hugo." Recherches sur l'Imaginaire 13 (1985): 37-56.

Mambrino, Jean. "'Hernani' de Hugo au Théâtre National de Chaillot." Etudes 372 (Jan. 1985): 500-01.

Mambrino, Jean. "L'intime immensité de Hugo [avec]: petite bibliographie hugolienne." Etudes 372 (Jan. 1985). 655-68.

Marfée, Aurélien. "Paul Foucher 'l'enfant gâté du Romantisme.'" A Rebours 32 (Summer 1985): 11-26.

Marquet, Jean-François. "Un syncrétisme philosophique." QL 448 (Oct. 1-15, 1985): 12-13.

Martin, Andrew. "Hugo." Pp. 65-81 in Andrew Martin, The Knowledge of Ignorance from Genesis to Jules Verne. Cambridge University Press, 1985. Pp. 259. $39.50.

Martín, Eutimio. "Presencia de Victor Hugo en F. García Lorca." Pp. 135-57 in Hommage à M. le professeur Claude-Henri Freches. (Publications de l'Université de Provence.) Marseille: J. Lafitte, 1984.

Massin, Jean. "Hugo et la photographie." QL 448 (Oct. 1-15, 1985): 18-19.

Massin, Jean. *Montreuil-sur-Mer dans "Les Misérables" de Victor Hugo.* Montreuil-sur-Mer: Lycée E. Woillez, 1984. Rev. by Pierre Dhainaut in *Nord* 5, supp. (June 1985): 24-26.

Maurel, Jean. *Hugo philosophe.* (Philosophies, 7.) Paris: Presses Universitaires de France, 1985.

Maurel, Jean. "Un sommeil songeur (la Dormition Hugo)." *RSH* 194 (1984): 71-83.

Mazaleyrat, Jean. "Victor Hugo et l'art de l'invective: à propos d'un passage des *Châtiments.*" Pp. 491-503 in Bernard Guidoux, bibliog., *Etudes de langue et de littérature françaises offertes à André Lanly.* Université de Nancy, 1980. Pp. 593.

Mazières, Jean. "Les idées religieuses de Victor Hugo dans 'Les Misérables' et 'La Préface philosophique.'" *Mémoires de l'Academie des sciences, inscriptions et belles-lettres de Toulouse* 145 (1983): 233-46.

Millet, Claude. "La politique dans *La Légende des siècles.*" *La Pensée* (May 1985): 59-69.

Minner, Lélia. "Bibliographie." *Livres-Hebdo* 7,2 (Jan. 7, 1985): 91-104.

Morvan, Jean-Baptiste. "Libre lecture de Victor Hugo." *Aspects de la France* 3 (Jan. 1985): 12.

Muela Ezquerra, Julián. "Observaciones sobre la temática hugoliana: 'Notre-Dame de Paris' como novela alegórica." *Textos* 3 (1983): 95-122.

Naux, Roger. "Ascendance maternelle de Victor Hugo." *Centre Généaologique de l'Ouest* 42 (1985): 8-26.

Naux, Roger. "Ascendances nantaises et vendéennes de Victor Hugo." *Bulletin de la Société d'études et de recherches historiques du Pays de Retz* 4 (1984): 77-84.

Niderst, Alain. "Victor Hugo à Jersey, du 20 au 30 avril 1854." *Etudes Normandes* 34,3 (1985): 25-33.

Olivé-Basso, Suzanne. *Victor Hugo en Provence.* (Hommes et récits du Sud.) Avignon: Alain Barthélemy, 1985.

Oliveira, M. do N. "Les traductions portuguaises de Victor Hugo au siècle dernier." *Récifs* 6 (1984): 57-76.

Onimus, Jean. "'Booz endormi' dans l'esthétique et la théologie de Péguy." *RLM* 731-34 (1985): 59-76.

Oxenhandler, Neal. "The Discourse of Emotion of Hugo's 'Demain, dès l'aube....'" *French Forum* 11 (1986): 29-39.

Analysis of polarities in the poem, its resistance to facticity, and its process of abreaction of grief shows the poem to be pivotal in the strategy of *Les Contemplations* and in Hugo's whole emotional economy.

Pagès, Alain. "Linguistique et pédagogie: la schématisation d'un champ lexical." *L'Information Grammaticale* 25 (March 1985): 11-14.

Pascaly, Josette. "Une lecture psychanalytique de 'L'Homme qui rit.'" *Littérature* 62 (May 1986): 25-47.

Takes the opposite point of view from Leon Cellier's reading of the novel as an initiation ending in triumph. The text remains dominated by what is archaic, and the hero's story as a whole is interpreted as a costly attempt to avoid the crucial trial of castration.

Patty, James S. "Hugo's Miniature Pyramid: 'Lettre,' *Les Contemplations*, 2, 6." *RomN* 26 (1985): 27-30.

Etymology of the word "contemplation" links the theme of birds to Hugo's poetic philosophy, thereby strengthening the unity of *Les Contemplations*.

Peeter, Guy. *Victor Hugo et Spa*. Brussels: Guy Peeters, 1985. Pp. 85.

Petrey, Sandy. "Must History Be Lost in Translation?" Pp. 86-94 in Marilyn Gaddis Rose, ed., *Translation Perspectives: Selected Papers, 1982-1983*. State University of New York at Binghamton, 1984. Pp. 130.

Treatment of history in English language translations.

Picon, Gaëtan. "Extrait de *Le Soleil d'encre*." *Cahiers Renaud-Barrault* 108 (1983): 41-47.

Pompilus, Pradel. "Notre Victor Hugo." *Conjonction* 166 (June 1985): 7-20.

Relationship to Haiti.

Poliakov, V.O. "Romantychna poetyka dramy V. Hiuho *Ernani*
u perekladi m.T. Ryl's'koho." *Inozemna Filoolohiia* 67
(1982): 113-19.

On Ukrainian language translation by Maksym Ryl'skyi.

Pouchain, Gérard, ed. *Chansons de Victor Hugo*. Pref. by
Guy Béart. Paris: C. Corlet, 1985. Pp. 359. Fr. 48.00.

Pouilliart, Raymond. "Victor Hugo et la critique actuelle."
RGB 121 (April 1985): 62-69.

"Pour mieux connaître Hugo: les livres du centenaire." *QL*
448 (Oct. 1-15, 1985): 22-23.

Prat, Marie-Hélène. "Aspects de la phrase hugolienne dans
'L'Homme qui rit.'" *L'Information Grammaticale* 23 (Oct.
1984): 24-29.

Prat, Marie-Hélène. "Victor Hugo ou 'L'Homme qui parle.'"
L'Information Grammaticale 24 (Jan. 1985): 28-32.

*Promenades dans l'Archipel de la Manche ... avec un guide nommé
Victor Hugo*. Pres. Gérard Pouchain. Condé-sur-Noireau,
1983.

Puts, Françoise. "Victor Hugo à l'école: Qu'en faisons-nous?"
Le Français d'Aujourd'hui 73 *(Histoire Littéraire 2)* (March
1986): 61-65.

Responses to a survey taken among teachers in "collèges,"
"lycées classiques," "lycées techniques," and "l'enseignement professionnel" about which Hugolian texts are studied,
what approaches are used, and what conclusions are drawn.

Ragon, Michel. "Les livres du peuple." *Magazine Littéraire*
214 (Jan. 1985): 40-42.

Rancière, Jacques. "L'archange et les orphelins." *QL* 448
(Oct. 1-15, 1985): 15-16.

Reichler, Claude. "Hugo déchiffreur des pierres." *RLMC* 39
(1986): 127-42.

Regnault, François. "Et puis on est bourgeois de Gand
[*Hernani*]." *L'Art du Théâtre* 1 (Spring 1985). (Actes Sud/
Théâtre National de Chaillot.)

Revol, Jean. "La gloire de Victor Hugo." *NRF* 396 (Jan. 1, 1986): 81-96.

Le Revue Musicale 378: *Victor Hugo et la musique.* Paris: 7 Place Saint-Sulpice, 1985.

> Brief rev. in *Europe* 683 (March 1986): 200.
> Contents: Julien Benda, "Victor Hugo et la musique" (1-6); Julien Tiersot, "Victor Hugo musicien" (7-36); Julien Tiersot, "La Esmerelda" (37-54); Jean Sergent, "Rythme poétique et musique" (55-72); Léon Kochnitzky, "'La Lyre Ouvrière'" (73-76); André Suarès, "Pensées sur la musique" (77-80); José Bruyr, "Victor Hugo mélophobe--ou mélophile" (81-83).
> Benda and Tiersot disagree about whether Victor Hugo was a music lover, Benda taking a negative stand, Tiersot using Hugo's correspondence with Berlioz, Liszt, Louise Bertin, Spontini, and Fétis to argue for Hugo's relationship with musicians and with music (especially German music and music composed for his own theatrical works). Tiersot's second article chronicles Hugo's adaptation of *Notre-Dame de Paris*, with score by Louise Bertin, and suggests reasons for the opera's lack of success. Hugo's remarks about Beethoven lead Sergent to conclude that if Hugo could not appreciate music as a musician, he could write about it as a philosopher and artist. Kochnitzky gives citations to show that Hugo was impressed by a concert given in his honor in Luxemburg on September 25, 1863. Suarès praises Victor Hugo's oratorical poetry as a form of music. Bruyr quotes brief passages from which the reader is to conclude that Victor Hugo was not a total "musicophobe."

Le Rhin: le voyage de Victor Hugo en 1840. Catalogue de l'exposition à la Maison de Victor Hugo, 25 mars-29 juin 1985. Commissaire de l'exposition, Jean Gaudon, avec la collaboration d'Evelyn Blewer.

> Rev. by Jacques Neefs in *Romantisme* 49 (1985): 118-19.

Rigolot, Carol. "Victor Hugo and Saint-John Perse: 'Pour Dante.'" *FR* 57 (1983-84): 794-801.

Roché, Déodat. "Victor Hugo poète et philosophe." *Cahiers d'études cathares* (Summer 1985): 51-60.

Rogers, Claire-Lise. "Bibliographie commentée de 'Quatre-vingt-treize' de Hugo." *RLM* 693-97 (1984): 165-88.

Röhl, Magnus. "Hugo et Eluard à la fenêtre: propos sur deux poèmes." *Moderna Språk* 79 (1985): 319-29.

Rosa, Annette. "Le manuscrit d'Adèle." *Magazine Littéraire* 214 (Jan. 1985): 29.

Rosa, Guy, and Jean-Marie Gleize, eds. *Les Châtiments*. (Le Livre de poche, 1378.) Paris: Librairie Générale Française, 1985.

Rosa, Guy, and Raymonde Debray-Genette. "Problèmes de l'édition critique des manuscrits, Hugo, Flaubert." *RHL* 85 (1985): 275-80, 281-84.

Rosolato, Guy. "A l'occasion d'un centenaire: entre Hugo et Mallarmé l'objet qu'on nomme RA de perspective." *Psychanalyse à l'Université* (July 1985): 473-82.

Ross, Werner. "Ein Napoleon der Literatur: Zum hundertsten Todestag Hugo's." *Frankfurter Allgemeine Zeitung* 114 (May 18, 1985):

Ross, Werner. "Wem gehört Hugo? Nachwort zu einer Jahrhundertfeier nach der Lektüre eines gescheiten Buches." *Dokumente* 41 (1985): 362-65.

Roubaud, Jacques. "Hugo, Ronsard, l'alexandrin." *QL* 448 (Oct. 1-15, 1985): 11-12.

Rougeron, Georges. "Victor Hugo et le Bourbonnais." *Les Cahiers Bourbonnais* (1985), 1er trimestre: 158-61; 2e trimestre: 189-95.

Sabiani, Julie. "'La Voix centenaire du vieil Hugo' ou Péguy palimpseste." *RLM* 732-34 (1985): 43-58.

Sabourin, Robert. "Victor Hugo: His Reasons for Leaving France." *Société jersiaise Annual Bulletin* (1985): 99-103.

Saint-Gérand, Jacques-Philippe. "Notes sur quelques-uns des titres de 'L'Homme qui rit.'" *L'Information Grammaticale* 25 (1985): 28-31.

Salgas, Jean-Pierre. "Entretien avec Pierre Henry et sa 'Hugo-Symphonie.'" *QL* 448 (Oct. 1-15, 1985): 16-17.

Salgas, Jean-Pierre. "Victor Hugo deux fois cent ans (1802-1985)." *QL* 448 (Oct. 1-15, 1985): 5.

Santa, Mª Angeles. "La narrativa hugoliana: de la acción
al mito." *Insula* 461 (April 1985): 3-4.

Savy, Nicole. "Victor Hugo féministe?" *La Pensée* (May 1985):
7-18.

Savy, Nicole, and Guy Rosa, eds. *Les Misérables*. Pref. by
Vercors. 3 vols. (Le Livre de poche, 964, 966, 968.)
Paris: Librairie Générale Française, 1985.

Schumann, Maurice. "Sur l'actualité de Victor Hugo." *RDM*
(Jan. 1985): 649-60.

Seebacher, Jacques. "L'Homme qui ruse." *Magazine Littéraire*
214 (Jan. 1985): 37-38.

Seebacher, Jacques. "Victor Hugo et Lamennais: autour de
Claude Frollo." Pp. 26-31 in Louis Le Guillou, ed., *Actes
du Colloque Lamennais (1982): Cahiers Mennaisiens* 16-17
(1983-84).

Seebacher, Jacques, and Anne Ubersfeld, eds. *Hugo le fabuleux*.
(Colloque de Cerisy-la-Salle du 30 juin au 10 juillet 1984.)
Paris: Seghers, 1985. Pp. 370. Fr. 95.00.

Seghers, Pierre. "Victor Hugo peintre: propos recueillis par
Vincent Landel." *Magazine Littéraire* 214 (Jan. 1985): 45.

Seghers, Pierre. *Victor Hugo visionnaire*. Paris: Laffont,
1983. Pp. 93; 54 illus.

Rev. by Jean-Claude Fizaine in *SFr* 39 (1985): 192-93.

Senart, Philippe. "'Angelo, tyran de Padoue' (Théâtre du Rond-
Point)." *RDM* (June 1984): 690-93.

Senart, Philippe. "'Hernani,' par Antoine Vitez, au Palais de
Chaillot." *RDM* (April 1985): 200-03.

Senart, Philippe. "'Mille francs de récompense' (Théâtre
Gémier)." *RDM* (July 1985): 718-20.

Simon, André. "Les obsèques de Victor Hugo, vues d'Avignon."
*Etudes Vauclusiennes: Bulletin de la Faculté des Lettres
d'Avignon* 34 (1985): 9-14.

Sinz, Dagmar. "Eine poetische Bildreportage: Hugo, Rheinreise
auf einer Pariser Ausstellung." *Neue Zürcher Zeitung* 112
(May 18, 1985): 53.

Sokologorsky, Irène. "L'accueil en Russie." *QL* 448 (Oct. 1, 1985): 21-22.

Soleil d'encre: manuscrits et dessins de Victor Hugo. (Exposition au Musée du Petit Palais, 1985.) Rev. by Jacques Suffel in *BduB* 4 (1985): 462-64.

Sorg, Jean-Paul. "Deux grands ecrivains alsaciens: Victor Hugo et Jean-Paul Sartre." *Revue Alsacienne de Littérature* 11 (Sept. 1985): 17-20.

Sozzi, Lionello. "Dante e Hugo." *Letture Classensi* 14 (1985): 45-61.

Suard, Claire. "Victor Hugo, dessins de voyages en Flandre (1837-1861)." *Nord* 5, supp. (June 1985): 15-24.

Suffel, Jacques. "L'amitié de Victor Hugo et de Théophile Gautier." *BduB* 4 (1985): 431-36.

Tabart, Claude-André. "'Crépuscule,' étude de texte." *L'Ecole des Lettres: Revue Pédagogique du Second Cycle* 65,8 (Jan. 15, 1984): 9-13.

Talon, Guy. "'Notre-Dame de Paris': la cathédrale dans l'univers hugolien." *RLM* 693-97 (1984): 139-55.

Tarantino Fraternali, Orsola. *La Famiglia Hugo: i giorni della ricomposizione e l'infanzia avellinese di Victor (Avellino 1807-1808).* Avellino: E.P.T., Comune di Avellino, 1985.

Teissier, Philippe. "Victor Hugo, 'Au Peuple.'" *L'Ecole des Lettres: Revue Pédagogique du Second Cycle* 77 (Oct. 1985): 11-17.

Thomasseau, Jean-Marie. "Le jeu des écritures dans 'Ruy Blas.'" *RLM* 693-97 (1984): 55-80.

Thomasseau, Jean-Marie. "Pour une analyse du para-texte théâtral: quelques éléments du para-texte hugolien." *Littérature* 53 (Feb. 1984): 79-103.

Tieghem, Philippe van. *Victor Hugo, un génie sans frontières: dictionnaire de sa vie et son œuvre.* Réédition remise à jour. Paris: Larousse, 1985. Pp. 256.

Tissier, André. "Victor Hugo, journaliste." *Ecrits de Paris* 460 (Sept. 1985): 72-78.

Trousson, Raymond. *Le Tison et le flambeau: Victor Hugo devant Voltaire et Rousseau.* Editions de l'Université de Bruxelles, 1985. Pp. 288. Bel. Fr. 875.00.

Rev. by Georges Cesbron in *L'Ecole des Lettres; Revue Pédagogique du Second Cycle* 78 (Nov. 1985): 50; by Vivienne Mylne in *FS* 40 (1986): 85.

Trousson, Raymond. "Victor Hugo et 'le Roi Voltaire.'" *Bulletin de l'Académie Royale de Langue et de Littérature françaises* 72 (1984): 240-56.

Ubersfeld, Anne. "'Chaos vaincu' ou la transformation." *RHL* 84 (1984): 67-76.

Ubersfeld, Anne. *Paroles de Hugo.* Paris: Editions Sociales/ Messidor, 1985. Pp. 190. Fr. 95.00.

Ubersfeld, Anne. "Un rire noir." *Magazine Littéraire* 214 (Jan. 1985): 36.

Vargas Llosa, Mario. "El último clásico: a proposito de 'Los Misérables.'" *Quimera* 30 (April 1983): 50-57.

Veck, Bernard. "Le génie aboli par excès." *Le Français Aujourd'hui* 73 *(Histoire Littéraire 2)* (March 1986): 43-49.

The figure "author" as given by Hugo in *William Shakespeare* leaves no room for God; authority derives from historical and social movement conceived as a double phenomenon of "délimitation et illimitation."

Verjat Massman, Alain. "Soledad del tribuno, soledad del poeta: Victor Hugo y la Segunda República (1848-1852)." *Insula* 461 (April 1985): 10.

Vernier, France. "Cela 'fait mal et ne touche pas.' [*Le Dernier Jour d'un condamné*]." *La Pensée* (May 1985): 41-57.

Victor Hugo: A Story of Resistance. (Catalogue of an exhibition held in the John Rylands University Library of Manchester, April 15-June 14, 1985.) Intro. by A.R.W. James. Manchester, 1985.

Victor Hugo, Bruxelles et la Belgique. (Catalogue de l'exposition, l'Hôtel de ville, 22 mars-28 avril 1985.) Pref. by

R. Leclercq, Jean-Pierre Poupko, Georges Sion. Brussels: Crédit communal de Belgique, 1985. Pp. 104.

Ville de Paris: Le Rhin: Le Voyage de Victor Hugo en 1840. (Exposition, Maison de Victor Hugo, 25 mars-29 juin 1985.) Commissaire: Jean Gaudon, avec la collaboration d'Evelyn Blewer. Paris: Maison de Victor Hugo; Paris-Musées, 1985.

Vitez, Antoine, et al. *Le Livre de Lucrèce Borgia: drame de Victor Hugo.* Paris: Actes Sud, 1986. Pp. 204. Fr. 79.00.

Vitez, Antoine. "Pour 'Hernani.'" Propos recueillis par Patrice Bollon. *Magazine Littéraire* 214 (Jan. 1985): 34-35.

Wentzlaff-Eggebert, Harald. "'Le Roi s'amuse' und 'Rigoletto': Zum Verhältnis zwischen romantischem Drama und dramatischer Oper." Pp. 335-49 in Angel San Miguel, Richard Schwaderer, and Manfred Tietz, eds., *Romanische Literaturbeziehungen im 19. und 20. Jahrhundert: Festschrift für Franz Rauhut zum 85. Geburtstag.* Tübingen: Gunter Narr, 1985.

Wilhelm, Frank. "Victor Hugo in Trier und seine Beziehungen zum Rheinland." *Kurtrierischer Jahrbuch* 24 (1984): 185-234.

Wolfromm, Jean-Didier. "Les trois coups: trois biographies pour ouvrir l'année du centenaire [Hubert Juin, Jean-François Kahn, Alain Decaux]." *Magazine Littéraire* 214 (Jan. 1985): 20-21.

XY. "Liminaire: le génie de Victor Hugo." *A Rebours* 32 (Summer 1985): 3-9.

See also Juden, Lasserre-Vergne, Macchia, Saffle, Scaiola, Stocker ("French 1. General"); Baudry ("Dumas"); Le Guillou ("Lamennais"); Picano ("Leroux"); Pichois ("Nerval"); Gardelles ("Stendhal"); Virtanen ("General 2. Criticism"); López Fanego ("Spanish 2. General").

Reviews of books previously listed:

BARRERE, Jean-Bertrand, *Victor Hugo, Poésies (1831-1840)* (see *RMB* for 1985, p. 237), rev. by Claude Gély in *Romantisme* 47 (1985): 126-27; in *SFr* 29 (1985): 599; BROMBERT, Victor, *Victor Hugo and the Visionary Novel* (see *RMB* for 1985, p. 238), rev. by Richard B. Grant in *NCFS* 13 (1984-85); 287-88; by John Porter Houston in *FR* 59 (1985-86): 621; by Carol A. Mossman in *French Forum* 11 (1986): 113-14; by Christopher Prendergast in *FS* 40 (1986): 224-25; by Charles J. Stivale

in *SubStance* 50 (1986):   116-19; by Keith Wren in *MLR* 81
(1986):   208-09; *La Gloire de Victor Hugo* (see *RMB* for 1985,
pp. 243-44, rev. by Gilbert Lascault in *QL* 452 (Dec. 1,
1985):   18-19; by Jacques Suffel in *BduB* 4 (1985):   460-62;
by Isabelle Tournier in *Romantisme* 49 (1985):   118; GRIMAUD,
Michel, ed., *Victor Hugo 1: Approches critiques et con-
temporaines* (see *RMB* for 1984, p. 266), rev. by Fernande
Bassan in *NCFS* 14 (1985-86):   399; by P.W.M. Cogman in *FS*
40 (1986):   86-87; by W.J.S. Kirton in *MLR* 81 (1986):   488;
KRAKOVITCH, Odile, *Hugo censuré: la liberté au théâtre au
XIXᵉ siècle* (see *RMB* for 1985, p. 245), rev. by Fernande
Bassan in *NCFS* 14 (1985-86):   401-02; by Rémi Gossez in
Romantisme 49 (1985):   123-26; ROUSSELOT; Jean, *Victor Hugo
avec nous* (see *RMB* for 1985, p. 248), rev. by Jacques
Gaucheron in *Europe* 672 (April 1985):   218; SEGHERS, Pierre,
Victor Hugo visionnaire (see *RMB* for 1983, p. 221), rev. by
Jean-Claude Fizaine in *SFr* 29 (1985):   192-93; UBERSFELD,
Anne, and Guy Rosa, eds., *Lire "Les Misérables"* (see *RMB*
for 1985, p. 250), rev. by Marius-François Guyard in *RHL* 86
(1986):   311-14; VERNOR-GUILLE, Françoise, ed., *Le Journal
d'Adèle Hugo*, vol. 3, *1854* (see *RMB* for 1985, p. 250), rev.
by Antoine de Gernado in *Europe* 678 (Oct. 1985):   214-15;
WIEGAND, Horst-Jürgen, *Victor Hugo und der Rhein* (see *RMB*
for 1983, p. 222), rev. by Robert Dumont in *RLC* 59 (1985):
354-55; by Klaus Heilmann in *RF* 96 (1984):   358-61; by Alain
Niderst in *Kritikon litterarium* 12 (1983):   7-9; WREN, Keith,
Victor Hugo: Hernani and Ruy Blas (see *RMB* for 1984, p. 271),
rev. by Claude Gély in *SFr* 29 (1985):   192; by Timothy Raser
in *NCFS* 13 (1984-85):   179-81; by Brian Rigby in *FS* 39
(1985):   354-55.

JANIN

Bandy, W.T. "Banville et Janin: une amitié peu exemplaire."
  Pp. 125-32 in Claudine Gothot-Mersch and Claude Pichois, eds.,
  Mélanges de littérature en hommage à Albert Kies. (Publica-
  tions des Facultés universitaires Saint-Louis, 34.) Brussels:
  Université Saint-Louis, 1985.

Soria, Andrès. "Alarcón y Janin. Notas para el estudio de
  los primeros escritos alarconianos." Pp. 359-88 in *Estudios
  ofrecidos a Emilio Alarcos Llorach*, vol. 5. Universidad de
  Oviedo, Servicio de publicaciones, 1983.

See also Frycer ("French 1. General"); Coniglio ("Borel").

JOUBERT

Dauphin, Jean-Luc. "L'année Joubert." *Etudes Villeneuviennes*
8 (1985): 98-99.

Magrelli, Valerio. "Per Joseph Joubert." *Nuovi Argomenti*
(July-Sept. 1985): 93-107.

Michaux, Didier. "Joubert homme de lettres." *La Nouvelle Revue
de Paris* 1 (March 1985): 135-48.

Pizzorusso, Arnaldo. "Joubert e l'osservazione della scrittura."
RLMC 39 (1986): 25-44.

Tessonneau, Rémy. "Une lettre inédite de Menu de Chomorceau
à Joseph Joubert (21 août 1789)." *Etudes Villeneuviennes*
8 (1985): 9-11.

   Also includes four unpublished quatrains and a note by
Joubert.

See also Société Chateaubriand, Bulletin 28 ("Chateaubriand").

Review of book previously listed:

TESSONNEAU, Rémy, ed., *Essais* (see *RMB* for 1983, p. 223),
rev. by Arlette Michel in *RHL* 86 (1986): 293-94.

JOUFFROY

Lefranc, Jean. "La critique du spinozisme dans le *Cours de
droit naturel.*" *Les Cahiers de Fontenay* 36-37-38 (March
1985): 223-27.

KOCK

Constans, Ellen. "'Votre argent m'intéresse.' L'argent dans
les romans de Paul de Kock." *Romantisme* 53 (1986): 71-82.

   Like Balzac's novels, those of Paul de Kock teach that
money is powerful, if not all-powerful--in theory, merit
triumphs over money. "Il n'empêche que tout au long de ces
récits gais, l'Argent devient un actant omni-présent et
puissant qui règle les modes d'existence des personnages
et le déroulement de leur existence romanesque. Signe des
temps et des moeurs de la France bourgeoise."

LACLOS

See De Jean ("French 1. General").

LACORDAIRE

Duval, André, O.P. "Comment Lacordaire présente l'Ordre à son pays." La Vie spirituelle (Jan.-Feb. 1985): 80-103.

Duval, André, O.P. "Lacordaire et Désiré Carrière en 1838." Le Pays Lorrain 4 (1984): 240-45.

Sainte Marie Madeleine. Pref. by Jean-Yves Leloup. Le Plan d'Aups, Sainte-Baume: Editions de l'Ouvert, Centre International de la Sainte-Baume, 1985.

LAMARTINE

Birkett, Mary Ellen. "Lamartine's 'Le Premier Regret': Manuscript, Poem, Commentary." KRQ 32 (1985): 341-46.

Studies changes from an unpublished manuscript version to final poem. These modifications indicate that in the writing of this elegy verbal revery is shaped to an ever greater degree by sound patterns. This permits new readings of the poem and of Lamartine's factually inaccurate but revealing version of how it came to be written.

Combaud, Louis. "Lamartine, marchand de vin." Annales de l'Académie de Mâcon 60 (1984): 155-59.

Croisille, Christian. "Quelques lettres inédites de Lamartine." Bulletin de la Société Théophile Gautier 7 (1985): 41-65.

Letters of varying importance written by Lamartine and his wife illustrating some fundamental aspects of his life as author, politician, and human being.

Domange, Michel. "Comment les Lamartine ont pressenti le Premier Empire." Annales de l'Académie de Mâcon 59 (1983): 124-34.

Favre, Robert. "La réception de Lamartine à l'Académie Française d'après le compte-rendu du 'Journal des Débats.'" Annales de l'Académie de Mâcon 59 (1983): 119-23.

Fraisse, Simone. "Tableau des citations de Lamartine et de Musset dans les 'Cahiers de la Quinzaine.'" RLM 731-34 (1985): 117-21.

Guyard, Marius-François. "Quand Claudel cite Lamartine."
   Pp. 275-80 in *Au bonheur des mots: mélanges en l'honneur
   de Gérald Antoine*. Presses Universitaires de Nancy, 1984.
   Rev. by Kurt Baldinger in *ZRP* 100 (1984): 606-10.

Iknayan, Marguerite. *"La Chute d'un ange*: Heaven and Hell
   on Earth." *NCFS* 13 (1984-85): 191-99.

   Reading of Lamartine's poem as a melodramatic epic bearing
   witness to the poet's anguish as he moves away from Christian
   faith toward Deism.

Kablitz, Andreas. *Lamartine's "Méditations poétiques":
   Untersuchungen zur Bedeutungskonstitution im Widerstreit
   von Lesererwartung und Textstruktur.* (Text und Kontext;
   Romanische Literaturen und Allgemeine Literaturwissenschaft,
   1.) Wiesbaden: Steiner, 1985. Pp. 259.

Lacoste, Claudine. "Lettres inédites d'Ernest Legouvé, de
   Jehan Duseigneur, de Lamartine, d'Arthur Stevens, de Judith
   Gautier." *Bulletin de la Société Théophile Gautier* 7 (1985):
   73-79.

   A short note of Lamartine's calling Gautier's attention
   to "Erigone" by the sculptor Jouffroy in 1851.

Lagarde, Jean. "Lamartine et Victor Hugo: deux parlementaires
   défenseurs de la Normandie maritime." *Etudes Normandes* 1
   (1985): 73-79.

Letessier, Fernand. "Un emprunt de Lamartine: du nouveau sur
   Milly." *Annales de l'Académie de Mâcon* 60 (1984): 175-83.

Letessier, Fernand. "Un texte retrouvé de Lamartine sur
   Chateaubriand." *Société Chateaubriand, Bulletin* 27 (1984):
   89.

   Letter to Aimé Martin of November 5, 1831, expressing
   "hargne" caused by Chateaubriand's *De la nouvelle proposition
   relative au banissement de Charles X et de sa famille.*

Machado, Alvaro Manuel. "Soares de Passos e Lamartine ou o
   paradoxo do ultraromantismo em Portugal." Pp. 353-60 in
   *Les Rapports culturels et littéraires entre le Portugal et
   la France: actes du colloque, Paris, 11-16 octobre 1982.*
   Paris: Fondation Calouste Gulbenkian, Centre Culturel
   Portuguais; Edition Jean Touzot, 1984.

Michel, Pierre. "Parole et pouvoir chez Lamartine." Pp. 155-
78 in Philippe Berthier, ed., *Stendhal: L'écrivain, la
société, le pouvoir; colloque du bicentenaire (Grenoble,
24-27 janvier 1983)*. Presses Universitaires de Grenoble,
1984.

Michel, Pierre. "*Prenez et lisez!* Lamartine et le livre
populaire." *Romantisme* 47 (1985): 17-30.

   Richly documented inventory of Lamartine's ideas about
the masses, about the kind of books appropriate for their
education, and about writing history and fiction for them.
Because Lamartine writes for a "peuple" that exists only
in his imagination, "la parole lamartinenne s'avance épurée
et masquée." (M.E.B.)

Morre, Ange. "Une visite à Lamartine." Pp. 115-23 in Jules
Huret, ed., *Interviews de littérature et d'art*. Vanves:
Les éditions Thot, 1984.

   Reprints an article from *Figaro*, March 2, 1895. The author
visited Lamartine three weeks before his death. He talked
about literature.

Reymond, Evelyne. "Lamartine en Dauphiné." Pp. 53-58 in
Evelyne Reymond, *Les Heures dauphinoises des écrivains
français*. Paris: Didier-Richard, 1984. Pp. 134.

See also Severino ("Italian 3. Manzoni").

Reviews of books previously listed:

   BIRKETT, Mary Ellen, *Lamartine and the Poetics of Landscape*
   (see *RMB* for 1982, p. 224), rev. by Willi Hirdt in *ZFSL* 96
   (1986): 186-88; FORTESCUE, William, *Alphonse de Lamartine:
   A Political Biography* (see *RMB* for 1983, p. 224), rev. by
   Fernand Letessier in *RHL* 86 (1986): 295-96.

LAMENNAIS

Antoine, Gérald. "Rome vue par Lamennais et Renan." Pp. 195-
207 in H. Gaston Hall et al., eds., *Mélanges à la mémoire de
Franco Simone*, vol. 3, *XIXe et XXe siècles*. Geneva: Slatkine,
1984. Pp. 822.

   Despite much that they had in common, the two writers reacted
very differently to the "Eternal City": Lamennais found it
"abominable"; Renan pronounced it "enchanteresse." This study,
then, involves more contrast than comparison.

Bedouelle, Guy-Thomas, O.P. "Fallait-il condamner Lamennais?"
Sources (Fribourg) (July-Aug. 1985):   145-58.

Cabanis, José, ed. *Affaires de Rome*. (L'Histoire partagée.)
Lyon: La Manufacture, 1986. Pp. 380. Fr. 120.00.

Cahiers Mennaisiens 16-17 (1983-84): "Actes du Colloque
Lamennais (1982)."

Unaccountably omitted from earlier volumes of *RMB*, this
symposium, to which eighteen specialists contributed, is
well reviewed by Fernand Rude in *SFr* 29 (1985): 405-07.

D'Ambrosio Mazziotti, Anna Maria. "Presenze di Pascal,
Bossuet e Lamennais nel mondo manzoniano." *CeS* 24 (April-
June 1985): 45-55.

Hilaire, Yves-Marie. "Les évêques mennaisiens dans la pensée
et à l'époque de Lamennais." Pp. 181-90 in *L'Evêque dans
l'histoire de l'Eglise*. Presses de l'Université d'Angers,
1984. Pp. 230. Fr. 90.00.

Hoffmann, Paul. "Lamennais lecteur de Rousseau: la question
de la vérité." *RHL* 86 (1986): 831-55.

Le Guillou, Louis. "Lamennais: A Happy Ending." *YFS* 71
(1986): 169-76.

On the satisfaction derived from editing Lamennais's
correspondence, plus a general apologia of Lamennais, "a
magnificent writer, a brilliant prophet of the modern world."

Le Guillou, Louis. "Lamennais et Joseph de Maistre en 1820
d'après des documents inédits." Pp. 209-23 in H. Gaston
Hall et al., eds., *Mélanges à la mémoire de Franco Simone*,
vol. 3, *XIXᵉ et XXᵉ siècles*. Geneva: Slatkine, 1984.
Pp. 822.

The two men never met; Maistre discovered Lamennais on his
return from Russia in 1817, i.e., it was the *Essai sur
l'indifférence* that introduced him to the younger writer.
They corresponded during the last two years of Maistre's
life (1820-21). Le Guillou explores their relationship as
revealed in their letters, providing needed annotation.

Le Guillou, Louis. "Victor Hugo, Lamennais et Montalembert
jusqu'aux *Paroles d'un croyant*." *RHL* 86 (1986): 988-98.

A new *mise au point* of the relationship between Hugo and
Lamennais, based on their correspondence and confirmed by

Montalembert's *Journal*. Hugo's strong sympathy for Lamennais
and his liberal Catholicism are made evident.

Prontera, Angelo. "Attualità del problema Lamennais." *Note
su Socialismo e Cristianesimo* 3,5 (March 1983): 56-71.
See résumé by Carlo Cordié in *Paideia* 39 (1984): 263.

Prontera, Angelo, and Peter Byrne, eds. *Lamennais e noi.*
(Incontri, 3.) Lecce: Milella, 1986. Pp. 196.

Valerius, Gerhard. *Deutscher Katholozismus und Lamennais. Die
Auseinandersetzung in der katholischen Publizistik 1817-1854.*
Mainz: Mattias-Grünewald-Verlag, 1983. Pp. xxxi+453.
DM 84.00.

Rev. by Jean-Marie Mayeur in *RHEF* 71 (1985): 374-75;
by Stephen J. Tonsor in *CHR* 71 (1986): 301-02.

See also Saffle ("French 1. General"); Seebacher ("Hugo");
Derré ("Saint-Simon"); Michaud ("Tristan").

LA MORVONNAIS

See Michaud ("French 1. General").

LASSAILLY

Pompili, Bruno. "'Mademoiselle, je vous aime comme la République.' Frenetismo e ironia in Charles Lassailly."
Pp. 175-83 in *Letteratura populare di espressione francese
dall''ancien régime' all'Ottocento. Roland Barthes e il
suo metodo critico.* (Quaderni della Società Universitaria
per gli studi di lingua e letteratura francese, 4.) Fasano:
Schena, 1983 [1984]. Pp. 346.

See résumé by Carlo Cordié in *SFr* 29 (1985): 594.

See also Frycer ("French 1. General").

LATOUCHE

Crouzet, Michel. "Monstres et merveilles: poétique de
l'androgyne. A propos de *Fragoletta.*" *Romantisme* 45 (1984):
25-41.

Société Chateaubriand, Bulletin 28 (1985). Special issue on
Latouche.

Relevant contents: Pierre Riberette, "Latouche, Chateau-
briand et Madame Récamier, avec des lettres inédites de
Latouche" (40-58); Georges Buisson, "Henri de Latouche,
éditeur d'André Chénier" (59-68); Edouard Guitton, "Latouche
'élève secret' d'André Chénier" (69-74); Renée Lemaître
"Latouche et Balzac" (75-80); Georges Lubin, "Latouche et
George Sand" (81-86); Fernand Letessier, "Henri de Latouche,
Charles et Marie Nodier" (87-91); Fernand Letessier, "Un
jugement inédit de Latouche sur Mme Récamier" (91-92);
Joseph-Marc Bailbé, "A propos de Léo: un épisode d'une vie
d'artiste" (101-06); Jean-Claude Berchet, "Latouche romancier
de la Révolution: Fragoletta" (107-15).

LEGOUVÉ

Offen, Karen. "Ernest Legouvé and the Doctrine of 'Equality
in Difference' for Women: A Case Study of Male Feminism in
Nineteenth-Century French Thought." JMH 58 (1986): 452-84.

Based on the lectures (free and open to the public) which
Legouvé gave in the spring of 1848. (In 1849 he published
Histoire morale des femmes; he later directed the Ecole
Normale Supérieure de Sèvres.) Offen's capsule formula for
Legouvé's feminist program: "radical ideas, expressed in
moderate language."

LEROUX

Barck, Karlheinz. "'Poetischer Materialismus' und 'Kult der
Kunst.' Perspektiven der Ablösung vom klassisch-humanistischen
Poesiebegriff bei Pierre Leroux und Emile Barrault." BRP 2
(1984): 187-98.

Le Bras-Chopard, Armelle. De l'égalité dans la différence: le
socialisme de Pierre Leroux. Paris: Presses de la Fondation
nationale des Sciences politiques, 1986. Pp. 464. Fr. 198.00.

Macherey, Pierre. "Leroux dans la querelle du panthéisme."
Les Cahiers de Fontenay 36-37-38 (March 1985): 215-22.

Picano, Jean. "De Pierre Leroux et de Victor Hugo." Note su
Socialismo e Cristianesimo 6-7 (Sept. 1983-March 1984):
11-17.

Van Slyke, Gretchen. "Riot and Revolution in the *Salon de 1846*." *French Forum* 10 (1985): 295-306.

Finds the influence of Leroux--his criticism of individualism and private property--in the penultimate chapter of Baudelaire's *Salon*, "Des écoles et des ouvriers."

Viard, Jacques. "Philosophie de l'histoire littéraire selon Pierre Leroux." *Lendemains* 37 (1985): 44-50.

See also Prontera ("Lamennais").

Review of book previously listed:

LA PUMA, Leonardo, *Il socialismo sconfitto* (see *RMB* for 1985, pp. 256-57), rev. by Peter Byrne in *SFr* 29 (1985): 409.

LEZAY-MARNESIA

Westerholt, Egon, Graf von. "Lezay-Marnésia et sa contribution à la connaissance de l'Allemagne en France." *CS* 37 (1985-86): 45-52.

Adrien de Lezay (1769-1814) was a member of Madame de Staël's circle. The author provides a solid sketch of his career, emphasizing his contacts with German culture (e.g., his translation of Schiller's *Don Carlos*, his travels and studies in Germany, his work as prefect at Coblentz and Strasbourg).

LOYSON

See Loyson ("Italian 3. Manzoni").

MAINE DE BIRAN

Azouvi, François, gen. ed. *OEuvres*, vol. 8, *Rapport des sciences naturelles avec la psychologie et autres écrits sur la psychologie.* Ed. Bernard Baertschi. (Bibliothèque des Textes philosophiques.) Paris: J. Vrin, 1986. Pp. xliii+451. Fr. 249.00.

Baertschi, Bernard, and François Azouvi. *Maine de Biran et la Suisse.* Avec des textes inédits de Biran et des extraits de la correspondance d'Ernest Naville. Lausanne: Cahiers de Théologie et de Philosophie, 1985. Sw. Fr. 20.00.

Bouzon, Sylvie. "Maine de Biran: de la réflexion à l'écriture intime." *Etudes de Lettres* (April-June 1985): 63-75.

Cavaciuti, Santino. *Il problema morale nel pensiero di Maine de Biran*. 2 vols. Milan: Marzorati, 1981.

Rev. by Gilbert Romeyer Dherbey in *RMM* 91 (1986): 253-54.

Cottier, Georges. "L'ontologie de Maine de Biran." *Studia Philosophica* 43 (1984): 201-06.

Perhaps a review of Bernard Baertschi, *L'Ontologie de Maine de Biran* (Fribourg: Editions universitaires, 1982; see *RMB* for 1983, p. 230).

Damiens, Suzanne. "Maine de Biran: les trois stades de sa vie." *Les Cahiers de Bergerac* (March-April 1985): 10-11.

Review of book previously listed:

EVEN, Lucien, *Maine de Biran critique de Locke* (see *RMB* for 1985, p. 257), rev. by Jean Bernhardt in *JHP* 24 (1986): 413-14.

MAISTRE (J. de)

Beffa, Massimo, ed. *Considerazioni sulla Francia*. Rome: Editori Riuniti, 1985.

Duret, Yves. "Joseph de Maistre et la Franc-Maçonnerie savoisienne." *Travaux de la Loge nationale de Recherches Villard de Honnecourt* (1984), 2ᵉ semestre, pp. 194-205.

Lebrun, Richard. "Les lectures de Joseph de Maistre d'après ses registres inédits." *Revue des Etudes Maistriennes* 9 (1985).

Vallin, Pierre. "Les 'Soirées' de Joseph de Maistre. Une création théologique originale." *Recherches de Science religieuse* 74 (1986): 341-62.

The author's résumé concludes: "Point by point, the article seeks to determine the sources, both contemporary and remote of this theology, which it ultimately categorizes as 'agnostic' as understood by the Greek Fathers."

See also Besnier, *Le Débat*, Michaud ("French 1. General"); Le Guillou ("Lamennais").

Review of book previously listed:

REBOTTON, Jean, ed., *Ecrits maçonniques de Joseph de Maistre et de quelques-uns de ses amis francs-maçons* (see *RMB* for

1983, p. 230), rev. by Jacques Brengues in *RHL* 86 (1986): 294–95.

MAISTRE (X. de)

Dumas, Pierre. "Xavier de Maistre peintre." *La Revue du Louvre* 33 (1983): 426–28.

MERIMEE

Avni, Ora. "L'Œdipe de la traduction: Lokis." *RSH* 189 (1983): 137–45.

Berthier, Patrick, ed. *Théâtre de Clara Gazul*. (Folio, 1626.) Paris: Gallimard, 1985. Pp. 384.

   Rev. by P.W.M. Cogman in *FS* 40 (1986): 340–41; by J. Landrin in *IL* 38 (1986): 51–52.

Biasotto, Ada. "L'elemente fantastico nelle novelle di Prosper Mérimée." *Letterature* 46 (May 1982): 13–27.

Biasotto, Ada. "'Les Ames du purgatoire': il miracoloso e il demoniaco." *Esperienze Letterarie* 9,2 (1984): 89–92.

Carmen. Paris: Actes Sud, 1986. Pp. 124. Fr. 9.00.

Carmen. (Poche Nathan, 329.) Paris: Nathan, 1985. Pp. 116. Fr. 19.00.

Carmen. Pref. by Bernard Leblon. Paris: Presses universitaires de France, 1986. Pp. 124. Fr. 49.00.

Ceserani, Remo, ed. *La narrazione fantastica*. Pisa: Nistri-Lischi, 1983. Pp. 414.

   Rev. by P. Pelckmans in *RHL* 86 (1986): 806–07.

Cooper, Barbara T. "Dramatized Prologues: The Space of Aesthetic Reflection in Works by Alexandre Duval and Prosper Mérimée." *Degré Second* 9 (1985): 33–41.

   On the "staged" representation (or shaping) of audience reaction as seen in the prologues of Duval's *Guillaume le Conquérant* and Mérimée's *Les Espagnols en Danemark*.

Crecelius, Kathryn. "Narrative as Moral Action in Mérimée's *Colomba*." *NCFS* 14 (1985–86): 225–37.

Examines *Colomba* as detective story. Central to the author's argument is the mystery that begs to be solved. The mythic dimension of the tale is dispelled for the author once the quest for vengeance is resolved. Although *Colomba*, like many works one could mention, bears a superficial resemblance to the detective story, the author's approach throws away much that is of deeper significance in the text. The "happy" ending in fact contains the seeds of Colomba's eventual triumph, and so promises a future tragedy. For a different and more detailed reading, see Jacques Chabot's *L'Autre Moi* (see *RMB* for 1983, p. 232). (E.F.G.)

Filius-Jehne, Christiane, ed. *Prosper Mérimees Novelle "Carmen": die Oper, die Filme. Faszination des Flamenco.* Munich: Heyne, 1984. Pp. 187

Fonyi, Antonia. "Carmen. Une histoire episode de l'Histoire: analyse narratologique et analyse sociologique de la nouvelle de Prosper Mérimée." *Récifs* 6 (1984): 39-56.

Imo, Wiltrud, and Mireille Mehlis. "Présentation et analyse d'un conte fantastique. 'La Vénus d'Ille' de Merimée." *Neusprachliche Mitteilungen* 38 (1985): 93-98.

Orlando, Francesco. "Il tema della 'méprise' nelle tre novelle paragine di Mérimée." Pp. 163-95 in Francesco Orlando, *Le costanti e le varianti. Studi di letteratura francese e di teatro musicale.* (Saggi, 243.) Bologna: Il Mulino, 1983.

First appeared in 1962, but not previously listed. The author traces in a traditional manner the use of mis-understanding in "Le Vase étrusque," "La Double Méprise," and "Arsène Guillot."

Reymond, Evelyne. "Mérimée à Vienne." Pp. 81-86 in Evelyne Reymond, *Les Heures dauphinoises des écrivains français.* Paris: Didier-Richard, 1984. Pp. 134.

Siebers, Tobin. "Narrative Unreliability and the Fantastic: The Case of Mérimée's 'La Vénus d'Ille.'" Pp. 57-77 in Tobin Siebers, *The Romantic Fantastic.* Cornell University Press, 1984. Pp. 194.

The notion of the unreliable narrator may be less useful than commonly thought, although central to the fantastic tale because there the narrator is unreliable by definition. The fantastic tale presents a conflict between the lover of lies and the doubter. The essential superstition in "La Vénus d'Ille" supplies the language by means of which is narrated a tale of the crimes of love, crimes whose punishment is inevitably violent.

Zolli, Paolo. "Mérimée a Venezia (con una lettera inedita)." *Quaderni Utinensi* 1-2 (1983): 107-09.

A letter from Mérimée to Jules Tascherau (August 9, 1858)-- a recommendation of abbé Giuseppe Valentinelli, of the library of St. Mark.

Review of book previously listed:

CHABOT, Jacques, *L'Autre Moi: fantasmes et fantastique dans les nouvelles de Mérimée* (see *RMB* for 1983, p. 232), rev. by A.W. Raitt in *JES* 15 (1985): 69-72.

MICHELET

Bellos, David. "Edition de l'histoire/histoire de l'édition. Le cas Michelet." *Romantisme* 47 (1985): 73-83.

Berriot, François, ed. *Leçons inédites de l'Ecole normale: histoire des XIVe, XVe et XVIe siècles.* Paris: Editions du Cerf, 1986. Pp. 384. Fr. 147.00.

Elseneur 4: *Révolutions?* (Publié par le Centre de la modernité.) Centre de publications de l'Université de Caen, 1986. Pp. 145. Fr. 50.00.

Edited by Pierre Barbéris, this symposium has as its theme the literary representation of revolution by Michelet, Flaubert, and others.

Fauquet, Eric. "Michelet partisan de l'unité italienne, 1848-1854." Pp. 359-70 in H. Gaston Hall et al., eds., *Mélanges à la mémoire de Franco Simone*, vol. 3, *XIXe et XXe siècles.* Geneva: Slatkine, 1984. Pp. 822.

Focusing on "la modernité" rather than on continuity in Michelet's long and many-faceted relationship with Italy and, in particular, on some unpublished or incompletely published texts of the period 1853-54 (*Le Banquet* and *Légendes de la démocratie*), Fauquet spells out Michelet's sympathy for Italy of the Risorgimento and for "un socialisme fort pratique."

Haac, Oscar A. "La Révolution comme religion: Jules Michelet." *Romantisme* 50 (1985): 75-82.

Traces Michelet's "second conversion" (i.e., to faith
in the Revolution of 1789) through the historian's lectures
at the Collège de France (1838-1851), "une série de textes
éloquents qui affirment et interprètent le mythe de 89."
We follow, also, the transformation of his conception of his
role as historian: "A mesure que l'historien élabore sa
philosophie républicaine, son patriotisme rejoint sa religion.... Sa foi d'historien comprend l'idéal religieux
et social."

Huet, Marie-Hélène. "La signature de l'histoire." *MLN* 100
(1985): 715-27.

Minerva, Nadia. "Sorcellerie et anthropologie: de Voltaire
à Michelet." Pp. 207-18 in Corrado Rosso, ed., *Transhumances
culturelles: mélanges.* (Histoire et Critique des Idées,
3.) Pisa: Goliardica, 1985. Pp. 317. Fr. 200.00.

Rétat, Laudyce. "Michelet et le Royaume des Mères." *Romantisme*
50 (1985): 83-96.

Borrows Goethe's formula of the "Realm of the Mothers"
(*Faust* 2) in order to "rendre compte de la présence fonda-
mentale dans l'oeuvre de Michelet des images féminines de
sens maternel."

Stadler, Peter. "Die Schweiz in Michelets Tagebüchern." Pp.
183-94 in *Cinq siècles de relations franco-suisses. Hommage
à Louis-Edmond Roulet.* (Le Passé présent, études et documents
d'histoire.) Neuchâtel: La Baconnière, 1984. Pp. 360.
Sw. Fr. 63.00.

Thierry, André. "Jules Michelet lecteur d'Agrippa d'Aubigné."
Pp. 967-74 in Michel Malicet, ed., *Hommages à Jacques Petit,*
vol. 2. (Annales littéraires de l'Université de Besançon,
série 2, 300.) Paris: Les Belles Lettres, 1985. Pp. 974.

Viallaneix, Paul. "Michelet et la Révélation de 1789."
Romantisme 50 (1985): 61-74.

"*L'Histoire de la Révolution* ... n'est rien d'autre que le
récit d'une Révélation moderne."

Viallaneix, Paul. "Michelet, le justicier." *Réforme,* March
23, 1985, pp. 107-10.

Viallaneix, Paul, and Edward K. Kaplan, eds. *Œuvres complètes,*
vol. 17, *L'Oiseau; L'Insecte.* Paris: Flammarion, 1986.
Pp. 544. Fr. 480.00.

See also Bollème, Bowman, Lasserre-Vergnes, Walch ("French 1. General").

Reviews of books previously listed:

BORIE, Jean, Mythologies de l'hérédité au XIXe siècle (see RMB for 1981, p. 216), rev. by Roddey Reid in ECr 26 (1986): 99-100; BUCUR, Marin, Jules Michelet et les révolutions roumaines (see RMB for 1984, p. 280), rev. by Odile Séjourne in RHL 86 (1986): 156; KAPLAN, Edward K., trans. and ed., Mother Death (see RMB for 1984, p. 281), rev. by Peter Byrne in SFr 30 (1986): 155; by Lionel Gossman in Clio 14,2 (1985): 209-13; by Arthur Mitzman in JMH 58 (1986): 943-48.

MONNIER

Reviews of book previously listed:

MEININGER, Anne-Marie, ed., Scènes populaires (see RMB for 1985, p. 262), rev. by Mireille Bossis in SFr 30 (1986): 159-60; by C.A. Burns in FS 40 (1986): 342-43; by Arlette Michel in IL 38 (1986): 133-43; by Jean-Marie Thomasseau in RHL 86 (1986): 1149.

MONTALEMBERT

Luirard, Monique. "Le Correspondant et la Pologne." Pp. 330-45 in Les Contacts religieux franco-polonais du Moyen Age à nos jours. Paris: Editions du Dialogue; C.N.R.S., 1985.

See also Le Guillou ("Lamennais").

MONTLOSIER

Cella, Paolo. "'Pouvoir civil' e 'pouvoir politique' nel pensiero di Montlosier." Il pensiero politico 16 (1983): 189-214.

According to Carlo Cordié (Paideia 40 [1986]: 114), outlines Montlosier's defense of a strong nobility as a buttress of the state. Cella calls his argument the "last line of defense of a declining class."

MUSSET

Cooper, Barbara T. "Breaking Up/Down/Apart: 'L'éclatement' as a Unifying Device in Musset's *Lorenzaccio*." *PQ* 65 (1986): 103-12.

Eclatements both of *forme* and of *fond*, whose similarities give the play an extraordinary aesthetic unity. The play is, moreover, a prototype of modern French dramatic works by its very *éclatement*, the "breakdown of causality and personality, of communication and community" (110).

Cordroc'h, Marie, Roger Pierrot, and Loïc Chotard, eds. *Correspondance d'Alfred de Musset*, vol. 1, *1826-1839*. (Centre de Recherche, d'Etude et d'Edition de Correspondances du XIXe siècle de l'Université Paris-Sorbonne [Paris 4].) Paris: Presses universitaires de France, 1985. Pp. 365.

Two hundred and twenty-eight letters by Musset. This publication completes the undertaking begun by Maurice Allem and continued by Jean Pommier. The edition provides a Musset chronology (1768-1839), a *table signalétique des lettres*, a table of correspondents (with biographical data, especially on their relationships with Musset), and an index of names cited in the letters.

Dominicy, Marc, and Thérèse Malengreau. "'Venise' d'Alfred de Musset: une analyse poétique." *FM* 53 (1985): 153-79.

Formal and thematic study to demonstrate that this "light" verse is far from frivolous. "Dans 'Venise' ... se profilent l'ensemble des tensions qui marqueront, bien plus explicitement, les longs poèmes de la maturité" (173).

Jeune, Simon. "'Gamiani' poème érotique et funèbre d'Alfred de Musset?" *RHL* 85 (1985): 988-1001.

Uses biographical, textual, and intratextual data to argue that "Gamiani" should indeed be attributed to Musset.

Noe, Alfred. "La ponctuation d'Alfred de Musset dans *La Confession d'un enfant du siècle*." *ITL: Review of Applied Linguistics* 65 (1984): 1-10.

Theater heute 26,11 (Nov. 1985).

The issue features *Lorenzaccio*, being staged in Munich and Cologne.

Zielonka, Anthony. "Images of the Poet in Musset's *Le Poète déchu*." *NCFS* 15 (1986-87): 87-93.

The unfinished work of 1839 presents Musset's ideal in regard to the poetic temperament and poetic expression: seriousness of purpose in both message and *métier*.

See also Rose ("Colet"); Daly ("Sand").

NERVAL

Aurélia. Paris: Lachenal et Ritter (diffusion: Distique), 1985. Pp. 196. Fr. 85.00.

Of no scholarly or critical interest.

Bony, Jacques. "Gérard de Nerval, *Sylvie*, *Les Chimères* et *Autres chimères*; *Aurélia*." *IL* 37 (1985): 174-75.

Selected bibliography intended for those preparing for the Agrégation de lettres et de grammaire.

Bony, Jacques. "Petit guide à l'usage du Nervalien amateur." *IL* 38 (1986): 72-76.

"Une série de sujets de réflexion et de directions de recherche ... quelques indications bibliographiques...." (See the preceding item.)

Bowman, Frank Paul. "'Mémorables' d'*Aurélia*: signification et situation générique." *French Forum* 11 (1986): 169-81.

Brix, Michel. *Nerval journaliste: 1826-1851. Problématique, méthodes d'attribution.* (Etudes nervaliennes et romantiques, 8.) Presses universitaires de Namur, 1986. Pp. 616. Bel. Fr. 1,800.00.

A rigorous and definitive sifting of the newspaper articles that have been attributed to Nerval, notably by Jean Richer, with important results for the establishment of the canon of Nerval's work and the dating of his correspondence. (J.S.P.)

Céard, Jean. "Habent sua fata libelli...." *Nouvelles du Livre ancien* 48 (Oct. 1986): 1-2.

On Nerval's borrowings from the Bibliothèque Nationale in 1830, in preparation for his anthology of sixteenth-century poetry (e.g., he was allowed to take out a copy of the original edition of the *Deffence et illustration*). He himself criticized this book loan policy in *Les Faux Saulniers*.

Deux lettres inédites à Ferdinand Sartorius. Paris(?):
Thierry Bouchard (diffusion: Distique), 1986. Pp. 16.
Fr. 21.00.

"Une lettre enfin complète, d'octobre 1853 et de la
clinique de Passy; une seconde complètement inconnue de juin
1854 de l'ultime voyage en Allemagne, toutes deux adressées
à l'éditeur Sartorius" (*Les Livres du mois*, Jan. 1987).

Françon, Marcel. "Réflexions sur quatre sonnets de Nerval."
Quaderni di Filologia e Lingue romanze (Macerata), n.s. 1
(1985): 209–14.

Guillaume, Jean, S.J. "*Le Christ aux Oliviers* de Nerval.
Essai de genèse." *ECl* 54 (1986): 386–88.

Certain details of the text of the sequence can be traced
to Nerval's readings in Hegel and the Gospel according to
St. Matthew.

Guillaume, Jean, S.J. "Gérard de Nerval." *ECl* 54 (1986):
375–82.

An overview of the new Pléiade edition and, especially,
the discoveries and corrections it offers.

Guillaume, Jean, S.J. "Liszt et Nerval." *Bulletin Baudelairien*
19 (1984): 85–86.

Finds traces of Liszt's presence in the last years of Nerval's
life, drawn, most likely, from the composer's article on
Tannhäuser (*Journal des Débats*, May 18, 1849).

Guillaume, Jean, S.J. "Sources d'*Aurélia*." *ECl* 54 (1986):
169–73.

Several passages in *Aurélia* are linked to episodes in
Gérard's friendship with Arsène Houssaye and to Etienne
Eggis's *Voyage aux Champs-Elysées*.

Guillaume, Jean, S.J. "Vers le texte d'*Aurélia*." *ECl* 54 (1986):
289–93.

Examining the four folio pages found on Nerval's body at
his death, the author reveals the changes made by the editor
who published part 2 of *Aurélia* in the *Revue de Paris*,
February 15, 1855, and suggests (as in the preceding item)
Nerval's interest in the death of Arsène Houssaye's wife.

Hristodorescu Loffredo, N. "Ipotesi di strategia analitica
testuale psicoestetica. Una lettura della poesia 'El Desdichado'
di Gérard de Nerval." *Francia* (Jan.–March 1982): 26–54.

Jay, Peter, trans. *Les Chimères--The Chimeras*. With essays
by Richard Holmes and Peter Jay. London: Anvil Press,
1984. Pp. 75. £6.95.

Rev. by A.L. Hendriks in *Agenda* 24,1 (1986):   42-45.

Kneller, John. "Anteros, Son of Cain?" Pp. 91-101 in Mary Ann
Caws, ed., *Writing in a Modern Temper: Essays on French
Literature and Thought in Honor of Henri Peyre.* (Stanford
French and Italian Studies, 33.) Saratoga, Calif.: ANMA
Libri, 1984. Pp. v+274.

Malandain, Gabrielle. *Nerval ou l'incendie du théâtre: identité et littérature dans l'oeuvre en prose de Gérard de Nerval.*
Paris: José Corti, 1986. Pp. 264. Fr. 135.00.

Rev. by R.P. in *Le Bulletin des Lettres* 457 (June 15, 1986):
243-44.

Milner, Max. "Délire et archaïsme dans *Aurélia* de Nerval."
Elseneur 3 (1984):   56-74.

Milner, Max. "Religions et religion dans le *Voyage en Orient*
de Gérard de Nerval." *Romantisme* 50 (1985):   41-52.

On the nature and, especially, the outcome of the religious
quest in the *Voyage*. Milner ably demonstrates that the writer
only achieved rather equivocal results; even his effort at
syncretism was not truly successful. The fictional episodes
do not contain Nerval's answer, either; rather, they betray
the "arrière-plans inquiétants" of his quest, the deep-seated
contradictions and conflicts within. "Le voyage en Orient
se confond dangereusement chez lui avec ce voyage 'vers
l'Orient' par lequel débute la première crise de folie relatée
dans *Aurélia*." (J.S.P.)

Mureşanu Ionescu, Marina. "Raconter/écouter dans *Emilie* de
Gérard de Nerval." *Analele stuntifice Universitatu 'Al.
I. Cuza' din Iasi,* Sectiunea 3, f. Literatura (1984):   59-64.

Pichois, Claude. "L'auteur et ses manuscrits: Hugo, Nerval,
Baudelaire." Pp. 15-21 in Michael Werner and Almuth Grésillons,
eds., *Hommage à Louis Hay.* Paris: Minard (Lettres modernes),
1985.

On these authors as collectors and preservers of their own
manuscripts. Hugo was much more efficient than the others,
thanks to his well-organized "atelier" (Juliette Drouet et
al.). The situation for Nerval and Baudelaire reflects their
more bohemian way of life.

Prendergast, Christopher. "Nerval: The Madness of Mimesis."
Pp. 148-79 in Christopher Prendergast, *The Order of Mimesis:*
Balzac, Stendhal, Nerval, and Flaubert. Cambridge University
Press, 1986. Pp. 288. $39.50.
    Rev. by Peter Brooks in *TLS*, July 11, 1986, p. 769.
    Draws on Barthes, Derrida, et al.

Richer, Jean. "La transfiguration du souvenir chez Nerval."
Pp. 387-403 in H. Gaston Hall et al., eds., *Mélanges à la*
mémoire de Franco Simone, vol. 4, *Tradition et originalité*
dans la création littéraire. Geneva: Slatkine, 1983.
Pp. 572.

    Attempts to bare the psychological process of Nerval's
memory at work in the major works of his last years. Richer
emphasizes "scènes retrouvées" and "clichés": the theme
of "amours enfantines" linked to that of "simulacre de
mariage"; an accidental fall into a river; round dances and
girls dancing; the arrest of the poet or one of his friends
in some suburban locality; certain symbols (lost horses,
swan, marsh).

Schneider, Marcel, ed. *Les Cent Plus Belles Pages de Gérard*
de Nerval. Paris: Belfond, 1985. Pp. 122. Fr. 59.00.

Smith, Anne-Marie. "Pandora's Quality of Figure." *Paragraph*
4 (Oct. 1984): 62-86.

Société des Etudes romantiques. *Le Rêve et la vie. Aurélia,*
Sylvie, Les Chimères de Gérard de Nerval. (Actes du colloque
du 19 janvier 1986.) Paris: S.E.D.E.S., 1986. Pp. 285.
Fr. 160.00.

    Contents: Béatrice Didier, "Nerval et Senancour ou la
nostalgie du XVIIIe siècle" (5-15); Anthony Zielonka, "L'expérience de la mélancolie et de la joie chez Nerval" (17-31);
Henri Bonnet, "Gérard de Nerval au rendez-vous de la civilisation grecque et romaine" (33-51); Jacques Bony, "*Sylvie,*
Aurélia: aux frontières de l'autobiographie" (53-63); Pierre
Brunel, "'Les cris de la fée'" (65-78); Jean Guillaume,
"Genèse des *Chimères*" (79-81); Vito Carofiglio, "Nerval entre
histoire et illusion: magie napolitaine et séduction
amoureuse" (83-96); Martine Bercot, "Poétique de l'ambiguïté
dans *Les Chimères*" (97-107); Norma Rinsler, "Gérard de
Nerval: *Le Christ aux Oliviers*" (109-14); L. Finas, "Le
péristyle: Gérard de Nerval: *Delfica*" (115-33); Serge
Meitinger, "Quelques hypothèses à propos de l'hermétisme
des *Chimères*" (135-47); Martine Reid, "Préface à un livre

dangereux" (149-56); Anne-Marie Jaton, "*Sylvie*: la rose
et le vert" (157-68); Monique Streiff-Moretti, "L'air et les
paroles: l'espace de l'ironie dans 'Sylvie'" (169-85);
Gabrielle Malandain, "*Sylvie*, 'dernière feuille'" (187-96);
J.D. Hubert, "Identité et écart dans *Sylvie*" (197-204);
Jacques Huré, "*Aurélia*, ordre et désordre" (205-11); Bruno
Tritsmans, "Ordre et dispersion. Les dynamiques d'*Aurélia*"
(213-31); Daniel Couty, "De la *Vita Nova* à la 'vie nouvelle'"
(233-36); Françoise Gaillarde, "*Aurélia*, ou la question du
nom" (237-47); Kurt Schärer, "Nerval juge d'*Aurélia*" (249-
60); Chiwaki Shinoda, "Origine et fonction du double dans
Aurélia" (261-73); Michel Jarrety, "Le retour et son exigence"
(275-83).

Tritsmans, Bruno. "Impasses narratives dans *Les Nuits d'octobre*
de Gérard de Nerval." *Neohelicon* 10,1 (1983): 133-63.

"Coïncidence du voyage avec la narrativité même (Brémond).
La comparaison du voyage réel par rapport au programme de
l'incipit, la liquidation du projet initial, témoigne de
l'impossibilité d'échapper au rétrécissement, à la cristalli-
sation des préoccupations de Nerval autour de la problématique
du moi" (*Bulletin signalétique 523*, 39,4 [no. 4333]).

Tritsmans, Bruno. "Nerval et l'indétermination textuelle."
Poétique 60 (1984): 423-26.

Tritsmans, Bruno. "Système et jeu dans 'Sylvie.'" *Poétique*
65 (1986): 77-89.

York, Holly Ulmer. "Nerval's *Aurélia*: à la recherche du signe
effacé." *French Forum* 11 (1986): 19-27.

See also Juden, Michaud ("French 1. General").

Reviews of books previously listed:

GUILLAUME, Jean, and Claude Pichois, *Gérard de Nerval.
Chronologie de sa vie et de son oeuvre, août 1850-juin 1852*
(see *RMB* for 1984, p. 286), rev. by Alfred DuBruck in *NCFS*
14 (1985-86): 170-71; by Norma Rinsler in *FS* 40 (1986):
90-91; GUILLAUME, Jean, and Claude Pichois, eds., *OEuvres
complètes*, vol. 2 (see *RMB* for 1984, p. 287), rev. by Monique
Streiff-Moretti in *SFr* 30 (1986): 160-61; HOLMES, Richard,
Footsteps (see *RMB* for 1985, p. 265), rev. by Robert M. Adams
in *NYRB*, April 10, 1986, pp. 36-37.

Le Bibliomane. Bordeaux: A Passage, 1985. Pp. 48. Fr. 48.00.
A deluxe printing of Nodier's tale, without any scholarly
or critical apparatus.

Cirrincione D'Amelio, Ludovica. "Per une definizione del
fantastique in Nodier." *Micromégas* (Jan.-Aug. 1984): 31-59.

Clause, Odile. "Procès et intercession dans les contes de
Charles Nodier." *Rocky Mountain Review of Languages and
Literatures* (1985): 107-12.

Hofer, Hermann. "L'Orient de Charles Nodier." Pp. 299-308 in
Exotisme et création en France du Moyen Age à nos jours.
Actes du Colloque international, Lyon, 1983. (Publications
de l'Université Jean Moulin.) Lyon: L'Hermès, 1986. Fr.
185.00.

Lambert, Marie-Sophie. "*La Fée aux Miettes*: une autre dimension." Pp. 713-33 in Michel Malicet, ed., *Hommages à Jacques
Petit*, vol. 2. (Annales littéraires de l'Université de Besançon, série 2, 300.) Paris: Les Belles Lettres, 1985. Pp.
974.

Pelckmans, Paul. "La folie et sa différence dans *Jean-François
les Bas-Bleus*." *OL* 41 (1986): 119-38.

Richer, Jean. "Charles Nodier et la Révolution française;
biographie, fiction et idéal." Pp. 109-22 in *Philosophes de
la Révolution française*. Paris: J. Vrin, 1984.

Rogers, Brian. *Charles Nodier et la tentation de la folie*.
Geneva and Paris: Editions Slatkine, 1985. Pp. 103. Fr.
135.00.

A study of the relation between dreams and madness in
Nodier's tales, especially *Smarra*, *Trilby*, and *La Fée aux
Miettes*. "Ses contes sont la transposition d'histoires
connues qui, après un début rassurant, s'orientent de manières
inattendues pour l'envelopper dans des expériences 'différentes'. Le démon du cauchemar, le lutin écossais, la
médaille à deux faces contenant le portrait de la fée aux
miettes, sont des symboles que l'écrivain rencontre dans une
écriture-folie qui l'attire."

Jean Sbogar. Pavillons-sous-Bois: Ressouvenances (diffusion:
Distique), 1986. Pp. 168. Fr. 70.00.

Steinmetz, Jean-Luc, and Jacques-Remi Dahan, eds. *La Fièvre et autres contes, suivis d'un poème et d'un essai d'auto-biographie; recueillis pour la première fois.* Paris (?): L'Homme au Sable; Thierry Bouchard, 1986. Pp. 55. Fr. 54.00.

A deluxe *plaquette* offering forgotten or unpublished texts by Nodier: four brief tales ("La Fièvre," "Une Heure," "Le Docteur Guntz," "L'Amulette"), a poem ("Le Vieux Marinier"— no kin to Coleridge's poem), and an autobiographical sketch. Steinmetz's "postface" is brief and sensible. Also provided is the essential bibliographical information. (J.S.P.)

Vartier, Jean. *Fanfan-la-Conspiration ou la vie aventureuse de Charles Nodier.* (Classiques de Nos Terroirs.) Nancy: Edition l'Est Républicain, 1986. Pp. 219. Fr. 135.00.

A popularizing biography and one that is hard to take seriously, what with a one-page bibliography. (J.S.P.)

See also Besnier, Steinmetz ("French 1. General"); *Société Chateaubriand, Bulletin* 28 ("Chateaubriand"); Baudry ("Dumas").

Reviews of books previously listed:

SANGUE, Daniel, ed., *Moi-même* (see *RMB* for 1985, p. 269), rev. by Roger Pearson in *FS* 40 (1986): 219-20; by Holly Ulmer York in *NCFS* 14 (1986): 391-92; VAULCHIER, Henri, *Charles Nodier et la lexicographie* (see *RMB* for 1985, p. 269), rev. by Jacques-Philippe Saint-Gérand in *Romantisme* 51 (1986): 114-15.

OZANAM

Barbiche, Bernard. "Frédéric Ozanam et la Pologne." Pp. 321-30 in *Les Contacts religieux franco-polonais du Moyen Age à nos jours.* Paris (?): Editions du Dialogue; C.N.R.S., 1985.

Launois, Pierre. "La vie inquiète et laborieuse de Théodore Pavie, grand voyageur et orientaliste." *Mémoires de l'Académie des Sciences, Belles-Lettres et Arts d'Angers* 1982-83 (1985): 209-25.

PIGAULT-LEBRUN

Campagnoli, R. "L'*Observateur* di Pigault-Lebrun." Pp. 159-74 in *Letteratura popolare di espressione francese dall''ancien régime' all'Ottocento. Roland Barthes e il suo metodo critico.* (Quaderni della Società Universitaria per gli studi di lingua e letteratura francese, 4.) Fasano: Schena, 1983 [1984]. Pp. 346.

See résumé by Carlo Cordié in *SFr* 29 (1985):   594.

PIXERECOURT

Carral, Pierre.   "Recherches pour une physionomie du mélodrame
au temps de Guilbert de Pixérécourt." *RHT* 36 (1984):   386-
91.

Résumé of a Sorbonne thesis (3ᵉ cycle) defended in 1977.

POTOCKI

Beauvois, Daniel.   "Jean Potocki's *Voyages*:   From Mythic Orient
to Conquered Orient."   Pp. 13-26 in Will L. McClendon, ed.,
*L'Hénaurme Siècle: A Miscellany of Essays on Nineteenth-
Century French Literature*.   (Reihe Siegen, 46.)   Heidelberg:
Carl Winter, 1984.   Pp. 242.

According to a review of the book (Robert T. Denommé in
French Forum 11 [1986]:   112), Beauvois "shows how the
author's travel studies gave kaleidoscopic movement to his
novel, *Manuscrit trouvé à Saragosse*."

Triaire, Dominique.   *Inventaire des oeuvres de Jean Potocki*.
Paris: Champion, 1985.   Pp. 348.   Fr. 200.00.

PROUDHON

Fitzpatrick, Maria.   "Proudhon and the French Labour Movement:
The Problem of Proudhon's Prominence." *EHQ* 15 (1985):   407-
30.

Kaltz, Barbara.   "Analyse d'un discours androcentrique: *La
Pornocratie ou les femmes dans les temps modernes* de Pierre-
Joseph Proudhon." *Atlantis* 10,1 (1984):   15-25.

On Proudhon's language.   After some background on the genesis
of Proudhon's book, "l'accent est mis sur les différentes
'stratégies discursives' (recours aux métaphores, aux oppositions sémantiques, à l'identification de termes non équivalents
entre autres).   Ces stratégies, intégrées dans un ensemble
de 'registres' alternants (scientifique, polémique, lyrique),
expliquent l'intensité du discours proudhonien sur la femme."

Reviews of books previously listed:

HAUBTMANN; Pierre, *Pierre-Joseph Proudhon.   Sa vie et sa
pensée (1809-1849)* (see *RMB* for 1982, p. 246), rev. by Antoine

Léon in *ASSR* 60,2 (1986):   259; VINCENT, K. Steven, *Pierre-Joseph Proudhon and the Rise of French Republican Socialism* (see *RMB* for 1984, p. 292), rev. by Benjamin F. Martin in *The Historian* 48 (1985-86):   449; by Jerrold Seigel in *JMH* 58 (1986):   328-30.

QUINET

Aeschimann, Willy.   *La Pensée d'Edgar Quinet: étude sur la formation de ses idées, avec essais de jeunesse et documents inédits.*   (Anthropos.)   Paris: Georg, 1986.   Pp. 700. Fr. 380.00.

Bernard-Griffiths, Simone.   "Edgar Quinet: réforme, révocation, révolution."   *Réforme*, March 23, 1985, pp. 111-14.

Furet, François.   *La Gauche et la Révolution française au milieu du XIXe siècle: Edgar Quinet et la question du jacobinisme, 1865-1870.*   Présenté par Marina Valensise.   Paris: Hachette, 1986.   Pp. 314.   Fr. 119.00.

Furet, François.   "Jules Ferry et l'histoire de la Révolution Française."   In François Furet, ed., *Jules Ferry, fondateur de la République.*   Paris: Editions de l'Ecole des Hautes Etudes en Sciences Sociales, 1985.   Pp. 256.   Fr. 98.00.

On the polemic (1865-66) over Quinet's history of the Revolution.

Histoire de la poésie; Des épopées françaises inédites du douzième siècle.   (Les Introuvables.)   Plan-de-la-Tour: Editions d'Aujourd'hui, 1986.   Pp. 156.   Fr. 74.00.

Weidenhammer, Dirk.   *Prometheus und Merlin.   zur mythischen Lebensbewältigung bei Edgar Quinet.*   (Bonner romanistische Arbeiten, 16.)   Frankfurt am Main and Bern: Peter Lang, 1982. Pp. 146.

Rev. by B. Guthmüller in *Archiv* 222 (1985):   451.

Reviews of books previously listed:

Le Christianisme et la Révolution française (see *RMB* for 1984, p. 293), rev. by Emile Poulat in *ASSR* 61,2 (1986): 304-05; CROSSLEY, Ceri, *Edgar Quinet (1803-1875)* (see *RMB* for 1983, p. 243), rev. by Simone Bernard-Griffiths in *RHL* 86 (1986):   932-35; by Peter Byrne in *SFr* 29 (1985):   600; by Robert T. Denommé in *FR* 59 (1985-86):   792-93; by D. Graham in *French Forum* 10 (1985):   113-14.

REMUSAT

See Welch ("French 1. General").

ROUSSEAU

Coleman, Patrick. *Rousseau's Political Imagination: Rule and
   Representation in the "Lettre à d'Alembert."* Geneva: Droz,
   1984. Pp. 193.

   Rev. by Ronald Grimsley in *ECS* 20 (1986): 118-20.

Jackson, Susan K. "Text and Context of Rousseau's Relations
   with Diderot." *ECS* 20 (1986-87): 195-219.

Marshall, David. "Rousseau and the State of Theatre."
   Representations no. 13 (1986): 84-114.

   Explores "the problem of theatricality in the *Lettre à
   d'Alembert*" and argues that "the issue for Rousseau is not
   whether a theatre should be established but whether theatre
   (in its many manifestations) can be avoided at all."

O'Neal, John C. *Seeing and Observing: Rousseau's Rhetoric
   of Perception.* (Stanford French and Italian Studies, 41.)
   Saratoga, Calif.: ANMA Libri, 1985. Pp. 144. $20.00.

   Rev. by Aubrey Rosenberg in *ECS* 20 (1986-86): 242-44.

See also Blum ("General 2. Environment"); De Jean ("French
   1. General").

ROYER-COLLARD

Cotten, Jean-Pierre. "Un libéral peut-il être un tyran
   domestique? Le cas de Royer-Collard." *Cahiers de Philosophie
   politique et juridique* 6 (1984): 191-207.

SAINTE-BEUVE

Finn, Michael R. "Proust and Sainte-Beuve: The Narrator as
   Journalist." *French Forum* 10 (1985): 175-87.

   All on Proust.

Guyoux, André, préfacier. *Volupté.* (Folio, 1755.) Paris:
   Gallimard, 1986. Pp. 512. Fr. 39.50.

Poulet, Georges. "Sainte-Beuve et l'indétermination."
  L'Ecriture 24 (Summer 1985): 27-30.

  Conclusion: the world of Sainte-Beuve is infinitely
  ambiguous, but it is not a world of pure confusion or of
  indetermination in the philosophical sense. "Il est plutôt
  celui de la multiplicité et de la variabilité des façons
  d'être et de vivre. Aucune pour lui n'est absolument
  déterminé ni indéterminé."

Vie, poésies et pensées de Joseph Delorme. (Les Introuvables.)
  Plan-de-la-Tour: Editions d'Aujourd'hui, 1985. Pp. 245.
  Fr. 68.00.
  Reprint of the original edition published in Paris, 1829.

See also Scaiola ("French 1. General").

Reviews of book previously listed:

  REGARD, Maurice, ed., *Volupté* (see *RMB* for 1984, p. 294),
  rev. by Robert T. Denommé in *FR* 60 (1986-87): 260-61; by
  Arlette Michel in *IL* 38 (1986): 48-49.

SAINTINE

Fongaro, Antoine. "Rimbaud et X.B. Saintine." *Parade Sauvage*
  3 (April 1986): 73-74.

  A reminiscence of *Picciola* in "Enfance II" (*Illuminations*)
  suggests that Rimbaud read this immensely popular novel by
  Saintine.

SAINT-MARTIN

Grasso, L. "Il 'désir' cratilista nel *Cahier des langues* di
  Louis-Claude de Saint-Martin." *Quaderno* 17 (1983): 99-126.

Konno, Kiroahito. "Louis-Claude de Saint-Martin et la vision
  illuministe de la Révolution française." *ELLF* 46 (1985):
  19-35.

SAINT-SIMON

Derré, Jean-René, and Roger Bellet, eds. *Regards sur le Saint-
  Simonisme et les Saint-Simoniens.* (Littérature et Idéologies.)
  Presses universitaires de Lyon, 1986. Pp. 200. Fr. 98.00.

Contents: Roger Bellet, "Avant-propos" (5-7); Jean-René
Derré, "Lamennais et la pensée saint-simonienne" (9-43);
Michel Espagne, "Le Saint-Simonisme est-il jeune-hégélien?"
(45-71); Christine Planté, "Les féministes saint-simoniennes.
Possibilités et limites d'un mouvement féministe en France
au lendemain de 1830" (73-102); Lucette Czyba, "L'oeuvre
lyonnaise d'une ancienne saint-simonienne: le *Conseiller
des femmes* (1833-1834) d'Eugène Niboyet" (103-41); Anne-Marie
Thiesse, "La chair de l'Utopie ou la vulgarisation de la
pensée saint-simonienne dans les romans d'Eugène Sue" (143-
60); Philippe Régnier, "De l'état présent des études saint-
simoniennes" (161-85); "Bibliographie du saint-simonisme de
1965 à 1984" (186-206).

Hoeges, Dirk. "Saint-Simon und die Theorie der Avant-Garde."
Lendemains 37 (1985): 37-43.

Locke, Ralph P. *Music, Musicians, and the Saint-Simonians.*
University of Chicago Press, 1986. Pp. xviii+400. $48.50,
paper $21.00.

   Rev. by John Warrack in *TLS*, March 27, 1987, p. 323.
   It would appear from the above review that the musicians
treated are Félicien David, Jules Vinçard, Berlioz, Mendelssohn
(who reacted to musical Saint-Simonisme with "sharp irrita-
tion"), and, especially, Liszt.

Zaganelli, Gioia. "L'école saint-simonienne: la donna messia,
profeta, madre." *SFr* 30 (1986): 81-85.

   Based on Maria Teresa Bulciolu, *L'Ecole saint-simonienne
et la femme* (see *RMB* for 1981, p. 229).

See also Armogathe, Biermann, Saffle, Walch ("French 1. General").

SAND

Bailbé, Joseph-Marie, ed. *Le Château des Désertes.* (Les
Œuvres de George Sand.) Meylan: Editions de l'Aurore,
1986. Pp. 192. Fr. 82.00.

   Rev. by René Bourgeois in *Présence de George Sand* 23 (1985):
51.
   "Un roman où se mêlent la magie du théâtre et l'envoûtement
de la fête, sur le thème de Don Juan" (*Les Livres du mois*,
June 1985).

Barry, Joseph. *George Sand ou le scandale de la liberté.*
Traduit de l'américain par Marie-France de Paloméra.

(Collection Points, série Biographie, Bl.) Paris: Editions du Seuil, 1982. Pp. 572.

Rev. by Simone Vierne in *Romantisme* 52 (1986): 124-26.
Joseph Barry is to George Sand what Ghislain de Diesbach is to Germaine de Staël. (His book was originally [1977] published under the title *Infamous Woman: The Life of George Sand*; see *ELN* 15, supp. 125.) (D.J.C.)

Bodin, Thierry, and Joseph Barry, eds. *Elle et lui*. Pref. by Joseph Barry. Meylan: Editions de l'Aurore, 1986. Pp. 229; illus.

Barry's preface (5-19) tells the story of the Sand-Musset affair. Bodin's excellent "Présentation" (21-36) relates the genesis of Sand's book and discusses the mixture of fiction and reality to be found in it (e.g., the chronology of the novel is minutely compared to that of the "real" events). Bodin also provides a detailed annotation (over 200 notes) and a generous choice of variants. Close to a critical edition. (J.S.P.)

Bonnat, Jean-Louis, and Mireille Bossis, eds. *Ecrire, publier, lire. Les correspondances: problématique et économie d'un "genre littéraire."* Actes du Colloque International, "Les Correspondances." Publications de L'Université de Nantes (diffusion: Distique), 1983. Fr. 120.00.

Rev. by Nancy Rogers in *Friends of George Sand Newsletter* 6 (1983): 80; by Kathryn Crecelius, *ibid*.: 70-71.
In its contents, six papers on George Sand as epistolary writer: Renate Karst Matausch, "George Sand épistolière. naissance d'un écrivain (1814-1832)"; Nancy Rogers, "Style, voix, et destinataire dans les lettres de George Sand avant 1837"; Kristina Wingard, "La correspondance entre le littéraire et le vécu--George Sand en 1834"; Simone Lecointre, "Pour une théorie du texte des correspondances (G. Sand)"; Mireille Bossis, "La correspondance comme figure de compromis--G. Sand"; Jean Delabroy, "A propos de la correspondance Flaubert-Sand."

Bozon-Scalzitti, Yvette. "George Sand: le bruit et la musique." *OL* 41 (1986): 139-56.

Byrne, Peter. "George Sand et Giuseppe Mazzini." *Note sul Socialismo e Cristianesimo* 6-7 (1983-84): 3-9.

Collister, Peter. "The Heritage of George Sand: Mrs. Humphry Ward's *The History of David Grieve*." *RES* 36 (1985): 501-21.

Corse, Sandra. "Henry James on Eliot and Sand." *SAR* 51
(1986): 57-68.

Crecelius, Kathryn J. "George Sand's Berry." *Laurels* 56
(1985-86): 149-56.

Daly, Pierrette. "Les récits autobiographiques de l'histoire
d'amour Sand-Musset." Pp. 171-74 in *Autobiography in French
Literature*. (French Literature Series, 12.) Department of
Foreign Languages and Literatures, University of South
Carolina, 1985. Pp. 227.

Desneuve, Alphonse. "Dix dessins pour illustrer *Le Chêne
parlant* de George Sand." *Les Cahiers de l'Imaginaire* 9
(1983): 17-27.

Friends of George Sand Newsletter 6,1-2 (1983). Pp. 83.

   George Sand Conferences proceedings, part 2, Bard College,
November 12-13, 1982: *George Sand and Her Contemporaries*.
Contents: Henriette Bessis, "George Sand, Eugène Delacroix,
reflets d'une amitié" (3-12); Roland A. Champagne and Pierrette
Daly, "The Rhetoric of Passion: Narration and Ideology in
George Sand's *Indiana* and Gustave Flaubert's *Madame Bovary*"
(13-20); Dominique Desanti, "George, Marie, Pauline, Flora
et les autres" (21-25); Mary P. Edwards, "Henry James and
George Sand: The Double Critical Standard" (26-35); Mary
Ann Garnett, "Pseudonym and Identity: Marie d'Agoult and the
Creation of Daniel Stern" (36-40); Howard N. Meyer, "The
Sisterhood of George Sand and Margaret Fuller" (41-46);
Tatiana Greene, "George Sand et le caché dans *Le Diable aux
Champs*" (47-51); Gabrielle Pascal, "La condition féminine
dans *La Ville Noire*" (52-57); Annabelle M. Rea, "George
Sand Misogynist?" (58-65); Benjamin Rountree, "George Sand's
Reflections on Children and Their Education" (66-69); Jean-
Louis Bonnat and Mireille Bossis, eds., *Ecrire, publier, lire
les correspondances* (Actes du Colloque international, Uni-
versité de Nantes), rev. by Kathryn Crecelius (70-71); Pierre
Reboul, *Errements littéraires et historiques*, rev. by Marie-
Jacques Hoog (72-74); Francis Steegmuller, ed., *The Letters
of Gustave Flaubert, 1857-1880*, rev. by Murray Sachs (75-77);
Simone Vierne, ed., *George Sand* (Colloque de Cerisy-la-Salle,
1981), rev. by David A. Powell (78-79); Conferences, Con-
ventions, Colloquia (80-82); "Publication News" (83);
"Seventh International Conference: George Sand; Hofstra
University" (84).

George Sand Studies (formerly, *Friends of George Sand News-letter*) 7,1-2 (1984-85).

Contents: George Sand Conference Proceedings, Missouri
Western State College, October 18-20, 1984. Sylvie L.F.
Richards, "Introduction" (1-2); Simone Vierne, "Music in
the Heart of the World: The Challenge of Music to Literature" (3-14); Marie-Jacques Hoog, "Le pic, le soc, le burin
et le stylet" (15-23); Gay Manifold, "George Sand: Mother
of Realism" (24-29); Dorothy Zimmerman, "George Sand and
Willa Cather: Their Pastoral Novels" (30-36); Eve Sourian,
"L'influence de Mme de Staël sur les premières oeuvres de
George Sand" (37-45); Isabelle Naginski, "*Lélia*: Novel
of the Invisible" (46-53); David A. Powell, "Discord, Dissen-
sion and Dissonance: The Initiation of *Les Maîtres Sonneurs*"
(54-61); Janis Glasgow, "George Sand's Use of Myths and
Symbols in *Le Géant Yéous*" (62-72); Annabelle M. Rea, "The
Art of Reading (in) Sand" (73-83); Pierrette Daly and
Roland A. Champagne, "The Semiotic Correspondence Between
Sand and Flaubert: Toward Heterosexual Thinking" (84-94);
Conferences, Conventions, Colloquia (95); "Publication
News" (96).

Glasgow, Janis, ed. *George Sand: Collected Essays*. (Selected
Papers from the Fourth International Conference: George
Sand: Her Life, Her Work, Her Circle, Her Influence. San
Diego State University, 1981, and the Modern Language Associa-
tion Convention, New York, 1983.) Troy, N.Y.: Whitston
Publishing, 1985. $30.00.

Lubin, Georges, ed. *Correspondance*, vols. 20-21. (Classiques
Garnier.) Paris: Garnier, 1985-86.

Rev. by Jean-Yves Mollier in *Bulletin de la Révolution de
1848 et des Révolutions du XIXᵉ siècle* 3 (1987): 124-26.

Mallion, Jean, and Pierre Salomon, eds. *Un Hiver à Majorque*.
(Les Œuvres de George Sand.) Meylan: Editions de l'Aurore,
1985. Pp. 216. Fr. 87.00.

Manifold, Gay S. *George Sand's Theatre Career*. Foreword by
Georges Lubin. Ann Arbor, Mich.: University Microfilms
International Research Press, 1985. Pp. xviii+188. $40.00.

Milner, Max, and Claude Pichois, eds. Pp. 86-89, 244-45 in
Max Milner and Claude Pichois, *Littérature française*, vol.
7, *De Chateaubriand à Baudelaire, 1820-69*. (Littérature
française/Poche.) Paris: Arthaud, 1985. Pp. 443.

Mitchell, Anne Marie. *George Sand ou les cheveux denoués*. (Rencontres.) Paris: Le temps parallèle, 1985. Pp. 125. Fr. 60.00.

Nagatsuka, Ryuji. *George Sand, ses oeuvres et sa vie.* Tokyo: Editions Yomiuri, 1977. (In Japanese.)

Pirotte, Huguette. *George Sand*. (Bibliographies.) Gembloux-Paris: Duculot, 1983.

Poli, Annarosa. "George Sand dans les journaux et revues de 1831 à 1833." Pp. 75-104 in *Ottocento francese*. (Quaderni dell'Istituto di Lingue e Letterature Neolatine, 3, seconda serie.) Milan: Cisalpino-Goliardica, 1983.

See *Francofonia* 9 (1985): 139-41, for a summary/review.

Poli, Annarosa. "Il viaggio reale e il viaggio immaginario nelle *Lettres d'un voyageur* di George Sand." Pp. 80-91 in *La letteratura e l'immaginario. Problemi di semantica e di storia del lessico franco-italiano.* Atti dell'XI Convegno della Società universitaria per gli studi di lingua e letteratura francese. Verona, 14-16 ottobre 1982. Milan: Cisalpino, 1984.

Présence de George Sand 22 (1985).

Contents: Yvonne Bargues-Rollins, "La Petite Fadette ou le verbe fait Femme" (4-14); Yvette Bozon-Scalzitti, "George Sand et le fantastique: *L'Homme de neige* ou la mort(e) qui revient" (15-27); Pierre Aubery, "George Sand dénonciatrice de l'imposture monastique" (28-37); Micheline Besnard, "Quelques repères structurels: les lieux dans *Valentine*" (38-46); Mihailo Pavlović, "Les thèmes yougoslaves dans l'œuvre romanesque de George Sand" (47-53); Kathryn J. Crecelius, "*Rose et Blanche*" la dernière œuvre d'apprentissage de George Sand" (54-57); Jean-Hervé Donnard, "Claudel a-t-il lu George Sand?" (58-62); V. Del Litto, "A travers les catalogues" (67).

Rambeau, Marie-Paule. *Chopin dans la vie et l'œuvre de George Sand*. (Histoire et Littérature françaises.) Paris: Les Belles Lettres, 1985. Pp. 394. Fr. 98.00.

See *RMB* for 1985, p. 278, for related article by Rambeau.

Reboul, Pierre, ed. *Lélia*. (Classiques Garnier.) Paris: Garnier, 1986. Pp. lxix+601. Fr. 80.00.

Richter, Anne. "George Sand ou la nostalgie du bois perdu."
Pp. 45-55 in *Le Fantastique féminin. Un art sauvage.*
Brussels: J. Antoine, 1984.

Sand, George. *Histoire de ma vie.* Nouvelle ed. Paris: Stock,
1985. Pp. 345. Fr. 43.00.

Sand, George. *Le Chêne parlant.* Illus. by Alain Durbec. Lyon:
Editions du Chardon bleu, 1986. Pp. 117. Fr. 46.00.

See *RMB* for 1985, p. 274: Berthier.

Sourian, Eve, ed. *Nouvelles.* Paris: Des Femmes, 1986. Pp.
441. Fr. 95.00.

Contains five short stories Sand wrote before she was 30:
La Marquise; *Lavinia*; *Metella*; *Mattea*; *Pauline.*

Van Runset, Ute. "Illuminisme et Lumières: impact sur les
idées sociales de George Sand." *SVEC* 216 (1983): 439-41.

See also *O&C* 10,1 (1985): 29-43.

Vierne, Simone, ed. *Jeanne.* (Les OEuvres de George Sand.)
Illus. by Robert Thuillier. Meylan: Editions de l'Aurore,
1986. Pp. 320. Fr. 98.00.

"Un roman peu connu de [George Sand], qui se situe dans
la Creuse, notamment au château de Boussac." (*Livres du
Mois*, Dec. 1986.)

Wentz, Debra Linowitz. *Fait et fiction: les formules pédago-
giques des "Contes d'une grand'mère" de George Sand.* Paris:
A.-G. Nizet, 1985. Pp. 296.

See also Claudon, Lasserre-Vergne, Michaud ("French 1. General");
Société Chateaubriand, Bulletin 28 ("Chateaubriand"); Bruneau
("Colet"); Prontera ("Lamennais"); Borowitz ("Staël"); Michaud
("Tristan").

Reviews of books previously listed:

JACOBS, Alphonse, ed., *Correspondance Flaubert-Sand* (see *RMB*
for 1981, p. 233), rev. by B.F. Bart in *RHL* 86 (1986): 935;
LUBIN, Georges, ed., *Correspondance*, vol. 18 (see *RMB* for
1985, p. 275), rev. by Jean Gaulmier in *RHL* 86 (1986): 306-
07; vol. 19 (see *RMB* for 1985, p. 276); rev. by Carlo Bronne
in *RG* (May 1985): 102; by Carlo Cordié in *SFr* 30 (1986):
158-59; vols. 19-20 (see *RMB* for 1985, p. 276), rev. by
Françoise van Rossum-Guyon in *Romantisme* 52 (1986): 118-24;

VAN ROSSUM-GUYON, Françoise, Recherches nouvelles sur George
Sand (see RMB for 1984, pp. 302-03), rev. by Simone Vierne
in RHL 86 (1986): 772-73; VIERNE, Simone, ed., George Sand,
Colloque de Cerisy-la-Salle (see RMB for 1983, pp. 252-53),
rev. by Mireille Bossis in RHL 86 (1986): 304-06.

SANDEAU

Bodin, Thierry. "Les métamorphoses d'Horace ou quelques avatars
romanesques de Jules Sandeau." L'Année Balzacienne 5 (1984):
15-36.

See also Leduc-Adine ("French 1. General").

SCRIBE

Gier, Albert. "Manon Lescaut als Fabel von der Grille und der
Ameise. E. Scribes Libretto für Daniel-François-Esprit
Auber (1856)." Jahrbuch für Opernforschung (1985): 73-89.

See also Gidel ("French 1. General").

SENANCOUR

Didier, Béatrice, ed. Oberman. (Le Livre de poche, 5959.)
Paris: Librairie Générale Française, 1984. Pp. 506.

Didier, Béatrice. "Oberman et l'art du discours." IL 38
(1986): 67-72.

Senancour's self-analysis follows patterns of "inventio,"
"dispositio," and "elocutio" because it is necessarily--and
uniquely--linguistic.

Didier, Béatrice. "Senancour, 'Obermann'" [Indications
bibliographiques]. Bulletin de la Société d'étude du XVIIIe
siècle 54 (July 1985): 13-16.

Didier, Béatrice. Senancour romancier: Oberman, Aldomen,
Isabelle. Paris: S.E.D.E.S., 1985. Pp. 351. Fr. 100.00.

An astute, well-documented analysis of the specificity
of Senancour's fiction: how it resembles autobiography and
self-portrait, how it borrows from such diverse literary
forms as epistolary writing, travel literature, novels of
initiation. Didier's conclusion is that none of these forms

of writing alone—and even their combination—wholly contains
Senancour's style, which seeks also to be philosophical
discourse and landscape description blended into harmony with
the consciousness of a monologuist. (M.E.B.)

Pizzorusso, Arnaldo. "'Oberman' et la conscience du temps."
Littératures 13 (Autumn 1985): 29-40.

Reviews of book previously listed:

MONNOYER, Jean-Maurice, ed., *Oberman* (see *RMB* for 1984, p.
306), rev. by Paul Lecoq in *RHL* 85 (1985): 1073-74; by Yves
Le Hir in *NRF* 39 (June 1, 1985): 63-64.

SISMONDI

Candaux, Jean-Daniel. "Deux lettres inédites de Sismondi rela-
tives aux notices italiennes de la Biographie Michaud."
Pp. 103-09 in H. Gaston Hall et al., eds., *Mélanges à la
mémoire de Franco Simone*, vol. 3, *XIXe et XXe siècles*.
Geneva: Slatkine, 1984. Pp. 822.

   Two letters (July 12, 1809; May 10, 1810) throw light on
Sismondi's negotiations with the Michauds and their assistant
Roux de Laborie about his contribution to the famous biographical dictionary (he ultimately contributed some 600 articles
on Italian figures).

Jost, François. "Aspects des relations franco-italiennes:
Simonde de Sismondi." Pp. 85-102 in H. Gaston Hall et al.,
eds., *Mélanges à la mémoire de Franco Simone*, vol. 3, *XIXe
et XXe siècles*. Geneva: Slatkine, 1984. Pp. 822.

   Jost defines his subject as follows: "comment Sismondi
a-t-il jugé ces deux pays et quels rapports a-t-il voulu
établir entre eux?" The question is studied especially on
the basis of Sismondi's major historical works (his *Histoire
des républiques italiennes* and *Histoire des Français*).
Jost concludes that Sismondi, "ce Genevois, ... cet Italien,
... ce Français ... demeure, par la sincérité de sa pensée,
la générosité de ses vues, l'une des figures les plus
attachantes de l'histoire du cosmopolitisme européen."

King, Norman. "Une collaboration libérale: Sismondi et Sir
James Mackintosh." Pp. 111-59 in H. Gaston Hall et al., eds.,
Mélanges à la mémoire de Franco Simone, vol. 3, *XIXe et XXe
siècles*. Geneva: Slatkine, 1984. Pp. 822.

Twenty-one letters from the correspondence exchanged between
Sismondi and his Scottish brother-in-law, Sir James Mackintosh (1765-1832). King has supplied an exemplary introduction
about the relationship between the two men (they met at Coppet
in September 1814) and their personal, literary, and political
affinities. The annotation is likewise exemplary. (J.S.P.)

Review of book previously listed:

Sismondi e l'agricoltura della Valdinievole nell'800 (see *RMB*
for 1985, p. 280), rev. by Carlo Cordié in *Paideia* 40 (1986):
265-66.

SOUVESTRE

Angenot, Marco. "The Emergence of the Anti-Utopian Genre in
France: Souvestre, Giraudeau, Robida, et al." *Science-
Fiction Studies* 12 (1985): 129-35.

A page is devoted to Souvestre's *Le Monde tel qu'il sera*
(1846), which is said to illustrate all the axioms of the
genre "with a kind of reactionary 'perspicacity' and by a
steadfast *reductio ad absurdum* reasoning--the radically
alienating logic which controls all attempts to speed up
social evolution or to reform social relationships."

Crossley, Ceri. "Emile Souvestre's Anti-Utopia: *Le Monde tel
qu'il sera.*" *NFS* 34,2 (1985): 28-40.

DE STAËL

Balayé, Simone. "*Delphine* de Madame de Staël et la presse
sous le Consulat." *Romantisme* 51 (1986): 39-47.

Behler, Ernst. "Das Wieland-Bild der Frau von Staël." In
*Christoph Martin Wieland, Nordamerikanisch Forschungsbeiträge
zur 250. Wiederkehr seines Geburtstages, 1983*. Tübingen:
Max Niemeyer Verlag, 1984.

Borowitz, Helen Osterman. "The Unconfessed *Précieuse*: Madame
de Staël's Debt to Mlle de Scudéry," and "Terpsichore and
Corinne: Two Nineteenth-Century Muse Portraits." Pp. 33-55,
56-74 in Osterman's *The Impact of Art on French Literature.
From de Scudéry to Proust*. University of Delaware Press;
London and Toronto: Associated University Press, 1985. Pp. 242.

Broglie, Gabriel de. *Madame de Genlis*. Paris: Librairie
Académique Perrin, 1985. Pp. 530. Fr. 125.00.

Already listed in *RMB* for 1985, p. 232, this biography
of Mme. de Genlis deserves inclusion here because of the
numerous references to Mme. de Staël.

Cahiers Staëliens (1984). "Hommage à Victor de Pange (1923-
1984)." Numéro spécial hors-série.

"Allocutions prononcées le 19 mai 1984 à la séance solen-
nelle de la Société des Etudes staëliennes, présidée par
M. Jean Gaulmier, professeur honoraire à la Sorbonne et vice-
président de la Société." This tribute to comte Victor de
Pange, on the occasion of his untimely death, comprises
encomia by Jean Gaulmier (3-4); by Norman King, "Un Anglais
de France" (5-10); by his life-long friend, Nicolaus Sombart
(11-19); and by Roland Mortier (21-25). Follow the "Homélies
prononcées à l'enterrement du comte Victor de Pange à
Champteussé-sur-Baconne et à la cérémonie religieuse à
Strasbourg," by Monsieur l'Abbé Gérard de Broglie (Champteussé,
2 février 1984) (29-33), and by Le Père Louis Christiaens,
S.J. (Strasbourg, February 23, 1984) (35-39). This special
issue ends with "Les travaux de Victor de Pange," a bibliography of his works (41-43).

Cahiers Staëliens 37 (1985-86): "Le Groupe de Coppet et
l'Allemagne. Actes du Colloque au Goethe Institut (10 et
11 mai 1985)."

Contents: Simone Balayé and Erika Tunner, "Introduction";
Roland Mortier, "Les retards et les obstacles à la révélation de la littérature allemande en France" (1-9); Manfred
Gsteiger, "Réalité et utopie de l'Allemagne staëlienne"
(10-22); Markus Winkler, "Quelques remarques de Mme de
Staël et de Benjamin Constant sur le 'genre naïf' dans la
littérature allemande" [cf. Winkler, *infra*] (23-44);
Graf von Westerholt Egon, "Lezay-Marnésia et sa contribution
à la connaissance de l'Allemagne en France" (45-52); Martine
de Rougemont, "'Hellénique ou romantique': les enjeux du
drame sous l'Empire" (53-64); Bernard Böschenstein, "Madame
de Staël, Goethe et Rousseau. Notes sur *De l'Allemagne*"
(65-79); Kurt Mueller-Vollmer, "Guillaume de Humboldt,
interprète de Madame de Staël: distances et affinités"
(80-96); Georges Solovieff, "Mme de Staël et August Wilhelm
Schlegel. Natures complémentaires et/ou antinomiques?" (97-
106); Kurt Kloocke, "Benjamin Constant, *De la religion*, et
Georg Friedrich Creuzer, *Symbolik und Mythologie der alten
Völker*, une étude épistémologique" (107-16); Monika Bosse,
"Esquisse de la réception du livre *De l'Allemagne*, en
Allemagne" (117-31).
Margaret R. Higonnet's paper, "*Lucinde et Adolphe*: écrire

au féminin" appeared in *Annales Benjamin Constant* 5 (1985):
17-35, in English, under the title "Writing from the
Feminine: *Lucinde* and *Adolphe*."

Fiorioli, Elena. *Madame de Staël e A.W. Schlegel. Il potere
al femminile*. Verona: Libreria universitaria editrice,
1983. Pp. 101.

"L'étude s'intéresse ici à Mme de Staël et à A.W. Schlegel
dans le but de montrer que le pouvoir est la vocation dominante
d'une femme pour qui l'ambition littéraire n'est que le
premier pas vers le pouvoir politique." (Alain Montandon,
RHL 86 [1986]: 927.)
See also Elisabeth Chevallier's synopsis in *RHL* 86 (1986):
103. Fiorioli's conclusion is to be read with caution.
(D.J.C.)

Folkenflik, Vivian, trans. and ed. *Selected Writings of
Madame de Staël*. Columbia University Press, 1986. Pp. 368.
$40.00.

Gutwirth, Madelyn. "Forging a Vocation: Germaine de Staël
on Fiction, Power, and Passion." *Bulletin of Research in
the Humanities* 86 (1983-85): 242-54.

Higonnet, Margaret R. "Madame de Staël and Schelling."
CL 38 (1986): 159-80.

Jasinski, Béatrice W., ed. *Correspondance générale de Madame
de Staël*, vol. 2, *Le Léman et l'Italie*. Paris: Hachette,
1985. Pp. xi+387. Fr. 400.00.

Rev. by Jean Gaulmier in *RHL* 86 (1986): 927-29.
Mme. Jasinski's impeccable new volume covers the period
extending from May 19, 1804, to November 9, 1805. The "highlights" of this impatiently awaited new contribution to Mme.
de Staël's general correspondence are her letters to Fourcault
de Pavant, her *notaire*, after the death of Necker April 9,
1804), a time for grief, but also a time for important
decisions to be made with regard to her father's estate,
a complex situation in which land speculations in North
America played no small part (hence the "surfacing" of names
such as Dupont de Nemours and Le Ray de Chaumont). Equally,

if not more, important are her letters to Monti, given here
by Mme. Jasinski, with perfect annotation. No fewer than
62 heretofore unpublished letters are contained in this
new volume. (D.J.C.)

Johnson-Cousin, Danielle. "Madame de Staël et le Groupe de
Coppet: expérimentation dramatique." *Ecriture* 25 (1985-
86): 103-16.

A brief introduction stresses that dramatic experimentation,
in the "Atelier de Coppet" (S. Balayé's expression), is part
of a clearly thought out, systematic plan bearing on the
group's own politics and culture. N. King speaks of the
"politique culturelle du Groupe," an apt expression to which
"culture politisée" should be added, or, better yet, "politique esthétique" (N. King). Proceeding chronologically,
from the *saison dramatique* of 1805-06 (Geneva) to the last
performances of 1814-16 (Coppet), the author shows Mme. de
Staël's *volonté d'expérimentation* in the theater, asserting
itself together with her undeniable adherence to the classical
and neoclassical repertory.
    In the second cycle of plays, appropriately called by Mme.
de Staël "essais dramatiques," which were specifically written
for experimentation (and, of course, entertainment) purposes,
Mme. de Staël's "testing out" of *modern* (Romantic) ideas on
stage is evident 1) in the form (prose) and contents (themes
and influences) of her plays; 2) in staging and in the careful choice of costumes; and 3) in personal expression and
acting (insistance upon individualism, simplicity, and
naturalness). Highlights Mme. de Staël's interest in the
then-developing *genre* of monodrama, attitudes, and "tableaux
vivants."
    Conclusion reveals that Mme. de Staël adapted some of
Byron's minor poems for the stage, which she acted out with
Louis-Albert Necker; Schlegel; Sismondi; Dumont, Sir
Humphry and Lady Davy; and others.

King, Norman. "[Une lettre de] Camille Jordan à Germaine de
Staël, Lyon, 29 janvier 1809." *Annales Benjamin Constant*
4 (1984): 68-71, 86.

    Apropos of Benjamin Constant's *Wallstein* (see *RMB* for
1985, p. 219; King).

Lauth, Reinhard. "J.G. Fichte et Madame de Staël: l'entretien de Madame de Staël avec Fichte, Berlin, mars 1804." *Archives de Philosophie* (Jan.-March 1984): 63-75.

Peterson, Carla L. "*Corinne* and *Louis Lambert*: Romantic Myth-Making." Pp. 37-81 in Carla L. Peterson, *The Determined Reader: Gender and Culture in the Novel from Napoleon to Victoria*. Rutgers University Press, 1986. Pp. x+264. $25.00.

   Rev. by Joan C. Kessler in *NCFS* 15 (1986-87): 231-33.

Poniatowski, Michel. *Talleyrand et le Directoire: 1796-1800*. Paris: Librairie Académique Perrin, 1982. Pp. 908.

   As one might expect, several references to Benjamin Constant and Mme. de Staël (in particular, pp. 29-30; 112-18; 135-40; 141-44; 150-54; 179-83; and 258-63).

Printz, Michel. "Chateaubriand et Madame de Staël à l'écoute du *Miserere* d'Allegri." *L'Ecole des Lettres*, Feb. 15, 1985, pp. 23-24.

Sato, Natsuo. "Le mysticisme de Mme de Staël." *Studies in Humanities* 83 (1982): 1-34. (In Japanese.)

   "Le premier chapitre (2-6) évoque les contacts que Mme de Staël e eus avec les mystiques des Ames intérieures, par l'entremise de Constant. Le second (6-12) traite du mysticisme dans *De l'Allemagne*. Le troisième (12-18) compare la conception staëlienne du mysticisme avec celle de Constant. Le quatrième (18-24) aborde la notion d'*enthousiasme* chez Mme de Staël, essentielle pour comprendre son idée du mysticisme. Une conclusion (24-26) situe la réflexion staëlienne dans le prolongement de celle de Shaftesbury, et souligne que Mme de Staël (à la différence de Constant, déchiré entre l'incrédulité du philosophe et le besoin de croire) ne cherche pas dans le mysticisme une échappatoire à la douleur, mais une force qui permettra l'éclosion d'un nouveau monde littéraire, celui du XIXe siècle 'romantique'" (Christian Viredaz, "Bibliographie," *Annales Benjamin Constant* 5 [1985]: 172).

Schlegel, Dorothea. *Corinna oder Italien*. Ed. Arno Kappler. Munich: Deutscher Taschenbuch Verlag, 1986.

   This famous translation of Mme. de Staël's *Corinne* had already been republished in 1979 by Winkler Verlag, in Munich--one of many signs of renewed interest in Germany for Mme. de Staël and her group.

Sofia, F. "Per una rilettura delle *Considérations* di
Madame de Staël." *Clio* 20 (1984): 305-21.

Solovieff, Georges. "Madame de Staël, les Schlegel et les
beaux-arts en Allemagne. 2. La sculpture, l'architecture,
la danse et la musique." *SFr* 30 (1986): 15-29.
Follows up on an article listed in *RMB* for 1985, p. 285.

Szabó, Anna. "Le sens d'un échec: *Delphine* de Madame de
Staël." *Analyses de roman. Studia Romanica Universitatis
Debreceniensis; Series litteraria* 11 (1985): 57-75.

Szabó, Anna. "Madame de Staël: *Delphine. Filologiai
Közlöňy, Bulletin de Philologie, Revue de l'Académie des
Sciences* (Budapest) 3-4 (1983).

Szmurlo, Karyna. "Le jeu et le discours féminin: la danse
de l'heroïne staëlienne." *NCFS* 15 (1986-87): 1-13.

Tenenbaum, Susan. "Liberal Heroines: Mme. de Staël on the
'Woman Question' and the Modern State." *Annales Benjamin
Constant* 5 (1985): 37-52 (abstract, p. 182).

Urfer, Selma. "Besuch bei der grossen Dame von Coppet.
Gegenwart und Vergangenheit an einem Sommertag: Über
Germaine de Staël." *Süddeutsche Zeitung* 130 (June 1985):
121.

Viredaz, Christian. "9e Journée de Coppet, 7 septembre 1985."
Annales Benjamin Constant 5 (1985): 178-79.

Viredaz, Christian. "Mme de Staël, Constant et le roman."
(Compte-rendu de la "Journée de Coppet.") *Gazette de
Lausanne* (Samedi littéraire), Sept. 21, 1985.

Viredaz, Christian. "Mme de Staël et l'Allemagne." (Compte-
rendu du Colloque de Paris, Institut Goethe, 10-11 mai
1985.) *Gazette de Lausanne* (Samedi littéraire), June 1,
1985.

Viredaz, Christian. "Madame de Staël, le Groupe de Coppet et
l'Allemagne. Colloque organisé par le Goethe-Institut de
Paris en collaboration avec la Société des Etudes Staëliennes,
Paris, 10-11 mai 1985." *Annales Benjamin Constant* 5 (1985):
163-65.

Wagener, Françoise. *Madame Récamier, 1777-1849*. Paris: Editions Jean-Claude Lattès, 1986. Pp. 545.

At long last, a contemporary, updated, comprehensive biography of this great friend of Mme de Staël. The most important work of this kind published since Edouard Herriot's *Mme Récamier et ses amis* (Paris, 1934), and, as one might expect, written in quite a different tone. (D.J.C.)

Winegarten, Renée. *Madame de Staël*. (Berg's Women's Series.) Lemington Spa: Berg, 1985. Pp. viii+144. $5.95.

Winkler, Markus. "Madame de Staëls Bemerkungen zum Idyllischen in Literatur und Leben der Deutschen." *Colloquium Helveticum* 4 (1986): 73-109 (abstract, pp. 109-10).

See also Becq, Peterson, Petit, Scaiola ("French 1. General"); *George Sand Studies* 7,1-2 ("Sand"); Higonnet ("German 3. Schelling").

Reviews of books previously listed:

BALAYE, Simone, ed., *Corinne ou l'Italie* (see *RMB* for 1985, p. 281), rev. by Arlette Michel in *IL* 38 (1986): 169-70; HOFMANN, Etienne, ed., *Benjamin Constant, Madame de Staël et le Groupe de Coppet* (see *RMB* for 1982, p. 261), rev. by Jean-Pierre Aguet in *Revue Suisse d'Histoire* 34 (1984): 155-56; by Carlo Cordié in *SFr* 27 (1983): 570-71; by Raymond Trousson in *DHS* 16 (1984): 423-24; by Dennis Wood in *MLR* 79 (1984): 193-95; MANSAU, Andrée, ed., *Réflexions sur le suicide* (see *RMB* for 1984, p. 310), rev. by Norman King in *RHL* 86 (1986): 764.

STENDHAL

André, Robert, ed. *Chroniques italiennes*. Paris: Collection de l'Imprimerie Nationale, 1986. Pp. 386.

An excellent edition, in luxury format, of the *Chroniques italiennes*. It contains the four *chroniques* that Stendhal completed, excludes the two unfinished ones ("Trop de faveur tue," "Suora Scolastica"), and adds, in appendix, the related story, "Vanina Vanini." André's general introduction discusses narrative technique in Stendhal and proposes that Stendhal's architectonic impotence is compensated by the use of preexisting plots and by an understanding of literature as a projection of personal experience. Each of the *chroniques* is given a separate introduction as well, and the editor provides a thorough history of the texts. There are ample and useful notes. The appendices include extracts from Shelley's *The*

Cenci (in French translation), Custine's *La Cenci*, and Artaud's *Les Cenci*. An important publication. (E.J.T.)

Arbelet, Paul. *Stendhal épicier*. Marseille: J. Lafitte, 1985.

Originally published in 1926.

Augendre, Jean-Charles. "La *Filosofia nova* dans l'histoire du matérialisme." *SC* 28 (1985-86): 255-69.

Taking Stendhal's early attempts at philosophy seriously, Augendre studies the "genealogy" of Stendhal's *Filosofia nova*, its early sources in Helvétius (soon repudiated in favor of Hobbes), its epicureanism, its preoccupation with autoanalysis, passion, and history. Useful survey. (E.J.T.)

Bennett, J.H.B. "*Le Rouge et le Noir* and the *Keepsake français*: Religious Expurgation Under the July Monarchy." *MLR* 81 (1986): 866-81.

Eight weeks after the publication of *Le Rouge et le Noir*, extracts from chapter 24 ("Une capitale") and chapter 25 ("Le Séminaire") of book 1 were published in *Keepsake français ou souvenir de littérature contemporaine*, a publication dedicated to the new Orleanist queen and meant for fashionable aristocratic and bourgeois readers. Bennett suggests that the omissions in the seminary episode (dealing with Julien's first encounter with l'abbé Pirard) were the result of the publisher's nervousness after Janin's review of the novel stressed its anticlerical side.

Bertelà, Maddalena. *Stendhal et l'autre: L'homme et l'oeuvre à travers l'idée de féminité*. Florence: Leo S. Olschki, 1985. Pp. 350.

Rev. by Elaine Williamson in *FS* 44 (1984): 471-72.

Berthier, Philippe. "Le Corneille de Stendhal." *FSSA* 15 (1986): 1-12.

Excellent discussion of the meaning of Corneille for Stendhal. The latter associated him with virility, with a period of French history not unlike that of the Italian Middle Ages, but above all with a sense of duty which, far from being repressive, represents a fidelity to the self. (E.J.T.)

Berthier, Philippe. "Qu'est-ce qu'un film stendhalien?" *Recherches et travaux* (Grenoble) 29 (1985): 19-21.

Stendhal's fiction is difficult to adapt to the cinema because Stendhal is not a visual writer. Places and people are left indeterminate so that each reader is free to imagine them as he wishes. Hence, the reader of Stendhal experiences a sense of betrayal when he sees a visualization of his imaginative construct. On the other hand, there are films having nothing to do with Stendhal which are Stendhalian in tone. Berthier lists films by Bertolucci, Visconti, and Rohmer as examples. Suggestive. (E.J.T.)

Berthier, Philippe, ed. *Stendhal.* Colloque de Cerisy-la-Salle, 1982. (Collection des mélanges de la bibliothèque de la Sorbonne, 2.) Paris: Aux amateurs de livres, 1984. Pp. 207.

Contains: Gilbert D. Chaitin, "Ce que parler veut dire: désir et parole chez Stendhal" (1-12); Jean-Jacques Hamm, "L'achèvement et son envers: de l'œuvre au lecteur" (13-32); Micheline Levowitz-Treu, "Considérations sur Stendhal: une possibilité d'approche psychanalytique" (33-48); Robert André, "Approche analytique de l'œuvre stendhalienne: l'image ambiguë du père. Ebauche d'un bilan" (49-56); Jean Delabroy, "*La Chartreuse de Parme* ou le problème de la position morale" (57-66); Pierre Barbéris, "*Armance*, Armance: quelle impuissance?" (67-86); Richard N. Coe, "La 'frivolité' de Stendhal" (87-102); Gérald Rannaud, "Le naturel et ses équivoques" (103-18); Béatrice Dider, "L'adresse au lecteur dans les textes autobiographiques de Stendhal" (119-34); Serge Sérodes, "Les blancs dans les manuscrits de la *Vie de Henry Brulard*" (135-50); Geneviève Mouillaud-Fraisse, "La question du destinataire dans l'écriture de Stendhal" (151-62); Kurt Ringger, "La 'véracité' de Stendhal ou le 'plaisir d'écrire'" (163-78); Didier Coste, "Discours de l'essai et discours narratif dans *De l'amour*" (179-92); Jean-Noël Marie, "L'invention de 'Stendhal' d'après Jean Prévost" (193-207).

Berthier, Philippe. "Topo-énergétique de *l'Abbesse de Castro.*" *SC* 28 (1985-86): 134-45.

Excellent topographical analysis of places in *L'Abbesse de Castro* and their relation to passion and energy. Special attention is given to the walled convent, the oasis-like garden, and the anarchic forest. (E.J.T.)

Binni, Lanfranco, ed. *Cronache italiane.* (I grandi libri Garzanti, 300.) Milan: Garzanti, 1983. Pp. xxvii+252. L. 6,000.00.

Birnberg, Jacques. "Energie et infamie ou la revitalisation
des stéréotypes: le thème du Juif." *SC* 28 (1985-86):
185-97.

Stendhal rarely speaks of Jews, but when he does, he does
not seem to accept all aspects of the traditional stereotype.

Bokobza, Serge. *Contribution à la titrologie romanesque:
variations sur le titre Le Rouge et le Noir.* (Collection
stendhalienne, 27.) Geneva: Droz, 1986. Pp. 150.

This book is important in a variety of ways: 1) as a complete and thorough review of all the interpretations of the
title, *Le Rouge et le Noir*, to date; 2) as an excellent
introduction to the problematics of novelistic titles and
to what Bokobza calls the "pacte de la titrologie"; and 3)
as an original and convincing discussion of the political
connotations to be found in the title. (E.J.T.)

Bokobza, Serge. "Littérature et idéologie: *Le Rouge et le
Noir*, chronique de 1830." *NCFS* 14 (1985-86): 19-27.

Reads *Le Rouge et le Noir* as descriptive of the struggle
between the working class and the bourgeoisie and sees Julien
as the victim, not of the aristocracy, but of the rising
middle class of the July Monarchy.

Bravo Castillo, Juan. "Stendhal hoy: uno de los nuestros."
Quimera 28 (1983): 41-45.

Discussion of the differences between Stendhal and writers
who were his contemporaries, and a survey of the growth of
Stendhal's reputation after his death. Bravo Castillo argues
that Stendhal's literary values (clarity, simplicity,
rapidity of action) and his insights into the modern world
(such as his recognition of the power of money and the press)
are responsible for his appeal today.

Brooks, Peter. *Reading for the Plot: Design and Intention
in Narrative.* New York: Knopf, 1984. Pp. 363.

Chapter 3, "The Novel and the Guillotine: Fathers and Sons
in *Le Rouge et le Noir*," is a revised version of Brooks's
1982 article of the same title (see *RMB* for 1982, p. 265).

Caramaschi, Enzo. "Le due donne di Julien Sorel." *RLMC* 37
(1984): 29-40.

Detailed discussion of Madame de Rênal and Mathilde and of
the role of love in *Le Rouge et le Noir*.

Caramaschi, Enzo. "Stendhal face à l'expérience musicale."
Micromégas (Jan.-April 1984): 217-38.

Carcich, Pierina. "The Idealized Voyage in Stendhal's *Rome,
Naples and Florence*." *EAS* 14 (1985): 13-22.

Remarks on the literary aspects of *Rome, Naples et Florence*,
with an emphasis on its similarities/dissimilarities with
the idealized archetypal voyage. Concludes that Stendhal's
narrative devices aim "at affirming the narrator-traveler
as a man of feeling."

Chantreau, Alain. "La découverte de l'énergie, la création
du mythe du rouge." *SC* 28 (1985-86): 103-12.

Traces the origins of Stendhalian energy, symbolized by
the color red, in *Vie de Henry Brulard*.

Chiaromonte, Nicola. *The Paradox of History: Stendhal,
Tolstoy, and Others.* University of Pennsylvania Press,
1985. Pp. 168. $13.95.

Chapter 1, "Fabrizio at Waterloo," is a penetrating essay
on Stendhal's understanding of history. Chiaromonte analyses
Stendhal's depiction of the battle of Waterloo and contrasts
it with Hugo's description of the same battle in *Les
Misérables*. Hugo believes in historical laws and expresses
an optimistic view of history, which is governed by a secret
yet rational law of progress. Stendhal is more interested
in single incidents in the lives of single individuals. He
sees no rationality in history nor even causal relations.
All we can know of history is its fragmentary and illusive
character. Chiaromonte's book was originally published in
England in 1970. (E.J.T.)

Claudon, Francis. "Stendhal et le néo-classicisme romain: un
autre romantisme." Pp. 83-95 in Massimo Colesanti et al.,
eds., *Stendhal, Roma, l'Italia*. Atti del Congresso Internazionale, Roma, 1983. (Quaderni di cultura francese, 23.)
Rome: Edizioni di Storia e Letteratura, 1985. Pp. 607.

Breaking with predecessors such as Chateaubriand and
Goethe, and with his own previous writings as well, Stendhal
emphasizes modern Rome in his *Promenades dans Rome*. He was
particularly sensitive to Roman neoclassicism, which he considered as Romantic because it signified progress while retaining the ideal of the *beau idéal*.

Colesanti, Massimo. "Stendhal et l'énergie romaine." *SC* 28 (1985-86): 113-20.

On Rome as a city of energy and on Roman energy in the *Chroniques italiennes.*

Colesanti, Massimo. "Un titolo: *Le Rouge et le Noir* (ou *L'imagination renversée*)." Pp. 415-31 in Massimo Colesanti et al., eds., *Scritti in onore di Giovanni Macchia*, vol. 1. Milan: Arnoldo Mondadori, 1983. Pp. 1062.

Establishes three conditions that any explanation of the title should fulfill: 1) it must account for the contrast implicit in the title; 2) it must be applicable to the novel as a whole and not to merely a few episodes; and 3) it must account for the other characters and not Julien alone. Colesanti sees the whole novel as operating on contrasts and contradictions and sees these same oppositions in the novel's characterization. Some valuable insights. (E.J.T.)

Colesanti, Massimo, et al., eds. *Stendhal, Roma, l'Italia.* Atti del Congresso Internazionale, Roma, 1983. (Quaderni di cultura francese, 23.) Rome: Edizioni di Storia e Letteratura, 1985. Pp. 607.

Contains essays by Claudon, listed above, and by Imbert, Marin, Rannaud, Rousset, Reid, and Seylaz, listed below. Also contains: Massimo Colesanti, "La Roma di Stendhal" (19-28); Victor Del Litto, "Stendhal e la critica italiana" (29-38); Leonardo Sciascia, "Stendhal e la Sicilia" (39-60); James Gerard Shields, "'Enricus Beyle, romanus': Le classicisme d'un romantique" (63-82); Albert Maquet, "Le rire et l'illusion (Stendhal aux marionnettes à Rome)" (97-114); Gian Franco Grechi, "Stendhal e 'monsignor' Sebregondi" (115-24); Letizia Norci Cagiano, "Teatri Romani" (125-35); Mario Arduini, "Nel mondo medico a cavallo di due secoli" (139-62); Michel Crouzet, "Stendhal et le coup de poignard italien" (163-238); Christopher W. Thompson, "Stendhal lecteur de Casanova" (255-78); Giovanni Marchi, "'Les Cenci' di Stendhal e di Artaud (ovvero dall'energia alla crudeltà)" (279-89); Kurt Ringger, "L'imaginaire de l'opéra chez Stendhal" (293-308); Mario Lavagetto, "La traccia di Ariosto" (309-30); Giuseppe Pintorno, "Fu musicologo Stendhal?" (331-38); Giuseppe Scaraffia, "Stendhal e il paradosso dell'attore" (339-45); Sergio Romagnoli, "I paesaggi della *Chartreuse*" (365-80); Vito Carofiglio, "Selvaggi, Turchi e intellettuali: il sud 'napoletano' di Stendhal" (381-400); Giovanni Saverio Santangelo, "Tre lettori siciliani di Stendhal: Borgese, Tomasi di Lampedusa, Vittorini" (401-16); Arnaldo Pizzorusso,

"Stendhal: occasioni e 'sensazioni attuali'" (431-44);
Lorenza Maranini, "Julien Sorel a cancello di Casa Rênal"
(445-63); Anna Maria Scaiola, "Ce qu'il y a de plus terrible
et de plus doux: Beatrice Cenci" (463-74); Christof Weiand,
"L'Abbesse de Castro et Lamiel ou le dépassement de l'italia-
nité chez Stendhal (475-84); Mariella Di Maio, "Interno
di un raconto: L'Abbesse de Castro" (517-28); Mechthild
Albert, "Le dollar et le bajoc: la fonction de l'argent
dans les Chroniques italiennes" (529-40).

Cook, Albert. "Stendhal: The Discovery of Ironic Interplay."
Pp. 110-24 in Albert Cook, Thresholds: Studies in the
Romantic Experience. University of Wisconsin Press, 1985.
Pp. 308.

Reproduces, with minor revisions, Cook's 1975 article of
the same title.

Crouzet, Michel. Quatre études sur Lucien Leuwen: Le jeu,
l'or, l'orviétan, l'absolu. Paris: S.E.D.E.S., 1985.

Rev. by W.A. Guenter in NCFS 14 (1985-86): 169-70.
Contains four substantial essays on Lucien Leuwen: "Jeu de
la vérité et vérité du jeu dans Lucien Leuwen" (5-25), which
treats Lucien Leuwen as a comic novel; "L'argent romanesque:
la bourse ou l'ironie" (27-65), a non-Marxist approach to
the problem of money in the novel; "'O toute puissance de
l'orviétan!': sur l'orviétan littéraire" (67-103), which
deals with charlatanism and the function of quotations and
clichés; "L'absolu romanesque" (105-30), which is the best
analysis of the character of Madame de Chasteller to date.
An important collection. (E.J.T.)

Crouzet, Michel. "Stendhal entre la gauche et la droite."
Revue des Sciences Morales et Politiques 139 (1984): 117-28.

Useful survey of the appropriations of Stendhal by the
political right (Barrès, Maurras, Bardèche) and the political
left (Aragon, Andrieux). (E.J.T.)

De Cesare, Raffaele, and Ilsemarie Brandmair Dallera. "Stendhal,
Manzoni, due articoli della Minerve française ed alcuni
dispacci del governo austriaco di Milano." Micromégas (Jan.-
Aug. 1984): 135-56.

Two unsigned articles critical of the Austrian regime in
Italy were suspected of having been written by Stendhal or
Manzoni. De Cesare and Dallera reproduce all the pertinent
documents and conclude that the author was probably neither
Stendhal nor Manzoni.

Dédéyan, Charles. "Stendhal et le Frioul." *Quaderni Utinensi* nos. 3-4 (1984): 106-24.

   Survey, with ample quotations, of Stendhal's acquaintance with Friuli. Emphasis on Stendhal's discussions of two Friulian painters, Giovanni d'Udine and Pordenone, whose works he seems to have known mainly through his readings of Lanzi.

Del Litto, V. "Autographes. Résurgences et affleurements." *SC* 28 (1985-86): 156-67.

   On the history of Stendhal's personal papers and on the acquisition by the Bibliothèque de Grenoble of some previously unknown documents dealing with the last years of Stendhal's life.

Del Litto, V. "Aux sources de l'énergie stendhalienne." *SC* 29 (1985-86): 97-102.

   On the origins of Stendhal's concept of energy and particularly the role played by Alfieri in the development of this concept.

Del Litto, V. "Bibliographie stendhalienne. Année 1985." *SC* 29 (1986-87): 73-91.

Del Litto, V. "Textes et documents." *SC* 28 (1985-86): 307-10.

   Newly found document showing an early pseudonym used by Beyle (h. Be Charles Englemann), and another reaffirming his youthful *jacobinisme*. A third section publishes Clémentine Curial's death certificate.

Del Litto, V., and E. Kanceff, eds. *Le Journal de voyage et Stendhal*. Actes du Colloque de Grenoble. (Biblioteca del viaggio in Italia, 24.) Geneva: Slatkine, 1985. Pp. 412.

Dettamanti, P. "Stendhal e Lecco." *Archivi di Lecco* no. 4 (Oct.-Dec. 1984): 663-77.

Didier, Béatrice, ed. *Souvenirs d'égotisme, suivi de Projets d'autogiographie et des Privilèges*. (Folio, 1430.) Paris: Gallimard, 1983. Pp. 253.

   Rev. by J.-J. Hamm in *NCFS* 12-13 (1984-85): 180-81.

Didier, Béatrice. "L'Italie dans l'autobiographie stendhalienne." *Bollettino del C.I.R.V.I.* 9 (Jan.-June 1984): 23-42.

Diefenbach, Dieter. "Stendhal: un pseudonyme et ses variantes."
    SC 29 (1986-87): 43-48.

    Interprets Henri Beyle's choice of Stendhal as a pseudonym
    as a consequence of his initiation into Freemasonry. Un-
    convincing. (E.J.T.)

Drouin, Jean-Claude. "Bordeaux et le mémorandum Gautier au
    moment du voyage de Stendhal (mars-avril 1838)." *Revue
    Française d'Histoire du Livre* 53 (1984): 483-504.

    On Bordeaux as it was when Stendhal visited it. Little on
    Stendhal, however.

Finney, Gail. "Garden Paradigms in Nineteenth-Century Fiction."
    CL 36 (1984): 20-33.

    An interesting and useful comparison of the garden image
    in *Le Rouge et le Noir* with the garden image in *Der Nachsommer*
    and *Great Expectations*. In Stendhal, the garden at Vergy
    "is typical of the Rousseauesque character of the garden image
    in much nineteenth-century French fiction: depicted as having
    retained a degree of the original, unself-conscious quality of
    prelapsarian nature, seemingly isolated from the effects of
    civilization, the garden setting furthers romantic activity
    which follows the dictates of nature rather than the laws of
    society." (E.J.T.)

Gardelles, Jacques. "Stendhal, Hugo, Gautier, Mérimée à
    Bordeaux: quatre 'romantiques' devant le patrimoine médiéval."
    Revue Française d'Histoire du Livre 53 (1984): 451-63.

    Stendhal viewed Bordeaux's medieval architecture from a
    neoclassical and Enlightenment perspective, though he
    occasionally revealed an ability to go beyond these constraints.
    Gautier and Hugo were more interested in the medieval heritage
    of Bordeaux, but were mainly fascinated by its irrational,
    fantastic side. Mérimée took a more detached view and re-
    jected some of Bordeaux's medieval architecture as belonging
    to a decadent stage of the Gothic.

Gohira, Takashi. "*Armance* et *Lucien Leuwen*: structure et
    signification." *ELLF* 48 (March 1986): 32-50.

Greshoff, C.J. "Le double héros du *Rouge et noir*." *FSSA* 15
    (1986): 13-20.

    Julien is really two characters. One, based on Berthet,
    is represented as ambitious and hypocritical (though in
    reality he is neither); the other, based on Stendhal himself,

is sensitive and generous. The double character explains the double ending of the novel. Not much that is new. (E.J.T.)

Hamon, Paul. "Les manuscrits de Stendhal de la Bibliothèque de Grenoble et leurs reliures." *SC* 28 (1985-86): 147-55.

On the history of Stendhal's manuscripts after his death, their donation to the Bibliothèque de Grenoble in 1861, and their physical condition since.

Imbert, Henri-François. "Les *Chroniques italiennes*: une expérience d'écriture beyliste." Pp. 488-500 in Massimo Colesanti et al., eds., *Stendhal, Roma, l'Italia*. Atti del Congresso Internazionale, Roma, 1983. (Quaderni di cultura francese, 23.) Rome: Edizioni di Storia e Letteratura, 1985. Pp. 607.

Argues that the *Chroniques* were for Stendhal in part a search for a novelistic style and a learning experience for the writing of novels.

Jackson, John E. "Henry Brulard et les fondements subjectifs de l'écriture chez Stendhal." *Versants* 8 (1985): 59-76.

Jacquelot, Hélène de. "Sur quelques contributions récentes à la bibliographie stendhalienne." *Micromégas* (Jan.-Aug. 1984): 239-51.

Jeune, Simon. "Stendhal et le gaillard curé de la Brède, ou une curieuse rencontre Stendhal-Balzac." *Revue Française d'Histoire du Livre* 53 (1984): 505-18.

Same article as that published in *SC* (see *RMB* for 1985, p. 298).

Kaplan, Carol L. "Une Extrême Energie: Julien's Romantic Writing Project." *FR* 59 (1985-86): 693-700.

Useful discussion of the role of Madame de Rênal in developing Julien's "literary medium," that is, the different kinds of internal monologue in which he expresses himself in the last pages of the novel. An analysis of these monologues shows that Julien has acquired a metaphorical language which he did not previously possess. (E.J.T.)

Knapp-Tepperberg, Eva-Maria. "Literatur, Gesellschaft, Geschichtlichkeit im Spiegel eines literarischen Motivs: Diderot--Stendhal--Maupassant-Proust." *Romanistische Zeitschrift für Literaturgeschichte/Cahiers d'Histoire des*

Littératures Romanes 8 (1984): 289-305.

Deals with Lucien Leuwen's attempts to use a horse as a status symbol.

Kurisu, Kosei. "Stendhal au Japon: bibliographie 1900-1945 (2)." *SC* 29 (1986-87): 63-72.

Continuation of Kurisu's bibliography, cited last year. This section lists works on Stendhal in the period covered.

Labia, Jean-Jacques. "Le recours au roman, ou l'impossibilité de la comédie au dix-neuvième siècle: l'expérience inaugurale de Stendhal." Pp. 11-15 in Douwe W. Folkema and Anna Balakian, eds., *Proceedings of the 10th Congress of the International Comparative Literature Association*, vol. 1. New York: Garland Publishing, 1985. Pp. xxi+516

On Stendhal's early attempts at theater, his reasons for abandoning them, and the theatrical dimensions of his first novel, *Armance*.

Le Yaouanc, Moïse. "Stendhal et les *Mémoires* de M. de Chateaubriand." *SC* 28 (1985-86): 239-54.

Argues that Stendhal knew of Chateaubriand's autobiography in progress.

Le Yaouanc, Moïse. "Stendhal et les *Mémoires* de M. de Chateaubriand (2)." *SC* 28 (1985-86): 311-25.

Continuation of the above. Argues that Chateaubriand's *Mémoires* served as a negative model for Stendhal's own autobiographical writings. The evidence is thin, though. (E.J.T.)

MacCannell, Juliet Flower. "Oedipus Wrecks: Lacan, Stendhal, and the Narrative Form of the Real." *MLN* 98 (1983): 910-40.

MacCannell argues that Stendhal's originality lies precisely in his deleting the Oedipal guilt for the origins of man's sexuality. Stendhal's great heroes die only *after* they have obtained the satisfaction that Oedipus ought to have denied them. (Reprinted, pp. 910-40 in Robert Con Davis, *Lacan and Narration: The Psychoanalytic Difference in Narrative Theory*. Johns Hopkins University Press, 1983.) Perceptive and original. (E.J.T.)

Magnani, Luigi. "Originalità del 'plagiario' Stendhal." Pp. 407-14 in Massimo Colesanti et al., eds., *Scritti in onore di Giovanni Macchia*, vol. 1. Milan: Arnoldo Mondadori, 1983. Pp. 1062.

In using "sources" Stendhal reduces borrowed material to the common denominators of his own original vision. Even when he is "plagiarizing," he is frequently giving life to arid texts. Magnani expands the discussion to include Stendhal's understanding of the arts and passion.

Maquet, Albert. "Les dossiers de l'Arioste des marionnettes." *Micromégas* (Jan.-Aug. 1984): 157-94.

An exhaustive dossier (identification of texts, minute comparisons of versions and editions, biographical data) on Stendhal and puppeteering in Italy.

Marchetti, Marilia. "A proposito dei *Privilèges*." *Micromégas* (Jan.-Aug. 1984): 121-34.

Les Privilèges, which can be seen as a final instrument of self-knowledge for Stendhal, are an extension of various aspects of Stendhal's personality such as his love of paradox and masks, his flirtation with dandyism, and his desire for metamorphosis.

Marin, Louis. "Bodies and Signs in Autobiography: Stendhal's *Life of Henry Brulard* (chaps. 2, 3, and 39)." *MLN* 99 (1984): 885-902.

The two passages in *Henry Brulard*, one at the beginning, the other at the end, in which Stendhal announces that he is "about to be born" frame the telling of his life. Both these texts signify births, the first from the mother according to bodies and indices, the second from the father according to signs and their representations.

Marin, Louis. "Stendhal et la peinture italienne dans la *Vie de Henry Brulard*." Pp. 349-63 in Massimo Colesanti et al., eds., *Stendhal, Roma, l'Italia*. Atti del Congresso Internazionale, Roma, 1983. (Quaderni di cultura francese, 23.) Rome: Edizioni di Storia e Letteratura, 1985. Pp. 607.

A lucid and intelligent discussion of the role of Italian painting in *Henry Brulard*. Marin is particularly interested in the *gravures* that Stendhal had placed in his text and focuses on the first of these, Garofalo's *The Resurrection of Lazarus*, in which the open tomb points to a narrative space--that of life and death--which is that of Stendhal's autobiography. (E.J.T.)

McWatters, K.G., and Renée Dénier, eds. *Chroniques pour l'Angleterre*. *Contributions à la presse britannique*, vol. 4. 2 vols. Grenoble: Université des langues et lettres, 1985. Pp. 506.

Rev. by Michel Arrous in *SC* 28 (1985-86): 269-72.

Mossman, Carol. "Les gravures de la *Vie de Henry Brulard*. Iconographie brulardienne: les figures de l'écriture." *SC* 28 (1985-86): 339-53.

An excellent discussion of the engravings (which, with one exception, are all of a religious nature) that Stendhal had selected for his *Vie de Henry Brulard*. Far from being a simple illustration of the text, these engravings assist in confounding the very notion of the integrity and the homogeneity of the personality. (E.J.T.)

Ono, Yushio. "Variabilité et identité du 'moi' dans la *Vie de Henry Brulard*." *ELLF* 48 (March 1986): 51-65.

Orlando, Francesco. "Il recente e l'antico nel cap. 1, 18 di *Le Rouge et le Noir*." Pp. 135-62 in Francesco Orlando, *Le costanti e le varianti*. *Studi di letteratura francese e di teatro musicale*. Bologna: Il Mulino, 1983. Pp. 423.

Detailed analysis of the chapter relating the arrival of a king at Verrières, which is seen as foreshadowing various aspects of Julien's life.

Purdy, Anthony. "Lieu commun et communauté: l'étiolement du discours chez Stendhal." *SC* 28 (1985-86): 198-208.

Good study of Stendhal's understanding of the relationship between language and class. Some pertinent remarks as well on Stendhal's authorial interventions. (E.J.T.)

Rannaud, Gérald. "L'Italie stendhalienne ou la société sans état." Pp. 239-53 in Massimo Colesanti et al., eds., *Stendhal, Roma, l'Italia*. Atti del Congresso Internazionale, Roma, 1983. (Quaderni di cultura francese, 23.) Rome. Edizioni di Storia e Letteratura, 1985. Pp. 607.

An original effort to see Stendhal's relationship to Italy as more than a predisposition of personality. In particular, Italy, which was at once in a post-revolutionary and a pre-revolutionary stage, offered Stendhal the possibility of speculation on types of government. In this way, Stendhal's "travel books" on Italy differ in an essential way from their predecessors. (E.J.T.)

Regaldo, Marco. "Un touriste 'idéologue': Stendhal à Bordeaux." *Revue Française d'Histoire du Livre* 53 (1984): 465-81.

Stendhal's treatment of issues such as climate, race, and the arts in *Mémoires d'un touriste* lead Regaldo to argue that this work is an example of a genre, which he calls "voyage anthropologique," whose rules were established in the late eighteenth and early nineteenth centuries by the Ideologues. Suggestive, although the argument for a new genre needs to be developed further. (E.J.T.)

Reid, Martine. "Correspondances stendhaliennes: les abîmes de la lettre." Pp. 541-51 in Massimo Colesanti et al., eds., *Stendhal, Roma, l'Italia*. Atti del Congresso Internazionale, Roma, 1983. (Quaderni di cultura francese, 23.) Rome: Edizioni di Storia e Letteratura, 1985. Pp. 607.

Letters are frequent in Stendhal's fiction and sometimes play a determining role in the plot. However, letters are not a satisfactory way for lovers to communicate with each other. Stendhal suggests a psychopathology of epistolary exchange in which the sender cannot control the semantic import of the message and the receiver, unable to break out of his personal preoccupations, misinterprets the message. Solid. (E.J.T.)

Rioux, Jean-Claude. "L'énergie au pouvoir ou le bon usage de la peine de mort." *SC* 28 (1985-86): 281-306.

On Stendhal's advocacy of the death penalty for homicide. Rioux discusses the possible sources for this support in Stendhal's own psychology, in his utilitarian concept of virtue, and in his readings of Bentham and the Ideologues.

Rollins, Yvonne Bargues. "Un pot-pourri de genres comiques: *Lucien Leuwen*." *FR* 59 (1985-86): 553-63.

Good study of various aspects of the comic in *Lucien Leuwen* and their relationship to theater (comedy, farce, vaudeville, comic opera). Some valuable links with Molière and Beaumarchais. (E.J.T.)

Rosa, George M. "Stendhal et Keats." *RF* 97 (1985): 47-49.

Stendhal probably got the notion that the *Quarterly Review* had caused Keats's death through his reading of Medwin's *Conversations of Lord Byron*.

Rousset, Jean. "La communication à distance dans *La Chartreuse de Parme*." Pp. 419-29 in Massimo Colesanti et al., eds., *Stendhal, Roma, l'Italia*. Atti del Congresso Internazionale, Roma, 1983. (Quaderni di cultura francese, 23.) Rome. Edizioni di Storia e Letteratura, 1985. Pp. 607.

Clear presentation of the various means of indirect communication between Fabrice and Clélia. (E.J.T.)

Rubino, Gianfranco. "*Armance*: segreto e communicazione." *Micromégas* (Jan.-Aug. 1984): 91-119.

After demonstrating that the refusal to divulge the secret in *Armance* is a decision not only of the character (as was the case in Duras's novel) and of the homodiegetic narrator (as was the case in Latouche's novel), but also of the heterodiegetic character, Rubino then undertakes to study the question of revelation/non-revelation in the broader context of forms of communication in the novel. Various forms of oblique communication, such as eye communication and physiognomy, are explored, as are qualities of voice such as tone and accent. Useful. (E.J.T.)

Rude, Fernand. "Le complot lorrain d'avril 1834 et sa résonance dans *Lucien Leuwen*." *SC* 29 (1986-87): 1-24.

Detailed narration of the republican conspiracy in eastern France in 1834, Stendhal's reactions to this conspiracy, and the subsequent trials and convictions.

Sallé, René. "Stendhal et la franc-maçonnerie." *SC* 28 (1985-86): 354-55.

More questions on Stendhal's possible links to Freemasonry.

Santangelo, Giovanni Saverio. "Borgese, Tomasi di Lampedusa e Vittorini lettori di Stendhal." *Micromégas* (Jan.-Aug. 1984): 195-216.

Thorough discussion of the relations between three Sicilian-born writers (Borgese, Tomasi di Lampedusa, Vittorini) and Stendhal. Santangelo takes into account the points of contact between Borgese's Filippo Rubè and Julien Sorel, but insists rather on the important presence of Stendhal in Borgese's critical discourse. Tomasi di Lampedusa, whose novel, *The Leopard*, has been compared to Stendhal's works and who wrote a book on Stendhal, seems to have seen in Stendhal a kind of narrative ideal. His *Lezioni su Stendhal* reveals a great deal about Tomasi di Lampedusa's own creative work. Vittorini, who wrote a number of essays on Stendhal beginning in the

1920s, was, of the three, perhaps the one to penetrate the most deeply into Stendhal's writings. (E.J.T.)

Sarocchi, Jean. "L'énergie syllabique ou l'ARA Energumène." *SC* 28 (1985-86): 209-20.

Discussion of the adversary relationship between the syllable RA and the syllable AR in Stendhal's works. Of dubious value. (E.J.T.)

Schacherl, Bruno, ed. *Storia della pittura*. Rome: Editori Riuniti, 1983. Pp. xxviii+460.

Rev. by Carlo Cordié in *SFr* 29 (1985): 407-08.
Italian translation of *Histoire de la peinture en Italie*.

Schork, R.J. "Stendhal's *Latinitas*." *CML* 6 (1985): 23-38.

Schork reviews Stendhal's abilities in Latin and concludes that he was a competent Latinist and student of ancient civilization. Then, he explicates the numerous Latin allusions in *Le Rouge et le Noir* and the fewer ones in *La Chartreuse de Parme*. A good deal of information given here is not found in critical editions. Useful. (E.J.T.)

Sciascia, Leonardo. *Stendhal et la Sicile. Suivi de Leçons sur Stendhal par Giuseppe Tomasi di Lampedusa*. Trans. Maurice Darmon. Paris: Maurice Nadeau, 1985. Pp. 179.

Translation of two Italian works.

Seylaz, Jean-Luc. "Lecture du prologue de *L'Abbesse de Castro*." *Saggi* 25 (1986): 221-37.

Detailed, solid analysis of the prologue highlighting the narrator's necessity to certify his knowledge and give his text a pedagogical importance. Stendhal above all wishes to link the Italian past with the present. (E.J.T.)

Seylaz, Jean-Luc. "Quelques romanciers italiens lecteurs de Stendhal." *SC* 28 (1985-86): 326-38.

Reflections on some twentieth-century Italian writers (Tomasi di Lampedusa, Vittorini, Sciascia, Carlo Levi, Savinio) who were admirers of Stendhal. Seylaz sees a link between their appreciation of Stendhal and their opposition to fascism. He also detects a Stendhalian influence in Savinio's and Sciascia's use of literary quotations.

Seylaz, Jean-Luc. "Une fiction stendhalienne: la France du touriste." Pp. 501-15 in Massimo Colesanti et al., eds.,

Stendhal, Roma, l'Italia. Atti del Congresso Internazionale, Roma, 1983. (Quaderni di cultura francese, 23.) Rome: Edizioni di Storia e Letteratura, 1985. Pp. 607.

Though not indicated as such, this article reproduces the author's essay of the same title in *Etudes de Lettres* in 1984 (see *RMB* for 1985, p. 303).

Shields, James G. "'Si fata sinant' ou la vertu de la virtualité chez Stendhal." *SC* 28 (1985-86): 121-33.

On the role of the concept of ancient Roman virtue in Stendhal's thought. The attraction of Roman virtue is in its virtuality more than its accomplishment.

Simon, Irène. "Religion et langage dans *Le Rouge et le Noir.*" *NCFS* 14 (1985-86): 201-13.

Argues that Stendhal's "religion" consists in a faith in the power of language. Julien Sorel can therefore be seen as a Christ figure who is persecuted because of his use of language. Although Simon does not seem to be aware of Richard B. Grant's essay on Julien as a Christ figure (1962), some of her perspectives (such as her presentation of the *Note secrète* episode as a political parody of the Last Supper) are original. (E.J.T.)

Sługocki, Leszek. "La falsification d'une lettre de Napoléon (Napoléon, Pierre Daru, Stendhal)." *Rivista italiana di studi napoleonici* 20 (1983): 65-70.

Sussmann, Hava. "Julien Sorel dans le sillage de Jean-Jacques Rousseau à Turin." *LR* 40 (1986): 127-32.

Argues that the second part of *Le Rouge et le Noir* is a development of an episode from book 3 of Rousseau's *Confessions*. This is the episode in which Rousseau relates his employment and stay at the home of Count Gouvon. A number of themes in this segment, including the return of the maternal woman, support the thesis. Plausible. (E.J.T.)

Suzuki, Shoichiro. "Du temps de l'histoire au temps du drame: les procédés d'invention de Stendhal dans *Henri III* (2)." *SC* 29 (1986-87): 25-42.

Detailed study of temporality in act 3 of Stendhal's unfinished *Henri III*. Stendhal seems to have solved the problem of presenting the four days of the "barricades" into a single act by situating his scenes mainly at night.

Teissier, Philippe. "Armance ou la genèse de l'univers stendhalien." *Annales de l'Académie de Mâcon* (1983): 73-82.

Broad, though solid, essay on *Armance*. Basing himself
on character analysis and the depiction of contemporary life,
Teissier argues that "*Armance* annonce les grands romans qui
suivront." (E.J.T.)

Théodoridès, Jean. "Ernst Jünger du côté de Stendhal." *Revue
Générale* (Brussels) 3 (March 1985): 17-28.

Affinities and influences.

Théodoridès, Jean. "Le personnage du médecin dans l'œuvre
romanesque de Stendhal." *Gesnerus* 42 (1985): 465-78.

Survey of physicians in Stendhal's works. Suggests that
the important role of doctors in *Lucien Leuwen* and *Lamiel*
is a result of Stendhal's own deteriorating health.

Tudesq, André-Jean. "Bordeaux, ses journaux et l'opinion
publique au moment de la visite de Stendhal en 1838."
Revue Française d'Histoire du Livre 53 (1984): 437-50.

Life in Bordeaux during the period described by Stendhal
in *Mémoires d'un touriste*. In his book Stendhal retains
those aspects of Bordeaux that correspond to his temperament.
Nothing new on Stendhal. (E.J.T.)

Viallaneix, Paul. "Mal du siècle et métier des armes." Pp.
379-92 in Paul Viallaneix and Jean Ehrard, eds., *La Bataille,
l'armée, la gloire, 1745-1871*, vol. 2. Actes du Colloque
Internationale de Clermont-Ferrand. Clermont-Ferrand:
Faculté des Lettres et Sciences Humaines, 1985. Pp. 657.

On the demoralization of the army since the end of the
Empire. Both Vigny (*Servitude et grandeur militaires*) and
Stendhal (*Lucien Leuwen*) demythify the old concept of Glory.

Wandruszka, Mario. "Stendhal explorateur de la conscience
verbale." Pp. 431-36 in Gilbert Boissier and Danielle
Bouverot, eds., *Au bonheur des mots: mélanges en l'honneur
de Gérald Antoine*. Presses universitaires de Nancy, 1984.
Pp. xxi+615.

Remarks on Stendhal's use of single words and expressions
as sociocultural indices.

Williamson, Elaine. "Stendhal et la comptabilité du Musée
Napoléon (documents inédits)." *SC* 28 (1985-86): 221-37.

One of Stendhal's functions as Inspecteur du Mobilier de

la Couronne was to audit the accounts of the Musée Napoléon
(today known as the Louvre). A number of previously unpublished documents reveal that Stendhal did a serious and
thorough job.

Winegarten, Renée. "Stendhal: The Enigmatic Liberal."
Encounter 65,3 (Sept.-Oct. 1985): 26-33.

Although there is no new information here, this is a
very competent discussion of Stendhal's political views,
which were often contradictory. (E.J.T.)

See also Finney, Peterson, Petit, Scaiola, Welch ("French 1.
General"); Willis ("Gautier"); Fido ("Italian 2. General").

Reviews of books previously listed:

BERTHIER, Philippe, ed., Stendhal: l'écrivain, la société
et le pouvoir (see RMB for 1985, p. 288), rev. by G. Strickland in FS 40 (1986): 220-21; by G. De Wulf in LR 40 (1986):
79; by Jean Decottignies in RSH 197 (1985): 160-61;
BERTHIER, Philippe, et al., eds., Le plus méconnu des romans
de Stendhal (see RMB for 1983, p. 263); rev. by Fernand Rude
in SFr 29 (1985): 187-89; COLESANTI, Massimo, Stendhal.
Le regole del gioco (see RMB for 1984, p. 313), rev. by
Kurt Ringger in RF 97 (1985): 479-80; by G. Benelli in RLMC
37 (1984): 266-68; CROUZET, Michel, Nature et société chez
Stendhal (see RMB for 1985, p. 291), rev. by Lucette Finas
in QL 453 (Dec. 16-31, 1985): 20; by Philippe Berthier in
SC 29 (1986-87): 56-58; by Charles Stivale in NCFS 15 (1986-
87): 192-93; CROUZET, Michel, La Poétique de Stendhal (see
RMB for 1983, p. 266), rev. by Louis Le Guillou in RHL 86
(1986): 301-02; DEL LITTO, V., ed., De l'amour (see RMB for
1980, p. 248), rev. by Carlo Cordié in SFr 29 (1985): 131-
36; DEL LITTO, V., ed., La Création romanesque chez Stendhal
(see RMB for 1985, pp. 293-94), rev. by Kurt Ringger in SC
29 (1986-87): 53-55; DEL LITTO, V., and Kurt Ringger, eds.,
Stendhal et le romantisme (see RMB for 1985, pp. 294-95),
rev. by G. Strickland in FS 40 (1986): 220-21; by F.W.J.
Hemmings in MLR 81 (1986): 207-08; by N. Morcovescu in AJFS
22 (1985): 87-96; by Jean Decottignies in RSH 197 (1985):
160; by Serge Bokobza in SC 27 (1984-85): 286-91; by P.A.
Borgheggiani in SFr 30 (1986): 152-54; FINCH, Alison,
Stendhal: La Chartreuse de Parme (see RMB for 1984, p. 316),
rev. by Kurt Ringger in RF 97 (1985): 323-24; by Gary M.
Godfrey in FR 60 (1986-87): 262-63; by Alison Fairlie in
RHL 86 (1986): 768-69; McWATTERS, K.G., and R. Denier, eds.,
Stendhal: Chroniques pour l'Angleterre (see RMB for 1984,
p. 220), rev. by C. Smethurst in MLR 81 (1986): 744-47;

MEININGER, Anne-Marie, ed., *Lucien Leuwen* (see *RMB* for 1983, p. 272), rev. by Murray Sachs in *FR* 59 (1985-86): 789-90; MOSSMAN, Carol A., *The Narrative Matrix* (see *RMB* for 1984, p. 321), rev. by Ann Jefferson in *FS* 39 (1985): 485-86; by Geoffrey Strickland in *MLR* 81 (1986): 1010-11; by Kurt Ringger in *ZFSL* 96 (1986): 105-06; by David Bell in *French Forum* 11 (1986): 118-19; by Stirling Haig in *FR* 59 (1985-86): 620; by Lloyd Parks in *NCFS* 14 (1986): 353-54; POLIAGHI, N.F., *Stendhal et Trieste* (see *RMB* for 1984, p. 321), rev. by Jean-Paul de Nola in *SFr* 30 (1986): 154-55; SOZZI, Lionello, *L'Italia di Stendhal* (see *RMB* for 1985, p. 304), rev. by S. Sérodes in *RHL* 86 (1986): 300-01; by C. Cordié in *SFr* 29 (1985): 408-09; TALBOT, Emile J., *Stendhal and Romantic Esthetics* (see *RMB* for 1985, p. 305), rev. by C.W. Thompson in *FS* 44 (1984): 472-73; by Micheline Levowitz-Treu in *NCFS* 15 (1986-87): 193-94.

SUE

Hülk, Walburga. *Als die Helden Opfer wurden: Grundlagen und Funktion gesellschaftlicher Ordnungsmodelle in den Feuilletonromanen "Les Mystères de Paris" und "Le Juif errant" von Eugène Sue.* (Studia Romanica, 61.) Heidelberg: Carl Winter, 1985. Pp. 423.

Verjat, Alain. "' ... et si je t'aime, prends garde à toi!' Le discours amoureux dans le mélodrame social d'Eugène Sue." Pp. 257-75 in Didier Coste and Michel Zeraffa, eds., *Le Récit amoureux.* (L'Or d'Atalante.) Seyssel: Champ Vallon, 1984.

Text of a lecture given at the Centre culturel international de Cerisy-la-Salle at a colloquium called "Raison du cœur, raison du récit." Concerns sublimated sexuality in *Les Mystères de Paris.*

Witkowski, Claude. *Eugène Sue et le trésor du juif errant.* (Monographies des éditions populaires, 9.) Beaumont: C. Witkowski, 1986. Pp. 18. Fr. 15.00.

See also Derré ("Saint-Simon"); *Cahiers I. Tourguéniev, P. Viardot, M. Malibran* 8 ("Viardot").

Reviews of books previously listed:

Letteratura populare di espressione francese dall''Ancien Régime' all'ottocento (see *RMB* for 1984, pp. 325-26), rev. by Carlo Cordié in *SFr* 29 (1985): 594-95; *Paris au XIXe*

siècle: aspects d'un mythe littéraire (see *RMB* for 1985,
p. 307), rev. by J. Guichardet in *RHL* 86 (1986): 778-80.

TÉNINT

Siegel, Patricia Joan. *Wilhelm Ténint et sa Prosodie de l'école
moderne. Avec des documents inédits.* Paris: Champion;
Geneva: Slatkine, 1986. Pp. 297.

A welcome reprint (but not in facsimile) of this unique
manifesto of Romantic versification, originally published
in 1843. The editor has unearthed a great many facts about
the hitherto unknown (and rather sad) life of Ténint (1817-
1879). Her footnotes identify the poetic examples cited by
Ténint and deal with other necessary matters. (J.S.P.)

TILLIER

"Dossier Claude Tillier." *Cahiers pour la littérature* 5 (1985).

Godeau, P. "Essai sur le village de Moulot décrit dans *Mon
oncle Benjamin* de Claude Tillier (1801-1843) avec des pré-
cisions, corrections et renseignements qui ne figurent pas
dans ce roman." *Bulletin de la Société scientifique et
artistique de Clamecy* (1984): 7-78.

Martin, Roger, ed. *Œuvres complètes.* 3 vols. Geneva and
Paris: Slatkine, 1985. Pp. 418, 392, 670. Fr. 1,828.00.

   Volume 1, *Mon oncle Benjamin*; *De l'Espagne.* Volume 2,
Belle-Plante et Cornélius; *Comment le chanoine eut peur,
comment le capitaine eut peur*; *Poésie.* Volume 3, *Pamphlets.*

TOCQUEVILLE

Jardin, André, ed. *De la démocratie en Amérique.* 2 vols.
(Folio/Histoire, 12.) Paris: Gallimard, 1986.

Jardin, André, ed. *Œuvres complètes*, vol. 3, part 2, *Ecrits
et discours politiques.* Paris: Gallimard, 1985. Pp. 767.
Fr. 280.00.

   Rev. by Jean Vidalenc in *RH* 558 (April-June 1986): 500-
01.

Kerr, A.P., and André Jardin, eds. *Œuvres complètes*, vol. 18,
*Correspondance d'Alexis de Tocqueville avec Adolphe de Circourt
et avec Madame de Circourt.* Paris: Gallimard, 1983. Pp.
600. Fr. 250.00.

Rev. by Paulette Enjalran in *RHMC* 33 (1986):   511-18.

Lawrence, George, trans. *Reflections on the French Revolution of 1848*. New Brunswick, N.J.:   Transaction Books, 1986. $19.95.

Mélonio, Françoise, et al., eds. *Œuvres complètes*, vol. 7, *Correspondance étrangère: Amérique et Europe occidentale*. Paris: Gallimard, 1986. Pp. 402. Fr. 230.00.

Perrot, Michelle, ed. *Œuvres complètes*, vol. 4, *Ecrits sur le régime pénitentiaire en France et à l'étranger*. 2 vols. Paris: Gallimard, 1984.

Shiner, Larry. "Writing and Political Carnival in Tocqueville's *Recollections*." *History and Theory* 25 (1986):   17-32.

"Thus despite Tocqueville's adherence to traditional rhetorical forms and the neoclassical restraint of much of his prose, the text of Part I of the *Recollections* is anything but 'monologic.' A countercurrent of satire, burlesque, and carnival breaks across its seriousness and decorum to divide it against itself and allow us to see some of the ways writing exceeds the intention of the writer."

Strout, Cushing. "Tocqueville and the Idea of an American Literature (1941-1971)." *NLH* 18 (1986-87):   115-17.

On the realization, by F.O. Matthiessen, Lionel Trilling, Richard Chase, and others, of Tocqueville's prophecy about the emergence of a distinctly American literature which would "illuminate by exaggeration, as he put it, 'certain dark corners of the human heart.'" The paradigm that emerged involved "desocialization of the novel," "metaphysical symbolism," and "mythicized characters," seen in the "classic American literature from Poe to James."

TÖPFFER

Histoire de M. Cryptogramme. (Grands Illustrateurs.) Paris (?): Agora, 1985. Pp. 80. Fr. 68.00.

Kunzle, David. "Goethe and Caricature: From Hogarth to Töpffer." *JWCI* 48 (1985):   164-88.

Goethe discovered Töpffer's drawings toward the end of his life and recorded his pleasure in them in an article published posthumously in the last issue of *Kunst und Alterthum* (his remarks in *Conversations with Eckermann* were not published

until after Töpffer's death). Kunzle holds that Töpffer's
satire appealed to the conservative, classicizing side of
the sage of Weimar because it "carried no real political
malice." Goethe must have appreciated the "mockery of a
tired romantic scenario in part II of *Jabot*."

Schaerer, Christian. "A propos de *Rosa et Gertrude*." *Bulletin
de la Société d'Etudes Töpfferiennes* 13 (Oct. 1984): 4-8.

Zurbuchen, Walter. "Le portefeuille de Rodolphe Töpffer."
Bulletin de la Société d'Etudes Töpfferiennes 12 (Oct.
1983): 3-6.

See also Pinkney ("French 1. General").

TRISTAN

Armogathe, Daniel, and Jacques Grandjonc, eds. *Union ouvrière;
Lettres*. (Ecrits d'Hier.) Paris: Des Femmes, 1986. Pp.
366. Fr. 90.00.

Michaud, Stéphane, ed. *Un fabuleux destin: Flora Tristan*.
Actes du premier colloque international Flora Tristan (Dijon,
3 et 4 mai 1984), suivis de lettres inédites de Flora Tristan.
Editions universitaires de Dijon, 1985. Pp. 263. Fr. 195.00.

　　Rev. by Roger Bellet in *Europe* 283 (March 1986): 198-200;
by Elissa Gelfand in *NCFS* 15 (1986-87); 233-34.
　　Contents: Jean Cassou, "Un fabuleux destin" (1-5); Lucien
Scheler, "Flora Tristan, cent ans après" (6-10); Magda Portal,
"Ma découverte de Flora Tristan" (11-14, 235); Denys Cuche,
"Le Pérou de Flora Tristan: du rêve à la réalité" (19-37);
Michel Baridon, "Flora Tristan peintre de la 'ville-monstre'
dans les *Promenades de Londres*" (38-51, 238-39); Peter Byrne,
"Daniel O'Connell vu par Lamennais et par Flora Tristan"
(52-64, 239-40); Pierre Lévêque, "Mission impossible? Flora
Tristan en Bourgogne vue par la presse locale" (65-81, 241-
46); Marie-Claire Hoocke-Demarle, "Le langage littéraire des
femmes enquêteuses" (95-106, 246-48); Christine Planté,
"Flora Tristan, écrivain méconnu?" (186-97, 256-57); Stéphane
Michaud, "En miroir: Flora Tristan et George Sand" (198-208,
257); Stéphane Michaud et Lucien Scheler, eds., "Lettres
retrouvées" (218-33, 257-61).

Ruggieri, Eve. *Eve Ruggieri racconte ... : Greta Garbo, Flora
Tristan, Eva Peron, Mata Hari, Maria Callas.* (J'ai lu.)
Paris: J'ai lu, 1986. Pp. 350. Fr. 22.00.

See also Michaud ("French 1. General"); Prontera ("Lamennais");
Friends of George Sand Newsletter 6,1-2 ("Sand").

Reviews of book previously listed:

MICHAUD, Stéphane, ed., *Flora Tristan (1803-1844)* (see *RMB*
for 1984, p. 327), rev. by Henriette Bessis in *Romantisme*
51 (1986): 123-24; by Brian Rigby in *FS* 40 (1986): 224-25.

VEUILLOT

Le Roux, Benoît. "Veuillot et les femmes." *Revue Universelle
des Faits et des Idées* 112 (March 1985): 35-39.

Rétif, André. "Louis Veuillot et les Ségur." *Au Pays
d'Argentelles* (Jan.-March 1985): 134-42.

See also Gough ("French 1. General").

Review of book previously listed:

LE ROUX, Benoît, *Louis Veuillot, un homme, un combat* (see *RMB*
for 1984, p. 327), rev. by Jean Albertini in *Europe* 685 (May
1986): 217-18.

VIARDOT

Cahiers I. Tourguéniev, P. Viardot, M. Malibran 8 (1984).
"Actes de la table ronde sur Louis Viardot (1800-1883).
Institut d'Etudes hispaniques de Paris, 5 mai 1983."

   Contents: Alexandre Zviguilsky, "Louis Viardot" (5-14);
Louis Miard, "Louis Viardot, traducteur du *Don Quichotte* ou
les secrets d'une 'belle infidèle'" (15-27); Henriette Lomne,
"Les provinces basques et leurs institutions dans les
Etudes sur l'Espagne" (29-35); Lucien Denon, "*Libre examen*
de Louis Viardot" (37-40); René Guise, "Une lettre d'Eugène
Sue à Louis Viardot" (41-44); "Catalogue de l'exposition
Louis Viardot. Institut d'études hispaniques de Paris, 5-6
mai 1983--Hôtel de ville de La Celle Saint-Cloud, 7-8 mai
1983" (44-48); Jacques-Paul Viardot, "Hommage à Louis Viardot,
Cimetière Montparnasse, 6 mai 1983" (5-51); Gustave Dulong,
"Pauline Viardot, tragédienne lyrique" [*MS* inédit, achevé
en 1856, introduction par Alexandre Zviguilsky] (53-104).

VIGNY

Association des Amis d'Alfred de Vigny 15 (1985-86). Pp. 79.

Contents: François Escoube, "Vie de l'Association" (3-4);
"Prix de Poésie Alfred de Vigny à Louis Amade, pour son
recueil 'Moi, je passais,' 14 janvier 1985" (4-7); Jean-
Pierre Lassalle, "Le séjour de Wanda en France: un journal
inédit (1843-1845) de la comtesse Alexandra Kossakowska"
(8-38); Loïc Chotard, "Un poème inédit d'Alfred de Vigny
révélé par sa correspondance" (39-42); André Jarry, "Un
poème inconnu de Vigny" (43-46); Claude Dietschy-Picard,
"Alfred de Vigny, arrière-petit neveu de Jean-François
Regnard" (47-49); Michel Cambien, "Le poète d'un journal:
une bio-graphie bien soutenue" (50-62); "Un texte de jeunesse
de Joseph Kessel sur Alfred de Vigny" (63-64); "Bibliographie"
(65); "Revue des autographes" (66-70); "Tables récapitulatives
des Bulletins 1 à 15" (71-79).

Bury, J.P.T. "A Glimpse of Vigny in 1830." *French Studies
Bulletin* 19 (Summer 1986): 8-10.

Vigny's tale of "La canne de jonc" (*Servitude et grandeur
militaires*) in another version, that of *Mémoires de mon
voisin par le Vicomte Edouard de Lamare.*

Chanteur, Janine. "Alfred de Vigny, lecteur de Spinoza."
Les Cahiers de Fontenay 36-38 (1985): 233-50.

Daniels, Barry V. "Vigny." Pp. 211-28 in Barry Daniels,
Revolution in the Theater: French Romantic Theories of Drama.
(Contributions in Drama and Theater Studies, 7.) Westport,
Conn., and London: Greenwood Press, 1983.

Dufresne, Marc. "Péguy lecteur de Vigny." *RLM* 731-34 (1985):
95-116.

Griffiths, D.A. "Alfred de Vigny et Constantin Pecqueur:
affinités intellectuelles à propos de 'La Maison du Berger.'"
RHL 85 (1985): 1044-49.

Parallels in thought concerning the social and humanitarian
role of railways.

Ikezawa, Katsuo. "Alfred de Vigny et La Rochefoucauld."
Language and Culture (Hokkaido University) 7 (1985): 91-166.

In Japanese with French summary.

Jarry, André. "Les lieux de l'écriture chez Vigny: étude de quelques manuscrits." *Litterature* 13 (Dec. 1983): 81-111.

Legrand, Yolande. "'Les grands pays muets ... ': de Vigny à Mauriac." *Travaux du centre d'études et de recherches sur François Mauriac* 18 (Dec. 1985): 23-58.

Legrand, Yolande. "Vigny, le mythe du changement et l'Affaire de l'Académie." Pp. 159-86 in Claude-Gilbert Dubois, ed., *L'Imaginaire du changement: conversions, modifications métamorphoses*, vol. 2. Presses Université de Bordeaux, 1985.

Rev. by Jean-Claude Margolin in *BHR* 47 (1985): 276-77.

Malinowski, Wieslaw Mateusz. "Vigny." Pp. 31-39 in *La Nouvelle historique en France à l'époque du Romantisme*. (Seria filologica románska, 9.) Uniw. Poznari, 1983.

Poli, Annarosa. "Giuseppe Mazzini e la traduzione del 'Chatterton' di Vigny." Pp. 327-44 in H.G. Hall et al., eds., *Mélanges à la mémoire de Franco Simone*, vol. 3, *France et Italie dans la culture européenne, XIXe et XXe siècles*. (Bibliothèque Franco Simone, 8.) Geneva: Slatkine, 1984. Pp. 822.

Prassoloff, Annie, ed. *Stello; Daphné*. (Folio, 1733.) Paris: Gallimard, 1986. Pp. 434. Fr. 37.00.

Saint-Gérand, Jacques-Philippe. "Les 'Mémoires' d'Alfred de Vigny et leur fonction métapoétique." *Lingua e Stile* 20 (1985): 397-408.

Sokolova, T.V. "Evolution de la méthode et la fortune du genre (éléments lyrique et épique dans le poème philosophique d'Alfred de Vigny)." *Zarubeziaja literatura* (Problema metoda; Leningrad) (1984, fasc. 2): 42-55.

Sokolova, T.V. "Problèmes de l'art et de l'activité politique dans l'œuvre de Vigny." *Literatura i obšcestvenno-politiceskie problemy epolkhi* (Leningrad) (1983): 6-18.

Sokolova, T. "Réminiscences de 'La Scienza Nuova' de Giambattista Vico dans l'œuvre de Vigny. ('La Sauvage')." Pp. 345-57 in H.G. Hall et al., eds., *Mélanges à la mémoire de Franco Simone*, vol. 3, *France et Italie dans la culture européenne, XIXe et XXe siècles*. (Bibliotheque Franco Simone, 8.) Geneva: Slatkine, 1984. Pp. 822.

Wren, Keith. *Vigny: "Les Destinées."* (Critical Guides, 44.)
London: Grant and Cutler, 1985. Pp. 98.

   Rev. by Ceri Crossley in *MLR* 81 (1986): 743-44; by Norma
   Rinsler in *FS* 40 (1986): 82-83.
   Not seen.

See also Viallaneix ("Stendhal").

Reviews of books previously listed:

   BASSAN, Fernande, *Alfred de Vigny et la Comédie-Française*
   (see *RMB* for 1985, p. 310), rev. by Barbara Cooper in *NCFS*
   14 (1985-86): 167-68; by Arlette Michel in *IL* 38 (1986):
   49; BUSS, Robin, *Vigny: Chatterton* (see *RMB* for 1984, p.
   328), rev. by Graham Chesters in *MLR* 81 (1986): 1011;
   Relire "Les Destinées" (see *RMB* for 1980, p. 236), rev. by
   Fernande Bassan in *O&C* 7,2 (1982-83): 97-98; VIALLANEIX,
   Paul, ed., *Les Destinées, Poèmes philosophiques* (see *RMB* for
   1983, p. 282), rev. by J.C. Ireson in *MLR* 79 (1984): 943;
   by Arlette Michel in *IL* 36 (1984): 229; by J.-Ph. Saint-
   Gérand in *RHL* 85 (1985): 313-14.

VILLEMAIN

Malavié, Jean. "Villemain et son temps d'après des correspondances inédites." *SFr* 29 (1985): 279-301.

   Based on extracts from 56 letters and notes from Villemain
to 27 correspondents, arranged, annotated, and linked so as
to display the major facets of Villemain's career: administra-
tor, *universitaire*, writer, academician (he was perpetual
secretary--"vraiment perpétuel," it was said--of the Académie
Française). These texts reveal the hidden side of "ce Rastigna
universitaire, moins cynique et plus spirituel que son frère
balzacien."

Wagner, Nicolas. "Le dix-huitième siècle de Villemain." *SVEC*
216 (1983): 441-42.

   "Ce que réfracte le *Tableau du XVIIIe siècle*, c'est un
siècle en tant que culture et non en tant que structure
rhétorique" (*Bulletin Signalétique 523*,39,4 [no. 4382]).
See *RMB* for 1985, p. 312.

See also Bonvallet-Mallet ("French 1. General").

VINET

Reymond, Bernard. "Regards neufs sur la théologie pastorale d'Alexandre Vinet." *Revue de Théologie et de Philosophie* 118 (1986): 269-79.

On the relevance of Vinet's pastoral theology today.

WEILL

Review of book previously listed:

FRIEDEMANN, Joë, *Alexandre Weill écrivain contestataire et historien engagé, 1811-1899* (see *RMB* for 1980, p. 265), rev. by Carlo Cordié in *Paideia* 39 (1984): 264-65.

GERMAN

(Compiled by Konstanze Bäumer, Syracuse University;
Christopher R. Clason, Duquesne University; William
Crisman, Pennsylvania State University, Altoona; Roger
Crocket, Texas A & M University; John F. Fetzer, Univer-
sity of California, Davis; Bernd Fischer, Ohio State
University; Wulf Koepke, Texas A & M University; Scott
McLean, University of California, Davis; Robert Mollenauer,
University of Texas, Austin; Jeffrey L. Sammons, Yale Uni-
versity; Leonard Schulze, Texas Lutheran College)

1. BIBLIOGRAPHY

"Annotierte Auswahlbibliographie germanistischer Dissertations-
schriften." *ZG* (Leipzig) 7 (1986): 119-22, 255-56, 380-83,
499-503.

*Arbitrium: Zeitschrift für Rezensionen zur germanistischen
Literaturwissenschaft.* Vol. 7, 1987. Ed. by Wolfgang
Frühwald and Wolfgang Harms. Munich: C.H. Beck.

A handy journal of book reviews. "Nachrichten aus dem
Fach," "Personalia," "Symposien, Kongresse," "Forschungs-
projekte," and a "Verzeichnis eingegangener Bücher."

Borck, Jim Springer, gen. ed. *The Eighteenth Century: A
Current Bibliography.* N.S. 8, for 1982. New York: AMS
Press, 1986. Pp. 603. Eds. for German: Barbara Becker-
Cantarino and John S. Pustejovsky.

Cazden, Robert E. *A Social History of the German Book Trade
in America to the Civil War.* Columbia, S.C.: Camden House,
1984. Pp. xvii+801.

Rev. by Christa Sammons in *JEGP* 85 (1986): 81-83 as
"indispensable."

*Deutsche Bücher: Referatenorgan germanistischer, belletris-
tischer und deutschkundlicher Neuerscheinungen* (vorm. *Het*

Boek) 16 (1986). Amsterdam: Editions Rodopi N.V.

Broad, selective coverage of recent critical works. Survey reviews in the concluding "Kurz berichtet."

"Doctoral Dissertations [U.S. and Canada]." *Monatshefte* 78 (1986): 348-50.

Faulhaber, Uwe K., and Penrith B. Goff, eds. *German Literature: An Annotated Reference Guide.* (Garland Reference Library of the Humanities, 108.) New York and London: Garland Publishing, 1979.

Not listed previously in the German section. A fine overview of the major research tools available, except for the most recent additions to the field. The evaluations are competent, and handiness is assured by the many sub-categories of the topical organization. (R.M.)

Germanistik: Internationales Referatenorgan mit bibliographischen Hinweisen. Jahrgang 27. 4 Hefte. Tübingen: Niemeyer, 1986-87.

For Romantism see "II. Allgemeines"; "XVII. Allgemeines zur Literaturwissenschaft"; "XXI. Deutsche Literaturgeschite, Allgemeines"; "XXIX. Goethezeit (1770-1830)"; "XXX. Von der Spätromantik bis zum Realismus (1830-1880)"; "XXXII. Volksdichtung [the Grimms, Märchen]." Books but not articles are reviewed. Articles and independent chapters within *Sammelbände* are cross-listed by epoch and author. Heft 4 includes the annual index of authors and topics.

Glass, D.C.K. "Literature, 1830-1880." *YWMLS* 43 (1981): 867-907; 44 (1982): 891-939; 45 (1983): 744-79; 46 (1984): 783-819; 47 (1985): 762-801.

Hartke, Werner, ed. *Deutsche Literaturzeitung für Kritik der internationalen Wissenschaft: Herausgegeben im Auftrage der Akademie der Wissenschaften der DDR (=DLZ).* Vol. 108, 1987. Berlin: Akademie-Verlag.

The monthly installments include a small section for *Germanistik.*

Hohnholz, J., ed. *Literature--Music--Fine Arts: A Review of German-Language Research Contributions on Literature, Music, and Fine-Arts (=LMFA).* (German Studies, Section III, edited by the Institute for Scientific Co-operation.) Vol. 20, Nos. 1 and 2, 1987.

English-language reviews of German-language studies in the three named fields, each section accompanied by a "Selected Bibliography."

Kossmann, Bernhard, and Monika Richter, eds. *Bibliographie der deutschen Sprach- und Literaturwissenschaft.* Vol. 25, 1985. Frankfurt am Main: Vittorio Klostermann, 1986. Pp. 856.

"XI. Goethezeit"; "XII. Romantik"; "XIII. 19. Jahrhundert." A continuation of the Eppelsheimer/Köttelwesch bibliography, integrated with the holdings and new acquisitions of the Stadt- und Universitätsbibliothek Frankfurt am Main.

Littlejohns, Richard. "The Romantic Era." *YWMLS* 46 (1984): 762-82; 47 (1985): 734-61.

Thompson, George A., Jr., ed., with the assistance of Margaret M. Thompson. *Key Sources in Comparative and World Literature-- An Annotated Guide to Reference Materials.* New York: Ungar, 1982. Pp. xv+383.

Rev. (pos. and neg.) by Gerhard R. Kaiser in *Arcadia* 20 (1985): 76.

Walker, C.A.S. "The Romantic Era." *YWMLS* 43 (1981): 837-66; 44 (1982): 861-90; 45 (1983): 720-43.

White, I.A. "The Classical Era." *YWMLS* 43 (1981): 803-36; 44 (1982): 809-60; 45 (1983): 684-719; 46 (1984): 722-61; 47 (1985): 706-33.

Zeller, Otto, and Wolfram Zeller, eds. *Internationale Bibliographie der Zeitschriftenliteratur aus allen Gebieten des Wissens (IBZ).* Vol. 22 (Pars 1 and 2, each in 6 vols.), 1986. Osnabruck: Felix Dietrich Verlag, 1986.

The article listings for each half-year are arranged in: A. Index rerum (Subject Index); B. Index systematicus (Keyword Index); C. Autores (Authors); D. Periodica (Periodicals). Since 1984 Dietrich Verlag has incorporated the listings of *IBR* (International Bibliography of Book Reviews), *IJBF* (International Annual Bibliography of Festschriften), and *IJBK* (International Annual Bibliography of Congress Proceedings). Dietrich has also entered into an arrangement with the University of Göttingen Library to load in a data bank all bibliographic material from the four bibliographies, permitting future online searches from that service: Bibliotheksrechen-

zentrum für Niedersachsen.   In addition to Lower Saxony, the
states of Bremen, Hamburg, and Schleswig-Holstein are taking
part in this project.   (R.M.)

2.   GENERAL

Bänziger, Hans.   *Schloß-Haus-Bau: Studien zu einem literarischen Motivkomplex von der deutschen Klassik zur Moderne.*
Bern and Munich: Francke, 1983. Pp. 219. Sw. Fr. 38.00.

Rev. by Rita Terras in *JEGP* 85 (1986): 315-15 as including
a "particularly impressive" essay on Kleist and a discussion
of Eichendorff, among other writers.
Not seen.

Benjamin, Walter.   *Le Concept de critique esthétique dans le
romantisme allemand.*   Trans. Philippe Lacoue-Labarthe and
Anne-Marie Lang. (La Philosophie en Effet.) Paris: Flammarion, 1986. Pp. 192. Fr. 95.00.

Benz, Ernst.   *The Mystical Sources of German Romantic Philosophy.*
Trans. Blair R. Reynolds and Eunice M. Paul. (Pittsburgh
Theological Monographs, n.s., no. 6.) Allison Park, Pa.:
Pickwick Publications, 1983. Pp. 132. $12.50.

Rev. by Bernard McGinn in *JR* 66 (1986): 92-93.

Bronfen, Elisabeth.   *Der Literarische Raum: Eine Untersuchung
am Beispiel von Dorothy M. Richardsons Romanzyklus "Pilgrimage."*
(Studien zur englischen Philologie, n.f., 25.) Tübingen:
Niemeyer, 1986. Pp. 373. DM 126.00.

Sometimes an unsolicited review book is so inappropriate
to your editorial concerns that returning it to the publisher
seems the only proper course.   Elisabeth Bronfen's study
of Dorothy M. Richardson's novel cycle *Pilgrimage* (1938) is
a twentieth-century and not a nineteenth-century concern,
and looking for even the word "Romantic" here is a hard
assignment.   It appears occasionally in connection with
"romance" and as the binary opposite of "realism." This
lucidly written and well-organized study is not the traditional
biographical, or lit-crit, aesthetic analysis of Richardson's
stream-of-consciousness "Miriam" novels.   It is modern meta-
criticism of the "new" psychological novel, involving with
prudence and precision such names as Bakhtin, Eco, Heidegger,
Eliade, Genette, Jakobsen, Barthes, as well as significant
specialists in architectural theory and the problem of space
in philosophy.   And it is done without puzzling jargon or

mysterious allusion to other modern critical theory. Syntagmatic (horizontal, denotative) and paradigmatic (vertical, connotative) are shown to be the structures of naming (*Benennen*) and being silent (*Schweigen*). And one understands why Dorothy M. Richardson rejects the notion of *stream* of consciousness and argues instead for a vertical *plunge* into the text as the key to textual spatiality. In Bronfen's words, "the tectonic principle underlying perception and understanding is examined" (concluding English summary, 365.) *In other words*, this is a study of the syntactic, metanymic, and metaphoric interplay between "Romantic" and "realistic." How else, really, can a writer like Kleist be understood? Thank you, Niemeyer Verlag. (R.M.)

Deutsches Literaturarchiv, ed. *Dichter Lesen: Von Gellert bis Liliencron*. (Marbacher Schriften, 23/24.) Marbach: Deutsche Schillergesellschaft e.V., 1984. Pp. 303.

A genially conceived cross-section of German intellectual history in the eighteenth and nineteenth centuries. This is fun scholarship from the staff of the deutsches Literaturarchiv at Marbach. From diaries, letters, reports, and works printed and unprinted they have put together a fascinating collection which reaffirms the importance of such institutions as the salon, the literary tea, and the writers' club. Informative background details accompany excerpts and series of items which were once read aloud, as well as reports of such readings. Romanticists and their kind are in abundance here. The insights provided are significant, often fun: [Fr. Schlegel to A. Böhmer, Oct. 1798] "Tieck ist sehr glücklich verheyrathet, nur klagt er, daß seine liebe Amalie nicht viel Kunstsinn hat. Sie schläft immer ein, wenn er ihr seine Sachen vorliest" (104). The provocative titles of the Romantic-oriented sections: "Geselliges Vorlesen in klassisch-romantischer Zeit" (94-136), "Romantische Reflexion" (137-43), "Stottern und Singen: Heinrich von Kleist und Clemens Brentano" (144-50). (R.M.)

Garland, Henry, and Mary Garland. *The Oxford Companion to German Literature*. 2d ed. Oxford University Press, 1986. Pp. 1019.

Big enough to go into detail; brief enough to allow such listings as individual poem titles, first lines, quotable lines. It thus is good for answering "who wrote that?" questions. The alphabetical format makes it a handy reference for terms, forms, persons (not characters), and periods—if one knows what to look for. The section on "Romantik" is sensible (division into "older" and "younger" rather than

three periods) and Kleist, Heine, and Hölderlin are accepted
as related figures. The slightest effort is made to treat
the concept(s) of Romanticism; perfectly understandable in
this format. One wonders ... why the entry a page later for
Generalfeldmarschall Erwin Rommel? (R.M.)

Goodbody, Axel. *Natursprache: Ein dichtungstheoretisches
Konzept der Romantik und seine Wiederaufnahme in der modernen
Naturlyrik (Novalis--Eichendorff--Lehmann-Eich)*. (Kieler
Studien zur deutschen Literaturgeschichte, Bd. 17.) Neu-
münster: Wachholtz, 1984. Pp. 384.

One might argue that after such studies as those by
Ziolkowski and Sørensen a new discussion of *Natursprache* is
unneeded. Indeed, Goodbody's work seems to fall back on
conventional Romantic intentions and arguments: nature presents
a secret, hieroglyphic language which speaks to the individual.
Goodbody acknowledges *Ideengeschichte* as a methodology and he
presents a twofold "definition" of Romantic *Natursprache*:
a. Nature is a language which reveals a higher essence, and
b. words are reflections of an original higher union with
things. The *Natursprache* reflects theological, linguistic-
philosophical, and poetological-aesthetic commitments. As
such it is a divine language. These three dimensions are
found in abundance in Novalis and Eichendorff.
The value of this study is the extension of this Romantic
argument to Lehmann and Eich in the twentieth century.
Convincing and clear distinctions are drawn between the
Romantic position (religious, signifying) and that of Goethe
(aesthetic, symbolic, classical). A final bonus is the short
consideration of the lyrics of Peter Huchel and Johannes
Bobrowski. (R.M.)

Greiner, Walter F., and Fritz Kemmler, eds. *Realismustheorien
in England (1692-1912): Texte zur historischen Dimension der
englischen Realismusdebatte*. Tübingen: Niemeyer, 1979.
Pp. 222. DM 22.00.

This handy text was designed for advanced work at German
universities. Obviously it could help English-only readers
as well, for it is a judiciously selected, chronological
ordering of excerpts from original texts, reviews of and
reviews by significant English writers from William Congreve
(1691) through Arthur Christopher Benson (1912). It seems
just about everybody expressed or had something said about
his "realistic" intentions before, during, or after the
Romantic period--including the Romantic writers included here:
Jeffrey, Scott, Dunlop, Austen, Hazlitt, and Whately. (R.M.)

Hay, Gerhard, ed., with an essay by Fritz J. Raddatz. *Deutsche Abschiede*. Munich: Winkler, 1984. Pp. 496.

The editor intends a cross-section of German intellectual history, provided through sketches of one writer by another. Of immediate concern to us: Tieck on Novalis, Jean Paul on Herder, Adam Müller on Kleist, Börne on Jean Paul, Heine on Börne, Schwab on Hölderlin, Hebbel on Tieck, Laube on Heine, Jacob on Wilhelm Grimm.

Hohendahl, Peter Uwe. *Literarische Kultur im Zeitalter des Liberalismus: 1830-1870*. Munich: C.H: Beck, 1985. Pp. 480.

Sections on "Heine" (166-70) and "Die Integration der Romantik" (183-93). The reception of *Klassik-Romantik* by Gervinus, Haym, Hettner, and Dilthey nicely demonstrated. (R.M.)

Klotz, Volker. *Das europäische Kunstmärchen: Fünfundzwanzig Kapitel seiner Geschichte von der Renaissance bis zur Moderne*. Stuttgart: Metzler, 1985. Pp. 412.

Rev. by Hans-Heino Ewers in *Arcadia* 21 (1986): 317-23; see also Wührl below.

In contrast to Wührl, who recognizes the complexity of the source (*Volksmärchen*) but then limits the literary by-product (*Kunstmärchen*) to the common denominator of *das Wunderbare*, Klotz keeps all the features in sight while nevertheless drawing sharp distinctions between folk and fantasy tale. Admittedly, his "definition" does not offer much more than Wührl's rejection of definition: "Kunstmärchen dagegen--so die vorläufige, noch sehr pauschale Definition--sind literarische, geschichtlich und individuell geprägte Abwandlungen der außerliterarischen, geschichtlich unbestimmten, anonymen Gattung Volksmärchen durch namhafte Autoren" (2). But here is an emphasis on the formal rather than on a single questionable content element, such as the fantastic (Wührl). Additionally, the communicative function of the *Kunstmärchen* form interests Klotz, and the author's own interpretative enthusiasm clearly becomes part of the communicative process. Wührl has a brief section on the Italian, French, and Oriental forebears of the German fantasy tale; the survey of origins by Klotz is little broader but more exhaustive in treatment. Klotz devotes a third of his attention to German writers, with chapters on Wieland, Musäus, Goethe, Novalis, Tieck, Fouqué, Contessa, Brentano, E.T.A. Hoffmann, Hauff, Mörike, Keller, and Kafka. The final third of his text focuses rather arbitrarily on Andersen, Dickens, Thackeray, Carroll, George MacDonald, Wilde, and Collodi, so that five national literatures in all have been represented: Italian, French, German, Danish, and English. One must ask if an American tradition-- with Poe and Faulkner, for example--might not have been considered as a meaningful extension of this European development. (R.M.)

Lehmann, Peter Lutz. *Von Goethe zu George: Heidelberger Essays.* (Beiträge zur Neueren Literaturgeschichte, Dritte Folge, 68.) Heidelberg: Carl Winter Universitätsverlag, 1986. Pp. 143.

This handsomely printed collection of addresses (*Reden*) reflects, by the author's own pronouncement, the several perspectives of summers spent in Heidelberg, a veneration for Stefan George, and a view of German literature from the distance of Chicago. Chapters on "Hölderlin and Heidelberg," "Klassische Romantik," and "Brentano" focus on Romantic concerns, yet the other essays--about Humboldt, Goethe, Stifter and Fontane, Bismarck, Gundolf, Stauffenberg, and George--also exude congenial references to the Romantic manner. The Hölderlin essay seems to lose focus at times, perhaps because Lehmann wants to show how far Hölderlin had distanced himself from the stances of both classicism and Romanticism. In the following essay Lehmann relates to two masters of German literary criticism--Fritz Strich and Richard Benz--to develop an admirable thesis for the complementarity of German *Klassizität* and *Romantik*, to the detriment of the former. Here he relates the longing of E.T.A. Hoffmann's obsessive Cardillac to the longing of Goethe's abstractly self-conscious Iphigenie in order to develop his argument for "klassische Romantik." Hindemith is summoned finally in order to demonstrate the greater viability of Hoffmann's hubris-figure over Goethe's. This is a high point of the book. The chapter on Brentano addresses itself to the reasons for the failure of Brentano's religious aestheticism--in comparison with models from antiquity--and the compensating abiding appeal of him as a folk favorite. (R.M.)

Loquai, Franz. *Künstler und Melancholie in der Romantik.* (Helicon: Beiträge zur deutschen Literatur, 4.) Frankfurt am Main: Lang, 1984. Pp. 398.

See Völker below.

Though nothing new is offered by the equation Romanticism = melancholy = insanity, Loquai's study is helpful for its concentration on the history of medicine in the Romantic period. Loquai builds on/against Schings's significant study of *Melancholie und Aufklärung*, where melancholy is seen as a tool against anti-rationalism. He sees in Romanticism the

attempt to use melancholy as a tool against philistine
rationalism. Of course, E.T.A. Hoffmann is central to this
investigation; further analyses of Wackenroder, Tieck, Fr.
Schlegel, Novalis, Hölderlin, and Bonaventura. (R.M.)

Lowenthal, Leo. *Literature and the Image of Man: Communication in Society, Volume 2.* New Brunswick, N.J., and Oxford:
Transaction Books, 1986. Pp. 344.

This study spans three decades of work but has not suffered
in sociological insight and consistency in the process. Part
II: "Studies on the German Novel in the Nineteenth Century"
was written originally in German while the author was associated with the Institute for Social Research in Frankfurt,
and is to be read as a complement to Part I: "Studies on the
European Drama and Novel from the Renaissance to the
Threshold of Modernity." From the "Afterword" by Helmut
Dubiel, editor of the German edition: "Assuming narrative
literature as his focus, the author traces the development
of bourgeois mentality peculiar to Germany in the nineteenth
century. The antimodernism of the romantics, the theoretical-
ly impoverished social critique of the "Young Germany,"
Mörike's neurotically disturbed embourgeoisement, Freytag's
bourgeois materialism, Conrad Ferdinand Meyer's glorification
of upperclass bourgeois 'heroic' style, and so on, are all
shown to be symptomatic of a single syndrome--that of the
miscarriage of a bourgeois revolution in Germany" (343-44).
A chapter in Part I first considers the German development
of a bourgeois mentality in discussions of Goethe's *Werther*
and *Wilhelm Meister*, and throughout Lessing is seen as a
touchstone for judging the writers of the age. Because of
its perspective, this is not a flattering picture of German
Romanticism. But it is fair for its humanistic concern.
It is less successful as a study of the nature of literary
genius than it is of the dependency of the human spirit--and
eventually of artists--on social and political change. (R.M.)

Martin, Stoddard. *Art Messianism and Crime: A Study of Anti-
nomianism in Modern Literature and Lives.* New York: St.
Martin's, 1986. Pp. 218.

You must read it to believe it--and the title is not altogether informative. This work reads as if it were written
under the influence of 218 pages of LSD, but the wealth
of material is a combination of startling insights presented
in a topical pointillism which will both inform and annoy.
Back to the title--but add the words lawlessness, nihilism,
disorder, magic and the occult, counter-culture, pop culture,
manichaeism, the Dionysian, Adolf Hitler and Charles Manson,
and see all of this as an expression of Romantic man. This

is not new. A.O. Lovejoy and, a few years back, Marxist critics traced everything bad about modernity back to German Romanticism. Martin's effort is faulted for the lack of any definition of Romanticism that would support his exposé. Nevertheless, his characterizations are so refreshing, so cleverly eclectic, and his insight into mass art (not the art usually merchandized by professors and critics) so persuasive that one begins to take his thesis of the "artist *manqué*" seriously. That is a person who turns his back on art to become a "man of action," and as such " ... is only one incarnation of Romantic man, who--like Goethe's Faust-- is ever striving, over-reaching, not-quite-achieving" (3). Even more insightful, perhaps, is: "Romantic man belongs to the era of capitalism, which institutionalizes mobility, rather than to feudalism or socialism, which attempts kinds of fixity" (4).

The sweep of Romantic characterization is also to be faulted for its stingy attention to texts (one poem: Yeats's "The Second Coming"). But Martin is compelled by the theme of justice, and therefore persons, artists turned actors, concern him. Christ was the finest exemplar of *human* behavior, and "Hitler must be discredited, Manson confined" (191). This is a superb analysis of the sickness of the 60s and 70s. It is worth cautious consideration as a testimony of the lingering Romantic spirit. (R.M.)

Mayer, Hans. *Das ungluckliche Bewusstsein: Zur deutschen Literaturgeschichte von Lessing bis Heine*. Frankfurt am Main: Suhrkamp, 1986. Pp. 635.

Hans Mayer always makes sense, even if one doesn't want to accept his superbly informed, rational, Marxist bias. This in addition to his plastic, lucid, sovereign style. Proceeding from a "given" that must rub Germans the wrong way, "das unglückliche deutsche Bewußtsein" ... "die deutsche Misere," Mayer builds on the bitter insights forcibly bestowed on such exile critics as Heine, Thomas Mann, Plessner, and himself when examining national sore spots: "Deutschland, wo liegt es?" Germany more than most nations, perhaps, has suffered under the conflicting aspirations of *Staatsnation* and *Kulturnation*. In its literature, since Kant, these have taken the form of a tension between *Innenwelt* and *Außenwelt*, *Subjekt* and *Objekt*, Romanticism and realism. Indeed, because of Kant, primacy was given to interiorization of the external reality.

Proceeding from an analysis of the "Bourgeois-aristocratic compromise" (Lessing, Wieland) through the "bourgeois-plebeian compromise" (Lenz, *Werther*, *Die Räuber*) to the "Endzeit des Ancien Regime," Mayer comes to a chapter dealing

with the possible Jacobin leanings of Hölderlin and Kleist
(also Goethe and Schiller). Throughout this work but
especially in Chap. 5, "Fragen der deutschen Romantik,"
Mayer comes to grips with the scholarship as well as the
primary literature. The easy answers of traditional *Germanistik* are repeatedly challenged with respect to their possible
escapist, unrealistic positions. Two of our favorite "Romanticists" are held back for a following chapter where their
realisms, their unsuitableness to the accepted brands of
either *Schlegelkreis*- or Brentano-irony is demonstrated:
Jean Paul and E.T.A. Hoffmann. The final chapter is devoted
to the "Nachtgedanken" of Börne and Heine--from the perspectives of "deutsche Misere" and "deutsche Ideologie" respectively.
An example of Mayer's fairness and insight: he explains the
negative positions taken by Goethe and Hegel toward E.T.A.
Hoffmann while also demonstrating why E.T.A. Hoffmann and
Heine nevertheless have become world literature. (R.M.)

Pizer, John David. *The Historical Perspective in German Genre
Theory: Its Development from Gottsched to Hegel*. (Stutt-
garter Arbeiten zur Germanistik, Nr. 160.) Stuttgart: Hans-
Dieter Heinz Akademischer Verlag, 1985. Pp. 328.

Though he invokes such more recent masters as Dilthey,
Lukács, and Benjamin, his study concludes with Romanticism
and Fr. Schlegel, "whose dynamic dialectical approach represents the climax of the evolution towards a historical perspective of the literary genres" (9). The book is unques-
tionably simple in its organization (I: Aufklärung--
Gottsched, Batteux; II: Sturm und Drang--Gerstenberg,
Herder; III: Klassik und Romantik--Goethe and Schiller,
Friedrich Schlegel) and written with a straightforward,
unpretentious style. Pizer takes issue with Szondi in particular, and he demonstrates his awareness of the pertinent
scholarship. A concluding section concerns itself with Hegel,
because of his attempted union of the historical with the
systematic. The typescript format has a pleasing appearance.
(R.M.)

Powell, Nicolas. "Imperial Biedermeier." *Apollo* 123 (1986):
30-33.

Sauer, Lieselotte. *Marionetten, Maschinen, Automaten: Der
künstliche Mensch in der deutschen und englischen Romantik.*
(Abhandlungen zur Kunst-, Musik- und Literaturwissenschaft,
Bd. 335.) Bonn: Bouvier Verlag Herbert Grundmann, 1983.
Pp. 513.

Rev. (negatively) by Lilian R. Furst in *Arcadia* 21 (1986): 323-24.

Treats Jean Paul, Bonaventura, Brentano, Achim von Arnim, and E.T.A. Hoffmann in some depth; Kleist in passing. Mary Shelley's *Frankenstein* is the only English text discussed, despite the promising subtitle. (R.M.)

Scheufele, Theodor. *Übergange zur Zukunft: Bewußseinserweiterung und deutsche Literatur um 1800.* (Europäische Hochschulschriften. Reihe I: Deutsche Sprache und Literatur, Bd. 871.) Frankfurt am Main: Lang, 1985. Pp. 201.

This is the sort of symphilosophizing which Fr. Schlegel and Novalis approved of but which vexes stuffy, traditional scholars. The publisher, Peter Lang, is easy. By the author's own admission he has avoided secondary texts and libraries in general and used his "own library." Thus G.H. Schubert's *Symbolik des Traumes* (that's O.K.), together with the *I Ching* and Capra's *The Tao of Physics* (hey wow!). Still, these essays are not mushy but informed, and their intention is to provoke rather than to prove. Scheufele searches for the confrontation between ratio and the mystic, unity through change, the tension between politics and myth, paradox, and various other typical Romantic concerns. Romanticists given major treatment: Hölderlin, Jean Paul, Kleist, Heine. The inspiration came from academic as well as meditative circles, and the study will surely find the audience it deserves. Typescript printing. (R.M.)

Schinkel, Eckhard. *"Süßer Traum der Poeten": Der Freiballon. Zu den Möglichkeiten und Grenzen der Motivuntersuchung.* (Forschungen zur Literatur- und Kulturgeschichte, Bd. 7.) Frankfurt am Main: Bern, New York: Lang, 1985. Pp. 238.

Section on Jean Paul, touches on Kerner and Günderode. Interesting for its unstuffiness. (R.M.)

Schubert, Bernhard. *Der Künstler als Handwerker: Zur Literaturgeschichte einer romantischen Utopie.* Königstein and Taunus: Athenäum, 1986. Pp. 289.

Though the style occasionally tends toward denseness, the subject is a welcome one. The Romantic era, beginning with Wackenroder and Tieck, sought to renew the utopian ideal of a pre-1800 unified aesthetic-moral world. The rise of capitalism and technology drove a wedge between art and functionality which affected all aspects of culture in the nineteenth century and eventually led to such programs of cultural regeneration as Hermann Muthesius's *Deutscher Werkbund* at the beginning of the twentieth century. Schubert analyzes works by Wackenroder, Tieck, Goethe, E.T.A. Hoffmann, Wagner, and finally Gottfried Keller and Thomas Mann to demonstrate a Romantic nostalgia for the *Handwerksmeister* who was also a Künstler. This was a unity that has been lost in the modern cleavage between the unaesthetic, pragmatic bourgeois and the creative artist who has been forced into a l'art pour l'art posture. In the section on Keller and Mann the author has enriched the argument with the critical observations of Georg Lukács. Yet another bonus: with respect to the idea of "craftmanship" in English "medievalism" a look at Ruskin, the Pre-Raphaelites, and Morris. A nicely conceived study, with Romanticism seen properly, i.e., broadly. (R.M.)

Sorg, Bernhard. *Das Lyrische Ich: Untersuchungen zu deutschen Gedichten von Gryphius bis Benn*. Tübingen: Max Niemeyer Verlag, 1984. Pp. vi+193. DM 46.00.

Rev. in German by Ruth E. Lorbe in *JEGP* 85 (1986): 72-75 as important for all students of lyric poetry.

Stallybrass, Peter, and Allon White. *The Politics and Poetics of Transgression*. London: Methuen, 1986. Pp. 228.

Though the focus here is on grotesque realism, occasional references to Romanticism depict it negatively as the adoptive manner of bourgeois culture. Bakhtin, Foucault, and Freud—carnival/fair, irony, and the grotesque—are clearly outlined in this well-organized and readable study. The grotesque as, variously: "The opposite of the classical ... the Other ..." and "... a process of hybridization or mixing of binary opposites, particularly of high and low, such that there is a heterodox merging of elements usually perceived as incompatible ..." (44). From Foucault's perspective, as interpreted by the authors: "By forcing the threshold and interrogating the liminal position, bourgeois romanticism and its modernist inheritors stage a festival of the political unconscious and reveal the repressions and social rejections which formed it" (200). The chapter about the pig is fascinating. (R.M.)

Vietta, Silvio, ed. *Die literarische Frühromantik*. *Mit Beiträgen von Wolfgang Frühwald, Heinz Gockel, Hans-Joachim Mähl, Horst Meixner, Lothar Pikulik, Gerhard Sauder, Silvio Vietta*. (Kleine Vandenhoeck-Reihe, 1488.) Göttingen: Vandenhoeck und Ruprecht, 1983. Pp. 223.

In this space it is impossible to dwell on the specifics of the several articles which make up this useful compendium.

The book results from a well-designed symposium at Mannheim
which sought, ambitiously, not just a reformulation of the
German early Romantic program but specifically a reinvestiga-
tion of a confused area of literary scholarship: the relation
between Enlightenment and *Frühromantik*. Silvio Vietta
addresses the keynote problem (7-84) and also concludes with
a study of the indebtedness of Romantic fantasy to the Enlightenment (208-20). Sauder on sentimentality ("Empfind-
samkeit") and the Romantic (85-111). Pikulik on Tieck's
Lovell and Fr. Schlegel's *Fragmente* (112-28). Frühwald on
A.W. Schlegel and the problem of communication (129-48).
Mähl on the (Christian) themes of chiliasm and utopia (149-
79). Meixner on the political ramifications (180-91). Gockel
on the "old new mythology" of the early Romantic program
(192-207). The separate articles retain the rhetorical
crispness of their symposium origins; their separateness
as symposium pieces has naturally allowed some overall
unevenness and overlapping. One could fuss about the exclu-
sion of studies specifically of the importance of music, of
the *Sturm und Drang*, and *Geniebegriff*, etc., but that which
is offered is tied to significant developments traceable to
the Enlightenment and therefore reasonably consistent.
(R.M.)

Völker, Ludwig, ed. *Komm, heilige Melancholie: Eine Anthologie
deutscher Melancholie-Gedichte. Mit Ausblicken auf die
europäische Melancholie-Tradition in Literatur- und Kunst-
geschichte. Mit 36 Abbildungen.* Stuttgart: Reclam, 1983.
Pp. 592. DM 22.80, paper DM 14.70.

   Rev. by Franz Loquai in *Arbitrium* 3 (1985): 122-23.
   See Loquai above.

Wais, Kurt. *Europäische Literatur im Vergleich: Gesammelte
Aufsätze.* Ed. by Johannes Hösle, Dieter Janik, Wolfgang
Theile. Tübingen: Niemeyer, 1983. Pp. 400. DM 228.00.

   Rev. by János Riesz in *Arbitrium* 3 (1985): 116-21.
   Chapters relating Hölderlin and Rousseau, E.T.A. Hoffmann
   and Balzac, and others.
   Not seen.

Wells, G.A. "Herder's Resistance to the Idea that Language Is
an Invention." *JEGP* 85 (1986): 167-90.

West, Evan. "The Musenalmanach and Viennese Song 1770-1830."
M&L 67 (1986): 37-49.

   These songbooks, edited by the likes of Tieck and the

Schlegels, provided a popular outlet for some major poets,
including Eichendorff and Rückert.

Wheeler, Kathleen M., ed. *German Aesthetic and Literary
Criticism: The Romantic Ironists and Goethe.* Cambridge
University Press, 1984. Pp. 259.

This is one of a series of three anthologies of German
aesthetic writing in translation, devoted to the period from
the second half of the eighteenth century to the early
nineteenth century. A lucid introduction gives sufficient
attention to the socio-historical background and gets on
properly with a brief and selective consideration of some of
the unique concerns of German aesthetics of the time. The
author fails in her attempt to justify the inclusion of Goethe
here; but then for non-Germans there is no need for such
justification. One could object to the inclusion of this
instead of that excerpt--a concern admitted by the author--
but the choices are representative. Especially helpful
to students of irony will be the sections on Solger and the
Tieck-Solger correspondence. Others covered: Fr. Schlegel,
Novalis, Tieck, Jean Paul, A.W. Schlegel, and Goethe. The
"Bibliography" is quite limited. This text will serve course
purposes as well as individual needs. (R.M.)

Williams, Simon. *German Actors of the Eighteenth and Nineteenth
Centuries: Idealism, Romanticism, and Realism.* (Contributions
in Drama and Theatre Studies, 12.) Westport, Conn., and
London: Greenwood Press, 1985. Pp. xii+197; 15 illus.
$35.00.

Rev. by Gloria Flaherty in *JEGP* 85 (1986): 630-32.
Romanticism and Romantic actors, like Ferdinand Fleck and
Ludwig Devrient, are treated in chapter 3.
Not seen.

Williams, Simon. "The 'Great Guest' Arrives: Early German
Hamlets." *TJ* 38 (1986): 291-308.

Following a successful and influential production in Hamburg
in 1776-1777, "the whole of German-speaking Europe can be
described as having been gripped by a veritable 'Hamlet-
fever.'"

Williamson, John. "The Revisions of Liszt's 'Prometheus.'"
M&L 67 (1986): 381-92.

An examination of how the 1855 symphonic poem developed
out of the earlier overture and choruses written by Liszt
for Herder's *Der entfesselte Prometheus*.

Wolpers, Theodor. "Die Romantik." Pp. 557-709, Book 6, in
Walter F. Schirmer et al., *Geschichte der englischen und
amerikanischen Literatur: Von den Anfängen bis zur Gegenwart.*
(Studienausgabe II, 1: Klassizismus und Romantik.) 6th rev.
ed. Tübingen: Niemeyer, 1983. Pp. 709. DM 18.80.

Now in its sixth edition, this literary history provides
a better than average survey because it is synoptic, discussing English and American literary development concurrently.
The introductory background sections are also serially multi-
perspective: historical-social, intellectual history, and
literary history. The generous bibliographical entry is extensively English language and the various sections are copiously footnoted. European Romanticism generally is a concern
of the coverage (e.g., transcendentalism). The style is
lucid. A bad feature, perhaps, is the organization by genre
(*Versdichtung, Roman, sonstige Prosa,* etc.), so typical of
literary histories. One also misses text citations--espe-
cially in the verse sections--and the evaluative emphasis
seems rather traditionally biographical-historical when
individual writers are treated. There is enough here for
students of German Romanticism (Gothic novel, Scott, Poe),
and the author makes clear why English literature did not
have the theoretical bent of German Romanticism: "Es geht
nicht mehre darum, wie vor allem Coleridge im Anschluß an
deutsche Romantiker und Goethe erläuterte, abstrakte Begriffe
in Bilder umzusetzen (wie in der älteren Allegorie), sondern
umgekehrt um die Andeutung einer allgemeineren, aber nicht
eindeutig definierbaren Bedeutung im Besonderen und Konkreten,
das dadurch zum Symbol wird" (574). Distinctions are ably
drawn between as well as within national/provincial traditions. The price is reasonable (it also gets you "Book V:
Der Klassizismus," by Erwin Wolf). An index would have been
useful. (R.M.)

Woodmansee, Martha. "The Interests of Disinterestedness: Karl
Philipp Moritz and the Emergence of the Theory of Aesthetic
Autonomy in Eighteenth-Century Germany." *MLQ* 45 (1984):
22-48.

Wührl, Paul-Wolfgang. *Das deutsche Kunstmärchen: Geschichte,
Botschaft und Erzählstrukturen.* (UTB für Wissenschaft: Uni-
Taschenbücher, 1341.) Heidelberg: Quelle und Meyer, 1984.
Pp. 370.

   Rev. by Hans-Heino Ewers in *Arcadia* 21 (1986): 317-23;
see also Klotz above.
   Wührl, whose experience with anthologies of *Kunstmärchen*

(with Insel: *Märchen deutscher Dichter*, 1964, and *Im magi-schen Spiegel*, 1978/81), claims in this instance to have produced the "erste umfassende Darstellung des deutschen Kunstmärchens von Wieland bis Peter Rühmkorf ..." (11): The problematic word here is "umfassend." Wührl's study despairs of the possibility of a definition of the *Kunst-märchen* but then declares all *Kunstmärchen* to be comprehendable as tales of the fantastic. Under the single rubric of *das Wunderbare* he organizes six chronological and unequal strands of investigation (*Längsschnitte*) which are to be considered fully symptomatic of this literary extension of the Märchen form: *das Wunderbare* as "Belustigung der Einbildungskraft," "symbolisches Traumbild," "philosophische ... Allegorie," "verfremdeter Alltag," "Dämonismus ... Nachtstück," and finally as "Travestie." This seems a coverup for a too narrow basic premise. It does not adequately account for science fiction or the various narrative forms dealing with horror and the grotesque. Wührl has suggested that his book might also be used as a *Nachschlagewerk* for analyses of individual *Kunstmärchen* (over 60), and that probably will be the best use to which it can be put. (R.M.)

Zach, Wolfgang. *Poetic Justice: Theorie und Geschichte einer literarischen Doktrin. Begriff--Idee--Komödienkonzeption.* (Buchreihe der Anglia: Zeitschrift für Englische Philologie, Bd. 26.) Tübingen: Niemeyer, 1986. Pp. 559. DM 178.00.

The earlier sections of this solid study trace the concept of "poetic justice" since antiquity. A unique and persistent association of the concept with comedy is established and this is examined from Aristophanes to Corneille, from Dryden to Steele, and then by means of an in-depth study of John Gay's *Beggar's Opera*--through 1800. Section IV broadens the discussion to poetics in general and England and Germany (some-what also to France) in particular. Three dimensions of the connection between "Poetic Justice" and comedy are seen: "weltanschaulich-religiös," "moralisch-didaktisch," and "ästhetisch-kulinarisch."

With the onset of a Romantic poetics in Germany and England moral purpose and the rationalistic-utilitarian world view of the mid-eighteenth century gave way to Romantic imagina-tion, sensuality, and moral freedom. Kant especially played a significant role in the uncoupling of aesthetics and ethics. "In der Romantik haben wir gerade das Vergnügen am Wilden, Abrupten, Bösen, Chaotischen, am Fragmentarischen und der Verfremdung als hohe ästhetische Werte bezeichnet gefunden" (439). The analysis of the rejection by English Romanticists of moral didactic intent is the more convincing for its coverage--Blake, Keats, Percy B. Shelley, Payne, Knight,

Byron, and John Stuart Mills. A.W. Schlegel and Kant are
summoned most often for the German argument against a need
for poetic justice. More attention to Kleist and Tieck would
have been welcome, but then they were practitioners, not
preachers of Romantic comedy. (R.M.)

See also Köhnke, Kunisch, Schwering, Zons ("German 3. Eichendorff"); Seibicke ("Fouqué"); Perraudin ("Heine").

3. STUDIES OF AUTHORS

ARNIM, ACHIM VON

See Sauer ("German 2. General"); Frühwald, Gajek, Püschel
("Arnim, Bettina von"); Köhnke ("Eichendorff"); Perraudin
("Heine"); Paulin ("Tieck").

ARNIM, BETTINA VON

Bäumer, Konstanze. *"Bettine, Psyche, Mignon": Bettina von
Arnim und Goethe.* (Stuttgarter Arbeiten zu Germanistik,
139.) Stuttgart: Akademischer Verlag, 1986. Pp. 315.

Bäumer begins with a review of recent efforts to correct
popular misconceptions about B. v. Arnim and her work.
Particularly *Goethes Briefwechsel mit einem Kinde* has
resisted proper interpretation by formal analysis because
it is a "mixed media" work in the best Romantic tradition:
autobiographical elements are combined with diary entries,
lyric poetry, anecdotes, travelogues, aphorisms, and recol-
ections of dreams. Of importance is also that the *Briefwechsel* is a work of Bettina's later years and thus influenced
by a historical perspective and by Bettina's more recent
friendships. Bäumer renders an in-depth analysis of significant factors determining the genesis and development of
the manuscript in relation to Bettina's view of Goethe and
his work. Her comparison of the *Briefwechsel* with Bettine's
subsequent work shows that the Goethe book served as a point
of departure for all of Bettina's subsequent literary efforts.
Interesting additional materials (such as the scores of
Bettina's compositions) and an excellent bibliography make
this book a superb addition to B. v. Arnim scholarship.
(Helene M. Kastinger Riley, Clemson University)

Frühwald, Wolfgang. "'Mephisto in weiblicher Verkleidung.'
Das Werk Bettine von Arnims im Spannungsfeld von Romantik
und sozialer reform (mit 1 Abb.)." *JFDH* (1985): 202-22.

In this stimulating and well-researched article with a
wide scope of rather loosely connected themes Frühwald
starts by discussing the painting "Io" by Correggio--a copy
of which Bettina kept in her study--as a metaphor for her
life and a leitmotif for her writing and thinking. In Achim
von Arnim's sonnet "Dichterliebe. Io von Correzzio," which
he inserted into his novel *Ariel's Offenbarungen* (1804), the
picture of Io served to express never-ending but always un-
fulfilled love. In the dual sense of loving poets (Goethe
and Arnim) or being loved by poets, and as a poetical symbol
for a love that thrives on remembrance and longing, "Dichterliebe" played a prominent role in Bettina's life. Frühwald
also provides us with a key to understanding Bettina's frequent use of biblical language in her writings. He sees it
as a tool which she used very effectively to promote social
criticism in her later years. Frühwald's contention, however,
that ·Bettina wronged Savigny and did great injustice to him
in connection with his handling of the Grimm affair is questionable. Finally, of interest is Frühwald's treatment of
Bettina's well-known love of nature, which he discusses with a
view to the Romantic topos of the tree as a symbol of life
and personal freedom for the individual. (K.B.)

Gajek, Bernhard. "Bettina von Arnim (1785-1859): von der
Romantik zur sozialen Revolution." Pp. 9-26 in Wolfgang
Böhme, ed., *"Die Liebe soll auferstehen"*: *die Frau im
Spiegel romantischen Denkens.* (Herrenalber Texte, 59.)
Karlsruhe: Evangelische Akademie Baden, 1985. Pp. 103. DM 5.80.

This article is yet another survey biographical study of
Bettina's "life and works"--old research rehashed. In connection with the 200th anniversary of Bettina's birthday, West
German researchers have "rediscovered" Bettina. Recently
quite a few attempts have been made to see her writings again
through a mainly religiously or mythologically tinted lens.
Gajek picks up the pieces of metaphysical Bettina research
where renowned postwar researchers like Schellberg/Fuchs and
Bergemann have left them. More contemporary sociohistorical
perspectives of Bettina from the GDR, or feminist views from
America, are largely ignored. Hence, some assertions re-
surfacing in this article have meanwhile been devalued or
even rejected by other researchers, e.g., the myth of Bettina's
happy and undisturbed childhood or her unflinching support
for the emancipation of Jews when she was still "ein halbes
Kind." Debatable from a feminist point of view is also
Gajek's assumption that the difficulties in Bettina's marriage
with Achim came largely from her wanting him to be a productive and successful writer, a desire Achim resisted. One
interesting aspect, though, is the reference to Sailer's

religious influence on the young Bettina in Landshut--even
though Schleiermacher's later influence in Berlin should be
weighted very carefully against it. Bettina von Arnim's
biography is by now certainly in need of a reevaluation.
However, recent international research should be taken into
account and there is also good reason to wait for the publication of further archival materials. (K.B.)

Gajek, Enid Margarete. "Bettine von Arnim und Goethe." Pp.
    27-44 in Wolfgang Böhme, ed., *"Die Liebe soll auferstehen"*:
    die Frau im Spiegel romantischen Denkens. (Herrenalber Texte,
    59.) Karlsruhe: Evangelische Akademie Baden, 1985. Pp. 103.
    DM 5.80.

    This is E.M. Gajek's second article about Bettina. The
first article about Bettina and Pückler--in style and content
similarly "hausbacken"--was published in the *Bettine von
Arnim Ausstellungskatalog des Freien Deutschen Hochstifts
1985*. Bettina's love story ("Die Geschichte der Liebe") with
Goethe is narrated on the basis of Bergemann's detailed earlier
research, with a heavy sprinkling of mythological and religious cross-references. Once again, Goethe (and likewise in
Gajek's other article, Pückler) is uncritically cast as
Bettina's "master," the main reason for her literary endeavors,
if not for her whole existence. Gajek seems to be unaware
of the existence of recent feminist research on Bettina, precisely challenging and modifying these assumptions of long
standing. *Goethes Briefwechsel mit einem Kinde*--the tangible
result of Bettina's involvement with Goethe--was certainly
not written just to express love and adoration for the "sage
in Weimar," but should also be recognized as an attempt at
female self-assertion and self-portrayal cast against the
background of Romantic thought and philosophy. Gajek's
article is at times also flawed by vague or misleading statements, such as the assertion that Bettina's monument of
Goethe never existed. All in all, this article reveals a
lack of in-depth understanding and familiarity with recent
critical research on Bettina. (K.B.)

Mattenklott, Gert. "Romantische Frauenkultur: Bettina von
    Arnim zum Beispiel." Pp. 123-43 in Hiltrud Gnüg and Renate
    Möhrmann, eds., *Frauen Literatur Geschichte: schreibende
    Frauen vom Mittelalter bis zur Gegenwart*. Stuttgart:
    Metzler, 1985.

Mattenklott attempts a very personal biographical portrait
of Bettina which is modeled with a view to convergence of
places of work and residence between himself and her--namely,
Marburg, Frankfurt am Main, and Berlin. In addition, Bettina
serves Mattenklott as a typical example of the women Romantics who created themselves by ceaseless letter writing.
By trespassing the boundaries of intimacy and confidentiality,
these women tried to achieve public trust, influence, and
recognition in a society that did not care very much about
granting them public positions. Mattenklott's article
displays a few captivating ideas, such as his sociohistorical
interpretation of a Bettina text passage about the destruction of the Berlin theater by fire. However, the article is
also flawed by some minor biographical errors such as naming
Wieland instead of Tieck as the person nursed by Bettina in
Munich. More serious is Mattenklott's flawed assumption--
persistently reiterated in West German research--that Bettina
was already in her youth an advocate for Jews and Jewish
rights, which he sees as an act of rebellion against her
bourgeois family. The truth of the matter is that it is
quite easy to find text passages that reveal that the younger
Bettina shared the anti-Semitic feelings of her time and
environment up to her late married years. Rahel Varnhagen
once poignantly spoke of Bettina's "Frankfurter Judenhaß."
(K.B.)

Patsch, Hermann. "'Ob Ich Dich Liebe, Weiss Ich Nicht':
Goethe und ein Wechselgedicht zwischen Bettina von Arnim
und Friedrich Schleiermacher." *ZDP* 104,4 (1985):   542-54.

Patsch, who is apparently preparing a book about "Schleier-
machers poetische Versuche," produced this well-documented
article about Bettina's relationship with Schleiermacher
as a by-product. Bettina's attitude toward Schleiermacher,
especially in her childlike self-portrayal, is reminiscent
of her bond with Goethe. Therefore it is very regrettable
that the bulk of the 14 letters that she wrote to Schleiermacher were auctioned off in 1929 and have been missing since
then. In July 1775 a short poem was published anonymously
in the literary journal *Iris*. It was attibuted by nineteenth-
century research to the young Goethe in connection with his
"Sesenheimer Lieder." This assumption lacks certainly and
is still controversial. Fifty-six years later, Bettina
wrote a poem on March 13th, 1831 (this date has been established by Patsch), which she sent to Schleiermacher as a
poetic answer to a public church sermon of his. Schleier-

macher responded immediately with a poem of his own, building
on the imagery Bettina had used. Part of Bettina's poetry
was obviously modeled--unconsciously, as Patsch thinks--on
this poem, which was supposedly by Goethe. Thus it needs to
be assumed that Bettina was acquainted with Goethe's poem,
in all likelihood from the time she spent with Sophie von
La Roche and her circle. (K.B.)

Püschel, Ursula. "Vor dem großen Kompromiß." NDL 33 (1985):
107-21.

　　Püschel's article about an important year in the life of
the young Bettina is rather essayistic in nature. In fact,
it can hardly be called a research paper since it lacks any
vital references such as footnotes or a bibliography. Nevertheless it is easily recognizable that Püschel draws heavily
from Sibylle von Steinsdorff's book about Bettina and Max
Prokop von Freyberg. In 1810 Bettina had come to an absolute
height in the development of her life. She stood in the
center of a network of affectionate affiliations which
included Goethe, Beethoven, and Achim von Arnim, as well as
Max Prokop, the latter two being in direct rivalry for her
love and commitment. Bettina's decision to marry Arnim and
have children with him came not without a good deal of hesi-
tation and wavering on her side. To this, and also to the
kind of skillful diplomacy Bettina employed in mediating
between her two suitors, Püschel draws special attention.
Her readable article presents nothing new but her own way
of putting the psychological pieces of these relationships
together. (K.B.)

See also Isselstein ("Varnhagen von Ense, Rahel").

BEETHOVEN

See Püschel ("Arnim, Bettina von").

BÖHME

See Anton ("Eichendorff").

BONAVENTURA

Brough, Neil, and R.J. Kavanagh. "Kreuzgang's Precursors:
Some Notes on the Nachtwachen des Bonaventura." GL&L N.S.
39 (1985-86): 173-92.

The learned and highly interesting essay traces the night watchman figure from sixteenth-century English literature, especially Dekker, and in the German tradition through the medieval *Tagelied*, Hans Sachs, and the Faust puppet plays. Astonishing is the extent to which Bonaventura synthesizes, "consciously or unconsciously," the features of the tradition: warning of Judgment Day, hindrance of illicit lovers, social satire, association with Hanswurst, combat with the immunity from the Devil, etc. (J.L.S.)

Pribic, Rado. "Kreuzgang: The Alienated Hero of the *Nachtwachen*." *ActaG* 17 (1984): 21-28.

Categorizes the narrator's alienation by citing and paraphrasing the text. A minor contribution, especially as it does not address the still potent force of a betrayed idealism against which the narrator's nihilism rebels. (J.L.S.)

Sammons, Jeffrey L. "In Search of Bonaventura: The *Nachtwachen* Riddle 1965-1985." *GR* 61 (1986): 50-56.

A review article on contemporary *Nachtwachen* scholarship with emphasis on the authorship problem, from which some conclusions are drawn concerning criticism's need for identifiable authors.

See also Loquai, Sauer ("German 2. General").

Reviews of books previously listed:

FLEIG, Horst, *Literarischer Vampirismus: Klingemanns "Nachtwachen von Bonaventura"* (see *RMB* for 1985, p. 327), rev. by A. Drijard in *EG* 41 (1986): 221-22; by Jeffrey L. Sammons in *GQ* 59 (1986): 651-53; HUNTER-LOUGHEED, Rosemarie, *Die Nachtwachen von Bonaventura: ein Frühwerk E.T.A. Hoffmanns?* (see *RMB* for 1985, p. 328), rev. by Horst Fleig in *MHG* 31 (1985): 102-05; by James M. McGlathery in *GSR* 9 (1986): 150-51; by Wolfgang Paulsen in *Seminar* 22 (1986): 264-65.

BÖRNE

See Hay, Mayer ("German 2. General"); Enzensberger ("Heine").

BRENTANO

Behrens, Jürgen, et al. *Clemens Brentano: Sämtliche Werke und Briefe*, vol. 22, 1: *Religiöse Werke* I, part I, *Die Barmherzigen Schwestern. Kleine religiöse Prosa.* Ed. Renate Moering. Stuttgart: Kohlhammer, 1985. Pp. 847.

Behrens, Jürgen, et al. *Clemens Brentano: Sämtliche Werke und Briefe*, vol. 24, 1: *Religiöse Werke III: Lehrjahre Jesu*, part I, *Erstes Lehrjahr, Mai bis Dezember 1821. Zweites Lehrjahr, Erster Abschnitt, Januar bis Juli 1822.* Ed. Jürg Mathes. Stuttgart: Kohlhammer, 1983. Pp. 475.

Rev. by Alfred Riemen in *Aurora* 45 (1985): 336-41.

This volume contains the first section of the middle part of Brentano's planned trilogy on the life of Christ based on his rendering of Anna Katharina Emmerick's visions. During his lifetime he edited part 3, *Das bittere Leiden unsers Herrn Jesu Christi*, and saw it through to published form (1833), and he prepared much of part 1, *Leben der heil. Jungfrau Maria* (which contains the youth of Christ) for publication, until death intervened in 1842 and this task was then completed by Pater Schmöger, who had been granted access to the poet's posthumous Dülmen papers. This central section is, therefore, the least reworked of the three volumes, and represents, stylistically speaking, the least unified. Entries for certain days are brief--some consisting of only a few key words--others more extensive, and others break off *in medias res*. The account concludes with the story of Jesus at the well with the Samaritan women. The full extent of Jürg Mathes's editorial expertise will only come to the fore when the entire critical apparatus appears. (J.F.F.)

Behrens, Jürgen, et al. *Clemens Brentano: Sämtliche Werke und Briefe*, vol. 22, 2: *Religiöse Werke III: Lehrjahre Jesu*, part I, *Zweites Lehrjahr, Zweiter abschnitt: August-Dezember 1822.* Ed. Jürg Mathes. Stuttgart: Kohlhammer, 1985. Pp. 531.

Boetius, Henning. *Der andere Brentano: Nie veröffentlichte Gedichte. 130 Jahre Literatur-Skandal.* Frankfurt am Main: Eichborn, 1985. Pp. 207. DM 28.00.

See Krättli, below.

According to the jauntily and somewhat irreverently written preface, Brentano's antipathy toward the publication of his poetry has led to both a scandal and puzzle among philologists; the scandal centers on the sad state of the extant editions of his verse--none of which are accurate--and the puzzle stems from speculation as to why this intolerable condition has been tolerated for such an inordinately long time. Boetius, a maverick critic and contentious gadfly for his one-time colleagues at the Freies Deutsches Hochstift, argues that by tailoring the poems in strictly philological and "philistine" fashion, the editors of the lyric volumes of the forthcoming historical-critical edition run the risk of stifling those very "Brentanesque" features (such as cascades

of puns and other modes of wordplay or linguistic by-play)
that constitute the life's blood of his uniquely idiosyncratic poet. In the four categories into which he divides
the over 50 previously little-known Brentano poems of varying
aesthetic quality ("Poetic," "Political," "Parodistic,"
and "Psychological"), Boetius displays some "Brentanesque"
qualities of his own, especially in the background commentary
and explanatory annotations printed along with the verses.
A brief "Postscript" compares and contrasts pictorial representations of the mercurial poet possessed of a "quicksilver"
personality. This book should engender considerable controversy, unless the targets of Boetius's invectives decide to
condemn their one-time collaborator to critical disdain or
scholarly death through disregard. (J.F.F.)

Brandstetter, Gabriele. *Erotik und Religiösitat: eine Studie
zur Lyrik Clemens Brentanos.* (Münchner Germanistische
Beiträge, 33.) Munich: Fink, 1986. Pp. 300. DM 58.00.

This is a very richly textured study with an overriding
thematic constellation which has been treated before (Schiel,
Gajek, Frühwald, et al.), but never in such depth, elaborate
detail and systematic fashion (sometimes leading to such a
plethora of major categories, minor subheadings, and mini-
segments that the reader runs the risk of losing the red-
thread, but, nevertheless, finds even in the fabric of the
ancillary material interesting minutiae). In the first of
the three main chapters the critic presents an overview
of the biographical and poetological bases for the symbiotic
association of eroticism and religiosity in Brentano's lyrics
in a fusion of prayer and poem, and includes some keen insights into his status as "poeta marianus" (speaking from the
female perspective), as a passive object rather than an ag-
gressive subject in the process of artistic creativity, and
on frequent interchanges of male-female role models in his
correspondence as a kind of "erotic play of communication,"
and his idealized projection of woman as intermediary or
mediatrix. At the other end of the spectrum is the contrasting second part, "seduction and conversion," focusing on the
poetry to prostitutes (the prototypical role model being the
magna peccatrix, Maria Magdalena, who stands at the crossroads
between Eve, the original seductress, and Mary, the epitome
of salvation). Brandstetter is at her best when she deals
with specific poems such as "Treulieb" and specific figures
(Violette, Älia Lälia Crispis, etc.), since she can illustrate
convincingly the ironic tones of lyrics linking fallen women
with the Devil; the facade of art and the deception of sex;
the sterility of the prostitute's life-style, and the poet's

desire to convert her to the right path as he, himself, would
soon be converted to Catholicism. The last and longest section of the study, "temptation and redemption," treats the
topic in a great variety of forms and in somewhat diffuse
fashion, so that the tempo bogs down considerably. Excursions into figural typologies (à la H. Meixner), emblematic
or parabolic contexts, patterns of teleological or theological thinking (a kind of antidote on Brentano's part to the
fetish of his Romantic confreres for the unique and interest-
ting) reveal a great breadth of knowledge and erudition on
the part of the critic, but tend to pall on the reader as he
wades through long excursions into interpolations from
Solomon's Song of Songs, modern linguistic-semiotic theories
(the "word becomes flesh" or the "transsubstantiation of
language"). One must, on the other hand, admire Brandstetter's
confidence in her own convictions: she does not accept un-
equivocally the views of more prominent mentors and critics,
but rather challenges them on the basis of textual evidence,
in many instances quite effectively. (J.F.F.)

Brentano, Clemens. *Italienische Märchen*. Postscript by
   Maria Dessauer. Frankfurt am Main: Insel, 1985. Pp. 377.

Brentano, Clemens. *Sämtliche Erzählungen*. Postscript by
   Gerhard Schaub. Munich: Goldmann, 1984. Pp. 494.

   Rev. by Helene M. Kastinger Riley in *CG* 17 (1984): 346–47;
   by Heinz Rölleke in *WW* 36 (1986): 314f.

*Clemens Brentanos Frühlingskranz: aus Jugendbriefen ihm selbst
   geflochten, wie er selbst schriftlich verlangte.* Postscript
   by Hartwig Schultz. Frankfurt am Main: Insel, 1985. Pp.
   367.

Hosch, Reinhard. "Eine unbekannte Quelle und biographische
   Hintergründe zur Geschichte des schönen Bettlers in Brentanos
   'Urchronika.'" *JFDH* (1986): 216–33.

   Parallels in motifs and story line reveal that not only the
Hero and Leander legend could have served as the source for the
story of the Handsome Beggar in the *Chronika*, but also Giovan
Straparola's *Le Piacevoli Notti*, not only in its original
sixteenth-century Italian version but also its later German
adaptations (all of which were in Brentano's library). Even
more interesting are the possible biographical ties of the
tale to Hannchen Kraus, one of Brentano's strong female interests, who lived hermetess-like on an island in the Lahn
(with Gritha Hundhausen serving as intermediary), so that
this literary production stems from an amalgamation of the

re-creative reception of works from earlier times, filtered
through the prism of immediate personal experience. Good
philology and a healthy degree of common-sense biographical
interpolation enter into a happy union here. (J.F.F.)

Isselstein, Ursula. "Rahel und Brentano: Analyse einer
mißglückten Freundschaft, unter Benutzung dreier unveröffent-
lichter Briefe Brentanos." *JFDH* (1985): 151-201.

In contrast to past practices with regard to Brentano's
previously unpublished correspondence, where a short commentary preceded a bulk of letters, we have here a detailed
introduction and analysis followed by just a few key epistles.
After recapitulating the events surrounding the infamous
anti-Semitic insults hurled at Rahel by Brentano and the
revenge of her fiance, Varnhagen, who confiscated the poet's
unfinished manuscript for *Aloys und Imelde*, Isselstein
launches into an interpretation of certain epistolary features,
perhaps the most intriguing of which is the view that Brentano
projected his own problems into Rahel's situation, producing
a cleverly concealed piece of autopsychoanalysis in the
process. Annoying, however, is the practice of whetting the
reader's appetite with provocative conjectures, which remain
only partially or obliquely resolved—such as continual
allusions to a spiritual crisis among the German intelligentsia
in the wake of the French Revolution, without full disclosure
of what that crisis entails. Very persuasive, however, is
the conclusion that Brentano's escape into the security of
dogmatic religion proved as futile as the pseudointegration
of Rahel into a societal structure that she could not respect
and that did not help solve her real dilemmas. (J.F.F.)

Janz, Marlies. *Marmorbilder: Weiblichkeit und Tod bei Clemens
Brentano und Hugo von Hofmannsthal*. Königstein and Taunus:
Athenäum, 1986. Pp. 218. DM 48.00.

If one can accept the psychoanalytical premise on which
this study is constructed—that Brentano's failed symbiosis
with his late mother (in Hofmannsthal's case, with his absent
father) proved to be a trauma leading to a crisis of identity
in the son, which the latter sought to combat and overcome
through aesthetic creativity—then many of the pieces in
the Brentano jigsaw puzzle begin to fall into place. Yet
occasionally, Janz seems to chide other critics for not
drawing her own conclusions: e.g., she notes that even though
Erika Tunner saw the underlying ambivalence between mother
and prostitute in a work such as *Godwi* with its redundancy of
stone monuments, Tunner failed to detect it in the sirenic
attributes of the "fallen woman" or the unconscious sublimated

homicidal tendencies on the part of the author (and his
surrogate, Maria). In conjunction with the thesis that the
mother in the patriarchially dominated family around 1800
was so overtaxed that her doleful status under such intolerable
conditions is subsumed in the image of the "bleeding wound,"
and that she was condemned literally (and figuratively) to the
silence of death (the symbol of such mortification being the
statues of the Mother and of Violette, Janz regards the
fatal allure of many female figures in terms of a kind of
womb-tomb syndrome. On numerous occasions the post-Freudian
conclusions drawn from this pre-Freudian literature give one
pause to reflect and ponder: for instance, does the drowning
of Marie and the concomitant fall of her son into the water
really constitute a reversal of the parturation process? Are
the sugar barrel and the death-skull necessarily to be equated
with the "uterus" and the "vagina dentata" respectively? Why
does the self-inflicted suicidal wound to the heart by
Biondetta in the *Romanzen* automatically qualify her a "mother
figure"? On the other hand, it is certainly true that sin
and immorality in the same work are more fascinating than
virtue and chastity; even though Brentano, after painting
a lush, even lurid portrayal of the desecration of Biondette's
body by the diabolic Moles, inserts the verse: "Ich
erschrecke und muß schweigen," isn't his sadistic voyeurism
almost a Brentanian variation of the tongue-in-cheek Brechtian
dictum: "Erst kommt das Schwelgen, dann kommt die Moral"?
Very incisive, on the other hand, is the analysis of "wild
discourse" in *Godwi* (as an adjunct to the unbridled nature of
the "unruly novel") and its ties to the bacchantian verbal
intoxication and Bakhtin-like carnival atmosphere with which
Brentano counters the staid morality of the contemporary
bourgeois world. The song of the weaver from the *Diary of the
Ancestress* exhibits similar traits, insofar as lavish language
enables the speaker, even if only momentarily, to overcome
the anguish of being bereft of all companionship, "mutterselig
allein." A frustrated maternal symbiosis is found to be at
the roots of Brentano's quest for women and wives who resembled
his mother; for the fictive mortification of females, as well
as for central concepts such as "das gezwirnte Kunstphantom"
in the *Romanzen* (the resurrection of Biodette's corpse as
the grotesque golem Alia Lalia Crispis); for the much-in-
terpreted "schöne Kunstfigur" of the *Gockel* tale; for the
perhaps most "liberated" of his females, Perdita, in the
Galeerensklave; and even for Brentano's perverse fascination
for the wounds of the stigmatic Emmerick and his immersion
in Catholicism during the age of Metternich in order to
establish a common bond with the suffering and sorrowing
community of the faithful.

In footnote 49, p. 204, Janz claims that she has not intended to engage in a strictly psychoanalytical interpretation; but her text, in spite of a host of good insights into
the dark and dense areas of Brentano's poetic world, "protests too much," offering a psychoanalytic approach which,
although all-pervasive, is not necessarily all-persuasive.
(J.F.F.)

Klotz, Volker. "Clemens Brentano." Pp. 181-95 in *Das
europäische Kunstmärchen: 25 Kapitel seiner Geschichte von
der Renaissance bis zur Moderne*. Stuttgart: Metzler, 1985.
Pp. xii+412.

Rev. by Hans-Heinz Ewers in *Arcadia* 21 (1986): 317-23.

In masterfully concise feashion, Klotz imparts more insights
into the essence of Brentano's two fairy tale cycles in their
European panorama and uniquely personal context than others
have accomplished in lengthy, learned tomes. The duality
of narrative perspective (adult as well as childlike), the
Boschian/Dalian surrealistic landscape of *Gockel*, the inter-
relationship of overriding time-space structures, and the
dominant mythic and demythologizing components and their
contemporary historical correlatives in the *Rheinmärchen* open
refreshingly new vistas of understanding and appreciation.
(J.F.F.)

Krättli, Anton. "Der wahre Bretano: zur historisch-kritischen
Ausgabe oder Philologen unter sich." *SM* 66 (1986): 530-34.

In essence, a sober and sobering review of Boetius's above-
mentioned book. Krättli takes Boetius to task for expressing
Schadenfreude at occasional philological shortcomings of the
staff editors of the poetry in the historical-critical edition (an enterprise in which Boetius himself formerly played
a major role). In spite of unmasking attempts by earlier
editors to "Goethe-ize" Brentano or to "embalm" the anything
but moribund writer (and thus deprive him of his most
"Brentanesque" features) Boetius, according to Krättli, over-
estimates the extent and impact of the "literary scandal"
which his renegade study ostensibly exposes. (J.F.F.)

Richter, Dieter. "Brentano als Leser Basiles und die
italienische Übersetzung des *Cunto de li Cunti*." *JFDH* (1986):
234-41.

As Rölleke and Solms have demonstrated over the past few
years, Brentano's borrowing from his sources gives philologists
headaches. The poet's freewheeling adaptation of myriad
source materials in this instance makes it impossible to consider the original Neapolitan text of Basile as the sole basis

for the Italian fairy tales. One must also consider how
the later translations and their alterations, in turn, were
modified and incorporated into Brentano's work. Does such
industrious scholarship, however, enhance in any way our
appreciation of the poet's talents or does it just constitute
a case of philological busy work? (J.F.F.)

Rölleke, Heinz. "Im Vorfeld der Grimmschen Märchensammlung:
Neun Volksmarchënskizzen Clemens Brentanos." Pp.
11-25 in *"Wo das Wünschen noch geholfen hat": Gesammelte Aufsätze
zu den "Kinder- und Hausmärchen der Brüder Grimm."* (Wuppertaler
Schriftenreihe Literatur, 23.) Bonn: Bouvier, 1985. Pp.
238.

See *ELN* 17, Supp. 192.

Schad, Brigitte, ed. *Die Aschaffenburger Brentanos: Beiträge
zur Geschichte der Familie aus unbekanntem Nachlaß-Material.*
Aschaffenburg: Geschichts- und Kunstverein, 1984. Pp. 233.

Schenk zu Schweinsberg, Karen, ed. *Meine Seele ist bey euch
geblieben: Briefe Sophie Brentanos an Henriette von Arnstein.*
Weinheim: Acta Humaniora, 1985. Pp. 227; 15 illus. DM
48.00.

The correspondence (1798-1800) between Brentano's one-eyed
sister--nevertheless the "apple of his eye"--and Henriette
von Arnstein contains some revealing perspectives on Clemens.
We learn, for instance, that his once very close relationship with this favorite sibling was not as intense at the
time of her death (1800) as he would like to have us believe,
and that a certain disaffection with her difficult younger
brother may have been a factor in Sophie's quest for a new
confidant in the aging father-figure Wieland. (J.F.F.)

Schlaffer, Hannelore. "Gitarre und Druckerei: Clemens Brentanos
Schwierigkeiten beim Publizieren." Pp. 51-58 in Klaus
Grubmüller and Günter Hess, eds., *Akten des 7. Internationalen
Germanisten-Kongresses, Göttingen 1985: Kontroversen, alte
und neue,* vol. 7: *Bildungsexklusivität und volkssprachliche
Literatur. Literatur vor Lessing--nur für Experten?*
Tübingen: Max Niemeyer Verlag, 1986. Pp. 237.

The guitar in the title is not only an instrument to accompany
the kind of improvisory song for which the poet was famous,
but it is also a metaphor for Brentano's antipathy toward
defiling the oral tradition in literature (so lauded by
Herder) by mummifying the living word once and for all in the
printed format. But if, in the iconographical tradition of
the guitarist (who, in turn, was replaced by the pianist),

then why does the critic not cite Werdo Senne from *Godwi* as a prime candidate for such displacement? Thought-provoking, however, is the comparison of the impromptu rendition of the guitarist and the precision-tooled mechanics of the piano with the unprinted and published text, respectively, as well as the shift in Brentano's own attitude from the poetic guitarist to the eidetic evangelist and faithful copyist of the Emmerick visions. (J.F.F.)

Schlaffer, Hannelore. "Mutterbilder, Marmorbilder: die Mythisierung der Liebe in der Romantik." *GRM* 67 (1986): 304-19.

The stone statue of the mother in *Godwi*, an intimate reflection of Brentano's own late mother, reveals how life determines literature. Interesting is the hypothesis of a syncretic fusion of the Virgin Mary and Venus Anadyome in this same figure, the latter concealed behind the fact that the former holds a child in her arms, thus sublimating sexual fantasy into metaphysical flights of fancy. Such "chaste sensualism" is traced briefly in Eichendorff's *Marmorbild*, in which mother-beloved and child coalesce, but in which the heathen, Venus components can only be checked by a chaste counterpart, Bianca, and finally in Stifter's Nausikae from *Nachsommer*, the last vestige of Brentano's Venus-mother. A drawing of A.K. Emmerick fusing features of the nun with those of Luise Hensel are claimed to represent an unsuccessful attempt to reverse the practice of *Godwi* and have literature determine life. (J.F.F.)

Tismar, Jens. "Ein sinnentstellender Fehler in Brentanos Gedicht 'Am Berge hoch in Lüften.'" *WW* 36 (1986): 1-2.

The printing error in question entails a gender change from "zu der Herzliebsten" to "zu dem Herzliebsten," and this certainly clarifies much confusion in the poem caused by the apparent misreading of "Zu dir Herzliebsten" (or possibly even "Herzliebstem"), as the line appears in a handwritten manuscript now in the Freies Deutsches Hochstift. (J.F.F.)

Zierden, Josef. *Das Zeitproblem im Erzählwerk Clemens Brentanos.* (Trierer Studien zur Literatur, 11.) Frankfurt: Peter Lang, 1985. Pp. 178. Sw. Fr. 41.00.

Regarding Staiger's catch-all concept of "torrential time" or Alewyn's counterpart of "cyclical or circular time" as inadequate to characterize Brentano's entire oeuvre, Zierden's heavily documented investigation attempts to delineate the

poet's temporal concerns in more finely nuanced categories
and gradations. There evolve, for instance, two modes of
"circling in time," one of which is "empty," a mechanical
eternal recurrence (à la Cisio Janus) devoid of meaning and
leading to ennui, and another which entails a "fulfilled,"
meaningful repetition (the seasons) as guarantor of permanence
and the integration of man into the divine plan.

In a similar fashion, a dialectical stance can also be
ascertained for "frozen time" (when embodied in an edifice
from the past such as the Straßburg Cathedral). "Reisende
Zeit," on the other hand, which dominates in early works
such as *Godwi* or the *Chronika*, is basically monodimensional,
a negative experience ensuing when an absolute, exclusively
egocentric perspective prevails; its positive counterweight,
however, "hovering time," is marked by a sense of harmonious
equilibrium or mediation between time and eternity, between
the past and the future in a meaningful present coexistence.
The fact that the ideal of hovering is achieved, if only
fleetingly and at isolated moments, already in an early work
such as *Godwi*, would seem to suggest a kind of stasis rather
than kinesis in the poet's spiritual evolution and gives
further credence to the Gajek school which argues for continuity over dichotomy or development. (J.F.F.)

See also Deutsches Literaturarchiv, ed., Klotz, Lehmann,
Lowenthal, Sauer ("German 2. General"); Perraudin ("Heine");
Paulin ("Tieck"); Isselstein ("Varnhagen von Ense, Rahel").

Reviews of books previously listed:

BEHRENS, Jürgen, et al., *Clemens Brentano: Samtliche Werke
und Briefe*, vol. 12 (see *RMB* for 1983, pp. 313-14), rev. by
Alfred Riemen in *Aurora* 45 (1985): 333-36; vol. 17 (see *RMB*
for 1985, p. 330), rev. by Alfred Riemen in *Aurora* 45 (1985):
336-41; by Helen M. Kastinger Riley in *CG* 19 (1986): 82-83;
vol. 28,2 (see *RMB* for 1983, p. 314), rev. by Alfred Riemen
in *Aurora* 45 (1985): 333-36; BLACKALL, Eric A., *The Novels
of the German Romantics* (see *RMB* for 1983, pp. 289-91), rev.
by Lilian R. Furst in *CL* 38 (1986): 205-06; by Gerhard
Hoffmeister in *MLN* 100 (1985): 668-70; FETZER, John, *Clemens
Brentano* (see *RMB* for 1981, p. 277), rev. by Siegfried E.
Heit in *GSR* 9 (1986): 151-52; NEMOIANU, Virgil, *The Taming
of Romanticism* (see *RMB* for 1985, pp. 319-20), rev. by John
Francis Fetzer in *GR* 61 (1986): 127-29; by Gerhart Hoffmeister in *YCGL* 34 (1985): 145-46; by W. Wolfgang Holdheim
in *Arcadia* 21 (1986): 102-05; RILEY, Helene M. Kastinger,
Clemens Brentano (see *RMB* for 1985, p. 337), rev. by John
Francis Fetzer in *GR* 61 (1986): 177-78; by Achim Hölter in

WW 36 (1986): 315-18.

BÜCHNER

See Mahlendorf ("General 3. Criticism").

CHAMISSO

Hagen, Waltraud. "Beträge zur Erschließung deutscher romantischer Dichtung." *Zeitschrift für Germanistik* 6 (1985): 338-43.

Hagen highly praises the 1981 DDR edition of Chamisso's works (eds. Feudel and Laufer). He claims that the volumes retained many features of historical-critical editions, such as a responsible textual reconstruction and a wealth of supplementary material, while offering the public a reader's edition, emphasizing concision and up-to-dateness in its presentation (including the modernization of spelling and punctuation). He calls for a new, expanded edition of Chamisso's works, based upon the Feudel and Laufer edition, which will take into consideration Chamisso's complicated method of composition as well as the difficult and obscure history of the texts themselves. (C.R.C.)

Kuzniar, Alice A. "'Spurlos ... verschwunden': 'Peter Schlemihl' und sein Schatten als der verschobene Signifikant." *Aurora* 45 (1985): 189-204.

Kuzniar brings the discussion of the lost shadow to the linguistic level: Schlemihl's search for identity becomes the search of the signified for a signifier, and a metonymic interplay among the self, an absent signifier, and an alienated self. Indeed, the quest for the shadow grows in meaning beyond the limits of the work, and parallels the quest for a cohesive interpretation, which has eluded readers since the story's publication. Kuzniar demonstrates the manner in which many images and episodes thematize the uncertainty of the interpreter, as well as the major role that rhetorical prowess (the manipulation of the spoken word), exhibited through deceit and lying, plays among such major characters as the devil figure and Schlemihl himself. This fine essay opens the door to new ways of regarding Chamisso's masterpiece from a metacritical viewpoint. While looking carefully at Chamisso's language, Kuzniar implicitly questions the methods of some earlier critics who have contributed little more than confusion to the "Schlemihl" discussion. (C.R.C.)

Pille, R.M. "La venue de Chamisso à Berlin." *EG* 41 (1986):
24-35.

   Pille's biographical article attempts to document the
circumstances surrounding the arrival of the Chamisso family
in Berlin during the last few years of the eighteenth century.
(R.C.C.)

Teucher, Eugen. "Sprachlich-literarische Wanderungen in die
Vergangenheit. 6. Folge: ein Franzose als deutscher
Dichter. Adelbert von Chamisso." *Sprachspiegel* 41 (1985):
173-74.

   Teucher's brief biographical sketch attempts to introduce
the general public to Chamisso. Teucher labels the Romantic
poet a "Klassiker," who never truly found a place among the
other Romantics of the Berlin circle. Chamisso's difficult
status as a French emigré on German soil becomes another
focal point. (C.R.C.)

CONTESSA

See Klotz ("German 2. General").

EICHENDORFF

Anton, Herbert. "'Geist des Spinozismus' in Eichendorffs
Taugenichts." Pp. 13-25 in Hans-Georg Pott, ed., *Eichendorff
und die Spätromantik*. Paderborn: Schöningh, 1985. Pp. 205.

   A very disjointed account that touches on *Taugenichts* from
time to time but that mostly consists of very long, unselective
quotations from Böhme, Goethe, Heine, and others. Indeed,
Anton quotes Goethe's "Wiederfinden" for a page and a half
only to conclude "but Eichendorff is not Goethe" (23). The
Spinoza part of the title comes from Jacobi's discussion of
the philosopher's unitary-but-impersonal God, and presumably
the essay is out to show that *Taugenichts* takes some stand
on this notion. Unfortunately, not even the concluding
abstract is very clear about what this stand is. (W.C.)

Bormann, Alexander von. "Kritik der Restauration in Eichendorffs
Versepen." Pp. 69-90 in Hans-George Pott, ed., *Eichendorff
und die Spätromantik*. Paderborn: Schöningh, 1985. Pp. 205.

   Surely echoing the response of many readers, von Bormann
wonders why Eichendorff in the verse epics "has to deliver
yet once again his message" about the inadequacies of pagan
nature (75). The answer concerns Eichendorff's political

dissatisfaction with Friedrich Wilhelm IV, whom David Friedrich Strauß labeled the "pagan Romantic" king.

The importance of von Bormann's article lies not so much in this limited point, but in his constant suggestion that Eichendorff's critique of paganism is more complicated than usually allowed. (W.C.)

Hartmann, Regina. "Eichendorffs Novelle 'Das Schloß Dürande': eine gescheiterte Kommunikation." *WB* 32 (1986): 1850-67.

Heiduk, Franz, and Wolfgang Kessler, eds. *Der Wächter und Eichendorff-Kalendar.* (Aurora Bücherreihe, 4.) Sigmaringen: Jan Thorbecke, 1985.

A full catalogue of Eichendorff articles in *Der Wächter* (1918-1961) and the *Eichendorff-Kalendar* (1910-1930), the principal organs of Eichendorff criticism before *Aurora* (1929-).

Holtmeier, Irmela. "Eichendorff-Bibliographie." *Aurora* 45 (1985): 328-33.

Hörisch, Jochen. "'Larven und Chraktermasken': zum elften Kapital von *Ahnung und Gegenwart.*" Pp. 27-38 in Hans-Georg Pott, ed., *Eichendorff und die Spätromantik.* Paderborn: Schöningh, 1985. Pp. 205.

A close reading of Eichendorff's critique of high society in the masked ball chapter. Hörisch's interest in the "Charaktermaske," a term from the commedia dell'arte tradition for costumes identifying specific people, goes beyond Eichendorff; indeed, a good part of the essay is not about Eichendorff at all but is an (albeit) fascinating account of East Germans' politically motivated suppression of the very word "Charaktermaske." (W.C.)

Köhnke, Klaus. "Eichendorff und Novalis." *Aurora* 45 (1985): 63-90.

A more accurate title might be "Eichendorff und die Früh-romantik," since significant parts of the article concern Wackenroder, Tieck, and A. von Arnim, as well as Novalis. Köhnke delivers a solid, biographically organized synopsis of Eichendorff's concept of the artist's role. Like the early Romantics, Eichendorff came to see the artist as a "translator" of nature's great "hieroglyphic book"; however, "in Eichendorff's conviction, the categories of meaning do not derive from the 'human heart,' on which Wackenroder and Tieck relied, a subjective feeling that easily perverts to

wild imagining or even erotic seduction; rather, they derive
from religion's 'firm principles of faith'" (86). Unfortunately, the study does not content itself with being the sound
comparison it could be and insists on trying to bill itself,
with fragile or no evidence, as an influence study. For
instance, Köhnke takes the presence of light-and-dark images
in "Marmorbild's" closing songs as doubtless signs of a
"conscious coming to terms" with Novalis's "Hymen an die Nacht"
(74f). Strangest of such frequent (and unneeded) implications
is Köhnke's suggestion that Romana's name in *Ahnung und Gegenwart* somehow comes from (has an "inner connection with" [76])
a Novalis fragment not published until 1901. (W.C.)

Kunisch, Dietmar. *Joseph von Eichendorff: Fragmentarische
Autobiogaphie: ein formtheoretischer Versuch*. Munich:
Wilhelm Fink, 1985. Pp. 115.

A critical by-product of Kunisch's considerable work on
the historical-critical edition. The modest title gives no
hint of how important this book is for students of Romanticism
generally as well as for literary theorists. The study goes
far beyond a useful description of the autobiographical fragments and their place in Eichendorff's career, though it certainly also performs these functions. At heart the study is
an investigation of "fragmentariness" as a nineteenth- and
twentieth-century aesthetic category. Kunisch takes issue
with the easy divide, derived from early Romantic theoretical
writers, between the intentional fragments of "Universal-
poesie" and the accidentally "open" fragments caused by sudden
change in an author's circumstance (death, MS loss, etc.).
This distinction does not cover such first-person literary
forms as the diary, which is "open" neither cleverly nor
accidentally; the distinction also does not cover cultural
causes of not being able to finish a first-person account,
like the increasing alienation of the speaker from himself.
The autobiographical fragment is not a Schlegelian "form";
on the other hand, it is also not merely the "bits and
pieces of some reconstructable, unified life-description"
(84).

Only one of Kunisch's suggestions that should keep literary
psychologists busy is that nineteenth-century writers create
symmetrical, "closed" works of fiction precisely because they
cannot create closed autobiographies. Eichendorff's autobiographical fragments, then, are not to be seen as distinct
from his famous "completed" works; rather, the fragments
instigate the completed works. (W.C.)

Lindemann, Klaus. "'Deutsch Panier, das rauschend wallt':
der Wald in Eichendorffs patriotischen Gedichten im Kontext
der Befreiungskriege." Pp. 91-131 in Hans-Georg Pott, ed.,
Eichendorff und die Spätromantik. Paderborn: Schöningh,
1985. Pp. 205.

A lengthy, illustrated catalogue of poems and paintings that
associate the forest with German patriotism in the wars against
the French. Lindemann attributes Eichendorff's appropriation
of this symbol directly to his readings of Friedrich Schlegel's
poetry and seems to think that the patriotic meaning is a
"message locked up" in a mysterious forest symbolism (121).
The reader has to wonder how "locked up" and mysterious the
symbolism is--and how much lengthy background one needs to
understand it--since most of the poems quoted pretty readily
decode their woodlands as patriotic loci. Still, the study
puts emphatically to rest any suspicion that Eichendorff's
forest poems are simply nature evocations. (W.C.)

Lüth, Christoph. "Arbeit und Bildung in der Bildungstheorie
Wilhelm von Humboldts und Eichendorffs: zur Auseinandersetzung Humboldts und Eichendorffs mit dem Erziehungsbegriff
der Aufklärung." Pp. 181-201 in Hans-Georg Pott, ed.,
Eichendorff und die Spätromantik. Paderborn: Schöningh,
1985. Pp. 205.

Only the last, five-page section of the essay concerns
Eichendorff. Lüth wonders if in Eichendorff "we can observe
the conflict of education and professional training that
[the rest of the essay has shown] is unjustly attributed to
Humboldt" (195). From both fiction and nonfiction works,
Lüth concludes unsurprisingly that in Eichendorff "the
claims of the individual, religious belief, and poetry are
directly opposed to professional education and professionalism"
(198). Left tantalizingly hanging for future scholarship
is the question of what Eichendorff would replace professional
training *with* in a real-world education. (W.C.)

Martens, Wolfgang. "Zu Eichendorffs Nicolai-Bild." *Aurora*
45 (1985): 106-20.

Nehring, Wolfgang. "Eichendorff und E.T.A. Hoffmann: Anta-
gonistische Bruderschaft." *Aurora* 45 (1985): 91-105.

Neubauer, John. "'Liederlichkeit der Gefühle': Kritik der
Subjektivität in Eichendorffs Studie zum deutschen Roman
des achtzehnten Jahrhunderts." *Aurora* 45 (1985): 149-63.

Polheim, Karl Konrad. "Das 'Marmorbild'-Fragment Eichendorffs
im Freien Deutschen Hochstift." *JFDH* 1986: 257-92.
Contains a reprint of the fragment.

Polheim, Karl Konrad. "Marmorbild-Trümmer: Entstehungsprozeß
und Überlieferung der Erzählung Eichendorffs." *Aurora* 45
(1985): 5-32.

An interesting piece of detective work in which Polheim
pieces together the scraps that became "Die Zauberei im
Herbst" and "Marmorbild" to produce a revised view of the
order in which Eichendorff composed the Novellen. Polheim's
specific, surprising conclusion is that the final version of
"Marmorbild" was not finished "until between middle October
and early December 1817" (32), in contrast with the usual
view that the story was finished by March 15, 1817, when
Eichendorff announced its conclusion to Fouqué. Though
Polheim perhaps too laboriously insists and reinsists that
Eichendorff *did* work hard on revisions, the Eichendorff
scholar can only be fascinated by the careful parallel passage
studies showing Eichendorff's reworking of G.E. Happel's
1687 "Die seltzahme Lucenser-Gespenst." (W.C.)

Pott, Hans-Georg, ed. *Eichendorff und die Spätromantik*.
Paderborn: Schöningh, 1985. Pp. 205.

A collection of essays, sometimes important, from the 1984
"Eichendorff Dazwischen" conference of the Eichendorff
Institut an der Universität Düsseldorf. As one might expect
from such a conference title, the essays as a group have no
coherent thematic ends; Pott's introduction confesses correctly that the title should not mislead one to expect a
unified literary-historical investigation of Eichendorff's
place in late Romanticism. The book, rather, is divided in
half between close readings of *Taugenichts*, *Ahnung und
Gegenwart* and the verse epics, and a (so-named) "kaleidoscopic" collection of essays, some not even about Eichendorff,
but about the writer's cultural environment. The papers in
this second section seem arbitrarily chosen, perhaps more in
an effort to include "big name" Eichendorff critics than to
identify, rank, and explore important influences on Eichendorff. Still, one need not be as editorially apologetic
as Pott is. The individual essays are often quite good.
Those with an identifiable bearing on Eichendorff are reviewed here separately. (W.C.)

Sammons, Jeffrey L. "'Welch ein vortrefflicher Dichter ist der
Freyherr von Eichendorff': Betrachtungen zu Heines Eichendorff-Urteil." *Aurora* 45 (1985): 137-48.

Schwering, Markus. *Epochenwandel im spätromantischen Roman: Untersuchungen zu Eichendorff, Tieck und Immermann.* (Kölner germanistische Studien, 19.) Cologne: Böhlau, 1985. Pp. 270.

The study of *Ahnung und Gegenwart* shows that Eichendorff finally cannot impose a historical "scheme" on the particulars of history. Schwering tries to propose this difficulty as a generic characteristic of the late Romantic novel in general. (W.C.)

Wittkowski, Wolfgang. "'Von der alten schönen Zeit': Eichendorffs 'Cupido' und Mörikes 'Mozart,' oder Morikes Mozart-Novelle, gemessen an Kategorien Eichendorffs." Pp. 133–55 in Hans-Georg Pott, ed., *Eichendorff und die Spätromantik.* Paderborn: Schöningh, 1985. Pp. 205.

The "old, beautiful time" in question is that of the rococo nobility before the French Revolution; the "Cupido" is a statue Eichendorff recalls in his 1857 essay "Der Adel und die Revolution." Wittkowski reads Mörike's story "as if" he were Eichendorff and finds that Eichendorff would disapprove of erotic matters toward which Mörike is more ambivalent. Very little here pertains to any given Eichendorff work. (W.C.)

Woesler, Winfried. "Frau Venus und das schöne Mädchen mit dem Blumenkranze: zu Eichendorffs 'Marmorbild.'" *Aurora* 45 (1985): 33–48.

The most important article on "Marmorbild" in some years. Woesler engages "what has up to now not been noted by any critic" (44), namely, that the Venus figure has a positive as well as a negative side, and that the "good" characters have ambiguous sides as well. The explanation for this--which Woesler might have tied together a bit more clearly at the end--seems to be: 1) that the Venus figure falls in a medieval tradition of conflating Venus and Diana, i.e., that she has chaste as well as voluptuous sides; 2) that following the Enlightenment exaltation of antiquity, Eichendorff could not simply discount pagan mythology, as traditional black-white readings of the Venus figure have done; and 3) that he particularly cannot discount such mythology when an artist figure like Florio is involved, who has to go through a "phase" of confused "fascination." This article should help put an end to stultifying, moralizing readings of the Novelle. (W.C.)

Zons, Raimar Stefan. "'Schweifen'; Eichendorffs *Ahnung und Gegenwart.*" Pp. 39–68 in Hans-Georg Pott, ed., *Eichendorff und die Spätromantik.* Paderborn: Schöningh, 1985. Pp. 205.

This article is really two in one, and the connection between them is largely left for the reader to intuit. On the one hand, Zons delivers one of the most important recent contributions to the study of landscape in Eichendorff. The "Schweifen" of the title refers to Eichendorff's practice of presenting landscape as an antisubjective flowing past the viewer, parallel to the view from a train or in a mechanical panorama. This type of viewing contrasts with two complementary forms that Eichendorff feared: being trapped *in* nature, and utterly departing nature ("Ausschweifen"). The second part of the essay hastily sketches an internalized, androgynous conflict Zons sees between the male and the female in Romanticism. Presumably the link between the two parts is that the "glance" of women and the "glance" of landscape are equivalent, as Zons tries to show in his analysis of the novel's opening scene. (W.C.)

See also Bänziger, Goodbody ("German 2. General"); Perraudin, Sammons ("Heine").

FICHTE

See Dürer ("General 3. Criticism"); Schmitz-Emans ("Jean Paul").

FOUQUÉ

Seibicke, Christa Elisabeth. *Friedrich Baron de la Motte Fouqué: Krise und Verfall im Spiegel seiner historisierenden Ritterromane.* (Sprach- und Literaturwissenschaften, 16.) Munich: Tuduv-Verlagsgesellschaft, 1985. Pp. 307.

While "Undine" secured Fouqué's popularity among the German masses, his reputation suffered greatly in the scholarly world as the result of his repetitious recalling of feudalistic and religious themes and concepts. Much of Fouqué's work has slipped into obscurity, and some texts are not readily available to the critic or student. Countering this trend, Seibicke evaluates some of his less well-known prose works, thus bringing them into a contemporary focus. Furthermore, she concentrates upon the strength of Fouqué's concrete images and upon the densely Romantic atmosphere that permeates his prose. Although Fouqué draws sometimes randomly from the standard pool of poular motifs, and although typically Romantic linguistic forms fill his writing, he nevertheless creates his own unique and fantastic images, and Seibicke

emphasizes this feature in her analysis.
She divides her study into three main parts. After out-
lining trends in Fouqué criticism, she directs her attention
to the following areas: firstly, to problems in the classification of Fouqué's novels; secondly, to the place Fouqué
holds in the intellectual-historical and "Ritterroman" traditions of the eighteenth century; and thirdly, to Fouqué's
magical atmosphere which opposes an inimical reality. She
concludes that Fouqué's novels occupy a position between
trivial literature and serious art. Although the reader's
path through Seibicke's book takes several detours, and
although her argument is sometimes difficult to follow (as
in the combining of several separate topics under a single
rubric, for example, in the second part), her contribution
to the literature on Fouqué, especially on his less popular
novels, proves to be very important. One hopes that her
generally positive assessment of her topic will spark new
interest in Fouqué's total production, and that this, in turn,
may make some of this Romantic author's obscure prose works
more readily obtainable. (C.R.C.)

See also Klotz ("German 2. General").

FREUD

See Jennings, Jennings ("Hoffmann, E.T.A."); Reeves ("Kleist").

GOETHE

See Goodbody, Klotz, Lehmann, Lowenthal, Mayer, Martin, Pizer,
Schubert, Wheeler ("German 2. General"); Bäumer, Frühwald,
Gajek, Patsch, Püschel ("Arnim, Bettina von"); Krättli
("Brentano"); Anton ("Eichendorff"); Perraudin ("Heine");
Tismar ("Hölderlin"); Birus ("Jean Paul"); Paulin ("Tieck");
Ragusa 3 ("Italian 3. Manzoni").

GRIMM, JACOB and WILHELM

See Hay ("German 2. General"); Rölleke ("Brentano").

GÜNDERODE

See Schinkel ("German 2. General").

HAUFF

See Klotz ("German 2. General").

HEBBEL

See Hay ("German 2. General.")

HEGEL

See Chase ("General 3. Criticism"); Mayer, Pizer ("German 2. General"); Brüggemann, Hosfeld ("Heine").

HEINE

Banuls, André. "Heine en vers français." Pp. 229-50 in Jean Moes and Jean-Marie Valentin, eds., *De Lessing à Heine: un siècle de relations littéraires et intellectuelles entre la France et l'Allemagne. Offerts à Pierre Grappin pour son soixante-dixième anniversaire.* Paris: Didier-Erudition, 1985. Pp. 340.

The original translations of Heine's poems into French were prose paraphrases. Banuls gives examples of 23 poems that he has translated into French verse with alternating rhyme. (J.L.S.)

Bark, Joachim. "'Versifizirtes Herzblut.' Zu Entstehung und Gehalt von Heines 'Romanzero.'" *WW* 36 (1986): 86-103.

In what looks like an introduction to an edition of *Romanzero* for the general reader, Bark makes perceptive observations on structure, genre, and themes. (J.L.S.)

Bellmann, Werner. "'Der Kaiser von China.' Anmerkungen und Materalien zu Heines Zeitgedicht." *WW* 36 (1986): 81-85.

New explanations for the allusions in Heine's satirical poem against Friedrich Wilhelm IV. (J.L.S.)

Betz, Albrecht. "Commodity and Modernity in Heine and Benjamin." *NGC* no. 33 (Fall 1984): 179-88.

Betz shadow-boxes with the nonproblem of why Benjamin, in his studies of nineteenth-century Paris and Baudelaire, ignored Heine, who had allegedly first described "the commodity as the new fetish of the bourgeois world." He blames Karl Kraus for damaging Heine's reputation (though

Kraus's essay was probably more a symptom than a cause) and
adds the psychological speculation that Benjamin may have
suppressed his affinity with Heine. (J.L.S.)

Briegleb, Klaus. *Opfer Heine? Versuch über Schriftzüge der
Revolution.* (Suhrkamp Taschenbuch Wissenschaft, 497.) Frankfurt am Main: Suhrkamp, 1986. Pp. 458. DM 24.00.

Rev. by Rüdiger Scholz in *Germanistik* 27 (1986): 632-33.
Briegleb's comprehensive book contains a number of previously published items; those that have been listed in this
bibliography are his essays on Heine and Prussia, on Marx
calling Heine a dog, on a comparison with Courbet and
Baudelaire, and on Briegleb's failure to make Heine's utopia
relevant (*RMB* for 1985, p. 353; for 1983, pp. 343-44). As
far as I can penetrate Briegleb's bizarre style, which is not
very far (I must confess I abandoned the effort to read the
whole book as an insupportable waste of my time), his thesis
is that Heine was a Wandering (literally, "Eternal"), ultimately
disinherited Jew who labored under a psyche distorted by his
repressive mother, and, as an Eulenspiegel and *flâneur*, with
sarcasm and irony acted out his disappointment at the failed
revolution and his anarchistic, destructive rage toward the
bourgeoisie and the liberal fools, ultimately sacrificing
himself in martyrdom as a sign of his own and of Jewish ob-
solescence in the face of the true revolutionary utopia.
But it might be something else.
Briegleb is the most eccentric of all of today's prominent
Heine scholars and for that reason was a poor choice as
editor of the practical, widely used Hanser edition. In a
sense he is beyond criticism because he does not actually
make arguments; instead he forms an allusive and metaphoric
web, almost as though he were writing a modernistic literary
work with Heine's texts as his resources. He has a vast
command of these texts, which he constantly cites and re-
shuffles out of context, often with tendentious manipulation.
Sometimes real insights flicker out of the stew: there *was*
a facet of anarchism and destructiveness in Heine, and a
masochism that expressed itself in fantasies of self-immolation. But in general all the fancy writing is applied to the
familiar purpose of presenting him as an uncompromising
revolutionary with a vision superior to that of all of his
contemporaries except, of course, Marx. When, for example,
Briegleb dissolves Heine's ambivalent attitude to King Louis-
Philippe (intimately connected to his own poetic self-understanding) in an insistence on ironic, sarcastic, uncompromising hostility, it is simply a falsification of the record.
He brings a fervid imagination to bear, but the result, I am

afraid, is an imaginary Heine. Meanwhile, he is threatening us with a biography. (J.L.S.)

Brüggemann, Heinz. "Der bare Ernst aller Dinge. Heinrich Heine: London." Pp. 114–39 in Heinz Brüggemann, *"Aber schickt keinen Poeten nach London!" Großstadt und litera- rische Wahrnehmung im 18. und 19. Jahrhundert: Texte und Interpretationen*. Reinbek: Rowohlt, 1985. Pp. 317.

A Marxist-inspired rhetorical analysis of Heine's account of London shows that he was overwhelmed by an urban experience that threatened a loss of self and, though unable to find a new concept of poesy adequate to the new reality, critically and ironically absorbed and allegorized its alienation of the individual and commodity fetishism. The highly abstract, thought-provoking discussion is made a little questionable by the misapprehension that Heine could have been influenced by Hegel's *Aesthetics*. (J.L.S.)

Derré, Jean-René. "Paris vu par Heinrich Heine dans *De la France*." Pp. 71–80 in Roger Bellet, ed., *Paris au xixe siècle: aspects d'un mythe littéraire*. Presses universitaires de Lyon, 1984. Pp. 170.

An essay on Heine's enduring love for the quality of Parisian life and confidence in the people's potential for liberty and revolution despite his ironies, critiques, and disappointments. (J.L.S.)

Enzensberger, Hans Magnus, ed. *Ludwig Börne und Heinrich Heine, ein deutsches Zerwürfnis*. (Die Andere Bibliothek, ed. Hans Magnus Enzensberger.) Nördlingen: Franz Greno, 1986. Pp. 381. DM 25.00.

A compendium of all the texts, public and private, pertain- ing to the relationship and eventual conflict of Börne and Heine, including the full text of Heine's book on Börne, along with the observations of contemporaries on the conflict through 1851 and excerpts from an oddly selected group of modern commentators. There is otherwise absolutely no commentary except for the rather silly remark that journalistic criticism was as bad in the 1830s as it is today and that it has been imaginative writers rather than scholars who have contributed most to the discussion. Thus there is no effort to explain to the reader who Börne was (by no means super- fluous today) or to place the conflict into any sort of larger retrospect. Consequently the utility of the publication may be doubted, except as a handy reference for those already well informed. (J.L.S.)

Espagne, Michel. "Le changement de paradigme dans les manuscrits." *Annali della Scuola Normale Superiore di Pisa:
classe di lettere e filosofia*, ser. 3,13 (1983):   785-816.

Texts of Heine (and some of Hölderlin) are employed to
illustrate the application of the theories of Thomas Kuhn to
shifts of genre paradigm within manuscript revisions.   (J.L.S.)

Forster, Leonard. "Zu Heines 'Wo?'" *MLN* 101 (1986):   695-96.

A note suggesting that reminiscences of Lucian and Cicero
in the poem were mediated by a passage in More's *Utopia*;
persuasive as the echo may appear, it puts considerable
demands on Heine's uncertain Latinity. (J.L.S.)

Franklin, Ursula. "Two German Poets 'Autour d'Hérodiade':
A Spark of Heine and a Georgean Afterglow." Pp. 175-86
in Will L. McLendon, ed., *L'hénaurme siècle: A Miscellany
of Essays on Nineteenth-Century French Literature*. (Reihe
Siegen, 46.) Heidelberg: Carl Winter, 1984.

Plausibly traces the Herodias motif from Heine's *Atta Troll*
to Mallarmé's *Scène* and from thence to Stefan George's
adaptation in 1905. (J.L.S.)

Futterknecht, Franz. "Vom Verstehen des Dichters zum Verständnis
seines Werks: Möglichkeiten der literaturwissenchaftlichen
Bibliographie am Beispiel Heinrich Heines." Pp. 571-88 in
Georg Stötzel, ed., *Germanistik--Forschungsstand und Perspektiven: Vorträge des Deutschen Germanistentages 1984*, part 2,
Ältere deutsche Literatur; Neuere Deutsche Literatur. Berlin
and New York: De Gruyter, 1985. Pp. 628.

A plea for a revival of biography under psychoanalytic
and sociopsychological auspices leads into a précis of the
principles governing Futterknecht's own biographical essay
(see *RMB* for 1985, pp. 355-56). Futterknecht makes many
interesting and some necessary observations, but I continue
to be skeptical of his faith in the universality of psychoanalytic theorems that allow us to retrace rule-governed
processes of repression and displacement in a writer of the
past. (J.L.S.)

Galley, Eberhard, and Alfred Estermann, eds. *Heinrich Heines
Werk im Urteil seiner Zeitgenossen*, vol. 2, *Rezensionen und
Notizen zu Heines Werken von 1830 bis 1834*. (Heine-Studien,
ed. Joseph A. Kruse.) Düsseldorf: Hoffmann und Campe, Heinrich Heine Verlag, 1985. Pp. 651. DM 124.00.

The somewhat improbable project of exhaustively documenting
the reception of Heine (see *RMB* for 1982, pp. 308-09) is

already beginning to face reality. While the original plan
was to include the documents for 1830 to 1841 in one volume,
this period will now require five volumes, of which the first
contains 393 items for five years, and we are here still in
a relatively modest phase of reception, focused primarily on
Buch der Lieder and the *Reisebilder*. Where this will end it
is difficult to say, but if the project is really carried out,
there will be many fat volumes, dwarfing Heine's own works in
bulk. Doubtless this is an important chapter in literary
history, and it is certainly convenient for the specialist
to have the materials collected in this way, but a shadow
of disproportionate gigantism hovers about the undertaking.
(J.L.S.)

Gilman, Sander L. "The *Farceur*: Heine's Ambivalence." Pp.
    167-88 in Sander L. Gilman, *Jewish Self-Hatred: Anti-Semitism
    and the Hidden Language of the Jews*. Johns Hopkins University
    Press, 1986. Pp. xiv+161. $28.50.

    With an ingenious and important probe into Heine's conflicted
sense of self, Gilman places the problem into a larger theory
concerning German-Jewish repression of the original Yiddish
language and its association with the Eastern European Jew.
The essay is too controversial and suggestive to be discussed
briefly; however, Gilman makes some claims about Heine that
cannot be substantiated and in a couple of places it would
have been better if he had gone to the original texts rather
than drawing upon secondary literature. But his ideas will
need to be considered in the growing study of Heine's Jewish
identity. (J.L.S.)

Gilman, Sander L. "Heine's Photographs." *Hebrew University
    Studies in Literature and the Arts* 13 (1985): 222-50.

    Expanding upon Prawer's essay on the subject (see *RMB* for
1981, p. 298), Gilman, in a subtle argument that draws upon
early social attitudes to photography, shows that Heine at
first rejected the daguerreotype as scientific, inartistic,
mimetic realism, then applied it positively as a metaphor
of his exact, implicitly satirical representation "of the
hidden truths of an age or an individual," or as an itself
colorless, awkward promise of a more hopeful future. Gilman
offers a speculative answer to the question of why there are
no photographs of Heine. (J.L.S.)

Gilman, Sander L. "Nietzsche, Heine, and the Otherness of the
    Jew." Pp. 206-25 in James C. O'Flaherty, Timothy F. Sellner,
    and Robert M. Helm, eds., *Studies in Nietzsche and the Judaeo-
    Christian Tradition*. (University of North Carolina Studies

in the Germanic Languages and Literatures, 103.) University of North Carolina Press, 1985. Pp. xii+393. $32.00. Similar to Gilman's previous article on this subject; see *RMB* for 1983, p. 347. (J.L.S.)

Grappin, Pierre. "Lessing, Saint-Simon, Heine." *Tijdschrift voor de studie van de Verlichting en van het vrije denken* 10 (1982): 203-12.

Heine's prophetic hopes for a third testament and a third age of mankind were encouraged by Lessing's *Erziehung des Menschengeschlechts*, which prepared him for the Saint-Simonian doctrine; the Saint-Simonians, for their part, had translated and propagated Lessing's essay in France. Grappin's thoughtful presentation will be helpful in making Heine's appropriation of Saint-Simonianism more precise. (J.L.S.)

Grubačić, Slobodan. "Heines Doppelstrategie: die literarische Exekution Platens." Pp. 215-49 in Franz Josef Worstbrock and Helmut Koopman, eds., *Akten des 7. Internationalen Germanisten-Kongresses Göttingen, 1985: Kontroversen, alte und neue*, vol. 2, *Formen und Formgeschichte des Streitens: der Literaturstreit.* Tübingen: Max Niemeyer Verlag, 1986. DM 31.00.

Deals with the rhetoric of the polemic against Platen as a grotesque, carnivalistic allegory, though without confronting the question whether the rhetoric was *persuasive.* (J.L.S.)

Haberly, David T. "Heine and Castro Alves: A Question of Influence." *RF* 97 (1985): 239-48.

Attempts to resolve the apparently contentious question of the influence of Heine's "Das Sklavenschiff" on the Brazilian poet's 1868 abolitionist poem by arguing that the latter is composed less in imitation of than in contrast to Heine's model. (J.L.S.)

Hansen, Volkmar. "'Männchen auf Männchen setzen': der Doppeldruck von Heines 'Vermischten Schriften.'" Pp. 337-54 in Georg Stötzel, ed., *Germanistik--Forschungsstand und Perspektiven: Vorträge des Deutschen Germanistentages 1984*, part 2, *Ältere Deutsche Literatur; Neuere Deutsche Literatur.* Berlin and New York: De Gruyter, 1985. Pp. 628.

Heinrich-Heine-Institut, Düsseldorf, ed. *Heine-Jahrbuch 1986* (= *HeineJ 1986*). Hamburg: Hoffmann und Campe, 1986. Pp. 240; 8 illus.

The quarter-century volume of the *Heine Jahrbuch* continues
in the well-worn paths of the last 25 years of Heine scholarship. Rudolf Drux analyzes the decline of the poetological
and political employment of the Prometheus image from Goethe
to Heine and beyond. Ugo Rubini measures Heine's contradictory views on economics and industrialization against a
sketch of the economic history of the times. Susan J. Ringler
gives a complete bibliographical description of the only
autograph manuscript of *Florentinische Nächte*, located in the
Huntington Library in California. With his customary attention to detail, Fritz Mende researches the initially collegial,
later hostile relations of Heine with the nationalist republican Jakob Venedey. Gerhard Weiss provides a note on the
literary occurrences and appearance of the Paris morgue
mentioned by Heine, and Fritz Mende another on a previously
unknown German edition Heine used for his book on Shakespeare.
The remainder concerns acquaintances and contemporaries of
Heine: Varnhagen (Konrad Feilchenfeldt), Ludwig Marcus
(Michel Espagne), and Hoffmann von Fallersleben (Joseph A.
Kruse); Helmut Hirsch appeals to the North American Heine
Society for a biography of the German exile Karl Louis Bernays,
who ended his career as a U.S. citizen. Heine society communications, book reviews, running bibliography, and chronicle
of Heine events as usual. (J.L.S.)

Henning, Hans. *Heines "Deutschland. Ein Wintermärchen" in der
zeitgenössischen Rezeption*. (Werk und Wirkung: Dokumentationen
zur deutschen Literatur, ed. Hans Henning, vol. 3.) Leipzig:
Zentralantiquariat der Deutschen Demokratischen Republik,
1985. Pp. 305. Sw. Fr. 47.80.

Reproductions of the text of the *Wintermärchen* in the *Neue
Gedichte* version and of contemporary reviews in German, French,
and English, with annotations, and an essay on the reception
of the poem. (J.L.S.)

Höhn, Gerhard. "Adorno face à Heine ou le couteau dans la
plaie." *Revue d'esthétique* N.S., no. 8 (1985): 137-44.

A critique of Adorno's sole commentary on Heine of 1956,
which reinforced, under reversed values, the traditional split
of him into poet and prose writer. Adorno failed to see
Heine's strategy under the exigencies of censorship and the
commodification of art. (J.L.S.)

Hörhammer, Dieter. "Heinrich Heines *Ideen. Das Buch Le Grand*."
Pp. 212-34 in Dieter Hörhammer, *Die Formation des literarischen
Humors: ein psychoanalytischer Beitrag zur bürgerlichen
Subjektivität*. Munich: Fink, 1984. Pp. 240.

The essay on *Das Buch Le Grand* is intended as an exemplary application of the author's theory, developed primarily with reference to Sterne and Jean Paul, of humor as a reflex of bourgeois alienation owing to the impossibility of achieving human freedom under the exchange values of capitalist society. It appears that Heine's allegedly disconnected and associated text exhibits an awareness of his own alienation and his location within its antinomies. (J.L.S.)

Hosfeld, Rolf. *Die Welt als Füllhorn: Heine. Das neunzehnte Jahrhundert zwischen Romantik und Moderne.* Berlin: Oberbaum, 1984. Pp. 223.

Rev. by M. Espagne in *EG* 40 (1985): 562-63; by Jean Pierre Lefebvre in *HeineJ 1986*, pp. 190-91.

In a dense, difficult work of uncommon originality, Hosfeld interprets Heine in terms of contemporary poststructuralist theories, with particular reference to Bakhtin's category of the carnivalesque. Examined are Heine's politicized cultural criticism; *William Ratcliff* (ingeniously read as a parody of the Gothic mode, exhibiting a dissociated self in a decentered reality); *Lyrisches Intermezzo* (the multivoiced cycles employ metonomy and parody rather than metaphor); *Das Buch Le Grand* as a Menippean satire; and the Italian *Reisebilder*. One theme is to distinguish Heine sharply from Hegel. Heine's texts are "dialogues of the non-contemporaneity of a disunited epochal consciousness" (83); being is not substance but a constellation, a disparate field of forces; his outlook is analytic, not speculative, dialogic, not universalistic; there are no characters with necessary actions, no circumstance with necessary consequences, no linear flow of time, no centered subject with an inner dialectic of consciousness, no three-dimensional causal world, and thus no organic work of art in Euclidean space. One might ask whether Heine is not being fashionably modernized here, in a way that refuses perception into his compositional order and his firm, not to say rigid, stock of presuppositional terms; when Hosfeld speaks at the end of modern montage, one wonders if traditional prejudices are not emerging from a new critical vocabulary. He says rightly that Heine's poems require to be treated in cycles, but he does not so treat them, that is, in succession and in their echo relationship to one another, but typologically, split up into noncontiguous categories. But the essays are intensely intelligent and absorbing, furthur evidence that Heine criticism is beginning to undergo a maturation. It is therefore unfortunate and eccentric that Hosfeld cites Heine from the wholly obsolete Karpeles edition of 1898. (J.L.S.)

Kahn, Lothar. "Heine's Jewish Writer Friends: Dilemmas of a
Generation, 1817-33." Pp. 120-36 in Jehuda Reinharz and
Walter Schatzberg, eds., *The Jewish Response to German
Culture from the Enlightenment to the Second World War*.
Hanover and London: University Press of New England, 1985.
Pp. xvi+362. $32.50.

   Discusses some similarities in the careers of Meyerbeer's
brother Michael Beer, Rahel Varnhagen's brother Ludwig
Robert, Daniel Lessmann, and Moritz Gottlieb Saphir, each of
whom was in his own way a mediocre figure indifferently related to Judaism (all but Beer were baptized) and seeking
accommodation to the dominant order. It is an exaggeration
to call them "friends" of Heine; except for Robert for a
short time, they were no more than acquaintances--Lessmann
was more a friend of Heine's brother Max--and all of them
regarded Heine quite critically. (J.L.S.)

Kossoff, Philip. *Valiant Heart: A Biography of Heinrich Heine*.
New York and London: Cornwall Books, 1983. Pp. 217. $14.95.

   This popularly written, undocumented biography of Heine
must have been published virtually in secret, for it took
three years for news of it to reach me. Modesty in this case
is well justified. The bibiliography lists only obsolete
sources in English, some of them of notorious unreliability;
the most recent is dated 1957. Kossoff cannot distinguish
between fact and fiction, and "in some cases [the incidents
and events] have been transmuted into dramatic form," i.e.,
Kossoff himself fictionalizes vigorously. Naturally there
are errors of fact and judgment on almost every page, some
inherited from the dubious sources, others contributed by
the author, a few of these howlers. The author may be an
amiable amateur with a genuine admiration for Heine and a
love of liberty and tolerance. But such a book is harmful,
for it perpetuates ignorance, and a responsible publisher
ought not to be associated with it. (J.L.S.)

Kruse, Joseph A. "Heinrich Heine, der Deutsche, und die
Deutschen." *Bulletin des Leo Baeck Instituts* 71 (1985):
3-19.

   A well-written essay (originally a lecture to the New York
Leo Baeck Institute in 1981) examines the complex semantic
field of "Germany" in Heine's texts and aims at a differentiate
view of Heine's intimate relationship to Germany and of
Germany to him in past and present. (J.L.S.)

Mende, Fritz. "Resumé 1847. Heinrich Heines Vorwort zu Alexander
Weills 'Sittengemälde aus dem elsässischen Volksleben.'" *ZG*
(Leipzig) 7 (1986): 26-32.

Heine's unwillingly written, hardly encomiastic preface to his friend Weill's stories has been little discussed by scholarship, but Mende shows how in it Heine once again develops his fundamental requirements for responsible and realistic political literature. (J.L.S.)

Murat, Jean. "Heine et Novalis: naissance d'un cliché." Pp. 251-62 in Jean Moes and Jean-Marie Valentin, eds., *De Lessing à Heine: un siècle de relations littéraires et intellectuelles entre la France et l'Allemagne. Offerts à Pierre Grappin pour son soixante-dixième anniversaire.* Paris: Didier-Erudition, 1985. Pp. 340.

Heine's devaluation, motivated by his anti-Catholic program, of Novalis in *De l'Allemagne* established a cliché in France of him as a soft, sick, misty poet and blocked the French perception of him for a long period. (J.L.S.)

Nationale Forschungs- und Gedenkstätten der klassischen deutschen Literatur in Weimar and Centre National de la Recherche Scientifique in Paris, eds. *Heinrich Heine Säkularausgabe,* vol. 3, *Gedichte 1845-1856,* ed. Helmut Brandt, Renate Francke, Fritz Mende, and Hans Böhm. Vol. 6, *Reisebilder 2 1828-1831,* ed. Christa Stöcker and Karl-Heinz Hahn. Berlin and Paris: Akademie-Verlag and Editions du C.N.R.S., 1986. Pp. 316, 256. DM 28.00, 24.00 (subscription price).

With volume 3 the texts of Heine's poetry are complete in the East German edition. The order of the volume has much to be said for it. The two late collections, *Romanzero* and *Gedichte 1853 und 1854,* are followed by individually published poems, then by the substantial corpus of unpublished poems, divided into those clearly written before 1848, those associated with *Romanzero,* those associated with the "Lazarus" cycles, political and autobiographical poems, "Bimini" (with the variant of the prologue in an appendix), fables, poems addressed to the "Mouche," and a little potpourri of mainly occasional poems. Since many of Heine's late poems cannot be dated exactly, this categorical arrangement seems wise and useful. Volume 6 completes the prose works of the *Reisebilder*: the Italian pieces, along with their paralipomena. It may be confusing to the reader that the volume also includes *Schnabelewopski*; although it more or less belongs here chronologically, it was published in the first volume of *Der Salon,* so that the uninformed reader is unlikely to look for it in a volume entitled *Reisebilder.* (J.L.S.)

Newman, Caroline. "Cemeteries of Tradition: The Critique of Collection in Heine, Nietzsche, and Benjamin." *Pacific Coast Philology* 19,1-2 (1984): 12-21.

Traces a line from Heine's "burial" of the "ghosts" of the
literary past in *Die Romantische Schule* to Nietzsche's demand
for the timeliness of history and Benjamin's critique of fixed,
official, tradition immured in antiquarian collection. (J.L.S.)

Oehler, Dolf. "Heines Frömmigkeit als List der Vernunft.
Die Lektion aus der Matratzengruft." *Merkur* 39 (1985):
968-79.

Oehler wishes to cleanse Heine's late utterances on religion
and politics of ambiguity. The device is the ascription of
irony: anything that does not suit Oehler is parodistic or
means its opposite. Thus Heine's "piety" is a joke on the
bourgeois reader, and he emerges as an unequivocal propagan-
dist of communism. A look into Heine's private letters at
this time should be sufficient to convince anyone that this
is just another of Oehler's mystifications. (J.L.S.)

Oehler, Dolf. "Mythologie parisienne. Lecture d'un poème de
Heine: *'Soucis babyloniens.'*" Pp. 81-92 in Roger Bellet,
ed., *Paris au xixe siècle: aspects d'un mythe littéraire.*
Presses universitaires de Lyon, 1984. Pp. 170.

"Babylonische Sorgen," in which Heine bitterly expresses
his fear for his wife's safety after his death, is associated
with Baudelaire and read against the grain, as an attack on
post-1848 politicians figured as beasts and insects and as
a parody of the reactionary clichés about Paris. Oehler does
not seem to realize that Heine asserted his anxiety about his
putatively frail wife in Babylon-on-the-Seine years before
1848. (J.L.S.)

Oswald, Stefan. "Heinrich Heine: *Reise von München nach
Genua*--Ironisierung eines Genres." Pp. 134-41 in Stefan
Oswald, *Italienbilder: Beiträge zur Wandlung der deutschen
Italienauffassung 1770-1840.* (*GRM* Beiheft, 6.) Heidelberg:
Carl Winter, 1985. Pp. 207.

Heine's account of his Italian journey ironically reflects
and politicizes its literary predecessors. (J.L.S.)

Perraudin, Michael. "'Anfang und Ende meines lyrischen Jugend-
lebens': Two Key Poems of Heine's Early Years." *Seminar*
22 (1986): 32-54.

Close readings of Heine's first published poem, "Die Weihe,"
and one of the latest of *Buch der Lieder*, "Im Hafen," show
that they are full of literary and private allusions (including masked ones to his Jewishness), exhibit the increase of
his maturity and confidence as a poet, and are linked by an

orientation on Goethe's *West-östlicher Divan*. Excellent and illuminating. (J.L.S.)

Perraudin, Michael. "The 'Doppelgänger' Poem and Its Antecedents: A Short Illumination of Heine's Creative Response to His Romantic Precursors." *GRM* 35 (1985): 342–48.

Heimkehr 20 is part of a subcycle, "the original and essential 'Heimkehr' sequence," and contains echoes of J.B. Rousseau, Wilhelm Müller, Uhland, Eichendorff, Kerner, and, behind them all, a *Wunderhorn* poem; Heine is consciously reflecting and elaborating these antecedents. (J.L.S.)

Perraudin, Michael. "Heine and Wilhelm Müller, a Poetic Relationship." *Archiv* 222 (1985): 22–46.

The most detailed examination yet undertaken of Heine's relationship to Müller, exhibiting an intertextuality consciously pursued by the author and very likely recognizable by contemporary readers. With his many echoes, Heine transcends the model through the creation of a more modern persona with a clearer sense of alienation and a philosophical awareness of the hubris of modern man, but retains a "wish to regain something like the ancient consciousness" he thought he detected in the folk spirit. (J.L.S.)

Prawer, S.S. *Frankenstein's Island: England and the English in the Writings of Heinrich Heine.* Cambridge University Press, 1986. Pp. x+357.

Prawer approaches Heine's relations with England and the English much in the same way as he did those with Judaism and the Jews (see *RMB* for 1981, p. 298), with great thoroughness, learning, and critical insight. The book draws upon and supersedes Prawer's inaugural lecture on Heine and Shakespeare (*ELN* 9, supp. 136) and his more recent one on Heine's habits of caricature (see *RMB* for 1984, pp. 370–71). This must be an uncomfortable topic for an Englishman owing to Heine's fierce invective against England and the English, but Prawer tries his best to relieve Heine of the charge of insuperable malice and to stress his moments of admiration and respect. While he may sometimes go too far in this, the book, like its predecessor, is instructive, stimulating, and gracefully written. (J.L.S.)

Sammons, Jeffrey L. "Heine as *Weltbürger*? A Skeptical Inquiry." *MLN* 101 (1986): 609–28.

A reexamination of Heine's cosmopolitanism, stressing its limitations, Heine's German-centered outlook, and the lack of empathy that made it difficult for him to appreciate sensitively foreign cultures and literatures.

Sammons, Jeffrey L. "'Welch ein vortrefflicher Dichter ist der Freyherr von Eichendorff.' Betrachtungen zu Heines Eichendorff-Urteil." *Aurora* 45 (1985): 137-48.

Endeavors to explain why Heine was not more critical of Eichendorff despite their great ideological differences.

Seyhan, Azade. "Poetic Discourse as Metanarrative: The Critical Map of Heine's 'Harzreise.'" *GQ* 59 (1986): 19-33.

It was only a matter of time until the deconstructionists got hold of Heine's complexly organized texts in order to deny their organization and read them as semiotically anarchic, dismantling conventional codes to imply a new freedom in reduplicated irony. Seyhan takes the text at its word that it is a fragment, arguing that it short-circuits "categorical statements about the world," undercuts its own experiments in Romantic organicism, and questions its own assumptions, transferring interpretation and completion to the reader. There are some thought-provoking observations here, but the project, which involves some rather wayward allegorizations and makes Heine into a proto-postmodernist, is, in my view, to be regarded with skepticism. (J.L.S.)

Shedletzky, Itta. "Im Spannungsfeld Heine-Kafka. Deutschjüdische Belletristik und Literaturdiskussion zwischen Emanzipation, Assimilation und Zionismus." Pp. in Walter Röll and Hans-Peter Bayerdörfer, eds., *Akten des 7. Internationalen Germanisten-Kongresses Göttingen, 1985: Kontroversen, alte und neue,* Vol. 5: *Auseinandersetzungen um jiddische Sprache und Literatur; Jüdische Komponenten in der deutschen Literatur--die Assimilationskontroverse.* Tübingen: Max Niemeyer Verlag, 1986. Pp. 265. DM 26.80.

In Jewish cultural periodicals in the nineteenth and early twentieth centuries there is a change in the estimate of Heine from outraged rejection to Zionist enthusiasm. This article is an abstract of a dissertation that at last, one may hope, will illuminate the imperfectly researched topic of Jewish Heine reception. (J.L.S.)

Tengler, Heinz F. "The Role of Judaism in Heine's Life and Work: Continuity in Change." *ActaG* 17 (1984): 53-68.

Another in the series of now obsolete efforts to claim Heine for some form of Judaism. This one is marked by careless argument, slovenly scholarship, simplistic judgments,

selective quotations, and misinformation. A self-respecting
scholarly journal should not accept such contributions.
(J.L.S.)

Traeger, Jörg. "Napoleon, Trajan, Heine: zur Malerei des
Ersten Kaiserreichs in Frankreich." Pp. 71–86 in *Jahres- und
Tagesberichte der Görres-Gesellschaft 1984*. Expanded with
illustrations and reference notes as "Napoleon, Trajan, Heine:
Imperiale Staatsmalerei in Frankreich." Pp. 141–206 in Hans
Bungert, ed., *Das antike Rom in Europa: Vortragsreihe der
Universität Regensburg*. (U.R.: Schriftenreihe der Universität
Regensburg, vol. 12, special printing.) Regensburg: Buch-
verlag der Mittelbayerischen Zeitung, 1986.

Traeger links Heine's mythifying figuration of Napoleon with
the propagandistic art that affirmed with traditional iconography the Emperor's royal authority and sacral aura. A
valuable contribution to our understanding of Heine's image of
Napoleon as well as of the way in which his imagination was
nourished by the visual arts. (J.L.S.)

Trilse, Christoph. *Heinrich Heine*. Leipzig: VEB Bibliogra-
phisches Institut, 1984. Pp. 199. DM 15.00.

Rev. by Slobodan Grubačič in *Germanistik* 26 (1985): 435;
by Joseph A. Kruse in *HeineJ 1986*, pp. 199–200; by Red. in
DU (East) 38 (1985): 318.
This undocumented *Bildbiographie* (89 illustrations) belongs
to a series that is an East German counterpart to the familiar
rororo Bildmonographien in the West. Probably one should not
bring many expectations to a product that is in the nature
of an extended encyclopedia article. The approach is generally
eulogistic (although one or two tender spots are brushed
upon), evasive of difficulties, in places simplistically
tendentious, and pinned into the crude categories of orthodox Marxist historiography. Some issues, such as Heine's
marriage, are not badly handled, but others are weakly
addressed, and the account of the inheritance feud is so distorted as to be almost silly. Surprising all the same is the
number of errors and old misconceptions; for example, the
marriage of Heine's parents is put into the wrong year, thus
silently perpetuating the legend of his illegitimate birth.
I counted over two dozen such inaccuracies. Altogether a
distinctly minor contribution to the understanding of Heine.
(J.L.S.)

Weber, Heinz-Dieter. "Heines Harzreise und der Tourismus."
DU (West) 38 (1986): 51–64.

Heine recognized tourism as an emptying of experience in
which everything becomes display, a loss of immediate natural
and aesthetic perception, but he was aware that he was a
tourist himself, and, though skeptical about nature mediated
by art, he saw that the traditional can be repressive and
primitive, and that the aesthetic experience of nature is
unavoidable in modern consciousness. (J.L.S.)

Weiss, Gerhard. "Heinrich Heines Bild von London: Beiträge
zu einem kulturhistorischen Kommentar." Pp. 336-42 in
*Staatliches Hohenstaufen-Gymnasium Kaiserslautern 1834-1984:
Festschrift zum 150jährigen Jubiläum.* Kaiserslautern:
Staatliches Hohenstaufen-Gymnasium, 1984.

A comparison with other writers on London affords examples
of what Heine perceived in a way similar to others and what
he saw with fresh eyes. Numerous interesting details on the
London of that time. (J.L.S.)

Werner, Michael. "Politische Lazarus-Rede: Heines Gedicht
'Im Oktober 1849.'" Pp. 286-99 in Günter Häntzschel, ed.,
Gedichte und Interpretationen, vol. 4, *Vom Biedermeier zum
Bürgerlichen Realismus.* (Reclams Universal-Bibliothek, 7893
[5].) Stuttgart: Reclam, 1983. Pp. 448. DM 11.50.

Werner interprets the poem by placing it in its historical
context, clarifying its allusions, describing its demontage
of conventional culture, and relating it to Heine's prostrate
but still revolutionary posture. (J.L.S.)

Windfuhr, Manfred, ed. *Heinrich Heine, Historisch-kritische
Gesamtausgabe der Werke,* vol. 7/1, *Reisebilder 3/4: Text,*
vol. 7/2, *Reisebilder 3/4. Apparat.* Ed. Alfred Opitz.
Hamburg: Hoffmann und Campe, 1986, Pp. 1,848 (paged through).
8 illus. DM 192.00 (subscription price).

The critical edition of the third and fourth volumes of
the *Reisebilder* is a major step forward. Any serious student
of Heine will learn from the painstaking accounts of their
complicated genesis, more thoroughly set forth than ever
before, and of the reception history, and from the detailed
annotation. Among the many valuable features is the attention
called to the first version of *Die Bäder von Lucca,* some of
which was scrapped to make room for the Platen polemic. A
great deal of space is naturally given to the latter problem
and its catastrophic echo. While there remains some room
for debate, the discussion is not only reasonably fair but
develops an independent and instructive perspective. Amidst
the tremendous learning in the commentary the amount of effort

that has been applied to the background and sources of the
Englische Fragmente and to the definition of the nature of
that text may be singled out for special praise. There is
an interesting essay on the British and American reception
of the *Reisebilder*, though here the English quotations seem
especially susceptible to misprints. In general, however,
the task of these volumes has been admirably executed, so
that they will be a major resource for all future Heine
studies. (J.L.S.)

Zinke, Jochen. "Amors bleierner Pfeil. Zu Heines Romanze
'Der arme Peter'"; "Tannhäuser im Exil. Zu Heines 'Legende'
'Der Tannhäuser.'" Pp. 69-81, 204-21 in Gunter Häntzschel,
ed., *Gedichte und Interpretationen*, vol. 4, *Vom Biedermeier
zum Bürgerlichen Realismus*. (Reclams Universal-Bibliothek,
7893 [5]). Stuttgart: Reclam, 1983. Pp. 448. DM 11.50.

Both interpretations are exemplary, informative close
readings that discuss models, show Heine's originality,
individuality, and modern social sensibility in reworking
traditional patterns, and touch on autobiographical aspects
without literalizing them. (J.L.S.)

See also Hay, Hohendahl, Mayer, Scheufele ("German 2. General");
Anton ("Eichendorff").

Reviews of books previously listed:

DRAPER, Hal, *The Complete Poems of Heinrich Heine* (see *RMB*
for 1982, pp. 307-08), rev. by Richard Gary Hooton in *HeineJ
1986*, pp. 186-87; EDERER, Hannelore, *Die literarische Mimesis
entfremdeter Sprache* (see *RMB* for 1980, p. 298), rev. by
Renate Böschenstein in *Germanistik* 26 (1985): 925-26;
ESPAGNE, Michel, et al., eds., *Cahier Heine 3* (see *RMB* for
1984, p. 363), rev. by Fritz Mende in *DLZ* 106 (1985): cols.
681-85; FRANCKE, Renate, ed., *Heinrich Heine: Buch der Lieder
zweiter Band* (see *RMB* for 1983, p. 346), rev. by Karl Pörn-
bacher in *Germanistik* 26 (1985): 933; FUTTERKNECHT, Franz,
Heinrich Heine: ein Versuch (see *RMB* for 1985, pp. 355-56),
rev. by Jeffrey L. Sammons in *IASL* 11 (1986): 303-07; by
Rüdiger Scholz in *Germanistik* 27 (1986): 633; GORDON, Jakob
Il'ič, *Heine in Rußland 1830-1860* (see *RMB* for 1983, p. 349),
rev. by Eberhard Reissner in *HeineJ 1986*, pp. 179-82; GRAB,
Walter, *Heinrich Heine als politischer Dichter* (see *RMB* for
1983, pp. 349-50), rev. by Jocelyne Kolb in *GQ* 59 (1986):
147-48; by Christoph Prignitz in *GRM*, 35 (1985): 358-59;
GRÉSILLON, Almuth, *La règle et le monstre: le mot-valise*
(see *RMB* for 1985, p. 356), rev. by Karlheinz Fingerhut in
Germanistik 27 (1986): 52-53; by Brigitte Nerlich in

HeineJ 1986, pp. 182–84; GUTJAHR; Herbert, *Zwischen Affinität und Kritik: Heinrich Heine und die Romantik* (see *RMB* for 1984, pp. 364–65), rev. by Gerd Heinemann in *Germanistik* 27 (1986): 634; GUY, Irene, *Sexualität im Gedicht: Heinrich Heines Spätlyrik* (see *RMB* for 1985, pp. 357–58), rev. by M. Espagne in *EG* 41 (1986): 226; by Gail K. Hart in *GQ* 59 (1986): 656–58; HÄDECKE, Wolfgang, *Heinrich Heine: eine Biographie* (see *RMB* for 1985, pp. 358–59), rev. by Rüdiger Scholz in *Germanistik* 27 (1986): 385–86; HOLUB, Robert C., *Heinrich Heine's Reception of German Grecophilia* (see *RMB* for 1982, p. 313), rev. by Michael Geisler in *Monatshefte* 78 (1986): 108–09; KLINKENBERG, Ralf H., *Die Reisebilder Heinrich Heines: Vermittlung durch literarische Stilmittel* (see *RMB* for 1981, p. 295), rev. by Wolfgang Monath in *Germanistik* 26 (1985): 934; KOPELEW, Lew, *Ein Dichter kam vom Rhein: Heinrich Heines Leben und Leiden* (see *RMB* for 1981, p. 296), rev. by Norbert Altenhofer in *Germanistik* 27 (1986): 634–35; MENDE, Fritz, *Heinrich Heine: Studien zu seinem Leben und Werk* (see *RMB* for 1983, pp. 356–57), rev. by Dieter Kliche in *WB* 31 (1985): 1753–56; by Jeffrey L. Sammons in *Arbitrium* 4 (1986): 68–71; NATIONALE FORSCHUNGS- UND GEDENKSTAETTEN, ETC., *Heinrich Heine Säkularausgabe*, vols. 7 and 7K (see *ELN* 9, supp. 135–36; *RMB* for 1983, pp. 358–59), rev. by Stuart Atkins in *JEGP* 85 (1986): 79–81; vols. 13K, 20–27R (see *RMB* for 1985, pp. 362–63), rev. by Helmut Koopmann in *Germanistik* 27 (1986): 142–43; OEHLER, Dolf, *Pariser Bilder 1: Antibourgeoise Ästhetik bei Baudelaire, Daumier und Heine* (see *RMB* for 1979, pp. 286–87), rev. by Karlheinz Fingerhut in *Germanistik* 27 (1986): 94; PONGS, Ulrich, *Heinrich Heine: sein Bild der Aufklärung und dessen romantische Quellen* (see *RMB* for 1985, p. 364), rev. by Joseph A. Kruse in *Germanistik* 26 (1985): 935; PRAWER, S.S., *Heine's Jewish Comedy* (see *RMB* for 1983, p. 360), rev. by Hans Reiss in *CG* 17 (1984): 349–51; by Carsten Peter Thiede in *Arbitrium* 4 (1986): 71–73; REISER, Andrej, *Heines Reise-Bilder* (see *RMB* for 1985, p. 364), rev. by Alfred Opitz in *HeineJ 1986*, pp. 187–88; RITZ, German, *150-Jahre russische Heine-Übersetzung* (see *RMB* for 1983, p. 361), rev. by Eberhard Reissner in *HeineJ 1986*, pp. 179–82; SPENCER, Hanna, *Heinrich Heine* (see *RMB* for 1980, p. 309), rev. by Franz Futterknecht in *Seminar* 22 (1986): 172–73; WEBER, Johannes, *Libertin und Charakter* (see *RMB* for 1985, pp. 366–67), rev. by Bernd Füllner in *HeineJ 1986*, pp. 200–01; by Slobodan Grubačić in *Germanistik* 27 (1986): 635–36; WERNER, Michael, ed., *Cahier Heine 2* (see *RMB* for 1982, pp. 319–20), rev. by Fritz Mende in *DLZ* 106 (1985): cols. 681–85; WINDFUHR, Manfred, ed., *Historisch-kritische Gesamtausgabe der Werke*, vol. 2 (see *RMB* for 1984, pp. 372–73), rev. by Helmut Schanze in *HeineJ 1986*, pp. 184–86.

HERDER

See Schmitz-Emans ("Jean Paul"); Paulin ("Tieck").

HOFFMANN, E.T.A.

Asche, Susanne. *Die Liebe, der Tod und das Ich im Spiegel der Kunst: die Funktion des Weiblichen in Schriften der Frühromantik und im erzählerischen Werk E.T.A. Hoffmanns.* (Hochschulschriften: Literaturwissenschaft, 69.) Königstein: Anton Hain, 1985. Pp. 239.

Rev. by James M. McGlathery in *GSR* 9 (1986): 645f.
Asche distinguishes the way in which Hoffmann discusses femininity from its treatment among the early Romantics. Friedrich Schlegel, she feels, tried to dominate his women readers dogmatically, whereas Hoffmann leaves open a variety of perspectives. As an observation on style, this point may be well enough taken, but how the variety of perspectives is any more available to women than to anyone else is hard to discern. (W.C.)

Becker, Alliene R. "'Alice Doane's Appeal': A Literary Double of Hoffmann's *Elixiere des Teufels.*" *CLS* 23 (1986): 1–11.

Projects Hoffmann's novel as a source of Nathaniel Hawthorne's short story. Becker's evidence is the "arabesque treatment" of Hawthorne's story (i.e., chapter breaks and shifting perspectives) and its "stylistic ambiguities." The article does not produce any new reading of Hoffmann, but it does present some original research into his American reception. Weighing Becker's claim for the close relation between Hoffmann and Hawthorne is hard because she either could not or did not print and discuss any of the "partial translation and summary" Hawthorne saw. (W.C.)

Crisman, William. "E.T.A. Hoffmann's 'Einsiedler Serapion' and 'Rat Krespel' as Models of Reading." *JEGP* 85 (1986): 50–69.

Gaskill, Howard. "Open Circles: Hoffmann's *Kater Murr* and Hölderlin's *Hyperion.*" *CG* 19 (1986): 21–46.

The article is a comparison, not an influence study. Gaskill concludes that despite their surface dissimilarity, Hoffmann's "comic masterpiece" and Hölderlin's "prose elegy" are works "which, whilst circular in structure, contrive to point beyond themselves to the reality of the infinite" (43). While this conclusion is of itself not revolutionary, along

the way Gaskill deftly shows the problems in some standard
Murr debates as those over the projected "third volume" and
Murr's philistines. (W.C.)

Jennings, Lee B. "Blood of the Android: A Post-Freudian
Perspective on Hoffmann's 'Sandman.'" *Seminar* 22 (1986):
95-111.

   By returning to psychoanalytic reading, Jennings tries
to supplant Wolfgang Preisendanz's view that "psychological
interpretations are pre-empted, or even rendered futile" by
assumed different levels of "reality-modes" in "Der Sandmann" (96). Exactly what he supplants Preisendanz's reading
with is hard to say, since Jennings concludes that Nathanael
suffers "failure of the timeless Ideal to interact with the
chaotic but fulfilling existence of the body and of nature"
(111)--a description that seems to hand the story's interpretation back to a conflict of "reality-modes." Still, Jennings
gives a good review along the way of psychoanalytic essays
on "Sandmann" after Freud's famous account. (W.C.)

Jennings, Lee B. "The Downward Transcendence: Hoffmann's
'Bergwerke zu Falun.'" *DVLG* 59 (1985):   278-89.

   In this enjoyably written essay, Jennings reacts against
an over-tendency to read all of Hoffmann's works as psychological dramas: "the somewhat naive idealistic approach of
older times has its merits also" (279). Elis in "Bergwerke"
finds the only sort of "transcendence" a person can find:
"his quest has not been in vain. In his own mind, at least,
he has attained an insight into the ultimate coherence of
things based ... on physical origins. He has glimpsed the
individual human psyche as part of an eros-driven unfolding
of nature" (287). This last sentence makes plain the difficulty of Jennings's task--how does one distinguish "just a
psychological reading," which Jennings opposes, from an
idealist vision of "eros-driven nature"? The answer to this
never comes quite clear. Still, the attempt is important.
(W.C.)

Oesterle, Günter. "E.T.A. Hoffmann: 'Des Vetters Eckfenster':
zur Historizierung ästhetischer Wahrnehmung oder der kalkulierte
romantische Rückgriff auf Sehmuster der Aufklärung." *DU*
39 (1987): 84-110.

   Oesterle sets out to ask if Hoffmann's story is "a precursor
of socialist realism" (85). While this question gets rather
lost--and is a bit difficult to understand to begin with--the
essay provides considerable information, accompanied by

illustrations, about the tradition of "city physiognomy" before Hoffmann. The material is a valuable aid to understanding Hoffmann's artistic representations in the story. (W.C.)

Stadler, Ulrich. "Die Aussicht als Einblick: zu E.T.A. Hoffmanns später Erzählung 'Des Vetters Eckfenster.'" *ZDP* 105 (1986): 498-515.

Stadler begins with the standard reading of the story as representing a new "poetic realism" in Hoffmann's work and tries to give this interpretation a precise statement by comparing the ideas of perception in "Eckfenster" with those in earlier Hoffmann works. "Eckfenster" develops a concept of "double distortion" that tries to rectify actual grotesqueness by rendering it even more grotesque, e.g., through the magnification of the cousin's telescope. The essay makes a good companion to Oesterle's (reviewed above) and covers some of the same source material to different effect. (W.C.)

Terpstra, Jan U. "Hexenspruch, Eierzauber und Feindkomplex in E.T.A. Hoffmanns Fragment 'Der Feind.'" *Euphorion* 80 (1986): 26-45.

Provides considerable cultural and historical material for understanding the "Eierschwank" anecdote with which Hoffmann's fragmentary story begins. Terpstra sees the witch's curse "tiefenpsychologisch" as a reflection of "an eruption of the elementary feminine, a regression of consciousness that has to be controlled by a male authority figure" (44). (W.C.)

See also Mahlendorf ("General 3. Criticism"); Klotz, Lahmann, Loquai, Mayer, Sauer, Schubert, Wais ("German 2. General"); Nehring ("Eichendorff"); Littlejohns ("Tieck").

HÖLDERLIN

Adler, Jeremy, trans. "Friedrich Hölderlin on Tragedy. Part 2: 'The Ground of Empedocles' and 'On the Process of Becoming in Passing Away.'" Pp. 147-73 in E.S. Schaffer, ed., *Comparative Criticism*, vol. 7. Cambridge University Press, 1985. Pp. 338.

The *Comparative Criticism* volumes issued by Cambridge University Press and edited by E.S. Schaffer have offered one of the most exciting and rigorous contemporary forums for interdisciplinary dialogue. Jeremy Adler has in the last three volumes contributed a series of translations from and commentaries to Hölderlin's poetry that not only serve to place

Hölderlin's work into a broader comparative context but which,
in that context, have reset analytical perspectives on
Hölderlin's poetry (see here especially his "Philosophical
Archaeology: Hölderlin's 'Pindar Fragments.' A Translation
with an Interpretation." See *RMB* for 1984, p. 376).

Adler continues in this translation and commentary the work
he began with his translations of the notes to Hölderlin's
Sophocles translations (see *RMB* for 1984, p. 376). The
commentaries by Adler are clearly written, balanced, informative, and intelligent, and the work of translation that he is
doing here, placing these difficult and central texts before
an English-speaking audience in the context of a comparative
discipline, is long overdue. (S.M.)

Bertaux, Pierre. "'Das fatale Nürtingen ...': Streitgespräch."
GRM 34 (1984): 148-66.

A controversial point, but one well within the compass of
Bertaux's research into the last 37 years of Hölderlin's life
and what has been circumspectly called his *Umnachtung*: that
the key to Hölderlin's psychic state in the second half of
his life is to be found in his relationship to his mother
(Bertaux himself makes reference to the outrage his pursuit
of this relationship aroused, noting that he was accused,
among other things, of having defamed Hölderlin's mother).
As always with Bertaux he raises questions that seem, after
he has posed them, obvious, but which needed to be raised and
had not been asked in any of the scholarship before Bertaux's
often biting queries. (S.M.)

Bertaux, Pierre. *Hölderlin-Variationen*. (Suhrkamp Taschenbuch,
1018.) Frankfurt: Suhrkamp, 1984. Pp. 210.

Rev. by Johannes Mahr in *Germanistik* 26 (1985): 640-41.
While the volume collects some earlier articles that have
appeared elsewhere ("Wozu Dichter in dürftiger Zeit"; "Höder-
lin--Sinclair: ein treues Paar?"--for both see *RMB* for 1983,
p. 366), Bertaux's last book does contain a wide range of
new essays, short observations, and critical reflections on
Hölderlin's work and its reception. Bertaux's demanding
readings of Hölderlin's work (both in their context and in
the context of our own times) reflect an acute historical
perspective (see especially "Friedrich Hölderlin, ein "Sohn
seiner Zeit'--und als solcher aktuell," or the note on
"Tinian") and a commonsense depth of perspective that has
rattled the Hölderlin scholarship and continues to do so,
even now that he has left us. These essays, reviews, notes,
and observations should be read like a series of related but
far-flung musical variations. (S.M.)

Constantine, David. "Translation and exegesis in Hölderlin."
MLR 81 (1986): 388-97.

Constantine's observations on the centrality of translation
to Hölderlin's poetic practice are inspired: in the compass
of this brief essay Constantine sees clear through to the
poetics of process that the terms of Hölderlin's poetry (as
singen and *deuten*) constantly underscore. But the process
itself yields, in Constantine's reading, a gesture of exegesis
in Hölderlin's poetry that is itself illusory: as he says,
Hölderlin's poems "contain many hints of the illusoriness of
their own most confident gestures." Constantine is not arguing here from a poststructuralist theoretical perspective.
The radicality of this reading he grounds in Hölderlin's own
practice: that poetry itself is, in its very act and performance, the point, and that any "acquisitive reading," any
attempt to reduce the poetry to some meaning outside the
boundaries of its own process, represents a distortion in
meaning. (S.M.)

Drewitz, Ingeborg. "Der Vaterlandsbegriff bei Hölderlin."
Pp. 72-96 in *Unter meiner Zeitlupe: Porträts und Panoramen*.
Wien: Europa Verlag, 1984. Pp. 215.

First published in 1981 (see *RMB* for 1983, p. 368), Drewitz's
essay offers a detailed analysis of Hölderlin's political
views and of the context in which those beliefs must be seen.
Drewitz is much indebted to Bertaux, but she really extends
the dimensions of Bertaux's readings in that she uses his
point of departure as a compass point to tackle one of the
thorniest of all issues in the *Rezeptionsgeschichte*:
Hölderlin's *Vaterlandsbegriff*. (S.M.)

Goodson, A.C. "Hölderlin and the Bounds of Romantic Metaphor."
Pp. 42-51 in Theodore G. Gish and Sandra G. Frieden, eds.,
Deutsche Romantik and English Romanticism. (Houston German
Studies, 1.) Munich: Wilhelm Fink Verlag, 1984. Pp. 77.

Goodson wants to situate Hölderlin's work outside a
"labyrinth of philosophic and theological controversy," and
seeks a description of Hölderlin's "voice." The author works
out a description of "romantic Metaphor" in Hölderlin and
Wordsworth that generates a deeper sense of the mutuality of
relations. This is an excellent reading of metaphor in
Hölderlin, subtle and insightful, stressing the limits of
metaphor, the silence beyond, and the range of possibilities
Hölderlin's metaphoric language opens in showing the "contingent relations" of the world. (S.M.)

Haverkamp, Anselm. "Error in Mourning--A Crux in Hölderlin:
'dem gleich fehlet die Trauer' ('Mnemosyne')." *YFS* 69
(1985): 238-53.

Haverkamp is looking for a crux in Hölderlin's work. Or
rather he is looking for a crux to Hölderlin's late poetry.
In any case, what is at stake here is really a correction of *
Beißner's reading of the line "dem gleich fehlet die Trauer"
in "Mnemosyne," and while a correction of Beißner's analysis
of this line is indeed necessary, this rereading gets lost
in the theoretical apparatus Haverkamp wields.
    Haverkamp stakes out his theoretical allegiances at the
same time that he makes the most incredible interpretive
capitulation. Citing de Man, he states that de Man risked
a paraphrase of the line in question that "leaves no further
insight to be wished." One wonders why all the bother then,
and with such labyrinthine circumambulations to say the most
simple things: "The subject concerned, though not the subject of this valedictory sentence, is the insisting force
of the afterthought, the poet." Really now. The line and
Beißner's gloss of it do cry out for rereading, but Haverkamp's
explication strains the bounds of what one should go through
to get to the meaning of any text, or its lack of meaning,
or its readability "only as an allegory of its unreadibility."
(S.M.)

Hoffmeister, Donna L. "Hölderlin-Biography, 1924-1982:
Transformations of a Literary Life." *Seminar: A Journal
of Germanic Studies* 21 (1985): 207-31.

    This is a learned review of fictional and scholarly
biographies, but it is also a first-rate meditation on the
very nature of biography itself, situating the biography
in the same field in which Adorno placed the essay--for
biography is, as Hoffmeister notes, an "uneasy synthesis of
the logical and the arbitrary." (S.M.)

Internationale Hölderlin-Bibliographie (IHB). A publication
of the Württemberg State Library, first edition, 1804-1983.
Ed. Maria Kohler. Stuttgart: Fromann-Holzboog, 1985.
Pp. 756.

    For those who have had the good fortune of receiving Maria
Kohler's help in the Hölderlin archives of the Württemberg
State Library, consulting this volume is the next best thing
to being there. The bibliography is exhaustive: one can
rest assured that listed here are virtually all publications

relating to Hölderlin that have appeared in the years 1803–
1983. The bibliography reproduces the *Schlagwort-Katalog*
of the archives: one may look up subjects such as *Welt* or
vaterländisch that would readily occur to one in the course
of research on Hölderlin, but one will also find listings
under topics such as *ordo inversus*, a listing that directs
one to an article on *ordo inversus* in Novalis, Hölderlin,
Kleist, and Kafka. There is a creative richness in the
arrangement of this bibliography, reflecting the richness
of the archives themselves, and this volume will long serve
as a standard for detailed, thorough, and clear-sighted
archival work. It is quite simply the finest aide to Hölderlin research ever published, and a real joy *to read!* (S.M.)

Jakobson, Roman, and Grete Lubbe-Grothues. "Two Types of Discourse in Hölderlin's Madness." Trans. by Susan Abrams.
Pp. 115-36 in Jaakko Hintikka and Lucia Vaina, eds., *Cogni-
tive Constraints on Communication: Representations and Processes*. Dordrecht: Reidel, 1984. Pp. xix+428.

A psycholinguistic analysis of the late Hölderlin's language
and of its schizophrenic aspects/tones, the essay follows
the lines of previous work by the authors (see *RMB* for 1984,
p. 379).

Klabes, Günter. "Political Reality and Poetic Mission:
Hölderlin's and Shelley's Heterocosm." Pp. 301-21 in James
Pipkin, ed., *English and German Romanticism: Cross-Currents
and Controversies*. Heidelberg: Carl Winter, 1985. Pp. 432.

Klabes interprets Shelley's "Ode to the West Wind" and
Hölderlin's "Dichterberuf" as paradigmatic texts, yielding
a poetics grounded in the necessary internalization of political revolution, an internalized "revolution of consciousness" structured by the realities of late eighteenth-century
European politics. While it is good to have Hölderlin's
poetry treated in such depth in a comparative study, the
"internalization" of politics Klabes pursues unfortunately
turns the interpretive clock backwards and tends to depoliti-
cize the very real political dimensions of Hölderlin's work.
(S.M.)

Maloney, Paul W. *Holderlins friedensfeier: Rezeption und
Deutung*. (European University Studies, series 1, vol. 823.)
Frankfurt: Peter Lang, 1985. Pp. 111.

Maloney offers a detailed meditation on the "Fürst des
Festes" in Hölderlin's "Friedensfeier," the main thesis of
which is that the "Fürst" is Christ. In Maloney's analysis
such an interpretation is the only justified reading of this

figure in the poem, and offers what Maloney calls the
"correct" understanding of the "Fürst" and of the poem (97):
Maloney gives a schoolmasterly review of the conflicting
interpretations of the "Fürst," and the thoughtfulness of his
close textual analysis is admirable; but one misses a clearly
articulated analytical center in this monograph. A lengthy
analysis of conflicting interpretations of the "Fürst" follows
Maloney's explication of the figure as Christ and seems, as
does the final chapter, "Ausblick," tacked on. And there are
methodological inconsistencies--Maloney insists, for instance, on a strict *textimmanente* interpretation of the poem,
only to make use of other texts when it is convenient.
     But the real point is this: Maloney states that Hölderlin's
Christusgestalt "lebt in einem Bereich abseits von jedem
Dogma und braucht sich folglich mit diesem nicht auseinander-
zusetzen." This is true, and should have served Maloney as an
analytic marker: Hölderlin's late work is syncretic and shuns
any simple reduction of its figures. It is a new mythology
Hölderlin is seeking to pull from the old. The figures, and
especially the figure of Christ, are intractable, but are not,
in the complex processes of the later poetry, simply to be
named with the old names. To do so misses, on one fundamental
level, the point of the poetry Hölderlin was writing. (S.M.)

Nägele, Rainer. *Text, Geschichte und Subjektivität in Hölderlins
Dichtung: "Uneßbarer Schrift gleich."* (Studien zur allgemein-
en und vergleichenden Literaturwissenschaft, 27.) Stuttgart: Metzler, 1985. Pp. 256.

     Rev. by Hans-Wilhelm Kelling in *GSR* 9 (1986): 420-21.
     I would rather read Rainer Nägele on Hölderlin than almost
any other contemporary scholar or critic. I may at times
strongly disagree with what he has to say, but there is more
subtlety, ingenuity, intellectual curiosity, and engaged
inventiveness in Nägele's analyses than in most everything
else that has appeared in the last ten years.
     Nägele's first chapter is devoted to an explication of
Szondi's critical methodology. But Nägele takes the analysis
of Hölderlin's work well beyond the application of a particular
methodology; Nägele's critical reflection, depth of reading,
and his finely tuned knowledge set his work apart and on a
level of its own. The opening chapter is followed by the finest
reading of "Brod und Wein" since Jochen Schmidt's, and the
third chapter, comprising almost half of the book, is devoted
to a subtle and rigorous analysis of the "subject" in the
late hymns. This is a benchmark study, a major contribution
to the Hölderlin scholarship and a model of critical
methodology. (S.M.)

Pott, Hans-Georg. "Schiller and Hölderlin. Die 'Neuen Briefe über die ästhethische Erziehung des Menschen.'" Pp. 290-313 in Jürgen Bolten, ed., *Schillers Briefe über die ästhetische Erziehung.* Frankfurt: Suhrkamp, 1984. Pp. 355.

Pott's essay is a substantial contribution to our understanding of Schiller's influence on Hölderlin, and of how that influence manifested itself in subtle ways. Pott rigorously pursues systematic interpretations of the complex relationships between philosophy and the arts that were so intensely explored in German idealistic philosophy, and he writes with exemplary personal engagement, clearly and with a firmly articulated graspo of his own methodological position. (S.M.)

Santner, Eric L. "Paratactic Composition in Hölderlin's 'Hälfte des Lebens.'" *GQ* 58 (1985): 165-72.

These two articles (see above) should be read together. Santner's point of departure is to be found in Adorno's famous essay on parataxis in Hölderlin's late poetry. Both "Andenken" and "Hälfte des Lebens" represent for Santner instances of a breakdown of what he calls "narrative vigilance" in Hölderlin's poetry--they are poems in which memories or "concrete particulars" are not assimilated into metaphysical narrative or philosophical argument. This fragmentation Santner sees as an instance of a radically different aesthetic undergirding Hölderlin's late poetry, an aesthetic that is an instance of a poetics of fragmentation. Santner's analyses are insightful and raise fundamental questions about relationships between subject and object in Hölderlin's later poetry. (S.M.)

Santner, Eric L. "Sober Recollections: Hölderlin's De-idealization of Memory in 'Andenken.'" *GR* 60 (1985): 16-22.

Sattler, D.E., ed. *Friedrich Hölderlin: Sämtliche Werke,* vols. 12 (*Empedokles 1,* manuscript facsimiles and transcriptions) and 13 (*Empedokles 2,* text). Frankfurt: Stroemfeld/Roter Stern, 1985. Pp. 525, 949.

Rev. by Hennig Boetius in *Germanistik* 26 (1985): 906-07. In his editing of the odes (volumes 4 and 5 of the Frankfurt edition; see *RMB* for 1984, pp. 380-81), Sattler divided the textual material into two separate volumes: he placed the manuscript facsimiles and the facing transcriptions in one volume, and the linear text transcription in the accompanying second volume. For the odes this proved, as have so many of the strategies Sattler has introduced, a stunning move,

for the centrality of the odes in the body of Hölderlin's
poetry became much clearer, and the process of his poetics
became much more accessible. Sattler has retained this
division for the Frankfurt *Empedokles*; volume 12 contains
the manuscript facsimiles and the transcriptions, and volume
13 the linear text sequence of the various stages of composition. The Frankfurt volumes of the *Empedokles* offer yet
another example of the value of Sattler's method in the study
of Hölderlin's work, as there are considerable discrepancies
between the Stuttgart and Frankfurt editions in the provisional
textual form. And we see in Sattler's editorial practices
the demonstration of an editorial *praxis* that itself partici-
pates in the poetics Hölderlin was mapping in his poetry and
in his theoretical writings, a poetics of process that under-
girds the very best of poetic developments in Western poetries
since the mid-eighteenth century. (S.M.)

Sieburth, Richard, trans. *Friedrich Hölderlin: Hymns and*
Fragments. Princeton University Press, 1984. Pp. 285.

   Rev. by W.S. Merwin in *The New York Times Book Review,*
Dec. 30, 1984: by Marjorie Perlogg ("Hölderlin our Contemporary") in *Parnassus: Poetry in Review* 13 (1986): 144-68.
   Sieburth translates the major hymns and a good selection
of the late fragments (most notably missing here is the
"Friedensfeier"). This collection represents a very welcome
addition to the English translations of Hölderlin. Sieburth's
volume will be particularly useful in advanced undergraduate
classes and in graduate seminars on European Romanticism.
Sieburth has a fine ear for nuance, and in rendering Hölderlin's late poetry and the difficult syntax of those poems
avoids an English that, were it to follow Hölderlin's German,
would be close to "Milton at his most stilted" (27). Sieburth
has more clearly Pound's models of translation in mind, and
tries "to convey the particular syntactical torque of Hölderlin's late hymns through means more native to American
cadence" (27-28). Sieburth offers a thoughtful if unwieldy
introduction. In his readings of the poems he stands in the
line of Adorno, de Man, and Foucault, stressing in the selection and in his analysis a "poetics of absence" in Hölderlin's
poetry.
   This is a fine book, and a significant addition to Princeton's Lockert Library of Poetry in Translation. (S.M.)

Tismar, Jens. "Herakles als Leitfigur bei Wieland, Goethe und
Hölderlin." *Text und Kontext* 13 (1985): 37-48.

   Tismar's is a comparative study of the figure of Heracles.
The author seeks to trace changes in European mytho-poetics

during the years 1770–1800, providing connections between
the spheres of *Geistesgeschichte* and *Sozialgeschichte*.
(S.M.)

Wackwitz, Stephan. *Friedrich Hölderlin*. (Sammlung Metzler,
M215: Abteilung D, Literturgeschichte.) Stuttgart:
Metzler, 1985. Pp. 157.

The volumes of the *Sammlung Metzler* have long served as
models of what literary handbooks should be: precise,
accurate, and with a thorough review of all relevant literature. Wackwitz's new volume in Hölderlin is all of this and
more: in the compass offered by the series, he not only
provides the *Realien* needed for further study of Hölderlin,
he also offers level-headed and clear commentaries in the
course of his exposition. Lawrence Ryan's volume on Hölderlin in this series first appeared in 1962, with a revision
that was issued in 1967. But these volumes appeared before
Bertaux's pioneering *Hölderlin und die französische Revolution*, and the developments in the Hölderlin scholarship that
followed from this and from Bertaux's later biographical
studies elicited such strong critical debate that one can
say, whether one agrees with Bertaux's theses or not, that
Bertaux's work changed the course of much of the Hölderlin
scholarship of the past 20 years. (One notes here, for example,
that Wackwitz adds two excursuses to his treatment of Hölderlin's biography: one on the question of Hölderlin's status
as a Jacobinian, the other on the question of Hölderlin's
sanity during his last years—both topics that were first
really raised by Bertaux.)

Wackwitz departs from an interwoven narrative of Hölderlin's
life and poetry, a commonplace of the monograph and a practice that Michel first established and that Ryan followed in
his Metzler volume. After a review of the text editions
of Hölderlin's work and a discussion of the institutions
and aids available for those pursuing research on Hölderlin's
work, Wackwitz separates the remaining chapters of his
monograph into separate *Leben* and *Werk* divisions, which he
then follows with a concise review of the *Rezeptionsgeschichte*.
This is an eminently simple and yet subtle strategy, for it
actually allows the lineaments of the poetry to be seen in
the context of Hölderlin's own biography much more clearly
than the earlier approaches.

Wackwitz's comments on the ongoing text editions (3) are
especially cogent. The biographical section of the text is
clear, straightforward, and incorporates the great wealth
of relevant secondary material that has appeared during the
last 20 years. And Wackwitz's brief analytical commentaries
on Hölderlin's work are models of precision. (S.M.)

Weisinger, Kenneth. "Hölderlin's 'Die Wanderung': Encomium
and Prophecy." *GSR* 7 (1984): 399-422.

There are two threads interwoven in this analysis: one is
Bloomian, an attempt to see Hölderlin's work through the
lense of anxiety, the other is comparative, an attempt to
contrast the encomiastic in Pindar and Hölderlin. The first
almost guarantees that the second come out in favor of Pindar,
and Weisinger sees Pindar's poetry as characterized by "supreme confidence" in the encomiastic task (clearly praising
the victors of athletic contests), whereas Hölderlin's poetry
is laden with anxiety, not just in light of the "precursor"
but with the knowledge that his own age fails to provide
Hölderlin with the "certainty of what is" that one sees as
the cultural fabric of Pindar's poetry. Careful reference
to Pindar is always helpful in reading Hölderlin, but the
Bloomian perspective "covers" the substance here: any
"discovery" implicit in "Die Wanderung" has its own terms of
reference, and to "measure" Hölderlin's later poetry by the
standards Weisinger proposes necessarily distorts Hölderlin's
meaning. (S.M.)

See also Hay, Lehmann, Loquai, Mayer, Scheufele, Wais ("German
2. General"); Espagne ("Heine"); Gaskill ("Hoffmann, E.T.A.").

Reviews of books previously listed:

FINK, Marcus, *Pindarfragmente: Neun Hölderlin-Deutungen* (see
RMB for 1983, p. 368), rev. by Jürgen Söring in *Arcadia* 20
(1985): 91-93; JAMME, Christoph, *"Ein ungelehrtes Buch":*
die philosophische Gemeinschaft zwischen Hölderlin und Hegel
in Frankfurt, 1797-1800 (see *RMB* for 1983, p. 370), rev. by
Michael Franz in *Germanistik* 26 (1985): 907-08; PETERS,
Uwe Henrik, *Hölderlin: Wider die These vom edlen Simulanten*
(see *RMB* for 1983, p. 374), rev. by Renate Reschke in *WB* 31
(1985): 152-55; PRILL, Meinhard, *Bürgerliche Alltagswelt und*
pietistisches Denken im Werk Hölderlins: zur Kritik des
Hölderlin-Biles von Georg Lukács (see *RMB* for 1983, p. 375),
rev. by Beth Bjorklund in *Monatshefte* 78 (1986): 400-01;
SATTLER, D.E., ed., *Friedrich Hölderlin: Sämtliche Werke*,
vols. 4 and 5 (see *RMB* for 1984, pp. 381-82), rev. by Hennig
Boetius in *Germanistik* 26 (1985): 906-07; SEIFERT, Albrecht,
Untersuchungen zu Hölderlins Pindar-Rezeption (see *RMB* for
1984, p. 382); rev. by Markus Fink in *Arcadia* 19 (1984):
90-92; by Jochen Schmidt in *Germanistik* 26 (1985): 602-03;
UNGER, Richard, *Friedrich Hölderlin* (see *RMB* for 1984, p.
383); rev. by Emery George in *GR* 61 (1986): 85-87.

HUMBOLDT, WILHELM VON

See Lehmann ("German 2. General"); Lüth ("Eichendorff").

JEAN PAUL

Bachmann, Asta-Maria. *Das Umschaffen der Wirklichkeit durch den 'poetischen Geist': Aspekte der Phantasie und des Phantasierens in Jean Pauls Poesie und Poetik.* (Europäische Hochschulschriften, series 1, vol. 891.) Frankfurt, Bern, and New York: Peter Lang, 1986. Pp. 221.

An examination of the pivotal role and mechanisms of the poetic imagination in Jean Paul's theory of literature and in his works, explaining positive and negative aspects of imagination and phantasizing. Besides an analysis of the idyllic imagination in *Wutz* and *Fibel* and the heroic enthusiasm of Charlotte Corday, the realms of dream and play ("Spiel") are explored. A good number of interesting insights, although the theoretical basis is not always very solid, and some of it repeats previous scholarship. (W.K.)

Birus, Hendrik. *Vergleichung: Goethes Einführung in die Schreibweise Jean Pauls.* (Germanistische Abhandlungen, 59.) Stuttgart: Metzler, 1986. Pp. 153.

Birus takes Goethe's section "Vergleichung" in the "Noten und Abhandlungen zu besserem Verständniß des West-östlichen Divans" and examines it in its place within Goethe's work, the context of the time, and how much it tells us about Jean Paul and his style. Especially the affinity of Jean Paul to the Orient is analyzed. From this vantage point, Birus is able to reexamine questions such as those about the "Poetische Enzyklopädie" and "Witzige Illumination" which have recently been debated, following the publications of Proß and Wiethölter. A new angle to the research on Goethe and Jean Paul with a thorough documentation. (W.K.)

Fürnkäs, Josef. "Aufklärung und Alphabetisierung: Jean Pauls 'Leben Fibels.'" *JJPG* 21 (1986): 63-76.

A new reading of Jean Paul's *Leben Fibels* from the point of view of authorship and the constitution of literature as well as its inherent dangers. It is a text on literature and its problematic relationship to life--a dominant theme in Jean Paul's late works. While this thesis is not new, it may help to bring into better focus the merits of this underrated text. (W.K.)

Jahrbuch der Jean-Paul-Gesellschaft (= JJPG). (Im Auftrag der Jean-Paul-Gesellschaft, Sitz Bayreuth, ed. Kurt Wölfel, 21. Jg.) Munich: C.H. Beck, 1986. Pp. 186.
Individual articles and reviews listed separately.

Kaiser, Herbert. "Jean Pauls 'Dr. Katzenbergers Badereise': zum Verhältnis von Subjekt und Ich." Literatur für Leser 4 (1985): 229-41.

Köpke, Wulf. "Agathons und Gustavs 'Fall': Wieland-Spuren in der 'Unsichtbaren Loge.'" JJPG 21 (1986): 7-22.

The seduction of Gustav in Jean Paul's first novel Die unsichtbare Loge has often been compared to the fate of Agathon. There is a strong case to be made for Wieland's influence on this aspect of Jean Paul's plot; but it needs to be better defined. Also, by creating this situation which he never repeated, Jean Paul got into an impasse with his story and never completed the novel. The comparison of Agathon and Gustav raises a number of interesting questions on politics and sexual psychology and allows us to see Jean Paul at work, learning his trade. (W.K.)

Koller, Hans Christoph. "Bilder, Bücher und Theater: zur Konstituierung des Subjekts in Jean Pauls 'Titan.'" JJPG 21 (1986): 23-62.

An examination of the role of pictures (paintings), books, and especially the stage and theater in the structure of the novel Titan, primarily from the perspective of the protagonist Albano. While the dominant function of art and artifacts, and Jean Paul's ambiguous attitude toward the aestheticism of classical Weimar and Romantic Jena have been widely recognized, the extent, and its significance, to which Jean Paul's positive figures are determined by this environment still deserves investigation. The study makes good use of Lacan, Foucault, and previous scholarship on Jean Paul. (W.K.)

Kuzniar, Alice A. "Titanism and Narcissism: The Lure of the Transparent Sign in Jean Paul." DVLG 60 (1986): 440-58.

A Lacanian exploration of the "double" in the novel Titan and the complex issues of identity, subjectivity, and the constitution of individuality, especially with reference to Schoppe and Roquairol; with a solid theoretical underpinning using the Vorschule der Ästhetik. One of the growing number of welcome investigations into the interrelation of language, poetics, and psychology, using approaches like that of Lacan. A convincing study. (W.K.)

Montandon, Alain. Intro., trans., and notes to *Levana ou
    traité d'education*. Lausanne: L'Age d'Homme, 1983. Pp.
    245.

    Rev. by Marie-Odile Blum in *EG* 41 (1986): 222.

Montandon, Alain. *La réception de Laurence Sterne en Allemagne*.
    (Publications de la faculté des lettres de Clermont 2, n.s.
    22.) Clermont-Ferrand: Faculté des lettres et Sciences
    Humaines de l'Université de Clermont-Ferrand 2, 1986. Pp.
    391.

    Rev. by Sabine Müller in *JJPG* 21 (1986): 147-54.

    An extract from Montandon's "Thèse" which offers an exhaustive
overview of the reception of Laurence Sterne in Germany, on
the basis of Jauss's reception aesthetics. The present publication excludes the heart of the matter, Laurence Sterne and
Jean Paul, which will be treated in a separate volume. There
are also some more theoretical parts of the *thèse* which are
left out. The main thread of the investigation is the path
from imitation of a model to its replacement by a new,
original form, developed pursuant to a reception of the model.
A fundamental contribution to a crucial topic. (W.K.)

Müller, Götz. "Jean Pauls Privatenzyklopädie: eine Untersuchung
    der Exzerpte und Register aus Jean Pauls unveröffentlichtem
    Nachlaß." *IASL* 11 (1986): 73-114.

    A thorough investigation of Jean Paul's famous excerpts,
their composition and structure, and examples for their use
in his works; with sample lists. An important contribution
from Jean Paul's unpublished materials, and an area that needs
to be investigated further. (W.K.)

Müller, Götz. "Die Literarisierung des Mesmerismus in Jean
    Pauls Roman 'Der Komet.'" Pp. 185-99 in Heinz Scholl, ed.,
    Franz Anton Mesmer und die Geschichte des Mesmerismus.
    Beiträge zum internationalen wissenschaftlichen Symposion
    anläßlich des 250. Geburtstags von Mesmer. Stuttgart:
    Steiner, 1985.

Nell, Werner. "Jean Pauls 'Komet' und 'Der Teutsche Don
    Quichotte': zum historischen Ort von Jean Pauls letztem
    Roman." *JJPG* 21 (1986): 77-96.

    Investigation of the "Don Quijote" reception in Jean Paul's
novel *Der Komet* with the help of a comparison with the novel
Der teutsche Don Quichotte of 1753. Although it remains
doubtful whether Jean Paul actually knew the earlier book,
the structural comparison throws new light on Jean Paul's

approach, on his original problems, and also on his much
deeper understanding of the poetological problems. (W.K.)

Och, Gunnar. *Der Körper als Zeichen: zur Bedeutung des mimisch-
gestischen und physiognomischen Ausdrucks im Werk Jean Pauls.*
(Erlanger Studien, 62.) Erlangen: Palm and Enke, 1985. Pp.
230.

Rev. by Ursula Naumann in *JJPG* 21 (1986): 160-63.
The interesting aspects of this study are the interpretations
of physiognomic and pathognomic expressions in Jean Paul's
works and in the context of novel literature of the later
eighteenth century. It is well known that the relationship
of body and soul is a central issue for Jean Paul, and that
he tried to characterize his figures by their physiognomic
expressions, while, on the other hand, maintaining the dichotomy of body and soul. The study contributes a good deal
to the exploration of this complex field. (W.K.)

Och, Gunnar. "'... und beschenkten sogar Moses': Jean Paul und
sein jüdischer Freund Emmanuel Osmund." *JJPG* 21 (1986):
123-45.

A biographical study which--finally--sheds some light on
Jean Paul's remarkable Jewish friend and their equally remarkable friendship. Emmanuel is seen as a representative
of his generation, trying to enter into German social and
cultural life. Also, the problems of communication between
the two friends and the limits of their mutual understanding
are explored. (W.K.)

Oschatz, Paul-Michael. *Jean Paulscher Humor aufgezeigt an den
Humoristen von den Jugendsatiren bis zum 'Komet.'"* (Kultur--
Literatur--Kunst, 3.) Essen: Verlag Die Blaue Eule, 1985.
Pp. 340.

Rev. by Ralf Simon in *JJPG* 21 (1986): 172-74.
A presentation of Jean Paul's humor and humorists, covering
the same ground as have many publications before, with a
number of good insights and many doubtful generalizations.
No significantly new perspectives. (W.K.)

Otto, Frauke. *Robert Schumann als Jean Paul-Leser.* Frankfurt:
Haag and Herschen, 1984. Pp. 179.

Jean Paul's writings inspired the composer's early literary
efforts.

Preaux, Alain. "Das Doppelgängermotiv in Jean Pauls großen
Romanen." *JJPG* 21 (1986): 97-121.

The "double" enters into German literature through Jean Paul, both as a word and as a phenomenon. It is a symptom of the identity crisis of the time and a sign of the hard struggle for a new orientation on the basis of the new subjectivism. The study follows the different embodiments of doubles in the novels from *Die unsichtbare Loge* through *Flegeljahre* and concludes that Jean Paul was able to cope with the underlying problems through and after a long struggle and process. A stimulating new perspective. (W.K.)

Schmitz-Emans, Monika. *Schnupftuchsknoten oder Sternbild: Jean Pauls Ansätze zu einer Theorie der Sprache*. (Literatur und Reflexion, N.F. 1.) Bonn: Bouvier, 1986. Pp. 477.

A thorough investigation into Jean Paul's ideas and reflections on language, comparing them to contemporary linguistic thought and tracing their origins. As expected, Herder's influence looms large, but Leibnizian ideas persist, and the comparison with Fichte yields surprising insights. Also, the different types of "language," including body language, are examined, and the various forms of communication and their literary expression. No "system" emerges, but this is a complex web of received and original ideas with some consequences for later linguistic thought. A very significant contribution to scholarship. (W.K.)

Wietholter, Waltraud. "Die krumme Linie: Jean Pauls humoristisches ABC." *JIG* 18 (1986): 36-56.

Explanation of Jean Paul's humor from the perspective of the narrator figure and the characters of writers in the texts, especially the "idyllic" texts *Wutz*, *Fixlein*, and *Fibel*; interesting exploration of the problems of subjectivity, intersubjectivity, narcissism, and the relationship of the author to his characters. (W.K.)

See also Michaud ("French 1. General").

Reviews of books previously listed:

MATZKER, Reiner, *Der nützliche Idiot: Wahnsinn und Initiation bei Jean Paul und E.T.A. Hoffmann* (see *RMB* for 1985, p. 382), rev. by Ralf Simon in *JJPG* 21 (1986): 175-78; MAURER, Peter, *Wunsch und Maske: eine Untersuchung der Bild- und Motivstruktur von Jean Pauls Flegeljahren* (see *RMB* for 1982, p. 329), rev. by Erhard Schüttpelz in *JJPG* 21 (1986): 155-59; MÜLLER, Götz, *Jean Pauls Ästhetik und Naturphilosophie* (see *RMB* for 1983, p. 385), rev. by Dennis F. Mahoney in *Monatshefte* 78 (1986): 404-06; PIETZCKER, Carl, *Einführung in*

die *Psychoanalyse des literarischen Kunstwerks am Beispiel
von Jean Pauls "Rede des toten Christus"* (see *RMB* for 1984,
p. 389), rev. by Jutta Osinski in *JJPG* 21 (1986): 164-71;
PIETZCKER, Carl, *Traum, Wunsch und Abwehr: Psychoanalytische
Studien zu Goethe, Jean Paul, Brecht, zur Atomliteratur und
zur literarischen Form* (see *RMB* for 1985, p. 383), rev. by
Helmut Schmiedt in *ZDP* 105 (1986): 305-08; SCHWER, Michael,
*Ex negativo: Dr. Katzenbergers Badereise als Beitrag Jean
Pauls zur ästhetischen Theorie* (see *RMB* for 1983, p. 386),
rev. by Erhard Schüttpelz in *JJPG* 21 (1986): 155-59; VIJN,
J.P., *Carlyle and Jean Paul: Their Spiritual Optics* (see *RMB*
for 1984, p. 36), rev. by Frederick Burwick in *CL* 38 (1986):
203-05.

See also Michaud ("French 1. General"); Hay, Mayer, Sauer,
Scheufele, Schinkel, Wheeler ("German 2. General"); Hörhammer
("Jean Paul").

KANT

See Mayer, Zach ("German 2. General").

KERNER

See Schinkel ("German 2. General"); Perraudin ("Heine").

KLEIST

Brüggeman, Diethelm. *Drei Mystifikationen Heinrich von
Kleists: Kleists Würzburger Reise. Kleists Lust-Spiel mit
Goethe. Aloysius, Marquis von Montferrat.* (Germanic Studies
in America, 51.) New York, Bern, Frankfurt am Main: Peter
Lang, 1985. Pp. 222. Sw. Fr. 46.00.

Rev. by Hansgerd Delbrück in *Germanistik* 27 (1986): 615;
cited previously without a review--see *RMB* for 1985, p. 385.
Despite the title this book does not deal with mystifications of Kleist but, rather testily, with constellations
of his life and work that have mystified readers. Brüggemann
seeks to show the inappropriateness or unacceptability of
theories concerning these constellations. In the case of the
Würzburg trip, he has nothing to offer in their place. His
contribution to the Goethe/Kleist unpleasantness suggests
that Kleist's contemporary reputation rests largely upon his
challenge to legitimate cultural forms. In this view, Kleist
becomes a focus for the shared resentment of everyone who
has ever been stung by rejection. In "Der Findling," Kleist

allegedly based his Nicolo on the historical figure of Aloysius Gonzaga, and then invented Colino to "negate" him. There is a lot of good scholarship here, but it seems to be in the service of contentious debunking of the "seriousness" of Kleist's reputation--as though he were some kind of spoiled trickster. What motivates Brüggemann is itself mystifying. (L.S.)

Cox, Jeffrey. "The Parasite and the Puppet: Diderot's *Neveu* and Kleist's 'Marionettentheater.'" *CL* 38 (1986): 256-69.

Dietrick, Linda. *Prisons and Idylls: Studies in Heinrich von Kleist's Fictional World*. (European University Studies 1, 585.) New York, Bern, and Frankfurt am Main: Peter Lang, 1985. Pp. 281.

A sensitive and wide-ranging study of the iconography of closure in Kleist's work, with extended readings of "Erdbeben," "Marquise von O ...," and *Kohlhaas*. Dietrick's well-wrought prose, her sustained but tactful pressure on the texts, and her insight into the philosophical significance of spatiality make this a good study that should be read by every student of Kleist. What keeps it from being a truly great critical work is that its vocabulary falters at crucial junctures. Statements such as " ... one is left with the sense that the positive and the negative have neither cancelled each other nor been resolved, but have only just balanced out," or "Kleist's fictional world is half open and half closed ..." (261) do justice neither to the depth of Dietrick's own insights nor to the complexity of Kleist's. Perhaps she will discover a terminology, say Adorno's "negative dialectics," that will serve her better. (L.S.)

Dybwad, Marie. *Ideologiebildung und Todestrieb bein Heinrich von Kleist: Betrachtungen zum Prinz von Homburg*. (Theorie und Forschung 6; Literaturwissenschaft 1.) Regensburg: S. Roderer Verlag, 1985. Pp. 157.

A patient, balanced study of the play that addresses its historical contexts (political, social, moral) as well as its formal and stylistic dimensions. The book is much broader than its title suggests. Only the last third specifically addresses "Ideologiebildung" and "Todestrieb," and is in many ways the weakest section of the book. It falls into unreflective jargon ("in-group," "out-group," "signifikant") and critical clichés ("der gescheiterte Konfliktlösungsprozess"). The earlier sections on various forms of emancipation and on sociopolitical changes underlying the tensions of the play are more rewarding. (L.S.)

Fairly, Barker. "Heinrich von Kleist." Pp. 187-210 in Rodney
Symington, ed., *Barker Fairley: Selected Essays on German
Literature.* (Canadian Studies in German Language and Litera-
ture, 29.) New York, Bern, Frankfurt am Main, and Nancy:
Peter Lang, 1984.

Like most of the essays in this collection from the works
of the British-born Canadian Germanist, this contribution
bears the marks of a more genteel age and more amiable assumptions about the role of literature in life than one is likely
to encounter in the works of contemporary scholars. It
originally appeared in 1916 as Fairley's first published
essay, and is characteristic of the psychobibliographical
criticism of the time. "Kleist's ability, then, to conceive
and organize dramatically is thus exactly in line with his
personal conviction about life. Just as he remained more
completely than most adults the center of a disorderly universe, so his natural tendency in play-writing was to throw
full energy into a single character and to surround it with
passive material ..." (207). While these sorts of claims
may still be found in Kleist criticism, the ease with which
they are universalized to exclude other concerns is astonishing. Of *Der Zerbrochne Krug,* for example, Fairley avers:
"There is not the faintest vein of social satire or criticism
in this delightful study of a country judge and his escapades"
(207-08). Worth reading, though, if only to savor Fairley's
aesthetics. (L.S.)

Grosjean, Jean. *Kleist.* Paris: Gallimard, 1985. Pp. 90.
Fr. 60.00.

Günzel, Klaus. *Kleist: ein Lebensbild in Briefen und zeitgenössischen Berichten.* Stuttgart: Metzler, 1985. Pp. 506.

    Issued under license from the original publishers, Verlag
der Nation (DDR), this volume delivers on its promise to
characterize Kleist through contemporary documentation. It
is, however, a layperson's version of Helmut Sembdner's
1977 *Heinrich von Kleists Lebensspuren,* on which it draws
heavily. Günzel provides interstitial narration that tends
to be a bit breathless and sentimental. On the whole, though,
very readable. (L.S.)

Harlos, Dieter. *Die Gestaltung psychischer Konflikte einiger
Frauengestalten im Werk Heinrich von Kleists: Alkmene, Die
Marquise von O ..., Penthesilea, Käthchen von Heilbronn.*
(Europäische Hochschulschriften 1, 796.) Frankfurt am Main,
Bern, New York, and Nancy: Peter Lang, 1984. Pp. 161.

Using the "Marionettentheater" essay as a theoretical base,
Harlos claims he finds in Kleist's female figures a parallel
celebration of unconscious graciousness. Like many others,
he fails to note the dialectical irony of the dialogue, and
fetishizes its transcendental moment. In this case, he also
fetishizes Kleist's view of women. The iconography of
gender in Kleist's life and work is problematic, but it never
occurs to Harlos that Kleist may be problematizing conventions
of the *Goethezeit*. He winds up attributing to Kleist precisely
the positions that the texts subject to scrutiny. (L.S.)

Harms, Ingeborg. "'Wie fliegender Sommer.' Eine Untersuchung
der 'Höhlenszene' in Heinrich von Kleists *Familie Schroffen-
stein*." *JDSG* 28 (1984): 270-314.

Hettche, Walter. *Heinrich von Kleists Lyrik*. (Europäische
Hochschulschriften 1, 859.) Frankfurt am Main, Bern, and
New York: Peter Lang, 1986. Pp. 298.

A 1985 dissertation written under the direction of Walter
Müller-Seidel and with the advice of Klaus Kanzog, Hettche's
work will probably serve, *faute de mieux*, for some time as
the standard study of Kleist's poetry. Eschewing theoretical
definitions of genre, Hettche sees Kleist's lyric as the
scene of fragmentary explorations of the loss of meaning and
orientation in the late Enlightenment. The work is thus
basically an extension of Müller-Seidel's perspectives on
Kleist into a relatively neglected portion of Kleist's
literary production. A workmanlike overview, familiar with
German secondary literature, but not much else. (L.S.)

Krueger, Werner. "Rolle und Rollenwechsel: Überlegungen zu
Kleists *Marquise von O....*" *AG* 17 (1984): 29-51.

Well-informed neostructuralist approach to the question of
the kind of "knowledge" the Marquise has concerning the father
of her child and the content of her own subconscious. Argues
that an emphasis on identifying that knowledge is misplaced,
for the play should be seen as a dramatization of structural
relationships in bourgeois society (despite the noble titles
involved). Such relationships as the nuclear family involve
strategies of sublimating and integrating libidinal forces
that are thus "known" differently in various contexts and
at various levels. Turgidly written, but intelligently
posed. (L.S.)

Nicholls, Roger A. "'Schlug meiner Leiden letzte Stunde?':
The Problem of the Resolution of Kleist's *Prinz Friedrich von
Homburg*." *CGP* 14 (1986): 45-54.

A brief *reprise* of the old issues involved in deciding whether the conclusion of *Homburg* represents resolution or discord. Nicholls argues that "the resolution is far from secure" (54). That may be true, but it is trivial in that he shows very little awareness of contemporary literary theory (the only vaguely theoretical reference cites Northrop Frye) or of the thought of Kleist's age (nary a glance at the *Pflicht/Neigung* dialectic. Useful perhaps to introduce undergraduates to the ambiguity of the play. (L.S.)

Perels, Christoph. "Ein unbekannter Brief Heinrich von Kleists an Christoph Martin Wieland." *JFDH* (1986): 179-86.

This letter, written from Fort de Joux on March 10, 1807, remains missing, but a 1933 typescript, prepared when the original was allegedly donated to the Freies Deutsches Hochstift, provides evidence that Kleist asked Wieland to read "ein Paar Manuscripte." It seems idle to speculate which works were involved. (L.S.)

Prandi, Julie D. *Spirited Women Heroes: Major Female Characters in the Dramas of Goethe, Schiller and Kleist.* Las Vegas, Bern, and Frankfurt am Main: Peter Lang, 1983. Pp. 146.

See also *RMB* for 1985, pp. 385-86.

Reeves, Nigel. "Kleist's Indebtedness to the Science, Psychiatry and Medicine of His Time." *OGS* 16 (1985): 47-65.

An attempt to counter predominantly Freudian readings of Kleist's "unstable personality," and to understand questions of health and illness as Kleist's contemporaries did. Kleist found patterns in the *Naturphilosophie* of Schubert and in J.C. Reil's *Rhapsodien über die Anwendung der psychischen Curmethode auf Geisteszerrüttungen.* But where such thinkers saw the possibility of therapy, Kleist saw irreconcilable opposition between facets or faculties of the mind. (L.S.)

Rohmer, Eric, and Heinrich von Kleist. *The Marquise of O--: Film by Eric Rohmer. Novella by Heinrich von Kleist.* New York: Ungar, 1985. Pp. 137.

Like all good documentaries, this volume is the occasion for reflection on the grounds of interpretation and representation. Notes by Rohmer on directing the 1976 film inform us why no screenplay exists: "the cinematic transposition takes place of its own accord" (8). Literary critics could learn from the sensibilities of Rohmer, who speaks eloquently of the dialogic nature of the narrative, of the impassive exteriority of its language, and of the semantic richness of gesture in the Kleistian world. The volume presents an English translation of the film's dialogue, along with Martin Greenberg's translation of Kleist's novella, and a "critical afterword" by Alan Spiegel. All in all, the multiple voices testify to a rich practical hermeneutic. One wishes Rohmer would do more Kleist. (L.S.)

Stephens, Anthony. "'Eine Träne auf den Brief': zum Status der Ausdrucksformen in Kleists Erzählungen." *JDSG* 28 (1984): 315-48.

Stephens, Anthony. "Name und Identitätsproblematik bei Kleist und Kafka." *JFDH* (1985): 222-59.

Stephens, Anthony. "'Was hilfts, dass ich jetzt schuldlos mich erzähle?': zur Bedeutung der Erzählvorgänge in Kleists Dramen." *JDSG* 29 (1985): 301-23.

Weiss, Hermann F. *Funde und Studien zu Heinrich von Kleist.* Tübingen: Max Niemeyer Verlag, 1984. Pp. xii+364. DM 138.00.

Rev. by James M. McGlathery in *JEGP* 85 (1986): 309-10 as frequently "tedious."

Professor Weiss has for some years been filling in our picture of Kleist through his relentless pursuit of realia that other scholars may consider peripheral. This volume, presenting results of his researches since 1981, is his most comprehensive offering so far. Yet, despite its length and range, it is not a book. It is rather a stroll through the archives, garnished with *aperçus* and informed by a very nearly pedantic passion to follow Kleist's footsteps where others have not. Weiss's description of his objective in the first essay, "Beiträge zu Kommentierung der Briefe Kleists aus Paris vom Jahre 1801," sets the tone of the work: "In lockerer Folge sollen eine Anzahl der von Kleist berührten Aspekte des Lebens in der französischen Haupstadt behandelt werden" (1). The second section, entitled "Studien und Funde zu Heinrich von Kleists Politischem Wirken 1808 bis 1809," is more substantive. (L.S.)

Wellberry, David E., ed. *Positionen der Literaturwissenschaft: Acht Modellanalysen am Beispiel von Kleists "Das Erdbeben in Chili."* Munich: C.H. Beck, 1985.

Wellberry, who has established himself as a student of semiotics (*Lessing's "Laocoon": Semiotics and Aesthetics in the Age of Reason*, 1984); has collected essays from representatives (often illustrious) of other schools of literary criticism: Friedrich Kittler on discourse analysis, Norbert

Altenhofer on hermeneutics, Karlheinz Stierle on pragmatics
(communication theory), Christa Bürger on institutional
sociology, Helmut J. Schneider on social history, and René
Girard on mythology and anthropology. Wellberry contributes
an essay on literary semiotics, and Werner Hamacher concludes
the collection with a postlude on the loss of representational
possibilities, entitled, representatively enough, "Das Beben
der Darstellung." Intelligent essays on an important text.
Could be used in an introductory graduate course. (L.S.)

See also Chase ("General 3. Criticism"); Bänziger, Bronfen,
Deutsches Literaturarchiv, ed., Mayer, Sauer, Scheufele
("German 2. General").

Reviews of books previously listed:

FISCHER, Peter, *Heinrich von Kleist* (see *RMB* for 1983, pp.
390-91), rev. by Hilda M. Brown in *Germanistik* 26 (1985):
643-44; HEINRITZ, Reinhard, *Kleists Erzähltexte: Interpretationen nach formalistischen Theorieansätzen* (see *RMB*
for 1985, p. 385), rev. by Peter Gebhardt in *Germanistik* 26
(1985): 909-10; McGLATHERY, James M., *Desire's Sway: The
Plays and Stories of Heinrich von Kleist* (see *RMB* for 1983,
p. 394), rev. by Hans Eichner in *SiR* 25 (1986): 583-85;
SEMBDNER, Helmut, *Das Detmolder "Kätchen von Heilbronn":
eine unbekannte Bühnenfassung Heinrich von Kleists* (see *RMB*
for 1981, pp. 339-40), rev. by Peter Gebhardt in *Germanistik*
27 (1986): 132-33; WEIDMANN, Heiner, *Heinrich von Kleist--
Glück und Aufbegehren* (see *RMB* for 1985, p. 387); rev. by
Waltraud Wiethölter in *Germanistik* 26 (1985): 414; WICKERT,
Gabriele M., *Das verlorene heroische Zeitalter: Held und
Volk in Heinrich von Kleists Dramen* (see *RMB* for 1983, p.
398); rev. by Hilda M. Brown in *Germanistik* 26 (1985): 644-45.

LA ROCHE, SOPHIE VON

See Patsch ("Arnim, Bettina von").

LAUBE

See Hay ("German 2. General").

LEIBNIZ

See Schmitz-Emans ("Jean Paul").

LESSING

See Lowenthal, Mayer ("German 2. General"); Grappin ("Heine").

MÖRIKE

See Klotz, Lowenthal ("German 2. General"); Wittkowski ("Eichendorff").

MÜLLER, WILHELM

See Perraudin, Perraudin ("Heine").

MUSÄUS

See Klotz ("German 2. General").

NOVALIS

Lenoble, Michel. "Novalis: une autre vision du texte." *CRCL* 13 (1986): 187-201.

See also Michaud ("French 1. General"); Goodbody, Hay, Klotz, Loquai, Wheeler ("German 2. General"); Köhnke ("Eichendorff"); Murat ("Heine").

PLATEN

See Grubačić, Windfuhr ("Heine").

REILL

See Reeves ("Kleist").

SAVIGNY

See Frühwald ("Arnim, Bettina von").

SCHELLING

Higonnet, Margaret R. "Madame de Staël and Schelling." *CL* 38 (1986): 159-80.

SCHILLER

See Mayer, Pizer ("German 2. General"); Pott ("Hölderlin");
Paulin ("Tieck"); Bottoni ("Italian 3. Manzoni").

SCHLEGEL, A.W.

Kurth-Voigt, Lieselotte E., and William H. McClain. "Three
Unpublished August Wilhelm Schlegel Letters in the Kurrel-
meyer Collection." MLN 101 (1986): 592-608.

Rougemont, Martine de. "'Hellénique ou romantique': les
enjeux du drame sous l'Empire." Cahiers Staëliens 37 (1985-
86): 53-64.

   On the reaction to A.W. Schlegel's famous comparison of the
two Phèdres.

Rougemont, Martine de. "Schlegel ou la provocation: une
expérience sur l'opinion littéraire." Romantisme 16,51
(1986): 49-61.

See also Fiorili ("French 2. Staël"); Vietta, Wheeler, Zach
("German 2. General"); Bosisio, Bottoni ("Italian 3. Manzoni").

Review of book previously listed:

PAULINI, Hilde Marianne, August Wilhelm Schlegel und die
vergleichende Literaturwissenschaft (see RMB for 1985, pp.
390-91), rev. by Frank Jolles in Germanistik 27 (1986): 898.

SCHLEGEL, FR.

Alford, Steven E. Irony and the Logic of the Romantic Imagination. (American University Studies, series 3: Comparative
Literature, 13.) New York: Peter Lang, 1984. Pp. 177.

   Rev. by David Simpson in BIQ 19 (1986): 185f.
   A comparison of Schlegel and William Blake, over half of
which is devoted to Schlegel. Alford admits he does "not claim
to have found an all-encompassing definition of [Schlegel's
irony] here"; rather, he has "tried to add something to the
critical literature" because he has "approached irony through
Schlegel's lectures on logic" and "limited ... consideration
to irony as a principle of style" (17). Alford is more
successful in achieving the first of these two goals; he
usefully summarizes Schlegel's explication and critique of

classical and modern philosophical logic. The treatment of
ironic style, in contrast, consists of a reading of "Über
die Unverständlichkeit" in which very long blocks of quoted
text are left to speak for themselves. Along the way, Alford engages what he considers two views of speech-act theory
and shows how they correspond, if only partly, to Schlegel's
view of language.

Finally, the reader has to note bibliographic skimpiness
here. While Alford quotes, among other unpublished secondary
sources, his own undergraduate class notes, he seems largely
unfamiliar with the "critical literature" to which he is
trying to add. (W.C.)

Hotz-Steinmeyer, Cornelia. *Friedrich Schlegels Lucinde als
'neue Mythologie': geschichtesphilosophischer Versuch einer
Rückgewinnung gesellschaftlicher Totalität durch das Individuum.*
(Marburger germanistische Studien, 4.) Frankfurt: Peter
Lang, 1985. Pp. 272.

   Rev. by Raymond Immerwahr in *Germanistik* 27 (1986):   371-72.
Not seen.

Immerwahr, Raymond. "Friedrich Schlegels Abhandlung über die
Selbstständigkeit: aufgegebenes Projekt oder Metamorphose?"
DVLG 60 (1986): 426-39.

   Amasses evidence that Schlegel's projected treatise is
really a preliminary version of "Gespräch über die Poesie."
An interesting speculation in textual history, but one that
leads to no new appraisal of Schlegel's thought. (W.C.)

Kraus, Gerhard. *Naturpoesie und Kunstpoesie im Frühwerk
Friedrich Schlegels.* (Erlanger Studien, 64.) Erlangen:
Palm und Enke, 1985. Pp. 437.

   Rev. by Hans Dierkes in *Germanistik* 27 (1986):   899f.
   "Nature" here is to be taken in the Romantic tradition of
"Nature's book," a "poem" composed by the divine. Kraus
traces Schlegel's model of human art as a redemptive complement to nature: as God's "poem," nature has sacrificed its
endlessness, which the human artist ultimately helps restore
through the ironic fragment. An interesting account that
moves Schlegel closer than usual to Schelling (perhaps because
so much of the account is *about* Schelling). (W.C.)

Kühn, Renate. "Der Leser—die Frauen: Resultate einer prag-
matischen Lektüre von Friedrich Schlegels 'Gespräch über die
Poesie.'" *JDSG* 30 (1986): 306-38.

Nakai, Chiyuki. "Die Religion des jungen Friedrich Schlegel."
   DB 76 (1986): 35-44.

Neubauer, John. "Time, Character, and Narrative Strategy in
   Tristram Shandy and Lucinde." Pp. 1023-39 in Joseph P.
   Strelka, ed., Literary Theory and Criticism: Festschrift
   Presented to René Wellek in Honor of His Eightieth Birthday.
   Bern: Peter Lang, 1984. Pp. 1462.

   Neubauer documents Schlegel's lukewarmness to Sterne and
claims that studying Lucinde is the only way to find Tristram
Shandy's true influence on Schlegel. The comparison produces
a few provocative suggestions, e.g., that the "unwelcome
visitor" who interrupts Julius's opening letter is patterned
on the various interruptions in Tristram. Neubauer concludes
that Lucinde differs from Tristram by portraying characters
who grow through time, but that Lucinde's playfulness represents "but one dimension in Sterne's richly orchestrated
novel"; there is "greater maturity and deeper wisdom in
Sterne's art" (1038). Despite the many good particular observations here, the reader has to wonder: in the absence
of any external evidence of Schlegel's trying to reproduce
Sterne, what is gained by considering Lucinde a "lesser"
Tristram Shandy instead of simply another sort of book? (W.C.)

Onuki, Atsuko. "Geschichtsbewußtsein und ästhetische Kategorie
   beim frühen Friedrich Schlegel." DB 77 (1986): 96-106.

Ridel, Volker. "Prometheus und Herakles: Fragen an Friedrich
   Schlegels 'Idylle über den Müßiggang.'" Impulse 8 (1985):
   231-41.

Sakata, Kenichi. "Ironie und Logik in der Gedankenwelt
   Friedrich Schlegels." DB 76 (1986): 24-34.

Schanze, Helmut, ed. Friedrich Schlegel und die Kunsttheorie
   seiner Zeit. (Wege der Forschung, 609.) Darmstadt: Wissenschaftliche Buchgesellschaft, 1985. Pp. 468.

   Despite Schanze's perplexing explanation in his brief introduction, the title of this volume remains a mystery. The
book is not a study of Schlegel and "art theory of his time."
Rather, it is an anthology of seminal Schlegel studies from
Joseph Körner (1927) to Günter Oesterle (1977). Such a
collection would be important for students of any author:
for Schlegel it is doubly important, since its overview of
twentieth-century criticism may offer a center to what is
becoming an increasingly decentered, repetitious, and para-
phrastic body of Schlegel studies. Though the study contains

no original essays, it could easily be the most important Schlegel publication in some time. (W.C.)

See also Handwerk, Pattison ("General 3. Criticism"); Beer, Fruman ("English 4. Coleridge"); *Cahiers Staëliens*, Pattison ("French 2. Staël"); Loquai, Pizer, Vietta, Wheeler ("German 2. General"); Lindemann ("Eichendorff"); Asche ("Hoffmann, E.T.A."); Paulin ("Tieck"); Littlejohns ("Wackenroder").

Review of book previously listed:

BEHRENS, Klaus, *Friedrich Schlegels Geschichtsphilosophie* (see *RMB* for 1984, p. 408), rev. by Hans Dierkes in *Germanistik* 25 (1984): 865.

SCHLEIERMACHER

Crouter, Richard. "Schleiermacher and the Theology of Bourgeoise Society: A Critique of the Critics." *JR* 66 (1986): 302-23.

Gerrish, B.A. *A Prince of the Church: Schleiermacher and the Beginnings of Modern Theology*. Philadelphia: Fortress Press, 1984. Pp. 79. $4.50.

Rev. by Richard Crouter in *JR* 66 (1986): 78-79.

Wyman, Walter E., Jr. *The Concept of Glaubenslehre: Ernst Troeltsch and the Theological Heritage of Schleiermacher*. Chico, Calif.: Scholars Press, 1983. Pp. xix+255. $14.05.

Rev. by Benjamin A. Reist in *JR* 66 (1986): 79-80.

See also Gajek, Patsch ("Arnim, Bettina von").

SCHUBERT, G.H.

See Scheufele ("German 2. General"); Reeves ("Kleist").

SCHWAB

See Hay ("German 2. General").

SOLGER

See Wheeler ("German 2. General").

STIEGLITZ, CHARLOTTE

Promies, Wolfgang. "Der ungereimte Tod, oder wie man Dichter
    macht: zum 150. Todestag von Charlotte Stieglitz." *Akzente*
    32 (1985): 560-75.

    The only virtue of this rather shallow biographically
oriented essay lies in the fact that reliable and readily
available data on Charlotte Stieglitz is still scarce.
Promies does not skip his opportunity to mention that Charlotte
as he perceives her has been neglected by recent feminist
research. In this connection Promies implies that a woman
like Charlotte, who committed suicide with a view to inspire
her husband Heinrich into accelerated poetic production,
hardly serves as a strong role model for feminists in search
of their forgotten past. In the end it seems, though, that
Promies himself has a hard time turning Charlotte into anything other than a "victim of a misguided female education."
(K.B.)

STRAUβ, D.F.

See Bormann ("Eichendorff").

TIECK

Crisman, William. "Names, Naming and the Presentation of
    Language in the Fairy Tales from Tieck's *Phantasus*." *MGS* 11
    (1985): 127-43.

    Crisman correlates an onomastic feature of the *Phantasus*
tales, the ease or reluctance with which Tieck names the
various characters, with the characters' relationship to
language in general. As examples he employs the extremes:
Der getreue Eckart und der Tannhäuser (most characters,
greatest ease in naming) and *Der Runenberg* (fewest characters,
greatest reluctance in naming). Eckart's moderate use of
and sober attitude toward the spoken word preserve his sense
of self, while Christian's exaggerated devotion to a nonverbal
language of nature relate to his loss of memory and identity.
The character Tannhäuser, however, seems to defeat the
correlation, for he is readily named, yet shares in Christian's
linguistic excesses and his fate. In general, an interesting
stimulation for future studies. (R.C.)

Hölter, Achim. "'Die sieben Weiber': ein handschriftlicher
    Entwurf Ludwig Tiecks zur Neufassung des 'Blaubart.'" *WW* 36
    (1986): 251-58.

A revised prose version of *Blaubart* planned in 1817-18
was never written. From Tieck's sketchy concept outline in
the "Berliner Nachlaß" it is clear that the actual Blaubart
tale was to be placed inside a frame, that is, read at seven
different locations on a journey by a traveler who is himself
searching for a lady. Similarities in the locations mentioned
in the outline to entries in a diary from the summer of 1803,
which formed the basis for the 1833 novella *Die Sommerreise*,
suggest that while Tieck gave up on the satire in 1818, he
later separated the frame from the Bluebeard plot and employed
the former for the *Sommerreise* novella. A good piece of
literary detective work. (R.C.)

Hölter, Achim. "Ludwig Tiecks Klopstock-Bild und Seine
'Kritik der Messiade.'" *JFDH* (1985): 187-215.

Hölter brings to light a previously unpublished manuscript
from the "Berliner Nachlaß" entitled by a cataloguer "Kritik
der Messiade." The manuscript, in the handwriting of Tieck's
secretary, is sketchy, with several gaps and illegible words,
but it clearly expresses Tieck's almost total rejection of
Klopstock's most famous work as empty bombast and an affront
to Christianity. Hölter further demonstrates in his commentary that Rudolf Köpke had originally intended to include
the "Kritik" in his edition of *Nachgelassene Schriften*, but
elected instead to excerpt the manuscript for use in the sixth
book of his Tieck biography to augment the few notes he had
made from an actual conversation with Tieck about *Der Messias*.
(R.C.)

Klussmann, Paul G. "Idylle als Glucksmärchen in der Romantik
und Biedermeierzeit: Bemerkungen zu Erzählungen und Taschen-
buchnovellen Ludwig Tiecks." Pp. 41-59 in Hans Ulrich Seeber
and Paul Gerhard Klussmann, eds., *Idylle und Modernisierung
in der europäischen Literatur des 19. Jahrhunderts*. Bonn:
Bouvier, 1986.

Littlejohns, Richard. "Tonelli und Tunelli: zu Ludwig Tiecks
Märchenparodie." *Euphorion* 80 (1986): 201-10.

Littlejohns has discovered in the British Library the
"Büchelein" which was the source for *Die merkwürdige Lebens-
geschichte Sr. Majestät Abraham Tonelli*. His textual
comparison exonerates Tieck of the charge of blatant plagiarism
leveled at him by Varnhagen, while demonstrating that not
only the bourgeoisie was the object of Tieck's satire, as
Gonthier-Louis Fink has contended, but, more importantly,
absolute monarchs. Influence of the parody on Hoffmann's
Kater Murr is also discussed. Ludidly written, logically
argued. (R.C.)

Loquai, Franz. "Lovells Leiden und die Poesie der Melancholie:
zu Ludwig Tiecks Gedicht *Melankolie.*" Pp. 100-13 in Wulf
Segebrecht, ed., *Gedichte und Interpretationen: Klassik
und Romantik.* (Gedichte und Interpretationen, 3.) Stuttgart:
Reclam, 1984.

   The poem "Melankolie," which appeared in the novel *William
Lovell* and later in a volume of Tieck's poetry, is interpreted
first as it relates to the novel and then out of context.
Within the novel it aids in the initial characterization of
William. It has oracular function, anticipating the disastrous
conclusion. The declaration of the hostile gods is relativized
because, through the poetic act, Lovell is able to create for
himself temporary consolation. Outside the novel the poem
presents an allegorical interpretation of negative melancholy,
unproductive because it bears no germ of creative genius
within itself and leads to no higher aspirations. (R.C.)

Paulin, Roger. *Ludwig Tieck: A Literary Biography.* Oxford:
Clarendon Press, 1985. Pp. xiv+434.

   Rev. by Dwight A. Klett in *MGS* 11 (1985): 209-11; by Ernst
Ribbat in *Arbitrium* 1 (1987): 70-72.
   Paulin's warts-and-all biography is as refreshing as it is
thorough. He has drawn on a wealth of sources, as the 56
pages of notes demonstrate, but where he cannot document he
is rightly hesitant to draw absolute conclusions, such as
to what may or may not have happened between Tieck and Henriette von Finkenstein in Ziebingen. Thus Paulin avoids
sensationalizing, but he is equally skillful in avoiding the
hagiographic excesses of Rudolf Köpke. We see instead a
poet of some genius who, for most of his life, was unable to
fulfill the grandiose plans he was constantly hatching. We
glimpse a less than totally devoted husband in constant need
of money, in debt to this friends, and relying frequently
on the generous advances by patient publishers who might get
the promised work years late if at all. Tieck's often stormy
family situation is related, but more important to this
literary biographer are Tieck's relationships to his contemporaries: Goethe, Schiller, and Herder in Weimar, the
short-lived and never unified Jena Circle, and the younger
generation of Romantics in Heidelberg. Tieck's reverence for
Shakespeare, his philological devotion to the Middle Ages,
and the novellas of the Dresden years are among the topics
treated skillfully and in depth. (R.C.)

Paulsell, Patricia A. "Ludwig Tieck's *Der gestiefelte Kater*
and the English Burlesque Drama Tradition." *MGS* 11 (1985):
144-57.

Der gestiefelt Kater is reexamined as a burlesque play in the tradition of Buckingham, Fielding, and Sheridan. Paulsell exposes elements of English burlesque in the comedy in an argument against the widely held notion that Tieck was consciously indulging in Romantic irony at this early stage of his career. It is instead, she claims, an intended satire against the poor taste of bourgeois audiences; pompous, dullwitted critics; hackneyed, conventional plots; and neoclassical standards in the theater. (R.C.)

See also Deutsches Literaturarchiv, ed., Hay, Klotz, Loquai, Schubert, Vietta, Wheeler ("German 2. General"); Mattenklott ("Arnim, Bettina von"); Köhnke, Schwering ("Eichendorff").

Review of book previously listed:

KREUZER, Ingrid, *Märchenform und individuelle Geschichte: zu Text- und Handlungsstrukturen in den Werken Ludwig Tiecks zwischen 1790 und 1811* (see *RMB* for 1985, p. 398), rev. by Alexander von Bormann in *GRM* 36 (1986): 116-17.

UHLAND

See Perraudin ("Heine").

VARNHAGEN VON ENSE, KARL AUGUST

See Heinrich-Heine-Institut, Düsseldorf, ed. ("Heine"); Little-Johns ("Tieck"); Isselstein ("Varnhagen von Ense, Rahel").

VARNHAGEN VON ENSE, RAHEL

Feilchenfeldt, Konrad. "' ... und da nahm sich der Himmel meiner an': zu Rahel Varnhagens religiösem Selbstverständnis." Pp. 45-55 in Wolfgang Böhme, ed., *"Die Liebe soll auferstehen": die Frau im Spiegel romantischen Denkens.* (Herrenalber Texte, 59.) Karlsruhe: Evangelische Akademie Baden, 1985. Pp. 103. DM 5.80.

The topic of Rahel's attitude toward religious issues was already widely discussed among her contemporaries and is still of interest to Rahel researchers nowadays. Rahel--in a pattern frequent among other prominent Jewish people of her time--converted to Christian belief shortly before her marriage to Varnhagen von Ense in 1814. She was baptized by Schleiermacher in Berlin. In her letters Rahel commented on this step toward assimilation and also spoke of her indebtedness to theosophical and mystical concepts which she acquired by

reading Jakob Böhme, Angelus Silesius, Saint-Martin, and
Tauler. In an essay entitled "Über Rahels Religiösitat,"
Wilhelm Neuman, a one-time friend of Varnhagen, discussed
as early as 1836 the quasi-religious impression that so
many readers gained from the posthumously published book
Rahel: ein Buch des Andenkens für ihre Freunde. The
Rahelbuch was then often read as an "Erbauungsbuch" obviously
in the tradition of the once so popular pietistic confessions.
Feilchenfeldt's final contention that Rahel's religiousness
showed strong signs of an apotheosis of herself remains,
however, unconvincing and in need of further verification.
(K.B.)

Isselstein, Ursula. "Rahel und Brentano: Analyse einer
mißglückten Freundschaft, unter Benutzung dreier unveröffent-
lichter Briefe Brentanos." *JFDH* (1985): 151-201.

Isselstein carefully traces the relationship between Rahel
and Brentano during the rather short time of their close
acquaintance in the summer of 1813 when both were in Prague.
The subject is pursued on two different levels. Isselstein
is telling a psychological story of mutual attraction and
rejection. At the same time, she views Rahel's and Brentano's
handling of their individual problems as paradigmatic struggles
for survival during a time of social and political upheaval
following the French Revolution. It is especially the
psychological insights, backed up by information from two
letters written by Brentano but never sent off to Rahel,
which prove to be very enlightening for the reader. Rahel
is portrayed as a person who knows about her worth and is
keenly aware of her many brilliant talents but is denied a
broader social arena for practicing her skills. While she as
a Jew and a woman suffered from lack of public appreciation
and recognition, Brentano, who never had to worry about social
status himself, struggled instead with the enemy within himself or--to put it in different words--with his split personality. Both felt initially attracted to each other, not
least on the grounds of talents they shared, such as wit,
sensitivity, emotionality, and verbal eloquence. It seems
that both also tried to make amends for the unpleasant scenes
they were involved in during their first encounter in Teplitz
in 1811, when Clemens apparently displayed a good deal of
anti-Semitism while Varnhagen, Rahel's fiancée at that time,
became physically abusive and confiscated Brentano's manuscript "Aloys und Imelde." However, when Rahel opened herself
up to Brentano in a long outpouring letter in 1813, Brentano
not only misunderstood but also misused her confidence, and
in a highly egocentric and offensive way set out to analyze

Rahel's situation in terms of his own problems. This response culminated in his total disregard and disrespect for Rahel's justified complaints about her treatment by society and in his attempt to point out individual sinfulness as the source of all evil. This response also exemplifies Brentano's growing preoccupation with the Catholic religion, which gradually became an all-encompassing passion for him. The relationship between Rahel and Brentano thus came to an abrupt end and was never revived, even though Bettina von Arnim in Berlin kept the lines of communication with the Varnhagens open until Rahel's death. (K.B.)

Weissberg, Liliane. "Writing on the Wall: Letters of Rahel Varnhagen." *NGC* 36 (1985): 157-73.

This well-formulated and interesting article based on the exchange of letters between Rahel and David Veit focuses on Rahel's quest for truth and authenticity. The close analysis of two letters in which Rahel discusses the relationship between speaking and silence, self-portrayal and self-disguise, serves as a paradigm for what Weissberg calls a "psychoanalytic discourse." Weissberg approaches her subject in a partly linguistic, partly psychological way. She succeeds in pointing out that "truth" in Rahel's understanding and in the context of her written language is a very complex and multiperspectival issue that needs still further investigation. An underlying distrust of established forms of language shared by many female authors of her time also surfaces in Rahel's writing. Weissberg concludes that Rahel attempts to deal with this distrust by constantly testing the boundaries of language in different settings during her lifelong dialogue with others. (K.B.)

See also Mattenklott ("Arnim, Bettina von"); Isselstein ("Brentano"); Heinrich-Heine-Institut, Düsseldorf, ed., Kahn ("Heine"); Littlejohns ("Tieck").

WACKENRODER

Littlejohns, Richard. "Die Madonna von Pommersfelden: Geschichte einer romantischen Begeisterung." *Aurora* 45 (1985): 163-88.

Variously attributed to Raphael, Leonardo, and Cornelius van Cleve, the Pommersfelder Madonna was largely responsible for igniting Wackenroder's passion for Renaissance painting and motivating the *Herzensergießungen, Phantasien über die Kunst,* and *Franz Sternbald.* It also strongly influenced

Friedrich Schelegel, the Boisserées, and Johann Karl Ludwig
Schorn. Despite the exaggerated reverence in which it was
held by the founders of German Romanticism, the painting
languishes in disrepair in a storeroom of the Alte Pinakothek.
(R.C.)

See also Loquai, Schubert ("German 2. General"); Köhnke
("Eichendorff").

WIELAND

See Klotz, Mayer ("German 2. General"), Mattenklott ("Arnim,
Bettina von"); Schenck zu Schweinsberg ("Brentano"); Tismar
("Hölderlin"); Köpke ("Jean Paul"); Perels ("Kleist").

ITALIAN

(Compiled by Augustus Pallotta, Syracuse University;
Daniela Bini, University of Texas, Austin)

1. BIBLIOGRAPHY

"Bibliografia manzoniana." *ON* 9,1 (1985): 240-58; 9,2 (1985):
268-91; 9,3-4 (1985): 310-81; 9,5-6 (1985), supp. 12-55.
Much of the bibliography included here pertains to interest
in Manzoni reflected in the *terza pagina* of Italian news-
papers, in regional publications, and in popular magazines
and cultural reviews.

Caserta, Ernesto. "Un decennio di studi manzoniani in America
(1974-83)." *AdI* 3 (1985): 61-63.
See Caserta's article by the same title reviewed below.

Chandler, S.B., et al. "Alessandro Manzoni. Rassegna biblio-
grafica essenziale." *RSI* 3 (1985): 96-113.

De Caprio, Vincenzo. "Aggiornamento bibliografico: Manzoni."
AdI 4 (1986): 249-69.
Contains: "Sei anni di bibliografia manzoniana: 1980-
85," which is limited to books on Manzoni and includes recent
editions of his works; a short review article by V. De Caprio
devoted to "Studi biografici e sui *Promessi sposi*" (255-62);
a shorter piece by Franca Fusco, "Edizioni commentate dei
Promessi sposi" (263-66); and a final piece by Luigi Trenti,
"Dai versi giovanili agli scritti linguistici" (266-69).
The book review approach used in these pages relies on concision and selectivity much the same way as the reviews in
RMB. (A.P.)

Fasano, Pino. "Primo Ottocento." *RLI* 90 (1986): 303-14.

Urbancic, Ann. "Ottocento." *RSI* 3 (1985): 235-44.

2. GENERAL

Bonadeo, Alfredo. *L'Italia e gl'italiani nell'immaginazione
romantica inglese*. Napoli: Società Editrice Napoletana,
1984. Pp. 135.

British critics and cultural historians have shown a
predominant interest in the Romantic vision of Italy fostered
by British writers. In the case of flawed scholarship (there
is no need to mention names), we have had a picture of Italy
twice removed from reality. The value of Bonadeo's study,
a study, that is, by an Italian (but we must not forget
Mario Praz in this context), is the corrective balance that
results from such an exercise. This is not to say that, in
examining Byron, Ruskin, and Lawrence, Bonadeo is more objective; only that he brings to the subject a different
perspective. He has no doubt, for instance, that Ruskin's
ethical and religious views prevented his full appreciation
of Italy. And, in discussing D.H. Lawrence, Bonadeo offers
a keen, if polemical, analysis of *Twilight in Italy* and of
the author's underlying psychological disposition. (A.P.)

Brand, C.P. "Dante and the Middle Ages in Neo-Classical and
Romantic Criticism." *MLR* 81 (1986): 327-36.

Fido, Franco. "At the Origins of Autobiography in the Eighteenth and Nineteenth Centuries: The *Topoi* of the Self."
AdI 4 (1986): 168-80.

Examines a large spectrum of European autobiographical
works--among them those by Chateaubriand, Stendhal, Alfieri,
and Goldoni--from the standpoint of their analogies and
differences. The analogies establish a sort of intertexual
dialogue in which stands out the presence of such *topoi*
as justification for the work, conditions of birth, relationship to family, and childhood. Another element typical
of autobiography examined with equal discernment by Fido
is a writer's reference to his literary models, a process
attesting to "a kind of intertextuality," that is, the
awareness that the authors "are working in common toward
instituting a new literary genre" (175). In sum, Fido
believes that autobiographical writing constitutes, above
all, an affirmation of the self, for "while writing a past
for himself," the writer "recovers consciousness of his
self" (178). (A.P.)

Petrocchi, Giorgio. "Carducci critico e il Romanticismo."
LI 38 (1986): 26-39.

Explores, through the poetry and critical writings, Carducci's deep antagonism toward Romanticism, his aversion to sentimentalism, the fantastic, and spiritualism--elements that prompted his dissociation from Manzoni, Leopardi, even Foscolo. Petrocchi seeks, of course, to place in evidence Carducci's negative perceptions of Romanticism as identified by the common traits shared by the three writers just mentioned. The problem with this approach is that, the differences among Leopardi, Foscolo and Manzoni being so substantial, such differences are minimized or blurred to bring to light their (much less important) Romantic affinities. (A.P.)

Ragusa, Olga. "Autobiografia italiana dell'Ottocento: orientamenti." *AdI* 4 (1986): 181-88.

Within a broad sociohistorical framework which enlightens the matter in question, Ragusa examines first the few anthological publications containing nineteenth-century Italian autobiographical works. She does so to draw attention to the limitations regarding the editions of available texts as well as the dearth of interest in what is commonly perceived by critics as "la marginalità e l'indeterminatezza del genere" (184)--two detrimental factors from which escape only a few works that "hanno le serietà della confessione e non la leggerezza dell'avventura" (184). A second cause relates to the entrenched sociocultural structures of the Ottocento ignored by traditional scholarship which nonetheless formed the matrix and often the object of memorialistic writing. Ragusa's insightful analysis and her sensible guidelines to upgrade critically this area of study constitute a valuable asset for those who accept the challenge. (A.P.)

See also Imbert ("French 3. Stendhal").

3. STUDIES OF AUTHORS

FOSCOLO

Barellai, Emanuela. "Sulla relazione di Ugo Foscolo ed il barone danese Herman Schubart." *RLI* 90 (June-Aug. 1986): 130-36.

Publishes a letter dated July 1813 from Foscolo to the Danish diplomat and Italophile H. Schubart in the wake of the unsuccessful staging of Foscolo's *Ricciarda* in Milan. Ample documentation on Schubart who lived in Italy for many years, met Alfieri, Foscolo, Mme. de Staël, and whose villa

in Livorno served as a meeting place for literati.   Important
source for students of cultural history.   (A.P.)

Ciardi, Roberto. "La cultura figurativa di Ugo Foscolo."
RiLI 3 (1985):   290-325.

Examines in depth Foscolo's position on the interaction
between literature and the plastic arts. The discussion
focuses on Canova's neoclassical sculptures toward which
Foscolo had ambivalent feelings because he objected to
Canova's heavily mediated representation of classical subjects. In Foscolo's aesthetics, visual arts "vengono collo-
cate nel gradino più basso dell'attività spirituale" (304)
because they tend to elicit sensations rather than rationality. Closer to Foscolo's aesthetic views, according to
Ciardi, are the works of Leonardo, Michelangelo, and
Raffaello, which were perceived as being far richer in intellectual content than neoclassical art. (A.P.)

Foscolo, Ugo. *Poesie e carmi. Dei sepolcri. Poesie postume.*
A cura di F. Pagliai, G. Folena, M. Scotti. (Edizione
Nazionale delle Opere di Ugo Foscolo, 1.) Firenze: Le
Monnier, 1985. Pp. xii+1,300.

A milestone in Foscolo studies, this critical edition
reflects nearly 25 years of assiduous philological scholarship by Pagliai. One of Pagliai's main objectives was to
correct the flaws of previous editions, especially the much-
used edition by Chiarini and Ferrari. As explained in the
introduction, Pagliai's work, left unfinished by his death,
was continued by Folena. A mine of philological learning
and a necessary point of reference for future Foscolo criticism. (A.P.)

Luti, Giorgio. "Poesie e carmi foscoliani." *NA* 121 (July-
Sept. 1986):   293-301.

Like Nencioni, whose article is reviewed below, Luti
praises the most recent edition of Foscolo's *Opere*, in
particular the methodology followed by F. Pagliai and M.
Scotti.

Matteo, Sante. *Textual Exile: The Reader in Sterne and
Foscolo.* New York: Peter Lang, 1985. Pp. 283.

Rev. by Douglas Radcliff-Umstead in *AdI* 4 (1986):   304-06.
Matteo's objective here is met by a difficult challenge:
to chart new territory in Foscolo studies by departing from
the traditional, author-oriented criticism (the essence of
which is summarized in the introduction) and undertaking

a new form of analysis centered on the text and its relationship to implied and real readers. To a large extent,
Matteo succeeds in conveying a fresh and mostly convincing
study of Foscolo's *Le ultime lettere di Jacopo Ortis* and
his translation of Sterne's *Sentimental Journey*. Supported
by the theoretical tenets of Iser, Jauss, Genette, and Eco,
among others, Matteo displays, quite skillfully, various
reading strategies, which are not limited to Foscolo and
Sterne. Chapter 3, for instance, is devoted to a polyvalent
reading of the *Roman de la Rose*. Among the fresh insights
gained from Matteo's reader-oriented criticism, one should
mention the problem of writing as a central concern in ·
literary analysis; the connection suicide-logocide, and
Jacopo's ambivalent attitude toward Teresa's father in
Jacopo Ortis, as well as Foscolo's efforts to expose Italian
readers to the bourgeois novel through his translation of
Sentimental Journey. Finally, the scornful attitude toward
philological or prestructuralist criticism that is found,
latently or explicitly, in much recent criticism, is nowhere
present here. At the very end of his study, Matteo remarks:
"Since an author-oriented approach has dominated for many
years, the advantage of a reader-oriented approach is not
that it is somehow better or more reliable, but simply that
it is newer and provides a new angle of vision which allows
texts ... to be perceived in slightly different ways" (230-
31). Very good bibliography. (A.P.)

Nencioni, Giovanni. "L'edizione critica delle *Grazie*." *NA*
121 (July-Sept. 1986): 270-92.

A comprehensive review of the recent critical edition of
Le Grazie included in the 1986 *Edizione Nazionale delle
Opere di Ugo Foscolo*, edited by F. Pagliai and M. Scotti.
Nencioni points out that the work brought to fruition by
the two editors goes well beyond the requisites of philology;
it integrates modern diachronic criteria as it does away
with "formule pseudostoriche e pseudologiche, le false
categorizzazioni critiche ed estetiche" (271) generated
by previous unscholarly editions. In appraising the work
of his colleagues, Nencioni manages to offer a remarkably
fresh study of Foscolo's poetry, a study that stands out
both autonomously and as a felicitous complement to the
critical edition that inspired it. (A.P.)

O'Neill, Tom. "Foscolo and Dante." Pp. 109-35 in E. Haywood
and B. Jones, eds., *Dante Comparisons. Comparative Studies
of Dante and Montale, Foscolo, Tasso, Chaucer, Petrarch,
Propertius, and Catullus*. Dublin: Irish Academy Press,
1985. Pp. 154.

Foscolo's "sdegno morale" toward his times is what links him most cogently to Dante: "If the style of the man was his and his alone, the moral indignation was universal. And this was the inheritance of Foscolo, but it was an inheritance which he translated into the language of his day and which in its vehemence he directed against the society of his day" (131). (A.P.)

Paolini, Paolo. "Foscolo e Manzoni: riconsiderazioni di un confronto obbligato." *ON* 9 (1985): 5-20.

Foscolo's uneasy relationship with Manzoni is placed in evidence through a series of biographical incidents (such as the lukewarm reception accorded to Foscolo in Paris in 1806) and, more importantly, through a comparative study of poetic texts in which the preeminence of Manzoni's art is established. (A.P.)

Velli, Giuseppe. *Tra letteratura e creazione. Sannazaro, Alfieri, Foscolo.* Padova: Antenore, 1983. Pp. 107.

Contains "Memoria letteraria e poiesi nel Foscolo giovane" (92-104) in which Velli studies vv. 10-12 of "Alla sera" ("E intanto fugge / questo reo tempo, e van con lui le torme / delle cure onde meco egli si strugge"), verses that are juxtaposed intertextually to the Virgilian "Fugit inreparabile tempus" (*Georgics*, 3,284) and Petrarch's *Bucolicum carmen.* Sound comparative analysis marked by an impressive knowledge of the classics. (A.P.)

See also Petrocchi ("Italian 2. General").

LEOPARDI

Ambrosini, Riccardo. "Per un'analisi linguistica dell'Infinito." *LeL* 1-2 (1983): 65-80.

This analysis, dedicated to Tristano Bolelli, aims at showing similarities between the images of the poem and astronomic and scientific texts, like those of Bruno, Galilei, and Viviani. The parallelism seems somewhat far-fetched, although nobody will deny the influence of scientific works on young Leopardi. Just as farfetched seems his idea about the strophic structure of the poem, which Ambrosini sees as a series of broken "terzine," the aim being to be anti-Dante and to turn Dante's message upside down. The critic concludes that knowledge of the infinite was Dante's source of beatitude whereas Leopardi's bittersweetness (he knew no beatitude) was caused by self-abandonment in the infinite, not by the knowledge of it. (D.B.)

Blasucci, Luigi. *Leopardi e i segnali dell'infinito.* Bologna: Il Mulino, 1985. Pp. 283.

Includes previously published essays (i.e., "Una fonte linguistica per i *Canti*: la traduzione del secondo libro dell'Infinito"; "I segnali dell''Infinito'"; "La posizione ideologica delle Operette morali"; "Capitoli di critica leopardiana"). Part of the third essay and the sixth are new ("Livelli e correzioni dell''Angelo Mai'" and "Linea della 'Sera del dì di festa'"); Blasucci will use them in an introductory chapter on a commentary of the *Canti*, still in a gestation phase. In chapter 3 Blasucci shows the presence of three different motives unfolding gradually in "Angelo Mai": the encomiastic, the patriotic, and the philosophical whose negative content undermines the other two and takes over. In chapter 5 the old question of the unity of "La sera" is answered not with the discovery of a theme, but rather of a dynamics of various motives whose climax consists in the song of the artisan which interrupts the poet's subjective reflection on his unhappiness. The phonic element aims at deviating the path of thought of the "I," in order to nullify it. (D.B.)

Bova, Anna Clara. "Leopardi e il 'sistema': Introduzione allo *Zibaldone*." *LCr* (Sept.-Dec. 1984): 57-131.

Bova sees the *Zibaldone* as a testimony of Leopardi's painstaking effort to explain scientifically the contrast between civilization and human misery. In his effort Leopardi had to overcome not only the separation claimed by the rationalists between man and nature, inserting man within the system of nature, but also the Romantic idea of a fusion of the two, that is, the idea of nature as a harmonic, vital organism. The study of the Ideologues and in particular of Cabanis was a necessary premise, but Leopardi's new approach found support in his friendship with the physicians Puccinotti and Tommasini. His need for a systematic understanding of nature moved him away from *ideology* and toward natural history, toward the study of animation and sensibility and to a definite physiological interpretation of life, defined as the material organization of sensibility. (D.B.)

Casoli, Giovanni. *Dio in Leopardi. Ateismo o nostalgia del divino?* Rome: Città Nuova, 1985. Pp. 250.

The question in the title is not answered. Many pages are
devoted to the development of Leopardi's thought in the
Zibaldone, especially the issue of Christianity. Casoli,
who wants to set his study off from contemporary Leopardi
scholarship, does not give any new insight into his philosophy. At the end of Leopardi's long pessimistic and nihi-
listic intinerary Casoli sees a positive end: the vocation
to love mankind, "il senso dell'animo di Plotino." This
message of solidarity, he says, is neither socialist, nor
liberal, nor strictly confessional; it is simply human.
(D.B.)

Cassata, Letterio. "Da Marchetti a Leopardi." *RiLI* 2 (1986):
247-51.

A brief note on the receptiveness of Leopardi's poetic
memory. Cassata shows how several verses by Count
Giovanni Marchetti, an acquaintance of Leopardi and the
author of a book of *Rime e Prose*, reappear with slight
variations in "A Silvia." The source, Cassata discovered,
was Marchetti's poem "La Speranza." In fact, hope had fallen
together with Napoleon. (D.B.)

De La Nieves Muñiz, Maria. "Verità come morte nell'ultimo
Leopardi." *CrL* 40 (1983): 557-80.

The scholar sees the polemic between Solmi and Timpanaro
as emblematic of the directions of Leopardi studies today.
On the one hand, there is the conviction of a continuity in
Leopardi's thought (Solmi) and the consequent necessity of
accepting, in the last phase, the coexistence of two contrasting ideas of nature; on the other, there is the overturn
of the initial system (Timpanaro); with its forced acceptance of the interrelation, at the end, between the idea of
a malignant nature and the revaluation of reason. Muñiz
wants to show that this polarization lies within Leopardi's
texts. The interpretation of "La ginestra," a symbol, she
claims, of nature at a vegetative state with which man should
try to identify, is weak. Muñiz seems to contradict herself
when, praising the "ginestra" for the acceptance of its fate,
she qualifies it as "voluntary and conscious." (D.B.)

Dell'Aquila, Michele. "Di Sinisgalli, di Leopardi e della
poesia." *ON* 9,2 (March-April 1985): 47-73.

Commenting on a paper read in 1972 by Sinisgalli for the
third *Convegno Leopardiano* on "Leopardi e il Novecento,"
Dell'Aquila briefly comments on the great affection and
respect that tie Sinisgalli to Leopardi despite their

apparent differences. He discusses their common interest
in the sciences and mathematics, the need for order, and
thus for a system, coupled, however, with the awareness of
the complexity of reality, which cannot be fitted into any
system. Finally, he notes their similar conception of the
poetic act, connected to study, to reading, and to the
physical immobility of the poet in a void which is the condition *sine qua non* for the creative act. (D.B.)

Derla, Luigi. "Leopardi: il bene, il vero, il bello."
ON 9,2 (March-April 1985): 5-25.

The essay begins with an extreme and ill-founded statement: that Leopardi's pessimism is not philosophical, but
sentimental. According to Derla, Leopardi promotes his
peculiar personal sorrow to the level of a universal principle. All his pessimistic statements do not leave the personal sphere. Thus Leopardi is still dependent on the
classical, hedonistic tradition. The solidarity he invokes
in "La ginestra," Derla claims, is, therefore, an ideological,
pathetic reaction, not a theoretical process. On the other
hand, the truth that the courageous soul must face is not
theoretical, but practical. Derla seems to read Leopardi
in Crocean terms when he concludes that the whole of his
philosophy is born from the "pathos della vita mortificata"
and that it expresses the revolt of feelings against reason.
Subjectivism, according to Derla, also underlies Leopardi's
aesthetics which is reduced to psychology: beautiful is
what pleases the subject. (D.B.)

De Silvestre, Tonino. *Leopardi oggi*. Poggibonsi: Antonio
Lalli, 1984. Pp. 61.

A very meager book with a strong moralistic aim, and no
scholarly qualities. In his crusade against our materialis-
tic times, De Silvestre uses Leopardi as a model of those
spiritual values that are totally lacking today, so he
claims. Leopardi, who better than anyone else diagnosed
the decay of man through his progress, teaches us how to
redeem ourselves through the spiritual values of art. This
process of redemption, he continues--but here it is hard to
follow him--postulates a return to the purity of childhood.
Thus, it coincides with the Christian message. (D.B.)

Di Benedetto, A. "Postilluminismo: Alfieri e Leopardi."
MC 54 (Jan.-March 1985): 5-16.

The essay stresses the ambivalent rapport that Leopardi
had with the Enlightenment: praise for the demystification

of superstitions and errors by means of reason, and criticism for reason was to coincide with misery. The basic
difference, in fact, between Leopardi and the thinkers of
the Enlightenment is the poet's total lack of conviction
that man can achieve happiness. Di Benedetto, however,
seems to doubt as well Leopardi's materialism. His doubt
rests on a few questions Leopardi asked himself, like those
in "Sopra il ritratto ..." ("Natura umana, or come / Se
frale in tutto e vile, / Se polve ed ombra sei, tant'alto
senti?") which in Di Benedetto's view prove the force of his
spiritualism. A weak proof! (D.B.)

Fasano, Pino. *L'entusiasmo della ragione. Il romantico e
l'antico nell'esperienza leopardiana.* Rome: Bulzoni,
1985. Pp. 135.

Two intelligent essays: "Leopardi controromantico,"
published in *Il Ponte*, 1971; and "Come gli antichi greci,"
published here for the first time. In order to answer the
old question: was Leopardi Romantic or classicist, Fasano
examines Leopardi's relationship with the Romantics in the
first essay and with the classicists in the second. The
most interesting aspect of this debate, says Fasano, is
Leopardi's attitude toward the issue, which was never dogmatic in either direction, but constantly open to dynamic
confrontation between the Romantic and the Ancient. The
second essay is of special interest. It points out the
importance of the translations in understanding this issue.
Fasano shows the development from early classicism (the
euphoria of creating poetry "alla maniera degli antichi")
to the later classicism of the translator and commentator
of the ancient philosophers. This later classicism helps
to prove the "absolute validity" of Leopardi's "filosofia
dolorosa." He can now tie together classicism and Romanticism. It is at this point, in fact, that Leopardi shows
the modernity and the "Romantic" quality of the ancient
thought. (D.B.)

Landoni, Elena. "Manzoni, Leopardi e il Romanticismo in
Europa." *Testo* 10 (July-Dec. 1985): 41-62.

Landoni distinguishes Manzoni's Romanticism with its
belief in the usefulness of the work of art, and in its

social application, from Leopardi's, which affirms the
autonomy of the work of art whose object is the beautiful,
not the useful. Manzoni's Romanticism was labeled "the
Italian Romanticism," different from its European counter-
parts insofar as it expressed the peculiarity of the Italian
social and political scene of the Risorgimento. Showing
similarities between Leopardi and German and English Romantic writers, Landoni points out that it was Leopardi's
Romanticism, unique on the Italian scene, that was closely
connected with European Romantic ideas. Perhaps, she concludes, it was because of this isolation from the Italian
literary scene that Leopardi could not only elaborate on an
aesthetical discourse which was immune to national preoccupations but also, paradoxically, become a pioneer in a
new poetical current. (D.B.)

Marchese, Angelo. "Radiografia di 'Alla luna.'" *ON* 9,2
(March-April 1985): 27-46.

A stylistic analysis of the phonic, metric, syntactic,
and semantic structures of the poem which aims at understanding its musical texture and thus the intention of the
poet's construction. In the perfect textual coherence and
unity of these four levels, none of these elements is found
to take over and dominate. At the end of his painstaking
analysis, Marchese concludes that Leopardi's elaborate
construction of the lines is not the skeleton or outline
of the message to be sent, but they are values in themselves
and melodic effects of that very poetical meaning. (D.B.)

Nemesio, Aldo. "Les différents masques de la légitimation
et les pièges du canon littéraire: réflexions sur le cas
des premiers *Canti* de Giacomo Leopardi." *EL* 2-3 (April-
Sept. 1985): 113-26.

After postulating the existence in nineteenth-century Italy
of literary canons--that is, a group of texts that a large
sector of intellectuals consider pertinent within a literary
system in a given historical period due to the unifying
efforts of the ruling class--Nemesio tries to show Leopardi's
dependence on them in his first *Canti*. He centers his
sketchy analysis on "Risorgimento," whose structure is constituted of binary oppositions. This was a fashion, he
claims, very much diffused in the 19th century (Nemesio
mentions Poerio but gives no examples). The main binary
opposition at work in the poem, that of past-present, transforms its apparent political message into a purely rhetorical
discourse, reduced to the binary opposition: good-evil.
Even at this early stage, he concludes, Leopardi's intention
was clearly literary, not political. (D.B.)

Parra Cristadoro, Diana. *Leopardismo e antileopardismo nel nostro 900: Ungaretti, Bacchelli, Montale.* Poggibonsi: Lalli, 1984. Pp. 57.

A poorly written essay with stylistic and editorial errors, which, despite the impressive title, has no beginning, development, or conclusion. The author speaks through quotations taken from Dolfi, Blasucci, and Solmi. Five pages are dedicated to the "Leopardism" of Ungaretti; no texts are examined, a few generalizations are made: what Leopardi and Ungaretti share is the belief in suffering as a source of poetry. Montale is brought in as an example, not proven, of "antileopardismo." Here, too, texts are not used. As for Bacchelli, the author examines a few superficial critical essays he wrote on Leopardi at the beginning of the century. One wonders what was the point of writing such a book and even more why it was published. (D.B.)

Potthoff, Elisabetta. "Rilke traduttore di Leopardi." *LL* 2 (May 1984): 191-98.

Rilke's translation of the "Infinito" and of ten lines of "La sera del dì di festa" begins a ten-year period (ca. 1910-1920) of poetry translation which coincides with Rilke's poetic silence. His efforts as translator are aimed at regaining his own poetic voice, which he had lost in those tragic years. The choice of these two poems reflects Rilke's long-standing obsession with silence. Leopardi seems to tell him that it is precisely nature's infinite silence that can stimulate the poetic imagination. (D.B.)

Ricciardi, Mario. *Giacomo Leopardi: la logica dei Canti.* Milan: Franco Angeli, 1984. Pp. 136.

By dividing the *Canti* into two groups: 1-9 ("All'Italia"--"L'ultimo canto di Saffo"), 12-16 (the *Idilli*) as Leopardi had done when he grouped them in two different books (*Canzoni* and *Versi*), Ricciardi points out the difference and the reciprocal dependence of the two. The poetic parabola shows the progressive extinction and transformation of the *Canzoni* into the *Idilli*, the passage from the political and public sphere to the sphere of the private and the sentimental. Three of the *Canzoni* constitute the focus of his analysis: "Ad Angelo Mai," with the emphasis on the renewed engagement of the modern humanist; "Bruto Minore," which represents the reflection on the end of the classical world of ethical values and virtues, that is, the end of the positive function of political messages; and "L'ultimo canto di Saffo," where matter defeats history and ethics, and the poet becomes the

speaker of the self. Thus the road is open to the *Idilli*,
the modern subjective poetry. (D.B.)

Righi, Stefania. "Gadda e Leopardi." *RLI* 89 (Jan.-April
1985): 148-56.

More caustic is Gadda's irony, more bitter his pessimism
(he lived through the experience of the war and of Fascism)
than Leopardi's; yet a basic similar philosophy sets both
against man's stupidity. The theme of knowledge seen as
suffering underlines all of Leopardi's work and becomes the
core of *La cognizione del dolore* where Gadda, quoting him
extensively, pays homage to Leopardi. Righi ends her comparison by pointing out what she claims is the main difference
between the two. Leopardi's final search for and faith in
men's solidarity, which she argues for by citing the much-
exploited "topos" of "La ginestra." This is a weak proof
indeed. Gadda's final isolation is, in fact, much closer
to Leopardi's position. The poet might have invoked some
solidarity among men, but he never deeply believed it could
be achieved. (D.B.)

Rigoni, Mario Andrea. "Leopardi et le vertige de la lucidité."
NRF 376 (May 1984): 76-86.

Rigoni calls Leopardi the only great poet-thinker Italy
has ever had--a poet who was ahead of his time and gave
voice to the drama of the modern conscience, the drama "de
la lucidité." More than 50 years before Nietzsche, he stated
that reason in its extreme lucidity is sheer folly and that
oblivion, in contrast to reason, is the only reasonable
attitude, for it allows us to live. Rigoni examines many
passages in the *Zibaldone* where Leopardi dwells on the paradox of two opposite and inseparable poles: the negation
of illusions and their defense. Regarding Leopardi, he claims,
we cannot talk of pessimism, but of nihilism, because only
he who has no illusions left loves illusions. Thus the
value of poetry--which creates illusions from the world of
all illusions. (D.B.)

Tellini, Gino. "Testo critico e autografi dei Canti leopardiani."
Paragone 35,616 (Oct. 1984): 71-77.

Ugniewska, Joanna. "La recezione di Leopardi nell'Ottocento
polacco." *RLI* 89 (Jan.-April 1985): 69-75.

The author bases her study on the belief that a literary
text is the result of the act of reading and using it, and
that it changes according to the reader (H.R. Jauss, H.

Weinrich, Gadamer, Habermas). This theoretical background
helps her to explain the initial resistance to Leopardi's
work by the Polish readers. At the begining of the 1800s
Polish culture was imbued with a patriotic and Catholic
ideology that made it more naturally receptive to Manzoni,
Pellico, and Mamiani. Ugniewska examines individual essays
where Leopardi's name appears and shows how slow the process
of acceptance was. Even toward the end of the 1800s, when
literature was recognized in its autonomy, Leopardi's
pessimism was still seen as the result of his personal life.
Only in this century have some Polish scholars, like S.
Brzozowski, understood the philosophical and existential
dimensions of Leopardi's message. A further difficulty was
the rendering in Polish of complex poems like "L'infinito."
(*Canzoni* like "All'Italia" were more easily translated.)
(D.B.)

Viani, Eva. "Ancora su Leopardi e i presocratici: Eraclito."
CI 6 (1984-5): 51-60.

   The epilogue of the "Dialogo della natura e di un Islandese"
seems to echo the end of Heraklitos's text as it was recorded
in the Byzantine *Suda*. Leopardi did, in fact, refer to this
text in the notes of the *Operette morali*. The purpose of
this brief essay is to point out the use by Leopardi of the
doxografic tradition. It would be hard, in fact, to consider
Heraklitos's fragments as a direct source for Leopardi.
(D.B.)

See also Petrocchi ("Italian 2. General").

MANZONI

Angelini, Cesare. *Con Renzo e con Lucia (e con gli altri).
Saggi sul Manzoni.* Ed. P. Gibellini and A. Stella. Pref.
by Maria Corti. Brescia: Morcelliana, 1986. Pp. 163.

   Contains 14 essays on Manzoni, the earliest of which was
written nearly 50 years ago. Angelini's source-oriented
criticism concerns itself primarily with the enduring
qualities of Manzoni's work. Maria Corti, the prominent
semiotician, would seem hardly the appropriate person to
introduce the volume. Yet she discharges the task with
admiring generosity. Invoking Lotman, she remarks that a
critic like Angelini "tenderà a usare i testi come stereotipi
e a identificare ciò che in un testo è valore eterno cioè
modello e sublime stereotipo." (A.P.)

Apollonio, Carla. "Edgar Allan Poe e *I promessi sposi*." *ON*
9 (1985): 237-46.

Attempts to relate Poe's review of Manzoni's novel,
published in the *Southern Literary Messenger* (1835) to
Poe's short story, "King Pest," which echoes in part Manzoni's
treatment of the bubonic plague. The matter is hardly original, having been treated to some degree by Cecchi, Getto,
and Olivero whose contributions are duly acknowledged in the
bibliography. (A.P.)

Bàrberi-Squarotti, Giorgio. "La storia impraticabile: le
tragedie del Manzoni." *FI* 19 (1985): 205-36.

Affording cogent textual documentation, the study traces
the gradual, though ultimately radical, change in Manzoni's
perception of the character and potentiality of literature,
from the initial preference for tragedy to the interest
in the novel to the total disillusion vis-à-vis the usefulness of letters in society. At the outset, Manzoni opted
for tragedy as the medium that enabled a Romantic writer
to strive for historical truth and combat the intensive emotional involvement associated with Neoclassical tragedy. In
the years that elapsed between the composition of *Adelchi*
and *Carmagnola*, and the first draft of the novel, the
preferential space assigned to tragedy was eroded by
disenchantment and a redimensioning attitude toward literature: "La storia non può essere l'oggetto privilegiato della
tragedia.... La tragedia, agli occhi del Manzoni, non è più
l'appello alla verità e alla giustizia che è pronunciato al
di la della storia e degli eventi" (225). Accordingly
Manzoni turns to the novel with temporary confidence until,
that is, in the historical research that accompanies the
Storia della colonna infame, he comes to the awareness that
no work of fiction can deal adequately with history: "A quel
punto la letteratura non avrà più significato per il Manzoni:
e incomincerà, infatti, il suo longo silenzio di scrittore,
che è una delle più radicali e lucide dichiarazioni di
impotenza e di inadeguatezza della letteratura che un secolo
di molta crisi della scrittura letteraria, quale è l'Ottocento,
presenti" (236). Clearly an important study, one that offers
further refinement of Bàrberi-Squarotti's ideas, contained
in his book, *Il romanzo contro la storia. Studi sui "Promessi
sposi"* (1980). (A.P.)

Basile, Bruno. "Dostoevskij, Manzoni e *I misteri del chiostro
napoletano*." *LI* 38 (1986): 233-41.

Examines the circumstances surrounding a *cause celèbre*:
the publication, in 1864, of *I misteri* by Enrichetta
Caracciolo, a Benedictine nun who offered a candid, albeit
anticlerical account of monastic life. In all likelihood,
the book was known to Manzoni and Dostoevski. Basile
claims that possibly it reminded Manzoni of Gertrude.
Dostoevski, who was in Florence in 1861 and 1868 and was
interested in women writers, brought the book to the attention of the readers of *Epocha*, a magazine he edited with
his brother. (A.P:)

Bezzola, Guido. "Il Manzoni e il sentimento della campagna."
NA 121 (April-June 1986): 240-53.

Links *Adda* and its idyllic images to Brusuglio, seen as
a privileged situs where Manzoni led a fruitful life as a
writer and botanist. The focus is on Manzoni as "gentilhomme
campagnard." (A.P.)

Bonora, Ettore. "Ancora sulla lettera a Marco Coen." *GSLI*
163 (1986): 27-43.

Marco Coen, the Venetian youth who wanted to study
literature while his father encouraged him to pursue a career
in commerce, elicited from Manzoni a letter which Bonora
places among "i documenti insigni della poetica manzoniana"
(28). Manzoni's poetics are linked to Parini, who believed
that literature has a relative value in society. In Coen's
system of values Manzoni rejected the egotistical pursuit
of fame identified with writing. Bonora is quite correct
in attributing Manzoni's attitude to a strong moral conviction according to which letters ought to serve the interests
of truth and society, not the interests of the self. (A.P.)

Borghini, Alberto. "La peste e la scopa: un'immagine
manzoniana ed alcuni paralleli folklorici." *RiLI* 3 (1985):
327-34.

Uses Don Abbondio's famous metaphor of the plague ("È
stato un gran flagello questa peste; ma è stata anche una
scopa ..." [ch. 38]) as a point of reference to single out
the fact that, as far back as ancient Greece and more
recently in several European countries, the act of sweeping
the house with a broom was associated with superstitious
omens of evil and death. Borghini does not tell us whether
Manzoni was aware of the genetic character of the metaphor.
In my view, the connection between Borghini's findings and
Manzoni's text is purely casual. (A.P.)

Bosisio, Paolo. *"Il Conte di Carmagnola* e la tecnica
teatrale del Manzoni." *ON* 9 (1985):   73-110.

   In spite of Manzoni's insistence that his plays were not
written to be staged ("non rappresentate né rappresentabili"),
Bosisio claims, arguably, that, in view of the Romantic
vision of the theater as "rappresentazione scenica," with
referential values to W.R. Schlegel, Manzoni did not dismiss
entirely the desirability of seeing his plays staged. Included are pertinent observations on the 1973 and 1985 representations of *Adelchi.* The second part of the study offers
a belabored analysis of *Adelchi* and *Carmagnola* centered on
their novelty with respect to neoclassical drama. Excellent
bibliography. (A.P.)

Bottoni, Luciano. "La conversione di un Innominato." *LI* 38
(1986):   338-61.

   Attempts an intertextual analysis of the Innominato,
calling into play Shakespeare, Schiller, Scott, and, above
all, the Bible. In spite of this ambitious critical frame,
hardly any light is shed on Manzoni's character, for Bottoni's
writing is clothed with incomprehensible verbiage. Here is
an example: "Abbiamo riscontrato come anche nella referen-
zialità topografica prevalga, nella descrizione della valle
e del castello, l'invenzione retorico-fantastica che recupera
metaforicamente i sottotemi nomenclatori di una originaria
matrice spaziale" (357). Conversely the concluding pages,
in which Bottoni addresses historical narrativity with
references to Murray Krieger, Hayden White, and others, are
quite stimulating. (A.P.)

Bottoni, Luciano. *Drammaturgia romantica. Il sistema
letterario manzoniano.* Pisa: Pacini, 1984. Pp. 222.

   A good share of the work is devoted to a comparative
discussion of A.W. Schlegel's *Cours de littérature romantiqu*
(1814) and Manzoni's dramatic works. The major topics,
treated with considerable skill but hardly for the first
time, include the theater as a sociocultural institution,
the moral dimension of dramatic works of the Romantic period,
and the active presence of Shakespeare as a model. (A.P.)

Brescia, Giuseppe. "Manzoni tra l'effimero e l'eterno."
ON 9 (1985): 185-92.

   Considerations on the bicentennial celebration of Manzoni's
birth are followed by critical notes of little consequence
inasmuch as they reiterate very familiar themes, Manzoni's
stress on morality and individual responsibility, among others.
(A.P.)

Carena, Carlo. "Manzoni lettore di Agostino." *Paragone.*
Letteratura 37 (April-June 1986): 8-15.

Manzoni was an assiduous reader of Augustine, but the
article deals with Manzoni's correspondence with J.F.
Poujoulat who, in researching his *Histoire de saint Augustin*
(1845) sought the modern name of Cassiciacum, a town in
Lombardy where Augustine spent a summer. Manzoni identified
the town with Casciago, near Varese. (A.P.)

Caretti, Lanfranco. "Le radici illuministiche di Manzoni."
NA 120 (Oct.-Dec. 1985): 238-55.

Faithful to the spirit of his earlier and very influential
essays, Caretti downplays the impact of the French Ideologues
on Manzoni and stresses instead "l'incidenza decisiva che
ebbe l'ambiente milanese sul carattere, sugli atteggiamenti
di vita, sulle convinzioni morali, sulla stessa struttura
mentale del Manzoni" (240). He remarks moreover that Manzoni's realism and ethical pragmatism are deeply rooted
elements of eighteenth-century Milanese culture. (A.P.)

Caserta, Ernesto G. "Un decennio di studi manzoniani in
America: 1974-83." *AdI* 3 (1985): 44-60.

A thorough and discerning account of Manzoni criticism
carried out in academic circles. Nearly all aspects of
Manzoni's oeuvre are represented in these contributions,
though critical interest, here as in Italy, stresses
I promessi sposi. The distinguishing mark of American
scholarship on Manzoni is its diversity--of the authors'
academic backgrounds, of methodological practice, and intellectual orientation. The results, according to Caserta,
are noteworthy: "Questi studi ... si muovono su un alto
livello critico: avanzano nuove proposte di lettura,
rettificano annosi e recenti pregiudizi estetico-critici,
approfondiscono e puntualizzano l'analisi testuale delle
opere manzoniane" (45). From a different angle, the number
of publications for the period in question--4 books, 29
articles, 16 book reviews, 5 doctoral dissertations--is
miniscule when juxtaposed to critical interest in writers
of Manzoni's stature, such as Flaubert, Balzac, Galdós,
and Dostoevski. In this perspective, Manzoni's case (but
the names of Foscolo, Leopardi, and Verga could be added)
attests to the relative insignificance of Italian letters
in the context of American culture. (A.P.)

Cattaneo, Giulio. "Colloqui col Manzoni." *Paragone. Lettera-*
tura 37 (1986): 137-39.

A review of N. Tommaseo, *Colloqui col Manzoni,* examined here.

Cavallini, Giorgio. *Lettura dell'"Adelchi." Ed altre note manzoniane.* Rome: Bulzoni, 1984. Pp. 112.

The nucleus of the book is Manzoni's tragedies, which Cavallini's synchronic reading connects, in terms of lyrical continuity, with *I promessi sposi.* Two other articles deal with Croce's well-known change of heart with regard to Manzoni's work. Of limited interest. (A.P.)

Cavallini, Giorgio. "Politica e giustizia." *AdI* 3 (1985): 114-22.

Reiterates what numerous critics have dwelt upon since the publication, in 1942, of A. Zottoli's *Umili e potenti nella poetica del Manzoni,* namely, that Manzoni's pessimism stems in part from the realization that it is at best problematic to seek social justice (as opposed to divine justice which Cavallini ignores) from those who wield power, for they have a vested interest in holding that power even at the cost of perpetuating social injustice. (A.P.)

Chandler, S.B. "Il motivo del timore nel pensiero del Manzoni e in alcuni suoi personnaggi." *Italianistica* 14 (1985): 393-99.

Fear of God, present to a significant degree in the writings of Nicole and Pascal (well known to Manzoni) gives way, in the eighteenth century, to a widespread interest in the nonreligious, psychological aspects of fear. As a consequence of this development, in *La morale cattolica* are reflected both types of fear. There follows an enriching discussion of Don Abbondio (physical fear) and Innominato (psychological fear). The article, which also takes issue with Getto's analysis of Don Abbondio, is grounded in solid scholarship. (A.P.)

Chandler, S.B. "The Concept of Confinement in Manzoni." *Italica* 62 (1985): 285-93.

Unlike Leopardi and many German Romantic writers who viewed life as a prison, Manzoni "uses the common Romantic concept of confinement in an original way" (292) endowing it with religious meaning. Very good bibliography of Italian and German sources. (A.P.)

Chandler, S.B. "The Motif of the Journey in the Eighteenth-Century Novel in Scott and Manzoni." *RSI* 3 (1985): 1-10.

Expanding on the source-related scholarship on Scott and
Manzoni by M.F. Meiklejohn, Chandler studies the journey in
I promessi sposi as a salient thematic motif. Cognizant
as well of past contributions (especially Ferrucci and
Bārberi-Squarotti), Chandler concludes sensibly that Manzoni
"takes the traditional motif of the journey but transforms
and elevates it in order to convey a far deeper view of life
and human beings" (8). (A.P.)

Chandler, S.B. "The Moral Formation of Characters in *I promessi
sposi*." *FI* 19 (1985): 237-46.

Shows that the seeds of Christian morality are planted in
every Manzonian character, good or bad, consistent with
orthodox Church teachings. The growth of moral responsibility,
or lack of it, unfolds in consonance with sociohistorical
conditions and individual choice. The article offers further
proof of Chandler's consummate familiarity with Manzoni's
work, especially with questions pertaining to ethics and
theology. (A.P.)

Chandler, S.B. "The Author, the Material, and the Reader in
I promessi sposi." *AdI* 3 (1985): 123-34.

Treats the triadic relationship author-text-reader with
intelligence and ample material documentation but without
much concern for the problematics of the matter. (The latter
approach is found in Illiano's studies, examined here.)
According to Chandler, in the use of sources or preexistent
narrative material (of which he provides numerous instances
drawn from *Tom Jones* and Scott's fiction) as well as in such
technical devices as shifting from one character to another,
Manzoni was more effective than his predecessors inasmuch
as he tried to bring together harmoniously historical and
fictional components of the narrative. One can readily
agree with Chandler regarding the structural, but not the
ideological, aspect of *I promessi sposi*. (A.P.)

Colombo, Angelo. "Manzoni nel *Racconto italiano* di Gadda."
ON 9 (1985): 19-39.

Offers further support to the significant nexus between
Manzoni and Gadda whose partly autobiographical story,
Racconto italiano di ignoto del Novecento, reveals, in the
light of Colombo's incisive reading, close ties with *I
promessi sposi*, ties distinguished by a similar existential
vision of profound disenchantment regarding human nature and
man's inability to strive for the moral betterment of society.
(A.P.)

Colombo, Umberto. "I silenzi del Manzoni." *ON* 9 (1985): 41-72.

Dwells in a very prolix fashion on such biographical aspects as Manzoni's silence on his "conversion," the relationships with his father and with Rosmini. Informative, but it covers familiar territory. (A.P.)

Cottignoli, Alfredo. "Muratori, Manzoni e la moralità del teatro." *Italianistica* 14 (1985): 401-05.

Muratori and Manzoni were led "a trattare in modi non dissimili, e del pari all'interno di un disegno di riforma teatrale, lo stesso problema della moralità del teatro" (401). To prove this central point, Cottignoli sheds considerable light on the intellectual impulses provided by Maffei, Nicole, and Bossuet--impulses which, in part at least, moved Muratori to defend theater as a vehicle of moral enlightenment. The section dealing with Manzoni is less significant because it builds on previous scholarship. (A.P.)

Dell'Aquila, Michele. *Manzoni. La ricerca della lingua nella testimonianza dell'epistolario. Ed altri saggi linguistici.* Bari: Adriatica, 1984. Pp. 420.

Manzoni's ideas on language are probed systematically and in four consecutive stages, from 1806 to 1873. Each phase in this evolutionary process attests to the complexities not only of a literary language, but of a unified social language deemed by the critic inseparable from the regional and economic realities of nineteenth-century Italy. Of remarkable interest is the essay, "Le piccole patrie e la grande patria nei contrasti linguistici del primo Ottocento" (353-82) which examines the factionalism, along socioideological lines, represented by Cesari (conservative), Porta (pro-dialect), Monti (moderate purist), and Manzoni (Romantic school). The latter, in his effort to reach a large readership, opposed dialects and regional aspirations in matters of literary expression. A solid contribution to both Manzoni criticism and the *questione della lingua.* (A.P.)

Dell'Aquila, Michele. "Le introduzioni al *Fermo e Lucia* e il groviglio non risolto della lingua." *Italianistica* 14 (1985): 347-64.

Characterizes the multiform concerns reflected in *Fermo e Lucia* as "un coerente programma romantico alla maniera lombarda ... nella ricerca di un pubblico più largo" (350).

Manzoni's ideas on the Italian language are said to evolve around the tenets of stability, homogeneity, and elasticity-- qualities that Manzoni found in the language of France. As a telling document in this respect, the critic cites a letter to Fauriel (November 1821) in which Manzoni formulated a *desideratum* for Italian in these terms: "le besoine d'une certaine fixité, d'une langue convenu entre ceux qui écrivent et ceux qui lisent." The study reaffirms, in convincing and eloquent terms, a matter of seminal importance in Manzoni's poetics. (A.P.)

De Rienzo, Giorgio. "L'innocenza della fede in Manzoni ed *Il Natale del 1833* di Pomilio." *IQ* 26 (1985): 117-20.

Of Manzoni's letters, which Pomilio studied closely while researching *Il Natale del 1833*, De Rienzo writes: "Le lettere sono fredde, si è detto, ma svelano a pieno la grande, lucidissima architettura di una mente, testimoniano l'infaticabile vigoria d'un pensiero: l'adorazione appunto della ragione" (120). (A.P.)

Di Mieri, Fernando. "Problemi della seconda estetica manzoniana." *RSI* 3 (1985): 11-23.

The term "seconda estetica manzoniana" refers to the attribution given by Romano Amerio, author of *A. Manzoni filosofo e teologo* (1958), to the nonfiction corpus of Manzoni's writings, in particular *Del romanzo storico* and "L'invenzione." Di Mieri argues that in his discussion of truth ("vero morale") Manzoni displays "rigorosa coerenza" whereas in his linguistic theories the influence of French Ideologues led him to perceive language as a vehicle of communication governed by usage. In so doing, Manzoni failed to tie together language and aesthetics, opting for a relationship between language and morality. The half-truths of Di Mieri's arguments can hardly diminish the significance Manzoni attached to the literary dimension of language, a dimension that is apparent to any close and judicious reading of the novel as well as his linguistic writings. (A.P.)

Di Pino, Guido. "Manzoni lirico e tragico: una storia di forme ardua e senza eredi." *Italianistica* 14 (1985): 365-78.

Argues that Manzoni's "formazione poetica di gusto elitario" represented a stumbling block to his quest for a mode of expression patterned on the Romantic tenets of simplicity and accessibility to a large readership. In discussing Manzoni's tragedies, Di Pino points to Alfieri as a powerful stimulus, so much so that he sees *Adelchi* and *Carmagnola* as betraying the "furore creativo dell'astigiano e l'indole naturalmente meditativa e analitica del Manzoni" (370). Di Pino's arguments are plausible enough, though they fail to demonstrate, along the lines he proposes, a connective thread between Manzoni's dramatic works and his poetry. (A.P.)

Dombroski, Robert. *L'apologia del vero: lettura ed interpretazione dei "Promessi sposi."* Padova: Liviana, 1984. Pp. 98.

Reviewed favorably in *MLR* 8 (1987): 217-18 by Conor Fay who regards the book as "extremely stimulating" and endowed with "acute observations." Not seen.

Dombroski, Robert. "Gertrude's Story: The Irony of Self-Discovery." *FI* 19 (1985): 247-58.

Dombroski attempts to identify "the ideological substance" of Gertrude's story and to this end he builds his arguments on several polemical premises, such as the all-important tenets that Gertrude's is "a kind of *dogmatic biography* produced in the service of a truth existing beyond the existence of the self" (254) and that "narrative authority serves a truth beyond the existence of the self" (257). These and similar propositions enable Dombroski, after considerable and remarkably deft intellectual footwork, to conclude that the biographical form of Gertrude's story reveals Manzoni's position toward the bourgeois values of his time, in particular the fact that "the pride and vanity that nourish Gertrude's self-deception threaten the stability of the traditional Christian social structure in which the novel is set" (257). One can easily admire Dombroski's sharply analytical mind; yet, paradoxically, his Marxist intellectuality is used to problematize Gertrude's figure to such an extent that, in the end, one can no longer recognize the original character. (A.P.)

Dombroski, Robert. "Manzoni on the Italian Left." *AdI* 3 (1985): 97-110.

A comprehensive review of Marxist criticism of Manzoni, updated and more precise than the equally important article by Gianni Scalia, "Manzoni a sinistra" (*Italianistica* 2 [1973]: 21-42). Understandably Dombroski looks to Marxist criticism as a valid approach to Manzoni's work—a view that is not widely shared. On the other hand, one can only welcome Dombroski's sense of balance and broadmindedness. He cites, for instance, the ideological differences among

Marxist critics, pointing to the moderate stance of
Sapegno and Salinari who view Manzoni as a progressive,
democratic thinker, and the radical position of Bollati
and Simonini, who see him as essentially a conservative
writer tied to the ideology of the ruling classes, and
more concerned with preserving the economic and political
interests of the bourgeoisie than in fostering the social
progress of the proletariat. One aspect of Manzoni criticism which, according the Dombroski, Marxism has not treated
adequately "regards the psychological character of the
audience on which Manzoni so painstakingly has inscribed
his work" (109). And the critic points out that in part
he has sought to fill that gap in his recent book, *L'apologia
del vero*, reported here. (A.P.)

Dotti, Ugo. "A proposito del Manzoni e del tema di Don
Giovanni." *GSLI* 162 (1985): 104–08.

Rejects as strained and inaccurate the conclusions of
P. Stoppelli's article on Manzoni and the Don Giovanni theme
(see *RMB* for 1984, p. 434).

Farina, Luciano. "Manzoni and the Microcomputer: *I promessi
sposi*: Chapter 9." *QI* 7 (1986): 223–46.

To a very large extent, the article illustrates the function and dynamics of the Linguistic Data Management System
(LDMS), seen as a remarkable research tool for scholars in
the humanities. Yet, at least with regard to Manzoni and
except for some marginal benefit of its word frequency
index, the system seems of negligible value. For a related
but more comprehensive study, see G. De Rienzo, "*I promessi
sposi* al computer" examined in *RMB* for 1984, p. 429. (A.P.)

Girardi, Enzo Noè. "Carattere e destino del personaggio
manzoniano." *RSI* 2 (1985): 24–36.

Girardi sees Don Rodrigo as a flat, one-dimensional
character, devoid of a strong individual identity. Thus
the soliloquy with his ancestors "mette in luce il suo
carattere di non-carattere" (28). Girardi adds: "Don
Rodrigo infatti non è nulla, come persona; quel che è come
personaggio gli viene tutto da [gli antenati]" (28).
Clearly Girardi fails to take into account that it is precisely this mode of characterization by allusion and under-
statement that renders Don Rodrigo's character uniquely
complex as it brings to light Manzoni's felicitous awareness
of what has become a commonplace in contemporary fiction.
(A.P.)

Giustiniani, Vito. "Il Manzoni e la lingua poetica italiana."
RSI 3,3 (1985): 37-49.

This study deals only marginally with Manzoni, its main
concern being the deterioration of the Italian language in
the Seicento (an example of which is found in the introduction to *I promessi sposi)* and the gradual revitalization of
Italian brought about by fresh interest in Latin and classical letters. The process begins with Alfieri, is strengthened
by Foscolo and Carducci, and ends with D'Annunzio. (A.P.)

Godt, Clareece G. "Multiple Perspective in *I promessi sposi*:
The Uprising in Milan." *FI* 19 (1985): 259-72.

In the description of the bread riots (chapter 13) the
reader witnesses, according to Godt's skillful analysis,
sudden shifts of authorial perspective from one narrative
segment to another, and these shifts generate polyvalent
textures of meaning marked by an underlying sense of contradictory irony. The microstructures examined here exemplify
a complex narrative process in which even "the smallest
details of word, gesture and movement imply an ever widening
context" (270). Perceptive and original. (A.P.)

Godt, Clareece. "Manzoni and Sigismondo Boldoni. A Note on
Two Versions of Landscape." *AdI* 3 (1985): 149-58.

A precise and well-written piece on Boldoni, a seventeenth-
century source utilized by Manzoni, particularly in *Fermo
e Lucia*. Boldoni's letters, with their eyewitness account
of the invasion of northern Italy by German mercenaries,
proved quite valuable to Manzoni. Godt, who goes beyond
the contributions of other critics, focuses on the use
Manzoni made of such letters and the plausible reasons
Boldoni became an unnamed source in the final version of
the novel. (A.P.)

Jones, Verina. "*I promessi sposi*: The Sources of Literacy."
RiLI 3 (1985): 335-63.

Examines five seventeenth- and eighteenth-century sources,
Ripamonti and Rivola among them, which proved essential to
Manzoni's understanding of literacy and illiteracy in the
Seicento. Jones's salient points: 1) "the relationship
between the novel and its sources changes significantly in
the transition from *Fermo e Lucia* to the published version"
(342); 2) *I promessi sposi* offers a hagiographic portrait
of Cardinal Borromeo with some regard to his role as chief
promoter of literacy among the poor; and 3) Renzo is consciously aware of the pen and inkwell as tools of literacy

associated with the upper classes, hence tools of oppression.
An important study, to be read in conjunction with Jones's
previous article, "Illiteracy and Literacy in *I promessi
sposi*," published in *RiLI* 1 (1983) and reported in *RMB* for
1984, pp. 431-32. (A.P.)

Illiano, Antonio. "Principi e procedure dell'arte del narrare
nei *Promessi sposi*." *Italianistica* 14 (1985): 407-17.

The essay focuses on key aspects of Manzoni's narrative
which Illiano characterizes as diegetic, triangular (manu-
script-narrator-reader), and permeated with "ironismo
autoriflessivo." Further, the text is said to betray a
narrative voice which unfolds in close interaction with
the author's demiurgic and omniscient presence. Under a
separate rubric, Illiano illustrates, with telling examples,
the function of paralepsis and digression as important means
in the narrator-reader relationship. The article elaborates
several complex and rather technical principles of the narrative discourse. However, the tenacious reader is rewarded
with an enhanced appreciation of the infrastructures and
internal dynamics of Manzoni's novel. (A.P.)

Illiano, Antonio. "Premesse a una definizione normativa
dell'autore-narratore manzoniano." *Italica* 62 (1985):
294-304.

In Illiano's lucid analysis of *I promessi sposi*, the
author-narrator relationship is examined in the light of
current critical thought on narrativity. Yet, unlike many
other critics, Illiano never forces or strains his arguments
to prove an important point. "Nella prassi manzoniana,"
he writes, "l'autore-scrittore non si occulta né si maschera,
non si fossilizza nell'irreducibilità del binomio *chi
scrive-chi è*" (295)--the latter with obvious reference to
Roland Barthes's famous dictum: "Qui parle (dans le récit)
n'est pas qui écrit (dans la vie) et qui écrit n'est pas
qui est" (*Communications* 8 [1966]: 20). Secondly, Illiano
sheds a great deal of light on the three introductions to
Fermo e Lucia and their underlying narrative principles,
one of them being organic coherence, coherence that is both
intertextual and intratextual. (A.P.)

Loyson, Charles. "L'enthousiasme poétique. Ode à M. Alexandre
Manzoni." *ON* 10, supp. (1986): 2-6.

Reprints the text of Loyson's *Ode*, published first in the
Lycée Français (1820), together with Victor Chauvet's negative
review of *Il Conte di Carmagnola*. The poem, which pulsates

with Romantic vigor and idealism, carries no internal
reference to Manzoni. But the dedication attests to
Manzoni's youthful reputation in French literary circles.
(A.P.)

Mantovani, Giorgio. "Tre lettere inedite di Leopoldo II ad
Alessandro Manzoni." *IQ* 26 (1985): 121-27.

Written in 1834, the letters are not devoid of biographical
interest with regard to the addressee. More important perhaps
is the first letter which reports Leopold's condolences
following the death of Enrichetta Blondel. (A.P.)

Manzoni, Alessandro. *Il Conte di Carmagnola*. Edizione a cura
di Giovanni Bardazzi. Milan: Fondazione Mondadori, 1985.
Pp. 104, 536.

Although it comes in the wake of the seminal work carried
out by Chiari, Ghisalberti, and Sanesi with regard to the
editions of Manzoni's tragedies, Bardazzi's critical edition of *Carmagnola* is neither unwelcome nor without merit.
It examines the historical sources thoroughly, including
Manzoni's debt to Sismondi, and it discusses the autograph
draft with precision and lucidity. But the salient part of
the introduction is the comparative study of the variants,
including the 1820, 1840, and 1845-55 (*Opere varie*) editions.
Here, departing from Ghisalberti and Sanesi, Bardazzi
prefers the 1820 edition, considering the remaining
editions too heavily influenced by Manzoni's pro-Florentine
linguistic position. (A.P.)

Manzoni, Alessandro. *Inni sacri. Il cinque maggio*. Trans.
Joseph Tusiani. *AdI* 3 (1985): 6-43.

Those who have had occasion to admire Tusiani's exceptional
skills as translator of the Italian masters will not be
disappointed by his delicate, resourceful, and largely
successful rendition of Manzoni's poetry. (A.P.)

Manzoni, Alessandro. *Los novios*. Trans. Maria Nieves Muñiz.
Madrid: Cátedra, 1985. Pp. 734.

The most recent Spanish translation of *I promessi sposi*,
it is preceded by a biocritical study of Manzoni. Reviewed
favorably by Tobia Toscano in *CrL* 14 (1986): 198.

Marchi, Gian Paolo. "La tenda insanguinata. Intorno a una
nuova edizione degli atti del processo alla Monaca di Monza."
Italianistica 14 (1985): 419-32.

A comprehensive review article of *Vita e processo di Suor Virginia de Leyva*. Marchi's generally favorable assessment of the book includes these reservations: "Sarebbe stato opportuno analizzare più a fondo le carte processuali, accordare maggiore attenzione al carattere di Suor Virginia e delle altre consorelle, sottolineare usi e costumi di vita quotidiana nel monastero" (426). (A.P.)

Mariani, Umberto. "Evoluzione dello storicismo manzoniano." *AdI* 3 (1985): 85-96.

Offers spirited and for the most part valid arguments in favor of a definitive characterization of Manzoni as "poeta della storia" rather than "poeta della Provvidenza." Thus the critic differs sharply with those who see a providential or divine design at work in Manzoni's narrative. He rejects as contradictory the common perception of Manzoni as both a religious and realistic writer: "O poeta della Provvidenza o poeta della storia.... Non si può continuare a chiamarlo tutti e due" (89). Finally, Mariani remarks, quite correctly, that history in Manzoni is the subtotal of individual actions and that divine intervention in history is drastically limited.

The effectiveness of these arguments is severely tested when they are juxtaposed to Manzoni's work which mediates and narrows, rather than separates, the boundaries between the historical and the divine. History in Manzoni, as Mariani recognizes, is a tangible record of human experience in which the operative qualifier, human, carries with it, inherently, the thrust of a dimension which is moral and divine. (A.P.)

Matteo, Sante. "I miei venticinque lettori: gli altri promessi sposi nei *Promessi sposi*." *Prometeo* 5 (1985): 116-38.

Matteo, who is fully conversant with reader-generated criticism (see his book on Foscolo included here), argues that in Manzoni's narrative one can discern two implied readers: the middle-class literate reader of the Seicento, and the refined reader that transpires from the pseudo-baroque passage in the introduction to the novel. In the elaboration of the work the two readers learn to coexist and communicate with one another. Transposed to the Otto-cento, the two readers reemerge through textual exemplifica-tion of high and low narratives. These narratives betray a process of reeducation engineered by the author to effect understanding and communication among the larger spectrum

of real readers. Matteo's provocative essay is bound to
disturb traditional Manzoni critics, but it will also cause
them to reflect seriously on the merits of different textual
approaches to *I promessi sposi*. (A.P.)

Nencioni, Giovanni. "A. Manzoni e l'Accademia della Crusca."
NA 121 (Jan.-March 1986): 279-302.

Documents the uneasy relationship between Manzoni and the
Crusca Academy of which he was made a corresponding member
in 1827. In the 1830s, under the influence of Niccolini
and Capponi, the academy stressed a correspondence between
spoken and written Italian which Manzoni endorsed. The
break occurred in the early 1840s when it became clear that,
as a national language, Manzoni advocated the Florentine
spoken by educated people. On the other hand, the academy
privileged, in Nencioni's words, "una lingua di secolare
tradizione *scritta* fondata su un canone di autori tosco-
fiorentini... e moderatamente aperta all'uso toscano
parlato" (292). Nencioni underlines the primary concerns
of both parties: Manzoni's, to promote language as a
vehicle of communication; the academy's, to guard language
against possible corruption. In retrospect, it would seem
that the academy's fears were not ill founded. Rigorous
research and a worthy contribution to the *questione della
lingua*. (A.P.)

Pandini, Giancarlo. "Nei libri la riscoperta del Manzoni."
RSI 3 (1985): 88-92.

Reviews several books on Manzoni, mostly of general
interest, published as a tribute to the bicentennial
commemoration of his birth.

Petrocchi, Giorgio. "Orazio in Manzoni." *Italianistica*
14 (1985): 379-85.

In addition to pointing out Manzoni's deep interest in
classical literature, Petrocchi shows that the most important
cause of Manzoni's attraction to Horace was the latter's
"umorismo bonario e un pō malinconico" (385). (A.P.)

Petrocchi, Giorgio. "Manzoni e il *De vulgari eloquentia*."
FI 19 (1985): 273-83.

Examines Dante's and Manzoni's divergent positions on the
Italian language. The article complements Petrocchi's
earlier study, "Dante in Manzoni" (in *L'ultima Dea*, 1977).
But, except for the comparative approach, nothing really
new emerges here, at least regarding Manzoni. (A.P.)

Pistelli Rinaldi, Emma. "Il cosiddetto 'miracolo di san Rocco' nella conversione del Manzoni." *Italianistica* 14 (1985):   433-58.

   A meticulous analysis of disparate sources relative to what is commonly, though inaccurately, known as Manzoni's conversion. Pistelli makes three points regarding Manzoni's return to Catholicism: 1) it was achieved "faticosamente, dopo lungo travaglio e neppure completamente a Parigi" (437); 2) it was not "di tipo giansenistico come Ruffini vorrebbe farci credere" (438); and 3) it did not entail anything miraculous. Pistelli's approach to Manzoni's "conversion" as a complex and gradual experience is praiseworthy. The same cannot be said for her elaboration, which is overly detailed and excessively long. (A.P.)

Puppo, Mario. "Problemi di cronologia manzoniana." *Italianistica* 14 (1985):   387-91.

   Defends the need for a critical edition of Manzoni's linguistic writings on the grounds that the work would reduce frequent inaccuracies found in Manzoni scholarship. In fairness to those who are called into question, the flaws cited by Petrocchi do not pertain to matters of substance. (A.P.)

Puppo, Mario. "Ancora sul rapporto 'poesia'-'verità' nel Manzoni." *AdI* 3 (1985):   111-23.

   An important note aimed at elucidating further a key point in Manzoni's poetics first broached in Puppo's *Poesia e verità. Interpretazioni manzoniane* (see *RMB* for 1980, p. 364), namely, the dichotomy, history-fiction which places the *Lettre à M. Chauvet* and *Del romanzo storico* at opposite ends of the critical discourse. In other words, Puppo points out that the *Lettre* betrays a position of youthful optimism, that poetic consideration of a historical character's inner life could ultimately strengthen the character's historicity. However, in time, Manzoni was to realize that such an objective was quite elusive, as reflected in *Del romanzo storico*. (A.P.)

Ragusa, Olga. "Alessandro Manzoni." Pp. 367-94 in *European Writers: The Romantic Century*, vol. 5. New York: Scribner's 1985.

   A biocritical essay intended for nonspecialist readers, who no doubt will appreciate the wealth of factual material, the clarity and precision with which it is presented, and, not the least, the critical insights investing all the seminal expressions of Manzoni's work. (A.P.)

Ragusa, Olga. "Due 'digressioni': ancora sull'unità dei *Promessi sposi.*" *FI* 19 (1985): 284-97.

The first "digression" concerns the passage in *Fermo e Lucia* in which the author justifies his refusal to dwell on the amorous aspect of the protagonists' relationship. Broadening the scope of the "digression," Ragusa suggests perceptively that its significance as a withholding narrative principle applied to Lucia's story can be understood in terms of the Proustian "raturer à l'avance." At the same time, the strategic structural position of the "digressione"--after the "Addio monti" and before Gertrude's story--invites the reader to bear in mind Manzoni's reflections in the course of the nun's story. The second part of the article studies the genesis of *La colonna infame* from its digressive function in *Fermo e Lucia* to a different and autonomous structure as "storia delle idee e delle parole" in its final form. With a sharp critical eye, Ragusa singles out the importance of narrative strategies identified with structural materials which others have viewed as mere digressions. (A.P.)

Ragusa, Olga. *Comparative Perspectives on Manzoni.* New York: S.F. Vanni, 1986. Pp. 35.

Text of a lecture given at Columbia University's Center for Italian Studies on January 28, 1986.

In placing Manzoni in a European perspective, Ragusa focuses on *I promessi sposi* as a problematic text barely understood outside Italy. The contexts in which these difficulties materialize--historical, social, political, academic--tell us a great deal about Manzoni's work. A different perspective concerns Manzoni's connection with French and German cultures which is anchored to two key figures, Fauriel and Goethe. The quality of scholarship here is what one has come to expect from Ragusa. Moreover, her remarks on Goethe's relationship with Manzoni are the most illuminating I have read. (A.P.)

Raimondi, Ezio. "Le bestemmie di Padre Cristoforo." *FeC* 10 (1985): 465-74.

Cristoforo's use of "parole troppo espressive" (textual reference found at the end of chapter 4, *Promessi sposi*) is treated by Raimondi, and convincingly so, as a euphemism for blasphemous expressions, albeit modified somewhat by the speaker. With this in mind, Raimondi juxtaposes *I promessi sposi* to *Tristram Shandy*, remarking that Sterne's prodigious manipulation of language may have stimulated

Manzoni (who probably read Sterne in the 1803 French
translation) to reflect on the duality of the written word.
(A.P.)

Scrivano, Riccardo. "Nella fabbrica dei *Promessi sposi.*" *FI*
19 (1985):   298-321.

A flat and inconclusive piece in which the use of un-
mastered structuralist and semiotic notions ("diegetic" is
the all-encompassing operative term here) is supposed to
lead to a new understanding of time and space in Manzoni's
novel.   In fact, the article has little to offer.   Scrivano's
hagiographic treatment of Lucia as a divine force and "il
vero cuore della favola" bears little resemblance to Manzoni's
Lucia.   The end-notes bespeak eloquently of the author's
unfamiliarity with Manzoni criticism.   (A.P.)

Severino, Roberto.   "Ad Angelica Palli: Manzoni improvvisatore
di versi encomiastici." *AdL* 4 (1986):   270-78.

Describes an interesting and little-known incident in
Manzoni's life: his acquaintance with Angelica Palli, a
gifted and attractive poetess at whose house in Livorno
Manzoni, in the company of Lamartine, he improvised an encomiastic poem (of negligible quality) dedicated to Palli.
The article is rich in biographical details and source-
related scholarship.   (A.P.)

Sovente, Michele.   "*Il Natale del 1833* di Mario Pomilio."
IQ 26 (1985):   103-10.

A dense and very perceptive study of Pomilio's acclaimed
novel centered on Manzoni's life (see *RMB* for 1983, p. 448).
In *Il Natale del 1833*, writes Sovente, "il dolore è l'asse
intorno al quale gravita sia la dimensione religiosa che
la dimensione letteraria dell'autore dei *Promessi sposi*"
(104).   Pomilio's text, permeated with grief and silence,
is seen as arising from an admiring mimetic effort to recap-
ture the nuanced texture of Manzoni's prose.   (A.P.)

Tommaseo, Nicolò, G. Borri, and R. Bonghi.   *Colloqui col
Manzoni*, a cura di Alessandro Briganti.   Rome: Editori
Riuniti, 1985.

The work, well known to Manzoni scholars, was last printed
in 1944.   This edition leaves out "Memorie manzoniane" and
"Una serata in casa Manzoni" by Cristoforo Fabris.   Briganti's
introduction gives a rich account of Manzoni's relationship
with Tommaseo; emphasized are the latter's jealousy and
generally untrustworthy character.   (A.P.)

Travi, Ernesto. "I tre tempi della 'suite' degli *Inni sacri*." *ON* 9 (1985): 99-123.

Travi dwells on biographical, historical, and metrical elements--the three *tempi* indicated in the title. However, nothing new or noteworthy emerges from the discussion. (A.P.)

V.A. *Vita e processo di suor Virginia de Leyva monaca di Monza.* Presentazione di Giancarlo Vigorelli. Milan: Garzanti, 1985. Pp. xx+958.

Following the publication, in recent years, of two biographies of Virginia de Leyva, this volume marks the most ambitious project regarding the historical figure that inspired Manzoni's Gertrude. Some of the contributions relate to the sociohistorical conditions in seventeenth-century Italy. Among these: Attilio Agnoletto, "Suor Virginia Maria de Leyva e il suo tempo" (95-114); and Enrico Cattaneo, "Le monacazioni forzate tra Cinque e Seicento" (145-95). With regard to the model of Manzoni's character, noteworthy are: Umberto Colombo, "La Gertrude manzoniana" (769-869); and Antonia Mazza Tonucci, "Virginia-Gertrude tra satira e romanzo: fascino e fortuna di un personaggio" (871-924). However, the lion's share of the volume (217-741) is taken by the "Atti del processo," the proceedings of Leyva's trial translated from Latin by Ermanno Paccagnini. No less useful is the "Bibliografia storica e letteraria" (925-55) compiled by Umberto Colombo. (A.P.)

Vallone, Aldo. "Le sospensioni e l'arte narrativa di Manzoni." *ON* 9 (1985): 5-17.

To my recollection, this is the first systematic study of incomplete sentences in *I promessi sposi*, that is, sentences marked by suspension points which are found quite frequently in the fictional parts of the novel. Significantly, they are virtually absent in historical descriptions. According to Vallone, the function of suspension points is complex, comprehensive, and quite effective in conveying "atteggiamenti di reticenza, candore, timore, viltà ... e così via" (17). The episodes studied as testing ground are the night of the Innominato and the encounter between Conte Zio and the Padre Provinciale, both in chapter 19. Original and effective. (A.P.)

Wis, Roberto. "Il Manzoni e la Svezia." *Italianistica* 14 (1985): 459-63.

In the nineteenth century Swedish readers showed some
genuine interest in Manzoni, but the 1951 translation of
I promessi sposi by Lisa Lundh drew a chain of "giudizi
balordamente negativi dei critici letterari svedesi" (461):
Wis, who wrote the introduction to the translation, remarks
that such negativism betrays a dismal ignorance of Italian
culture on the part of Swedish readers as well as nationally
respected critics such as Svan Stolpe and Arthur Lindqvist.
More importantly, the response reveals an obstinate resistance to Manzoni's religious ideas. (A.P.)

Zatti, Sergio. "Il cavallo del Père Canaye e la mula di Don
  Abbondio." *AdI* 3 (1985): 135-48.

To the phenomenally large list of real and supposed sources
of *I promessi sposi* Zatti adds the name of Saint-Èvremond
whose *Conversation de M. Le Marechal d'Hocquincourt avec
le Père Canaye* (1692) contains the description of a horse
ride by a skeptical clergyman named Père Canaye. The episode
reminds Zatti of Don Abbondio's hilariously contentious experience with his mule (chapter 23). The analogies between
the two scenes are indeed remarkable. But Zatti is able to
show as well that "scaricando la satira evremondiana dei
suoi veleni di polemica anticlericale," Manzoni draws from
the French writer "strumenti razionalistici e ironici di
indagine" (145) which are masterfully woven into the texture
of the novel. (A.P.)

See also Capentari, Messina, Sansone ("French 3. Fauriel");
  Petrocchi ("Italian 2. General"); Landoni ("Leopardi");
  Paolini ("Foscolo").

Review of book previously listed:

MANZONI, Alessandro. *On the Historical Novel* (see *RMB* for
  1984, p. 433), rev. by Donald M. Schurman in *QQ* 93 (1986):
  196-98.

PORTA

See Maquet ("French 3. Stendhal").

SPANISH

(Compiled by Brian J. Dendle, University of Kentucky)

1. BIBLIOGRAPHY

Departamento de Bibliografía de la Universidad Complutense de Madrid. *Repertorio de impresos españoles perdidos e imaginaros*, vol. 1. Madrid: Ministerio de Cultura, 1982. Pp. 333.

The listing of over 5,000 vanished books includes some nineteenth-century items.

Menarini, Piero, Patrizia Garelli, Félix San Vicente, and Susana Vedovato. *El teatro romántico español (1830-1850). Autores, obras, bibliografía.* Bologna: Atesa Editrice, 1982. Pp. 263.

Comprehensive bibliographies of Spanish Romantic dramatists, original theatrical works, translations, *sainetes*. Indexed. An invaluable tool.

Rall, Dietrich. *La literatura española a la luz de la crítica francesa 1898-1928.* Trans. Marcos Romano. Universidad Nacional Autónoma de México, 1983. Pp. 323.

The French vision of Spanish literature in the early years of this century (the war years are excluded). A useful work, although dealing mainly with contemporary literature. Indeed, if we are to believe Rall, there was no interest in Spanish Romanticism. Regrettably, no onomastic index.

Thomas, Diana M. *The Royal Company of Printers and Booksellers of Spain: 1763-1794.* Troy, N.Y.: Whitson, 1984. Pp. xii+ 198.

Rev. by D.W. Cruickshank in *Library* 7 (1985): 379-82.

2. GENERAL

Balcells, Albert. *Historia contemporánea de Cataluña.*
Barcelona: EDHASA, 1983. Pp. 441; illus.

Chapter 1, "La revolución burguesa en Cataluña (1833-1876)"
(11-89), includes a brief, but intelligent, overview of the
Renaixença. Indexed.

Caldera, Ermanno. "L'età della ragione." Pp. 7-22 in *Teatro*
romantico spagnolo. (Quaderni di Filologia Romanza, 4.)
Bologna: Pàtron Editore, 1984.

The different portrayals of aged characters in the works
of eighteenth-century dramatists, Gorostiza, Martínez de la
Rosa, Gil y Zárate, Grimaldi, Javier de Burgos, and, above
all, Bretón, to whom Caldera devotes the greater part of this
illuminating analysis.

Charnon-Deutsch, Lou. *The Nineteenth-Century Spanish Story.*
Textual Strategies of a Genre in Transition. London:
Támesis, 1985. Pp. 176. £19.60.

A brief introduction to the stories of Mesonero, Estébanez
Calderón, Fernán Caballero, and Larra. Examines the treatment
of the northern European folk motif of Death and the doctor
by Fernán Caballero (*Juan Holgado y la muerte*), Antonio
Trueba (*Traga-aldabas*), and Alarcón (*El amigo de la muerte*).

Delgado Illo, José ("Pepe-Illo"). *La tauromaquia o arte de*
torear. Intro. by Manuel Chaves. Granada: Biblioteca de
la Cultura Andaluza, 1984. Pp. 251; 250 illus.

A biography of Pepe-Illo and documents concerning his
career; the text of *La tauromaquia* (including a glossary of
bullfighting terms); and the texts of poems on the deaths
of nineteenth-century bullfighters. A welcome edition of a
curious and interesting work.

Díez Garretas, Rosa. *El teatro en Valladolid en la primera*
mitad del siglo XIX. Valladolid: Diputación Provincial,
1982. Pp. 226; illus.

A description of the Casa-Teatro; its financial and legal
standing; and lists of works performed in 1803, 1824, and
1842. Bibliography.

Dowling, John C. "The English Chaplain and the Spanish Colonel:
Edward Young, José Cadalso, and the Growth of Spanish Romanticism." *Dieciocho* 9 (1986): 126-37.

The popularity of Young's *Night Thoughts* and of Cadalso's *Noches lúgubres* in nineteenth-century Spain.

Esteban, José. *El Madrid liberal.* Madrid: Editorial El Avapiés, 1984. Pp. 159; illus.

The Madrid of the *trienio.* Includes treatment of the press, theater, literature, popular customs, and cultural societies.

García Castañeda, Salvador. "De 'figurón' a hombre de pro: el montañés en la literatura de los siglos XVIII y XIX." Pp. 89-98 in Douglas and Linda Jane Barnette, eds., *Studies in Eighteenth-Century Spanish Literature and Romanticism in Honor of John Clarkson Dowling.* Newark, Del.: Juan de la Cuesta, 1985.

The *hidalgo* from the Cantabrian Mountains is no longer a figure of fun in the works of María Rosa Gálvez, Gorostiza, and Gil y Zárate.

Garelli, Patrizia. "Conquista, conquistatori e conquistati sulla scena romantica spagnola." Pp. 43-64 in *Teatro romantico spagnolo.* (Quaderni di Filologia Romanza, 4.) Bologna: Pàtron Editore, 1984.

The conquest of the Americas, as portrayed in dramas by Escosura, Gorostiza, and Sánchez de Fuentes.

Gates, David. *The Spanish Ulcer.* New York and London: Norton, 1986. Pp. xiv+557; illus.

A fascinating history of military operations during the the Peninsular War. The atrocious communications and problems of supply are stressed.

Gil Novales, Alberto. "Madrid en la fama del general Riego." *CHA* 426 (Dec. 1985): 181-88.

Riego, *pace* Galdós, did not die in a cowardly manner and was not mistreated by the Madrid populace.

Glendinning, Nigel. "Tendencias liberales en la literatura española a fines del siglo XVIII." *Dieciocho* 9 (1986): 138-52.

Gold, Hazel. "From Sensibility to Intelligibility: Transformations in the Spanish Epistolary Novel from Romanticism to Realism." Pp. 133-43 in Gilbert Paolini, ed., *La Chispa '85. Selected Proceedings.* Tulane University Press, 1985.

Professor Gold briefly touches on: the feminization of the epistolary novel (and Ochoa's belittling of the same); the use of letters in didactic essays (Alvarado, Balmes, Miñano, Larra, Bécquer) rather than in the novel; the passive manner of communicating in such epistolary novels as *Cornelia Bororquia* and Segunda Martínez de Roble's *Las españolas náufragas* (1831); and Cosca Vayo's moralistic *Voyleano* (1827).

Jiménez de Gregorio, Fernando. *El Ayuntamiento de Toledo en la Guerra por la Independencia y su entorno, de 1809 a 1814.* Toledo: Diputación Provincial, 1984. Pp. 242; illus.

La Parra López, Emilio. *El primer liberalismo español y la Iglesia. Las Cortes de Cádiz.* Prologue by Antonio Mestre Sancho. Alicante: Instituto de Estudios Juan Gil-Albert, Diputación Provincial, 1985. Pp. 320.

Lapesa, Rafael. "El lenguaje literario en los años de Larra y Espronceda." Pp. 345-79 in *Homenaje a Julián Marías.* Madrid: Espasa-Calpe, 1984.

Fascinating analysis of the language of such Romantics as Mesonero Romanos, Espronceda, Larra, and Enrique Gil, including treatment of neologisms, the Romantic lexicon, grammatical change, colloquialisms, regionalisms, and the consciousness of political and generational change.

Lechner, Jan. "El campesino como tema literario (Literatura y realidad rural durante el siglo XIX)." Pp. 26-40 in Claude Dumas, ed., *L'homme et l'espace dans la littérature, les arts et l'histoire en Espagne et en Amérique Latine au XIXe siècle.* Université de Lille 3, 1985.

The peasant rarely appears in nineteenth-century Spanish literature; when he does he is portrayed as a brute or in idyllic terms.

López Fanego, Otilia. "Los dramas 'españoles' de Victor Hugo." *CHA* 426 (Dec. 1985): 117-38.

Hernani, Ruy Blas, and *Torquemada* have their sources in Spanish literature. The source of *Torquemada* (1869) was Juan Antonio Llorente's *Historia crítica de la Inquisición en España.*

Menarini, Piero. "La statistica commentata. Vent'anni di teatro in Spagna (1830-1850)." Pp. 65-89 in *Teatro romantico spagnolo.* (Quaderni di Filologia Romanza, 4.) Bologna: Pàtron Editore, 1984.

A statistical analysis to establish the proportion of original and translated works performed, 1830-1850.

Moliner Prada, Antonio. "Las Juntas corregimentales de Cataluña en la 'Guerra del francés.'" *Hispania* (Madrid) 44 (1984): 549-82.

Montero, Alonso, José. *Amores y amoríos en Madrid.* Madrid: Editorial El Avapiés, 1984. Pp. 174; illus.

Sketchy treatment of the loves of Joseph Bonapart, Espronceda, Larra, and la Avellaneda.

Pérez Gómez, Antonio. *Murcia en los viajes por España.* Ed. and intro. by Cristina Torres Suarez. (Biblioteca Murciana de Bolsillo, 55.) Murcia: Academia Alfonso X el Sabio, 1984. Pp. 287; illus.

The introduction includes a bibliography of Pérez Gómez's works. A discussion of the vision of Murcia in the works of 14 eighteenth- and nineteenth-century English travelers.

Picoche, Jean-Louis. "Les décors du drame romantique espagnol." Pp. 95-109 in Claude Dumas, ed., *L'homme et l'espace dans la littérature, les arts et l'histoire en Espagne et en Amérique Latine au XIXe siècle.* Université de Lille 3, 1985.

Romantic drama required frequent and expensive changes of scene. Preferred settings were palace rooms, streets, prisons, and convents; rural décors were rare.

Pinilla Navarro, Vicente. "La conflictividad social en Zaragoza durante el bienio progresista." *Hispania* (Madrid) 44 (1984): 583-98.

Pino, Enrique del. *Historia del teatro en Málaga durante el siglo XIX.* 2 vols. Málaga: Editorial Arguval, 1985.

Volume 1 covers the theater in Málaga from the eighteenth century to 1869. Chapter 3 discusses Málaga in the Romantic period; chapter 4 treats the drama of "la nueva generación" (1840-1856) and includes the theatrical works of Ramón Franquelo Martínez (143-47), Tomás Rodríguez Rubí (147-53), and Luis and José de Olona y Gaeta (154-58). Volume 2 includes an index of the works and dramatists cited.

Rodríguez, Rodney T. "Continuity and Innovation in the Spanish Novel: 1700-1833." Pp. 49-63 in Douglas and Linda Jane Barnette, eds., *Studies in Eighteenth-Century Spanish Literature and Romanticism in Honor of John Clarkson Dowling.* Newark, Del.: Juan de la Cuesta, 1985.

A succinct introduction to the Spanish novel of the eighteenth and early nineteenth centuries, in which Rodríguez
discerns three trends: "the survival of a native picaresque
tradition, the proliferation of a moral or exemplary novella,
and the introduction into Spain of French *sensibilité* and
of the British sentimental novel." The works of Eugenio de
Tapia, Antonio San Román, Agustín Pérez Zaragoza Godínez,
Vicente Rodríguez de Arellano, Montengón, Mor de Fuentes,
and Estanislao de Cosca Vayo illustrate Rodríguez's thesis.
A useful essay.

Romero, Carmelo, Carmelo G. Encalvo, and Margarita Caballero.
La provincia de Soria entre la reacción y la revolución,
1833-1843. Soria: Excma. Diputación Provincial, 1985.
Pp. xix+303; illus.

Includes a treatment of the social and demographic background, the cultural life of Soria, and its journals (such
as the literary publication *El Numantino*). Bibliography;
index.

Rubio Cremades, Enrique, and María Angeles Ayala. *Antología*
costumbrista. Barcelona: Ediciones El Albir, 1985. Pp.
450; 1,500 Ptas.

The detailed introduction discusses problems of genre and
chronology, the nature of the *cuadro de costumbres*, authorial
perspective, the xenophobia of the *costumbristas*, and *cos-*
tumbrista collections. Bibliography. Texts of *costumbrista*
articles by Mesonero Romanos, Estébanez Calderón, Larra,
Fermín Caballero, Gil de Zárate, Ochoa, Rivas, Flores, and
Pérez Galdós ("Aquel"). A most useful anthology.

Rubio Jiménez, Jesús. *El teatro en el siglo XIX.* Madrid:
Editorial Playor, 1983. Pp. 157.

Includes a brief treatment of the major authors of the
Romantic period; and the lexicon, imagery, and characteris-
tics of Romantic drama. Commentary of sample texts of
La viuda de Padilla (Martínez de la Rosa) and *Don Juan*
Tenorio (Zorrilla). Bibliography.

San Vicente, Félix. "El mensaje sin secreto. Tipología del
título en el teatro español (1830-1850)." Pp. 91-133 in
Teatro romantico spagnolo. (Quaderni di Filologia Romanza,
4.) Bologna: Pàtron Editore, 1984.

A thematic analysis of the titles of dramas performed,
1830-1850.

Schinasi, Michael. "The History and Ideology of Calderón's Reception in Mid-Nineteenth-Century Spain." *Neophil* 70 (1986): 381-96.

Placing the reception of Calderón in the socio-ideological context of nineteenth-century Spain, Schinasi demonstrates that even such admirers of Calderón as Lista, Durán, Hartzenbusch, and Gil y Zárate expressed reservations. Three *loas--Derechos póstumos* (Hartzenbusch), *Apoteosis de don Pedro Calderón de la Barca* (Zorrilla), and *La tumba salvada* (Ventura de la Vega)--reflect nineteenth-century values. An interesting discussion, especially valuable for its treatment of Ventura de la Vega.

Sebold, Russell P. "Nuevos Cristos en el drama romántico español." *CHA* 431 (May 1986): 126-32.

In an interesting discussion of the Romantic interpretation of Christian symbols, Sebold argues that Rugiero (*La conjuración de Venecia*) and Don Alvaro (*Don Alvaro*) have parallels with Christ.

Seminario de Historia Moderna. *Documentos del Reinado de Fernando VII*, vol. 8, *Los agraviados de Cataluña*. (Colección Histórica de la Universidad de Navarra, 26.) 4 vols. Pamplona: Ediciones Universidad de Navarra, 1972.

My apologies for the tardiness of this listing.

Tudela, Mariano. *Zumalacárregui. La primera guerra del norte.* Madrid: SILEX, 1983. Pp. 212.

Novelized biography of the Carlist hero. Rudimentary bibliography.

Urquijo y Goitia, José Ramón de. "Represión y disidencia durante la primera guerra carlista." *Hispania* (Madrid) 45 (1985): 131-86.

Urquijo y Goitia, José Ramón de. *La revolución de 1854 en Madrid.* Prólogo de Manuel Espadas Burgos. Madrid: Consejo Superior de Investigaciones Científicas, 1984. Pp. xxi+594; illus.

Includes a treatment of the background to the revolution, details of the rising, the condition of the Madrid working class in 1854, the impact of the cholera epidemic, and the role of the Milicia Nacional. The appendices offer a wealth of statistical information on the period. Bibliography; index.

Valverde Rodao, Valentina. "'Lo que son trigedias' o la
parodia dramática de 1830 a 1850." Pp. 135-61 in *Teatro
romantico spagnolo*. (Quaderni di Filologia Romanza, 4.)
Bologna: Pàtron Editore, 1984.

Parodies of Romantic drama.

Vaquero Iglesias, Julio Antonio, and Adolfo Fernández Pérez.
"Estructuras familiares y sistemas hereditarios en la sociedad
rural tradicional asturiana: el Concejo de Caso en el siglo
XIX (1775-1875)." *Hispania* (Madrid) 44 (1984): 517-47.

Vedovato Ciaccia, Susana. "Los artistas en las tablas.
Trayectoria de un tema en la época romántica." Pp. 163-77 in
Teatro romantico spagnolo. (Quaderni di Filologia Romanza,
4.) Bologna: Pàtron Editore, 1984.

Fourteen Romantic plays in which the protagonists are
artists or writers.

See also Aymes ("French 1. General").

3. STUDIES OF AUTHORS

ALCALA GALIANO

See Aymes ("French 1. General").

ALVARADO

See Gold ("Spanish 2. General").

AMADOR DE LOS RIOS

Amador de los Ríos, José. *Historia social, política y
religiosa de los judíos de España y Portugal*. Madrid:
Ediciones Turner, 1984. 3 vols.

Facsimile of 1875 edition.

ASQUERINO

García Castañeda, Salvador. "Los hermanos Asquerino o el uso
y mal uso del drama histórico." Pp. 23-42 in *Teatro
romantico spagnolo*. (Quaderni di Filologia Romanza, 4.)
Bologna: Pàtron Editore, 1984.

The ideologically biased historical dramas of the republicans Eusebio and Eduardo Asquerino.

AVELLANEDA

Schlau, Stacy. "Stranger in a Strange Land: The Discourse of Alienation in Gómez de Avellaneda's Abolitionist Novel *Sab*." *Hispania* 69 (1986): 405-502.

See also Montero Alonso ("Spanish 2. General").

BALMES

See Gold ("Spanish 2. General").

BECQUER

Bécquer, Gustavo Adolfo. *Desde mi celda*. Ed. Darío Villanueva. Madrid: Castalia, 1985. Pp. 217; illus.

The comprehensive introduction includes an account of Bécquer's visit to Veruela, a commentary on the text of the *Cartas*, and a selected bibliography. Annotated text.

Bécquer, Gustavo Adolfo. *Historia de los Templos de España*. Madrid: Ediciones El Museo Universal, 1985. Pp. xii+124; illus.

The introduction by María Dolores Cabra Loredo usefully treats the circumstances of publication of the *Historia de los Templos*. The text is a facsimile of the 1857 edition and includes numerous color plates. Since this is the first time since 1857 that the text and illustrations are united in a complete edition, the present publication will indeed be welcomed not only by Bécquer scholars but by connoisseurs of nineteenth-century art.

Bécquer, Gustavo Adolfo. *La Ilustración de Madrid*. Ed. and intro. by María Dolores Cabra Loredo. Illus. by Valeriano Bécquer. Madrid: Ediciones El Museo Universal, 1983. Pp. 302; illus.

The texts of articles by and concerning Bécquer published in *La Ilustración de Madrid*, 1870 to 1871, with the illustrations of Valeriano Bécquer. The combination of excellent typography and magnificent illustrations make this a volume of beauty, for which Ediciones El Museo Universal deserve to be congratulated.

Billick, David J., and Walter Dobrian. "Bibliografía selectiva
y comentada de estudios becquerianos, 1960-1980." *Hispania*
69 (1986): 278-302.

   One hundred and ninety-eight items are listed for the
   period!

Mantero, Manuel. "La *vida como relámpago* de Bécquer en la
poesía española de posguerra (Aleixandre, Hidalgo, Otero,
García Nieto)." Pp. 177-86 in Douglas and Linda Jane
Barnette, eds., *Studies in Eighteenth-Century Spanish
Literature and Romanticism in Honor of John Clarkson Dowling.*
Newark, Del.: Juan de la Cuesta, 1985.

Pageard, Robert. "L'évocation d'atmosphère dans les écrits
de Gustavo Adolfo Bécquer (1836-1870). La relation Bécquer-
Azorín." Pp. 41-51 in Claude Dumas, ed., *L'homme et l'espace
dans la littérature, les arts et l'histoire en Espagne et
en Amérique Latine au XIXe siècle.* Université de Lille 3,
1985.

   Brief notes for a lengthier study, which will compare
   Bécquer and Azorín.

Rodríguez, Alfred, and Shirley Mangini González. "El amor y la
muerte en *Los ojos verdes* de Bécquer." *Hispano* 86 (1986):
69-73.

   The archetypal fusion of Love and Death in *Los ojos verdes.*

Villanueva, Dario. "Ponz, Jovellanos, Bécquer. Originalidad
y unidad de las cartas *Desde mi celda.*" Pp. 215-34 in H.L.
Boudreau and Luis T. González-del-Valle, eds., *Studies in
Honor of Sumner M. Greenfield.* Lincoln, Neb.: Society of
Spanish and Spanish-American Studies, 1985.

   A competent discussion of the travel literature of Ponz,
   Jovellanos (a pre-Romantic), and others. Discusses the
   predominance of the "yo romántico" in Bécquer's *Cartas.*

See also Gold ("Spanish 2. General").

BLANCO WHITE

Murphy, G. Martin. "Blanco White y John Henry Newman: un
encuentro decisivo." *BRAE* 63 (1983): 77-116.

   The theological controversies of yesteryear are resurrected
   in Murphy's detailed account of the friendship, and later
   estrangement, of Blanco White and Newman. Blanco White resided

in Oxford for several years after being awarded an Oxford
M.A. in 1826; Newman was among his young friends in Oriel
College. However, Blanco came under attack for defending
Catholic emancipation and was accused of unorthodoxy in
the affair of the Bampton Lectures. Later, Blanco believed
that Newman sought to impose theocracy; his reading of, and
opposition to, Blanco's *Life* contributed to Newman's conversion to Rome.

BRETON DE LOS HERREROS

See Caldera ("Spanish 2. General"); Gies ("Larra").

BURGOS

See Caldera ("Spanish 2. General").

CASTRO, ROSALIA DE

Alonso Montero, Xesús, ed. *En torno a Rosalía.* Madrid:
Júcar, 1985. Pp. 471.

One hundred essays, written from the nineteenth century
to the present, concerning the life and works of Rosalía.

Poullain, Claude. "Rosalía de Castro y las inundaciones de
Padrón en 1881." *Iris* 2 (1986): 162-87.

Four articles by Rosalía in *La Ilustración gallega y
asturiana.*

CHESTE

See Martín ("Larra").

COSCA VAYO

See Gold, Rodríguez ("Spanish 2. General").

DONOSO CORTES

Donoso Cortés, Juan. *Ensayo sobre el catolicismo, el liberalismo
y el socialismo. Otros escritos.* Intro. by Manuel Fraga
Iribarne. Ed. and notes by José Luis Gómez. Barcelona:
Planeta, 1985. Pp. xliv+367.

Includes bibliography and texts.

DURAN

See Schinasi ("Spanish 2. General").

ESCOSURA

See Garelli ("Spanish 2. General").

ESPRONCEDA

Polt, J.H.R. "Espronceda's 'Canto a Teresa' in Its Context."
Pp. 167-76 in Douglas and Linda Jane Barnette, eds., *Studies
in Eighteenth-Century Spanish Literature and Romanticism in
Honor of John Clarkson Dowling.* Newark, Del.: Juan de la
Cuesta, 1985.

The "Canto a Teresa" seen in relation to the wider context
of *El diablo mundo.*

See also Lapesa, Montero Alonso ("Spanish 2. General").

ESTEBANEZ CALDERON

See Charnon-Deutsch, Rubio Cremades ("Spanish 2. General").

FERMIN CABALLERO

See Rubio Cremades ("Spanish 2. General").

FERNAN CABALLERO

See Charnon-Deutsch, Rubio Cremades ("Spanish 2. General");
Sebold ("Hore").

FLORES

See Rubio Cremades ("Spanish 2. General").

FLOREZ ESTRADA

Lancha, Charles. *Alvaro Florez Estrada 1766-1853 ou Le
libéralisme espagnol à l'épreuve de l'histoire.* Grenoble:
Université des Langues et Lettres, 1984. Pp. 308.

Florez Estrada's activities during the *Cortes* of Cádiz,
during the *trienio*, as an *emigrado* before and after the
trienio; his political, social, and economic ideology.

FRANQUELO MARTINEZ

See Pino ("Spanish 2. General").

GALVEZ

See García Castañeda ("Spanish 2. General").

GARCIA GUTIERREZ

García Gutierrez, Antonio. *El trovador*. Ed. Antonio Rey Hazas. Barcelona: Plaza y Janés, 1984. Pp. 312.

The life and works of García Gutiérrez; the influence of *Macías* on *El trovador*; the structural and thematic analysis of the drama; a brief bibliography; the annotated text of *El trovador*; Larra's review.

GIL, ENRIQUE

See Lapesa ("Spanish 2. General").

GIL Y ZARATE

See Caldera, García Castañeda, Rubio Cremades, Schinasi ("Spanish 2. General").

GOROSTIZA

See Caldera, García Castañeda, Garelli ("Spanish 2. General").

GOYA

Bull, Duncan, and Enriqueta Harris. "The Companion of Vélazquez's *Rokeby Venus* and a Source for Goya's Naked *Maja*." *BM* 128 (Sept. 1986): 643-54. 5 illus.

According to the authors, this was a painting (once attributed to Titian) of a frontally reclining Venus, paired with Vélazquez's averted figure in the Godoy collection and hence accessible to Goya.

Glendinning, Nigel, and Rolfe Kentish. "Goya's Country House in Madrid: The Quinta del Sordo." *Apollo* 123 (1986): 102-09.

Helman, Edith. "El desastre núm. 69 de Goya (Visto contra el
trasfondo político-literario de 1811-1814)." Pp. 255-76 in
Homenaje a Julián Marías. Madrid: Espasa-Calpe, 1984.

Lafuente Ferrari, Enrique. "Humanismo y filosofía en Goya."
Pp. 297-331 in Homenaje a Julián Marías. Madrid: Espasa-
Calpe, 1984. Illus.

Soufas, C. Christopher. "'Esto si que es leer': Learning to
Read Goya's Los Caprichos." Word and Image 2 (1986): 311-
30. 14 illus.

Taking Capricho 43 as the key to the whole series, Soufas
sees in the famous ambiguous inscription ("el sueño de la
razón produce monstruos") a parody of the "empiricist mind
model": without recourse to sense experience, images either
are produced from memory by the active imagination (if reason
is sleeping), or are projected upon the imagination by the
understanding itself (if reason is dreaming). Accordingly,
Soufas proposes that the etchings be read by the viewer in
two different ways: in chronological order (with eyes
"open"), as "an exposé of the irrational vices of society,"
as "an investigation of Goya's personal obsessions" after
his unhappy love affair with the Duchess of Alba. (I.H.C.)

Review of book previously listed:

MULLER, Priscilla E., Goya's "Black" Paintings: Truth and
Reason in Light and Liberty (see RMB for 1985, p. 417), rev.
by Lawrence Gowing in BM 128 (July 1986): 506-08; 1 illus.

GRIMALDI

Gies, David Thatcher. "'Inocente estupidez': La pata de
cabra (1829), Grimaldi, and the Regeneration of the Spanish
Stage." HR 54 (1986): 375-96.

The astounding success of Grimaldi's La pata de cabra
(1829); "its popularity brought money into the coffers of
the theaters and helped to form an audience prepared for the
extravagances of Romantic drama."

See also Caldera ("Spanish 2. General"); Gies ("Larra").

HARTZENBUSCH

See Schinasi ("Spanish 2. General").

HORE

Sebold, Russel P. "La pena de la Hija del Sol. Realidad, leyenda y romanticismo." Pp. 295-308 in Luis T. González-del-Valle and Dario Villanueva, eds., *Estudios en honor a Ricardo Gullón*. Lincoln, Neb.: Society of Spanish and Spanish-American Studies, 1984.

The pre-Romantic poet María Gertrudis Hore (1742-1801) ("La Hija del Sol") was influenced by Young's *Night Thoughts* and inspired a Romantic legend related by Fernán Caballero.

LARRA

Cano, Vicente. "Los ensayos de Larra y Alberdi. Paralelos y puntos de contacto estilísticos." Pp. 37-47 in Douglas and Linda Jane Barnette, eds., *Studies in Eighteenth-Century Spanish Literature and Romanticism in Honor of John Clarkson Dowling*. Newark, Del.: Juan de la Cuesta, 1985.

Parallels between Larra and his Argentinian contemporary, Alberdi ("Figarillo").

Gies, David T. "Larra, Grimaldi, and the Actors of Madrid." Pp. 113-22 in Douglas and Linda Jane Barnette, eds., *Studies in Eighteenth-Century Spanish Literature and Romanticism in Honor of John Clarkson Dowling*. Newark, Del.: Juan de la Cuesta, 1985.

Protests by Larra and Bretón de los Herreros at the incompetence of Spanish actors; Grimaldi's attempt to reform the Spanish stage.

Lorenzo-Rivero, Luis. "La estructura del ensayo en Ortega y Larra." Pp. 169-80 in *Ortega y Gasset Centennial*. Madrid: Ediciones José Porrúa Turanzas, 1985.

An attempt, relying too much on the findings of earlier critics, at establishing affinities between Larra and Ortega.

Martín, Gregorio C. "Larra y el teatro: Censura, crítica e historia (I)." *RQ* 33 (1986): 431-37.

Two of Larra's articles on the theater in late 1832 were inspired by the quarrel between the actor Nicanor Puchol and the dramatist Juan de la Pezuela (el Conde de Cheste). Larra's attacks on Puchol's incompetent acting in the summer of 1833 resulted in legal action against *La Revista Española*. A useful article, illuminating the context of Larra's theatrical criticism, 1832-33.

Rodríguez, Alfredo. "Larra, Ortega y las casas de Madrid."
Pp. 181-85 in *Ortega y Gasset Centennial*. Madrid: Ediciones
José Porrúa Turanzas, 1985.

Sketchy treatment of coincidental similarities between
Larra's "Las casas nuevas" (1833) and Ortega's "Nuevas casas
antiguas" (1926).

See also Gold, Lapesa, Montero Alonso, Rubio Cremades ("Spanish
2. General"); García Gutiérrez ("García Gutiérrez").

LISTA

See Schinasi ("Spanish 2. General").

LLORENTE, JUAN ANTONIO

See López Fanego ("Spanish 2. General").

¡MADRID!

¡Madrid! *Indicaciones de una española sobre inmoralidades y
miserias presentes, y su remedio.* Madrid: Méndez Editores,
1984. Pp. xxxv+220; illus.

Facsimile of a curious work of 1833, written by a woman,
in large part a reply to Mesonero Romanos's *Manual*.

MARCHENA

Volney, C.F. *Las ruinas de Palmira*. Trans. by Joseph Marchena.
Madrid: Ediciones El Museo Universal, 1984. Pp. 250; illus.

Reprint of Marchena's translation.

MARTINEZ DE LA ROSA

Mayberry, Nancy K. "Martínez de la Rosa and the Adverse Fate
Theme." Pp. 251-58 in Gilbert Paolini, ed., *La Chispa '85.
Selected Proceedings*. Tulane University, 1985.

The theme of failed revolution in Martínez de la Rosa's
dramas, his abhorrence of fatalism, the source of fate (a
literary device) in *La conjuración de Venecia* to be sought
in Sophocles' *Oedipus Rex*; Martínez de la Rosa's Christian
morality.

See also Caldera, Rubio Jiménez, Sebold ("Spanish 2. General").

MARTINEZ DE ROBLE

See Gold ("Spanish 2. General").

MESONERO ROMANOS

Mesonero Romanos, Ramón de. *Mis ratos perdidos o Ligero bosquejo de Madrid en 1820 y 1821*. Madrid: Méndez Editores, 1984. Pp. 63; illus.
Facsimile of the 1822 edition.

Mesonero Romanos, Ramón de. *Recuerdos de viaje por Francia y Bélgica*. Madrid: Miraguano, 1983. Pp. 291.
Facsimile of the 1881 edition.

Museo Municipal. *Mesonero Romanos (1830-1882)*. Madrid: Ayuntamiento de Madrid, Delegación de Cultura, 1982. Pp. 159; illus.

A handsomely illustrated volume to commemorate the centennial of Mesonero's death. It includes essays by Federico Carlos Sainz de Robles (15-28), Ricardo Donoso Cortés (31-65), Antonio Matilla Tascón (on Mesonero's financial affairs) (67-88), and Eulalia Ruiz Palomeque (on Mesonero's proposals to reform Madrid) (89-134), and a bibliography, by María del Carmen Herrero and Mari Cruz Seseña, of Mesonero's works published during his lifetime (135-56).

See also Charnon-Deutsch, Lapesa, Rubio Cremades ("Spanish 2. General"); ¡Madrid! ("Spanish 3. ¡Madrid!").

MIÑANO

Martín, Gregorio C. "Un conflicto editorial del siglo XIX." Pp. 179-86 in Gilbert Paolini, ed., *La Chispa '83. Selected Proceedings*. Tulane University, 1983.

Miñano's skill in settling legal problems in connection with the publication of the *Gaceta de Bayona* (1828) and a proposed translation of Thiers's *Histoire de consulat* (1844).

See also Gold ("Spanish 2. General").

MONTENGON

Montengón, Pedro de. *Eusebio*. Ed. Fernando García Lara. Madrid: Editora Nacional, 1984. Pp. 1112.

This welcome edition of the famous pre-Romantic work is
preceded by an account of Montengón's life and works, a detailed treatment of the *Eusebio*, a listing of editions (half
of which are from the Romantic period), and a bibliography.

See also Rodríguez ("Spanish 2. General").

MOR DE FUENTES

Hafter, Monroe Z. "Mor's Achievement of Realism in *La Serafina*."
Dieciocho 9 (1986): 153-63.

See also Rodríguez ("Spanish 2. General").

MORA

See Aymes ("Spanish 2. General").

OCHOA

See Gold, Rubio Cremades ("Spanish 2. General").

OLAVIDE

Dufour, Gérard. "Le village idéal au début du XIXe siècle selon
El evangelio en triunfo de Pablo de Olavide." Pp. 11-25 in
Claude Dumas, ed., *L'homme et l'espace dans la littérature,
les arts et l'histoire en Espagne et en Amérique Latine au
XIXe siècle.* Université de Lille 3, 1985.

Olavide's *El evangelio en triunfo* was a best-seller in the
first half of the nineteenth century (14 Spanish editions
between 1797 and 1848; 15 French editions between 1805 and
1861). Volume 4 offered a revolutionary proposal for rural
reform.

OLONA Y GAETA

See Pino ("Spanish 2. General").

PARREÑO

Parreño, Florencio Luis. *Jaime Alfonso el Barbudo.* 2 vols.
Elche: Manuel Pastor Torres, 1983.

Reprint of the text (illustrated) of the 1895 edition.

PEREZ ZARAGOZA GODINEZ

See Rodríguez ("Spanish 2. General").

RIVAS

Sanchez, Roberto G. "On Staging *Don Alvaro* Today." Pp. 133–43
    in Douglas and Linda Jane Barnette, eds., *Studies in Eighteenth-
    Century Spanish Literature and Romanticism in Honor of John
    Clarkson Dowling.* Newark, Del.: Juan de la Cuesta, 1985.

See also Rubio Cremades, Sebold ("Spanish 2. General").

RODRIGUEZ DE ARELLANO

See Rodríguez ("Spanish 2. General").

RODRIGUEZ RUBI

See Pino ("Spanish 2. General").

ROSELL

Rosell, Cayetano. *Crónica de la provincia de Madrid.* Madrid:
    Comunidad de Madrid, 1983. Pp. 248; illus.
    A facsimile of the 1883 edition.

SAN ROMAN

See Rodríguez ("Spanish 2. General").

SANCHEZ DE FUENTES

See Garelli ("Spanish 2. General").

TAPIA

See Rodríguez (Spanish 2. General").

TRUEBA

See Charnon-Deutsch ("Spanish 2. General").

VENTURA DE LA VEGA

See Schinasi ("Spanish 2. General").

ZORRILLA

Mas-López, Edita. "El Don Juan del Romanticismo poético del
    Siglo 19 y el Don Juan realista del Siglo 20." *CA* 264,1
    (Jan. 1986): 190–201.

    Zorrilla's Don Juan Tenorio is a lover and adventurer who
    seeks salvation through a perfect woman; by way of contrast,
    Shaw's Don Juan is an intellectual.

Menarini, Piero. *Don Juan canta Don Juan*. Bologna: Atesa
    Editrice, 1982. Pp. 39.

    Operatic versions of *Don Juan Tenorio*, including numerous
    parodies. Bibliography.

See also Rubio Jiménez ("Spanish 2. General").